Map of the European Union

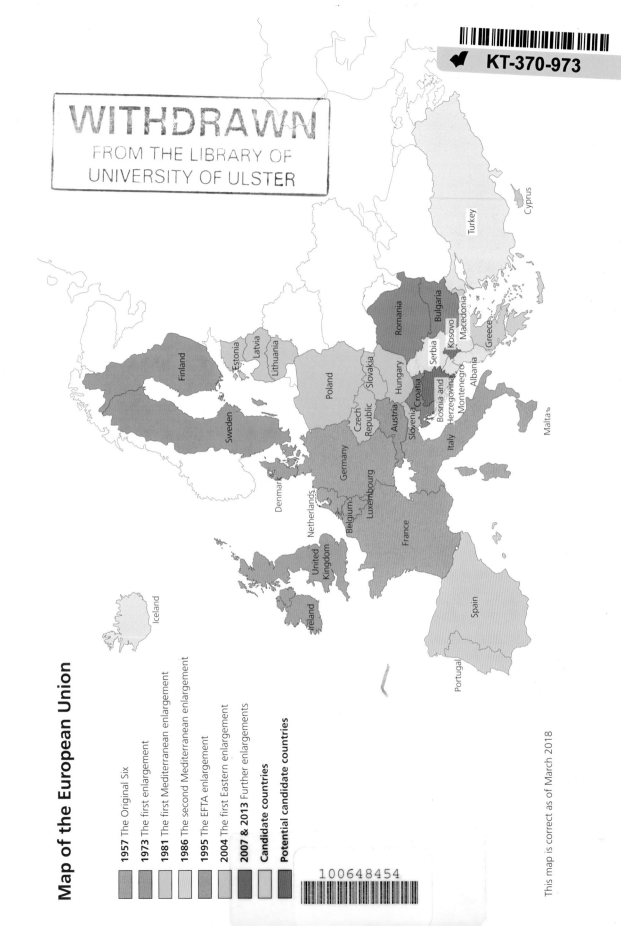

1957 The Original Six
1973 The first enlargement
1981 The first Mediterranean enlargement
1986 The second Mediterranean enlargement
1995 The EFTA enlargement
2004 The first Eastern enlargement
2007 & 2013 Further enlargements
Candidate countries
Potential candidate countries

This map is correct as of March 2018

EU Law

DIRECTIONS

6th Edition

NIGEL FOSTER, FRSA

Visiting Professor of European Law, the Europa Institut,
Universität des Saarlandes, Saarbrücken, Germany

Academic Director and Lecturing Professor, LLMs in
International Business & International Commercial Law,
Robert Kennedy College, Zürich, Switzerland

Module Leader for the Online courses on EU law for the
SEE EU Cluster of Excellence in European and International
Law (Saarbrücken & Belgrade).

OXFORD
UNIVERSITY PRESS

OXFORD
UNIVERSITY PRESS

Great Clarendon Street, Oxford, OX2 6DP,
United Kingdom

Oxford University Press is a department of the University of Oxford.
It furthers the University's objective of excellence in research, scholarship,
and education by publishing worldwide. Oxford is a registered trade mark of
Oxford University Press in the UK and in certain other countries

Third edition 2012
Fourth edition 2014
Fifth edition 2016

Impression: 1

Published in the United States of America by Oxford University Press
198 Madison Avenue, New York, NY 10016, United States of America

British Library Cataloguing in Publication Data

Data available

Library of Congress Control Number: 2018932380

ISBN 978–0–19–881653–9

Printed in Great Britain by
Bell & Bain Ltd., Glasgow

This book is dedicated to my two elder brothers,
Graham and Michael

Guide to the book

EU Law Directions is enriched with a range of special features designed to support and reinforce your learning. This brief guide to those features will help you use the book to the full and get the most out of your study.

Learning objectives

Each chapter begins with a bulleted outline of the main concepts and ideas you will encounter. These provide a helpful signpost to what you can expect to learn from the chapter.

□ LEARNING OBJECTIVES

This chapter will help you to become familiar with the institutions of the European Union (EU), the work that they do, and how they work together. The following topics will be considered:

● the institutional framework;
● the European Commission;
● the Council (of Ministers);

Further information boxes

Allow you to take your study further by supplying important detail and key insights for you to consider.

The overuse of the general powers, referred to as the 'competence creep', has been criticised and resisted by the member states. It was addressed both in the Constitutional Treaty and Lisbon Treaty, by more clearly establishing the division of competences. This topic is considered in Chapter 3. The Lisbon Treaty also specifically empowers the Union to accede to the ECHR, which is now provided in the amended Article 6(2) TEU.

2.2.6 **COREPER and the Council General Secretariat**

Case close-up boxes

Identify and explain key influential cases.

See, for example, **Cases C-6 and 9/90** *Francovich and others v Italy,* in which the establishment of liability on the part of member states for a breach of EC law could never have been derived from a literal reading of the Treaty or secondary law.

These Community (and now Union) methods of interpretation are applied in addition to the usual array of methods of interpretation found in the member states' legal systems, including the logical, literal, purposive means of interpretation, although any strict use of such methods has often been rejected by the Court as unsuitable in the Community and now Union context.

Definition boxes

Key terms are highlighted when they first appear and are concisely explained in definition boxes. These terms are found in the online resources that accompanies this book.

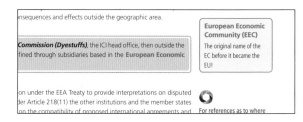

nsequences and effects outside the geographic area.

Commission (Dyestuffs), the ICI head office, then outside the fined through subsidiaries based in the **European Economic**

on under the EEA Treaty to provide interpretations on disputed der Article 218(11) the other institutions and the member states on the compatibility of proposed international agreements and

European Economic Community (EEC)
The original name of the EC before it became the EU!

For references as to where

Thinking points

Thinking points encourage you to reflect on the implications of legislation and cases and the reasoning behind them.

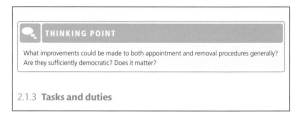

💬 THINKING POINT

What improvements could be made to both appointment and removal procedures generally? Are they sufficiently democratic? Does it matter?

2.1.3 **Tasks and duties**

Chapter summaries

The central points and concepts covered in each chapter are distilled into summaries at the ends of chapters. These reinforce your understanding and can be used for quick revision.

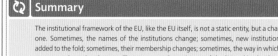

⟳ Summary

The institutional framework of the EU, like the EU itself, is not a static entity, but a char one. Sometimes, the names of the institutions change; sometimes, new institution added to the fold; sometimes, their membership changes; sometimes, the way in which operate and act also changes. They too are a dynamic part of the EU and its developr Certainly, the powers they enjoy also change: in particular, the changes to function power of the only directly elected body, the EP, need to be understood, especially in co tion with the discussion about the democratic deficit in the EU. Having a good backgr

Cross-references

Crucial connections between topics are carefully cross-referenced to provide a fully integrated understanding of the subject. Links are highlighted to aid quick and accurate navigation through the book.

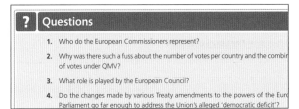

of appointing a new Commission is that the Commission President is
ed by qualified majority voting (QMV) by the European Council, after
account the elections to the EP under Article 17(7) TEU (Figure 2.1).
pproval by the EP by majority of members' vote. This more politicised
mission President than was originally established was one of the very
om the constitutional Treaty to the Lisbon Treaty. The current President,
e choice of the European People's Party, the largest party in the EP, and
ention to be complied with. In 2014 though, two member states voted
he European Council, which in fact voted by simple majority. This pro-
d EP approval arguably injects indirect democracy into the Commission

▶ CROSS REFERENCE
QMV is considered in detail
in section 2.2.4.3.

End-of-chapter questions

Self-test questions at the end of each chapter help you develop analytical and problem-solving skills. The online resources that accompany this book suggest approaches to answering these questions. These will help you develop your own successful approach to assessments and examinations.

? Questions

1. Who do the European Commissioners represent?
2. Why was there such a fuss about the number of votes per country and the combir of votes under QMV?
3. What role is played by the European Council?
4. Do the changes made by various Treaty amendments to the powers of the Euro Parliament go far enough to address the Union's alleged 'democratic deficit'?

Further reading

Selected further reading is included at the end of each chapter to provide a springboard for further study.

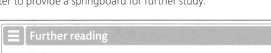

☰ Further reading

Books

Beck, G. *The Legal Reasoning of the European Union Court of Justice*, Hart Publi Oxford, 2013.

Burrows, N. and Greaves, R. *The Advocate General and EC Law*, Oxford University Oxford, 2007.

Christiansen, T. 'The European Union after the Lisbon Treaty: an elusive "institutiona ance"?' in Biondi, A., Eeckhout, P., and Ripley, S. (eds) *EU Law after Lisbon*, Oxford Univ

Guide to the online resources

The online resources that accompany this book provide ready-to-use learning resource to help further support your studies. They are free to use and are designed to complement the book and maximise your learning.

 www.oup.com/uk/foster_directions6e/

Interactive timeline and map of Europe

Allows you to trace the development of the European Union (EU) through a series of key dates and events, providing a useful overview of the history of the EU, and summarises each county's involvement.

Author podcast: study and examination technique guidance

Useful tips from the author on how to learn, prepare for, and pass exams.

Answers to end-of-chapter questions

Suggested approaches are given for the end-of-chapter questions in the book. These will help you to develop your skills in constructing a well-balanced argument.

Web references

Further information and web links as referenced in the book.

Self-test questions

Multiple-choice questions for each chapter provide instant feedback to help consolidate your knowledge and identify areas for further study ahead of assessments.

New to this edition

- Fully revised to take account of new legislative and case law developments
- In Chapter 1, consideration of the consequences of the second UK Referendum on continuing EU membership and the progress of Brexit and Brexit negotiations
- In Chapter 4, further extensive rearrangement and coverage of human and fundamental rights provision
- In Chapter 5, the much-amended sections on EU law in the UK in view of Brexit
- In Chapter 12, reordering of material on extended persons' rights, in particular those relating to educational rights
- In Chapter 13, some reordering of the material relating to Article 101 TFEU
- Additional cross-references and web links pointers, plus additional and up-to-date further reading advice

Preface

Dear Reader

At the time of this sixth edition the landscape of the European Union (EU) has started a process of radical change as a result of the historic vote by a slim majority of the UK electorate who voted in the 2016 UK Referendum to leave the EU.

This edition has benefited from some very good and helpful reviews of the previous editions—thanks very much! There have been rearrangements of material in certain chapters, as noted above in the 'New to this edition' section. In addition, there has been the usual general updating and amendments to take account of new legislative and case law developments.

The biggest changes to this edition though, are, with no surprise to you I am sure, the impact of Brexit, and Chapters 1 and 5 have been amended significantly. However, as I am sure will be equally readily understood, the Brexit process is a moveable mystery feast held on shifting sand! As I write, the United Kingdom has only just moved on to negotiating the future trade relationship with the EU and issues from the initial talks still need further clarity and substance, in particular those relating to the Irish Border. No doubt I will need to make even further changes to the original material from the fifth edition and also to the amendments already made in this edition as the Brexit discussions and negotiations progress (or not, as the case may be). Continuing updates will be posted to the dedicated OUP online resource pages on Brexit, which will be reviewed regularly.

As with the previous editions, I would like to thank a few people who have been involved and who have helped me along the way.

Thanks are due to the staff of Oxford University Press: for their continued excellent assistance and attention to this sixth edition, in particular to Emily Hoyland. Thanks also to the production staff led by Aishwarya Panday for their assistance and to Fiona Barry and Jeremy Langworthy at copy-editing and proofreading stages, respectively. Thanks also to the reviewers of the book, who made numerous very positive and constructive comments, many of which have helped my decisions in updating and amending this edition. Thank you very much.

My thanks to 30+ years' worth of students, who must now easily number over 10,000 all told, I would think. I learn new things and find new ways of expressing some aspect of law with each new cohort of students.

Finally, for all readers, I hope that this book serves your purpose and that you find it a useful addition to the material available on EU law. Please let me know either way, and whilst I cannot promise to make any changes you suggest, I will certainly give them some thought. Thanks in advance.

Best regards
Nigel Foster
Buckingham
April 2018

Outline contents

Detailed contents

Table of cases

Court of Justice cases-numerical

Table of legislation

Regulations

Directives

Decisions

PART 1
INSTITUTIONAL LAW

1

The establishment and development of the European Union

□ **LEARNING OBJECTIVES**

This chapter first of all provides an overview of why and how the European Union (EU) was established and how it developed. In doing so, it pays special attention to the two parallel developments in the history of the Communities and the EU known as 'widening' and 'deepening'. After considering these developments, the chapter then explores the relationship with the UK and for this edition concentrates on Brexit and its possible consequences, although at the time of writing this is still far from clear. Finally, it considers the external relations of the EU. Hence this chapter will enable you to understand:

- why the Union (at first called the Communities) was originally set up;

- how the Communities were first established;

- the perceived aims and goals, and how those aims and goals have continued to change;

- the expansion and development of the Communities and Union;

- the increase in policies and integration;

- the UK's role in this history and possible future relations;

- the external relations of the EU; and

- where we are today with the EU—developing news.

Introduction

Reasons for considering EU history

As with many things, particularly legal rules, they are easier to understand and rationalise if you are aware of why they were established in the first place. Any study of the law on courses of 'European Union law' and, as it was previously entitled, 'European Community law', must start with a consideration of the history and development of the Union. Without this, it will be much more difficult. Looking at the past helps us to understand why the EU has taken the form it has today, the pressures involved in this process, and why certain decisions were taken along its history. In any subject, merely learning the rules does not help you to understand the purpose for which they were enacted and the reasons that led to them. This is even more the case with the EU. Many of the laws, whilst clearly aimed at specific topics such as ensuring free movement of goods or persons, or requiring the equality of treatment of different groups, or regulating the recognition of a profession in the member states, are a compromise of different perspectives. In the EU, these perspectives come from the different member states, the different cultural under-standings, different histories, and different social and economic backgrounds, hence the treaties and laws that have been produced under the Treaties are often achieved only as a compromise. On their own, the individual rules may not make a great deal of sense; with an understanding of the history and development, hopefully, they might make a great deal more sense.

Section 1.4 considers in more depth two particular aspects of this development: namely, the expansion and further integration of the Communities and Union, which are referred to as 'widening and deepening'.

Explanation of the terms 'European Communities' and 'European Union'

A brief mention needs to be made here in respect of the terms 'European Union' and 'European Community' because their use can be confusing. The term 'European Union' was brought in by the Treaty on European Union (TEU, which is also known and referred to as the Maastricht Treaty—just to make matters more complicated!), and describes the extension by the member states into additional policies and areas of cooperation. Even though the Lisbon Treaty, following its amendment of the European Community (EC) and EU Treaties, has now established definitively that the EU be known exactly as that, this was not always the case, and whilst the history and development sections that follow make this clear, it is nevertheless useful now to outline the previous terms used, as you will come across them. Prior to the changes brought about by the TEU, three original Com-munities existed: the European Coal and Steel Community (ECSC), the European Economic Community (EEC), and the European Atomic Energy Community (EURATOM). The TEU brought these together under one so-called 'pillar' and renamed the EEC Treaty simply as the European Community (EC) Treaty. It also added two further pillars, dealing with Com-mon Foreign and Security Policy (CFSP) and Provisions on Police and Judicial Cooperation in Criminal Matters. Note that the ECSC has now expired and no longer exists and the organisation in three pillars, which was often illustrated in the form of a classical Greek temple, has now been abandoned.

》 CROSS REFERENCE

We will come back to the discussion about why the Communities evolved in this way in section 1.5.8.

When the Lisbon Treaty came into force on 1 December 2009, the term 'Community' was re-placed by the term 'Union' and it is now correct to refer only to the EU. Most EU law courses, and indeed books, did not consider matters previously in the old second and third pillars in any depth, if at all. Following the Lisbon Treaty, the three-pillar structure was broken up. CFSP has been retained in the EU Treaty, and freedom, security, and justice matters, which were in the third pillar, are now organised in a Title of the Treaty on the Functioning of the EU (TFEU). Hence, for the most part, the term 'Community' has been replaced by 'Union' in this book, except where the context demands otherwise. It remains to be seen whether EU law courses will be expanded to incorporate freedom, security, and justice matters.

1.1 Why was the Union set up? The motives for European integration

This section will go through the various factors that combined to persuade at first two European states, and then six, to enter into the process of European integration.

1.1.1 Reaction to the World Wars: the desire for peace

Even a cursory glance at European history will reveal just how long Europeans have been fighting and killing each other. The ultimate in the series of wars was, of course, the Second World War, in which some 55 million souls worldwide, but mostly in Europe and on the Russian front, lost their lives. There have been centuries of invasions, occupations, and dictatorial rule in most, if not all, of the countries of Europe at some stage. With this firmly in mind, it should come as no surprise that the very strong reaction after the Second World War to this death and destruction was a very important and motivating factor in the moves to create a more peaceful and stable European environment in which countries could develop and prosper without resorting to the obliteration or subjugation of others. It is all too easy, in this period of relative European peace and stability now, to understate this motive. Of course, there are reasons underlying the violence, and featuring large is the desire to unify Europe, and, in pursuit of this goal, for one country or ethnic group to impose its culture, often including language or religion or government, on others. Unfortunately, most of these attempts have not been peaceful and, over the ages, these attempts have affected the majority of the citizens of Europe. Generally, the attempts to unite, from the Romans to the Second World War, have led to wholesale loss of life, even attempted genocide and that ghastly modern euphemism for the same, 'ethnic cleansing'. It is therefore this bleak, but simple and understandable backdrop that led to an increased desire to do something to stop the cycle of wars that caused so much death and destruction. Whilst, over the centuries, there had been ideas and discussions to unite European nations, particularly following the First World War, it was only after the Second World War that these desires and expressions found substantive fruition.

For more details on this section visit the online resources.

1.1.2 Security against the rising Soviet threat

At the time, a further and developing factor that considerably influenced the desire on the part of the European nations to cooperate was the deteriorating relations between the former Allied powers. It was not long after the Americans, British, and Russians had met victoriously in the streets of Berlin in 1945 that the understandings between those countries broke down and they became increasingly suspicious of each other. UK Prime Minister and war premier Winston Churchill described in March 1946 in Fulton, Missouri, the situation of increasing Soviet influence and control

For more details on this section visit the online resources.

over Eastern Europe, in a borrowed phrase that was taken up generally, as a kind of 'Iron Curtain' that had descended between Western and Eastern Europe. This led in 1949 to the establishment of the North Atlantic Treaty Organisation (NATO) and to the Western EU in 1954, primarily for the defence of Europe against possible Soviet aggression.

The general situation came to be described as the 'Cold War' and lasted in lesser and greater states of tension until the collapse of Communism in Europe in 1989–90. With this increased fear of the possible expansion and domination of Europe by the Soviet Union, combined with the then existing Soviet strict control over the countries of Eastern Europe, the tension mounted in the late 1940s and throughout the 1950s. At its worst, in the 1960s, the Cold War threatened the nuclear annihilation of the opposing parties. It thus became increasingly important that the countries of Western Europe integrate among themselves to form a bulwark against further Soviet expansion. The Cold War was thus a clear and real catalyst for Western European integration.

1.1.3 Political willingness

The period following the Second World War saw a number of moves towards the integration of European nation states. Political and economic cooperation and development between nations was regarded as crucial to replace the economic competition that was viewed as a major factor in the outbreak of wars between European nation states. Some of these moves were taking place within a worldwide effort for greater political cooperation between nation states, the most notable being the establishment of the United Nations (UN) in 1945 and the Council of Europe in 1949.

1.1.4 Economic development

There were also inherently economically motivated steps towards international cooperation that resulted in the establishment of such organisations as the International Monetary Fund (IMF), the General Agreement on Tariffs and Trade (GATT), and, most notably, in 1947, the Marshall Plan, which funded the establishment of the Committee of European Economic Cooperation (CEEC) and the Organization for European Economic Cooporation (OEEC), which later became the Organisation for Economic Co-operation and Development (OECD), designed initially to distribute the finance for the post-war reconstruction of Europe.

1.1.5 Summary of underlying motives and initial goals

For more details on this section visit the online resources.

When we come to the three European Communities, which were the forerunners of the EU that we have today, the ultimate goals are not so distinctly discernible. As remains the case today, even before the foundation of the Communities, there was a conflict of opinion between those who wished to see European integration take the form of a much more involved model, such as a federal model, and those who wished merely to see a purely economic form of integration, such as a free-trade area. The first steps were, predictably, a compromise between the political, economic, and social desires of various parties. The scene was set by the address by Winston Churchill at the University of Zurich in September 1946, with his call to build 'a kind of United States of Europe' and in particular the brave (for the time) call for a partnership between France and Germany. However, even within that speech, Churchill and the UK did not envisage a role as a key participant and instead saw the UK as being outside any general European integration, alongside the United States and Russia, observing and assisting the rise of a European state from the ashes of the destruction of the Second World War.

》 CROSS REFERENCE

A longer look at the relationship between the UK and the EU will be taken in section 1.6.

These motives, which were the catalyst for European integration and the creation of the EU, find themselves reflected in the reasons given for the award to the EU of the Nobel Prize for peace in 2012. The individual reasons are referred to further in the text following.

1.2 The founding of the European Communities

This section looks at the mechanics of how the Communities and the Union were established.

1.2.1 The Schuman Plan (1950)

The climate was certainly ready for a greater form of integration in Europe, and the first direct impetus for the Communities came in the form of the plan proposed in May 1950 by the French Foreign Minister, Robert Schuman, in conjunction with the research and plans of Jean Monnet, a French government official. They proposed the linking of the French and German coal and steel industries, which would be taken out of the hands of the nation states and put under the control of a supranational body. This would not only help economic recovery, but would also remove the disastrous competition between the two states. It aimed to make future war not only unthinkable, but also materially impossible, because it put control over coal and steel production—vital then for the production of armaments and thus the capability of waging war—in the hands of a supranational authority, and not the individual states. The plan was deliberately left open for other European countries to join in its discussions. The UK, however, was reluctant to involve itself, even in the negotiations, although it did send observers. The plan was readily accepted by Germany under Chancellor Adenauer, which reconciliation of France and Germany after the Second World War is the first of the five achievements of the EU which was cited as justifying the award of the Nobel Peace Prize in 2012. Belgium, the Netherlands, and Luxembourg, which form the Benelux nations, had already moved ahead with their customs union and also saw the benefits to be gained from membership and this form of integration. Italy also considered it to be in its economic interest to join and, perhaps more importantly, considered it to be a resistance to further Communist gains in the state. Therefore, six nations went ahead to sign the European Coal and Steel Community (ECSC) Treaty in Paris in 1951, which entered into force on 1 January 1952. This first form of integration was thus both politically and economically motivated.

1.2.2 The European Coal and Steel Community

The ECSC Treaty was a mix of both intergovernmental and supranational integration, as the institutions set up included both the High Authority (which was later renamed the 'European Commission' by the 1965 Merger Treaty), a supranational body, and the Council of Ministers from the member states—an essentially intergovernmental body. Whilst the Community as established did not fulfil all the wishes of Jean Monnet, who was a federalist, he was appointed the first President of the High Authority. The degree of integration that it achieved was, without any doubt, a very important and indispensable first step from which further integration could follow. Indeed, it was assumed by some—the so-called neofunctionalists—that further integration would be inevitable, as successful integration in one area was assumed to spill over into other areas of integration. The ECSC Treaty expired in 2002, but its enduring tasks and commitments were assumed by the EC Treaty and eventually by the TFEU.

1.2.3 The proposed European Defence Community and European Political Community

The Schuman Plan, which formed the basis of the ECSC, was not the only proposal for integration being discussed and negotiated at the time. Monnet also put forward a proposal (the 'Pleven

> **CROSS REFERENCE**
> Customs unions are defined in Chapter 10, section 10.2.2.

> **CROSS REFERENCE**
> Intergovernmentalism, supranationalism, and federalism are defined at section 1.3.1.1.

For more details on this section visit the online resources.

Plan') for a European Defence Community (EDC) in 1952. In addition, because it was argued to be politically and practically necessary, in support of the EDC, a European Political Community (EPC) was also proposed in 1953, to provide overseeing political control and foreign policy for the EDC. The proposals and the negotiations proved to be complex and were drawn out because they were surrounded by other political considerations such as the expansion of Communism in South-east Asia and fears in respect of the rearmament of West Germany. Both of these proposals, with hindsight, were premature and far too ambitious for the time. They faced opposition from outside the ECSC—from the UK in particular—and from within the Community, most notably and fundamentally France, which, after some prevarication, failed to ratify the EDC in the National Assembly. Even today, the prospect of a common European army and political union is very radical; then, it was probably just unrealistic. Having said that, the other five countries had approved both proposals.

1.2.4 Progress to the EEC and EURATOM Treaties

It might have been thought that the unfortunate failure to agree the EDC would have put paid to any further attempts at European integration, and it was without doubt a blow to the European federalists. However, rather than jeopardise any such attempts, it appeared to strengthen the resolve of some of the original six member states to take matters further. Once again, Jean Monnet was centrally involved. He had resigned as President of the ECSC High Authority in order to promote European integration. Working in particular with the Benelux nations, it was proposed that rather than leave the integration to two industries, the nations should integrate the many more aspects of their economies. Thus, following the Messina Intergovernmental Conference (IGC) in 1955, the Spaak Report (named after the former Belgian Prime Minister and Foreign Minister at the time of the report) was prepared to consider the establishment of an Economic Community and an Atomic Energy Community for energy and the peaceful use of nuclear power. There were also additional external catalysts for further integration, including the Algerian war of independence, the Soviet suppression of the 1956 Hungarian Uprising, and the Suez Canal invasion by France and the UK. This last event served to highlight the real politics at play in the world in the 1950s and the precarious position of individual nation states in Europe, which no longer wielded the influence that they had done prior to the Second World War. All of this assisted in bringing the European Treaty negotiations to a much quicker and more successful conclusion. Thus, in 1957, the Treaties of Rome were agreed by the same six nations establishing the EEC Treaty and the EURATOM Treaty. The latter is still in operation and remains a separate and distinct Community and Treaty.

At first, all three Communities each had their own institutions, but shared a Court of Justice (CoJ) and the Parliamentary Assembly. The separate institutions were later merged under the Treaty, establishing a single Council and a single Commission of the European Communities (the Merger Treaty) in 1965, which entered into force in 1967 and the provisions of which have been incorporated into the present Treaties. Due to the range of subject matters and policies covered, the EEC Treaty was the most important.

> The ECSC Treaty, established for 50 years only, expired in 2002 and the EC Treaty (now TFEU) then took over the obligations and responsibilities arising under the ECSC Treaty, whereas the EURATOM Treaty remains in force. It is assumed that the UK will also exit from this Treaty in March 2019 if both the plans and timetable for exit remain the same.

1.3 The basic objectives and nature of the Communities

1.3.1 Was there an ultimate federal goal for the Union?

With the initial three Treaties established, what the Communities were intended to do and how they were supposed to function should be considered. The formal aims of the Communities can readily be seen by looking at the preambles to the original Treaties. The stated general aims included the creation of the Common Market, which was to be achieved by abolishing obstacles to the freedom of movement of all of the factors of production: namely, goods, workers, providers of services, and capital. The EEC Treaty also provided for the abolition of customs duties between the member states and the application of a common customs tariff to imports from third countries. There were to be common policies in the spheres of agriculture and transport, and a system ensuring that competition in the Common Market was not distorted by the activities of cartels or market monopolists. A limited start was also made with a social policy and a regional policy. Apart from these formally set-out objectives, there has been a debate older than the Communities themselves as to whether there was a grand plan for the integration of Europe. Even if it was not originally clear that the 'pooling of resources', as then termed, by a transfer of sovereign powers meant that the Communities took over in certain agreed areas, this was made clear not long afterwards by the CoJ in its landmark decisions in *Van Gend en Loos* and *Costa* v *ENEL*.

▶ CROSS REFERENCE

These cases are fully explored in Chapter 5, section 5.1.1.

At this stage, some terms of integration need to be considered.

1.3.1.1 Intergovernmentalism, supranationalism, and federalism

The terms **intergovernmentalism**, **supranationalism**, and **federalism** are employed to describe the forms of integration.

---

intergovernmentalism

This is the normal way in which international organisations work, the decisions of which require unanimity and are rarely enforceable, and if so only between the signatory states and not the citizens of those states. The clearest examples are the UN or the World Trade Organization (WTO).

supranationalism

This describes the fact that the decision-making takes place at a new and higher level than that of the member states themselves and that such decisions replace or override national rules.

federalism

This is a flexible term in that it can refer to a fairly wide band of integration models, but essentially, for the purposes of this discussion, it is used to mean that there will also be a form of political integration whereby the constituent states transfer sovereign powers to the federation, which will control the activities of the members from the centre. There are plenty of examples of states set up on a federal basis in the world, including the United States, Germany, Canada, Australia, Switzerland, and Belgium. Certain local issues are still regulated by the constituent states, such as education, culture, and land management, but most economic and political power is transferred to the centre, including, most notably, defence and trade.

 THINKING POINT

What relevance do these terms have in the discussion on the 'Future of Europe'?

1.3.1.2 **Integration in the Communities and EU**

A debate continues as to whether the Communities were supposed to integrate only in the specific areas as originally set out in the ECSC and EEC Treaties and arguably confined largely to free trade, or whether something more dynamic was intended. It was originally considered that because there was success in certain policies, this would automatically lead to a spill-over from one area to another, thus bringing about increasing integration. This is termed 'functional integration' or 'neofunctionalism'. Others have described this as 'creeping federalism'. In fact, it was considered that, in order for the original policies to work properly, there had to be continuing integration, otherwise the whole project would probably first stagnate and then roll backwards to collapse. Thus, sector-by-sector integration and the process of European union was regarded as an inevitable process.

For example, the setting of common trade tariffs and the establishment of the Common Market for the free circulation of goods would require and lead to exchange rates being stabilised to ensure that production factors and costs in the member states were broadly equal. This in turn requires monetary union to be established to ensure that exchange rates do not drift apart, and this requires full economic union to be achieved so that the value of different components of the common currency is not changed by different economic and fiscal policies in different countries. Clearly, then, the fiscal policies must be integrated, and this economic integration would require that political integration would have to follow in order to provide stable and consistent policy control over the economic conditions applying in the Union. The difficulties experienced by Greece and the Eurozone from 2010 onwards and the attempts to impose stricter financial and economic rules—in other words political control over them—in 2011–14 highlight this aspect.

According to this view, federalism, in some form, would thus seem to be the probable outcome of this process. Such an outcome, however, is a highly contested one. Only a few persons have argued openly for this degree of integration, although some of the founding fathers of the Community— Monnet, Schuman, and Spaak—had expected that sector-by-sector functional integration would lead slowly to ever greater degrees of federalism. It is also arguable that an agenda of federalism has been buried under the euphemisms 'a closer' or 'ever closer' Union, which are terms that have been used in the EEC Treaty (which became the EC Treaty in 1993) and in the TEU, in order to make the progress to the ultimate destination of the Communities and Union more acceptable, although it is unclear, and arguably deliberately so, whether they refer to federalism or something short of that. The TEU, as amended by the Lisbon Treaty, carries on in this vein by using the words 'continue the process of creating an ever closer Union'. In 2013, David Cameron, the UK Prime Minister, proposed that the removal of this term might be one of the matters he would raise in any possible re-negotiation of UK membership, although he would, of course, have to get the agreement of 27 other member states to secure that.

It shows, however, the highly political nature of the concerns and debate. The original plans put forward by Monnet for the ECSC may have been much more federal in nature and openly so, particularly as the Community was to be governed by a supranational High Authority only, but it was at the insistence of the member states that the original ECSC Treaty established a Council of Ministers, clearly intergovernmental, and a Parliamentary Assembly of member state representatives. This mixed model was followed in both the EURATOM and EEC Treaties. Therefore, while the Communities and some of its institutions do operate on the supranational level, it does not signify an inevitable move to federalism.

❱ **CROSS REFERENCE**

For the latest on this issue, see the discussion on the UK EU in/out referendum in section 1.6.6.

❱ **CROSS REFERENCE**

This topic is considered further in the end-of-chapter Summary after the developments to date have been outlined.

Increasingly, as none of the terms defined above individually fits the EU, the term 'multilevel governance' is used, which essentially acknowledges the complexity in the EU in that the degree of integration and the decision-making process varies according to the particular policy pursued with a number of different means existing side by side. It includes not only the EU member states and institutions in this form of governance, but also all participants that influence decision- and law-making in the EU including, notably, all the pressure and lobbying groups and international organisations. Whether it is any more helpful in summarising or describing the EU is difficult to say.

Despite the failure of the EDC and EPC, the ECSC remained successful and was complemented in 1957 by the other two Communities. The EEC proved immediately to be a success under the leadership of the first EEC Commission President, the German Walter Hallstein, and it was far more political in outlook and operation—despite the contrary view of de Gaulle—as to how the Communities were and should be organised and governed. The success of the EEC seemed to give support to the neofunctionalist view that success in one sector would lead inevitably to success in other sectors and assist the process of European integration. Indeed, the success in the area of the common customs tariff appeared to work as envisaged by the neofunctionalists/federalists and led to spill-over into other areas, and in particular to further pressure for the reform of the Common Agricultural Policy (CAP). This form of functionalism was adopted deliberately by the High Authority and later the EEC Commission as the way in which to achieve further progress with European integration in the manner by which these bodies put forward linked package reforms for the Communities. Since then, the Communities and Union have moved on with numerous Treaty revisions, which are highlighted in section 1.4.

The agreed decision by the member states in June 2007 at the Brussels European Council Summit to abandon the Constitutional Treaty (CT) and to replace it by a Reform Treaty, which is argued to be far less supranational in nature, may be seen as providing a clear and deliberate halt to progress to a federal Europe, although that too could change in time. The Brussels Summit and the Lisbon Treaty are considered in section 1.5.13.

Furthermore, it appears that, as more states join, there may be more resistance to deeper integration, with some states actually calling for a rolling back of the degree of integration already achieved in view of Brexit and the more widespread Euroscepticism today.

1.4 Developments following the original Treaties

The member states made considerable progress under the original Treaties and the Communities were very successful in achieving the aims set out and promoting economic growth in the member states, in contrast with countries such as the UK. The dismantling of customs duties was achieved by the original six member states, and the Common Market for the free movement of goods was largely achieved ahead of the target year of 1969, set down in the EEC Treaty. Additionally, competition policy and the CAP—successful in terms of guaranteeing production, but the object of criticism ever since because its price-support mechanisms have generated overproduction—are both regarded as successes. However, the Communities did not expand until 1973, nor integrate any further until 1986, much of which was to do with the rejection by de Gaulle of the UK

For more details on this section visit the online resources.

▶ **CROSS REFERENCE**

The Luxembourg Accords are considered under section 1.5.2.

applications and the national veto established under the Luxembourg Accords. However, in 1969, a fresh start for the Communities appeared to take place. Whilst in itself it did not lead to massive or immediate change, it did allow for a new agenda for change.

The member states held a summit in The Hague in 1969 to try to get the Communities moving again, which set as its goals the completion, widening, and deepening of the Communities. Although the completion of the Common Market, which should have been fully achieved by 1969, took considerably longer and actually had to wait until 1992, the widening and deepening of the Communities were processes always intended to be ongoing. The terms **widening** and **deepening** are those used then and they still survive in Community and EU jargon to describe developments in two ways.

---

deepening

This term refers to the degree of integration in terms of how integration takes place. By this is meant the extent to which integration is intergovernmental or supranational, but deepening can also apply to integration in new policy areas because it would consider the extent to which the Communities have encroached into previously exclusively held areas of the member states' competences.

widening

This term refers primarily to the process of the expansion to include new member states, but can also apply to the extension into new policy areas and in developing new sectors for integration.

To some extent, the terms are overlapping; and the same development, it can be argued, fits into both categories. At a fairly simple level, however, they refer in turn to the quantitative and qualitative changes over the years.

1.4.1 The widening of the Communities

The original founding member states—Belgium, France, West Germany, Italy, Luxembourg, and the Netherlands—remained the only six member states from 1952 to 1973.

- 1973—first expansion of members: Denmark, Ireland, and the UK
- 1981 and 1986—second expansion: Greece, Portugal, and Spain
- 1990—due to the reunification of Germany, East Germany is assimilated
- 1995—expansion: Austria, Finland, and Sweden
- 2004—expansion: Cyprus, the Czech Republic, Estonia, Hungary, Latvia, Lithuania, Malta, Poland, Slovakia, and Slovenia
- 2007—expansion: Bulgaria and Romania
- 2013—expansion: Croatia

1.4.1.1 First expansion

The Paris IGC of 1972 finally paved the way for the first expansion of the member states, which took place in 1973, when the UK, Ireland, and Denmark joined. Two earlier attempts by the UK, Denmark, and Ireland to join were thwarted by de Gaulle's veto of UK entry.

▶ **CROSS REFERENCE**

UK entry attempts are considered in brief in section 1.6 below.

Norway was also to have joined at this time, but a referendum of the Norwegian electorate on the eve of membership resulted in a majority against and Norway failed to become a member—not for the last time!

1.4.1.2 Second expansion

The second expansion actually consisted of two smaller expansions spread over five years, when Greece joined in 1981 and, after protracted periods of negotiation, Spain and Portugal entered in 1986. None of these three countries were economically in a strong position in relation to the existing member states, and in view of this all were regarded by some as unfit for membership. Politically, however, their acceptance into the Communities was regarded as crucial to support the recently emerged democracies in all of these countries after varying periods of authoritarian or dictatorial right-wing rule, and further, to act as a counter force to any possible violent reaction to the Left and possible establishment of governments sympathetic to Moscow. The Cold War still featured prominently in this period of history; hence, entry was facilitated sooner than economic conditions might have permitted. Indeed, this support for new democracies in Greece, Portugal, and Spain in the 1980s is the second of the five achievements of the EU that was cited as justifying the award of the 2012 Nobel Peace Prize.

> Note that, in 1985, Greenland withdrew from the EC after a consultative referendum. As part of the Danish realm, Greenland had become a member of the EC when Denmark joined. After being granted home rule, Greenland opted to leave the EC.

1.4.1.3 East Germany is assimilated

A smaller automatic expansion took place in 1990, with the reunification of West and East Germany as the first concrete change to result from the fall of the Communist regimes in the Soviet Union and Eastern European countries.

> This automatic assimilation of a previously independent country results from the separation of the single-state Germany after the Second World War and the view that East Germany was not a new member state, but that the areas in the former German Democratic Republic simply became part of a larger Federal Republic of Germany and thus automatically a part of the Communities.

1.4.1.4 Setting terms for future expansions

The German mini-expansion awakened the Communities to the possibility of a number of the former Eastern European states seeking membership and prompted a longer-term evaluation of the conditions required of aspirant member states. This led to criteria being agreed at the Copenhagen Summit in June 1993, which outlined the requirements for new members. These included the need for stable government and institutions guaranteeing democracy, the rule of law, human rights, and the protection of minorities. Economically, applicant states would need to have a functioning market economy and the ability to cope with life in the single market. The applicants would have to accept the *acquis communautaire* in its entirety, including the overall political, economic, social, and monetary aims of the Union, such as eventual adoption of the euro; no easy task, even for the existing member states at that time.

> **acquis communautaire**
> The term given to describe the accumulated body of Community and Union law, including treaties, secondary legislation, and judicial developments.

The next and fourth enlargement took place sooner than expected as a result of the changes in Eastern Europe and the economic success facilitated by the Single European Act (SEA).

1.4.1.5 The European Economic Area (EEA)

After observing, in the late 1980s, the economic benefits of the SEA enjoyed by the member states of the Communities, other European states, most of which had cooperation or association agreements with the Communities and were members of the European Free Trade Association (EFTA), started to make overtures to the Communities for greater cooperation and some for possible membership. Initially, further expansion was not favoured by the Commission, because it was thought that it would stifle plans for deeper integration of the then existing member states, in particular progress on the single market and possible further progress to monetary union. Additionally, prior to the collapse of Communism in Europe in the late 1980s, some of the EFTA member states were uncertain for various reasons, including their neutrality and post-Second World War constitutional position, whether full membership was politically feasible or possible. Therefore, a lesser form of integration was proposed by the European Commission, in which the participants could benefit from the advantages of the single market and the competition policy, but not be involved in the other economic or political aspects of the Communities, including decision-making. This offer was open to all of the then existing members of EFTA. However, the negotiations for this new form of cooperation were very drawn out and subject to considerable delays. They were also taking place against the backdrop of the collapse of Communism in Eastern Europe.

One of the consequences of this was that the previous objections or difficulties that might be raised by Eastern Bloc countries and the Soviet Union in particular—that full Community membership of militarily neutral countries, such as Austria, Finland, and Sweden, would not be compatible with their status as neutral countries—were effectively resolved and disappeared. It is to be noted that the neutral state Ireland was already a member.

In October 1991, the EFTA member states—Austria, Finland, Iceland, Liechtenstein, Norway, Sweden, and Switzerland—signed an agreement with the EEC on the creation of the EEA. The agreement reached was that the EFTA members were not represented in the Community institutions and would take no part in the decision-making processes of the Community. They would be subject to all Community law relating to the single market, as defined by the CoJ. However, an additional problem was encountered whilst negotiations were being finalised and shortly before the Treaty was to come into force on 1 January 1993. The Swiss electorate rejected membership of the EEA in a referendum in December 1992, which caused considerable political and legal difficulties because Liechtenstein, with which Switzerland has a monetary union, had agreed to join. Without Switzerland, the remaining six EFTA states went on to sign and ratify the agreement, which came into force on 1 July 1993. It was soon clear, however, that, as far as business confidence was concerned, full membership of the EU was the status that attracted investment, and not membership of the EEA. Indeed, both the concept and the consequences of the EEA might not, in any case, have been fully understood by outside interests. Hence, almost before the ink had dried on the signatures to the EEA Treaty, Austria, Finland, Norway, and Sweden applied for full membership of the EC.

1.4.1.6 **The 1995 expansion**

In view of the fact that most of the bargaining had already been done for the EEA, entry terms were easily and rapidly decided and the four applications were quickly accepted. On 1 January 1995, therefore, the Union was joined by Austria, Finland, and Sweden, bringing the number of member states to 15. This is sometimes referred to as the Scandinavian expansion, although, of course, Austria is some way from Scandinavia. The Norwegian electorate, however, once again chose to reject membership in a referendum in December 1994 and Norway again failed to join the Communities. The entry of the three former EFTA members meant that the remaining EFTA states—Iceland, Norway, and Liechtenstein—were now the only remaining EFTA members of the EEA. Following the economic crisis of 2008–09 and its economic near-collapse, Iceland made a membership application and commenced entrance negotiations in July 2010. The other two EEA states do not have membership applications pending. Switzerland remains outside both the EC and the EEA. Its application for full membership, lodged in 1992, was put on hold following the EEA rejection. A special series of bilateral agreements have been negotiated with Switzerland instead, covering many, if not most, of the aspects of the EEA.

1.4.1.7 The 2004 expansion

The expansion that took place on 1 May 2004 was the largest in the history of the EU, and 10 new states joined in one go, comprising Cyprus, the Czech Republic, Estonia, Hungary, Latvia, Lithuania, Malta, Poland, Slovakia, and Slovenia. The overall time taken to resolve terms of entry was surprisingly quick considering the number of states involved and their differing economic and social circumstances. The haste was fuelled by the political events unfolding in the world, in particular by the break-up of the Soviet Union and the bloody fragmentation of the former Communist state of Yugoslavia. The 10 new countries were thus brought into the fold much more quickly than economic conditions alone would have allowed owing to the political desire to lock these countries into a Western liberal democratic club of nations, and fears again that not doing so would create conditions of political unrest and possible rise of extreme Left or Right movements in any countries not accepted for a number of years. Support for former Communist states in the 1990s is the third of the five achievements of the EU that was cited as justifying the award of the 2012 Nobel Peace Prize. The accession agreements with all of the member states were concluded and the entry terms settled for the Treaty of Accession, which was signed in Athens on 16 April 2003. The 10 new member states duly joined on 1 May 2004.

1.4.1.8 The 2007 expansion

In September 2006, the EU Commission expressed its view that Bulgaria and Romania were ready for accession, as originally planned in the Accession Treaty concluded in April 2005. Entry into the Union of these two countries took place on 1 January 2007, once again with similar concerns that entry was economically premature but politically justified.

1.4.1.9 Croatian entry 2013

Croatia joined the EU on 1 July 2013, an accession process that included some postponement of negotiations caused by the failure to cooperate with the UN Balkans War Crimes Tribunal in handing over a suspected war criminal. With this apparently overcome, negotiations were concluded and Croatia joined the EU as planned, but just three days before entry amended the law on the European Arrest Warrant effectively to give immunity from prosecution to an ex-secret police chief and 20 others suspected of an assassination in Germany. Following the threat of EU financial sanctions, the law was subsequently removed and Perkovic was extradited to Germany in January 2014.

1.4.1.10 Future expansion

At present, five countries are official candidate states: Turkey, Albania, the former Yugoslav Republic of Macedonia, Montenegro, and Serbia. There are two potential candidate countries: Bosnia and Herzogovina, and Kosovo but progress is understandably slow, particularly with Brexit occupying so much of the time and work of the Commission.

For more details on this section visit the online resources.

With regard to Turkey, a candidate country since 1999, the Commission recommended on 6 October 2004 that the EU should open entry negotiations; in December 2004 the Brussels European Council Summit approved this position and negotiations were started on 3 October 2005. Without doubt, these negotiations will be the most controversial in the history of the Union. The difficulties are the recognition and reunification of Cyprus, the predominantly Muslim population of Turkey, the human rights record of Turkey, and the fact that, quite simply, geographically, most of the Turkish land mass lies in Asia and not in Europe. Its economic situation is also regarded as problematic; however, it may be argued that the entry of Turkey is exactly what the EU should come to terms with to create a multi-ethnic, multicultural, and multi-religious Union. The support for the modernisation of Turkey is the fourth of the five achievements of the EU that was cited as justifying the award of the 2012 Nobel Peace Prize. Negotiations on 15 **chapters** were taking place, plus one which was provisionally completed, but further progress was stalled due to Turkey's restriction on trade with Cyprus and failure to fully implement the Additional Protocol to the Ankara Association Agreement. As a consequence of the European refugee crisis in the second half of 2015, Turkey's humanitarian aid for Syrian refugees, and renewed support for talks on Cyprus, negotiations recommenced with a cautious approach to opening new chapters but no further chapters will be closed, and with no fixed timetable for overall completion, negotiations may still take many years. Political developments and mass arrests in Turkey in 2016 and 2017 and the possibility of the introduction of the death penalty cast further doubt on any progress being made for the foreseeable future, and indeed are likely to end Turkey's bid for membership.

For more details on this section visit the online resources.

> **chapter** The name given to each of the various policy areas covered by the Treaties with which Turkey (or another candidate state) must fully conform before it can be accepted for membership. There are about 35 chapters in total to be negotiated and closed.

Following the economic recession in 2008–9, Iceland, already a member of the EEA, made an application in July 2009 for full membership of the EU. It was envisaged that a fast-track negotiation might take place in view of the existing conformity of Iceland with the EU through EEA membership; however, the now more favourable economic conditions, and a change of government has halted this. In March 2015, Iceland requested that it should not be regarded as a candidate country and that is where it remains at the end of 2017.

The Former Yugoslav Republic of Macedonia made an application to join in March 2004, and was considered as of 17 December 2005 to be a candidate country. Entry negotiations were recommended by the Commission in 2009, but have not yet commenced, which remains the case up to the end of 2017. Internal political difficulties, concerns about press and speech freedom, and the country's name are three matters causing concern and preventing formal progress with accession.

Montenegro applied for membership in 2009 and was granted candidate status in December 2010. Access negotiations commenced in June 2012 with, at the time of writing, two chapters provisionally closed, and another 22 in progress. Serbia was granted candidate status on 1 March 2012 and membership negotiations commenced in January 2014, with eight chapters open, of which two were provisionally closed. Peace-building in the Western Balkans is the final of the five achievements of the EU that was cited as justifying the award of the 2012 Nobel Peace Prize. Albania was added as a candidate status country in June 2014. As to other possible members, there are the remaining Balkan states, presently considered to be potential candidate countries, as well as the possibility in the future for the states of the former Soviet Union that border the EU. The countries of Bosnia and Herzegovina and Kosovo have been formally recognised by the EU as those eligible for future EU membership, but only if they prove themselves to the satisfaction of the EU and existing member states to be fit for membership. One or two other countries have previously made applications, but have either withdrawn these or put them on hold. Norway has twice concluded entry negotiations, only for entry to be rejected by the Norwegian electorate at the eleventh hour. At present it has no application pending, but the possibility of future membership remains high on the political agenda, with opinion polls showing a majority of Norwegians in favour of full membership.

The rejection by the Swiss of membership of the EEA in 1992 also led to the suspension of its application for full membership. Even though Swiss governments have expressed the view that Switzerland will eventually apply for full membership, that aim was severely dented, at least for a few years, by the categorical rejection by the Swiss electorate of EU membership negotiations in a private initiative referendum in March 2001 when 77 per cent of those voting said 'No'. This has subsequently been followed up by a second referendum negative to the EU in 2014 in which the Swiss voted to restrict Croatian migrant entry and to control immigration generally, including that from the EU, despite the fact that there was a free movement of persons' agreement with the EU. This has led to the suspension of certain EU programmes that were also open to Switzerland. Therefore, there are presently no plans to revive the dormant application by Switzerland, although significant governmental and other elements consider membership of the EU to be necessary, and indeed inevitable, if not immediately, then at some stage in the future.

1.4.1.11 The future of enlargement

The fact that the EU is conducting accession negotiations with Turkey invites a final consideration in respect of further widening and enlargement: what is the limit? The answer to this is as much driven by the answer to the question 'What is Europe—politically and geographically?' Two Mediterranean island states have already pushed the geographical border of the EU further: Cyprus lies closer to the Middle East and is nearer to Asia than Europe, and Malta is not much further away from Africa than it is from other parts of Europe. Indeed, there are existing parts of some member states that are clearly beyond any usual definition of Europe. The Canaries (Spain) lie off the west coast of Africa, French Guyana is completely in another continent in South America, the Azores and Madeira (Portugal) are in the Atlantic, and the French islands of Guadeloupe, Martinique, and Reunion lie in the Caribbean. Greenland was part of the EU until it was granted home rule from Denmark in 1979 and left the EU in 1982.

In fact, there are not many European states left to apply, depending on the definition of 'Europe': only Norway, Liechtenstein, the smaller states of Andorra and Monaco, and perhaps parts of the former Soviet Union, such as the Ukraine, Belarus, and Moldova, some of which are deliberately pursuing pro-European policies.

An application by Morocco in 1987 to join was rejected on the geographical ground that Morocco was in Africa and could not be considered as being Europe. There is now also perhaps the more focused question of whether the present citizens of the EU want a bigger Europe. At the time of writing, there appears to be more reticence than support for further expansion, and the migration crises from 2015 only serve to increase that reticence.

THINKING POINT

Is there a finite country membership of the EU, and if so, what is that? If not, then how long can the EU expand?

1.4.1.12 Accession preconditions

Regardless of which state is a candidate, all existing and new member states are required to accept and adopt the entire body of EU law—that is, the *acquis communautaire*—which includes the Treaties, Protocols, Declarations, conventions, and agreements with third countries, secondary legislation, and the judgments of the CoJ. This requirement was previously noted under Article 2 TEU, but is now to be found indirectly in Article 20 TEU (post-Lisbon). Since the TEU, the criteria for membership have been much more clearly spelled out.

Article 49 TEU

Any European State that respects the principles set out in Article 2 and is committed to promoting them may apply to become a member of the Union.

The principles of Article 2 are human dignity, freedom, democracy, equality, the rule of law, and respect for human rights. In addition, potential member states will be required to satisfy a number of criteria provided at Copenhagen in 1993 that were established with the membership applications of the newly emergent democracies in Eastern Europe in mind. The criteria were essentially a refinement of previous practice. The 1999 Helsinki European Council Summit added a form of 'good neighbour' requirement for entrant states: that disputes with neighbouring countries be resolved before entry. It might have been a good idea, but the most visible case requiring the application of that policy was Cyprus; however, the Greek and Turkish parts of the island were not able to resolve fully their differences prior to the entry of Cyprus to the EU on 1 May 2004. Thus, although the whole island of Cyprus is in the EU, EU law is applied only in the southern, Greek half of the island, despite the fact that a referendum vote in Cyprus to reunite the island was approved by the Turkish side but rejected by the Greek Cypriot electorate. Note, though, that Turkish Cypriots are citizens of a member state—the Republic of Cyprus—even though they live in the northern part of Cyprus; therefore, their personal rights as EU citizens are not affected.

Potential border disputes existing between Estonia and Latvia and the Russian Federation were also not resolved prior to accession. The Helsinki Summit additionally marked a realisation that the Copenhagen criteria could not be strictly applied and that some flexibility had to be exercised. The Laeken European Council Summit in December 2001 also emphasised that membership was dependent on candidate countries ensuring that their judicial institutions were capable of meeting the requirements of EU membership. The applicability of the criteria for deciding whether an eligible candidate can become an admissible one was confirmed at the Copenhagen Summit, which took place in December 2002.

The good neighbour principle has now found Treaty expression in Article 8(1) TEU:

The Union shall develop a special relationship with neighbouring countries, aiming to establish an area of prosperity and good neighbourliness, founded on the values of the Union and characterised by close and peaceful relations based on cooperation.

1.5 The deepening of the Communities

This section charts the increasing degree of integration entered into by the member states, from the original Treaties establishing the Communities to the present position following the entry into force of the Lisbon Treaty in 2009.

For more details on this section visit the online resources.

1.5.1 **The primary Treaties**

The first and fundamental movement on the path of integration was, of course, the ECSC Treaty, now expired, which was soon followed by the agreement and ratification of the EEC and EURATOM Treaties by the original six member states. It was clear at the time of negotiation that a transfer of power was involved, particularly in the climate of the time and the clear federalist intentions of the main protagonists of the plan, Schuman and Monnet. The only amendments that were made to the primary Treaties for the first two decades were minor ones, brought about first by the decision to merge the institutions of the three Communities, and then by the Accession Treaties required for the new member states. Prior to the Merger Treaty of 1965, each of the Communities had its own Council and High Authority/Commission; however, the CoJ and the Parliamentary Assembly had both been shared by all three Communities from the outset. The merger of the institutions was a practical step to provide common coordination and to avoid the duplication of effort and resources. It was nothing more significant than that. The first Accession Treaties for Denmark, Ireland, and the UK dealt specifically with the details of accession of the new member states, or merely made the changes to the Treaties considered necessary for it to continue working in the same way as previously, but with adjustments to reflect the increase in member states and the composition of the institutions: for example, to Council voting numbers and to Commission, European Parliament (EP), and CoJ memberships. The fundamental constitutional core of the Communities and how they worked remained untouched until 1986.

1.5.2 The 1960s and the Luxembourg Accords

Initially, the Communities were very successful in achieving the aims set out and promoting economic growth in those member states, in contrast with slower economic growth in countries such as the UK. The dismantling of customs duties was achieved by the original six member states before the target date set down in the EEC Treaty. Additionally, competition policy was seen to be working and the CAP was clearly successful in terms of guaranteeing production. It was, however, the subject of criticism because its price-support mechanisms led over time to the massive overproduction and stockpiling of commodities such as butter, milk, sugar, and wine. These stockpiles cost the Community not only a great deal of money to dispose of, but also political ill-will in the world as developing world agricultural products had severely reduced chances of entering the heavily protected EC market.

However, following this initial period of success and achievement, any chance of either further expansion or deeper integration was stifled. The brake on such progress was applied most effectively to the Commission and the Communities in 1965 by de Gaulle, the French President, by a boycott of the institutions that caused lasting damage for decades. In 1965, the Commission proposed that the Communities move to a system of own resources and that the Council move to majority voting, which was no more than originally envisaged by the Treaty of Rome in 1957. It was further proposed that the Parliamentary Assembly should have some control over the expenditure of the Communities. These proposals were categorically opposed and vetoed by de Gaulle who, when the other member states were not opposed, adopted a policy of non-attendance at the Community institutions by the French representatives, which became known as the 'institutions boycott' or the 'empty chair policy'.

⟫ CROSS REFERENCE

Qualified majority voting (QMV) is also considered in Chapter 2, section 2.2.4.3.

The boycott of the EU institutions by French President de Gaulle was the way in which France objected to an increase in the Communities' own resources and powers.

All progress, indeed everything in the Communities, simply halted. The compromise agreement that broke the deadlock was the infamous Luxembourg Accords, in essence an 'agreement to disagree'. This basically provided that where the member states were not able to agree a proposal and where a vital national interest of any member state was at stake, that member state could finally veto the proposal in Council. There was no definition of a vital interest, and so member states were left to define a vital interest themselves.

> **'Majority Voting Procedure', Extract from the Luxembourg Accords (1966) 3 EEC Bulletin 9**
>
> (I)   Where, in the case of decisions which may be taken by majority vote on a proposal of the Commission, very important interests of one or more partners are at stake, the Members of the Council will endeavour, within a reasonable time, to reach solutions which can be adopted by all the Members of the Council while respecting their mutual interests and those of the Community, in accordance with Article 2 of the Treaty.
>
> (II)   With regard to the preceding paragraph, the French delegation considers that where very important interests are at stake the discussion must be continued until unanimous agreement is reached.
>
> (III) The six delegations note that there is a divergence of views on what should be done in the event of a failure to reach complete agreement.
>
> (IV) The six delegations nevertheless consider that this divergence does not prevent the Community's work being resumed in accordance with the normal procedure.

1.5.3 Stagnation and 'Eurosclerosis'

The whole unfortunate episode surrounding the Luxembourg Accords resulted in stagnation in the decision-making process for many years to come. It led to the long, slow, painful period of the Communities that has become known as the period of 'Eurosclerosis', and which lasted from 1966 until the early-to-mid-1980s. The basic problem was the near-inability of the member states to reach decisions on Community legislation, and widespread dissatisfaction at the slow pace at which the goals of the EEC were being achieved. Whilst much of the blame can be laid at the door of the French boycott and the Luxembourg Accords, the ability to reach decisions was made much more difficult by the doubling of member states between 1973 and 1986 to 12.

> In 1973, Denmark, Ireland, and the UK joined the Communities, followed in 1981 by Greece, and in 1986 by Spain and Portugal.

Trying to obtain the unanimous agreement of first six, then nine, then ten, and then all 12 members proved at times to be simply impossible. Among the main concerns were the time taken by the Community institutions to make new laws and the amount of work with which the Council was faced, partly because particular provisions were presented many times as the Commission made amendments to make them acceptable to all member states. A notorious example of this is Directive 85/384, which did nothing more controversial than harmonise the training requirements for architects, but which took the institutions 17 years to agree and finally enact. Further concerns related to the lack of representative democracy in the decision-making process of the Community and the delays experienced by litigants to the CoJ. It was clear to everyone that some change had to be brought about. Whilst it was true that some adjustments had been made in the form of amendments to the original Treaties, these were of a limited nature. More significant were the direct elections to the EP, which first took place in 1979 and the increase in its powers in the budgetary process by the Budgetary Treaties of 1970 and 1975. Otherwise, little further progress had been achieved in this period. However, before looking at the re-launch of the Communities, in the background the CoJ was going about its business of judging cases and, in doing so, laying down some extremely important principles of law.

1.5.4 The Court of Justice and integration

Whilst the Community institutions were busily going nowhere on the path to European integration, the CoJ appeared not to be affected by the 'Eurosclerosis' and had, from a very early date, adopted a very supranational tone in its judgments, including the far-reaching decisions on direct effects and supremacy in Case 26/62 *Van Gend en Loos* and Case 6/64 *Costa* v *ENEL*. These judgments contributed greatly not only to building a separate Community legal system, but also to enhancing the supranational status of the new European legal order and constitutionality of the Communities. A formal Constitution of or for the EU per se is not, though, something acknowledged by the member states, despite the view of the CoJ that the Treaties do in fact represent the constitutional basis expressed in Case 294/83 *Parti Ecologiste (Les Verts)* v *Parliament*.

▶ CROSS REFERENCE

This development and these cases will be fully considered in Chapters 5 and 8.

1.5.5 Revival attempts

In 1969, following the resignation of de Gaulle and the change in West Germany to a Social Democrat government, a summit of the heads of state and government was arranged in The Hague expressly to re-launch European integration. The 1969 Hague Summit established the system of EPC, but it was deliberately intergovernmental in nature and sat outside the formal Treaty set-up. As such, it can be regarded as another move away from supranationalism and the neofunctionalists' dream of progress on European integration. It was also unfortunate, but the reforms and the re-launching of the Communities envisaged at The Hague were severely disrupted by the world economic situation, which grew steadily worse in the early 1970s. The Middle East wars and ensuing oil crises led to very high inflation and stagnation in the world economies and to the unwinding of the first attempt at some sort of monetary union, the European Monetary Unit (EMU), which bound European currencies into a flexible relationship with each other.

The year 1973 also saw the entry of three new member states, two of which, the UK and Denmark, were even then the least federal-minded member states in the European Communities. There were nevertheless further attempts to revive the flagging fortunes of the Communities. A further summit in Paris in 1974 led to the formalisation of the previously informal European Council Summit meetings to provide an overriding political guide to the Communities. This, however, tended to further strengthen the intergovernmental hand of control over the Communities rather than to provoke deeper integration. The Paris Summit also, for the first time, allowed the Commission a role in the summitry, something pressed for by the new Commission President, Roy Jenkins. The Summit also made the decision that the EP should be directly elected as from 1978, although this could not take place until 1979 due to difficulties in the UK in preparing the legislation. Finally, the European Monetary System (EMS) was established in 1978, despite the collapse of the previous attempt (the EMU). The EMS proved to be stable and, with the establishment of the European Currency Unit (ECU), became the precursor to monetary union and the euro (€).

These limited successes, however, did little to counter the generally prevailing malaise that hung over the Communities and institutions. This was not helped by the attitude and activities of certain member states. When de Gaulle disappeared from the international scene in 1979, the new UK Prime Minister, Margaret Thatcher, appeared to take up the baton of intergovernmentalism and the bolstering of purely national interests. Whilst the UK may well have had a case in arguing for a more equitable budget contribution and neither Mrs Thatcher nor, indeed, anyone else has gone as far as de Gaulle in disrupting the work of the Communities, the negotiating style and public pronouncements of Thatcher were abrasive. These budget wrangles and the sheer lack of progress generally in the Community dragged on seemingly endlessly into the mid-1980s. The stagnation and intergovernmentalism not only thwarted any moves to more integration, but also engendered a period of national protectionism, which itself was threatening to undermine some of the basic goals of the European Communities already achieved. Notably, the Common Market was not being completed

⟫ CROSS REFERENCE

See section 1.6 for more on the relationship between the UK and the EU.

as envisaged and, if anything, was becoming more fragmented. The situation in the 1980s was that both the stagnation of the Communities and the lack of international competitiveness of Europe in relation to American and Japanese industrial and commercial progress had been clearly recognised. It was abundantly clear and understood that reform, and indeed radical reform, of the Community and institutions was necessary.

Numerous reports and studies were conducted by the different Community institutions and additionally many external reports had been commissioned over the years that had all recommended changes. A number of areas in which improvements were required had already been identified by those reports in the lifetime of the Communities. The fact that there were so many of these speaks volumes for their (in)effectiveness in tackling the deep-rooted problems of European stagnation. However, whilst individually they did not provide a solution, collectively all of them, especially the latter ones, helped finally to establish and develop the climate for the eventual changes brought about by Treaty change and in particular by the SEA, which led in turn to the TEU ('the Maastricht Treaty'), the Treaties of Amsterdam and Nice, and finally the 2009 Lisbon Treaty. In particular, these concerns were taken up by the new Commission President, Jacques Delors, who brought a package of reforms to the member states with the measures considered necessary for the completion of the single market. Whilst there remained opposition to any significant institutional changes recommended, especially by the UK, the single market completion was the carrot that brought the Eurosceptic governments on board, particularly the UK and Germany, as the proposals were hailed as a shining example of trade liberalisation. Although the other member states were undoubtedly also interested in the trade and economic aspects of the reforms proposed, the smaller states in particular had a greater desire to see the institutional reforms recommended. In 1985, a sufficient head of steam had built up for the member states to accept, albeit some reluctantly, that the necessary changes were ones that could effectively be undertaken only by substantively amending the founding Treaties.

1.5.6 The first Intergovernmental Conference (IGC) and the Single European Act (SEA)

Intergovernmental Conference

This is a conference of the member states outside the Treaty and Communities (now Union) set-up, which is established to discuss and agree Treaty change.

An **Intergovernmental Conference** took place in 1985 to discuss the decision-making of the Council of Ministers, the legislative powers of the EP, the executive power of the Commission, the policy areas of the Community, and the delays before the CoJ.

The SEA was the product of the IGC and came into force in May 1987. The preamble to the SEA states that it is 'a step towards European Union'. It amended the EEC Treaty in several important respects, perhaps most importantly changing the legislative process affecting some Treaty Articles and generally extending the Community's competence and concern in new policy areas.

The SEA is the first significant amendment of the primary Treaties. It is an important watershed in the historical development of the Communities and is not to be underestimated in its importance, although it was underestimated at the time, not only by external observers and commentators, but also by the heads of state and government who signed up to it. It is sometimes difficult to grasp its importance because it is the first of a series of package-deal changes to the Treaties that not only added new areas of competence, but also simultaneously made various institutional changes and policy amendments.

The SEA proposals that put the primary focus on market liberalisation were enthusiastically welcomed by the member states, but were linked to the institutional changes, and it is probably fair to say that the far-reaching political consequences of these were seriously downplayed by the EC Commission. Even its title underplays the significance of the matter: an 'Act' suggests something less than a new Treaty; it suggests secondary legislation rather than primary treaty material, which it is. So, in 1985, the draft SEA was put to and debated at the IGC. It was agreed by the 10 member states in December 1985 and came into force in July 1987, after signature and ratification by all 12 states.

Portugal and Spain had joined the Communities in January 1986, during this ratification process.

1.5.6.1 Achievements and evaluation of the SEA

Whilst the SEA had its critics and was condemned by some parties, its success lay not in what it actually changed, although there was considerable progress with the internal market; its true success lay in its longer-term influence in reinvigorating integration.

The SEA amended the EEC Treaty in several important respects, and although not massive changes in themselves, they proved to be a catalyst for further European integration. Perhaps most important was the change of the legislative process affecting 10 Treaty Articles and generally the extension of the Community's competence and concern in new policy areas. The SEA also introduced provisions that made it possible to make changes to the judicial structure in the future by supplementing the CoJ with a Court of First Instance (CFI), which was regarded as being vital to cope with the significant increases in the number of cases reaching the Court and the increased delay being caused as a result. The SEA also made formal the existence of the European Council of Heads of State and Government, which was originally established as the EPC. The SEA reintroduced and extended qualified majority voting (QMV) in the Council, introduced the cooperation procedure in law-making, which provided the EP with more than just a consultative role for the first time, and increased Commission powers.

▶ CROSS REFERENCE
All of these matters are further considered in Chapters 2 and 3.

It is certainly the case that the SEA did not represent a radical shift to supranational or federal integration. In contrast to the original Treaties, the member states were the ones constructing its agenda, and not the federalist visionaries of the immediate post-war period. Also, in view of the preceding 15–20 years, which had seen a complete standstill on any such progress, it is not surprising that the changes introduced by the SEA can be regarded as modest, and even disappointing. But to view the limited, mainly intergovernmental changes brought by the SEA as a backward step on the integration road misses the point somewhat. The preamble to the SEA states that it is 'a step towards European Union' and it therefore represented forward movement at a time of massive political conservatism in Europe; perhaps as important was the fact that, for the first time, the original primary Treaties had been substantively amended. Although this has happened on a number of occasions since then and thus has the appearance of being something not too difficult to achieve, at the time it was, without any doubt, a significant development. The original legal and constitutional base was shown not to be cast in stone and thus set for all time to come; it could be altered—and not just once, but as many times as deemed necessary. For most, if not all, of the states, especially the UK, signing up to and joining the Communities in the first place was a massive and historic commitment. Changing that original deal was not something to be taken lightly and could even be regarded as being as important as the CT, which failed to gain universal member state approval and was ultimately abandoned. The very substance of the original Treaties was being altered and, in order to amend a treaty, another treaty is needed, so despite its name the SEA is a true amending treaty agreed by the member states. Also, after a 20-year delay, it introduced real majority voting in the Council of Ministers, albeit within limited fields for clear and obvious benefits, but it allowed the member states to become comfortable with QMV and thus it prepared the ground for the future use of majority voting in other areas.

▶ CROSS REFERENCE
These aspects were considered earlier in sections 1.4.1.5 and 1.4.1.6.

The success of the SEA and benefit to the Communities was also observed externally at that time as other European states on the outside of the Communities were able to witness the increase in investment from outside Europe into the EC and indeed away from their own countries. They also wished to join in this success and, initially, plans were made to accommodate them in association agreements with the European Communities and, later in an extended form of these, with the EEA. It led much more quickly than originally envisaged to the further widening of the Communities.

1.5.7 Beyond the SEA

For more details on this section visit the online resources.

It was realised very soon after the signing of the SEA that this was only part of the answer and it was advocated, largely by the Commission, that further institutional changes were required. As a result, even before the deadline of 1992 had passed, plans were being put forward by the Commission President Delors for further Treaty reform, especially on economic and monetary union and social policy. A further IGC was planned and was set up to debate the adoption of common monetary and fiscal policies, which were deemed necessary to cement in the gains achieved by the largely successful completion of the single market. This further proposal for integration and, again, for the IGC to debate it, were opposed by the UK. However, external political events were moving rapidly in the world. Margaret Thatcher (nicknamed 'the Iron Lady') was deposed by her own party as Conservative Party leader and thus as UK Prime Minister. The 'Iron Curtain' was also being dismantled, changing the political situation in Europe radically and leading very quickly to German reunification. The planned IGC for 1991 to discuss and provide for greater economic integration was supplemented by a parallel second IGC to consider political reform and to produce proposals for a new constitutional basis for the Communities. It was also considered necessary that political decision-making should be integrated further in order to lock in any decisions reached on monetary union; otherwise, it was feared that any gains or decisions reached for monetary and economic union would be lost if the political decisions supporting them could still be taken independently by each member state. This, in turn, would lead to a drifting apart of the economic conditions in the member states and is a clear example of functionalist integration in action, in that integration in one area demands, or inevitably leads to, integration in another area in order to maintain the initial integration.

▶ **CROSS REFERENCE**

Refer to section 1.3.1.1 for explanation and further details.

The parallel IGCs commenced work in December 1990, but were subject to delays as a result of the economic problems in Europe, inflation in Germany due to the cost of unification, and the considerable political social and economic change taking place across Europe.

> In 1990, Germany was reunified and the area comprising the former East Germany joined the Communities.

1.5.8 The Maastricht Treaty on European Union (TEU)

The two IGCs of the early 1990s can be regarded effectively as one, particularly because they resulted in proposals for a single amending Treaty. However, the Treaty that was drafted and eventually accepted by the member states considerably complicated the constitutional base of the Communities and Union, not only because it amended the existing Treaties and most notably the EEC Treaty, but also because it added another Treaty to complement and supplement the existing treaties and to remain in force alongside the existing Treaties. It also proved to be a huge compromise, with its opt-outs in some matters for some of the member states, such as the social policy opt-out for the UK.

Chief among the main changes introduced by the Treaty were the timetable and convergence criteria to move to a single economy and monetary union, complete with a single currency. It provided more political cooperation, especially in the areas of foreign policy, security, home affairs, and justice. The EEC Treaty title was changed to 'European Community (EC)' to represent the changes that had taken place and the huge expansion in the range of topics and policies covered by the Treaty. A new overall term—the 'European Union (EU)'—was introduced to describe the extension by the member states into additional policies and areas of cooperation. The Union consists of three pillars comprising the existing Communities (the three original Treaties), a CFSP, and Cooperation in the fields of Justice and Home Affairs (CJHA).

A large part of the problem facing European governments trying to sell this Treaty at home was that the European public had not been taken on board during the period of negotiation. Whilst European citizenship was introduced to the EC Treaty (Articles 17 and 18 EC, now 20–21 TFEU), this status was really only given teeth later by the CoJ. There were further improvements for the EP in the law-making process, but the TEU also represented a backward step as far as progress towards deeper integration was concerned. The other two pillars, as first established, were intergovern-mental in nature, with decisions having to be taken unanimously by the member states. Very little had been done to increase the democratic credentials of the Communities; the powers of the most intergovernmental body—the Council—were left largely untouched except where they were actu-ally strengthened in respect of the two new pillars.

> **CROSS REFERENCE**
> See the generous interpretation of this by the CoJ in Chapter 12, section 12.7, on citizenship.

> The TEU also led to new jargon, which was the result of the new complex shape of the Union and the difficulties in getting the Treaty ratified in all member states, and reflected the frustra-tions of some member states not being happy about the more reluctant states—hence the terms 'European architecture' to describe the new three-pillar structure and 'variable geometry' to describe the way in which combinations of member states might integrate deeper and cer-tain states could opt out of certain policies. This is also described in the term 'multi-speed Eu-rope'. For example, the UK was able to opt out of the social policy chapter and economic and monetary union.

The Treaty did contain an expression of commitment to the rule of law and democracy, but failed to provide for any significant democratic accountability of the EU and the rule of law itself. The EP had no effective voice in the intergovernmental pillars. There was also an attempt to define the relation-ship between the Union and the member states by the introduction of the term 'subsidiarity', which was written in the new EU Treaty (Article B) and which was further defined in Article 5 EC (now 5 TEU), also discussed in Chapter 3, section 3.4.2. However, its true import was vague. It was sup-posed to delineate the respective powers of the Union and the member states, but instead has merely confused them, and as such is regarded as somewhat reflective of the ambivalence of the member states at the time.

> **CROSS REFERENCE**
> These issues and the democratic deficit are considered in detail in Chapter 2, section 2.4.3.1 and Chapter 3, section 3.5.

The TEU was also supposed to redress the serious concerns about the democratic deficit: that the EP was the only directly elected institution, but had less law-making power than the Council. The TEU increased the power of the EP by the introduction of the co-decision procedure to a limited number of Treaty Articles. Whilst this was an important step, in the beginning it amounted to little more than a parliamentary veto and did not establish real democratic decision-making in the Com-munities. Furthermore, this had the effect of increasing, once again, the range and complexity of law-making procedures in the Community. It was a modest start, which has been extended consid-erably since.

The TEU was agreed by the member states in February 1992 and was due to come into force on 1 January 1993. However, the process was thrown into confusion on being rejected by a slim Danish majority in a referendum. As a result, further compromises had to be found in order to appease the Danish electorate. The Edinburgh Summit in December 1992 agreed to allow Denmark various Protocols and Declarations to opt out of participation in stage III of economic and monetary union, the single currency, and the defence arrangements of Maastricht, whilst not actually changing the Treaty itself. The Treaty finally came into force in November 1993. However, the experience of cre-

> **CROSS REFERENCE**
> See, however, the comments on the Amsterdam and Nice Treaty IGC Summits and the 2007 Brussels Treaty Summit in sections 1.5.9, 1.5.10, and 1.5.13.

ating this Treaty was clearly an unhappy one and the European leaders promised that it would be better handled next time.

There was not much time to learn the lessons from Maastricht: the 'next time' was just around the corner. In 1992, mindful of the political changes in Europe, further expansion had already been contemplated by the existing member states, and the Copenhagen Summit laid down criteria that would have to be met by aspiring member states, considered in section 1.4.1.12.

Whilst politically the TEU was supposed to be an attempt to tidy up the constitutional base of the Communities, the end result was far from this. It is criticised for its complex three-pillar construction, which involved a mix of intergovernmental and supranational elements of governance. The TEU also started a trend that was continued subsequently by the attachment to the Treaties of numerous Protocols and Declarations, which help in many cases to define further some provisions of the Treaties themselves and outline the reservations and opt-outs of some member states. Justifiably, this too has been criticised for making the Union and its legal powers too opaque and splintered. Furthermore, the Union established was only an 'ever closer one' and not the federal union originally mooted, suggesting far greater integration than the reality agreed by the member states; hence, the end product was more intergovernmental cooperation.

> In 1995, a further expansion took place, with Austria, Finland, and Sweden joining the Union.

1.5.9 The Amsterdam Intergovernmental Conference and Treaty

As a part of the agreement for the TEU and specified in the EU Treaty, a timetable was planned for the further revision of the Treaties by providing that another IGC be constituted in 1996 with a view to signing a further amending Treaty in Amsterdam in 1997. It was given the objectives of proposing changes to reform the institutional structure in preparation for enlargement, revising social policy, and reviewing the intergovernmental pillars, in particular the CFSP, especially in respect of the rights of the free movement of persons. However, due to the delays in ratifying the Maastricht Treaty, the agenda was increasingly hijacked by new items, foremost being the preparations required for the eastern expansion of the Union. The political landscape for the Union had changed greatly in a very short time. One of the few things upon which sufficient member states were agreed was the opening up of entry negotiations with the new democracies of Eastern Europe. Hence, the focus of attention soon shifted to further institutional reform for the next, and probably much larger, expansion of the Union. The focus thus became narrowly concentrated on the size of the Commission, the EP, QMV, and the rotation of the presidency of the Council of Ministers.

The negotiations were highly problematic. Each member state, with its own agenda to defend, did so vigorously and some member states were prepared to push their positions to the limit. The UK government even sought to reopen previous Treaties, to curb the powers of the CoJ, and to reverse some of the decisions not favoured by the UK government. Hence, in this climate, the IGC dragged on into April 1997. However, in the UK, the Labour Party won the May 1997 general election and formed a new government with fewer objections. As a result, final negotiations were soon wrapped up and the Treaty was concluded in Amsterdam in June 1997. It was signed by all member states at a late-night summit in October 1997 and, following a slow, but less troublesome, ratification by all member states, it entered into force on 1 May 1999.

Whilst not as dramatic as those brought about by the TEU, a number of changes were introduced in the Treaty of Amsterdam. Unfortunately, some of these have considerably complicated the structure of the Union and the Treaties.

Following the 1997 landslide Labour victory in the UK, the Protocol and Agreement on Social Policy, previously lying outside of the Treaty structure, was accepted by all 15 member states and therefore a revised and extended chapter on social policy could be contained within the EC Treaty in the then Articles 136–145. A new section on employment was introduced, which provided, as one of the first examples of a more open method of coordination, that the member states can develop cooperative ventures to combat unemployment. Whilst it retained broadly the division between the supranational EC pillar and the intergovernmental nature of the other two, part of the Justice and Home Affairs (JHA) pillar, concerned with the free movement of persons, was moved within the EC pillar, with opt-outs for the UK, Ireland, and Denmark. It was also agreed that the EU would incorporate the Schengen Agreement on the elimination of all border controls for 12 states, in a new Title IV in the EC Treaty, but not for the UK, Ireland, and Denmark, which secured more opt-outs in this area. The CoJ and the EP were also given a greater role in the JHA pillar, now renamed the Provision on Police and Judicial Cooperation in Criminal Matters.

The institutional reforms were far more modest. The proposals to extend QMV in Council were severely restricted. However, the variety of legislative procedures, which were getting out of hand, were slightly reduced and the EP's powers were modestly increased by the moderately extended use of the co-decision procedure. The number of Commissioners was capped at 20, but subsequently amended upwards in line with the number of member states as further IGCs and enlargement re-opened this issue along with other institutional matters.

> **CROSS REFERENCE**
> Considered in section 1.5.13 and in Chapter 2.

The various changes were consolidated within both the EC and EU Treaties, and unhelpfully these were renumbered as a result, something that has done little to promote the clarity of Union law. Regrettably, the Treaty of Amsterdam added even more Protocols, thus making even more obscure an overall picture of EU and EC law.

The Treaty of Amsterdam, according to some, achieved very little; others regard it as a necessary consolidation of European political union, although the tangible benefits and progress are hard to discern. Additionally, the Treaty of Amsterdam seemed to throw a spanner in the works of further integration, by the replacement of further supranational integration, with the possibility of allowing some member states to cooperate further, but without all member states having to do so. It introduced into the EC Treaty Article 11, and into the TEU a section (Articles 43 *et seq*, now 20 TEU) on 'closer cooperation', which allows any number of member states that so wish to integrate in other areas. This seemed to make the fragmentation of the Communities even more possible and allow for the possibility that the body of Community law known as the *acquis communautaire*, which applies in all member states in the same way, could be undermined as different combinations of member states go their own way with particular policies. Thus far, this has not been taken advantage of, although a revised form of enhanced cooperation was introduced by the Lisbon Treaty (Articles 20 TEU and 326–334 TFEU).

> **CROSS REFERENCE**
> See sections 1.5.14 and 1.6.5.

The Treaty of Amsterdam, as finally agreed, proved to be far from the solution needed for preparing for enlargement, consolidating the political union and establishing a firm basis for European governance. It did little to restore public faith and confidence in the Union. As a result of the fact that Amsterdam failed to resolve the institutional reforms considered essential for the next enlargement of the EU, there was so much left over that had to be addressed before enlargement could take place that yet another IGC was deemed necessary and was called.

1.5.10 The Nice Intergovernmental Conference and Treaty

The Nice IGC was convened in February 2000 with the more tightly drawn objectives of institutional change ahead of enlargement, to deal with the so-called 'Amsterdam Leftovers'. Whilst the preparatory negotiations were relatively short-lived, the summit in December 2000 proved to be exceedingly difficult. The member states wrangled mainly over the extension of QMV and voting weights in Council, and the conclusions reached were neither conclusive nor satisfactory, despite the various statements of success following the summit. The size of the Commission was also a contentious issue. The QMV discussions were, however, seized on by the member states to defend national positions as rigidly as possible. QMV was extended to 27 more Treaty Articles, but not in as many areas as proposed by the Commission. The discussions were also drawn out because of arguments over the combinations of country votes to get a qualified majority or a blocking minority, and even qualifications on a majority were devised defining a minimum number of states and/or a percentage (62 per cent) of population of the EU required. In particular, the three big member states, France, Germany, and the UK, were fighting, against the wishes of many of the smaller states, to retain their level of influence, and whilst agreement was reached at Nice on the voting formula, it was very much an imperfect one, and this was soon shown to be the case. The co-decision procedure was extended again for the EP, so that the cooperation procedure became even less important, applicable in only six Articles largely concerning monetary union.

The ultimate maximum size of the Commission was also postponed again, and the temporary agreements reached were put into a Protocol on the Enlargement of the EU, which detracted further from the transparency of the rules governing the Union. The Treaty of Nice was signed by the member states in February 2001, but did not enter into force until 1 February 2003 because of its rejection by a single member state once again, this time Ireland in June 2001. When the Irish government was returned to power with an increased majority, a second referendum was organised, resulting in a positive endorsement of the Treaty by the Irish electorate (c. 63 per cent in favour).

> One policy that was tightened was the 'closer cooperation' provision introduced by the Treaty of Amsterdam, which was rather open-ended and which enables certain states to proceed to further integration outside of the Treaty (ex Article 11 EC—now 20 TEU and 326–334 TFEU).

Other changes agreed at Nice was that a Charter of Fundamental Human Rights should be included within the Union, although the member states did not or could not agree whether it should formally be a part of a treaty or of the Union and it was not initially legally binding on the member states. Note though that it is now legally binding via Declaration 1 attached to the Treaties post-Lisbon Treaty.

The Nice Treaty also introduced a provision designed to do something about the situation in which there was a clear risk of a serious breach by a member state of one of the respected principles of liberty, democracy, respect for human rights and fundamental freedoms, and the rule of law contained in Article 6 TEU. Article 7 TEU provided that a risk of breach can be determined and recommendations to deal with the situation can be agreed by a four-fifths' majority decision of the member states in Council, including suspension of voting rights of the member state where a persistent breach has been determined. Both of these Articles were carried forward with the same numbers into the amended TEU in 2009.

The Nice Summit also saw the agreement of the member states to move on to the next stage of integration, but it was to be done in a different way, the details of which were to be decided at a later summit of the member states.

1.5.11 **The 2001 Laeken Summit**

The Laeken Summit in December 2001 was the start of an ultimately unsuccessful attempt to put the EU on a new constitutional footing. It set up the agenda for a 'Convention on the Future of Europe', which was headed by a praesidium of 12 members, led by Valéry Giscard d'Estaing, a former French president. It further consisted of representatives of the heads of state and government of the 15 member states and the 13 candidate countries, 30 representatives of the national parliaments and 26 from the candidate countries, 16 members of the EP, and two members from the Commission.

It laid out in a Declaration the goals for making the EU more democratic, transparent, and efficient. In particular, attention would be paid to the governance of the Union, institutional preparations for the forthcoming expansion, the division of competences, and democratic participation in the decision-making processes of the Union.

There was to be a better definition and understanding of subsidiarity, to determine the status of the Charter of Fundamental Rights, and to simplify the Treaties and numerous Protocols and Declarations (thus finally admitting the complexity of the Treaties as they had accumulated and indeed been added to by the agreements at Nice). Other issues to be addressed included how national parliaments feed their legitimacy into the Union, and finally the Convention was charged with establishing a 'Constitutional' Treaty for the EU.

> **CROSS REFERENCE**
> This is considered further in Chapter 3, section 3.2, on the division of competences.

The Convention worked until June 2003, when it wrote up its report and a draft CT was finalised and presented to the European Council in Greece on 18 July 2003. This was subsequently considered by the IGC that commenced in October 2003 and the draft CT was presented to the Heads of State and Government Summit in Rome in December 2003, with a view to agreement and ratification prior to the forthcoming expansion of 10 new member states.

1.5.12 The Constitutional Treaty for Europe

The main features of the CT were a new President of the European Council and a Foreign Minister, a smaller Commission, the formal inclusion of the Charter of Human Rights, new simplified legislative tools, and more involvement for national Parliaments in law-making. Whilst agreeing on almost everything, the member states failed to agree about the QMV numbers in the Council, with a side argument on the number of Commissioners, and the Rome Summit broke down without agreement on these points.

> **CROSS REFERENCE**
> Council voting, and in particular QMV, are considered in detail in Chapter 2, section 2.2.4.

Subsequently, 10 new member states joined on 1 May 2004 on the basis of the Nice Treaty, and this event, combined with the low turnout in the EP elections in early June 2004, refocused the attention of the member states on reaching a compromise on the voting figures, considered further in Chapter 2, section 2.2.4.4. Thus, after some delay, the CT was signed in October 2004 by all member states and handed over to each of the member states to ratify it by parliamentary approval or referendum or both, according to the constitutional or legal requirements of each state. However, in 2005, during the ratification process, the CT was rejected by the electorates of France and the Netherlands, which threw the ratification process into confusion. The member states agreed that there should be a period of reflection, although some states continued the ratification process, taking the total that had ratified to two-thirds.

> There was a contingency plan in a Declaration (No. 30) attached to the CT, which provided that in the event that one or more countries, up to 20 per cent of the countries, did not ratify the CT, then all member states could meet in the European Council to decide how to go forward and adopt a political solution. Ratification did not go far enough for this Declaration to be invoked before the CT was abandoned.

After being put on ice for two years, the CT was considered at a further summit in June 2007 to see if it could be rescued or replaced—by which time the EU had grown to 27 members with the entry of Bulgaria and Romania at the beginning of 2007. The German presidency had the task of either making the CT more palatable or coming up with something in its place that nevertheless addressed the institutional challenges of enlargement. Following another late night of summit discussions, however, it was agreed to abandon the CT entirely and to replace it.

Even though the CT was abandoned, it is worthwhile listing the agreements reached, because most of the matters agreed found expression in the Lisbon Treaty, although slightly altered or in a more complex form. These agreements covered:

- changes to the institutional architecture of the Union and its powers, decision-making procedures, and institutions;
- the transfer of power to the EU on 15 new policy domains;
- the transfer of 40 Article bases, ranging from unanimity to qualified majority;
- making the Charter on Fundamental Rights legally binding;
- providing the EU with the status of a legal person to negotiate international agreements for all member countries;
- the establishment of a longer-serving and independent President for the European Council;
- a smaller Commission, comprising two-thirds of the number of member states;
- the creation of a common EU Foreign Minister to lead a joint foreign ministry with ambassadors;
- QMV for the election of all high-positioned officials;
- the commencing of a project of a common EU defence;
- an express statement that Union law shall have primacy over the national law;
- procedures for adopting and reviewing the Constitution, some without the need for another IGC; and
- an exit clause for member states.

However, the most controversial change may have been including in its title the term 'Constitution', which was probably a mistake, as it was arguably just another Treaty.

For more details on this section visit the online resources.

1.5.13 **The 2007 Brussels Summit and the Lisbon Treaty**

The member states returned to considering the next move in Brussels in June 2007. This meant that everything was potentially up for renegotiation and some member states in particular wanted to change or amend the things that had previously been agreed at Nice and in relation to the CT. Poland in particular wanted to change the voting arrangements in Council. The German presidency wanted to restrict discussion to more structural aspects of the Union, to ensure that member states' powers were retained, and to remove any symbolism in the Treaty that suggested statehood, such as the flag and anthem. The CT was then officially abandoned and an agreement was reached for a new amending treaty, originally called the 'Reform Treaty', to be signed in Lisbon, which would not replace the existing Treaties but would amend them. A new IGC was convened in July 2007 to hammer out the details, although many of the features agreed for the CT were incorporated into the 2007 Lisbon Reform Treaty.

The main changes can be summarised as follows.

(1) The Union was to get its legal personality, the EC Treaty to be renamed as the 'Treaty on the Functioning of the Union' (elegant, eh?) and the term 'Community' to be replaced throughout by 'Union'.

(2)   The proposed Union Minister for Foreign Affairs was to be called the 'High Represen-tative of the Union for Foreign Affairs and Security Policy'.

(3)   The European Council was to be established as a full institution as envisaged by the CT and a European President was to be established.

(4)   The names and types of secondary law 'Regulations, Directives, and Decisions' were to be kept, but given slightly changed definitions.

(5)   The Charter on Fundamental Rights was to become legally binding, but with an opt-out for its internal application in the UK and Poland and with a similar opt-out agreed for the Czech Republic, which was negotiated later. This is now contained in Declaration 53 attached to the Treaties.

The TEU was to be turned more into an overview Treaty, with the EC Treaty being converted into a Treaty dealing with substantive issues; both, however, were to concern the institutions.

> Hence, far from consolidating the Treaty, Protocols, and Declaration, the European leaders have made the constitutional architecture of the Union even more complicated and fragmented. The Treaty was signed in Lisbon on 13 December 2007 by all 27 member states and subjected to the required ratification process by all 27 member states.

The ratification process of this Treaty was also interrupted by the rejection of the electorate of one state, because in June 2008 the Irish voters for the second time voted against an amending Treaty. Following a period of consideration and negotiation, in exchange for the agreement by Ireland to hold a second referendum, EU leaders agreed to provide legal guarantees respecting Ireland's tax-ation policies, its military neutrality, and ethical issues. More controversially, they also agreed that each state should maintain one Commissioner, contrary to the Treaty itself, thus keeping one per member state. Constitutional challenges in other states such as Germany, the Czech Republic, and Poland were resolved, and the deliberate delay by the Czech and Polish presidents in completing the constitutional ratification process was overcome. The Treaty was finally ratified by all 27 states in November 2009 and entered into force on 1 December 2009.

The Union quickly appointed its full-time European Council President and its High Representative of the Union for Foreign Affairs and Security Policy (the Foreign Minister, but referred to as the 'High Representative') in time for the Lisbon Treaty coming into force. It amended the EC and EU Treaties significantly.

> CROSS REFERENCE
>
> The meaning of these posts and full institutional changes are addressed in Chapter 2, and other changes brought about by the Lisbon Treaty are considered wherever appropriate.

1.5.14 An overview of developments to date and the future

The institutional changes needed for the expansion of the Union in 2004 are now well established and the governance of the Union has been put on a new footing by the new Treaty set-up, albeit far less cleanly than originally planned. The prior concerns of the Union, which were the further widening and deepening of the Union, are no longer top of the agenda, having been replaced by the continuing economic and financial crisis in the world, and in the Eurozone in particular and the mass inward migration to the EU. Whilst five states are currently candidate states, they, along with the prospective candidate states, are unlikely to be accepted for many years. The further widening of the Union has already been considered in detail in this chapter, but does represent a serious challenge to the cohe-sion of the Union, particularly in respect of the attitudes already voiced about possible Turkish and even wider membership. Further deepening, in the form of taking integration even further forward,

For more details on this section visit the online resources.

is also very unlikely in view of the difficulties experienced in bringing the Lisbon Treaty into force and the expected exit of the UK. However, as a response to the prolonged economic and financial difficulties among southern Eurozone member states during 2008–14 (Greece in particular), a European Stability Mechanism has been established, which is essentially a bailout fund. The UK Prime Minister, David Cameron, declared that the UK would not participate, however, thus forcing the Eurozone countries (the Eurogroup of 19 following Lithuanian entry to the Eurozone on 1 January 2015) and the other eight (excluding the UK) non-Eurozone countries to conclude their own intergovernmental treaty to put in place the necessary laws, leaving the UK once again isolated in the EU. The Treaty on Stability, Coordination and Governance in the Economic and Monetary Union (TSCG) entered into force on 1 January 2013, with the exception of the Czech Republic and the UK. It is also known as the Fiscal Compact. Only the Eurozone members have ratified all of the titles in the Treaty, but it is open to non-Eurozone member states for ad hoc participation in financial assistance operations.

1.6 The relationship of the UK with the European Union

This section may or may not receive attention in all EU law courses. It concerns the rocky relationship between the UK and the European Communities and Union. This section in this edition has been considerably amended in view of Brexit.

For more details on this section visit the online resources.

1.6.1 The early relationship (up to the 1970s)

As noted in section 1.1.5, in the late 1940s and early 1950s, the UK was also initially keen to see a united Europe, but without its direct participation. It had at the time a historical legacy that involved different economic and social ties, including the Empire and Commonwealth and the Atlantic alliance, both of which featured strongly in the then recently won Second World War. These ties of security and common language are often overlooked, but played no small part in the attitude of the UK to European integration in the immediate post-war years. The UK also regarded its status as being one of remaining a world power, the sovereignty and independence of which might be compromised by membership of such an organisation. Also, immediately after the Second World War, the UK Labour government was more concerned with taking control of prime industries by nationalisation and not giving away power over them to supranational bodies. As well as having the offer to participate in the ECSC negotiations, the UK was also invited to participate in the EEC and EURATOM negotiations. However, it played no significant or indeed useful part and withdrew after minimal participation. Instead, with Austria, Switzerland, and other nations, the UK embarked in 1958 on what may have seemed a potentially unhelpful path of establishing the apparent competitor organisation, EFTA, which involved no supranational or political aims and was intended merely to set up a free-trade area for goods. It was not long, however, before UK governments had changes of heart and policy, which could be regarded as a tacit admission of the error of not joining in the first place, but with the second EU referendum a second reversal attitude has now taken place.

1.6.2 Two applications rejected

Within months of the entry into force of the EEC Treaty and the establishment of EFTA, the Macmillan Conservative government led the UK application for associate membership and, very shortly after that, on 9 August 1961, the UK application for full membership. The reasons for previously not wishing to join had been undermined. Among the changes were the demise of the UK's previous world power status, the fact that direct links with most of the world had been weakened by the economic demise of the UK, the Suez climb-down, and the continuing conversion of the Empire into a Commonwealth of independent states. Trade patterns were also shifting towards Europe and the Atlantic alliance was less prominent—pointedly so after the disagreement over how to handle the Suez crisis. More than anything, the UK had observed the much faster economic progress made by the existing six members and this provoked its desire for membership. Whether the UK was ever interested in the entire Community package is not clear. It had now, however, to bargain from the outside and its applications both for associate and full membership were steadfastly rejected by Charles de Gaulle, the French President. The 1967 application by the Wilson Labour government was similarly vetoed. De Gaulle's opposition to the potentially distorting influence of the UK in the Community was clearly expressed at the time.

1.6.3 Third application accepted

In 1970, following the resignation as president and withdrawal from politics of de Gaulle in France, the entry application by the Conservative Prime Minister Edward Heath was successful. Thus, the UK joined the EEC in 1973, as did Ireland and Denmark, mainly because of their trade dependency with the UK. However, soon afterwards, the UK sought to renegotiate entry terms and held a referendum on membership.

1.6.4 The timing of the entry

The timing of the 1973 entry was, in fact, unfortunate. Instead of the UK being able to participate equally in the post-war boom and recovery, the world economy and that of Europe had received a severe setback and the UK, along with the rest of the Western world, became the hostage of massive oil price increases. Instead of a period of economic prosperity, the 1970s witnessed high inflation and economic stagnation (sometimes termed 'stagflation'). To aggravate matters still further, the high and arguably inequitable level of the UK budget contribution became the focus of attention. It did not take long before disquiet over the terms of entry arose. It seems that the UK paid too high a price to join the club, and that the budget wrangles that both then and in the future were to polarise opinion in Europe and the UK were inevitable.

> The pattern of trade in the UK, which initially favoured imports from Commonwealth non-EEC countries, coupled with having to pay the higher food prices regulated under the EEC CAP, meant that British contributions were extremely high and added to the then severe UK domestic economic problems.

To recap for a moment, in the context of the UK entry, the Community was spawned in the aftermath of the Second World War. For membership, the original states exchanged some sovereignty and monetary contribution for security, the stability of democratic nationhood, and economic progress. It was argued that the UK did not need the first two, and the third proved illusory in the 1970s and 1980s. Hence when, in 1974, a new government was elected in the UK, a renegotiation of the terms of entry was begun, which did not require Treaty amendment. This culminated in the clear-cut (over 67 per cent in favour) approval of the British public in the then unprecedented 1975 referendum, which not only *post facto* approved membership, but also the renegotiated terms and specifically the revised budget contributions. However, it was only a partial cure for the level of contributions, and this dispute was later reopened by UK Prime Minister Margaret Thatcher. Its effect was, however, to cast the UK firmly in the role of reluctant partner and troublemaker in Europe. Viewed politically, the UK had decided to cast its lot with the EC, aware that some loss of sovereignty was involved and that a potentially high monetary contribution was required. One side of the bargain was not, as with other member states, the security of nationhood or the stamp of approval and stability of the democratic political system that membership gave. The fact that the UK, with a little help from its friends, had won the war and had centuries of stability meant that these were so well secured in the UK that the European Communities could never seriously be considered for these advantages. The other side of the bargain was to share in the spoils of European economic progress. Given the changing circumstances, this proved to be a dubious, or even illusory, economic gain. No wonder there was a feeling by some, which still remains, that membership had sold the UK short.

1.6.5 **1980 to 2015**

For more details on this section visit the online resources.

From the 1980s on, there was a growing scepticism towards the EU from certain sections of UK politics and society, in particular from the right wing of the Conservative Party encouraged by an increasingly Eurosceptic Prime Minister, Margaret Thatcher, who had originally supported EC membership.

In 2007, in the negotiations for the Lisbon Reform Treaty, further opt-outs were secured by the UK Labour government, in particular from the Charter of Fundamental Rights, which, under Protocol 30 attached to the Lisbon Treaty, confirm that the Charter will not apply internally in the UK.

For more details on this section visit the online resources.

A further development in the relations between the UK and the EU was the stance taken by David Cameron, the UK coalition government Prime Minister, in Brussels in December 2011 when he refused to participate in the economic and fiscal Treaty proposals, wielding in effect the UK veto. Furthermore, the UK Conservative Leader David Cameron pledged in 2013 that if the Conservative Party won the next election outright, it would renegotiate terms of membership and hold an in/out referendum on continuing EU membership, which became known as Brexit or Remain. This was regarded as more of an attempt to unite the Conservative Party and stem the increase in the support of the United Kingdom Independence Party (UKIP) to whom some Conservative Party supporters were drifting.

1.6.6 **The second UK Referendum on continuing EU membership**

When the Conservatives did in fact win an outright majority government victory in the 2015 election, a referendum on Europe was one of the first things outlined in the Queen's Speech on the opening of Parliament.

For more details on this section visit the online resources.

The second referendum on EU membership was held on 23 June 2016. The result was that overall the electorate in the referendum voted to leave by 51.9 per cent to 48.1 per cent to remain in a turnout of 72.2 per cent and with over 30 million people voting. England voted to leave by 53.4 per cent to 46.6 per cent, and in Wales, Leave received 52.5 per cent of the vote and Remain 47.5 per cent. Scotland and Northern Ireland went with pre-referendum forecasts and both voted overall to remain. In Scotland 62 per cent to 38 per cent, voted Remain to Leave and in Northern Ireland the figures were respectively 55.8 per cent Remain and 44.2 per cent Leave.

Internally in the UK there was a period of significant political upheaval. Prime Minister Cameron announced his resignation immediately following the vote and was soon replaced when only one leadership contender emerged from the leadership campaign. The unopposed Tory leadership candidate and former Home Secretary, Theresa May was appointed as the new Prime Minister.

As a consequence, the Leave vote and subsequent exit may lead to the break-up of the United Kingdom. Internally with Scotland now very pro-European, the overall UK vote to withdraw contrasted with Scotland and Northern Ireland, which voted regionally to stay in. As a result, Scotland, a part of the UK Union since 1707, was considering holding another referendum on their independence as the means to stay in the EU; however, this has been put on hold following the snap 2017 general election result in which the Scottish Nationalist Party lost some support. Theresa May called an election in June 2017 in order to increase the slim majority of the Conservative government and provide her with a stronger negotiation mandate, but the gamble failed and instead the Conservatives were returned as a minority government propped up by the Northern Ireland Democratic Unionist Party.

In order to fulfil the promise to exit the EU, the UK had first to give formal notice under Article 50 TEU to leave.

For more details on this section visit the online resources.

1.6.7 Article 50 TEU

Prior to 2009, there was no EU Treaty Article facilitating the exit of a member state from the EU; however, Article 50 TEU does now provide for a member state to withdraw, following a two-year negotiation period to agree the terms of withdrawal. This was the first time that Article 50 has been invoked.

Article 50

1. Any Member State may decide to withdraw from the Union in accordance with its own constitutional requirements.

2. A Member State which decides to withdraw shall notify the European Council of its intention. In the light of the guidelines provided by the European Council, the Union shall negotiate and conclude an agreement with that State, setting out the arrangements for its withdrawal, taking account of the framework for its future relationship with the Union.

The terms of withdrawal then have to be agreed with the EU, with negotiations led by the European Council with the input also of the EP and Commission and the agreement reached will be subject to the approval of the Council of Ministers and the EP. Article 50 TEU was triggered on 29 March 2017 and the two-year clock started ticking. The further consequence of this is the internal measure needed to exit, considered in section 1.6.8. The two years on paper—i.e. as envisaged in Article 50—may not prove long enough. In the meantime, and up to formal withdrawal, all EU Treaties and laws remain legally binding and in force in the UK. The negotiation period for withdrawal can, however, be extended under Article 50(3) TEU, but only if the European Council unanimously decides to extend it with the agreement of the UK. The Article does not provide for any further time periods, so presumably that would also be subject to negotiation and agreement with the UK. Presently a transition has been agreed ending on 31 December 2020, which is when the present EU five-year budget period expires, despite the UK expressing earlier that this should extend until 29 March 2021. Whichever date is agreed, some or all EU laws may apply, as negotiated and agreed until the end of that period.

Exit negotiations are progressing, albeit slowly and the first three issues have been agreed, at least in principle. These are the border between the Republic of Ireland and Northern Ireland, the right of EU citizens in the UK and vice versa, and the Exit financial settlement. A Joint Report on this agreement was issued on 8 December 2017.

For more details on this section visit the online resovurces.

The Irish border issue though remains a puzzle, with the UK seemingly committed to retaining an open or soft border with the Republic of Ireland, including the free movement of citizens, but at the same time committed to exiting the internal market and free movement and the customs union, including removing the right of free movement of citizens.

Exit negotiations have now moved on now to establishing the new trading relationship between the EU and the UK. In view of the fast moving and ever changing nature of these negotiations it is best that the online updates are consulted.

1.6.8 Exit and the Repeal Bill/Act

In order to arrange the exit internally, the UK has to repeal the most important Act of Parliament standing it its way. This is the European Communities Act 1972, the Act which facilitated accession and membership, which will be replaced by the proposed Great Repeal Bill which is formally now called the European Union (Withdrawal) Bill.

As this is rather complicated and only affects the UK, suffice it to say that it seeks to nationalise EU law in one go, but it will be highly difficult to sort out which pieces of EU can be easily converted and which need amendment. It has now been announced and decided, partially by an amendment to the above bill, that the eventual agreement with the EU will be put within another bill, presently entitled The Withdrawal Agreement and Implementation Bill, which will then be put before the Commons and Parliament for approval or rejection. That is assumed to be sometime in early 2019.

For more details on this section visit the online resources.

1.6.9 The new relationship with the EU

What sort of relationship would the UK have with the EU? Would it join the EEA and still be subject to EU rules but not participate in the decision-making process like Norway and Iceland, or negotiate a number of bilateral agreements, in the way that Switzerland has done? Both alternatives have a sticking point and that is to do with the free movement of persons, one of the cornerstones of the internal market and something that has been robustly defended by the EU and other member states and is likely to continue to be insisted upon. It was, however, the main reason—and for many people the only reason—they voted 'Leave'. The same would apply to trying to remain part of the single market or having an association agreement—both would almost certainly also require free movement. Maybe the UK will have no specific relationship, so the UK would be like non-European and non-association countries, simply trying to get ad hoc agreements on countless issues and be subject to WTO rules only with the world.

There are a number of options out there, described as lying somewhere between a soft Brexit and a hard one, and at present (April 2018), a hard Brexit looks the most likely as in March 2018 Prime Minister May ruled out both the customs union and the single market. A bespoke or specialised trade deal is the preferred option as of April 2018. This makes the border with the Irish an even more difficult issues to resolve as both the UK and Ireland are committed to a soft border.

As this is a fast-moving issue, especially on the alternative trade relationship which emerges, for more details on this issue visit the online resources.

Regardless of the outcome, a further question raised is whether it is likely to settle the EU question in the UK. The answer, like last time in 1975, is probably no. A sizeable part of the electorate who voted still wish to remain, as do many politicians and businesses. This is a moveable feast and is likely to remain so.

1.7 The EU and the world: external relations

The EU has diverse roles to play in the world order. Not surprisingly, given the more limited original political scope of the Communities, trade relations with the rest of the world feature most prominently, but not exclusively. However, because these roles and obligations in the areas of external relations have been spread over the various Treaties, an overview has been difficult to achieve. Also, the competences to undertake external relations had been granted in different terms under the three original Treaties: for example, the ECSC Treaty expressly granted the legal capacity to make external agreements generally in pursuit of the objectives of the Treaty, and the EURATOM (EAEC) Treaty also allowed for general agreements to be concluded, whereas the EC Treaty (Article 281 EC) provided that whilst the EC had been given legal personality, it was provided with powers to conclude specific types of agreement only, such as commercial agreements under the common customs tariff (Articles 131–133 EC, now 205–207 TFEU) or the association agreements. Article 300 EC (now 218 TFEU) provided an express power to conclude international agreements in areas already clearly within the competences of the EU, such as the common customs tariff, agriculture, and fisheries. However, the Council of Ministers must first give the Commission the go-ahead and the EP must finally assent to the agreement. As a result, there is a confusing array of trade agreements, association agreements, and development aid agreements with third countries that have been negotiated by the Commission under a mandate from the Council, but finally concluded by the Council on the basis of a qualified majority. With the entry into force of the Lisbon Treaty, the Union competences in its various relations with the rest of the world have been set out more clearly. These are introduced in Articles 3 and 8 TEU, and provided in greater detail in Articles 21–46 TEU and in a new Part Five of the TFEU, 'External Action by the EU', Articles 205–222, although the policies themselves will not change. In addition, Article 47 TEU also expressly conferred legal personality on the EU. External relations are now coordinated by the new High Representative of the Union for Foreign Affairs and Security Policy, who is appointed by the European Council (but is a Vice-President of the Commission) and who chairs the Foreign Affairs Council. In support of the High Representative a European External Action Service (EEAS) has been set up by Council Decision 2010/427. Its prime duty is to ensure consistency in the EU's external action.

> **CROSS REFERENCE**
>
> International agreements are also considered as a source of law in Chapter 4.

An extensive chapter on CFSP is now to be found in Articles 23–46 TEU, which also spell out in more detail the roles of the European Council and its relationship with the Council, although in view of the specialised nature of this area it is unlikely to be covered in most EU law courses. Equally, the details of the various external relations set out in Articles 205–222 TFEU will not be considered in this text.

The three-pillar organisation of the EU has now therefore been dismantled, with the JHA aspects subsumed into the supranational TFEU, and the CFSP remaining intergovernmental, but within the EU Treaty. Until their various roles are fully clarified over time, there will be some overlap in external representation by the European Council President, the High Representative, the Commission, the rotating Council presidency, and the still remaining Trade Commissioner.

The further details of this vast area of the EU's affairs are omitted as it is unlikely to be a part of undergraduate EU studies.

⟳ Summary

The process of further integration has continued with the Lisbon Treaty, which seems for the moment to have settled the argument about whether the EU was moving towards a form of Federal Union or something less than that. At present, the EU enjoys the transfer of considerable powers from the member states, its own institutions and law-making powers, an internal market, a division of powers and competences, the supremacy of EU law, its own catalogue of fundamental rights, its own Parliament, and also some of the more symbolic external trappings of statehood, such as a currency, a flag, an anthem, and a national day, although these aspects have not now been formalised in the Treaties. Note, though, that 16 member states agreed Declaration 52 attached to the Treaties that the flag, anthem, motto, euro, and Europe Day would continue as symbols to express the community of the people in the EU and their allegiance to it. The EU has a citizenship, but no *demos*—that is, no coherent European population who identify themselves with an embryonic European state. It has been shown in this chapter that the path to European unity is not straight and wide, and is far from certain. It is not planned in advance, and any plans that are put in place can easily be hijacked by rapidly evolving European and world political events, such as oil price increases, world economic crises, currency collapses, the collapse of Communism in Europe, the terrorist attacks of 11 September 2001, or rejections of new Treaties by the electorate of a single member state.

The EU consisting of 28 states today but maybe 27 in 2019 when the UK leaves, but equally possibly as many as 34 states if all of the candidate and potential candidate states were to join, will play an ever more important role in world affairs, not just economically, but politically as well, if for no other reason than because of its economic size. It needs to adapt to do this and, internally also, it still needs to address the issues of governance and democracy, until now not properly dealt with. However, European integration was regarded from the beginning as a process and not an end in itself. The 2007 Lisbon Treaty may be regarded as both an example of further deeper integration because it represents a far more comprehensive ordering of the Union and member states, and also as a brake on further unwelcome integration because of its clearer delineation of competences. It makes matters clearer and sets discernible boundaries on the exercise of Union power. It might have been thought also that there would be no appetite for further integration, but the Eurozone financial crises have seemingly forced upon the EU the need to integrate more closely economically and fiscally. The latest challenge to European integration is one that has been forced upon it, once more from external sources and is that of the mass inward migration of refugees and economic migrants from the troubled countries of the Middle East and Africa. It is a situation that has severely tested the frontier-free Schengen area and the EU ideal of an area of free movement.

Brexit may also lead to more instability and possible disintegration in Europe, but at this stage it is difficult to say.

Clearly, the integration of European states into the EU remains an unfolding story and the end is not yet written; what the end is will no doubt also continue to be the subject of considerable debate.

For more details on this section visit the online resources.

For more details on this section visit the online resources.

THINKING POINT

Which member states have rejected a Treaty? What were their reasons? How were the rejections overcome?

? ## Questions

1. What were the main concerns of the planners of the European Communities after the Second World War? Are these issues relevant to Europe today?

2. What is meant by the terms 'integration', 'intergovernmental', 'supranational', 'functional integration', and 'federalist'?

3. What are the meanings of, and the distinction between, the EU and TFEU?

4. Why do you think the UK wished to exit the EU in 2016?

5. How far can the EU keep expanding and integrating or disintegrating?

For more details on this section visit the online resources.

Sample exam Q&A

The **2007 Lisbon Treaty**, having eventually been ratified by all of the member states at the time, was a much poorer substitute for the **2004 CT,** whilst essentially making the same institutional and other changes to the EU.

Discuss.

For guidance on how to tackle this specimen exam question and to read a suggested model answer, visit the online resources. www.oup. com/uk/foster_ directions6e/

Further reading

Books

Bache, I. *Europeanization and Multilevel Governance: Cohesion Policy in the European Union and Britain*, illustrated edn, Rowman & Littlefield Publishers, New York, 2008.

Bache, I. and George, S. *Politics in the European Union*, 2nd edn, Oxford University Press, Oxford, 2006 (especially Chapters 1–17 and 31).

Barnard, C. and Peers, S. (eds), *European Union Law*, 2nd edn, Oxford University Press, Oxford, 2017.

Blair, A. *The Union since 1945*, 2nd edn, Pearson Longman, Harlow, 2010.

Cini, M. and Borragan, N. *European Union Politics*, 3rd edn, Oxford University Press, Oxford, 2009.

Craig, P. *The Lisbon Treaty: Law, Politics and Treaty Reform*, Oxford University Press, Oxford, 2010.

Craig, P. 'Development of the EU' in Barnard, C. and Peers, S. (eds) *European Union Law*, 2nd edn, Oxford University Press, Oxford, 2017, p. 9.

Dinan, D. *Ever Closer Union: An Introduction to European Integration*, 4th edn, Oxford University Press, Oxford, 2010.

Duchene, F. *Jean Monnet: The First Statesman of Interdependence*, W. W. Norton & Co., New York, 1996.

Eeckhout, P. *EU External Relations Law*, 2nd edn, Oxford University Press, Oxford, 2011.

Fabbrini, R. *The Law and Politics of Brexit*, Oxford University Press, Oxford, 2017.

Prechal, S. *Reconciling the Deepening and Widening of the European Union*, Cambridge University Press, Cambridge, 2008.

Szyszczak, E. and Cygan, A. *Understanding EU Law*, 2nd edn, Sweet & Maxwell, London, 2008.

Tatham, A. *Enlargement of the European Union*, Kluwer Law International, London, 2009.

Ward, I. *A Critical Introduction to European Law*, 3rd edn, Cambridge University Press, Cambridge, 2009 (especially Chapters 1, 2, and 7).

Articles

Aubelj, M. 'Theory of European Union' (2011) 36 EL Rev 818.

Barratt, G. 'The King is dead, long live the King: the recasting by the Treaty of Lisbon of the provisions of the Constitutional Treaty concerning national parliaments' (2008) 33 EL Rev 66.

Craig, P. 'The Lisbon Treaty: process, architecture and substance' (2008) 33 EL Rev 137.

Craig, P. 'The European Union Act 2011: locks, limits and legality' (2011) 48 CML Rev 1915.

Dougan, M. 'The Treaty of Lisbon 2007: winning minds, not hearts' (2008) 45(3) CML Rev 609.

Gatti, M. and Manzini, P. 'External representation of the European Union in the conclusion of international agreements' (2012) 49 CML Rev 1703.

Majone, G. 'Unity in diversity: European integration and the enlargement process' (2008) 33 EL Rev 457.

Schütze, R. 'From Rome to Lisbon: "Executive Federalism" in the (New) European Union' (2010) 47 CML Rev 1385.

Website

Europa.eu containing multiple links to other pages on the EU: in particular, for this chapter, its history.

http://europa.eu/about-eu/index_en.htm

http://europa.eu/about-eu/eu-history/index_en.htm

2 The Union institutions

LEARNING OBJECTIVES

This chapter will help you to become familiar with the institutions of the European Union (EU), the work that they do, and how they work together. The following topics will be considered:

- the institutional framework;
- the European Commission;
- the Council (of Ministers);
- the European Parliament;
- the European Council and President;
- the European Court of Justice;
- the Court of Auditors;
- the European Central Bank and other Union bodies.

Introduction: the institutional framework

The institutional framework of the Union was originally laid down in the European Coal and Steel Community (ECSC) Treaty (considered in Chapter 1, section 1.2.2), which established a mix of supranational and intergovernmental institutions in a tripartite system consisting of the Council of Ministers, the Commission (then called the High Authority), and the European Parliament (then called the Assembly). These three bodies are the main policymaking and law-making bodies in the Union, but this institutional foundation has been added to and refined considerably. There is now an overall policy-steering body, the European Council, which has been formalised as a main institution (Article 13 Treaty on European Union (TEU)), and additional consultative bodies—the European Economic and Social Committee (EESC) and Committee of the Regions (CoR)—which gather the opinions of public interest groups and regional opinions and feed these into the decision-making process. From 1965, a unitary set of four 'official' or principal institutions served the original three Communities. Following the entry into force of the Maastricht Treaty on European Union (TEU), these were expanded to five with the addition of the Court of Auditors and, in 2009, when the Lisbon Treaty entered into force, the European Council and European Central Bank (ECB). There is no formal or classical 'separation of powers' built into the institutional set-up of the EU, since powers are often shared—the most notable being legislative authority, which can be exercised by the Council, European Parliament, and Commission. In view of the piecemeal and sometimes ad hoc development of the EU and institutions, whereby powers may be increased, as with the European Parliament, or new powerful institutions established, such as the European Council, this lack of separation of powers is not really surprising. The judicial branch is the most visibly separate, although, by Article 13 TEU, an institutional balance is required whereby each institution must not act beyond those powers conferred upon them by the Treaties.

Article 13 TEU states that the Union's institutions shall be the European Parliament (EP), the European Council, the Council, the Commission, the Court of Justice (CoJ), the ECB, and the Court of Auditors.

Article 13 TEU requires that each institution shall act within the limits of the powers conferred on it by the Treaty. Article 13(4) provides for two advisory bodies, the EESC and the CoR, as part of a secondary group of bodies completing the institutional structure and which presently include the Committee of Permanent Representatives (COREPER), the European Investment Bank (EIB), and the European System of Central Banks (ESCB). Detailed provisions on the Institutions are contained in Articles 223–287 Treaty on the Functioning of the European Union (TFEU).

The general Articles of the TEU set out a number of general duties applicable to all of the institutions, which include: Article 5, respect for the principles of subsidiarity and proportionality; Article 9, equal attention to all citizens; Article 11, giving citizens and representative associations the opportunity to exchange views on Union action; Article 12, keeping national parliaments informed: and Article 15 conducting their work as openly as possible.

2.1 The Commission

For more details on this section visit the online resources.

This section considers in turn the composition, appointment, and removal of the Commission, and its tasks and duties. The Commission fulfils the role of an executive administration for the Union and was given the sole right as the proposer of legislation. This makes the Commission more powerful than a straightforward civil service bureaucracy carrying out the will of an elected government. It is not to be confused with a government itself. It is, however, able to formulate policy within the parameters of the agreed areas contained in the Treaties and to make proposals for legislation to realise this. The real power of initiative is somewhat compromised by the overall policy formulation and guidance provided by the Council of Ministers and more so now by the European Council, which was made a full institution by the Lisbon Treaty. This is considered further in section 2.3. The Commission also has its own powers of decision-making and is able to exercise powers and enact delegated and implementing legislation under powers provided by the Council of Ministers and EP (Articles 290 and 291 TFEU). This is discussed in section 2.1.3 below. Although not presented first in the Treaties, the Commission is a much more visible institution in the eyes of the public and, as initiator of legislation, is a good place to start a tour of the institutions.

2.1.1 **Composition of the Commission**

The composition, tasks, and functions of the Commission are determined by Articles 17 TEU and 244–250 TFEU. It was agreed during the Nice Treaty and 2004 accession negotiation discussions for Bulgaria and Romania that numbers of the Commissioners should be reduced to two-thirds of member states. Although Article 17(5) TEU still formally commits to this reduction of the number of Commissioners from 2014, the guarantees given to Ireland to encourage it to hold a new referendum on the Lisbon Treaty in 2009 reinstated the principle of one Commissioner per state; hence, there are currently 28 EU Commissioners, although this is due to be reviewed again before the next Commission appointment in 2019 or before the EU membership reaches 30 member states. Article 17(5) does, however, empower the European Council, acting unanimously, to alter that number, and Article 244 TFEU provides detail of how the reduced number of Commissioners will be decided.

The Commissioners, although nominated representatives of the member states, are required under Articles 17(3) TEU and 245 TFEU to be completely independent in the performance of their duties and neither take nor seek instructions from any government or any other body. Too often they are regarded as each member state's representative in Brussels. However, to counterbalance this view, it is suggested that, after spending some time in Brussels, a member state's Commissioner has a tendency to 'go native'—in other words to take on a much more Union, rather than national, perspective on things. Article 17(3) TEU also states that the members of the Commission shall be chosen on the ground of their general competence and European commitment.

The Commission is assisted by about 23,000 staff working directly in the Commission Directorates, and whilst this sounds a high number, the Union itself asserts that this is fewer than in most medium-sized city councils in Europe. The Commission, then, is not a massive bureaucracy. In the member states, there are hundreds of thousands of civil servants, with some single departments employing far more than the entire European Commission. Part of the reason for the much lower numbers in the EU is that most of the work covered or generated by EU legislation is, in fact, carried out by the national agencies, particularly in respect of the Common Agricultural Policy (CAP).

2.1.2 **Appointment and removal of the Commission**

The first part of the process of appointing a new Commission is that the Commission President is considered and then proposed by qualified majority voting (QMV) by the European Council, after consultations and taking into account the elections to the EP under Article 17(7) TEU (Figure 2.1). He or she is then subject to approval by the EP by majority of members' vote. This more politicised method of electing the Commission President than was originally established was one of the very many changes carried over from the constitutional Treaty to the Lisbon Treaty. The current President, Jean-Claude Juncker, was the choice of the European People's Party, the largest party in the EP, and this now is set to be the convention to be complied with. In 2014 though, two member states voted against his appointment in the European Council, which in fact voted by simple majority. This process of European Council and EP approval arguably injects indirect democracy into the Commission President appointment and thus also the status of the Commission overall.

> **CROSS REFERENCE**
> QMV is considered in detail in section 2.2.4.3.

> QMV is one of the ways by which the Council votes on legislation.

The Commission President-elect and the member states in Council then jointly propose the other Commissioners, with the exception of the High Representative of the Union for Foreign Affairs and Security Policy, who is selected and appointed independently by the European Council (Article 18(1) TEU), but who is simultaneously a Commission Vice-President (Article 18(4) TEU).

Although the member states chose to reject the term 'Foreign Minister', which was used in the Constitutional Treaty in favour of the more politically acceptable but far more cumbersome and unwieldy term 'High Representative of the Union for Foreign Affairs and Security Policy', it appears that the terms 'HR', or 'High Rep', or 'High Representative' are being used, or that he or she might be informally referred to as the 'Foreign Minister'. The term 'High Representative' will be employed in this volume.

For more details on this section visit the online resources.

The Commission is then subject to the consent of the EP en bloc and then formally appointed by the European Council. This makes the rejection of a single Commissioner designate technically, although not practically, impossible, as was seen in 2004 by the objection of the EP to the Italian nomination because of the latter's genuinely held, but incongruous, views on homosexuality and the role of women. The Commission President-designate Barroso decided not to submit the Commission for approval for fear of a probable rejection of the entire Commission. Instead, he reshuffled the proposed Commission, without the original Italian nomination, which was then approved by the EP and appointed by the Council. In 2014, each of the Commissioners designated were questioned by the EP about the portfolio they had been proposed for. As a result, the Hungarian nominee was not approved for the portfolio originally proposed but was accepted for a different one. The Slovenian nominee, however, was rejected outright wholly on political rather than legal grounds and a new nominee had to be proposed and approved.

❯ CROSS REFERENCE

The High Representative is considered in section 2.3.2.

The 'High Representative' is appointed by the European Council by QMV with the agreement of the Commission President. This position is special and unique because the appointee is automatically a Vice-President of the Commission and also presides over the Foreign Affairs Council in conducting the Union's foreign and security policies.

The term of office for all Commissioners is for a renewable period of five years (Article 17(3) TEU). There are seven Vice-Presidents in the second Barroso Commission, whose office will run from 2010 to 2014. The number of Vice-Presidents is no longer specified by the Treaty (Article 17(6) TEU), as was previously the case.

Figure 2.1 Commission appointment flow chart

Commission President proposal agreed by QMV by European Council.

Proposal sent to EP for majority vote approval.

Council and Commission President-elect agree list of other Commissioners, including name of High Representative (previously appointed by European Council by QMV).

President, High Representative, and other members as a body are subject to a vote of consent by the EP.

Commission then appointed by European Council by QMV.

The Commission can be removed by a vote of censure by the EP, but only collectively (Articles 17(8) TEU and 245 TFEU) and, until the replacement Commission is appointed in its entirety, the old Commission stays in office. It is therefore something of a blunt instrument if the activities of only one Commissioner are objected to, although there is the procedure under Article 247 TFEU for the CoJ, on an application of the Council and by a simple majority of the Commission (but not the EP), compulsorily to retire a Commissioner for serious misconduct, or where he or she no longer fulfils the conditions required for the performance of his or her duties. However, under a slightly amended procedure now contained in Article 17(6) TEU, a member of the Commission shall resign if requested to do so by the President. Article 17(6) TEU contains a summary of the management powers of the Commission President, first introduced by the Nice Treaty.

> Special rules apply to the removal and resignation of the 'High Representative': see Articles 17(6) and (8) and 18(1) TEU and 246 TFEU.

Censure of the entire Commission was threatened in 1999 following a damning report of an independent committee of experts appointed by the EP that exposed serious fraud, cronyism, and incompetence on the part of individual Commissioners. Whilst it did not come to a vote of censure, it forced the resignation of the entire Santer Commission on 15 March 1999 as the only way in which to oust the culpable Commissioners. A new Commission was approved by the EP in September 1999 under the presidency of Prodi, who required from the individual Commissioners a promise to resign on demand, thus increasing the power of the President within the Commission. A follow-up case to this episode, Case C-432/04 *Commission* v *Edith Cresson*, confirmed not only that Commissioner Cresson had breached her duties as a Commissioner, but also that the CoJ had an independent discretionary right to hear such actions, free of any influence of national courts. The Belgian criminal courts had cleared Cresson of any criminal wrongdoing.

In view of the possibilities under Articles 17(6) TEU and 247 TFEU to remove or require the resignation of a single member of the Commission, it would seem less necessary for a vote of censure of the whole Commission to be threatened in order to tackle the excesses or breaches of individual Commissioners, unless the Council or Commission President refuse or fail to take action.

 THINKING POINT

What improvements could be made to both appointment and removal procedures generally? Are they sufficiently democratic? Does it matter?

2.1.3 Tasks and duties

Article 17 TEU imposes on the Commission the general duty of promoting the general interest of the Union and of taking initiatives to reach that end. The Commission is a collegiate body and is responsible collectively for all decisions taken, although the proposals are prepared by a Commissioner and his or her particular Directorate. Decisions are taken by consensus or simple majority, if voting is deemed necessary.

The Commission has a number of main functions within that general duty, as follows.

(1) It must ensure that the provisions of the Treaty and the measures taken by the institutions under them are applied. The Commission is described as the 'guardian' or 'watchdog' of the Communities, because it is given the task of bringing to the European CoJ breaches of the

Treaty by member states under Article 258 TFEU, other institutions under Article 263 TFEU, and individuals under various provisions of the Treaty and secondary law, such as Regulation 1/2003 in respect of competition policy.

(2) It formulates and proposes policy initiatives and legislative proposals by way of recommendations or opinions on matters as expressly provided for by the Treaty or as the Commission considers necessary. Here, the Commission is acting as the initiator of legislation. The Commission has the sole right to propose legislation (Article 17(2) TEU), although it may now be requested to submit legislative proposals by either the Council (Article 241 TFEU) or the EP (Article 225 TFEU). The TEU, as amended by the Lisbon Treaty, now also provides for a European Citizens' Initiative (ECI) whereby if at least one million citizens from a minimum of seven member states come together, they may request the Commission to submit a legislative proposal (see Articles 11 and 241 TFEU). ECIs are now regulated in detail by Regulation 887/2013 and have been available since 1 April 2012. Whilst a number (c. 30 at the last count) have been rejected as not coming within the criteria, withdrawn, or failing on procedural grounds, four have been accepted. This does not mean that any action on the part of the Commission will necessarily result. However, an ECI concerning water rights did cause the Commission to remove proposed regulation of water supply from a concessions Directive.

(3) It has limited powers of independent decision-making by participation in the shaping of measures taken by the Council of Ministers and by the EP. This was outlined previously in Article 211 EC; and although this Article has now been repealed by the Lisbon Treaty and not directly replaced, there is no suggestion that the power has been removed, because Article 17 TEU provides that the Commission shall take appropriate initiatives to promote the general interest of the Union.

(4) It has powers under the delegated and implementing legislation procedures conferred on it by the Council of Ministers and the EP for the adoption of the non-legislative or otherwise-termed administrative or Regulatory acts (Articles 290 and 291 TFEU).

> Implementing powers are regulated by Regulation 182/2011, which provides for supervision by a range of committees, known collectively as 'comitology' and which are determined by the Council under Article 291 TFEU.

(5) The Commission is also responsible for the external representation of the Union and negotiation of international agreements under Articles 207 and 218 TFEU, with the exception of the Common Foreign and Security Policy (CFSP), where the High Representative undertakes negotiation.

(6) The Commission also plays a leading part in drawing up the Union's annual budget (Articles 314–316 TFEU) and its implementation (Articles 317–319 TFEU).

The Commission is regarded as the most federal institution of the EU, owing largely to its independence from direct national influences. Its decision-making process, under Article 250 TFEU (ex 219 EC), provides that it can decide matters collectively by a majority, but the practice is to try to decide by consensus. All members of the Commission are expected to abide by Commission decisions.

Commission activity is most pronounced in the fields of competition policy and in the management of the CAP, Common Customs Policy, and competition policy because of the high degree of day-to-day decision-making that is necessary. It is also very much involved in representing the Union in international organisations such as the General Agreement on Tariffs and Trade (GATT) and the World Trade Organization (WTO), and in concluding international agreements on behalf of the Union, such as the association agreements with various countries.

For more details on this section visit the online resources.

For more details on this section visit the online resources.

CROSS REFERENCE
This is considered further in Chapter 1, section 1.7, and Chapter 4, section 4.5.

In view of the strengthening of the positions of the EP, by a greater and almost equal involvement in the legislative process, and the European Council, now formally at the political helm or apex of the institutional hierarchy, the position of the Commission may have been weakened following the Lisbon Treaty. This will be considered in brief in this chapter, but it may take time for this to be confirmed in reality.

2.2 The Council (of Ministers) of the EU

The Council of Ministers has undergone a few name changes, presently being called simply 'the Council' in contrast previously to being 'the Council of Ministers'. Furthermore, there is also the 'European Council', and the Council should not be confused with this other body, or indeed with the Council of Europe in Strasbourg. This section considers the functions and powers of the Council of Ministers, as well as its role and forms of voting procedures within the legislative procedures and its general law-making powers. Furthermore, although strictly speaking COREPER and the Council Secretariat are not main institutions and should be considered in the section on other EU bodies, they will be considered here because of their direct connection with the work of the Council.

For more details on this section visit the online resources.

Although there have been various changes to the processes by which Union legislation is enacted that have given more power to the EP, notably more so after the Lisbon Treaty reforms, the Council remains, marginally on paper but not so much in practice, the main legislative organ of the Union. Its tasks, composition, and functions are outlined in Article 16 TEU and Articles 237–243 TFEU.

For more details on this section visit the online resources.

The Council consists of representative ministers of the member states, depending on the subject matter under discussion, who are authorised to act on behalf of their represented states and to commit that state to discussions and votes taken in Council (Article 16(2) TEU). Thus different configurations of the Council take place, with the foreign ministers attending the General Council, and agriculture or finance ministers, for example, attending the specialist Councils. There are presently 10 different council configurations following the Lisbon Reforms, which provide now, under Article 236 TFEU, that the European Council shall decide the configuration and presidencies of the Council. The General Affairs Council is attended by the foreign ministers and coordinates the work of the other Council configurations, except the Foreign Affairs Council, which is chaired and coordinated by the High Representative but which does not enjoy legislative powers (see Article 24 TEU). Previously the Council could have been constituted by the heads of state and government. However, whilst this is still theoretically possible, the elevation of the European Council, which has the same membership, as a full institution of the Union, renders this unnecessary and unlikely.

> **CROSS REFERENCE**
>
> The European Council is considered under section 2.3.

This explains why Article 214 EC, previously regulating the Council constituted by the heads of state and government, was repealed and replaced when appointing the Commission. The appointment of the Commission is now found in Article 17(7) TEU, placing that right clearly within the prerogative of the European Council.

2.2.1 Functions and powers

Article 16(1) TEU imposes on the Council the general requirement to carry out policymaking and coordinating functions as laid down in the Treaties, as well as jointly with the EP, exercising legislative and budgetary functions. The Treaty gives the Council the power to take decisions and, with the EP, to delegate some decision-making and implementing powers to the Commission under Articles 290 and 291 TFEU.

▶ CROSS REFERENCE

The ordinary legislative procedure is considered in Chapter 3, section 3.6.1.1.

Following the Lisbon Treaty reforms, the Council decides on the adoption of legislative proposals predominantly by the co-decision procedure, now referred to as the 'ordinary legislative procedure' (Article 289 TFEU), which provides the EP with an equal input and a final right of veto, as detailed in Article 294 TEU. The Council, with the EP, is also responsible for the adoption of the annual budget (Article 314 TFEU). When acting in its legislative capacity, the Council is now required to meet in public (Article 16(8) TEU).

The Council is also now able to request that the Commission undertakes studies that the Council considers desirable to attain objectives and to submit proposals on the same. It may do this by simple majority. This compromises the Commission's original sole right of initiative in proposing legislation. The Commission must state reasons if it decides not to submit a proposal (Article 241 TFEU).

The Council also agrees the EU budget, jointly with the EP (Article 314 TFEU).

2.2.2 The presidency of the Council

The Council of Ministers is chaired by a presidency, which is held by each of the member states in turn for a period of six months only (Articles 16(9) TEU and 236 TFEU).

> The European President chairs and coordinates the work of the European Council; both are considered below.

The Foreign Affairs Council is chaired by the 'High Representative'; the President usually hails from the state holding the rotation governed by Articles 16(9) TEU and 236 TFEU.

> Even prior to the Lisbon Treaty reforms, the very short period of Council presidency of six months made it clear that greater continuity between presidencies was required. Hence, a current president and both the previous and succeeding presidents coordinated to a greater degree to work in conjunction, particularly in the pursuit of international relations. The term *Troika* has therefore been used to describe the 18-month rolling Council governance to provide continuity in policy, although it remains the case that each presidency can outline and pursue particular policy objectives that it has identified as its priorities, although these must have been outlined in advance and essentially comply with the 18-month rolling programme previously agreed. Furthermore, with the formalisation of the European Council and the establishment of the European President, any Council programme must inevitably also not be in conflict with the European Council agenda. The Council no longer represents the EU externally, however, clearly reducing the overall role and impact of this institution.

2.2.3 Role and voting in the legislative procedures

▶ CROSS REFERENCE

The legal base is outlined in Chapter 3, section 3.5.1.

The many institutional reforms over the years, especially in increasing the EP's participation in law-making, has meant that the Council's pre-eminence in deciding on and enacting secondary legislation is now only a narrow one on paper and more equal in practise. The Council now decides extensively by co-decision with the EP. The actual process used to enact legislation and the degree of participation by the EP and/or other bodies depends on the particular Treaty provision under which legislation is enacted—in other words, the legal base.

In broad terms, the political institutional balance has seen a number of changes over the decades, mostly in favour of a power shift from the Council to the EP in the law-making process. However, it is not only the EP that participates with the Council. The Council may have to consult the EESC and/ or the CoR before legislation can be enacted. If it fails to do so, the legislation subsequently enacted may be challenged and annulled. Even when enacting legislation with the EP, there are different processes by which the legislation can be enacted. The Council may consult the EP or co-decide with the EP, or require the EP's consent.

CROSS REFERENCE

See Chapter 9, section 9.1 for more on Article 263 TFEU (ex 230 EC) annulment actions.

2.2.4 Forms of voting

The Council does not simply vote in one way on all of the decisions it makes—that is, it does not vote only by a majority or unanimously on everything. In contrast to the previous Treaty provision on voting, the new Article 16(3) TEU is a much more accurate reflection of both law and practice.

CROSS REFERENCE

The legislative procedures will be explained in Chapter 3, section 3.6.

> Article 16(3) TEU provides that the Council shall act by a qualified majority except where the Treaties provide otherwise. Previously, Article 205 European Community (EC) Treaty provided that, subject to Treaty exceptions, the Council would vote by a simple majority. In fact, it was even the case from the very beginning that the exceptions were the rule (or the rule was the exception) and voting was mainly either by a qualified majority or by unanimity.

Following the Lisbon Treaty reforms, the rule is reflected in fact and QMV is by far the most common method of voting, although it would be usual practice for the Council President to attempt to gain the consensus of all member states before proceeding to make a decision, and if a consensus view is achieved, the Council may not vote at all. A requirement of unanimity is now much rarer.

2.2.4.1 Unanimity

The meaning of 'unanimity' is clear: all member states must agree, which means that, as from 2013, all 28 member states must agree! This is where a single member state can wield a veto and prevent a particular legislative proposal from being enacted: see, for example, Article 19 TFEU requiring unanimity on the part of the Council to enact measures outlawing different forms of discrimination. The more that voting is done by unanimity, the less potentially and probably will be accomplished; hence a move to more majority voting is crucial. Member states that abstain from voting do not prevent the others from agreeing a measure unanimously, which is then binding on all member states (Article 238(4) TFEU). Unanimity is still used in a considerable number of Treaty Articles, especially following the Lisbon Treaty amendments, which brought within the TFEU areas of law lying previously purely within the intergovernmental EU Treaty, such as CFSP and policing.

For more details on this section visit the online resources.

2.2.4.2 Simple majority voting

Simple majority voting, whereby a measure is enacted by an arithmetic majority, such as by 15 states with 13 against, is rare and is required for only eight Articles of the TFEU, concerned mainly with the setting up of advisory committees and the institutions.

> Article 238 TFEU defines this requirement as follows: 'Where it is required to act by a simple majority, the Council shall act by a majority of its component members.'

2.2.4.3 Qualified majority voting

In 1965, when the Communities still consisted of only six member states, the Council was due to move from unanimity voting to QMV for certain subject areas of the Treaty. This was objected to by

President de Gaulle of France, and the ensuing dispute led eventually to a boycott of the institutions by the French members. It was resolved only when a compromise—the 'Luxembourg Accords' or 'Luxembourg Compromise'—was reached (considered in Chapter 1, section 1.5.2).

> The Luxembourg Accords were essentially an 'agreement to disagree', but provided that where a member state identified a very important national interest, all member states should try to reach a unanimous decision rather than overrule that member. The six member states could not, however, agree on the consequence of a failure to agree. The conclusion, which was certainly that of the French and generally accepted, was that an objecting member state effectively had a veto over the decision.

The legal position of the Accords was always uncertain, but despite the provision in the Treaty for both majority voting and QMV, the Council denied itself these forms of voting for many years. Successive enlargements and the difficulties in reaching a consensus every time led the Council to realise that it could no longer make progress using only unanimity. Thus, particularly for and after the Treaty revisions of the Single European Act (SEA) and TEU, the Council has moved slowly, but significantly, to using QMV in more and more areas (12 more occasions with the SEA and 30 more with the TEU in 1992)—so much so that the continued applicability of the Luxembourg Accords has been brought into doubt. The Amsterdam and Nice Treaties extended QMV to another 70 instances.

> Despite the further considerable move to QMV following the Lisbon Treaty in some 44 more instances, unanimous voting will be retained for a few matters, particularly when measures may be considered necessary to fulfil certain Union aims, but for which express powers have not been foreseen. Unanimity has been retained for the areas of CFSP and defence policy, taxation, social security matters, and some budgetary matters, involving about 40 Treaty Articles.

For more details on this section visit the online resources.

QMV has been an exceptionally important issue in the Council. To agree that it is to be used more often has often involved much horse-trading—after all, any increase in the use of QMV also represents a further transfer of sovereign competences to the EU. However, more use of QMV is regarded as necessary because it allows votes to be taken by majorities. The possible alternative—to take decisions by simple majority—is not a real option because it is not politically acceptable for most member states that a simple majority should dictate a policy for the whole Union. This is particularly the case where the majority could consist of smaller states only, the population of which represents a clear minority of the overall EU population. Thus, the use of QMV enhances both democracy and efficiency in law-making in the EU where otherwise decisions would be extremely difficult to reach in a Council of 28 possible vetoes. It also encourages debate and consensus, because it is no longer possible for a state or states to fall back on a veto.

2.2.4.4 How QMV works

To reiterate that mentioned earlier in the chapter, new Article 16(3) TEU states that the Council shall act by QMV unless otherwise stated within the particular Treaty base concerned with the subject matter of the required legislation.

For more details on this section visit the online resources.

> It is worth noting that four countries—Germany, France, the UK, and Italy—had just over 57 per cent of the EU-25 population and in the EU of 28, the big four still have *approximately* 53 per cent of the population (around 270 from 506 million). This will of course be changed radically when the UK, with a population of *c.* 65 million, exits the EU.

Unlike the old Article 205 EC, which provided, within the Treaty, the numbers of votes that each member state has, the EU Treaty and TFEU no longer contain those figures, which are now contained in Protocol 36 on Transitional Provisions, Title II, as further qualified by Declaration 7 on Articles 16(4) TEU and 238 TFEU, both attached to the Treaties.

If voting were undertaken by simple majority based directly on population, it would mean that the four large states could always outvote the other 24 states combined. This would not be acceptable to the rest of the Union; therefore, the QMV voting rules and numbers contained compromises that seek to achieve a balance between facilitating a form of majority decision-making, and also providing that a sizeable minority of states can block decisions. Hence instead of a simple majority of states or votes or population representations being able to secure a result, a predetermined majority of votes has to be achieved from the sum of the blocs of votes of the member states.

France, Germany, Italy, (UK until exit, but not presently attending or voting)	29
Spain, Poland	27
Romania	14
The Netherlands	13
Belgium, Czech Republic, Greece, Hungary, Portugal	12
Austria, Bulgaria, Sweden	10
Croatia, Denmark, Finland, Ireland, Lithuania, Slovakia	7
Cyprus, Estonia, Latvia, Luxembourg, Slovenia	4
Malta	3
TOTAL	352

The qualified majority with 28 member states is 260 votes (73.86 per cent) from a possible total of 352. Thus a blocking minority of 92 votes will prevent a proposal from being passed. If voting on a proposal that has been introduced by the Council rather than the Commission, an additional requirement is imposed that a minimum of two-thirds (that is, essentially 19) of the member states must have voted in favour. Note, though, that the system was subject to a permanent change in 2017, which does pay more attention to population and the effect of the UK exit, which changes are noted below.

The rationale behind QMV is the idea that the number of Council votes per country should in some way, even if very crudely, represent the populations and thus usually the gross domestic product (GDP) of the countries—or, if you like, their political and economic clout! However, if this was straightforwardly or directly proportionately represented, the big four would have the majority and, if not actually dominating Europe, would certainly result in the fear of domination of Europe by a few large states over the wishes of numerous smaller states. Hence the votes for each country for a qualified majority were deliberately biased for the protection of smaller states and to ensure more of a consensus view. Of course, it is also possible to overcompensate the smaller states so that they hold the balance of power, and the Treaty of Nice went some way towards addressing the over-representation of the smaller states, by giving the larger member states a higher proportion of votes. To some extent, the acceptance of this change by all states is argued to have been regarded as fair compensation for the loss of a second Commissioner by the large states. However, it was not accepted without further condition because this change meant that a smaller combination of larger states could outvote the small states, something with which the smaller member states were not happy. Hence the reforms of QMV were hotly contested issues, with the discussions first concentrating on the number of votes per member state, and then on the additional requirements on the number of states voting and the populations of those states. The issue is one that was revisited a number of times, in particular at the June 2007 summit, and finally agreed in the Lisbon Treaty, which now provides for two transitional periods. QMV is now governed by Article 16 TEU, Article 238 TFEU, and Protocol 36 on Transitional Provisions, and was added to by a Decision within Declaration No 7 also attached to the Treaties! This is far from transparent.

For more details on this section visit the online resources.

It was originally agreed that new rules lowering the requirements of states or population to 55 per cent for either would apply, but this was postponed until 2017. The compromise resembles the Ioannina compromise, which was employed in the 1990s to allow a large, but not sufficient, blocking minority under QMV to ask the Council to consider further a matter before it and to try to reach a consensus view rather than adopt it. The reweighing of votes by the Treaty of Nice effectively ended this compromise, only for it to be brought back following representations by Poland during the negotiations on the Lisbon Treaty. It now finds expression in Declaration No 7 attached to the Treaties, whereby member states with a vote that is not sufficient to constitute a blocking minority can ask the Council to continue to discuss an issue to find a satisfactory solution without proceeding on the matter.

> The Ioannina compromise was established in 1994 as a result of the concerns that it would be harder to form a blocking minority following the move to QMV after the introduction of the SEA and the expansion in the member states. It essentially required the Council to think again, but, if insisted upon, to reduce the number of votes needed to form a blocking minority (Official Journal (OJ) 1994 L105/1).

For more details on this section visit the online resources.

> Following Lisbon:
>
> * from 1 April 2017, a single state can no longer ask for the previous rules to be imposed, and the double majority (55 per cent of Council members comprising at least 16 states and 65 per cent population) will apply to represent the minimum votes required to enact a measure which is subject to opposition. However, the revised Ioannina Compromise in Article 4 of Declaration 7 provides that member states representing 55 per cent of population or of the member states that constitute a blocking minority, who oppose the Council taking a decision by QMV can ask the Council to continue discussions. Article 5 of the Declaration provides that the council find a solution in a reasonable time.

So, in order to try to understand QMV today, one needs to have in mind the Treaties (Articles 16 TEU and 238 TFEU), the Treaty-altering Protocol 36 *and* Declaration No 7 attached to the Treaties, which modifies the rules again, to see the full picture. This is truly deplorable and something that only politicians could have dreamt up! Of course, most legislative decisions are, and will be, reached either by consensus or by a clear majority, but the exception-riddled rule on QMV makes it exceedingly difficult to gain a clear and straightforward understanding of the rules. Of course, after Brexit, the UK's 29 votes will disappear and new voting totals will have to be established with perhaps also new blocking percentages, yet to be determined.

 THINKING POINT

For what reasons are the rules and arithmetic for QMV so complicated?

2.2.5 Council general law-making powers

Apart from specific powers to enact legislation under the particular titles and Articles within the Treaty—the form of voting for which is specified in those Articles—the Council also possesses general powers to enact legislation. Article 113 TFEU empowers the Council, acting unanimously, under a special legislative procedure, to adopt provisions for the harmonisation of legislation concerning turnover taxes, excise duties, and other forms of indirect taxes (VAT) where harmonisation is deemed to be necessary to ensure the functioning and establishment of the internal market. Article 114 TFEU provides that the Council shall act by a qualified majority on a proposal that has as its object the establishment and functioning of the internal market. Article 115 TFEU, as an exception to Article 114, provides for the approximation of laws to complete the internal market which are not catered for by any of the specific parts of the Treaty and requires unanimity by the Council in consultation with the EP and EESC. Further, Article 352 TFEU provides generally that the Council may enact measures to attain the objectives of the Union. These general powers have been used extensively by the Council, particularly for measures not originally sanctioned elsewhere—for example, in 1976, to support the enactment of the Equal Treatment Directive 76/207. The Directive went much further than original Article 119 EC (ex Article 141 EC, now 157 TFEU) which was concerned narrowly with equal pay matters only. Article 308 EC (now Article 352 TFEU) was often used to enact environment measures before the Treaty was amended to include a title on environment. However, its proposed use to accede to the European Convention for the Protection of Human Rights and Fundamental Freedoms (ECHR) was prevented by the CoJ, which stated in Opinion 1/96 that it could not be used as the basis for acceding to the Convention as it was not within the contemplation, then, of the Treaty objectives.

> The overuse of the general powers, referred to as the 'competence creep', has been criticised and resisted by the member states. It was addressed both in the Constitutional Treaty and Lisbon Treaty, by more clearly establishing the division of competences. This topic is considered in Chapter 3. The Lisbon Treaty also specifically empowers the Union to accede to the ECHR, which is now provided in the amended Article 6(2) TEU.

2.2.6 COREPER and the Council General Secretariat

The Council is not a unitary and permanently constituted body, and in all configurations meets on only about 90 occasions per year. Hence it requires assistance to deal with its workload and to prepare for, and ensure some continuity between, meetings. This help comes in two forms. First, COREPER was established, consisting of representatives of the member states who may be part of the ambassadorial delegation or other civil servants on secondment. It is now formally established within Articles 16(7) and 240(2) TFEU. This body was brought in to reduce the workload of the Council, to balance the result of the delegation of decision-making power to the Commission, and to sift the Commission proposals. It also oversees and, to a lesser extent, controls the numerous management committees that were set up to supervise the delegation of power to the Commission. It receives assistance from numerous working groups of national experts and effectively takes many of the lesser important decisions for the Council itself, which then just rubber stamps those decisions.

Article 240(2) TFEU also provides for a permanent Council Secretariat made up of national civil servants to undertake much of the more mundane work of the Council, such as the organisation of and preparation for meetings, and it will also assist the European Council (Article 234(4) TFEU) and the High Representative in the new External Action Service (Article 27(2) TEU).

2.3 The European Council

Following the entry into force of the Lisbon Treaty, the European Council was elevated to a full Union institution (Articles 13 and 15 TEU). It now comprises the 28 heads of state and government, and in addition the European President and the President of the European Commission (Article 15(2) TEU), although these last two do not have voting rights (Article 235(1) TFEU). The High Representative will also participate in its meetings, also without voting rights. The European Council developed from the summit meetings of the heads of state and government of the member states who met from time to time to discuss matters outside the formal scope of the Community Treaties. Among other initiatives, it acted, or tried to act, in common response to international crises. After this informal start, Article 2 SEA placed the European Council on a legal basis and formalised European political cooperation in the areas of foreign policy consultation and monetary cooperation. These moves were further formalised and brought into the EU framework by Article 4 TEU, which stated that the European Council shall provide the Union with the necessary impetus for its development and shall define the general political guidelines, which are carried into Article 15(1) TEU today. Note, though, that legislative functions are specifically excluded (Article 15(1) TEU). The European Council therefore enjoys a much broader role than the Council of Ministers, which is restricted to matters included in the Treaties. Its overall function is set out in Article 22 TEU and specialised functions in other Treaty articles, for example, Article 68 TFEU, which provides that it define the strategic guidelines for legislative and operational planning within the area of freedom, security, and justice. In certain areas, draft legislation in sensitive matters, which more member states consider would affect their national systems and law, can refer to the European Council to review that matter whilst the ordinary legislative procedure is suspended. See, for example, Article 48 TFEU relating to the social security concerns. The European Council is also charged with overseeing membership applications and withdrawals (Articles 49 and 50 TEU).

❱❱ CROSS REFERENCE

The European President is considered further at section 2.3.1.

The European Council will meet at least twice every six months and member states' ministers may also take part, as may an assistant to the Commission President (Article 15(3) TEU). It meets now in Brussels, in a building constructed for it, rather than in each of the member states that in turn hold the Council presidency.

Previously, decision-making was entirely by consensus; now, whilst consensus is prescribed as the norm under Article 15(4) TEU, in certain areas as provided by the Treaty and as noted in this volume, it also decides by QMV. One of the most notable instances of this—which is also one of the, if not *the*, most notable institutional changes introduced—is the establishment of the new position of the European President. It appoints the High Representative by qualified majority (Article 18 TEU), jointly decides with the EP on the membership and appointment of the Commission, and decides on both the composition of the EP and its membership by unanimity (Articles 14(2) TEU, 17(5) and 18 TEU, and 244 TFEU, respectively).

The European Council has been criticised for being a purely intergovernmental organisation and for presenting a distinctly intergovernmental attitude at the top of the Union institutional hierarchy. Whilst it has, at times, provided the necessary political will and impetus to achieve very notable goals, such as economic union and the euro, it is feared that trying to achieve the agreement of 28 heads of state or government will prove very demanding. It is, though, regarded as having gained power following Lisbon, not least because of the continuity and leadership provided by the more permanent and independent chair, which has assisted decision-making and is considered next.

2.3.1 The European Council President

New to the Union, brought forward from the Constitutional Treaty to the Lisbon Treaty, is the creation of a President for the European Council, known as the 'European President'. The election of this person is by the European Council by qualified majority for a period of two-and-a-half years, renewable once.

Herman Van Rompuy was elected and stood down as premier of Belgium to comply with the requirement of independence (Article 15(6) TEU). He was re-elected unopposed by the European Council for a second term on 1 March 2012 with a term of office ending 30 November 2014, and was succeeded by former Polish Prime Minister Donald Tusk, who was elected unanimously.

The President is provided with the tasks of chairing the European Council, and driving forward and organising its work in cooperation with the Commission and General Affairs Council. He or she shall seek to obtain consensus by the European Council and report to the EP after each of the meetings (Article 15(6) TEU). He or she shall also oversee the external representation of the Union, without prejudice to the powers of the High Representative.

2.3.2 The High Representative of the Union for Foreign Affairs and Security Policy

The High Representative is, first of all, chosen from among the proposed Commissioners, then elected by the European Council by qualified majority, and automatically becomes a Commission Vice-President (Article 18 TEU). He or she conducts the CFSP, attends relevant European Council meetings, chairs the Council foreign affairs meetings, and leads the Commission in external relations. The present High Representative is assisted by an External Action Service set up for this purpose (Article 27 TEU). The idea of the role is to coordinate the conduct of the EU's external relations, although getting the 28 member states to come to a consensus on particularly sensitive political developments in the world can be understandably difficult.

2.4 The European Parliament (EP)

As originally conceived and constituted, the EP was called the 'Assembly', and consisted of members nominated by and largely from the member states' parliaments. It was arguably more aptly named at that time because it was not a true legislative body capable of law-making in its own right and it consists of only one chamber. However, the term 'Parliament' was used by its members from 1962, and with more authority following the direct election of its members for the first time in 1979. The name is now clearly sanctioned by Article 14 TEU. The EP is governed by Articles 14 TEU and 223–234 TFEU, and has enjoyed significant incremental increases in its powers and functions with each amending Treaty. It is still required, by agreement of the member states and now under Protocol 6 attached to the Treaties, to transit between three cities, holding most plenary sessions in Strasbourg and additional sessions in Brussels, but having its supporting Secretariat travelling in from Luxembourg.

For more details on this section visit the online resources.

Sections 2.4.1–2.4.5 consider the membership, elections, political groupings, functions, and powers of the EP.

2.4.1 Membership

Following the expansions of 2004, 2007, and 2013, the number of members of the European Parliament (MEPs) has been fixed under the Lisbon Treaty to a maximum of 750 plus the President (Article 14(2) TEU). Post Brexit, these figures must be revised.

MEPs are elected to serve the electorate in constituencies and are organised into cross-border political groupings rather than according to member state. Whilst the total number per state should be crudely in proportion to population, the broad political deal reached at Nice was that those member states that had gained in the QMV numbers lost more MEPs, whereas those member states regarded as losing out under QMV either retained the previous numbers of MEPs or lost proportionately fewer MEPs, compared with other member states. As a result of these changes, the constituencies of the larger states are considerably larger than those of the smaller states.

2.4.2 Elections and political groupings

Article 223(1) TFEU requires a common election system to be set up for the EP. Whilst all member states now, including the UK, have used proportional representation (PR) voting systems for the EP elections, this is still not a single common system, and although the same four-day period of Thursday into the weekend is used, the actual polling day(s) are different in different member states according to election day traditions: for example, the UK prefers a Thursday, whereas other member states have always used a Saturday or Sunday as polling day. Turnout for the EP elections is overall low and varies across the member states, but some national general elections also see low turnouts such as in Lithuania, Poland, Romania, and Switzerland. Once elected, MEPs sit in the transnational political groupings, recognised under Article 224 TFEU, although there is a strong national element and organisation within these, particularly as a result of national political party discipline. There are seven distinct groups and a final group for those members not wishing to be aligned to any of the specific groups. Obviously post Brexit, these figures will be revised.

The European (and UK) membership of the nine groups of MEPs is as follows.

(1) Group of the European People's Party (Christian Democrats) (PPE)	215 (0 in the UK)
(2) Group of the Progressive Alliance of Socialists and Democrats in the European Parliament (S&D)	190 (20 in the UK)
(3) European Conservatives and Reformists (ECR)	74 (21 in the UK)
(4) Group of the Alliance of Liberals and Democrats for Europe (ALDE) 65	(1 in the UK)
(5) Confederal Group of the European United Left–Nordic Green Left (GUE/NGL)	51 (1 in the UK)
(6) Group of the Greens/European Free Alliance (Verts/ALE)	51 (6 in the UK)
(7) Europe for Freedom and Democracy Group (EFD)	44 (20 in the UK)
(8) European Nations & Freedom Group	37 (1 in the UK)
(9) Non-attached members (NI)	18 (3 in the UK)
TOTAL	745 total seats

2.4.3 Functions and powers

Apart from the obvious function of a Parliament, which is that of a discussion and debate forum, the EP has the following powers and functions.

2.4.3.1 Legislative powers

Before the SEA was negotiated, as far as legislative participation was concerned, the EP had advisory and consultative powers only. Original Article 137 of the European Economic Community (EEC) provided that the Assembly shall 'exercise the advisory and supervisory powers which are conferred on it by this Treaty'. The Treaty originally specified only 17 instances in which the EP had to be consulted before legislation could be adopted by the Council. Its participation in the legislative process was increased by the conciliation procedure of 1977 and the introduction of the cooperation procedure by the SEA.

> Note that the cooperation procedure was removed entirely by the Lisbon Treaty.

The present authorisation for the EP's law-making role is Article 14(1) TEU, which empowers the EP to exercise legislative and budgetary functions jointly with the Council. It was the TEU that gave the Parliament its most extensive role in the legislative process by introducing the co-decision procedure, which has been extended in line with the extension of QMV in the Council of Ministers and has become the most widely used procedure. The Lisbon Treaty extended it very considerably in more than 40 instances, although not as far as in the draft Constitutional Treaty, which, as originally drafted, removed unanimity entirely. It is referred to now as the 'ordinary legislative procedure' (see Articles 289 and 294 TFEU) and accounts for about 90 per cent of law-making, including, since Lisbon, the areas of freedom, security, and justice, and in budgetary matters.

⟩ CROSS REFERENCE
This is considered in Chapter 3, section 3.6.1.1.

> The recent extension may affect the long-running debate about the EP's legislative role, whether it remains as limited as it was, and whether the term 'democratic deficit' can arguably still be used to describe the unsatisfactory degree of democratically legitimised participation in the law-making process in the EU by the EP, the only directly elected Union institution.

Finally, the EP has a power of consent (previously assent), which is a prerequisite for the accession of new member states or the entry of the Union into association agreements, the ECHR, and international agreements (Articles 49 TEU and 218 TFEU, replacing the powers contained in ex 300 and 310 EC). The EP can also ask the CoJ whether a proposed international agreement is compatible with the Treaties under Article 218(11). The EP has a new power of veto over delegated Acts (Article 290 TFEU), which answers the criticism that the EP had been left out of the procedure when decision-making powers are delegated by the Council to the Commission. This not only avoids some of the complexity of the previous comitology procedures, but also answers the 'lack of democratic input' criticisms levelled at this form of decision-making in the EU.

⟩ CROSS REFERENCE
Considered in Chapter 3, section 3.6.1.3.

The EP has also now been provided a right of participation in the revision of the Treaties, under Article 49 TEU by submitting a proposal for a Treaty revision to the European Council and to consent to intergovernmental conferences (IGCs) or conferences of government representatives being called.

2.4.3.2 Supervisory roles

The EP has, through various Treaty amendments, gained powers of appointment and removal of the Commission, as well as a general role of the scrutiny of the work of the Commission and other institutions.

Appointment of the Commission

Starting with appointment, the Treaty of Amsterdam introduced the requirement that the President of the Commission be nominated by the member states; after Lisbon, he or she is now nominated by the European Council by QMV and is then approved by the EP, despite the clear statement in

Article 14 TEU that the EP shall elect the President of the Commission. However, in 2014 the will of the EP was recognised by the European Council, who accepted the Commission President candidate who had secured a majority of votes of the EP. Then, the whole Commission, as selected by the member states in the Council and nominated in conjunction with the President-elect of the Commission, is subject to the approval of the EP (see now Article 17(7) TEU). The political strength gained by the EP by such changes was demonstrated in 2004, when the proposed new Commission had to be reconstituted because the EP took objection to the nomination of a particular Commissioner. In order to avoid a likely vote not to appoint the entire Commission, Barroso, the Commission President-designate, instead withdrew his proposed team and resubmitted it a couple of weeks later, having replaced the offending person.

Censure/removal of the Commission

At least on paper, the most powerful weapon of the EP would seem to be its power to censure the Commission, which means in effect to require it to resign from office. Articles 17(8) TEU and 234 TFEU provide that a two-thirds vote of the majority of the members is needed, but the Commission is required to resign in its entirety. The censure motion cannot be used against individual Commissioners, which is regarded as unfortunate. For example, in 1999, under the Santer Commission, certain Commissioners were accused of financial improprieties and fraud. A censure motion against the entire Commission failed, but following the very critical report of a committee of independent experts set up by the EP and Commission, the entire Commission resigned without a further vote of censure taking place. Whilst the end result was that which was required—that is, that certain Commissioners were removed from office—the result is criticised because the particular Commissioners were able to hide behind the collective resignation and not be singled out. Until new Commissioners are approved, the censured Commissioners remain in office. So far, no motions of censure have been adopted. Whilst not a right of the EP, the Commission President can require an individual member of the Commission to resign (Article 17(6) TEU), and no doubt the EP could bring its political pressure to bear if sufficiently motivated.

Other powers of scrutiny now available to the EP include:

- the ability to set up a committee of inquiry to investigate the alleged contravention or maladministration in the implementation of Union law (see Article 226 TFEU);
- the ability to question, orally or in writing, the Commission and the Council under Article 230 TFEU; and
- the right to discuss the Commission's annual general reports under Article 233 TFEU.

By political practice, the Council and now the European Council submit to the EP their work programme and annual reports for debate. The ECB is also now required to submit an annual report for debate. The EP is also entitled to request the Commission to submit proposals that the EP considers necessary for the implementation of the EC Treaty (Article 225 TFEU), although the Commission is not obliged to do anything about such a submission except inform the EP of its reasons for not submitting a proposal. Finally, under Articles 227–228 TFEU, EU citizens can petition the EP and complain to the Parliamentary Commissioner (the Ombudsman) to investigate maladministration by the institutions.

2.4.3.3 Budgetary powers

From the 1970s, the EP was given budgetary powers in the form of the final say over some limited aspects of expenditure. Furthermore, under the Budgetary Treaty of 1975, Parliament was given the power to reject the budget entirely, which it did in 1979 and 1984 (see Article 314 TFEU) and on a number of occasions subsequently. The 1979 rejection was partly in response to the increase in democratic legitimacy that the Parliament gained as a result of being directly elected in that year for the first time. However, rejection is not so drastic as it sounds because if the budget is rejected, the so-called 'one-twelfth rule' comes into operation, which means that until the new budget is approved, the Commission can spend per month up to one-twelfth of the previous year's head of expenditure (Article 315 TFEU). In order to try to avoid future, nevertheless disruptive, budget rejections, from 1988 various inter-institutional agreements have been agreed by the institutions to improve the functions of the budgetary procedure and financial planning. Thus the EP now discharges the Commission's implementation of the budget on an annual basis, although this has become more of a political show event as an opportunity to question and thus hold the Commission to account.

For the latest version of the inter-institutional agreements, see the online resources.

> The Lisbon Treaty provided full parity of the Council and EP in adopting the budget, and removed the distinction between compulsory and non-compulsory expenditure (Articles 314–315 TFEU).

2.4.3.4 Right to litigate

The EP was not originally named as one of the privileged applicants for the purposes of taking actions against the other institutions under Articles 263 and 265 TFEU. The CoJ held, however, in the *Transport* case (Case 13/83 *European Parliament* v *Council*) and in *Chernobyl* (Case C-70/88 *European Parliament* v *Council*), that the EP was able to bring an action against the other institutions under Article 232 EC (now 265 TFEU) where the other institutions had a duty to act, but had failed, and whilst originally it was held not to have a general right to challenge legislative acts under Article 263 TFEU (ex 230 EC), in the *Comitology* case (Case 302/87 *European Parliament* v *Council*), the EP was held to have the right to take action to protect its own prerogative powers.

> See also in this respect **Case C-295/80 *European Parliament* v *Council* (Students Residence Directive).**

Acts of the Parliament that have legally binding consequences can also be challenged under Article 263 TFEU by others: see Case 294/83 *Les Verts* v *European Parliament* and Case 34/86 *Council* v *European Parliament (Budgetary Procedure)*. The TEU amended Articles 230 and 232 EC (now 263 and 265 TFEU) to specify that the acts or omissions of the EP can be challenged, and the Treaty of Nice provided express confirmation that the EP is one of the privileged applicants able itself to challenge acts of the other institutions under Article 263 TFEU without any restriction in its *locus standi*.

⫸ CROSS REFERENCE

The details of all of these cases are considered in Chapter 9.

2.5 The Court of Justice of the European Union (CJEU or CoJ)

The CoJ, once a single-body institution, now comprises the CoJ, the General Court (formerly known as the Court of First Instance, CFI), and now the possibility of setting up specialised courts. These were first permissible following the Treaty of Nice in 2003, and initially called 'judicial panels'. The CoJ is governed and regulated by Articles 19(1) TEU and 257 TFEU and Protocol 3 on the Statute of the Court of Justice of the European Union and the Rules of Procedure. Note though that the only specialised Court, the Civil Service Tribunal, has been merged with the General Court by Regulations 2015/2422 & 2016/1192.

⫸ CROSS-REFERENCE

The Statute and Rules of Procedure can be found in Foster, *EU Treaties and Legislation*, Oxford University Press, Oxford, published annually.

The CoJ is a self-standing independent EU court; it is not in a hierarchical relationship with the national courts as in a system of appeal. Article 19(1) TEU outlines the general function of the CoJ, which is to ensure that, in the interpretation and application of the Treaties, the law is observed. In slightly more detail, Article 19(3) provides that the court shall:

(a) rule on actions brought by a Member State, an institution or a natural or legal person;

(b) give preliminary rulings, at the request of courts or tribunals of the Member States, on the interpretation of Union law or the validity of acts adopted by the institutions;

(c) rule in other cases provided for in the Treaties.

▶ CROSS REFERENCE
The specialised courts are considered in section 2.5.7.

This section considers the composition and organisation of the Court, the main aspects of procedure, its jurisdiction, and its methodology. The results of the expansion of the Court to a General Court and the specialised courts is also included.

2.5.1 Composition and organisation

The CoJ presently consists of 28 judges, one for each member state (as from 1 July 2013) and 11 Advocates-General (AGs) (as from 7 October 2015) (Article 252 TFEU), nominated and appointed by unanimous agreement by the governments of the member states for a renewable period of six years. As far as the AGs are concerned Poland will, as is already the case for Germany, France, Italy, Spain, and the UK, have a permanent AG and no longer take part in the rotation system, while the existing rotation system will involve the rotation of five AGs instead of three. Brexit will probably amend these numbers by the withdrawal of all UK members from the CoJ and the General Court.

The judges must be chosen from persons whose independence is beyond doubt and who possess the qualifications necessary for appointment to the highest judicial office in their own countries, or from academic lawyers who, in their own countries, may be appointed to the highest courts (see Articles 253–254 TFEU). The Lisbon Treaty also provides that future appointments must take account of the opinion of an advisory panel comprising former members of the CoJ (Article 255 TFEU).

The Court can sit as a full court with a quorum of 17 judges, a Grand Chamber of 15 judges with a quorum of 11 to hear cases involving either member states or Union institutions, or in chambers of three or five judges and of which there are 10 in total.

The TEU introduced an amended Article 221 (now 251 TFEU) that reduces the occasions on which the Court may need to sit in plenary session. This now occurs when a member state or a Union institution, as a party to an action, requests plenary jurisdiction.

2.5.2 Procedure

The Court is faced with a large number of cases, which can arise ad hoc from any of the member states in one of the now 24 official languages acceptable to the Court, but the Court operates internally in French as its only working language. The procedure of the Court is governed by a Protocol containing the Statute on the Court of Justice and by its Rules of Procedure. Its Rules generally reflect civilian law procedure, with the emphasis on written proceedings rather than oral, as is the case in the UK and other common law systems.

See the latest report of the CoJ on the online resources.

There are essentially four stages to proceedings: written proceedings, can now be filed online via the e-Curia website (http://curia.europa.eu/), followed by investigation and preparatory work on the case; then oral proceedings, including the AG's opinion, which can be omitted in certain circumstances. The final stage is the judgment, which follows deliberation in secret in French. Judgments of the CoJ are delivered in a single ruling. Article 2 of the Statute on the Court provides that, before taking up judicial office, each judge shall, in open court, take an oath to preserve the secrecy of the Court's deliberations. Arguments in favour of the single opinion of the Court include: that it supports its authority and that of the EU legal system; that it helps to build up new a common European law and to avoid reliance on the laws of particular states; and that it provides for more authoritative decision-making for the future. Arguments against include: that it often results in terse and cryptic judgments, with little evidence of reasoning; that it stifles true legal argument; and that it may inhibit judges and the development of law. To some extent these criticisms may be countered by the existence and role of AGs, who are to assist the Court by giving an opinion, in complete independence and impartiality, on the legal issues of a case to be examined in depth and by reviewing critically the jurisprudence of the Court on the subject. Although the opinion of the AG is not binding on the Court, it carries weight and adds to the development of EU law. Thus, an opinion of the AG acts like a first-instance decision subject to an automatic and instant appeal. He or she can adopt a public view or the parties' views, but cannot be bound to present any particular view. It is no longer a mandatory requirement that the opinion of the AG be heard before every judgment is given. According to Article 20 of the Statute of the Court of Justice, the Court may decide in a case that raises no new point of law, after hearing the view of the AG, that the case be determined without a submission from the AG. This possibility has been used increasingly, as demonstrated by the statistics of the Court in which it was estimated that about 30 per cent of the cases in 2004, increasing to 52 per cent of the cases in 2009 and 50 per cent in 2010, were decided without an opinion of an AG.

Note now that the expedited procedure under Article 62a of the Statute and Article 105 of the Rules of Procedure omits the part of the procedure comprising the chance to reply and rejoinder the original application or defence in a case, and interventions may be refused by the President in order to render a judgment in much less time and in as little as two months. These account for less than 18 applications in any year and only about half of them are granted. Figure 2.2 illustrates the procedure of the CoJ.

Figure 2.2 Procedure before the Court of Justice

Source: http://curia.europa.eu/

Procedure before the Court of Jusctice		
Direct actions and appeals		*References for a preliminary ruling*
Written procedure		
Application Service of the application on the defendant by the Registry Notice of the action in the Official Journal of the EU (C Series) [Interim measures] [Intervention] Defence/response [Objection to admissibility] [Reply and Rejoinder]	[Application for legal aid] Designation of Judge-Rapporteur and Advocate General	National court's decision to make a reference Translation into the other official languages of the European Union Notice of the questions referred for a preliminary ruling in the Official Journal of the EU (C Series) Notification to the parties to the proceedings, the member states, the institutions of the European Union, the EEA States, and the EFTA Surveillance Authority Written observations of the parties, the states, and the institutions
The Judge-Rapporteur draws up the preliminary report General meeting of the Judges and the Advocates General Assignment of the case to a formation [Measures of injuiry]		
Oral stage		
[Opinion of the Advocate General] Deliberation by the Judges Judgment		

For more details on this section visit the online resources.

2.5.2.1 The form of judgments

The report is drafted first in the language of the case, which is chosen from the 24 official languages by the parties or the defending member state. The full report, as required by the Rules of Procedure of the Court, comprises a brief summary of judgment, followed by the report for the hearing drawn up by the Judge Rapporteur, and containing the facts and procedure, and a summary of the arguments of the parties. The next part of the report contains the opinion of the AG, although this does not form an official part of the report. The final part contains the reasons or grounds for the judgment presented in numbered paragraphs, and the usually very succinct single ruling of the Court.

2.5.2.2 The reporting of cases and electronic reporting

There was until recently only one official set of reports of cases emanating from the CoJ and the General Court. These were the European Court Reports, cited up to the end of 2011 as 'ECR' and preceded by the year of publication. These are published in all of the official languages. They are divided into Part I, containing the judgments of the European Court of Justice (ECJ), Part II, containing the judgments of the General Court, and ECR-SC, containing staff cases, which are no longer automatically translated into all of the official languages. Until 2003, all cases were published, but thereafter a selective publication policy was adopted whereby, under Article 20 of the Statute of the CoJ, cases can be decided without an AG opinion and not subsequently published in paper form, although they will always be available electronically. Summaries of cases can also be found in the Official Journal, now official in the electronic version only, and full cases can be found on the Curia Internet website (http://curia.europa.eu/). The Court reports themselves are also as from 1 January 2012 published exclusively in digital format on the EUR-Lex site, at http://eur-lex.europa.eu/homepage.html. Furthermore, the citation for cases has also been revised by the adoption of the European Case-Law Identifier (ECLI) system, which will apply to national cases also concerned with EU law, which will carry the ECLI prefix. The system was adopted to make electronic tagging of cases, and thus access, both uniform and easier and works as follows as far as EU CoJ cases are concerned. The case name and number in the Court Register are retained, to which are added additional elements as demonstrated by the example provided by the Court of Justice.

> The ECLI of the judgment of the Court of Justice of 12 July 2005 in Case C-403/03 *Schempp* is the following: 'EU:C:2005:446'.
>
> It is broken down as follows:
>
> - 'EU' indicates that it is a decision delivered by an EU Court or Tribunal (for decisions of national courts, the code corresponding to the relevant member state appears in the place of 'EU');
> - 'C' indicates that this decision was delivered by the CoJ. Decisions delivered by the General Court are indicated by the letter 'T' and those of the Civil Service Tribunal by 'F';
> - '2005' indicates that the decision was delivered during 2005;
> - '446' indicates that it is the 446th ECLI attributed in respect of that year.

Note the prefix ECLI is not being added to CoJ decisions. It is being backdated to all cases from 1954 and is being used by the CoJ as from 2014. How it will be adopted for cases prior to 2014 in text books remains to be seen, particularly whether it replaces or is used alongside the existing cases before then.

For more details on this section visit the online resources, but as the URL is quite short the www case list is: http://curia.europa.eu/en/content/juris/c2_juris.htm.

The principal alternative in which cases are reported very soon after judgment is the Common Market Law Reports, cited as 'CMLR' and published by Kluwer. These provide reports in English of not only the judgments of the Community and now EU courts, but also of cases from the national courts of member states that have considered or applied important points of Community (EU) law or which have demonstrated the attitude of the national courts to such Community (EU) concepts as supremacy or direct effects.

2.5.3 Jurisdiction

Article 19 TEU provides that the CoJ, including the General Court and the specialised courts, each within their jurisdiction, shall ensure that the law is observed in the interpretation and application of the Treaties. The Court's factual jurisdiction is determined by Articles 19(3) and 256–279 TEU. The Court's geographic jurisdiction is limited by the Treaties to the area of the member states, but a judgment of the Court can have consequences and effects outside the geographic area.

> For example, in **Case 48/69 *ICI* v *Commission (Dyestuffs)***, the ICI head office, then outside the territory of the Community, was fined through subsidiaries based in the **European Economic Community (EEC)**.

European Economic Community (EEC)

The original name of the EC before it became the EU!

In addition, the Court has jurisdiction under the EEA Treaty to provide interpretations on disputed rules under the EEA Treaty, and under Article 218(11) the other institutions and the member states may obtain the opinion of the CoJ on the compatibility of proposed international agreements and Treaties with the TEU and TFEU.

For references as to where further information on these specialised aspects can be found, visit the online resources.

Article 275 TFEU excludes the jurisdiction of the CoJ on matters decided under the CFSP, except those relating to compliance monitoring under Articles 40 TEU and 263 TFEU. Article 276 excludes jurisdiction over police and law enforcement agency operations or actions.

2.5.3.1 Division of jurisdiction

The Court's jurisdiction can be divided in a number of ways that can be helpful in understanding what the CoJ does. One way is to look at the broad types of action available under Union law and adjudicated by the Court. This division also considers the parties to the actions, and three main categories can be established: actions taken against the member states, such as Article 258 TFEU; actions concerned with the review of acts of the Union institutions, such as Article 263 TFEU; and preliminary rulings under Article 267 TFEU.

CROSS REFERENCE

Details of all these actions can be found in Chapters 8 and 9.

Certain other aspects of the Court's work, such as interim measures and appeals from the General Court, stand outside such a division and have to be considered separately. One can also consider the way in which the Court is acting, for example as a constitutional court when considering the powers of the institutions and member states or the relations between them. It acts as an administrative court in cases of judicial review of acts of the institutions. It acts as an appeal court in hearing cases from the General Court. It also acts to determine the scale of fines against those offending against competition law and also against the member states when they breach Union law obligations. Finally, it acts as a kind of advisory court when providing rulings to national courts in response to preliminary ruling references.

The jurisdiction can also be divided into the following two much more commonly found classifications:

(a) direct judicial control, whereby the Court interprets a rule and applies it to decide the case itself; and

(b) indirect judicial control, whereby the Court interprets and rules on the validity of provisions, not the subject of an action before the Court. (This jurisdiction is mainly concerned with the preliminary rulings on the request of national courts.)

2.5.3.2 Direct actions

Direct actions are also termed the 'contentious jurisdiction' of the Court, under which the Court upholds the lawful exercise of the Union legislative and executive powers in actions against the Union institutions under Articles 263–265 TFEU concerning the judicial review of legally binding acts. The Court also upholds compliance of the Union obligations by the member states via Articles 258–260 TFEU and conformity with Union law by individuals via various Treaty Articles and secondary legislation, for example Article 103(2)(a) TFEU and Regulation 1/2003 concerning competition policy. Articles 268 and 340(2) TFEU confer non-contractual (delictual) jurisdiction and Article 270 TFEU gives the CoJ jurisdiction over staff cases, now effectively handed over to a specialised court with limited appeal rights, which is considered in section 2.5.7. The Court has a preventative judicial control intended to block the conclusion of an envisaged agreement by the Union with a third state or international organisation considered incompatible with the TFEU under Article 218. It can also be called upon to adjudicate in contractual disputes between Union institutions and contractual partners if called to do so under an arbitration clause in the contract (Article 272 TFEU). Finally, under Article 277 TFEU, the CoJ hears indirect challenges to Union legislation in proceedings already taking place before the CoJ.

2.5.3.3 Indirect actions

▶ CROSS REFERENCE

Such indirect actions are considered in further detail in Chapters 6 and 8.

Indirect judicial control is exercised by the preliminary ruling proceeding of Article 267 TFEU, whereby references are made from the courts of the member states for judicial rulings by the Court.

2.5.4 Methodology

A consideration of the methodology of the work of the Court is helpful in understanding the very pro-integrationist stance, also referred to as the Court's 'judicial activism', which has often been adopted in judgments, and how these judgments have helped to build a new European legal order.

2.5.4.1 Interpretation

The European Treaties and some of the secondary legislation are framework measures that often require considerable amplification and interpretation. This has given a wide scope to the CoJ to engage in expansive interpretation of the texts. From the beginning, the Court has taken a very proactive role at times in European integration, often to the consternation of some of the member states. Notable judgments are those concerned with what are now fundamental decisions of the Court, including direct effects, supremacy, and the liability of the member states. In these respects, the cases of *Van Gend en Loos, Costa* v *ENEL*, and *Factortame* (involving Spanish fishermen and the UK) are very good examples. The criticisms of the Court's integrationist stance were most strongly voiced during the negotiations for the Treaty of Amsterdam, with a report prepared by the UK government advising a curb on the activity of the Court. However, this was not taken any further and, in any case, the then Conservative government was voted out of office before the Amsterdam Treaty negotiations were concluded. Indeed, it could be argued that if it were not for the lead given by the Court in certain fundamental questions of then EC law jurisprudence, the Union legal system would not have obtained the coherency or strength that it has today and, as a result, the Union itself would be less secure. The Court has, as a result, been highly instrumental in European integration and in confirming the constitutional basis of the Union.

THINKING POINT

What arguments are for and against the Court engaging in such judicial activism?

The style of interpretation is described as 'teleological', 'far-looking', or 'forward-looking', in that the Court tries to determine, in the light of the aims and objectives of the Treaties and legislation, what was intended and what result would assist those goals. The Court often refers to the 'spirit' of the Treaty, the Community and now Union project itself, the preamble, and to general provisions of the Treaty, notably Articles 2, 3, 10, and 12 EC (now 3–6 TEU and 18 TFEU), in order to assist it in reaching a particular conclusion. As such, then, these represent a form of contextual approach, taking many things into account to justify a particular result in a particular judgment.

> For example, look at [71]–[75] of the judgment in **Case 26/62 *Van Gend en Loos,*** in which virtually all of the above justifications are covered by the ECJ in reaching its conclusions that EC law (as then termed) was capable of giving rise to direct effects, despite there being no express words to that end in the Treaty itself.

The Court often refers to the concept of *effet utile*, or the 'useful effect' of Community (and now Union) law, which would be undermined if a particular provision were not interpreted in a much more expansive way, more in line with the objectives of the Treaty rather than the actual words used.

» CROSS REFERENCE

For a full discussion and reasoning of direct effect, see Chapter 8, section 8.1.3.

> See, for example, **Cases C-6 and 9/90 *Francovich and others v Italy,*** in which the establishment of liability on the part of member states for a breach of EC law could never have been derived from a literal reading of the Treaty or secondary law.

These Community (and now Union) methods of interpretation are applied in addition to the usual array of methods of interpretation found in the member states' legal systems, including the logical, literal, purposive means of interpretation, although any strict use of such methods has often been rejected by the Court as unsuitable in the Community and now Union context.

> See, for example, **Case 6/60 *Humblet*** and **Case C-70/88 *Chernobyl***, in which direct use of the literal and historical intent methods, respectively, were rejected.

2.5.4.2 **Precedent**

Whilst there is no formal system of precedent, the CoJ, just like courts in civil law jurisdictions, tries to maintain consistency in its judgments. Past decisions are often cited in court and do therefore carry some persuasive, rather than any formal, authority. In particular, whilst all rulings of the Court are binding within the case itself, certain decisions are regarded as forming a sort of precedent for the national courts.

> For example, in **Cases 28–30/62 *Da Costa*** it was decided that references do not need to be made to the CoJ where the materially identical question had already been answered by the CoJ—in that instance, in the *Van Gend en Loos* case heard shortly before.

Furthermore, leading cases in Community law, such as *Van Gend en Loos* and *Costa* v *ENEL*, have acquired a higher, more authoritative, status than other cases, dealing, for example, with an interpretation of one of the common custom tariff classifications or some other mundane item of Community secondary legislation. This is so much so that this difference in status has now been more formally recognised by the decision no longer to publish all cases in the official series of courts reports, the ECR. Those from the chambers of three are not to be published, nor are rulings from chambers of five in which there has been no opinion of the AG, but this does not include Article 267 TFEU (ex 234 EC) preliminary rulings.

There are instances, however, in which the courts use the terminology of precedent.

> See, for example, **Case C-310/97 P *Commission* v *Assidomän***, in which the CoJ mentions *ratio decidendi* at [54], and both identifies previous precedents and distinguishes past cases relied on by one of the parties (at [54]–[62]).

❱ CROSS REFERENCE

These cases are dealt with in detail in Chapter 11.

Furthermore, judicial review cases often refer back to the leading Case 25/62 *Plaumann* v *Commission*: in Case C-263/02 P *Commission* v *Jego-Quere*, the *Plaumann* test was virtually held to dictate the result in subsequent cases. Hence, unofficially, the case law developed by the CoJ increasingly seems to resemble a true case law system relying on precedents to be taken forward to new cases. It must also be made clear, though, that the CoJ will not be constrained by previous case law it if considers that a change in the law is required.

> For example, see **Case C-267/91 *Keck***, which expressly sought to modify a previous ruling (**Case 120/78 *Cassis de Dijon***).

2.5.5 **The General Court**

For more details on this section visit the online resources.

The first measure to attempt to tackle the growing case load and thus to address the long delay in proceedings before the CoJ was the setting up of a CFI in 1986 by the SEA and now governed under Article 256 TFEU (ex 225 EC). The CFI commenced operation on 1 September 1989 and was re-named by the Lisbon Treaty as the General Court. It has presently 47 members as of 19 September 2016 due to the expansion agreed by the member states in December 2015, which was also in-volved with the assumption the Civil Service Tribunal. A further nine appointments will be made in September 2019. One of the judges may act as an AG where considered necessary in complex cases (Article 254 TFEU). The Court is divided into chambers of three and five judges, but can sit in Grand Chamber of 13 judges or a full court. Article 50 of the Statute of the Court of Justice has allowed for a single judge to hear cases in the General Court.

❱ CROSS REFERENCE

The specialised courts are considered at section 2.5.7 but the only existing specialised court, the Civil Service Tribunal, was abolished in 2016.

The jurisdiction was initially limited, but has been slowly expanded to any area of jurisdiction in-cluding, from 2004, direct actions under Articles 263, 265, and 340 TFEU, but only annulment applications brought by natural and legal persons and the member states, not those brought by the Union institutions. It has also been extended to include Article 267 TFEU preliminary refer-ences unless there is a risk to the unity of EU law, in which event the case should be referred to the CoJ. However, although the ability to hear preliminary rulings is given by Article 256(3) TFEU, this ability has not yet been designated and remains presently dormant. Article 256 TFEU allows for future changes of jurisdiction of the General Court to be made by amendment of the Protocol containing the Statute of the Court of Justice rather than by Treaty amendment. The General Court also has jurisdiction to hear appeals from the specialised courts (Article 256 TFEU), should any more be established, because the Civil Service Tribunal was dissolved in 2016 and its judges and jurisdiction transferred to the General Court, and applications for interim measures under Article 279 TFEU.

Appeals from the General Court may be made on points of law only to the CoJ. Three grounds are given:

(a) Lack of competence by the General Court;

(b) breach of procedure; and

(c) the infringement of a Union provision or rule of law by the General Court, or an error in the interpretation or application of law.

2.5.6 **Length of proceedings**

Despite the low numbers of appeals in the early years and optimism that the bringing into operation of the CFI would significantly reduce the backlog and length of proceedings, the continued increase in the numbers of cases being lodged at the CFI and the large numbers of cases that were transferred to it by the CoJ meant that the overall backlog of cases pending judgment before the CFI and the CoJ nevertheless increased. After years of increasing case-loads and growing backlogs, the expansion of the EU and CoJ in 2004, which saw a large influx of new judges, but (at least at first) few new cases from the new member states, combined with the increased jurisdiction of the then CFI, enabled the Court to make inroads into the backlog. This is no longer the case and, as was noted above, a Regulation was enacted in December 2015 to double the number of judges by September 2019, partly by merging the Civil Service Tribunal with the General Court.

> In 1998, there were over 1,000 cases pending before the CoJ. In 2005, this was reduced to 740, with only a slight rise to 767 in 2008. With these figures, the length of proceedings, which had increased over the years, also changed for the better, with Article 234 TEU (now 267 TFEU) references, direct actions, and appeals all showing annual reductions in the length of proceedings, more so in the period 2009–11, from 25.5 to 16.1 months, from 24.7 to 16.7 months, and from 28.7 to 14.3 months, respectively.

2.5.7 **The specialised courts**

The Treaty of Nice made changes to the organisation of the Community Courts and also provided for the establishment of judicial panels (now called 'specialised courts' following Lisbon) attached to the CFI (now the General Court) to relieve that Court of some of its case law (Article 257 TFEU, ex 225a EC). Judges are appointed by the Council acting unanimously under Article 257 TFEU. These courts will operate as first-instance courts, with an appeal to the General Court. The first decision under the new power was taken by the Council of Ministers in November 2004 (Decision 2004/752) and an EU Civil Service Tribunal comprising seven judges was established, but now abolished and assumed by the general Court. Staff cases were an apparently not inconsiderable load on the Court and 117 cases were transferred to the then judicial panel from the then CFI at the end of 2005. The possibility of establishing more tribunals for specialist subjects is now very unlikely in view of two more recent changes. The first is the decision to merge the Civil Service Tribunal with the General Court in September 2016, which was given legal effect by Regulation 2015/2422 (OJ 2015 L341/14). The second is that a possible EU Patent Court, which might have been constituted as a specialised court, was established outside of the CJEU structure and is considered briefly next.

2.5.7.1 **The Unified Patent Court**

Twenty-five member states (without Spain, Italy, and Croatia), have agreed the establishment of a Unified Patent Court (UPC), with exclusive jurisdiction to adjudicate disputes relating to the European Patent and now the Unified European Patent for those 25 states. It is not sure at this stage whether Brexit will mean the withdrawal of the UK from this Court and the cancellation of the proposed establishment of London, one of the three proposed locations of the Court.

For more details on this section visit the online resources.

2.5.8 **The European Central Bank (ECB)**

The ECB was set up in Frankfurt under the TEU to achieve price stability in the Union and is responsible for monetary policy, regulating eurozone interest rates, and the euro (€). Following the entry into force of the Lisbon Treaty, it became a full institution of the EU and is governed by Articles 13

TEU, Articles 282–284 TFEU, and Protocol 4 attached to the Treaties. It has its own legal Personality. It also cooperates with the national central banks in the Eurosystem, or ESCB.

2.5.9 The European Court of Auditors

While the Court of Auditors was made a full institution by the TEU and is regulated under Articles 13 TEU and 285–287 TFEU, it is not one usually covered in any detail in textbooks and will be mentioned here only briefly. The Court of Auditors, with a member from each member state, was established under the 1975 Budgetary Treaty, and audits the expenditure of the institutions for legality and sound financial management. It produces an annual report, which is forwarded to the EP to debate and to provide the Commission with a discharge if the expenditure is correct (Article 319 TFEU). The amended Article 263 TFEU provides that the Court of Auditors can take action to protect its prerogatives in judicial review actions against acts of the main legislative institutions.

2.6 The Union's advisory bodies

For more details on this section visit the online resources.

The following bodies are not full institutions named in Article 13 TEU, but advisory bodies to assist the main institutions and now established by a new Article 300 TFEU.

2.6.1 The Economic and Social Committee (EESC)

The EESC, previously also known under the acronym ECOSOC, was introduced to serve in an advisory role to represent various sectional interests, and must be consulted for the adoption of certain legislation as determined by the Treaty—although, once received, its opinion may be ignored by the Council. However, failure to consult would open up the legislation enacted to annulment, by analogy with the Article 263 TFEU (ex 230 EC) action by the EP in Cases 138 and 139/79 *Roquette and Maizena* v *Council*. Its members are appointed in a personal capacity along national lines by the Council voting by QMV and are drawn from various sections of society to provide a wide-ranging array of views on legislative proposals. They are also able to give opinions on their own initiative without invitation from the Council, Commission, or EP. The Committee is governed by Articles 301–304 TFEU.

2.6.2 The Committee of the Regions (CoR)

▶ CROSS REFERENCE

See Article 8 of Protocol 2, considered in Chapter 3.

A much later Community body, the CoR, was established by the TEU and is also an advisory body set up to represent regional and local bodies, and to meet the criticisms that the Union fails to recognise regional interests, particularly those of federal states. Usually, only the central or national bodies of federal states are formally represented in the Union institutional set-up—that is, in the Council of Ministers, which draws its members from the state governments. The Committee must be consulted for the enactment of certain legislation—see, for example, Articles 153, 165–168, and 173 TFEU—and is governed by Articles 305–307 TFEU. In the UK, membership is drawn from local authorities and the devolved forms of government in Scotland, Wales, and Northern Ireland. The CoR has been given the right to defend its prerogatives under the amended Article 263 TFEU and to issue proceedings when it considers that subsidiarity has not been complied with in instances where its consultation was compulsory in the legislative process.

2.7 Other Union bodies

Note that there is also an EIB, under Article 308 TFEU, to channel funding into European projects, and a number of advisory bodies. These include a Transport Committee (Article 99 TFEU), an Economic and Financial Committee (EFC, or ECOFIN) to advise the Council and Commission on internal market coordination matters (Article 134 TFEU), a European Social Fund Committee (Article 163 TFEU), and a Political and Security Committee (PSC, or POLISEC) to advise the Council and the High Representative on international situations under Article 38 TEU. In addition, there is an extensive list of further specialised EU bodies and agencies too numerous to include in this volume. When and if the UK exits the EU and all the institutions and bodies, adjustments to the membership and compositions of the institutions will take place.

For more details on this section visit the online resources.

Summary

The institutional framework of the EU, like the EU itself, is not a static entity, but a changing one. Sometimes, the names of the institutions change; sometimes, new institutions are added to the fold; sometimes, their membership changes; sometimes, the way in which they operate and act also changes. They too are a dynamic part of the EU and its development. Certainly, the powers they enjoy also change: in particular, the changes to functions and power of the only directly elected body, the EP, need to be understood, especially in connection with the discussion about the democratic deficit in the EU. Having a good background to these developments is not only something that is pertinent to this chapter, but is also relevant to an understanding of other aspects of EU law, which will be considered in the following chapters, such as the numerous inter-institutional disputes that have arisen from the law-making procedures. The Lisbon Treaty too has had a further profound effect on the institutional balance, perhaps more so than anticipated, introducing the European Council as a full institution, creating the European President and High Representative, and increasing significantly QMV in Council and co-decision for the EP. As a result, the EP and European Council are regarded as being much stronger now, but consequently, the Council and the Commission have much reduced power and influence. The next few years will see how they all settle into the new institutional order.

For suggested approaches to answering these questions, visit the online resources.

Questions

1. Who do the European Commissioners represent?

2. Why was there such a fuss about the number of votes per country and the combination of votes under QMV?

3. What role is played by the European Council?

4. Do the changes made by various Treaty amendments to the powers of the European Parliament go far enough to address the Union's alleged 'democratic deficit'?

5. Who or what is the European President and what function is played by the European President?

For guidance on how to tackle this specimen exam question and to read a suggested model answer, visit the online resources. www.oup.com/uk/forster_directions6e/.

6. Who or what is the High Representative for Foreign Affairs and Security Policy and what does he or she do?

7. What are the merits or otherwise of: (a) the CoJ delivering a single opinion when giving judgment (as opposed to separate and dissenting opinions); (b) the system of AGs?

 ## Sample exam Q&A

'The Council of Ministers is by its very nature the federal institution of the Community' (Walter Hallstein).

Discuss.

 ## Further reading

Books

Beck, G. *The Legal Reasoning of the European Union Court of Justice*, Hart Publishing, Oxford, 2013.

Burrows, N. and Greaves, R. *The Advocate General and EC Law*, Oxford University Press, Oxford, 2007.

Christiansen, T. 'The European Union after the Lisbon Treaty: an elusive "institutional balance"?' in Biondi, A., Eeckhout, P., and Ripley, S. (eds) *EU Law after Lisbon*, Oxford University Press, Oxford, 2012, p. 228.

Corbett, R., Jacobs, F., and Shackleton, M. *The European Parliament*, 8th edn, John Harper, London, 2011.

Earnshaw, D. and Judge, D. *The European Parliament*, 2nd edn, Palgrave, Basingstoke, 2008.

Foster, N. *EU Treaties and Legislation*, Oxford University Press, Oxford, yearly.

Hayes-Renshaw, F. and Wallace, H. *The Council of Ministers*, 2nd edn, Palgrave, Basingstoke, 2006.

Nugent, N. *The Government and Politics of the European Union*, 7th edn, Palgrave, London, 2010.

Peers, S. 'The EU's political institutions' in Barnard, C. and Peers, S. (eds) *European Union Law*, 2nd edn, Oxford University Press, Oxford, 2017, p. 37.

Peterson, J. and Shackleton, M. (eds) *The Institutions of the European Union*, 3rd edn, Oxford University Press, Oxford, 2012.

Puetter, U. *The European Council and the Council: New Intergovernmentalism and Institutional Change*, Oxford University Press, Oxford, 2014.

Wallace, H., Pollack, M. A., and Young, A. (eds) *Policy-making in the European Union*, 6th edn, Oxford University Press, Oxford, 2010.

Ward, I. *A Critical Introduction to European Law*, 3rd edn, Cambridge University Press, Cambridge, 2009.

Werts, J. *The European Council*, Harper, London, 2008.

Articles

Barents, R. 'The Court of Justice after the Treaty of Lisbon' (2010) 47 CML Rev 709.

De Waele, H. and Broeksteeg, H. 'The semi-permanent European Council presidency: some reflections on the law and early practice' (2012) 49 CML Rev 1039.

Gatti, M. and Manzini, P. 'External representation of the European Union in the conclusion of international agreements' (2012) 49 CML Rev 1703.

Horsley, T. 'Reflections on the role of the Court of Justice as the "motor" of European integration: legal limits to judicial lawmaking' (2013) 50 CML Rev 931.

Solanke, I. '"Stop the ECJ"?: an empirical analysis of activism at the Court' (2011) 17 ELR 764.

WEBSITE

http://curia.europa.eu/

3

Transfer of powers, competences, and law-making

LEARNING OBJECTIVES

In this chapter, you will learn about:

- the transfer of power and competences from the member states to the Union;

- the division of competences between the member states and the Union;

- the principles of proportionality and subsidiarity and other methods of controlling that competence transfer; and

- the processes by which binding secondary EU laws are made.

Introduction

This chapter has as its focus the topic of the transfer and division of power, otherwise termed competences, from the member states to the European Union (EU). The question of whether the EU has the competence for a certain subject area also determines the logic of the supremacy of Union law. However, in order to have competence in the first place, the EU needs to have power transferred to it. Hence the logical way in which to introduce these topics is to outline first the transfer, and then the division and control of competences between the Union and the member states. In this context, the principles of subsidiarity and proportionality play an increasingly important role as additional elements of the ways in which the member states are seeking to control the use of transferred powers and competences. Thus, the division of competences and the principle of subsidiarity are both political solutions to the very emotive questions about how power is shared between the Union and the member states. Subsidiarity is a way of determining where the line between Union and member states' competences should be drawn. The chapter commences, however, with the start of this process, which is the transfer of powers to the EU. It then considers the principal reason for the transfer of competences, which is to provide the EU institutions with law-making powers by which the Union is able to carry

> **CROSS REFERENCE**

The supremacy of Union law is considered in Chapter 5.

out its tasks as laid down in the Treaties. A part of law-making is concerned with using the correct legal base for those laws, a topic allied with competences; hence legal base as well as law-making are considered in this chapter.

The relationship between transfer, competence, and supremacy

The original Treaties, and indeed those now applicable, do not provide a clear-cut expression of the relationship between the law of the EU—that is, the Treaties and the laws created by the institutions, on the one hand, and the national laws or domestic laws of the member states, on the other. There is no Treaty Article or rule to say which, in the event of conflict between laws covering the same subject matter, should take priority. Neither did the original Treaties make any expression as to their own status: were they constitutional rules or just another international treaty between signatory states?

THINKING POINT

Why do you think that the very important issue of supremacy was omitted? Do you think that it was done intentionally or merely overlooked?

Whilst the question of supremacy was quickly and clearly settled by the Court of Justice (CoJ), at least from the Union standpoint, the matter of competence is not so easily dealt with. In order for Union law to be supreme, the Union must first possess a competence to act. If it does not have the competence to act in a certain way or to create laws to facilitate its actions, then by logic such laws cannot take priority over member states' national law. This interlinked relationship between supremacy and competence can be observed in Case 22/70 *Commission v Council (ERTA)* ([30]–[31]) and in Opinion 1/94, in which it was held that if the (then) Community has competence, the member states cannot act contrary to it. This is now confirmed in Article 2 TFEU, considered below in section 3.2. Furthermore, there are circumstances whereby even when member states exercise their own exclusive competences, these may be held to be subject to EU law if they impact on or restrict EU laws in some way. See, for example, Case C-438/05 *Viking*, in which the CoJ held that when exercising their own competence, member states must nevertheless comply with EU law. Hence, the possibility of a clash of views in this area is quite possible and easy to foresee.

If you think about it, this is another way of saying that, in such circumstances, EU law is supreme.

First in this relationship, however, is the transfer of power from the member states that provides the competences.

3.1 The transfer of sovereign powers

When the Union was first established, it was in full recognition that to be able to achieve the goals set for it, the member states had to pool their resources in the new entity—in other words, they needed to transfer some of their sovereign rights to the Union and its institutions for them to be able to carry out their tasks. This was facilitated by the member states providing the competences for the Communities (Union) to make their own laws, a process that was later acknowledged clearly by the CoJ in the seminal *Van Gend en Loos* case, but with the proviso that the power transfer or transfer of sovereignty was carried out only within limited fields and was not a general transfer of power. A general transfer would include the ability to redefine competences without reference to any other body, the most obvious and important other body in this context being the member states. There was not a general transfer of powers by the member states to the Communities.

> This judgment in *Van Gend en Loos* by the CoJ in fact met the comments and criticisms that were to be raised subsequently by national constitutional courts, especially a German court, many years later, and was therefore very prescient of the Court. The general transfer of power is often discussed using the German term '*Kompetenz-Kompetenz*'. See Chapter 5 on supremacy for details.

Any power that the Communities and Union have been provided is only there by virtue of the transfer by the member states. However, the Communities, as developed into the Union, were not static; they have developed considerably since first being established and the competences have grown hand in hand with the complexity of the Union. Each successive Treaty amendment has transferred further powers to the Union, with a corresponding loss of sovereignty for the member states in those areas as agreed by the member states. For details, see Chapter 1. The member states, however, remain the bodies that decide whether the competences of the Union should be increased at all. It is to be noted that, so far, the Union has only an incomplete external competence, and there is no single Union body that makes law and represents the Union externally, as would the government of a federal state. The creation of the 'High Representative' is perhaps, though, a move in this direction. How competence and competences are divided between the member states and the Union and exercised by the institutions of the Union is considered next and involves the introduction and initial discussion of another European term: 'subsidiarity'.

3.2 The division of competences

For more details on this section visit the online resources.

One of the most fundamental elements of an organisational order is the division of competence or power between the central body and the constituent parts of the state or organisation in question. The transfer of powers and thus competences from the parts to the centre, from the EU member states to the Union itself, should in theory be a clear-cut process whereby any exercise of these powers by the institutions of the Union can only be within the terms granted by the member states and contained and clearly set out in the Treaties. In other words, there should be nothing done by the Union institutions that is not expressly permitted by the Treaties.

The division between member states and the Union is termed the vertical division of competences. A horizontal division exists between the institutions and the EU; these relationships are considered in Chapter 2.

The logical consequence of this is that what is attributed to the Union by the member states is necessarily removed from member states' competence. In other words, the member states no longer have competence in the fields transferred.

This principle of **attributed, or conferred competence** finds expression in Articles 1, 4, and 5 of the Treaty of the European Union (TEU) or Maastricht Treaty. Article 4(1) states that 'competences not conferred upon the Union in the Treaties remain with the Member States'. Article 5(1) provides that 'The limits of Union competences are governed by the principle of conferral' and Article 5(2) amplifies a general statement to the same effect as that in Article 4 that:

the Union shall act only within the limits of the competences conferred upon it by the Member States in the Treaties to attain the objectives set out therein. Competences not conferred upon the Union in the Treaties remain with the Member States. The limits of conferral also apply to each of the institutions by Art 13(2) TEU.

Article 2 of the Treaty on the Functioning of the EU (TFEU) backs that up by outlining the exclusive and shared competences, as set out in sections 3.2.2.1 and 3.2.2.2.

> **Attributed, or conferred competence**
> Union law terminology for the competence transferred from member states to the Union.

3.2.1 Express policies, powers, and legal base

The range of actions to be undertaken by the Union and competences are now set out in Articles 3 TEU and 2–6 TFEU, which list the objectives and activities of the Union, but do not specifically detail any one of them. This is left to specific titles and chapters in the TFEU. Where the Treaty specifies a particular object, it invariably provides a power to achieve that object. This may also be expressed by the concepts of express policies, powers, and legal base, all of which are covered in further detail during the course of this chapter. The express policies are those objectives outlined in the Treaties; the power to achieve them and thus simultaneously the legal base for secondary EU law to achieve the objectives will also be provided within a Treaty Article.

For example, Articles 45 and 46 TFEU set out respectively the objective and power of achieving the free movement of workers in the Union. Article 45 provides the policy, and Article 46 the power and legal base, to enact secondary legislation to achieve the policy aims.

3.2.2 The split between exclusive, concurrent, and complementary competences

If the division of competences were clearly set out, there would be no particular difficulty; but in 1957 this was not so. However, at that time, the initial Treaties were much more limited in scope, and therefore this was less of a concern. The Communities were not, however, intended to be a static, one-off creation, but a long-term and evolving one. The initial expectation was that integration in one area was expected to spread to other areas and that powers would be needed to regulate those new areas. In addition, the Community would have to react to events in the world as they unfolded and affected it. Hence, it was anticipated that the competences and their division needed to be dynamic and equally evolving, and not static. This meant that the Communities (and now Union) would also have to be reactive and the competences capable of expansion. It is necessary, therefore, to consider what the competences were, how they developed, how the member states considered and reacted to this, and what measures were taken to control the **competence creep** that was observed.

▶ CROSS REFERENCE

Competence creep was discussed in Chapter 1 and is explored further in section 3.4.

> **Competence creep**
>
> The term given to the slow assumption of competences by the Commission and institutions generally to carry out the policies of the Union. Their power to do so is not expressly granted by the member states, but the Commission and/or Union is seen to both increase the use, and take advantage, of implied powers.

Competences are divided initially into exclusive and concurrent or shared competences, and until the reforms brought about by the Lisbon Treaty this division was vague. Now, it is much clearer and is expressly set out in the Treaties, as will be noted in section 3.2.2.1. Furthermore, a revised Declaration (No. 18) on competences has been attached to the Treaties, which confirms the respective rights of the member states and Union, the latter represented by the Commission in these matters. The clarification of this division is one of the answers to competence creep. In addition to the three categories considered next, there are also special categories of competence that should be briefly noted, such as those within the Common Foreign and Security Policy (CFSP) (Article 24 TEU).

3.2.2.1 Exclusive competences

The Union enjoys exclusive competences in a few areas only, the customs union and internal market being the most obvious and important area and parts of the Common Fishing Policy. The exclusive competences and thus power to adopt legally binding acts are defined in Article 2(1) TFEU:

> **Article 2(1) TFEU**
>
> 2. When the Treaties confer on the Union exclusive competence in a specific area, only the Union may legislate and adopt legally binding acts, the Member States being able to do so themselves only if so empowered by the Union or for the implementation of Union acts.

Those exclusive competences are then set out in Article 3 TFEU. In these areas, the member states no longer have the right to enact laws. Inevitably though, there can be an overlap with those areas in the shared list, such as customs union and internal market.

> **Article 3 TFEU**
>
> 1. The Union shall have exclusive competence in the following areas:
>
>   (a) customs union;
>
>   (b) the establishing of the competition rules necessary for the functioning of the internal market;
>
>   (c) monetary policy for the Member States whose currency is the euro;
>
>   (d) the conservation of marine biological resources under the common fisheries policy;
>
>   (e) common commercial policy.
>
> 2. The Union shall also have exclusive competence for the conclusion of an international agreement when its conclusion is provided for in a legislative act of the Union or is necessary to enable the Union to exercise its internal competence, or in so far as its conclusion may affect common rules or alter their scope.

The second paragraph was to make express that the EU has external competence to achieve matters that the member states had empowered the Union to regulate internally, as will be seen with the cases in section 3.3.3.

3.2.2.2 Concurrent competences

In other areas—that is, in most areas—the dividing line is not so clear and competence is concurrent between the member states and the Union.

> This is also termed 'shared', or 'non-exclusive', competence.

Shared competence is, however, initially defined by Article 2(2) TFEU, which provides:

Article 2(2) TFEU

2. When the Treaties confer on the Union a competence shared with the Member States in a specific area, the Union and the Member States may legislate and adopt legally binding acts in that area. The Member States shall exercise their competence to the extent that the Union has not exercised its competence. The Member States shall again exercise their competence to the extent that the Union has decided to cease exercising its competence.

Following the Lisbon Treaty reforms, the areas covered by shared competences are set out in Article 4 TFEU. Once the EU has acted, the member states power to legislate in the same area is denied, which is termed 'pre-empted' in EU jargon and is also mentioned below at the end of this section. Note, though, Protocol 25 on the Exercise of Shared Competence, which seeks to limit the extent of shared competence by restricting it to specific actions and not whole areas of competence.

> **CROSS REFERENCE**
>
> This is considered in section 3.4.4.

Article 4 TFEU

1. The Union shall share competence with the Member States where the Treaties confer on it a competence that does not relate to the areas referred to in Articles 3 and 6.1.
2. Shared competence between the Union and the Member States applies in the following principal areas:
    (a) internal market;
    (b) social policy, for the aspects defined in this Treaty;
    (c) economic, social and territorial cohesion;
    (d) agriculture and fisheries, excluding the conservation of marine biological resources;
    (e) environment;
    (f) consumer protection;
    (g) transport;
    (h) trans-European networks;
    (i) energy;
    (j) area of freedom, security and justice;
    (k) common safety concerns in public health matters, for the aspects defined in this Treaty.

The TFEU makes clear that the Union also has a shared competence with the member states in the development of common foreign, security, and defence policies (Article 2(4) TFEU).

3.2.2.3 **Complementary or coordinating competences**

Areas of law outside those exclusive and concurrent competences remain the competence of the member states, although, following Lisbon, the Union may support, complement, or coordinate (Article 2(3) TFEU) member states' activities in relation to economic policy, employment, and social policy (Article 5 TFEU). In addition, the Union may also support, coordinate, or supplement the member states in areas sanctioned by Article 6 TFEU.

Article 6 TFEU

The Union shall have competence to carry out actions to support, coordinate or supplement the actions of the Member States. The areas of such action shall, at European level, be:

(a) protection and improvement of human health;

(b) industry;

(c) culture;

(d) tourism;

(e) education, vocational training, youth and sport;

(f) civil protection;

(g) administrative cooperation.

It is in the area of shared competences that most difficulties arise, where it can still be unclear whether the Union or the member states have the competence for a particular action. Furthermore, the degree of sharing also alters according to the subject matter: for example, in areas such as the internal market, as soon as the Union acts under its competence, it assumes exclusive power to act and the member states are then deprived of the power to act in conflict. If, however, the Union chooses not to act, the member states retain the power to act.

This assumption of competence is known as 'pre-emption'.

⟫ CROSS REFERENCE

The free movement of goods will be considered in Chapters 10 and 11.

A good example can be seen from the area of the free movement of goods by the following case.

The CoJ held in the leading case of **Case 120/78 *Rewe-Zentral AG* v *Bundes-monopolver-waltung für Branntwein (Cassis de Dijon)*** that only where the Community had not acted could the member states act independently, and even then, if concerned with a general area, the member states could act only within prescribed limits.

As a result, it is possible for there to be a genuine grey area between what is within the Union competence and what is still within the member state competence.

This is a matter that has troubled the EU time and again, in particular as it became clear from the progressive judgments of the CoJ that the Community (and now Union) had taken over from the member states even in areas to which the member states were either not sure they had agreed, or indeed to which they were of the conviction that they had not agreed, or even where they considered that they had excluded that particular matter from EU competence.

For example, in **Case C-262/88 *Barber***, private pension scheme payments were held to be pay, and therefore within the European Community (EC) equal pay competence and not therefore a matter of state competence and exclusive regulation. (See Article 7 of Directive 79/7, which reserved pension age matters to member states.) It was considered, however, that state pension policy was a matter still within the exclusive competence of the member states.

Another good example is Case C-135/08 *Rottmann*, which was concerned with a decision about the withdrawal of national citizenship, which should, it would seem, fairly obviously be a matter for the member states alone. However, the CoJ advised that when making such a decision, the member state should take into account the consequence for EU citizenship.

As a result, there has been a reaction by some of the member states, which considered that the Commission and Community and now Union were and are extending their competences by stealth and not with the agreement of the member states. We now consider how competences could be and were extended, and what measures were developed by the member states to control this.

3.3 Extension of competences

In the traditional understanding of international law, the only way in which to add competences to a specific international organisation is where all signatories to the Treaty agree to Treaty amendment. Whilst Treaty amendment has taken place in the EU, it is only one of three ways in which the competences of the Union can be extended, which include the express increase in competences as sanctioned by the member states, the exercise of residual competence-creating powers provided by the member states and contained within the existing Treaties, and implied competences, which are those declared by the CoJ, for the most part, as necessary to undertake existing obligations under EU law. All three will be explained in turn.

For more details on this section visit the online resources.

3.3.1 **Express by Treaty amendment**

Treaty amendment, the first of these ways, is deliberate and clear-cut. The areas of Union competence have expanded greatly as a result of the member states assigning additional competences to the Union, with successive Treaties adding, for example, a chapter on environmental policy to the EC Treaty by means of the Single European Act (SEA), or economic and monetary policy by means of the Maastricht Treaty. The Lisbon Treaty also contains the agreement of the member states to extend areas of Union competence further into intellectual property rights, sport, tourism, and civil protection, amongst others. Article 48 TEU also allows for an increase in competences, either by the ordinary legislative procedure, if they are considered as minor, or if not, following a Convention of the Parliaments, member states, Commission, and European Parliament (EP) to consider them. Equally competences may be reduced.

The second and third ways are not express and have led to the use of the term 'competence creep' to describe the manner in which the institutions' competences have advanced incrementally. This has been by the use of general or otherwise termed, residual powers and implied powers by the institutions, notably the Commission. This process of extension by implied powers has been subject to the review of the CoJ, highlighting that, as a dynamic and evolving area of Union law, the limits of its development and extension must be judicially controlled, especially where not expressly provided for in the Treaty.

3.3.2 **Residual powers**

The second way by which competences have been expanded is via the residual or general law-making powers, which include both specific and general kinds defined in context in sections 3.3.2.1 and 3.3.2.2.

3.3.2.1 **Specific**

Specific residual powers are those that grant subsidiary law-making powers to complete goals in specific areas, in particular to complete the internal market. Articles 114 and 115 TFEU provide for the approximation of laws affecting the establishment or functioning of the internal market and measures for the completion of the internal market.

> Note also in this context Article 113 TFEU, which provides a residual specific power for the Council, acting unanimously and consulting the EP and the European Economic and Social Committee (EESC), to adopt harmonising legislation in the areas of turnover taxes, excise duties, and indirect taxes where necessary to ensure the establishment and functioning of the internal market and to avoid distortion of competition.

> **CROSS REFERENCE**
>
> For details of the voting procedures in Council, see Chapter 2, section 2.2.4.

Article 114 TFEU (ex 95 EC) provides that to achieve the objectives of the internal market, set out in Article 26 TFEU, where powers are not otherwise provided by the Treaty, action can be taken by qualified majority voting (QMV) under the ordinary legislative procedure, as well as consultation of the EESC. In other words, action can be taken outside of the express and exclusive granting of powers to the Union by a majority and not by the agreement of all of the member states. Article 114(2), though, excludes the adoption of measures relating to fiscal provisions (catered for by Article 113 TFEU, noted above), the free movement of persons, and the rights and interests of employed persons.

Article 115 TFEU (ex 94 EC) is an exception to the powers granted in Article 114 TFEU, which is a general power to enact harmonising legislation. It does, however, contain safety measures so that member states and institutions do not go too far: the Council must act by unanimity and only need consult the EP and EESC.

> **THINKING POINT**
>
> What is the consequence of the Union using these powers to enact a harmonising measure (which is binding)? The states lose competence, and if it happens a lot, states lose a lot of competences. Hence this is important, because any use or misuse of Article 115 TFEU may be seen as part of the competence creep problem.

It has been held, though, by the CoJ that these Articles should not be used where other Articles are more appropriate. In the following case, the question was essentially whether the measure enacted was an internal market measure or enacted for another reason.

> In **Case C-376/98 Germany v European Parliament and Council (Tobacco-Advertising I)**, Article 95 EC (now 114 TFEU) was used as the legal base to enact a Directive banning the advertising of tobacco products, but was held to be inappropriate and thus lacking the competence to enact a measure which was basically aimed more at the protection of health than at completing the internal market.

However, in **Case C-210/03 *R v Secretary of State for Health, ex p Swedish Match***, the European Court of Justice (ECJ) held that if obstacles to trade emerge, the Commission can intervene to harmonise even if the internal market is not the prime motive—that case being concerned with the banning of a type of snuff. The ban in one country was projected as causing disparities in the internal market.

Finally, in the second Tobacco Advertising case, **C-380/03 *Germany v European Parliament and Council***, Article 95 EC (now 114 TFEU) could be used to enact the second attempt Directive to restrict the advertising of tobacco products, where differences in the national laws relating to this advertising would have the effect of creating obstacles to free trade, thus elevating the internal market aspect of the legislation. The Directive was thus held necessary to harmonise the internal market to allow it to function properly. Whilst Article 114 as conceived was for the harmonisation or approximation of laws, and not for completely new laws, the CoJ has been flexible in its interpretation of that. In Case C-217/04 *UK v EP & Council* (ENISA) it held that Article 114 could be used to create a new EU body which itself contributed to the process of harmonisation by providing assistance to member states in assimilating their laws to harmonisation legislation already in existence.

> **CROSS REFERENCE**
>
> These cases concerned with competence are related to or the same cases dealing with where an incorrect legal base has been employed, which are considered in section 3.5.1.

3.3.2.2 General residual power

The general kind of residual power is Article 352 TFEU (ex 308 EC), which provides that, in furtherance of any of the objectives of the Treaty and where no specific power exists, the Union may act by means of the Council acting unanimously with the consent of the EP. Note that previously it was only necessary to consult the EP. In other words, where the EU has no other options it should be a measure of last resort.

> **Article 352 TFEU**
>
> If action by the Union should prove necessary, within the framework of the policies defined in the Treaties, to attain one of the objectives set out in the Treaties, and the Treaties have not provided the necessary powers, the Council, acting unanimously on a proposal from the Commission and after obtaining the consent of the European Parliament, shall adopt the appropriate measures.

A new Article 352(2) TFEU requires the Commission to draw such proposals also to the attention of the national parliaments in accordance with the subsidiarity principle, which is considered in section 3.4.2.

Article 352(3) TFEU expressly does not permit harmonisation of member states' laws nor, under Article 352(4) TFEU, does it apply to the areas of CFSP; the member states have backed this up in Declaration Nos 41 and 42, considered further at the end of this section. As these are residual powers, use of Article 352 has led to problems regarding just how far it sanctions Union activity in the face of member states' competence claims. However, it has been generously interpreted by the CoJ. Article 308 EC (now 352 TFEU) was used as the Treaty base for the original Equal Treatment Directive 76/207 because, at the time, the relevant Treaty base (ex Article 119 EC) extended only as far as equal pay. Article 308 EC (now 352 TFEU) was also used extensively to introduce legislation concerned with environmental matters for which there was not, at the time, a Treaty Article base available and at a time when Treaty amendment was unlikely. Article 352 TFEU was used recently for the adoption of Regulation 216/2013, which promoted the electronic version of the Official Journal as the only official version, thus replacing the printed version.

The use, overuse, or improper use of Article 352 TFEU and its predecessors has been subject to criticism that the Council was by-passing both the EP, which originally only needed to be consulted, and the national parliaments, which would have participated in Treaty revisions. Hence, limits on its use were established.

> A limit to such use was found when the CoJ held in its Opinion 2/94 of 1996 that Article 235 TEU (ex 308 EC, now 352 TFEU) could not be used to accede to the European Convention on Human Rights and Fundamental Freedoms (ECHR) because of the profound constitutional impact it would have on the Community and the member states, which was not envisaged nor indeed sanctioned by the Treaty, especially where such action would in effect amount to an unsanctioned amendment of the Treaty. Note that there is now an express power to access the ECHR by Article 6 TEU.

Furthermore, the use of Article 308 EC (now 352 TFEU) would be improper if a specific Treaty base was shown to exist (see Case 8/73 *HZA Bremerhafen* v *Massey-Ferguson*) and which should therefore have been used instead. More recently, in Cases C-402/05 P and C-415/05 *Kadi* v *Council*, a challenge to the use of Article 308 EC (now 352 TEU) was made following a freezing of the assets of persons whom the United Nations (UN) considered to be related to terrorists following the 9/11 attacks. It was argued that this was beyond the competence of the EU, but this argument was not accepted by the ECJ, which linked the economic action of the Council to the Common Market—a link that seems somewhat tenuous. It would seem therefore that even very weak links to the Union and its activities will suffice to justify the use of Article 352 TFEU. Article 352 TFEU can now also be used in pursuit of the objectives of the Union, as opposed previously to only those of the EC, so its potential scope for use is much wider. This is countered by the requirement that measures taken under this Article will be subject to the same procedure as that required for the monitoring of subsidiarity, requiring consultation of the national parliaments, and that whilst it still restricts the EP's role, it does at least now require the consent of the EP, and not just mere consultation. It is also countered by the member states' attachment of Declaration Nos 41 and 42 to the Treaties, which seek to prevent both a general widening of the scope of Union powers, especially those which would resemble Treaty amendments and thus beyond those expressly conferred, and specifically not to permit its use in pursuit of CFSP objectives. It remains to be seen whether the CoJ will regard Article 352 TFEU as being so constrained.

3.3.3 Implied powers

The exercise of implied powers is the third means of extending competences. This was recognised by the CoJ in cases dealing with both internal and external powers of the Commission, where, in the absence of express powers in the Treaty, powers are nevertheless required to achieve a Union goal and are thus implied. This development is also referred to as 'parallelism'. Implied powers to carry out internal competences can also be used to support external powers, although no such express external powers are provided in the Treaty.

The Court of Justice confirmed the validity of implied powers in the Union legal order as early as Case 8/55 *Federation Charbonniere* and in subsequent cases.

3.3.3.1 Internal implied competences

> In **Cases 281, 283–285, and 287/85 Commission v Germany (Migration Policy)**, a Treaty Article (Article 153 TFEU, but then Article 118 EEC) provided for cooperation between member states in a social field and was used by the Commission to enact a decision requiring the member states to supply information on migration figures. When the decision was challenged by Germany, arguing that the Decision concerned its competences, the CoJ held that where an Article of the EEC Treaty confers a specific task on the Commission, it must be accepted if that provision is not to be rendered wholly ineffective, and that it confers on the Commission necessarily and per se the powers that are indispensable in order to carry out that task, such as the gathering of information.

3.3.3.2 Impact on external competence from internal competences

Where existing internal powers have been acted upon by the EU, the member states are also prevented from acting externally in those areas in which such action would impact on the internal policy. Under its external trade policy, the Union alone is in a position to carry out the contractual obligations towards third countries.

In **Case 22/70 *Commission* v *Council (ERTA)***, the then six member states had negotiated independently a road transport agreement, which was then adopted by Resolution of the Council, but subsequently challenged by the Commission because there was no express right for the Council to do this and because the Commission itself was empowered to conclude international agreements. The CoJ held that it was the authority of the Community to negotiate international agreements, which authority arose not only from express conferment, but could also be implied from other Treaty provisions providing express internal competences in the same area. In the particular case, because the member states' negotiations were the continuance of agreements reached originally before the internal policy was formulated, it was held that the member states collectively within the Council were entitled to act for the Community (now Union). However, they could not subsequently act collectively outside of the Community (now Union) without impacting on the implied exclusive rights of the Union.

See also one of the air transport cases, **Cases 4, 6–9/98 *Commission* v *Finland and others***, in which it was confirmed that where the Community has acted in pursuit of exclusive internal powers that it possesses, any action by the member states in adopting an international agreement (in this case, bilateral agreements with the United States) affecting the common Community rules is an unlawful intrusion on Community competence. There was no express power to regulate air transport with consequences outside the EU; however, that power was nevertheless implied in view of the impact on the internal exclusive power that there would have been if the member states were to go it alone.

The most complex agreements are the multilateral trade liberalisation agreements entered into by member states of the organisations of the World Trade Organization (WTO) and the General Agreement on Tariffs and Trade (GATT). These cover so many aspects of external trade that a different view was taken by the CoJ of the extent to which the Union could be said to have taken over competence.

Opinion 1/94 was concerned with the competence of the Community or member states acting with the Community to conclude the General Agreement on Trade in Services (GATS) and Trade-Related Aspects of Intellectual Property Rights (TRIPS) Agreement elements of the WTO talks, but the ECJ held that implied powers operate only between the member states and the Community and not the Commission and the Council; hence, whilst there was joint competence in these areas, there was not an exclusive Community competence.

In Opinion 1/03 in considering EC competence in respect of joining the Lugano Convention, the CoJ held that where the EC had already exercised its powers internally in the area, this would also then provide it with an exclusive external competence in the same area where necessary to preserve the effectiveness of EC law and the proper functioning of the systems established by its rules. Following the entry into effect of the Lisbon Treaty, Article 3(2) TFEU effectively puts into statutory form and, indeed, strengthens the position reached already in the jurisprudence of the CoJ by providing:

> The Union shall also have exclusive competence for the conclusion of an international agreement when its conclusion is provided for in a legislative act of the Union or is necessary to enable the Union to exercise its internal competence, or in so far as its conclusion may affect common rules or alter their scope.

This is effectively repeated in Article 216(1) TFEU:

> 1. The Union may conclude an agreement with one or more third countries or international organisations where the Treaties so provide or where the conclusion of an agreement is necessary in order to achieve, within the framework of the Union's policies, one of the objectives referred to in the Treaties, or is provided for in a legally binding Union act or is likely to affect common rules or alter their scope.

It remains to be seen whether the member states will react to the exercise of external powers taken under these provisions and the degree to which the Court of Justice will regard these two provisions as covering the same ground.

 THINKING POINT

What is it about the competence creep that motivates the member states so much to take action to prevent or hinder it?

3.4 Tackling the competence creep

These increases in the competences of the Union, without express Treaty sanction, have been increasingly criticised and challenged. Even the use of the residual powers, in general democratic terms, is suspect, because if using either Articles 115 or 352 TFEU—both requiring unanimity on the part of the Council—they require consultation or consent of the EP only and not its greater participation in the ordinary (co-decision) legislative procedure. Even Article 114 TFEU, which allows the use of QMV in Council, may be subject to a challenge by one or more aggrieved member states that do not agree with the final Act. Hence, there have been challenges before the CoJ to some proposed and completed Union actions against the Council's choice of legal base and, more formally, by amendments to the Treaties to try to curb this development.

> Generally, Article 1 TFEU provides: 'This Treaty . . . determines the areas of, delimitation of, and arrangements for exercising its competences.'

3.4.1 Restrictive drafting

Legal bases have been drafted restrictively so that the Commission cannot use the base for further legislative intervention.

See, for example, Article 168(5) TFEU (ex 152 EC), which provides for action to promote cooperation in public health matters, but 'excluding any harmonization of the laws and regulations of the member states'. In other words, the Union can take action provided it does not interfere with the existing laws in the member states.

Another method, in addition to specific Treaty Article amendments to control the extension and exercise of competences, is the introduction of the principles of subsidiarity and proportionality, which now find formal Treaty expression. These are designed to address the concerns of the member states about how implied competences were being employed by the Commission, albeit without much clear success thus far.

3.4.2 **The principle of subsidiarity**

The principle of subsidiarity requires that decisions be taken at the most appropriate level and, in the EU context, this focuses on whether a decision should be taken at the level of the Union or by or within the member states. The wish to regulate activities within the Union should not insist on action at the Union level when it is not necessary. Whilst there was arguably always the view that legal measures that were taken centrally by the Union institutions should only be taken where necessary and that, if not suitable, member states should be allowed to regulate matters individually, this understanding did not find formal expression in any Treaty provision. There are implied examples of its use, such as the discretion given to the member states to meet the requirements of a Directive or the principles of mutual recognition and the rule of reason established by the CoJ in the *Cassis de Dijon* case. Subsidiarity made its first express appearance in the Community legal order among the 1986 SEA Treaty amendments. Essentially, it provided that the Union should take action only where objectives could be better attained at the Union level than at the level of individual member states. It was subsequently introduced generally into the Union legal order by the TEU.

> **CROSS REFERENCE**
> The rule of reason and the principle of mutual recognition are discussed in Chapter 11.

Article 1 of the TEU provides that decisions are to be taken as closely as possible to the citizen; Article 5(1) TEU provides that 'The use of Union competences is governed by the principles of subsidiarity and proportionality' and further provides in Article 5(3) TEU that:

in areas which do not fall within its exclusive competence, the Union shall act, only if and in so far as the objectives of the proposed action cannot be sufficiently achieved by the member states, either at central level or at regional and local, but can rather, by reason of the scale or effects of the proposed action, be better achieved at Union level.

Thus it is clear that it does not apply in the area of exclusive competences.

The exact meaning of Article 5(3) TEU is, however, far from clear, particularly regarding where the line may be drawn between the competence of the Union and the competences of the member states. The introduction of this concept and proportionality has not proved to be the instant fix desired by the member states, let alone a concept that is readily understandable, or indeed translatable into a clear-cut process by which it is decided whether Union or member states' action is appropriate and thus lawful within the terms of the concept. It seems to suggest that decision-making that might be accumulated in the centre—that is, by the institutions—but which is not actually necessary at this level should instead be taken by the member states. Thus, EU action needs to be shown to be necessary, in that the member states are unable to achieve the same objectives, and shown to provide greater benefits at the Union level.

> **CROSS REFERENCE**
> Article 5 TEU and the principle of subsidiarity build on the principle of conferral and are discussed at section 3.2.

In support of Article 5 TEU is Article 13 TEU, which requires that each institution acts within the limits of the power conferred on it.

One of the main difficulties with this principle of subsidiarity remains: who decides when to apply it, and whether it has been observed in the decision-making process. If the matter is one within the exclusive competence of the Union, subsidiarity does not apply. The problem is, however, that 'exclusivity' itself is not a clear-cut term. The practice has arisen now that, in order to justify taking the action, the Commission needs to outline why it has competence to take the particular action, and does so in the preamble and recitals to proposed legislation.

> See, for example, Directive 2002/14 on employee consultation, recital 17 or recital 36 from Directive 2006/54:
>
> > Since the objectives of this Directive cannot be sufficiently achieved by the Member States and can therefore be better achieved at Community level, the Community may adopt measures in accordance with the principle of subsidiarity as set out in Article 5 of the Treaty. In accordance with the principle of proportionality, as set out in that Article, this Directive does not go beyond what is necessary in order to achieve those objectives.

It may therefore give rise to considerable litigation to determine whether the principle and its requirements have been adhered to correctly. Whilst the principle itself was not disturbed by the Treaty of Amsterdam, it did add a Protocol as an attempt to clarify its meaning, which has been amended and expanded by the Lisbon Treaty and attached to the present Treaties as Protocol No. 2 on the Application of the Principles of Subsidiarity and Proportionality in which the national Parliaments can take a view and advise on whether they consider whether proposed legislation confirms with the principle in the so-called 'early warning mechanism'. There is also another Protocol (No. 1) on the role of national parliaments, which also outlines how national parliaments, when considering draft EU legislation, should also be involved in the adjudication of whether the principle of subsidiarity has been complied with.

> Protocols have Treaty status, under Article 51 TEU (ex 311 EC).

Article 12 TEU now outlines formally the contribution of the national parliaments in the good functioning of the Union and specifically in relation to this section:

> (a) through being informed by the institutions of the Union and having draft legislative acts of the Union forwarded to them in accordance with the Protocol on the role of national Parliaments in the European Union;
>
> (b) by seeing to it that the principle of subsidiarity is respected in accordance with the procedures provided for in the Protocol on the application of the principles of subsidiarity and proportionality;

Protocol No. 2 requires the Commission to consult widely before formally proposing legislation and, in an amendment brought in by the Lisbon Treaty, draft legislative Acts shall be forwarded to the national parliaments at the same time as to the EP and Council. The Commission must accompany drafts with detailed statements as to how the proposal complies with the principles of subsidiarity and proportionality, and must provide evidential support to demonstrate that Union action is required and the general and financial impact of the proposed legislation. The Council is also required to take account of the principle when considering and amending Commission proposals, as should the EP also, as well as the views as expressed by the national parliaments.

Articles 6 and 7 of Protocol No. 2 further outline the Council members' national parliaments' ability to object to the proposal and the procedure involving how those objections are further considered by the Union institutions in the legislative processes, and how the Commission must issue a reasoned opinion if it wishes to maintain the proposal for further consideration in the legislative process. National parliaments have eight weeks to comment, each having two votes to object, and if votes amounting to one-third of the total votes object, the Commission is 'yellow carded' and is required to reconsider its proposal. This happened in 2012 when the Commission proposal for a Posted Workers Directive was objected to. The Commission subsequently amended the proposal and a watered-down version (Directive 2014/67) was adopted. Subsequently, the yellow card system was used to object to a Commission Proposal to establish a European Prosecutor's Office; however, the Commission nevertheless proceeded.

For more details on this section visit the online resources.

If, consequently, a majority of the member states' parliaments consider subsidiarity to have been breached and the Commission continues, it must rebut this by reasoned opinion, which is forwarded under 'an orange card procedure' to the EP and Council to vote on, either of which can decide that the proposal should no longer be considered.

As a last resort—previously impliedly, but now expressly under Article 8 of the Protocol—legislative Acts may be challenged under Article 263 TFEU for infringing the principle. Whilst no challenges have yet reached the CoJ under the amended Protocol, challenges previous to the changes taking place have been made. In view of the fact now that it is an established principle of EU law, it is likely also to be raised in Article 267 preliminary ruling references from the national courts. Article 267 is considered in Chapter 6.

3.4.2.1 Challenges for non-compliance with the principle

Non-compliance with the subsidiarity principle has been cited as a ground for annulment under an Article 230 EC (now 263 TFEU) judicial review action before the CoJ for an infringement of an essential procedural requirement. In its previous form, however, the principle received little judicial guidance, or indeed support. This is no surprise given the obscurity of the principle, which involves the balancing of economic and political priorities with which the CoJ is reluctant to interfere. It remains to be seen whether the amended Protocol clarifies this.

▶ CROSS REFERENCE
For details of this action, see Chapter 9, section 9.1.

> In **Cases C-84/94 *UK* v *Council (Working Time Directive)*** and **C-377/98 *Netherlands* v *European Parliament and Council (Biotechnology Directive)***, arguments raised by the member states in the cases that subsidiarity had not been observed were roundly rejected by the CoJ. In the *Working Time Directive* case, the Court of Justice dismissed this part of the action with little discussion, merely to confirm that the Council had a clear power to act on working hours as an issue of the health and safety of workers. In other words, if it had the competence to act, it could not be prevented from acting, and only in cases of manifestly exceeding the discretion would the CoJ intervene.

> However, in **Case C-376/98 *Germany* v *Parliament and Council (Tobacco Advertising Ban Directive)***, the harmonising Directive 98/43 banning most forms of tobacco advertising was enacted under what was then Article 95 EC (now 114 TFEU) as an internal market measure. This was challenged by Germany, which argued that the measure was more closely allied to a public health measure and thus should have been enacted under the then Article 152 EC (now 168 TFEU), which expressly prohibited harmonising legislation. The CoJ held that measures under (the then) Article 95 must have the primary object of improving conditions for the establishment or functioning of the internal market and that other Articles of the Treaty may not be used as a legal basis in order to circumvent the express exclusion of harmonisation. It held further that to construe the internal market Article as meaning that it vests in the Union legislature a general power to regulate the internal market would be incompatible with the principle embodied in (the then) Article 5 EC that the powers of the Union are limited to those specifically conferred upon it. The CoJ thus held that, as a measure doing little to enhance the internal market, the use of the legal market Treaty base was inappropriate, and it therefore annulled the measure entirely.

» CROSS REFERENCE
See further details on the legal base in section 3.5.1.

The latter judgment was not a definite endorsement that subsidiarity is a clearly justiciable issue; more that it is another confirmation that where an incorrect legal base is used, or where no powers have in fact been conferred, this provides grounds for the annulment of the measure. The Tobacco judgment is regarded, however, as a reply to national courts, in particular the German Federal Constitutional Court, which might have been minded to take Union law into its own hands, by showing that the Court of Justice is prepared to police incursions into the member states' competences by the EU's institutions. This topic is considered in Chapter 5, section 5.3.1.

> **Cases C-154/04 and C-155/04 *Alliance for Natural Health*** provide another view of the Court of Justice that arguments based on a possible breach of subsidiarity will not allow it to interfere with decisions that are the result of the exercise of legislative discretion.

> Even in **Case C-58/08 *Vodafone and others***, the Court of Justice did not interfere with the Regulation 717/2007 on the basis of either subsidiarity or proportionality. It was argued that roaming charges should be capped only by each individual country, and not by EU action. The CoJ held that the power to act had been conferred on the EU and that the need for Union action to maintain the smooth functioning of the internal market and competition was clear. The exercise of the discretion by the EU legislature had not been disproportionate.

Thus, it would seem that if a measure is concerned with the internal market, which can arguably only effectively be regulated on an EU-wide basis by the EU, it will be extremely difficult for this to be challenged on the ground of a breach of subsidiarity. Almost inevitably, the CoJ will be invited to come up with a clearer and more workable definition or judgment on the availability and application of the principle in actions that seek to challenge EU legislation. It is possible that the principle of subsidiarity will also join the ranks of general principles of Union law, although it is one introduced deliberately by the member states rather than created or introduced by the CoJ.

 THINKING POINT

Is the way in which the principle of subsidiarity has been pleaded in the Court more to do with the member states' concerns rather than those of the citizens?

3.4.3 **Proportionality**

Proportionality, apart from being a legal principle in its own right and often employed by individuals in challenges to Union action, is also contained in Article 5 TEU and is linked to the subsidiarity principle, because both are concerned with the control and exercise of powers by the institutions. Proportionality applies, though, to all measures, including those coming within exclusive competences.

> **Proportionality** Article 5(4) TEU defines proportionality as follows: 'Under the principle of proportionality, the content and form of Union action shall not exceed what is necessary to achieve the objectives of the Treaties.'

Like subsidiarity, it too is subject to Protocol 2, and Union Acts are open to possible challenges if they breach proportionality. Draft legislation must also state how it complies with the principle of proportionality.

It was, for example, raised in **Case 84/94 *UK* v *Council (Working Time Directive)*** by the UK under the argument that the restrictions imposed on working time were not minimum requirements, but were excessive—that is, disproportionate. This view was rejected by the ECJ on the grounds that unless there had been a manifest error or misuse of powers, the Council must be allowed to exercise its discretion in law-making involving social policy choices.

The extent to which proportionality can be employed to challenge Union law in an action to annul a harmonisation measure dealing with food supplements was shown to be limited.

See **Cases C-154/04 and C-155/04 *Alliance for Natural Health*** for the view provided by the CoJ that arguments based on a possible breach of proportionality will not allow it to interfere with decisions that are the result of the exercise of legislative discretion. Legality can be affected only as a result of the legislative act being manifestly inappropriate.

This was confirmed in similar terms in the follow-up case, **Case C-344/04 *R* v *Department of Transport, ex p International Air Transport Association and European Law Fares Airline Association***. At [80] of that judgment:

> With regard to judicial review of the conditions referred to in the previous paragraph, the Community legislature must be allowed a broad discretion in areas which involve political, economic and social choices on its part, and in which it is called upon to undertake complex assessments. Consequently, the legality of a measure adopted in those fields can be affected only if the measure is manifestly inappropriate having regard to the objective that the competent institution is seeking to pursue.

However, in Case C-310/04 *Spain* v *Council (Spanish Cotton Subsidies)*, the CoJ held that the Council in legislating had failed to take into account all the relevant matters and in particular labour costs, and had thus as a consequence not complied with the principle of proportionality. The case remains as a rare example of success in pleading proportionality and in the *Vodafone* case, considered also earlier in respect of subsidiarity, proportionality was also tested and satisfied in that no other means was considered to be available to the Commission to ensure there was no distortion in the functioning of, nor to competition in, the internal market, other than the reduction in roaming charges.

Note, however, that the early warning mechanism and the yellow card system for national parliaments, mentioned at the end of section 3.4.2 above, are not available to object on the grounds of proportionality.

 THINKING POINT

This is a little like the considerations taken into account by the Court of Justice in deciding *locus standi* in Article 263 TFEU actions and in the *Schöppenstedt* formula in Article 340 TFEU actions. These are both considered in Chapter 9, and proportionality is considered in more detail as one of the general principles in Chapter 4, section 4.6.1.6.

3.4.4 **Further competence controls**

Finally, in the attempt to counter the competence creep, the Lisbon Treaty has introduced a requirement in Article 296 TFEU that relates to the competence and legal base issues, and states that:

'When considering draft legislative acts, the EP and the Council shall refrain from adopting acts not provided for by the relevant legislative procedure in the area in question.'

Furthermore, Protocol 25 and three Declarations attached to the Treaties also address these issues. Protocol 25 provides that 'when the Union has taken action in a certain area, the scope of this exercise of competence only covers those elements governed by the Union act in question and therefore does not cover the whole area'. The protocol also provides that one or more member states may request the Commission to submit proposals to repeal a legislative Act.

A revised Declaration (No. 18) on competences confirms the respective rights of the member states and Union, the latter represented by the Commission in these matters; and Declaration Nos 24 and 42 are also pertinent here in that they seek to prevent further competence creep arising from the conferral of legal personality on the EU as a whole and the use of the general law-making power under Article 352 TFEU.

Allied to subsidiarity, in as much as the Commission is required to make a case for legislation is the impact assessment which must be carried out before new initiatives are proposed. It is not restricted to harmonising legislation under Article 114 TFEU, but certainly would include those.

The revisions made by the Lisbon Treaty actually allow for a reduction in the competences of the EU under Article 48 TEU by the ordinary revision procedure whereby member states (or EP or Commission) submit a proposal to the Council, which is then submitted to the European Council and the national parliaments are notified. This has not happened yet, so the further details can be consulted in the Treaty Article itself.

For more details on this section visit the online resources.

3.4.5 **Summary**

As means by the member states to correct the perceived competence creep of the Union and its institutions, the principles of subsidiarity and proportionality alone still do not appear to be very effective. However, when considered alongside the raft of measures available and introduced, including the right to challenge legal bases, the Treaty amendments, Protocols, and Declarations, and the reaction of some member states courts, the institutions, and the Commission in particular, may be forced at least to think longer about the justifications for EU action. The impact assessment process is yet another process in itself to add to all of the others, which serve to show how EU action is necessary and justified. It remains to be seen, however, whether the Court of Justice will change its stance on this topic and be more amenable to arguments claiming a breach of the principles or whether as a result of all of these measures member states are assured that competences are no longer being increased by stealth.

3.5 The participation of the institutions in the legislative processes

This section deals with how the binding secondary law of the Union is enacted. These forms of law now constitute the vast bulk of Union law, and their enactment has unfortunately become complex over the years, involving principally three institutions, but, according to the process required, often more of the Union bodies. The Lisbon Treaty did, though, make good progress in rationalising the legislative processes, although the Constitutional Treaty (CT) would have gone further. First, an allied issue needs to be addressed in order to provide a complete picture and to explain what determines the particular process that should be employed in any given circumstance.

3.5.1 The legal base for legislative proposals

Articles of the Treaties that empower the EU institutions to enact further legislation to carry out the policies of that title or chapter provide the key to the legislative procedure that must be used to enact the laws. In view of the reforms introduced by the Lisbon Treaty, this topic has been considerably simplified, although an awareness of it is still required.

Treaty Articles that set out a policy objective either provide details of the procedure themselves or refer to another Treaty Article, which provides the details of the procedure to be used.

> For example, Article 59 TFEU, dealing with the liberalisation of specific services, provides that 'the European Parliament and Council, acting in accordance with the ordinary legislative procedure and after consulting the Economic and Social Committee shall issue directives'.
>
> Alternatively, as an example, Article 48 TFEU refers to the ordinary legislative procedure, which is outlined in Article 294.

The Treaty Article providing the power is known as the 'legal base', which thus determines the participants in the procedure and the level of their participation. Law-making always involves the Commission and Council plus the EP, and sometimes, as noted in section 3.6.1, the EESC or the Committee of the Regions (CoR). The Treaty base is fundamental to the relative powers and ability of the other institutions to affect the content of Union law. For example, the use of QMV in the Council of Ministers is extremely important to the Commission, which stands a greater chance of having proposals accepted by a majority than by all member states in Council. Minority or marginal views can thus be ignored, rather than taken into account at the draft stages. The legal base is also vital to the level of participation of the EP in the legislative process—that is, whether it is merely consulted, or gives its consent, or whether the co-decision procedure is used, in which case the EP has more power.

> **CROSS REFERENCE**
> If in doubt about what QMV means, refer back to Chapter 2, section 2.2.4.3.

> For example, measures in support of the single market under Article 114 TFEU require QMV rather than unanimity in the Council.

As indicated, because this makes life easier for the Commission, it has tried to exploit this by introducing as much legislation as possible under Article 114 TFEU (ex 95 EC), whereas the Council or one or more member states have argued often that proposals should have as their legal base other Articles requiring unanimity (such as Article 115 TFEU, concerned directly with approximating legislation for the internal market). Looked at from another point of view, a single member state that objects to a particular measure would wish to veto it and would want unanimity voting in Council to have that chance. It would object to the Council deciding to adopt the measure under a legal base requiring QMV if there were even an outside chance of another Treaty Article base being relevant—that is, one requiring unanimity. For the most part, the particular Treaty legal base is clear, in that the subject matter of the proposal is clearly within the subject matter of a specific Treaty Article, and therefore base. However, the subject matter may straddle different Treaty subject areas and thus lend itself to more than one Treaty base. Hence, there is sufficient ground for differences of opinion as to which is the correct Treaty base to use, and the institutions and member states have fought often over this. In particular, in view of the democratic deficit argument and its long campaign to attain greater involvement in the legislative process, the EP has not refrained from challenging the Council for the use of an allegedly incorrect legal base and has brought a number of cases before the CoJ.

 THINKING POINT

Note that, in order to fully appreciate the importance of these cases in the law-making procedures, you need to read about the procedures themselves. For the moment, though, read through the case examples here and come back to them later, if need be, after reading about the procedures in more detail.

Note that there have been two complete changes of Treaty Article numbers, once when the Amsterdam Treaty came into force and a second now that the Lisbon Treaty is in force, and a number of other less extensive changes and amendments also. This means that cases such as the following, many of which were decided prior to Amsterdam, are now completely adrift from the present Treaty Article numbers, and some of the Articles themselves have been amended substantially, and even removed. Rather than use three sets of numbers for these cases, in which often the old versions of the Treaty Articles themselves also are needed, only the original Article numbers will be given. The value of the cases is in the issues arising rather than showing what the new numbers are.

An early example, and one likely to be in materials books, is **Case 68/86 *UK v Council (Hormones)***, which concerned a Directive banning growth-producing hormones. This first case was based on an earlier Article 43 concerned with measures in support of the Common Agricultural Policy (CAP), which required a qualified majority only. This was objected to by the UK, which argued that it should have been based on an earlier Article 100 Treaty of the European Economic Community (EEC)—a single-market measure that required unanimity. The question raised was whether this was free movement, as argued by the UK, and thus a single-market measure, or whether it concerned agricultural policy, in which case the Treaty Article under that section would be the most appropriate. The CoJ held that the CAP Article was the appropriate one because it lent itself more to the subject matter concerned.

Similarly, in **Case C-155/91 *Commission v Council (Waste Directive)***, the Waste Directive 91/156, adopted by the Council under an old Article 130s EC (an environment measure legal base then requiring unanimity), was challenged by the Commission on the basis that the old Article 100a EC, which was concerned with the internal market, requiring majority voting only, should have been used as the legal base. On this occasion, the Court disagreed and held that the protection of the environment, as stated in the Directive, was the real reason and not the free movement of waste. Therefore, the challenge by the Commission was rejected. The issue was not so much the right to move waste around, but the promotion of the most efficient way of dealing with waste to protect the environment. This was, however, to be achieved by removing any prevention of movement, so that the most efficient operators or disposers of waste could handle it, regardless of where they were situated.

THINKING POINT

One might argue that to transport waste to recycle or to dispose of it is not particularly environmentally friendly.

A further case concerned the adoption by the Council in June 1993 of a Directive specifying a minimum working week, albeit with the ability of workers to work longer voluntarily. The UK, which was opposed to this, was unable to veto the proposal because it was introduced under the health and safety of workers provision under the old Article 118a EEC, requiring a qualified majority in the Council. In **Case C-84/94 UK v Council**, the UK formally requested the CoJ to annul the Directive, arguing that it would have been more appropriate to base the measure on the original Article 235 EEC (the flexibility clause that is now Article 352 TFEU) or the old version of Article 100 EEC, either of which would have required unanimity on the part of the Council, thus allowing the UK the chance to veto the measure before its possible enactment. The CoJ was, however, satisfied with the choice of Article 118a EEC as a health-and-safety matter.

In **Case C-295/90 European Parliament v Council (Students' Residence)**, Parliament successfully challenged the adoption of Directive 90/366 on the free movement and right to residence of students that the Council adopted under old Article 235 EEC, requiring only consultation, rather than under old Article 7 EEC (prohibition of discrimination on the grounds of nationality), which would require the old and now removed cooperation procedure to be used, which provided the greater participation of the EP. The Directive was annulled and has been re-enacted as Directive 93/96. The EP had no objection to the rights provided by the measure itself; merely to the way in which it had been enacted, which denied it its full participation.

A final case here to focus on the issues raised above is **Case C-300/89 Commission v Council (Titanium Dioxide Directive)**. The Council adopted a Directive on the basis of old Article 130s EC as an environmental measure, which then required unanimity in Council and only consultation of the EP, despite the protests of the EP. The Commission argued that it should have been adopted using old Article 100a EC as a single-market measure, which then required QMV and the cooperation procedure instead. Whilst the Court acknowledged that both could be valid bases, the use of old Article 130s EC instead of old Article 100a EC deprived the EP of its greater role in the legislative process. Even if both were used, as suggested by the Council, it would still have to decide unanimously and be able to overrule any objections of the EP.

What emerges from this case law is that the view of the CoJ is essentially that the democratic process in law-making, which now involves the EP, demands that where two legal bases are available requiring differing procedures, the one allowing the EP the greater role must be used so as not to deprive the EP and the Union of its democratic right, unless it can be shown that the matter is primarily more concerned with a particular Treaty base.

In view of the simplification of the legislative procedures by the Treaties of Amsterdam and Nice, and particularly the Lisbon Treaty, many more Treaty subject areas have moved under what is now termed the 'ordinary legislative procedure'. As this is by far the most prominent procedure, increasingly there is less room for a dispute as to the correct legal base, and therefore less scope for argument and less possibility for Court action in the future.

CROSS REFERENCE

See section 3.6.1.1 for more on the ordinary legislative procedure.

A warning to observe the correct legal base is also now provided in Article 296 TFEU, which provides that: 'When considering draft legislative acts, the EP and the Council shall refrain from adopting acts not provided for by the relevant legislative procedure in the area in question.'

There have been two more recent cases in which the appropriateness of the chosen legal base was challenged.

> In Case C-210/03 *R v Secretary of State for Health, ex p Swedish Match*, the CoJ held that if obstacles to trade emerge, the Commission can intervene to harmonise even if the internal market is not the prime motive. That case concerned the banning of a type of snuff.

> In the second tobacco advertising case, **C-380/03 *Germany v European Parliament and Council***, Article 95 EC could be used, under the new justifications provided by the Commission for its use, to enact Directive 2003/33 restricting the advertising of tobacco products, where it was argued that differences in the national laws relating to this advertising would have the effect of creating obstacles to free trade. Thus, the Community Directive was held necessary to harmonise the internal market to allow it to function properly.

3.6 Law-making principles and procedures

For more details on this section visit the online resources.

A number of factors have influenced, first, the establishment of the law-making procedures and, secondly, their expansion and evolution. From relatively straightforward beginnings, these have mushroomed into numerous and complex forms and procedures, which were considerably rationalised by the Lisbon Treaty in 2009. The issues provoking such change include the democratic deficit of the law-making procedure overall, the expansions in the number of member states, voting arrangements in the Council, and the establishment and subsequent removal of the two intergovernmental pillars by the TEU and Lisbon Treaty. Hence, there have been numerous Treaty amendments both increasing and complicating the legislative procedures. Whilst the Treaty of Amsterdam made an attempt to rein in the prolixity and complexity of these procedures, it is the Lisbon Treaty that has done most, but unfortunately not to the extent originally proposed by the CT.

Three institutions are principally involved in law-making. However, it is worth noting that, before law-making even commences, the overall policy is decided by the member states during both Treaty negotiation and amendment, and on an ongoing basis by the European Council in making recommendations and requesting actions by the main institutions—notably the Council, but also the Commission. The principal three institutions, which are the Commission, the Council, and the EP, are also in dialogue throughout the process and may conclude inter-institutional agreements under Article 295 TFEU to assist them in the law- and decision-making processes. Delegated law-making is also considered in section 3.7 in this chapter.

> See, for example, the Joint Declaration on practical arrangements for the co-decision procedure.

3.6.1 **The law-making procedures**

There are at present essentially three law-making procedures in the EU, plus the delegated legislative power of the Commission. Following the Lisbon Treaty reforms, there has been a radical renaming of these and a clear leading law-making procedure has been established from these three:

- the ordinary legislative procedure;
- special legislative procedures; and
- the consent (formerly known as assent) procedure.

Most law-making procedures start with the Commission, which prerogative is contained in Article 17(2) that 'Union legislative acts may only be adopted on the basis of a Commission proposal, except where the Treaties provide otherwise.' The Commission puts policy into effect by means of preparing and proposing legislative instruments, although, following the entry into force of the Lisbon Treaty, suggestions and recommendations for legislative acts may also come from the Council and the EP (Articles 241 and 225 TFEU), the European Council, the member states, the European Central Bank (ECB), the CoJ, the European Investment Bank (EIB), and EU citizens (Articles 11–12 TEU and 24 and 289 TFEU). It is the Council that makes most use of the power under Article 241 TFEU to request that the Commission might introduce legislative proposals for a particular issue or give reasons for not doing so. There are limited exceptions to the prerogative of Commission proposal, which include the right under Article 281 TFEU for the CoJ to propose amendments to the Statute on the Court and matters falling within the area of judicial cooperation in criminal matters and police cooperation may be proposed by one-quarter of the member states (see Articles 82–89 TFEU).

> **CROSS REFERENCE**
>
> The European Citizens' Initiative (ECI) is considered in Chapter 2, section 2.1.3.

The Council and Parliament, for the most part, then dispose of these legislative proposals—that is, they decide the final shape and enact the legislation. The actual details of each procedure varies according to the way in which the Council votes and the different forms of participation of the EP. Additionally, for some procedures, other institutions are involved, most notably the EESC and the CoR. The institutions, and the extent to which they are involved, are determined by the Treaty. First, Article 289 TFEU provides details of the procedures available to enact Union legislation.

Article 289 TFEU

1. The ordinary legislative procedure shall consist in the joint adoption by the European Parliament and the Council of a regulation, directive or decision on a proposal from the Commission. This procedure is defined in Article 294.

2. In the specific cases provided for by the Treaties, the adoption of a regulation, directive or decision by the European Parliament with the participation of the Council, or by the latter with the participation of the European Parliament, shall constitute a special legislative procedure.

3. Legal acts adopted by legislative procedure shall constitute legislative acts.

4. In the specific cases provided for by the Treaties, legislative acts may be adopted on the initiative of a group of Member States or of the European Parliament, on a recommendation from the European Central Bank or at the request of the Court of Justice or the European Investment Bank.

Which particular process is employed depends on the subject matter for which legislation is required and then, in turn, the Treaty Article(s) which is/are the legal base governing those matters—that is, legislation is enacted under a particular prescribed procedure.

> **CROSS REFERENCE**
>
> The legal base, discussed at section 3.5.1, is the Treaty Article covering the subject matter of the legislation under consideration.

For example, Article 46 TFEU, which empowers legislation to be enacted for the free movement of workers, requires that the ordinary legislative procedure be used (detailed in Article 294 TFEU, previously 'co-decision' in Article 251 EC).

In addition to the procedures themselves, we need to consider why they have become so convoluted and the consequences of this, although it is not necessary to learn the fine details and points of each and every legislative process. This, apart from being tedious, is not very productive and, like many sets of rules, will simply change over time.

3.6.1.1 The ordinary legislative procedure

Article 289 TFEU (ex 249 EC) has been amended over the years to provide that the EP act more extensively with the Council and Commission in the legislative process, notably by the introduction of the co-decision procedure and its renaming as the ordinary legislative procedure, detailed in Article 294 TFEU. It provides for the enhanced participation of the EP to the extent that the EP now essentially enjoys equal law-making power with the Council (see Articles 14(10) and 16(1) TEU). This use of co-decision may be argued to represent a check and balance between the power of the Council and the EP. Note that, in the procedure, the Council votes mainly by QMV, but at times, according to some Treaty Articles and parts of the procedure itself, it must vote unanimously.

The following description takes into account the amendments made to the procedure by the Treaties of Amsterdam and Lisbon, which ironed out some of the initial teething troubles and delays originally experienced in the operation of the procedure. The description has been marked with reference numbers that relate to Figure 3.1.

The main stages of this procedure are that the Commission proposal (1), taking into account the opinions of the national parliaments (1A) and other bodies where specified (1B), is forwarded simultaneously to the EP for its opinion and the Council for consideration. The EP can, at first reading (2), either approve the proposal or amend the proposal by a simple majority or, although not strictly allowed under the procedure detailed in Article 294 TFEU, reject or substantially amend the proposal, in which case the proposal is returned to the Commission for an amended proposal (3). The Council, at first reading (4), can either, within three months, approve those amendments by a qualified majority (5), in which case the act can be adopted (6), or, if there have been no amendments (7), it can simply adopt the act by a qualified majority (8). This often involves considerable exchanges of views between the three institutions to reach an agreement at first reading, but, where successful, disposes of the need to spend time on the rest of the procedure. Instead, the provision can be enacted without further ado. Otherwise, the Council adopts a common position (9) on which the Commission comments (10).

The proposal then goes to the second reading by the EP (11), which can, within three months and with a possible one-month extension, either approve the common position or, for whatever reason, do nothing within the time limit (12), in which case the act is deemed to have been adopted (13). If, however, the EP rejects, by an absolute majority, the common position (14), the Act is deemed not to have been accepted (15)—that is, the proposal will not become law and the procedure ends. The EP, however, may propose amendments to the common position (16), which are forwarded to the Commission for comment (17) and the Council for a second reading (18).

At second reading (18), the Council may, within three months plus a one-month extension, approve the EP amendments by a qualified majority or unanimously if the Commission has issued a negative opinion (19), in which case the act is adopted as amended (20). If, on the other hand, the Council does not accept the amended common position (21), the matter is referred, within six weeks, to a conciliation committee to attempt to achieve a compromise also within six weeks, with a possible two-week extension (22 and 23). The committee comprises members of the Council with an equal number of members of the European Parliament (MEPs) and the Commissioner responsible.

If a joint text is approved by the committee (24), the Council, by qualified majority (unless the Treaty base requires unanimity), and the EP, by a simple majority, may adopt the provision together within

Figure 3.1 The co-decision procedure

Source: http://ec.europa.eu/codecision/stepbystep/diagram_en.htm=

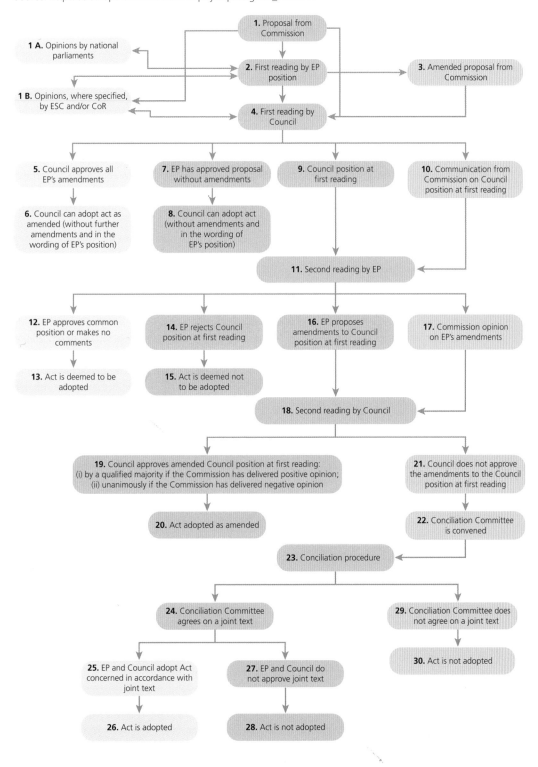

six weeks (25) and the Act is adopted (26). If, however, there is no approval of the joint text (27), or no agreement by the conciliation committee on a joint text within the time limit in the first place (29), then in both cases the procedure comes to an end and the act is deemed not to have been adopted (28 and 30).

As will be seen, this procedure is not for the faint-hearted, and despite the fact that the powers of the EP have been increased clearly and significantly, it cannot enforce its own positive view over the Council. If they cannot agree, the EP can defeat the proposal, as it did early in 2010 by rejecting the 'Swift' data-sharing agreement with the United States. The procedure was extended by the Amsterdam, Nice, and Lisbon Treaties into many new areas of the Treaty and as the co-decision procedure was made subject to a joint declaration on it use. However, despite its complexity on paper, most legislation is enacted at points 6 or 8 in Figure 3.1 (i.e. relatively quickly in the procedure). It is also now by far the most frequently employed legislative procedure in the Treaty and, in the 2009–14 legislative term, it was employed in about 90 per cent of all secondary law enactment. Of those c. 85 per cent were first reading agreements, with only a handful of proposals having to be carried over to the conciliation procedure. It is calculated by the Commission that the Treaties provide 83 instances of the use of this procedure. There is the possibility of a so-called 'emergency brake' procedure whereby a single member state, which considers a proposal affects a fundamental aspect of its legal system, asks for a suspension of the procedure and a referral to the European Council to allow for further reflection.

For more details on this section visit the online resources, which includes an updated Guide to how the EP co-legislates from December 2014.

3.6.1.2 Special legislative procedures

This second category is really a bundle of procedures that may be referred to in the Treaties variously as 'the' or 'a' special legislative procedure, and essentially groups together a number of procedures that differ in one or more elements from the ordinary legislative procedure (Article 289(2)–(4) TFEU). Instead of QMV, the Council may vote by unanimity or the EP may just be consulted or asked for its consent rather than co-deciding. Other bodies, such as the EESC, CoR, or ECB, may also be included in the process. It often incorporates the original consultation procedure, which originally featured only in a limited number of Treaty Articles (17) and provided that the Council was required to consult the EP as to its opinion before coming to a decision on Community secondary law. Under this procedure, the Commission proposes legislation that it deems necessary to fulfil a Union aim; the EP is then consulted and it offers its opinion; and the Council decides on the matter, by QMV, but usually unanimously. However, on receipt of the opinion of the EP, the Council could proceed to ignore it and override any view given by the EP.

> See, however, **Cases 138 and 139/79 Roquette and Maizena v Council**, in which the Court annulled a Regulation because the Council had failed to consult or obtain the opinion of the EP before it passed the legislation.

> Furthermore, in **Case C-65/93 European Parliament v Council**, it was held that if the Commission proposal has been substantially altered, the EP must be consulted again, and failure to do so will also result in annulment of the measure, which occurred in this case.

It is argued that, without express authority, these considerations will continue to apply to measures adopted under a special legislative procedure that fails to consult the EP when required. Unanimity of Council combined with consulting the EP appears to be the most common form of this procedure. Note though that Article 48(7) TEU, the *passerelle* clause, allows that the European Council voting unanimously with the consent of the EP may adopt measures normally requiring a special legislative procedure, instead under the ordinary legislative procedure, providing no national Parliament objects.

❱ CROSS REFERENCE

See section 3.6.1.4.

For examples of special legislative procedures, see Articles 19, 22, 126, 115, 192, and 332 TFEU, which include the unanimity of Council and consultation of the EP alone or with others; Articles 25 and 252 TFEU on the unanimity of Council and consenting of the EP; or Article 223 TFEU under which the EP takes the lead, consults the Commission, and obtains the consent of the Council. The Council can legislate alone, on a Commission proposal under Article 26 TFEU regulating the Common Customs Tariff, Articles 108 and 109 TFEU in respect of aid grants, and Article 207 TFEU on matters within the common commercial policy. Apart from its delegated powers of legislating, considered in section 3.7, the Commission can also legislate alone under Article 45(3) TFEU on workers' rights to remain and under Article 106(3) TFEU on member states' grants to companies. There is also the budgetary decision-making procedure as a special legislative procedure under Article 314 TFEU. All of the uses of the procedure take into account in some way matters or areas where the member states were less keen to hand over complete competence to the EP and the Council under the ordinary legislative procedure. If the Treaty for the Constitution for Europe had entered into force unamended, then all legislative procedures were destined to be governed by the ordinary legislative procedure.

3.6.1.3 The consent procedure

The consent (previously referred to as 'assent') procedure was introduced by the SEA and extended under the TEU and Lisbon Treaty, so that the EP's consent is required by the Council in respect of membership and withdrawal applications to the EU, the Union's membership of international agreements and organisations, and for association agreements with third countries (Articles 49 and 50 TEU, and 218 and 217 TFEU): in total, in 15 instances. In the event of disagreement, the EP has effectively a right of veto, but there are no formal mechanisms built in by which a dialogue between the two institutions can be initiated in the event of a disagreement on any aspect of or an entire agreement. In reality, though, any such dispute would have been subject to debate and discussion behind the scenes. Consent may also be employed to confirm serious and persistent breaches by a member state (Article 7 TEU), to approve anti-discrimination legislation (Article 19(2) TFEU), in establishing a procedure for the revision of the Treaties (Article 48 TEU), to approve the budget (Articles 311–12 TFEU) and for the flexibility clause (Article 352 TFEU). The procedure has not been made subject to time limits.

 THINKING POINT

Why does the EU not move to only one law-making process?

3.6.1.4 *Passerelle* provisions

It is possible without Treaty amendment, under Article 48(7), to change the legislative procedure required in specific instances from a special legislative procedure to an ordinary legislative procedure by a so-called *passerelle* provision. To do so, though, requires a special procedure itself of unanimity in the European Council and consent by a majority of the component members of the EP. However, national parliaments must be given six months to consider this, and a single member state can veto any such proposal.

There are special *passerelle* possibilities in Articles 81, 153, and 192 TFEU.

3.6.2 Why so many changes to the legislative procedures?

As was noted at the beginning of this section, the increase of and subsequent changes to the decision-making procedures are the product of a number of developments in the EU: the democratic deficit, the various expansions of member states' voting arrangements in the Council, the movement and expansion of the EU into new policy areas, and as a response to the international regulation of pan-European or even global problems such as the environment or business regulation. One of the unfortunate consequences of the increase in procedures is that it led to legal disputes between the member states and institutions, and between the institutions themselves, about whether the correct legal procedure and legal base has been used and not, for the most part, the substance of the final legislative act. Many cases were more concerned with the degree of power wielded by the EP or individual states in the Council. As a result, the procedures have become even further removed from a sensible understanding of the legislative processes by lawyers, yet alone laypersons, hence the desire to reform the procedures, in addition to the desire to reform the type and number of legal instruments.

> Under the original proposal for the abandoned Constitutional Treaty, the co-decision route was to become the only procedure; however, the member states insisted on retaining the consultation procedure, within the new umbrella term of 'specialist legislative procedure', requiring Council unanimity in the areas of tax, some aspects of social and environmental policy, some bases of CFSP, and Justice and Home Affairs (JHA) issues.

3.7 The delegation of powers

For more details on this section visit the online resources.

Changed from the earlier EC Treaty, delegation is now regulated by Article 290 TFEU, which specifies that a legislative Act (those enacted under the ordinary and special legislative procedures of Article 289 TFEU) may delegate to the Commission the power to adopt non-legislative acts of general application. In addition, Article 291 TFEU regulates implementing powers.

In order for day-to-day decision-making to be effective, in most, if not all, democratic systems of government, some form of executive action is required, either to implement or complete legislative acts or to be used in respect of detailed, technical issues not requiring the debate or input of the main legislators.

Delegation can be in the form of wide discretionary powers, including legislative, as well as administrative forms of secondary legislation. Delegation may, however, be subjected to confirmation, or limits or rules laid down by the delegating authority, or the delegating authority may retain the right to rescind the act adopted. This latter right is usually subject to a time limit by which the delegating authority must act. In the Union legal order, a system of committees was set up to supervise the exercise of delegated power whereby the Council retained control over the delegated power.

This set-up and system was originally outside the Treaties, but approved by the CoJ initially in Case 25/70 *Köster*, but has now been amended by the Lisbon Treaty in that Article 290 TFEU now provides the power for the Council and EP to delegate powers to the Commission to enact non-legislative acts of general application, the objectives, content, scope, and duration of which must be expressly defined in the empowering legislative act. Furthermore, Article 290(2) TFEU provides that the empowering act may either provide for the EP or Council to revoke the delegation or only enter into force if no objection has been expressed by the EP or Council within a period set in the empowering act. This replaces part of the committee structures set up in the past to oversee delegated and implementing powers exercised by the Commission, in terms of the regulatory committees.

> This system of management committees was known collectively as 'Comitology'. An overview of the changes can be found in Council press release 6378/11, 14 February 2011, available at http://www.consilium.europa.eu/uedocs/cms_data/docs/pressdata/EN/genaff/119270.pdf. See also the Common Understanding Memorandum 8753/11 of 10 April 2011.

Delegation and the management committees were considered by the CoJ as early as 1958.

In **Case 9/56 *Meroni* v *High Authority***, the CoJ stressed the necessity of preserving the balance of powers in the institutional structure of the Communities as envisaged by the Treaties and which would therefore not allow the delegation of discretionary powers involving policy decisions.

A ruling confirmed in Case 98/80 *Romano*. The *Meroni* and *Romano* cases have subsequently been upheld as good law by the CoJ in Case C-270/12 *UK* v *EP & Council (Short Selling)*, in which specific powers were delegated to a body created to respond to financial difficulties in some member states to prevent short selling in the financial markets. The UK objected, claiming a breach contrary to the earlier cases, but the CoJ held that the powers delegated were sufficiently delineated as not to offend the previous *Meroni* judgment, in particular that Lisbon Treaty changes to Articles 263 and 277 TFEU now specifically envisage the delegation of general law-making powers to other EU bodies and agencies.

In **Case 25/70 *Köster***, the delegation of power to the Commission within the management committee procedure was challenged on the ground that the procedure disturbed the institutional balance of the Community contrary to the Treaty and undermined the independence of the Commission. The Court observed that the management committee could not take decisions itself, but merely provided options for implementation, and therefore the power balance was not disturbed.

Thus, provided the empowering legislation is adopted by the procedures envisaged by the Treaty, the details can be delegated to the Commission.

The CoJ held further in **Case 23/75 *Rey Soda***, that implementing powers under old Article 211 EC must be interpreted widely, especially under the CAP, where actions must often be taken on a day-to-day basis and discretion is necessary to cope with changing circumstances.

In **Case 16/88 *Commission* v *Council (Management Committee Procedure)*** concerning the Commission's power of implementation under old Article 274 EC, the Council delegated power to conclude certain contracts to the Commission subject to a management committee procedure. The Commission argued that implementation under old Article 274 concerning budgetary procedure was not subject to management committees. The Court held that as the Commission was also legislative in character, it was validly subject to the management committee procedures.

It was argued that, since the formalisation of the comitology procedures, too much power has been given to the committees and was consequently lost from the Commission and the EP. The EP attempted to challenge the committee management structure in the Comitology Decision (Case 302/87 *European Parliament* v *Council*), particularly because the Council failed to state in which circumstances particular procedures would apply, but the challenge failed due to the inadmissibility, at that time, of the direct challenge by the EP. These criticisms were fed into the revisions undertaken by the Lisbon Treaty, which resulted in the new systems established by Article 290 TFEU, considered above, and Article 291 TFEU, considered next. In addition, the EP, Council, and Commission agreed a Common Understanding on Delegated Acts (Official Journal (OJ) 2016 L123/1).

3.7.1 Implementing acts

Article 291 now provides separately and expressly for acts that are to be implemented uniformly in the member states, but the overall control of such powers is retained by the member states. It further provides that powers delegated to the Commission to implement legally binding EU acts are subject to a revised comitology procedure. To that end, Regulation 182/2011 was enacted setting up a new form of committee structure comprising two forms of Committee, comprising Advisory, which are similar to those set up by the old Comitology Decision, and Examination committees, which are the equivalent of the previous management and regulatory procedures.

The CoJ has at times been asked to decide whether a particular delegated/implementing act has been appropriately enacted by the Commission as they are subject to different oversight procedures and involvements of the Council and EP. See, for example, Case C-427/12 *Commission v EP and Council* concerning Regulation 528/12, in which the CoJ was prepared to outline the distinction between the two. For delegated legislation, the Commission may amend the governing act in non-essential matters, whereas for implementing acts, the Commission may only add details to ensure uniform implementation in the member states. The CoJ, though, was not prepared to determine whether the type chosen by the EU legislature was the correct one because of the discretion it enjoyed in its choice, unless it was manifestly in error. The ruling of the court is regarded as a sensible one, which will thus prevent frequent claims from individuals suggesting that the wrong procedure was chosen and thus rendering the delegated/implementing act void.

In other specific circumstances, the Commission has further powers of its own under Article 105 TFEU competition law exemptions and under Article 106 TFEU concerned with state aids.

 Summary

The Communities and now Union were established by a transfer of powers by the member states to enable them to act independently of those member states and to create their own laws and legal system. However, the transfer was not a complete transfer of competences, but only a transfer of competences in those areas agreed by the member states. In some areas, exclusive competence was agreed where considered necessary; in others, competence was to be shared. In addition, in order to operate effectively, it was necessary that additional residual and general powers were granted if needed to complete particular aspects without having to have recourse to the member states on each and every occasion. This led to a perceived competence creep by the member states, which considered the Commission to have overstepped the mark. Thus, the attention turned to considering the attempts by which this competence creep might be curbed, notably through the principles of proportionality and subsidiarity, but also through other Treaty amendments and by Protocols and Declarations added to the Treaties.

As outlined in this chapter, there are a number of shifting dynamics in the policymaking and law-making procedures of the EU. The most notable remains the balance between the direct democratic legitimacy of the EP in the face of the still legislative superiority of the Council, although clearly under the Lisbon Treaty things have moved further in the direction of the

EP. The problem, however, with increasing the input and power of the EP still further or including national parliaments to a greater degree is that it would certainly increase democratic participation, albeit indirectly, although that might jeopardise the present level of efficiency of the law-making process. Whilst it is far from perfect at the moment, it does seem to have achieved a relatively happy medium of getting most things done, albeit sometimes slowly. An increase in the power of the EP truly to rival that of the Council or increasing the participation of the national parliaments may have the knock-on effect of creating conflicts between the institutions, which may result in stalling the law-making processes—and if nothing ever gets done, it would hardly be a useful democratic input. In other words, too much participation by the EP or the national parliaments may lead to a slowing down of the legislative processes. So, should efficiency be sacrificed for the sake of democracy? The concern presently is whether democracy is being sacrificed for the sake of efficiency.

> Under the changes brought about by the Lisbon Treaty, national parliaments have been given a formal say in any future Treaty amendment proposals and new membership applications (Articles 48–49 TEU). The difficulty with this is that the national parliaments may then become a rival for power with the EP and it may also reduce efficiency in the law-making processes if the views of 28 national parliaments have to be obtained before progress can be made.

? Questions

1. What role do the principles of subsidiarity, proportionality, and attributed competence play in the process of EU law-making? Who should rule on the question of whether these principles are being respected?

2. What is the legal base of a Union law? Why is it important to know this and why have so many disputes arisen as to the proper legal base?

3. Why are there so many law-making procedures?

For suggested approaches to answering these questions, visit the online resources.

▢ Sample exam Q&A

The transfer of power to the EU and control of competence in the EU is now firmly regulated by the Treaties following the Lisbon Treaty reforms.

Please discuss.

For guidance on how to tackle this specimen exam question and to read a suggested model answer, visit the online resources. www.oup.com/uk/foster_directions6e/.

☰ Further reading

Books

Azoulai, L. (ed.) *The Question of Competence in the European Union*, Oxford University Press, Oxford, 2014.

Bergström, C.F. and Ritleng, D. (eds) *Rulemaking by the European Commission—The New System for Delegation of Powers*, Oxford University Press, Oxford, 2016.

Bradley, K. 'Legislating in the European Union' in Barnard, C. and Peers S. (eds) *European Union Law*, 2nd edn, Oxford University Press, Oxford, 2017, p. 97.

Corrias, L. *The Passivity of Law: Competence and Constitution in the European Court of Justice*, Springer Press, Amsterdam, 2011.

Garben, S. and Govaere, I. *The Division of Competences Between between the EU and the Member States*, Bloomsbury, London, 2017.

Konstantinides, T. *Division of Powers in European Union Law: The Delimitation of Internal Competences between the EU and the Member States*, Kluwer Law International, London, 2009.

Sieberson, S.C. *Dividing Lines between the European Union and its Member States*, Cambridge University Press, Cambridge, 2008.

Articles

Conway, G. 'Conflicts of competence norms in EU Law and the legal reasoning of the European Court of Justice' (2010) 11(9) GLJ 966.

Craig, P. 'Subsidiarity: a political and legal analysis' (2012) 50 JCMS 72.

Cygan, A. 'The parliamentarisation of EU decision-making? The impact of the Treaty of Lisbon on national parliaments' (2011) 36 EL Rev 480.

Davies, G. 'Subsidiarity: the wrong idea, in the wrong place, at the wrong time' (2006) 43 CML Rev 63.

Davies, G. 'Legislative control of the European Court of Justice', (2014) 51 CML Rev 1579.

Harbo, T.-I. 'The function of the proportionality principle in EU law' (2010) 16 ELJ 158.

Horsley, T. 'Subsidiarity and the European Court of Justice: missing pieces in the subsidiarity puzzle' (2012) 50 JCMS 267.

Weatherill, S. 'Better competence monitoring' (2005) 30 EL Rev 23.

Weatherill, S. 'Competence creep and competence control' (2005) 24 YEL 1.

4 Sources and forms of EU law

LEARNING OBJECTIVES

In this chapter, you will learn about:

- the form and nature of the EU legal system;
- the EU's own sources of law;
- other external sources that also contribute to the body of Union law that exists today;
- fundamental and human rights in the EU legal order as well as general principals;
- the different Treaty-based forms of Union secondary law;
- EU procedural law and delegated law forms.

Introduction

As noted above in the learning objectives, the main focus of this chapter are the various forms of law which today make up so-called *acquis communautaire* (the overall body of European Union (EU) law, which term we met in Chapter 1). Essentially this comprises, primarily, of the EU's own law, which in turn consists of the Treaties, EU secondary legislation, EU-delegated and implementing laws, and the now extensive case law of the Court of Justice (CoJ). Then, subsequently but equally important, is a range of law sources external in origin to the EU consisting of various forms of international agreements, general principles, fundamental and human rights, and procedural law and laws of natural justice. Following the entry into force of the Lisbon Treaty, the terms 'EU law' and 'EU legal system' will now apply to what was previously termed 'Community law' and 'Community legal system'. Both sets of terms, though, are referring to the same things, which is the subject of the rest of this chapter, and indeed, this book.

4.1 The EU legal system

This section will introduce the founding Treaties, which provide the basis of other forms of Union law, but it is to be noted immediately that the EU and its Court, the CoJ, have also used external sources for some of its laws, notably fundamental rights and general principles, which are considered in this chapter. Furthermore, the individual style of Union law is highlighted.

For more details on this section visit the online resources.

The Treaty on European Union (TEU) and the Treaty on the Functioning of the European Union (TFEU) are, following the entry into force of the Lisbon Treaty, the principal sources of law for the Union and those with which we are most concerned. As will be clear from Chapter 1 of this book, the Treaties and Union law are not static bodies of law, but are amended from time to time as the member states agree, as can clearly be seen by the changes introduced by the Single European Act (SEA), the Maastricht Treaty (TEU), and the Treaties of Amsterdam, Nice, and Lisbon. In establishing the basic format of the Communities at the time of their founding, legal models were sought on which to build the legal system for the Communities and now Union. At that time, there were no member states from common law jurisdictions and it is therefore to be expected that the initial Community legal system would broadly resemble a civil law system and, in particular, follow legal structures found in the French and German legal systems. For example, much of the procedure of the Courts is based on French administrative law, as are actions for damages under the second paragraph of Article 340 TFEU. In turn, looking over the longer-term development of Community and now EU law, this has been influenced both by the legal structures and the principles of law in the member states, and in turn Community and now EU law influences the development of law in the member states.

The founding framework Treaties provide broad principles and aims, which reflect the way in which civil law countries approach legislative enactment with codified law. They commence with general abstract principles, such as the Preamble and Articles 2 and 3 TFEU.

Preamble TFEU

DETERMINED to lay the foundations of an ever closer union among the peoples of Europe,

RESOLVED to ensure the economic and social progress of their countries by common action to eliminate the barriers which divide Europe,

AFFIRMING as the essential objective of their efforts the constant improvements of the living and working conditions of their peoples,

RECOGNISING that the removal of existing obstacles calls for concerted action in order to guarantee steady expansion, balanced trade and fair competition,

---

Article 2(3) TFEU

The Member States shall coordinate their economic and employment policies with arrangements as determined by this Treaty . . .

Indeed, this approach has been strengthened by the latest amendments and rearrangement of the Treaties and their content. The TEU has been made into a general overview Treaty providing the broad basis for the former EC Treaty, which has become, as it is inelegantly titled, the Treaty on the Functioning of the European Union (TFEU). This Treaty provides the details of the overall policies set out in the EU Treaty. It too, though, retains its general introduction and Articles.

The TEU also has a general Preamble and Articles 2 and 3 providing a list of objectives including, for example, under Article 3(4), that 'The Union shall establish an economic and monetary Union whose currency is the euro.' It also includes something with which lawyers from civil law countries are familiar: a form of good faith clause, included in Article 4(3) TEU (ex 10 EC), which imposes an obligation on the member states both to act positively to achieve the goals of the Treaty and not to act in any way that would jeopardise those aims.

Article 2(3) TFEU

The Member States shall take any appropriate measure, general or particular, to ensure fulfilment of the obligations arising out of the Treaties or resulting from acts of the institutions of the Union. The Member States shall facilitate the achievement of the Union's tasks and refrain from any measure which could jeopardise the attainment of the Union's objectives.

The rest of the TFEU, although putting the broad aims into greater detail, nevertheless provides merely an outline for the areas of law that the member states agreed should be integrated. It provides, for example, the basic legal regime for free movement of goods and workers, competition law, and agriculture. Some sections are more detailed than others, and whereas free movement of goods has required little secondary legislation, competition law and agriculture have been subject to considerable legislative regulation. Thus, for the most part, the Treaties require completion by detailed Regulations and Directives. The areas agreed by the member states can and have been added to; for example, environmental protection and research and technology were added by the SEA, and new policy areas were introduced by the TEU, notably economic and monetary union, public health, and consumer protection.

Apart from the secondary legislation needed to put into effect the goals of the various policies, any gaps and ambiguities in the legislation and interpretation of the Treaty and secondary legislation are resolved by the CoJ. As a result, a body of case law has slowly arisen, itself relying on a variety of internal and external sources, such as general principles and fundamental rights.

4.1.1 The style of the EU legal system

Before moving on to consider the individual elements of the Union legal system, it is worthwhile considering how the legal system is intended to work. Similar to the civil law systems, the Union legal system is essentially a deductive system; therefore, the result in a particular case is achieved by working from the general to the particular—that is, from the broad framework Treaty rules, which have in the past often included the Preamble, Articles 2, 3, 10, and 12 EC (now Articles 1, 8, and 18 TFEU and Articles 3 and 4 TEU), to the relevant provisions of the specific Chapter or Title of the Treaty.

Undoubtedly, this will continue with the Treaty base, as amended by the Lisbon Treaty, providing an enhanced general introduction and provision. Consider the Preamble and Articles 2–4 TEU and the Preamble and Articles 2–13 TFEU.

Then, any applicable general principles and secondary legislation on the topic can be considered and, finally, the relevant case law on the interpretation and application of the Treaties or other legislative provisions can be evaluated to help to determine the outcome of a particular case.

As will be demonstrated in the following chapters, the interpretation techniques of the CoJ also follow the approach of taking into account the general aims to help to decide in particular cases.

CROSS REFERENCE

Interpretation was considered in Chapter 2, sections 2.5.4.1 and 2.5.4.2.

The Court will often make reference to the Preamble and general provisions of the Treaty to justify a particular decision, and applies law in the scope of the Treaty as a whole, in the light of the basic aims and objectives of the Treaties and not only the specific legislation. Examples from the old Treaties include:

- Article 2 EC is referred to in Case 7/75 *Mrs and Mrs F. v Belgian State* concerning social security;
- Article 3 EC in Case 6/72 *Europemballage and Continental Can v Commission*; and
- Case 14/83 *Von Colson* was very strongly argued on the basis of Article 10 EC (now 4(3) TEU).

> **Cases C-6 and C-9/90 *Francovich*** was also argued strongly on the basis on Article 10 EC to establish, for the first time under Community law, state liability for the failure of the member state to implement a Directive.

Article 18 TFEU (ex 12 EC), the general prohibition of discrimination on the grounds of nationality, is also relevant to all areas of EU law and is used on particular occasions as a general tool of the CoJ to reach just results that might not otherwise have been reached by the application of more specific provisions.

> For example, Article 18 TFEU has been used to extend the equality of law requirement in respect of vocational training and fees into more mainstream education, as can be seen in **Cases 24/86 *Blaizot*, 263/86 *Humbel*, 39/86 *Lair*, and 293/83 *Gravier***, among others.

4.1.2   The classification of the elements of EU law

EU law can be divided broadly into three main components and it may be that your course makes a similar division that helps to make EU law more accessible. The division is usually along the lines of institutional law, procedural law, and substantive law.

4.1.2.1   Institutional law

Institutional law is also called the 'constitutional law' of the EU. It concerns the structure of the Union, the regulation of the main institutions and other bodies of the Union, the sources of EU law, and the special principles of EU law, including supremacy and direct effects. Institutional law also concerns the relationship of the institutions among themselves, the relationship of the Union with the member states, and its external relations with other countries and international organisations. The institutions are the bodies responsible for the legislative and budgetary processes and, as their relationship alters in time due to Treaty amendment, disputes arise over the boundaries of the powers and duties of the institutions and their relationships to each other. Such disputes have had to be settled by the CoJ as the institutions seek to protect their powers or legally to extend them: for example, the Court has assisted the European Parliament (EP) in gaining increased litigation rights to reflect its democratic power in the Community, now formally recognised by Treaty amendment (Article 263 TFEU). Generally, also, the CoJ's pronouncements on the status and effects of the provisions of EU law have resulted in the establishment and development of ground-breaking, and now fundamental, leading principles of EU law, including direct effects, supremacy, and state liability, the details of which can be found in Chapter 8.

4.1.2.2   Procedural law

Procedural law is sometimes referred to as the 'administrative law' of the Union and includes actions for judicial review by the CoJ and the various other actions that can be taken by the institutions, member states, and natural and legal persons under rules provided by the TFEU (see Articles 258–260, 263, 265, 267, 277, and 340 TFEU). These actions, then, are mainly concerned with the enforcement of rights against the Union institutions, the member states, and individuals. Procedural law covers a range of remedies, and indirect actions involving the national courts and direct actions at the level of the Union, considered in Chapters 6–9.

4.1.2.3 Substantive law

Substantive law comprises the legal rules established to carry out the broad policy areas of law agreed under the Treaties, and can be distinguished from the law relating to the institutions and the procedural law of the Union. The substantive law is largely secondary law and takes effect predominantly in the member states and not at the Union level, despite its primary base in Treaty Articles. The substantive law of the Union has also been described previously as 'economic law' or the 'law of the economy of the Community', and even as 'Community (now Union) private law'. However, this is not a particularly meaningful label because the concept of economic law varies from state to state and between political systems. Additionally, this does not reflect the considerable extension of the EU into new policy areas. The Union is now concerned with far more than the setting up of a regulatory framework for limited aspects of the economies dealing only with free-trade rules. More recently, far more social concerns and policies are being given voice in the EU legal order and Treaties: see, for example, the much-expanded Titles on social policy, education, culture, public health, and consumer protection in the TFEU (Articles 151–169) brought about by Treaty amendment and intergovernmental agreements. Further evidence can be found in the statements made by the CoJ that the Union places social concerns above economic considerations, for example as in Case C-324/96 *Deutsche Telekom* v *Vick*.

The substantive law chapters following (Chapters 10–14), however, will deal with four topics only, all of which were within the original policies of the Community, although to a different extent, social provision being at the time very limited. Those included are the free movement of goods, free movement of workers and persons, sex equality law, and competition law.

4.2 The sources and forms of Union law

What should be mentioned at the outset of this particular section of the book is the term *acquis communautaire*. This refers to, or is a way of describing, the whole body of EU law that has been built up over the life of the Communities and now Union, and which comprises all of the sources of law considered in this chapter. It is more likely to be heard in connection with the entry of new member states, which are now required to accept in total the *acquis communautaire*, which is non-negotiable (i.e. the member states have to accept all elements of the *acquis* in its entirety). It was estimated that this amounts now to about 80,000 pages of legal text.

For more details on this section visit the online resources.

The Commission in 2011 estimated the *acquis* to consist of some 8,863 Regulations and 1,185 Directives. In 2015, a different estimate suggested there were more than 40,000 various EU legal Acts.

For more details on this section visit the online resources.

Figure 4.1 Hierarchy of EU law sources

The Treaties, Protocols, Declarations, secondary legislation, international agreements, case law, and development of legal principles by the CoJ all contribute to the *acquis communautaire*. Whilst no formal hierarchy of these various sources of laws is set out in the Treaties, some clarification has been provided by reforms introduced by the Lisbon Treaty. The Treaties remain clearly at the apex of the hierarchy and with them now the EU Charter of Fundamental Rights (see Figure 4.1). In second rank, previously ascribed to EU secondary legislative acts, are general principles and fundamental rights, some of which, though, are also part of the primary source of law as they are contained in either the Treaties or in the Charter of Fundamental Rights. General principles are accorded this ranking because they may lead not only to the annulment of secondary and other lower-ranking legal rules but also used to interpret provisions of primary law, but not their annulment. Then follow international Treaties, which are ranked above a further major category: secondary EU law, which has its own internal hierarchy of norms. Finally, we need to consider the jurisprudence or case law of the CoJ. It is not universally acknowledged as a formal source of law, which is surprising since it is through the case law of the CoJ that some of the leading and strongest general principles have been recognised or introduced into the EU legal order, such as supremacy, direct effects, state liability, equality, and very many of the general principles considered already in either the first- or the second-ranking category of sources. As a result of this somewhat schizoid and boundary-crossing classification, general principles are introduced in rank order below in section 4.4, but the details of the general principles themselves are considered with the rest of the judicial developments and case law of the CoJ in section 4.6.

4.3 EU primary law

4.3.1 **The Treaties**

⧫ CROSS REFERENCE

See Chapter 1 for further details.

The Treaties are the primary source of law in the Union, with two main Treaties now of equal standing: the TEU and the TFEU (see Article 1 of both) and the European Atomic Energy Treaty (EURATOM). The original Treaties were amended and supplemented considerably by a number of

Treaties, including the 1965 Merger Treaty and the various Treaties or Acts of Accession providing details for the entry into the Communities and Union of new member states. More fundamentally, they were amended by the SEA, the TEU, the Treaty of Amsterdam, the Treaty of Nice, and, finally and most fundamentally, the Lisbon Treaty in 2009.

> All of the Treaties of the Union are drawn up in all of the official languages of the Union, which are equally authentic. Any difficulties that arise from the fact that different meanings may, despite all attempts, arise between languages are usually overcome by the CoJ applying the teleological interpretation of the spirit of the provision, rather than the letter. A comparison of a number of language versions may be necessary in order to discern the true meaning of a particular provision.

> See, for example, **Case C-106/89 *Marleasing SA v La Comercial Internacional de Alimentacion SA*** and **Case C-149/97 *Institute of the Motor Industry v Customs and Excise Commissioners,*** in which the different language versions of the Sixth VAT Directive were discussed.

The special nature of these Treaties is encapsulated within the concept of direct applicability, which means that, on the accession of a member state to the Union, all of the provisions of the Treaties automatically become part of the generally binding law of the member state. The provisions are applicable not only to the member states, but also to the citizens of each country. This form of law is also known as 'self-executing law', a term previously recognised in international law. This describes the way in which some provisions of law have legal validity in the member states, in that no further action need be taken by a member state to incorporate or transform the Treaty into the national legal order once it has ratified the Treaty. Some member states, however, such as the UK, may need an introductory Act formally to mark the presence of the Treaty, but even then, would not reproduce the text of the Treaty into a national Act. Self-executing law, such as the Treaties, does not rely on the way in which the member state has incorporated it for its validity.

> The early **Case 26/62 *Van Gend en Loos*** is confirmation of the deeper impact of this directly applicable Community law because, in this case, the CoJ made it clear that Community law is also the legal concern of individuals and not only of the member states, and although it was related to international law, it was a new legal order in international law.

The Treaties are framework Treaties in that they lay down broad guidelines for the pursuit of certain agreed aims and objectives. They do not provide extensive details for the implementation of these policies, which is left for the most part to secondary legislation of the Union or, failing that, to the CoJ, which will rule on what was intended by the Treaty provision. The Treaties have often been described as the constitutional basis of the Union and notably so by the CoJ in the leading cases of *Van Gend en Loos* and *Costa v ENEL*.

The scope of the Treaties has expanded considerably since their establishment and now covers wide areas of the economic and social life of the member states, including economic and monetary policy, culture and tourism, humanitarian aid, judicial and police cooperation, and foreign policy, among many others, although not all to the same level of integration and control.

The Lisbon Treaty did not add to these areas of Union influence, with the exception of making the catalogue of human rights binding (Article 6(1) TEU), but not a part of the Treaty, and with opt-outs for the UK and Poland and exemptions from specific aspects of it for Ireland and the Czech Republic.

Treaty amendment is usually achieved by the signing and ratifying of an amending treaty after discussion and agreement of the member states in an Intergovernmental Conference (IGC). The Lisbon Treaty has changed the procedure by which the Treaties are amended by providing now in Article 48 TEU for both an ordinary and a simplified revision procedure. Under the ordinary procedure, proposals for amendment may come from any member state, the EP, or the Commission, which submits it to the Council, which in turn notifies the European Council and the national parliaments. If the European Council, having consulted the EP and Commission, considers that a proposal should be taken forward, it will convene a convention, attended by representatives from the national parliaments, heads of state, or government, the EP, and the Commission, which shall adopt by consensus a recommendation which will be discussed in an IGC; further agreement, signing, and ratification takes place in the usual form. Alternatively, the European Council may decide by simple majority, with the consent of the EP, that the changes do not justify a Convention and may then proceed directly to an IGC. The simplified revision procedure, which applies only to Part Three of the TFEU—internal policies and action— allows first under Article 48(6) TEU for the European Council to decide unanimously after consultation of the EP and Commission on Treaty amendments, which are then subject to ratification in the usual way by all member states. The simplified revision procedure also allows the European Council acting by unanimity to change the voting procedures of Treaty Articles, except those concerned with defence or military matters, from unanimity to qualified majority voting (QMV) and from a special legislative procedure to the ordinary legislative procedure. This requires the approval of the national parliaments and is termed a *passerelle* provision. Whilst the validity of the Treaties is clearly beyond the jurisdiction of the CoJ, it has nevertheless considered in Case C-370/12 *Pringle*, whether the procedure under the simplified revision procedure was validly followed.

4.3.2 The Protocols attached to the Treaties

The TEU and TFEU do not represent the entirety of primary Union law because, following an unfortunate practice of limited beginnings, each successive IGC has added what has now amounted to a complex range of Protocols to the Treaties.

4.3.2.1 Status of the Protocols

▶ CROSS REFERENCE

See Chapter 1 for the Treaty amendments.

Article 51 TEU declares Protocols to be an integral part of the Treaties, which means that they possess Treaty status and are endorsed by the CoJ. However, by the addition of so many Protocols, the Treaty constitutional set-up has become increasingly complex. Whilst some steps have been attempted to consolidate them, this has been very limited and half-hearted.

In international law, Protocols would be regarded as a lesser form of international law than Treaties, but no less binding.

One of the aims in drafting the Constitutional Treaty (CT) was that this matter would be looked at and, as with the Treaties themselves, considerably simplified. However, that simplification amounted only to consolidating the then existing Protocols and Declarations, which would then be attached as a list of Protocols to the CT. Since the CT was rejected, the Lisbon Treaty has done nothing more than the same, and perhaps worse, by adding more Protocols. In total, there are 38 Protocols now attached to the Treaties, the last one being the Irish Protocol added in 2013.

THINKING POINT

Should member states be allowed opt-outs? What might be the consequences, if it was decided they should no longer be allowed?

4.3.3 Declarations

In addition to the various Protocols, further attached to each subsequent Treaty is usually a list of Declarations of the member states, sometimes by all member states, but mainly by a few or only one, which makes a unilateral declaration on a particular matter, for example the Declaration by Austria and Luxembourg on credit institutions that was attached to the Amsterdam Treaty. These Declarations need to be noted because, like the Protocols, they may alter our view or perception of the meaning or application of Treaty provisions. However, unlike the Protocols, they enjoy no express Treaty status, and their status in EU law is not clear.

For more details on this section visit the online resources.

The Lisbon Treaty has added more Declarations, so this unfortunate aspect of the EU legislative base has been made worse and not better. There are now 65 Declarations attached to the Treaties.

Without making any clear-cut express statement as to the status, the European Court of Justice (ECJ) held in **Case C-192/99 *ex p Manjit Kaur* v *Secretary of State for the Home Department*** that, in order to determine UK nationality, it was necessary to refer to the 1992 Declaration No. 2 on Nationality attached to the Treaties, which declared that the determination of nationality of a state was a matter of each state alone and not a matter of EU law. The judgment thus acknowledged the instrument without, however, expressly declaring it to be binding in the EU legal order.

Note now that Declaration No. 2 is no longer to be found attached to the Treaties.

Further judicial advice on the value of Declarations has been received in Case C-354/04P *Gestoras* in as much as no legal binding effect was accorded to them by the CoJ.

4.3.4 The EU Charter of Fundamental Rights

The EU Charter, first established in 2001, has now been appended to the Treaties by Declaration No. 1, which, with Article 6(1) TEU, declares that it has Treaty status and is fully binding in the member states—hence its classification as primary law within the hierarchy of EU law sources. There are exceptions to the scope of its application internally within Poland and the UK, agreed in Protocol 30

For more details on this section visit the online resources.

and in the Czech Republic by Declaration No. 53, although Article 6(1) TEU makes it clear that the Charter does not extend the competences of the Union.

> **Declaration No. 1 concerning the Charter of Fundamental Rights of the European Union**
>
> The Charter of Fundamental Rights of the EU, which has legally binding force, confirms the fundamental rights guaranteed by the European Convention for the Protection of Human Rights and Fundamental Freedoms and as they result from the constitutional traditions common to the member states.
>
> The Charter does not extend the field of application of Union law beyond the powers of the Union or establish any new power or task for the Union, or modify powers and tasks as defined by the Treaties.
>
> The Charter is reproduced in full in Foster, *EU Treaties and Legislation*, Oxford University Press, published yearly.

The EU Charter was not intended to replicate the rights contained within the European Convention on Human Rights (ECHR), but rather, to provide a catalogue of rights relevant to the EU brought together largely from the existing case law of the CoJ, the constitutions of the member states, and international conventions from the Council of Europe including the ECHR, the United Nations (UN), and the International Labour Organisation (ILO). It nevertheless overlaps with some of the rights provided in the ECHR. It is divided into seven chapters covering: dignity, freedoms, equality, solidarity, citizens' rights, justice, and general provisions—the so-called 'Horizontal Articles'.

The freedoms and equality rights are to be expected and for the most part lend themselves well to the EU context. The workers' rights in the solidarity chapter, which also includes general social and economic rights, are more in line, however, with policy areas now catered for to some extent in the EU legal order. This chapter also contains environmental protections which are expressed only in general terms and rely on other provisions of EU law to provide the details of the rights. The fifth chapter contains citizens' rights, which are restricted to EU citizens and which for the most part reproduce the rights contained in Articles 20–25 TFEU, although the right of access to documents is also included. The final substantive rights chapter on justice contains rights of natural justice and procedural law rights, many of which had already featured in the jurisprudence of the CoJ.

The seventh chapter contains the general rights of to whom and how the Charter applies. Article 51 of the Charter defines the scope of the application of the Charter as addressed to the institutions and bodies of the Union only when they are applying EU law, and not extending to the member states when not implementing EU law. Furthermore, the Charter does not extend the field of application of EU law, nor does it modify its powers and tasks, a proviso that is repeated in Declaration No. 1, reproduced above.

CROSS REFERENCE

See for example in the case of *Hauer* v *Rheinland Pfalz,* considered in section 4.3.5.

Article 52(1) contains a derogation clause, similar to those found in the ECHR in that derogations will only be permitted if provided for by law. They must meet the essential rights contained in the Articles, be proportionate, and are only acceptable if they are necessary and genuinely meet objectives of general interest or the need to protect the rights and freedoms of others. As with the provisions of the ECHR, a court faced with conflicting rights will have to balance the rights of those rights-holders, but this is something the CoJ has already been doing with cases involving a claim to the protection of fundamental rights.

Articles 52(2)–(4) and 53 essentially provide rules of conflict in the event of clashes with the protection regimes of the EU Treaties, the member states, and the ECHR. Article 52(5) suggests that there is a distinction between rights, actionable without further ado before the courts, and principles that are declared to be enforceable only via implementing legislation and are justiciable only as persuasive interpretations.

A lot of case law has already made mention of the Charter, with a 2011 report by the Commission stating that 42 rulings in 2011 referred to the Charter, up from 27 in 2010.

Notable rulings include **Case C-236/09 *Test-Achats***, in which the Court invalidated a derogation in EU gender equality legislation that enables insurers to differentiate between men and women in individuals' premiums and benefits, which was found to be incompatible with sex equality also contained within the Charter. See also **Cases C-411/10 and 493/10 *NS* v *Secretary of State for the Home Department* and *ME* v *Refugee Applications Commissioner (the Dublin Convention)***, in which the member state responsible for the assessment of an asylum seeker who first entered the EU through Greece before seeking asylum in the UK was determined. The CoJ stressed that member states are under the obligation to respect the Charter when they establish the responsibility for examining an asylum application. In particular, member states must not transfer an asylum seeker to another member state if they cannot be certain that systemic deficiencies in the asylum procedure and reception conditions may amount to substantial grounds for believing that person would face a real risk of being subjected to inhuman or degrading treatment. This case also considered Protocol 30 and whether that indeed had the effect of exempting the UK from the application of the Charter. The CoJ held that the Protocol was not an 'opt-out' but a document clarifying the interpretation of the Charter and that the case, in fact, involved EU law in the shape of the Dublin Convention established precisely to determine which EU member state should be responsible for determining asylum applications.

In **Case C-617/10 *Fransson***, Article 51 and the scope of the application of the Charter were considered by the CoJ. The Court held that when member states are putting into effect the requirements of EU Directives, the national law transposing them is also subject to the Charter; hence the conclusion is that the Article provides not just a narrow understanding on the scope of EU law but also its implementation in the member states.

The Charter was also obliquely raised in **Case C-399/11 *Melloni***, in which a national court asked if Article 53 of the Charter allowed national courts to apply stricter standards than provided by EU law in the event of difference. The CoJ, relying on previous case law on supremacy held that not to be the case.

In **Case C-258/13, *Sociedade Agricola***, the Court of Justice made it quite clear that where a case did not involve EU law but just national law, the Charter would not apply and could not be relied on, which was the expected interpretation and indeed, as far as the member states are concerned, the hoped-for interpretation.

The Charter will no doubt be a rich source of human rights case law to come.

4.3.5 **Human or fundamental rights**

This section regards 'human' and 'fundamental' rights as synonymous terms. Whilst human or fundamental rights may be considered as a completely separate source of law, they nevertheless take a higher hierarchy now in the Union legal order. The Communities and the EU were established as a direct response to the wholesale abuse of rights in the Second World War. Originally, fundamental rights were completely absent from any of the Treaties, although some isolated Articles provided rights that either coincided with general principles or helped in the development of general principles of Community and now Union law.

Previously, most of these Articles were contained solely in the EC Treaty, but now, given the redistribution of some of the Articles between the TEU and TFEU, both Treaties are home to general provisions.

> Previously, the EC Treaty contained Articles 2 (social protection, the standard of living, and quality of life), 3 and 39 (the free movement of persons), 12, 34, and 39(2) (discrimination), 137 (social provision), and 141 (equal pay). Similar Articles with enhanced provision are now to be found in Articles 2–3 and 6 TEU and 8–10, 18–19, 40, 45, 153, and 157 TFEU.

At the start of the Communities, there was no specific and binding set of obligations imposed by the Treaty on the Community institutions to guarantee the individual rights of citizens. This initial apparent lack of commitment to human rights was in turn reflected in the early decisions of the CoJ when faced with arguments or pleas raised by litigants based on basic or human rights. Hence the early case law of the CoJ presents the view of a Community unsympathetic to the fundamental human rights of individuals.

> The following cases were all decided before the Lisbon Treaty came into effect; hence, the term 'Community' is retained. In the present context, this should be taken to read 'Union'.

> In **Cases 1/58 *Stork* v *High Authority*** and **40/64 *Sgarlata* v Commission**, arguments based on individual rights were clearly rejected in favour of upholding Community law.

This position can be contrasted with the then six member states' positions regarding human rights. Following the Second World War, Western European nations were more than ever ideologically committed to the concept of protecting human rights. The German and Italian Constitutions were rewritten with very strong commitments to basic rights contained within a rights catalogue. By 1955, all of the original members of the EEC, except France, had ratified the ECHR. The Community and Court were thus morally, if not legally, obliged to observe fundamental human rights. Thus, the CoJ could not maintain its unsympathetic stance and adopted, from the late 1960s, a new response.

> In **Case 26/69 *Stauder* v *City of Ulm***, a German citizen protested that his fundamental right of human dignity, protected by Article 1 of the German *Grundgesetz* (its 'Basic Law', or Constitution) was being infringed by having his name on the coupon when claiming reduced-price butter by the Community. The CoJ held that the Community legislation did not require his name, but the Community law itself had not prejudiced his fundamental rights, which were 'enshrined in the general principles of Community law and protected by the Court'. This recognition of the right of human dignity in the EU legal order was confirmed by the CoJ in **Case C-36/02 *Omega***.

After the French ratification of the ECHR in 1974, the CoJ referred also to the ECHR as an example of the member states' commitment to fundamental rights. Further encouragement came from the

Joint Declaration by Community Institutions on Fundamental Rights of 5 April 1977, which stressed the importance of national constitutions and the ECHR.

Hence, for the first time, in **Case 44/79 _Hauer_ v _Land Rheinland-Pfalz_**, the CoJ considered in some detail a provision (Article 1 of Protocol 1) of the ECHR to help it to decide the case. Although it recognised the right of property in the case, its exercise was subject to overriding Community interests.

Thus, despite recognition of the fundamental rights, previously cases were usually resolved on the basis of either Community law applying or the rights being subject to limitations mainly of the Community interest.

In a number of cases, the Court reaffirmed its statement that fundamental rights form part of the general principles based on the constitutional traditions of member states.

For example, **Case 11/70 _Internationale Handelsgesellschaft_** showed the potential for conflict and ultimate harm to the Community legal order if the Community were to fail to uphold human rights provisions because of a potential clash, in this case, of Community law with the German Constitution. The German Constitution had claimed the exclusive right to decide on cases involving a clash between Community law and the German Constitution. In fact, the CoJ had declared that there was no breach of the Community law in question. No self-respecting legal system in Europe could ignore or be seen to be ignoring such ideologically important rights as these and, in the case, the Court gave a guarantee that members states' constitutions will not be infringed despite the superiority of Community law because of the commitment of the Community to human rights and the fact that they form part of the Community legal order.

In **Case 63/83 _R_ v Kirk**, a fine imposed on a fishing boat captain by a UK court that was based on a national UK statutory order was held to infringe the principle of non-retroactivity, because the order was supposedly validated only by later Community legislation. The CoJ held that such an action violated the principle of non-retroactivity of criminal law enshrined in Article 7 ECHR and now a principle of Community law.

▶ CROSS REFERENCE
Non-retroactivity was also confirmed as a principle of Community law in _Kolpinghuis Nijmegan_, considered further in section 4.6.1.4 and in Chapter 8.

In **Case 222/86 _UNECTEF_ v _Heylens and others_**, the Court was able to refer to Articles 6 and 13 ECHR to support the right to judicial review and the right to be heard in support of a claim for an additional right—the right to free access to employment. In **Case 5/88 _Wachauf_**, the Court extended its support of fundamental rights by holding that the actions of member states in implementing Community measures must also comply with the requirements of human rights provisions.

A very strong support for the respect for human rights in the EU legal order can be found in **Joined Cases C-402/05P and 415/05P _Kadi and Al Barakaat_,** which were concerned with the translation into EU Regulations of UN measures against the support of terrorism, namely the freezing of assets of persons listed by the UN as suspected of being involved. The applicants, Kadi and Al Barakaat, challenged the Regulation, which contained and was the cause of

▶ CROSS REFERENCE
This case is considered further in Chapter 5.

the alleged infringements of human rights, including the right to be heard and the right to an effective remedy. The CoJ made clear that neither the member states nor the EU institutions can avoid review of the conformity of their acts with the basic constitutional charter, the EC Treaty, which established a complete system of legal remedies and procedures designed to enable the Court to review the legality of acts of the institutions. Furthermore, a guarantee of fundamental rights forms an integral part of the EU legal order, and their respect is a condition of the lawfulness of EU acts and that, as constitutional principles of the EU, this status cannot be affected by any international agreement or the fact that EU acts are based on an international obligation. A review of the validity of any Community measure in the light of fundamental rights must be considered to be the expression, in a Community based on the rule of law, of a constitutional guarantee stemming from the EC Treaty as an autonomous legal system. The Resolution and thus the Regulation were held patently to breach the right to be heard and to an effective remedy in the inclusion in the list of the applicants' names without recourse to any form of judicial review. The CoJ acknowledged that security interests may justify the secret compilation of the list but will not exclude a judicial review of the lawfulness after publication (see [281–4], [292], [296], and [316]).

The CoJ continues to refer to the ECHR in support of its judgments.

> **CROSS REFERENCE**
Article 8 ECHR is considered further in Chapter 12, sections 12.3.1 and 12.3.2.2.

For example, see recent cases from the area of the free movement of persons **C-413/99 Baumbast, C-459/99 MRAX**, and **C-109/01 Akrich**, which all featured Article 8 ECHR, the right to family life.

4.3.5.1 The status of the ECHR and its relationship with EU law

> **CROSS REFERENCE**
The Charter itself is considered under primary EU law in section 4.3.4.

The elevated status given to the ECHR and to fundamental rights generally by the CoJ has been reflected in a greater status within the Treaty base and strengthened further by the Lisbon Treaty. Article 2 TEU declares that the Union is founded on the respect for human rights. Article 6(1) TEU now provides that the Union recognises the rights in the EU Charter of Fundamental Rights as having the same legal status as the Treaties, although the Charter itself is not contained within the Treaties; it is referred to in Declaration No. 1 attached to the Treaties.

Article 6 TEU further settles years of debate as to whether the EU should or could accede to the ECHR. In 1996, the CoJ gave Opinion 2/94 that, under the Treaties at the time, the Union did not have the power to accede. Now that the EU has its own catalogue of rights, in the form of the Fundamental Rights Charter, but still outside the Treaty base, it may be argued that membership is more acceptable, but conversely, with its own catalogue of rights, there may be no further need for either the debate or accession to the ECHR. However, Article 6(2) clearly provides that the Union shall accede to the ECHR and declares in any event that those rights contained in the ECHR shall constitute general principles of the Union's law. This may seem now to be superfluous and even confusing, and prone to conflict in view of the introduction of the EU's own catalogue of rights. However, a Protocol (No. 8) requires the accession agreement to ensure the preservation of the special characteristics of Union law and not to affect the competences or powers of the Union or institutions. Further, Declaration No. 2 specifically notes that dialogue between the CoJ and the European Court of Human Rights (ECtHR) should both continue and be reinforced when the EU accedes to the Convention. A considerable amount of work was put into drafting an accession agreement in view of the consequences of the EU joining and being subject to the jurisdiction of the ECtHR in Strasbourg. Ultimately, though, following accession, the Union will subject its laws to the review of the ECtHR as far as their compliance with rights and freedoms guaranteed by the ECHR are concerned, which is a considerable step for the Union to have made. The draft agreement has now been finalised but before any further progress can be made to actual accession, the CoJ was asked whether it considered the Agreement to be compatible with the Treaties.

The main features of the agreement as submitted for the opinion of the CoJ are as follows. Decisions of the ECtHR will be binding on the EU, including the CoJ. The agreement will become part of EU law and be legally regarded in the legal order in the same way and status of other international agreements. Article 3 of the draft agreement would introduce to the Convention a co-respondent procedure to cater for circumstances whereby both the EU and one or more member states were the subject of proceedings instigated initially against only one of them. The EU or one or more member states may then be called to join the proceedings as a co-respondent. This will cover situations where it may be unclear to the applicant whether the EU, which enacted an Act or a member state, who implemented it, is responsible when that act is alleged to have breached the applicant's rights, in addition to the existing principle of the exhaustion of local remedies, whereby applicant parties are required to pursue their claims in their domestic courts first before being permitted to bring a complaint action before the Commission and Court of Human Rights in Strasbourg. This means cases must be brought to the CoJ first before access to the machinery of Strasbourg is permitted and the Agreement supports this with a prior involvement procedure. This provides that before any review by the Strasbourg Court may take place both the national courts and EU courts must be allowed to review an applicant's complaint. If the EU courts were not given this right, a case from a member state involving EU law or action may bypass the CoJ and adjudicate on EU law contrary to the autonomy of EU law, a principle which the EU negotiators required to be observed. The EU will have its own judge at the Court in Strasbourg, members of the EP will be entitled to participate in the Parliamentary Assembly of the Council of Europe, and, whilst the EU will not become a member of the Council of Europe or its Committee of Ministers, the EU will be consulted on matters discussed and decided by the Strasbourg Committee of Ministers.

However, before any further progress could have been made to actual accession, the CoJ was asked whether it considered the agreement to be compatible with the Treaties. It decided in December 2014 in Opinion 2/13, that the agreement was not compatible with the EU Treaties for the following reasons taken from the 258-paragraph Opinion. The CoJ considered that the agreement was liable to adversely affect the specific characteristics and the autonomy of EU law in so far as it does not ensure sufficient coordination between the ECHR and EU legal orders. Further, it is liable to affect Article 344 TFEU, which requires member states not to submit disputes under EU law to any other forum, in so far as the Accession Treaty does not preclude the possibility of disputes between member states or between member states and the EU concerning the application of the ECHR being brought before the ECtHR. It also held that it does not lay down arrangements for the operation of the co-respondent mechanism and the procedure for the prior involvement of the CoJ that enable the specific characteristics of the EU and EU law to be preserved. It would have provided the ECtHR with jurisdiction over EU Common and Foreign Policy, something largely denied the CoJ itself. Finally, in this comment on it, it fails to have regard to the specific characteristics of EU law with regard to the judicial review of acts, actions, or omissions on the part of the EU in Common Foreign and Security Policy (CFSP) matters in that it entrusts the judicial review of some of those acts, actions, or omissions exclusively to a non-EU body.

So presently, quite a bit more work remains to be done in amending the agreement and then re-negotiating those amendments with the Council of Europe and its 48 member states, 28 or probably 27 in the near future of which, though, are EU member states. It was never going to be easy and it will certainly not be a process completed soon, as the Court's objections must be overcome. It is not even clear at this stage if there is the political will in sufficient strength on the part of the member states to take this forward.

Article 218(8) TFEU provides that when accession is to be approved, the Council shall act unanimously and the member states separately by their constitutional requirements.

For more details on this section visit the online resources.

THINKING POINT

In view of this robust rejection by the CoJ and the fact that the EU's own Charter of Fundamental Rights is gaining prominence, is there still a real need to accede given the complex legal relationships and problems accession seems to have generated?

Article 6(3) TEU re-confirms that in any case, the rights contained within both the ECHR and constitutions of the member states shall be recognised as general principles in the EU legal order.

Any applicant states wishing to join the EU are now obligated by Article 49 TEU to have respect for human rights, and any member state that seriously and persistently offends human rights may have its rights under the Treaties suspended by the other member states under Article 7 TEU. Furthermore, Article 3(5) TEU provides that the Union shall promote, inter alia, the protection of human rights in its external relations.

THINKING POINT

What have proved to be the difficulties or problems of the EU acceding to the ECHR?

4.3.6 Equality and non-discrimination

The prohibition of discrimination is catered for in the Treaties under a number of Articles: Article 18 TFEU, on non-discrimination on the grounds of nationality; Article 157 TFEU, on non-discrimination between men and women with regard to pay and equal treatment; Article 40(2) TFEU, on non-discrimination between consumers and producers under the Common Agricultural Policy (CAP); and Article 45(2) TFEU, on non-discrimination with regard to the free movement of workers. Non-discrimination has also become a general principle recognised by the CoJ. It applies in all areas of EU law, especially to the fundamental freedoms.

For example, in **Cases 75 and 117/82 *Razzouk and Beydoun* v *Commission***, the Court held that a Commission decision that discriminated between men and women in relation to a certain pensions payment should be annulled as being contrary to the fundamental right of equal treatment of sexes.

The principle was applied in **Case 114/76 *Bergman* v *Grows-Farm (Skimmed Milk Powder)***, in which the Court held that a scheme to force animal feed producers to incorporate skimmed milk powder in animal feed discriminated against non-dairy farmers.

It was also applied to religious discrimination in **Case 130/75 *Prais* v *Council***, although, on the facts involving a Community competition for a post held at a Jewish religious festival, the Council was held not to have breached the general principle of equality. It was nevertheless held by the CoJ that, wherever possible, Community employees and citizens should have the general principle of non-discrimination in respect of religious freedom upheld in their favour.

In **Case C-144/04 *Mangold***, the principle of non-discrimination was applied by the CoJ as a general principle in the absence of an enforceable specific equality right: although there was such a right in the background, its lack of direct effects prevented its direct employment.

The Union moved further towards the development of a general principle of equality or at least non-discrimination in a range of issues in an amendment made to the EC Treaty by the Treaty of Amsterdam. Article 19 TFEU provides that the Council may take appropriate action to combat discrimination based on sex, racial or ethnic origin, religion or belief, disability, age, or sexual orientation, and the Council issued Directives 2000/43, 2000/78, and 2004/113 under this Article.

》 CROSS REFERENCE

Direct effects are considered in Chapter 8, and the *Mangold* case is considered further both in Chapter 8 and in Chapter 14 on equality law.

> The existence and value of a general principle of equal treatment has been acknowledged and confirmed by the CoJ in a number of cases, including, for example, **Case C-149/10** *Chatzi*, in which the Court held that the principle of equal treatment is one of the general principles of EU law and is now affirmed by Article 20 of the EU Charter of Fundamental Rights. In that case, it was applied to support the right to parental leave on an equal basis.

4.4 General principles

General principles are those principles of law which are adopted mainly from a wide variety of external sources, some of which have now been given primary status as they have been incorporated within the Treaties or the Charter of Fundamental Rights, for example the principles of subsidiarity and proportionality in Article 5 TEU, which were considered in Chapter 3, and the general right to equality in Article 20 of the Charter. Apart from those codified deliberately into primary law, general principles have been introduced into the EU legal order predominantly by the CoJ. They are employed to assist the Court to interpret and assess the EU's own laws, including Treaty provisions and to provide guidance on the application of EU law. They may also be pleaded or relied on by parties challenging EU law or the actions of EU institutions and additionally the actions of the member states in the application of EU law. Apart from the general justifications, outlined above, there are three particular Treaty Articles that also justify the introduction of general principles.

》 CROSS REFERENCE

See, for example, Articles 263 and 265 TFEU and the extension of judicial review rights to the EP, considered in Chapter 2, section 2.4.3.4 and Chapter 9.

Article 19 TEU provides that the CoJ shall ensure that, in the interpretation and application of the Treaties, the law is observed. It is a general guideline set by the Treaty for the functioning of the Court. This is taken to mean law from outside the Treaty rather than some duplicated reference back to the Treaty. Article 19 has thus been employed to justify the introduction of very many different general principles of law, most notably human rights.

Two Articles of the Treaty specifically mandate the Court to take account of general principles of law. Article 263 TEU refers to the infringement of any rule of law relating to the application of the Treaty as one of the grounds for an action for the challenge to the validity of EU law. Article 340 TEU is concerned with damages claims against the Union institutions and allows the consideration of claims on the basis of the general principles of the laws of the member states. Whilst these are specific to the claims raised under those Treaty Articles, they serve to reinforce the CoJ's claim that it can rely on general principles as a source of law in the EU legal order. The sources of general principles are the national legal systems, in particular the constitutions of member states and the many rules of natural justice, often found in a majority of the member states. Other sources have been developed from the Treaty, for example Article 12 EC (now 18 TFEU) involving the prohibition of discrimination on the grounds of nationality, which has been one of the foundations for a general principle of equality and non-discrimination.

Whilst some are clearly of higher rank, others are not, and rather than trying to conduct an exercise of sorting and ranking them all, which may well just reflect my view on where they should be treated, I merely note a few prominent examples here. The equality rights, various fundamental rights, and principles of legal certainty and non-retroactivity stand out as prominent examples and are considered in section 4.6 on the case law contribution of the CoJ.

> A specific principle was elevated to a general principle in **Cases T-74, 76, 83 en-rule 85,132,137, and 141/00 *Artegodan et al v Commission***. The 'precautionary principle' which was only to be found in the environmental chapter of the EC Treaty (Article 174) has been held by the Court of First Instance (CFI, now the General Court) to be a general principle to be employed outside of the strict confines of environmental policy. The process of recognition of the status of general principles was considered by the CoJ in **Case C-101/08 *Audiolux SA v GBL***. It held that in order to be recognised as a general principle, a principle of law has to possess a general and comprehensive character, which is naturally inherent in general principles. It refused to recognise an equal treatment protection of minority shareholders' principle from company law because of its limited and specific nature.

4.5 Secondary sources of EU law

4.5.1 **International agreements and conventions**

Legal Personality

This is a characteristic of a body establishing that it is capable of entering into formally binding agreements.

Within the Treaties, there are provisions that empower the Council and the Commission to conduct external relations, the agreements of which are binding on both the Union and the member states (Article 216 TFEU), which as such then form a further source of EU law. This is possible because the entire Union, following the entry into force of the Lisbon Treaty, also has **legal personality** (Article 47 TEU).

The Union is usually represented by the European Commission in negotiations, in coordination with the High Representative, who is responsible for negotiating agreements relating to the CFSP.

The express treaty-making powers of the Union can be found in three principal Treaty Articles. Article 207 TFEU provides that EU commercial and trade policy is conducted by the Commission under the authority of the Council. Under this provision, the EU behaves as a single entity, and the European Commission (EC) negotiates trade agreements and represents European interests on behalf of the 28 member states. The Council concludes the agreements and can thus bind the member states to agreements ranging from bilateral trade agreements with individual countries to the multiparty World Trade Organization (WTO) agreements and the General Agreement on Tariffs and Trade (GATT), although, as will be seen, much of the subject matter of the WTO agreements falls outside the express and exclusive competence of the Union.

> Confirmation that particular provisions of the GATT can be binding on the Community was confirmed by the CoJ in **Cases 21–24/72 *International Fruit***.

Article 217 TFEU provides for the conclusion of association agreements with non-member states that can be regarded as either a precursor to membership or as agreements in their own right without any view to future membership of the EU. These can be concluded by the Council with the consent of the EP, with either individual third countries or within more extensive multinational agreements to govern, among other things, various aspects of the trade relations between them. The most important agreements are the Agreement on the European Economic Area (EEA); the association agreements with candidate member states (at present, Turkey, Iceland, Macedonia and Montenegro, and Serbia); the agreements with the potential candidate countries of Albania, Bosnia and Herzogovina, and Kosovo; the bilateral agreements with Switzerland and the Mediterranean countries; and the preferential treatment agreements that have been concluded with the Mediterranean countries. Furthermore, there are the very comprehensive Yaounde and Lomé Conventions and the Cotonou Agreement (2000) with 78 African, Caribbean, and Pacific (ACP) countries, all of which provide binding rules for the EU.

> For example, in **Case 181/73 *Haegemann v Belgium***, provisions of the association agreement between the Community and Greece were held to be binding on the member states even though such agreements were not envisaged by Article 249 EC (now 288 TFEU). A more recent example is the free movement case, **Case C-265/03 *Simutenkov***, which concerns rights provided under the 1997 EC–Russian Federation partnership agreement and the right of a Russian football player employed by the Spanish club Deportivo Tenerife. In a similar manner to the ruling in **Case C-415/93 *Bosman***, the number of players that could be fielded from non-EEA countries was restricted in national competitions. The judgment followed the *Bosman* ruling with the interpretation by the CoJ that the partnership agreement contained directly enforceable free movement rights.
>
> The ranking of international agreements above EU secondary laws was made clear by the CoJ in **Case 40/72 *Schroeder v Germany***.

CROSS REFERENCE
See Chapter 12, section 12.1.3.2.

Finally, the TFEU provides under Article 218 a power for the conclusion of international agreements with non-member states in matters covered by areas of the Treaty not specifically catered for by Articles 207 and 217 TFEU. In furtherance of this, Article 220 TFEU requires the Union to maintain appropriate relations with international organisations such as the United Nations (UN), the Council of Europe, and the Organisation for Economic Co-operation and Development (OECD). The Union is to be represented by the Commission and the High Representative. In many of these areas, however, the EU must act with the member states because the subject matters of the agreements often straddle matters coming both within and outside Union competence. However, even agreements and international agreements entered into by the member states alone can bind the Union.

> See **Case 214/72 *International Fruit Company***, for example, in which the CoJ held that the provisions of the GATT concluded by the member states prior to membership of the then Community or prior to the assumption of responsibility for the agreement by the Community bind the Community.

CROSS REFERENCE
The direct effects of these agreements are considered in Chapter 8, section 8.1.3.7. For general information on international agreements, see also Chapter 1, section 1.7.

4.5.2 **EU secondary legislation**

In the EU, secondary legislation arises entirely subject to the authority, higher rank, and procedures provided for in the Treaties. Article 288 TFEU provides the means by which the Union institutions are able to enact secondary legislation, which are also a binding source of law for the member states. The acts of secondary legislation consist of Regulations, Directives, and Decisions.

The Lisbon Treaty did not change this aspect, but introduced a distinction in Articles 289–290 and 297 TFEU between legislative and non-legislative acts; thus, all forms of secondary legislation can be both legislative acts of the Union law-makers per se and the non-legislative acts, which are essentially the delegated administrative and implementing acts of the Commission and other Com-

For more details on this section visit the online resources.

munity bodies, both under the authority of enacted legislative Acts. The delegated and implementing acts can also take the form of a Regulation, Directive, or Decision. The choice of which particular act to adopt may be determined by the legal base specifying either Regulation, Directive, or Decision, but where this is not the case, which is more frequent, Article 296 TFEU provides that the institutions shall select it on a case-by-case basis. In some limited circumstances, the Treaty requires certain forms of legislation to be used, for example Article 24 TFEU requires Regulations to be adopted to organise the citizens' initiatives and Article 50 TFEU specifies Directives for rights of establishment. Article 296 also requires legal acts to state reasons and any preparatory materials and preliminary acts which led to them. Whilst not expressly requiring the legal base to be cited, the CoJ has held in Case 325/91 *Commission* v *France* that this is also a requirement, the failure to comply with which would render the act open to challenge and annulment.

For more details on this section visit the online resources.

All EU secondary legislation is published in the Official Journal (OJ), which, as its name suggests, is the official publication of the EU and is published in two main parts with a supplement. The L Series (legislation) contains the binding legislative Acts. The C Series (information and notices) contains a very wide range of documents that are not binding as such, and include notices, draft legislative acts, press releases, job advertisements, and all other non-legally binding publications, with the exception of the public procurement notices, which are published in the S Series (supplement). The OJ is officially authentic as from 1 July 2013 only in its electronic form and can be found in this format online, but still in printed form in libraries and official documentation centres.

4.5.2.1 Regulations

Regulations

This is defined in Article 288 TFEU: 'A regulation shall have general application. It shall be binding in its entirety and directly applicable in all member states.'

Regulations are general provisions of legislation applicable to the entire Union, member states, institutions, and individuals, rather than to specific individuals or groups. Regulations are detailed forms of law so that the law in all member states is uniform—in other words, exactly the same. As far as implementation is concerned, like Treaty provisions, Regulations are directly applicable or self-executing. This is the mode of incorporation of law that is generally or universally binding. Regulations become legally valid in the member states without any need for implementation on the date specified or on the twentieth day after publication in the OJ (see Article 297 TFEU).

Implementation of a Regulation is normally prohibited.

> For example, in **Case 39/72 *Commission* v *Italy***, it was held that member states cannot subject the Regulation to any implementing measures other than those required by the Act itself. **Case 34/73 *Variola* v *Amministrazione delle Finanze*** also confirms this point.

There may, however, be circumstances in which the member states are required to provide supporting measures to ensure the effectiveness of the Regulation.

> See **Case 128/78 *Commission* v *UK (Tachographs)***, in which administrative rules had to be implemented concerning the enforcement and sanctions for failure to install tachographs in lorry cabs, the installation of which was the requirement in the Regulation.

4.5.2.2 Directives

Directives

These are defined in Article 288 TFEU: 'A directive shall be binding as to the result to be achieved, upon each member state to which it is addressed, but shall leave to the national authorities the choice of form and methods.'

Directives are binding on those to whom they are addressed and can be targeted if desired to specific member states, although in practice they are addressed to all member states. Directives set out aims that must be achieved, but leave the choice of the form and method of implementation to the member states. This was done to ease the way in which national law could be harmonised in line with EU law and to give the member states a wider area of discretion to do this. If, for example, a member state considers that the existing national law already conforms with the requirements of a new Directive, then it need not do anything, apart from the requirement now in Directives that the member state inform the Commission of measures taken to implement the Directive. The Commission monitors this every two months and failure to notify may prompt the Commission to open infringement proceedings for non-implementation, considered in Chapter 7.

Directives enter into force either on the date specified or 20 days after publication, which is rare (see Article 297 TEU). Member states are given a period in which to implement Directives, which can range from one year to five years or more, depending on the complexity of the subject matter and the urgency for the legislation, but two years is usual. Some Directives, especially if consolidating and adding rules to an existing area of EU law, may contain more than one date for entry into force, to take account of the law that should already have been enacted and the new provisions for which the member states are given a further implementation period (see, for example, Directive 2004/38 on the free movement of persons).

4.5.2.3 Decisions

Decisions are specific binding and enforceable acts of law, which are normally, but not necessarily addressed to individual member states or to specific individuals, for example in the area of competition law, to notify a determination about whether the agreements between companies are in conformity or in conflict with EU competition law rules. They can, though, be addressed to all member states at the same time, such as Decision 87/327 which established the Erasmus student mobility programme.

> **Decisions**
> This is defined in Article 288 TFEU: 'A decision shall be binding in its entirety. A decision which specifies those to whom it is addressed shall be binding only on them.'

4.5.2.4 Inter-institutional agreements

Whilst not listed in Article 288 TFEU, inter-institutional agreements which regulate the positions of the Council, Commission, and EP with each other and in relation to specific topics such as budgetary agreements may also, according to Article 295 TFEU constitute binding acts.

4.5.2.5 Other acts producing binding legal effects

Article 288 TFEU is not exhaustive of the legally binding acts that can be created by the institutions.

4.5.2.6 Delegated and implementing legislation

The Commission is empowered to create non-legislative but nevertheless binding acts, which may be in the form of Regulations, Directives, or Decisions, under the delegated and implementing powers granted respectively by Articles 290 and 291 TFEU (these are considered in Chapter 3, section 3.7).

4.5.2.7 Unique acts

The CoJ has held that it can review all measures taken by the institutions, whatever their nature and form, which are designed to produce legal effects. Thus, such acts need not stem from the specific acts listed in Article 288 TFEU and are often termed *sui generis*, meaning literally 'in a class of its own' or 'unique'.

> See **Cases 8–11/66 *Noordwijks Cement Accord***, in which a Commission letter not formally labelled as a Regulation, Directive, or Decision could nevertheless be challenged under Article 173 EEC (now 263 TFEU), which is the action to challenge the validity of binding acts of Community law. This was accepted by the CoJ because the letter had led to a change in legal status of applicant companies, rendering them subject to competition law liability from which they had previously been immune.

> See also **Case 22/70 Commission v Council (ERTA)**, in which a Decision of the member states outside of the Council of Ministers was nevertheless held to be a reviewable act of the Community.

❯ CROSS REFERENCE

See these cases also in the context of Article 263 actions in Chapter 9, section 9.1.1.2.

> In **Case C-106/96 UK v Commission**, even a press release was found to have legal effects and was consequently annulled for lacking a legal base.

Article 295 TFEU now puts on a statutory basis the inter-institutional agreements that have for a long time played a role in establishing the ground rules for the EP, Council, and Commission to work together, in particular in areas such as delegated powers or better law-making. These may now be made formally binding under Article 295 TFEU.

4.5.2.8 Recommendations, opinions, and soft law

❯ CROSS REFERENCE

See section 4.3.5.1 in this chapter for further details.

Under Article 288 TFEU, recommendations and opinions do not have any binding force, but it was established in Case 322/88 *Grimaldi* that, despite this, national courts are required to take recommendations into account when interpreting national law based on Union law. An opinion of the CoJ, when specifically asked for, has the effect of being binding, for example, Opinion 2/13 on the Accession Agreement of the EU to the ECHR, which had the effect of causing the application to be abandoned.

Recommendations, in particular, often provide a gloss on a Regulation or Directive, or extend its scope of application, and as such then may be regarded as a form of soft law.

> See, for example, the randomly selected Commission Recommendation 2011/696 of 18 October 2011 on the definition of nanomaterial.

For more details on Soft Law and the OMC visit the online resources.

Soft laws come in the form of guidelines, which very often indicate how binding law should be applied. A good example of soft law input is the practice of the Commission when issuing communications following a leading judgment, or series of judgments, of the Court of Justice. By doing so, the Commission advises how it considers the judgment should operate in practice and it seeks to shape member states' behaviour without recourse to legislative enactments to do so. See the Commission Practice Note on import prohibitions following the leading Case 120/78 *Cassis de Dijon*. Within the category of soft law is also the Open Method of Coordination (OMC) as a way of creating standards which member states should comply with. This once threatened to become more popular but has not, so will not be discussed further here.

4.5.2.9 Procedural requirements

Article 296 TFEU requires that the legal acts of institutions shall state the reasons on which they are based and shall refer to any proposals or opinions that were required to be obtained. In practice, this means that the Treaty base must also be cited. Failure by the institutions to comply with these requirements will give rise to grounds for judicial review and possible annulment of the measure under Article 263 TFEU.

For example, it was held in **Case C-325/91** *France v Commission* that there was a require-ment to state the Treaty base, without which the measure is void.

The Lisbon Treaty has introduced a new requirement in Article 296 TFEU, which relates to the competence and legal base issues. It states that, 'When considering draft legislative acts, the European Parliament and the Council shall refrain from adopting acts not provided for by the relevant legislative procedure in the area in question.' This is another attempt to curb the competence creep and/or use of the incorrect legal base, which was considered in Chapter 3, section 3.2.

Article 297 TFEU provides the rules concerning the publication of legislative and non-legislative acts. Regulations, Directives, and Decisions adopted under the ordinary legislative procedure must be signed by the Presidents of the European Parliament and the Council, and published in the OJ. They become valid on the specified date, in the absence of which they become valid on the twentieth day following publication.

The Lisbon Treaty clarified the position of legislative and non-legislative acts—in other words, administrative types of act. The shake-up was designed to replace the very many different, less formal, types of act that have been developed over the years or specifically introduced under the TEU. The general non-legislative acts—that is, the delegated acts under Article 290 TFEU—must be signed by the President of the institution that adopted them and shall also be published in the OJ.

Article 297(2) TFEU specifies that 'Other directives, and decisions which specify to whom they are addressed, shall be notified to those to whom they are addressed and shall take effect upon such notification.' These need not be published in the OJ, but it was previously held in Case 98/78 *Racke* that an act cannot produce legal effects unless it comes to the knowledge of its addressees.

4.6 The Court of Justice's contribution to the sources of law

Whilst the CoJ's role in introducing general principles within the hierarchy of EU law sources has been considered in section 4.4, this section looks in further detail at the overall range of general principles in the EU legal order. First, though, a look at the process of this.

When the EC was first established, the Community legal system was to be found only in the Treaties and the limited secondary legislation that existed at the time. However, because the Treaties are largely framework Treaties, they require substantial supplement. Whilst much of this is provided by the secondary legislation, both the secondary legislation and the founding and primary Treaties'

Articles may need to be interpreted. There is, then, much scope for judicial activity by the CoJ. Furthermore, as with all legal systems, codified or written law cannot possibly cater for all economic and social developments that can take place, and the judges must at times either adapt existing rules to fit the situation or introduce new rules to settle the matter judiciously. The CoJ has previously determined that the EC Treaty (now TFEU) and secondary legislation must be interpreted and applied according to the scheme of the Treaty as a whole and in the light of the broad principles of the Preamble and Articles 2, 3, 10, and 12 EC (now 3 and 4 TEU and 8 and 18 TFEU) to achieve the result required. The case law or jurisprudence has been developed by the CoJ from a wide variety of law sources and is not restricted in origin to the words or phrases from EU legislative provisions, and very many general principles have been borrowed and adopted from those present in the member states' legal systems. The CoJ has also developed additional fundamental doctrines and principles of Union law, including direct effects, supremacy, and state liability, which are considered in Chapters 5 and 8.

For more details on this section visit the online resources.

In particular, the CoJ has drawn inspiration from, and even adopted extensively, principles from outside, including general principles, fundamental rights, and national procedural rules. In some instances, the principles have been directly influential in bringing about Treaty changes well before the formal Treaty amendment of such provisions by the member states. The decisions of the CoJ are binding on the member states not only where the Court decides strictly on the basis of Union treaties or secondary law, but also where it decides on the basis of legal rules that it has applied or used as inspiration that originate from outside the Union or which have been instrumental in developing a new Union rule. To back up this position, Article 280 TFEU provides that judgments shall be enforceable.

⟫ CROSS REFERENCE

See also the CoJ methodology section in Chapter 2, section 2.5.4.

These additional sources of law are sometimes classified into broad groupings. Whilst they are far from definitive in terms of establishing clear-cut categories because of the diversity of principles and the degree of overlap, presenting them in this way may, however, aid accessibility. They can therefore be divided into three groups:

- human or fundamental rights;
- equality principles; and
- those relating to general procedural rights.

⟫ CROSS REFERENCE

Fundamental rights were covered in section 4.3.5 and Equality was covered in section 4.3.6 and in Chapter 14, which just leaves general procedural rights to be considered in section 4.6.1.

4.6.1 General principles of procedural law and natural justice

A number of principles are closely associated with the administrative law principles found in many of the member states, but may also be classified under the rules of natural justice and due process. These can be found in differing forms in the member states' legal systems, for example as common law rules in the UK or within the ECHR or, for example, as a part of the Constitution in Germany, Articles 101–104 *Grundgesetz* (GG). A very general principle is the principle of the rule of law, which is effectively an umbrella term for a number of the following general principles. The Community was held to be based on the rule of law in Case 294/83 *Les Verts* v *Parliament*.

For more details on this section visit the online resources.

> Judicial review, confidentiality/legal privilege, legal certainty, non-retroactivity, legitimate expectation, and proportionality have been selected here as broad categories of general principles that have been identified and applied by the CoJ.

4.6.1.1 The right to judicial review

A general right to have administrative decisions, as opposed to legislative Acts, reviewed by a court exists, as well as to have reasons for such decisions. The CoJ bases its view on the constitutions of

For more details on this section visit the online resources.

the member states, and notably on Article 6 ECHR, dealing with a fair and public hearing, and Article 13 ECHR, requiring an effective judicial remedy.

> Cases 222/84 *Johnston* v *Chief Constable RUC* and 222/86 *UNECTEF* v *Heylens* are examples. In the latter case, the CoJ had already determined that free access to employment was a fundamental right that should be respected in the Community. It thus becomes essential that there must be a remedy of a judicial nature against any decision of a national authority refusing the benefit of that right. The *UNECTEF* case established that the duty to give reasons was a general principle to be recognised in the Community legal order.

> In **Case 17/74 *Transocean Marine Paints Association* v *Commission***, the principle of the right to a fair hearing (under the maxim *audi alterem partem*, meaning literally 'hearing the other side') was introduced by the Advocate-General (AG). He argued that, in the absence of being allowed to present its view on the condition imposed in a decision, the Commission's decision would be in breach of a general principle of law, clearly applicable in the UK and other legal systems. This was upheld by the Court.

> The Court held also in **Cases 33 and 59/79 *Kuhner*** that where a person's rights were affected, he or she must be given the opportunity to make his or her views known, and the right to be heard must be upheld as a general principle of good administration.

4.6.1.2 Confidentiality/legal privilege

> In **Case 175/79 *A M & S* v *Commission***, a company refused to hand over certain documents during a raid by Commission officials under the rules on competition law, on the grounds that, by doing so, the principle of legal privilege would be breached. The CoJ held that the principle was recognised in the Community legal order, provided that it was in relation to or preparation for a client's defence, but it must be between a party and an independent lawyer.

> Supporting and extending this principle are **Cases 136/79 *National Panasonic*** and **T-30/89 *Hilti***. The *Hilti* case decided that the privilege extends also to the in-house lawyer's reports of the independent lawyer's findings, but not the stand-alone work of the in-house lawyer.

> In **Case C-36/92 P *Samenwerkende***, a refusal to hand over documents considered to be confidential was held to be unjustified in the light of the existing protections in Community law under which the Commission is required to notify undertakings of the documents that it intends to release to the national authorities and thus give the undertakings the chance to seek judicial review to protect these documents. As such, the refusal to supply would be unjustified.

> **Case C-550/07 P *AKZO*** was appealed on various points to the CoJ, which confirmed the earlier case of **Case 175/79 *A M & S v Commission***, to the extent that the CoJ confirmed that the principle of legal privilege does not extend to in-house lawyers. It held that it made no difference even if the in-house lawyer was a member of the relevant national Bar or Law Society and was subject to the same rules of professional conduct and discipline as an independent lawyer.

The CoJ and the General Court must, however, be the final arbiters of what is privileged. Cases 209/15 *Dow Benelux*, 218/78 *Van Landewyck*, and 53/85 *AKZO*, now backed up by Articles 27 and 28 of Regulation 1/2003, provide that the principle of professional secrecy does not apply to allow a company to protect documents from the Commission, but to ensure that information received by the Commission in an investigation is not disclosed to competitors.

4.6.1.3 **Legal certainty**

The basic concept underlying legal certainty incorporates a number of ideas concerned with the boundary between legality and illegality or lawfulness and unlawfulness, which should be marked clearly in advance. Additionally, the existence of sanctions or punishment for a breach of a rule or what constitutes overstepping the boundary should also be reasonably ascertainable: not the exact punishment, but at least the type and scope or range of punishment applicable. As such, the principle of proportionality is included in this category. Textbook and writers' considerations of EU law differ in their classification of general principles; therefore, proportionality may be classified as a distinct and separate category. The different treatment accorded it is not really important. The point is that it is nevertheless recognised as a general principle by the CoJ and is often quoted in cases to defeat the arguments of the member state or the Commission in justifying action or behaviour that has affected the rights of others, mainly individuals in the EU context. Legal certainty thus includes the underlying concepts of legitimate expectations, protection of vested rights, proportionality, and non-retroactivity. Legal rules not published cannot under the EU legal regime be enforced against individuals held the CoJ in Case C-345/06 *Heinrich* when he was denied boarding to a plane because he had a tennis racquet in his cabin luggage. The Annex to Regulation 622/2003 listing the banned items was not, however, published in the OJ, so passengers could not avail themselves of the list of prohibited cabin items. Thus, the Annex carried no legal status and the ban was therefore unlawful.

> Legal certainty was first acknowledged by the CoJ in **Case 43/75 *Defrenne v Sabena (No. 2)*** and later confirmed in **Case 262/88 *Barber v Guardian Royal Exchange*** to support the Court's argument that the judgment should not be retroactively effective, although there is an argument to suggest that if a Treaty Article is held to be directly effective, as in the *Sabena* case, it must have been so from the outset of the Community—that is, from 1957—and not from the date of judgment of the CoJ.

Allied to legal certainty is the concept of *res judicata*, which embodies the principle that once appeal time limits have expired, a judgment becomes definitive and beyond challenge. It was expressly confirmed in Case C-224/01 *Köbler*.

4.6.1.4 **Non-retroactivity**

▶ **CROSS REFERENCE**

See Chapter 9, section 9.1, for details of cases claiming a breach of those principles.

The principle of non-retroactivity is seen in its purest form in Case 63/83 *R v Kent Kirk* and Case 262/88 *Barber*, noted at 4.6.1.3 and is firmly established as a general principle of EU law. Simply put, law should not retroactively impose punishments or be the legal base for punishments, particularly with regard to criminal sanctions, nor should it be the basis for a change in legal status or administrative sanctions.

> **Case 80/86 *Public Prosecutor* v *Kolpinghuis Nijmegan*** is also a very good example of the principle being cited by the CoJ in defence of the rights of the individual. In this case, the principle was used to protect the company from being prosecuted by the Dutch authorities on the strength of retroactive Community law validating national law where Holland had failed to implement the Directive correctly into national law.

Civil or non-criminal law retroactivity may also occur when a person's actual rights or expected rights are altered, redefined, or totally removed.

> See, for example, **Cases 106 and 107/63 *Töpfer* v Commission** dealing with the retroactive validation of import licence refusals by the German authorities, which provided Töpfer with the right and *locus standi* to challenge the decision and have it reviewed by the CoJ.

The principle of non-retroactivity may take on more subtle forms in civil law application to remove the difficulties created by the alteration or withdrawal of rights by EU legal measures. These cases also involve the principle of legitimate expectations of the individual, which are often argued to have been infringed by the Union measure complained about, particularly where the Commission is trying to regulate a very difficult market in goods. This means that, provided the legitimate expectations of the parties affected have been respected, even a measure that is retroactive in effect may be upheld.

> In **Case 98/78 *Racke* v *HZA Mainz***, which concerned the regulation of the wine market then producing massive surpluses and the so-called 'wine lake', regulations with retroactive effect were nevertheless upheld by the ECJ on the basis that the situation was so serious that it demanded such and that the legitimate expectations of the parties had been taken into account.

4.6.1.5 Legitimate expectation or vested rights

The legitimate expectations of affected parties must be observed, especially when they pre-date an EU provision affecting their rights; hence, there is some degree of overlap with non-retroactivity.

> In **Case 88/76 *Sugar Export* v *Commission***, a Regulation was enacted by the Commission on 30 June 1976, which removed the right of sugar exporters to cancel licences previously granted when refunds payable on sugar exports, to reduce the overproduction of sugar in the Community, dropped in value. The date of entry into force was set as 1 July 1976, but the Regulation was not published until 2 July 1976. Sugar exporters who applied for a cancellation on 1 July 1976 were refused by the Commission. The Court interpreted the Regulation as coming into force on 2 July 1976 and held that whilst there was no intention of retroactivity, the rights vested in the applicant, applicable as on 1 July 1976, had to be protected.

The principle was confirmed by the CoJ in Case 112/77 *Töpfer* v *Commission* under similar factual circumstances dealing with the sudden removal of the right to cancel an export licence.

> In **Case 81/72 *Commission v Council (Staff Salaries)***, the principle was employed in different circumstances when the Council adopted a three-year experimental period for a system of staff salary payments, but changed this after only nine months. Despite the view that the Council could not bind itself as such—that is, it could not bind itself never to make changes—the CoJ held that the employees had a reasonable or legitimate expectation that the Council would abide by its decision.

4.6.1.6 Proportionality

The principle of proportionality embodies the concept that the punishment should fit the crime and not go further, or must be reasonable in the circumstances, and puts the question to the relevant authority of whether the same result could have been achieved by other methods or means less harmful to the party concerned. In the Union context, it means that individuals should not be affected by actions beyond those necessary in the public or Union interest and that any fines or punishment must be in proportion to the seriousness of any breach. It occurs frequently throughout all areas of EU law and especially to the internal market. It was invoked in Cases 11/70 *Internationale Handelsgesellschaft* and 36/75 *Rutili*. Examples from specific areas of law are Cases 159/79 *R* v *Pieck*, in respect of the free movement of persons, and 178/84 *Commission* v *Germany (Beer Purity)*, in relation to the free movement of goods.

> A good example is **Case 181/84 *R* v *Intervention Board for Agricultural Produce, ex p Man***, in which a company was required to give a security deposit to the Intervention Board when seeking a licence to export sugar outside the Community. The applicant was late, but only by four hours, in completing the relevant paperwork. The Board, acting under a Community Regulation, declared the entire deposit of over £1.5 million to be forfeit. The Court held that the automatic forfeit of the entire deposit in the event of any failure was too drastic in view of the function of the system of export licences—that is, it was disproportionate to the aims.

 CROSS REFERENCE

See Chapter 3, section 3.4.3, for further details.

The principle of proportionality has now been given statutory recognition in the Treaties. Article 5 TEU applies to the relations between the Union and the member states in ensuring that any action at the Union level must be in proportion to the aims of the Union and not go beyond those strict aims.

> Article 5 TEU provides that 'the content and form of Union action shall not exceed what is necessary to achieve the objectives of the Treaties'.

⟲ Summary

The category of general principles is already a wide one and potentially capable of great expansion. Indeed, in keeping with a system of law in which case law is regarded as important and can supply legal principles that become general principles to be applied in future cases, other new principles—in addition to those considered in this chapter, which are the most frequently raised—can arise. Subsidiarity could also be included here, because it is so connected to the division of competence. Among those knocking on the door of more widespread recognition is 'transparency', although the CoJ has been equivocal about its status as a possible general principle: see Cases C-58/94 *Netherlands* v *Council* and C-353/99 P *Hautala* v *Council*. Its present status in the legal system has now been endorsed by statutory intervention, first in a number of Decisions, but now by Regulation 1049/2001, which provides a right of access to Community and Union documents. Another example of a potential general principle is 'good faith', which received support as a general principle of EU law.

> See **Case 366/95 *Steff-Houlberg Export***, which concerned the recovery of exports refunds that had been found to have been unduly paid. The export company was not responsible for the breach of rules and had acted in good faith. Under national law, and also in view of the time elapsed, the refunds should not be recoverable. The CoJ held this to be the position under EC law also.

Finally, 'unjustified enrichment' is a principle well established in civil law legal systems and has made its entrance into the EU legal order in a few cases, one of the leading ones being Case C-309/06 *M&S* (although *Steff-Houlberg Export* could also be regarded in that category).

> In 1973, in **Case C-309/06 *M&S***, chocolate-covered teacakes sold by Marks & Spencer were designated as 'biscuits' by UK tax authorities and therefore value added tax (VAT) was charged on them at the standard rate. However, in the mid-1990s, the tax authorities realised their mistake and re-designated the teacakes as 'cakes'. Cakes are zero-rated for VAT purposes and Marks & Spencer therefore attempted to recover the VAT previously paid. In their defence, the Commissioners of Customs & Excise argued that any repayment should be capped (at 10 per cent), because the VAT had been passed on to Marks & Spencer's customers in the price of the teacakes and therefore would result in Marks & Spencer being unjustly enriched. The House of Lords referred the following questions to the ECJ for preliminary ruling:
>
> (1) Is there a right, derived from principles of Community law, to refund wrongfully paid VAT?
>
> (2) If so, can the right to repayment of wrongfully paid VAT be restricted on the basis of unjust enrichment?
>
> The Court answered the first question in the affirmative—that is, that a right to repayment of wrongfully paid tax derives from the principle of fiscal neutrality. In response to the second question, the Court held that the application of an unjust enrichment defence against a claim was not contrary to Community law, but that the unjust enrichment defence should be regarded as an exception to the right of repayment of wrongfully paid tax and therefore should be interpreted strictly 'following an economic analysis in which all relevant circumstances are taken into account'.

Overall, it can be seen that the EU draws the laws applicable in the EU legal order from a variety of sources, the specific EU sources representing the formal and official sources of Treaties, Protocols, Declarations, and EU secondary law mentioned in Article 288 TFEU. The other sources are much more varied and far wider in scope, consisting of a number of forms of international agreements and the vast potential of general principles and fundamental rights that can so easily be added to. Finally, at some stage, the EU will become a signatory to the ECHR, which will formally add that body of law to the sources of EU law.

For the suggested approach to answering these questions visit the online resources.

? Questions

1. Are you able to outline the range of sources of EU law?

2. What forms of EU secondary law exist? Are they all equally binding?

3. How are EU laws transformed into the member states' laws?

4. What is the status of Protocols and Declarations in the EU legal order?

5. What is the justification for the inclusion of general principles in the EU legal order?

For guidance on how to tackle this specimen exam question and to read a suggested model answer, visit the online resources www.oup.com/uk/foster_directions6e/.

☐ Sample exam Q&A

Identify the sources of law (other than Treaty provisions and secondary EU legislation) invoked by the CoJ. What is the justification for the recognition and application of such sources in the EU legal order?

≡ Further reading

Books

Bernitz, U., Nergelius, J., and Cardner, C. *General Principles of EC Law in a Process of Development*, Kluwer Law International, London, 2008.

Birkinshaw, B. *The European Legal Order after Lisbon*, Kluwer Law International, London, 2010.

Gragl, P. *The Accession of the European Union to the European Convention on Human Rights*, Hart Publishing, Oxford, 2013.

Morano-Foadi, S. and Vickers, L. (eds) *Fundamental Rights in the EU*, Hart Publishing, Oxford, 2015.

Peers, S., Hervey, T., Kenner, J., and Ward, A. (eds) *The Charter of Fundamental Rights: A Commentary*, Hart Publishing, Oxford, 2014.

Schütze, R. *European Constitutional Law*, Cambridge University Press, Cambridge, 2015.

Spaventa, E., 'Fundamental rights in the European Union' in Barnard, C. and Peers, S. (eds) *European Union Law*, 2nd edn, Oxford University Press, Oxford, 2017, p. 227.

Tridimas, T. *The General Principles of EU Law*, 2nd edn, Oxford University Press, Oxford, 2007.

Articles

Barrata, R. 'Accession of the EU to the ECHR: the rationale for the ECJ's prior involvement mechanism' (2013) 50 CML Rev 1305.

Bast, J. 'New categories of Acts after the Lisbon Reform: dynamics of parliamentarization in EU law' (2012) 49 CML Rev 885.

Craig, P. 'Delegated Acts, implementing Acts and the new Comitology Regulation' (2011) 36 EL Rev 671.

Douglas-Scott, S. 'The European Union and human rights after the Treaty of Lisbon' (2011) 11 HRLR 645.

Fabbrini, F. and Granat, K. '"Yellow card, but no foul": the role of the national parliaments under the Subsidiarity Protocol and the Commission proposal for an EU Regulation on the right to strike' (2013) 50 CML Rev 115.

Harbo, T.-I. 'The function of the proportionality principle in EU law' (2010) 35 EL Rev 158.

Hofmann, H. 'Legislation, delegation and implementation under the Treaty of Lisbon: typology meets reality' (2009) 15 ELJ 482.

Iglesias Sanchez, S. 'The Court and the Charter: the impact of the entry into force of the Lisbon Treaty on the ECJ's approach to fundamental rights' (2012) 49 CML Rev 1565.

Lock, T. 'Walking on a tightrope: the Draft ECHR Accession Agreement and the autonomy of the EU legal order' (2011) 48 CML Rev 1025.

Mendes, J. 'Delegated and implementing rule making: proceduralism and constitutional design' (2013) 19 ELJ 22.

Sarmiento, D. 'Who's afraid of the Charter? The Court of Justice, national courts and the new framework of fundamental rights protection in Europe' (2013) 50 CML Rev 1267.

Spaventa, E., 'A very fearful Court? The protection of fundamental rights in the European Union after Opinion 2/13' (2015) 22 Maastricht Law Journal 35.

5 Supremacy of EU law

LEARNING OBJECTIVES

In this chapter, you will learn about:

- how the principle of supremacy was established in the European Community/EU legal order;
- how it was developed further by the Court of Justice;
- how in particular the supremacy of EU law takes precedence over all forms of law of the member states;
- how it also applies to different forms of international law; and
- how EU law has been received in the UK and other member states.

Introduction

This chapter has as its focus the status of European Union (EU) law in the member states, in particular the reasons for the supremacy of EU law and its development by the Court of Justice (CoJ), not only over all forms of member states' national laws, but also all forms of international law. The chapter then goes on to consider whether the supremacy as outlined and developed by the CoJ has been accepted in the same way, or at all, in the member states. However, the review of the member states is necessarily limited for reasons of space, and only a selection of states is included. The topic of the transfer and division of competences, which was considered in Chapter 3, provides the starting point for a consideration of supremacy.

5.1 The supremacy of EU law

For more details on this section visit the online resources.

The supremacy or priority of EU law can be considered from two perspectives: first, from the point of view of the Union; and, secondly, from the point of view of the member states, although dealing with this latter aspect in a Union of 28 or 27 states must of necessity be very selective. Therefore, only a sample of the member states will be chosen, concentrating on the older or larger member states. As with the doctrine of direct effects, considered in Chapter 8, it is through the decisions and interpretation of the Court of Justice of the European Union (CoJ) that the reasons and logic for the supremacy of Community law and now EU law have been developed, and that is the view considered here first. Note, though, that sometimes the word 'primacy' is used also. This is referring to the same thing (i.e. that EU law prevails over national law).

5.1.1 The view of the Court of Justice

There is, despite the reforms introduced by the Lisbon Treaty and the inclusion of an express statement in the abandoned Constitutional Treaty (CT), still no express declaration or specific legal base for the supremacy of EU law in the Treaties. It can be argued that some of the Articles of the Treaties impliedly require primacy: for example, Article 4(3) TEU, known as the fidelity or good faith and also the solidarity clause and the principle of cooperation, which requires member states to comply and not hinder the objectives of the Union; Article 18 TFEU, on the general prohibition of discrimination on the grounds of nationality; Article 288 TFEU, on the direct applicability of Regulations; and Article 344 TEU, on the reservation of EU and not national dispute resolution for matters coming within the scope of the Treaties. In the initial absence of an express statement written into the Treaties, another route was needed to establish this supremacy of EU law over national law.

> Note that the Lisbon Treaty sidestepped the direct expression of supremacy that was contained in Article I-6 CT by adding a Declaration (No. 17) that instead supports supremacy by reference to the case law of the CoJ on supremacy, and referring to the Opinion of the Council Legal Service, which confirmed the same conclusion.

From the outset, the Communities included their own supreme CoJ, which is the equivalent of a constitutional court, to adjudicate on disputes between the institutions of the Union and between the member states and the institutions. Without an express statement of priority, the CoJ took the lead in providing basic constitutional principles on which the new legal order was based.

CROSS REFERENCE

For further details of the Court, see Chapter 2, section 2.5.

> The CoJ's view on supremacy is straightforward. In the first pronouncement dealing with this, the Court held, in **Case 26/62 Van Gend en Loos**, that the member states had limited their sovereignty, albeit within limited fields as agreed in the Treaty, and held that individuals in the Community could uphold rights under Community law in the national courts and in the face of conflicting national law.

> The language of the earlier case law will be retained, but where the term 'Community' is used, this is to be read now as also meaning 'Union'.

From its progressive case law, notably Cases 26/62 *Van Gend en Loos*, 6/64 *Costa v ENEL*, and 106/77 *Simmenthal*, it is clear that Community (EU) law was assumed to be an autonomous legal order that is related to international law and national law, but nevertheless distinct from them and thus subject to its own logic in relation to supremacy over the law of the member states.

THINKING POINT

The CoJ in the *Van Gend* case did not mention supremacy of EU law. Why is this case then one that supports that conclusion?

▶ CROSS REFERENCE

See also the case coverage of *Van Gend en Loos* in Chapter 8, section 8.1.3.1.

Case 26/62 *Van Gend en Loos*, as the leading case in the development of the doctrine of direct effects, substantially prepared the ground for the CoJ to build its argument for supremacy of Community law. The case affirmed the Court's jurisdiction in interpreting Community legal provisions, the object of which is to ensure uniform interpretation in the member states. The case established the direct effect of Community law in the national legal orders. The Court held that:

> the Community constitutes a new legal order of International law for the benefit of which the States have limited their sovereign rights, albeit in limited fields, and the subjects of which comprise not only member states but also their nationals.

It was not long, though, before this supremacy over national law was stated expressly by the CoJ, and further elaboration of the new legal order in *Van Gend en Loos* was provided in **Case 6/64 *Flaminio Costa v ENEL***. This case primarily concerned the payment, or in fact the attempt not to pay, an electricity bill of a very low value (then approximately £1). In 1962, the Italian government passed an Act to nationalise the electricity industry, and the newly nationalised industry sent out bills to recover debts previously outstanding. Mr Costa claimed that the action was in conflict with then Article 37 of the European Economic Community (EEC) Treaty concerned with state monopolies, and he refused to pay his bill. The case, however, also raised the wider issue of whether a national court should refer to the CoJ if it considers that Community law may be applicable or, in the view of the Italian government, simply apply the subsequent national law.

In addressing this question, the Court again stressed the autonomous legal order of Community law:

> By contrast with ordinary international treaties the EEC Treaty has created its own legal system which became an integral part of the legal systems of the member states and which their courts are bound to apply. By creating a Community of unlimited duration, having its own institutions, its own personality, its own legal capacity, and more particularly real powers stemming from a limitation of sovereignty or a transfer of powers from the states to the Community the member states have limited their sovereign rights and have created a body of law to bind their nationals and themselves.

The Court also established that Community law takes priority over all conflicting provisions of national law, whether passed before or after the Community measure in question:

> The integration into the laws of each Member State of provisions which derive from the Community, and more generally, the terms and spirit of the Treaty, make it impossible for the states, as a corollary, to accord precedence to a unilateral and subsequent measure over a legal system accepted by them on the basis of reciprocity. Such a measure cannot therefore be inconsistent with that legal system.

As additional justifications, the Court also invoked the use of some of the general provisions of the EEC Treaty: old Article 5 EEC (now 4(3) Treaty of the European Union (TEU)) on the requirement to ensure the attainment of the objectives of the Treaty and old Article 7 EEC (now 18 Treaty on the Functioning of the European Union (TFEU)) on the prohibition of discrimination, both of which would be breached if subsequent national legislation were to have precedence; and old Article 189 EEC (now 288 TFEU), regarding the binding and direct application of Regulations, which would be meaningless if subsequent national legislation could prevail. The Court summed up its position:

> It follows . . . that the law stemming from the treaty, an independent source of law, could not because of its special and original nature, be overridden by domestic legal provisions, however framed, without being deprived of its character as Community law and without the legal basis of the Community itself being called into question.

Therefore, the conclusion must be that EU law must be supreme over subsequent national law.

Later, in **Case 106/77 *Simmenthal***, the CoJ ruled that:

> A national court which is called upon, within the limits of its jurisdiction, to apply provisions of Community law, is under a duty to give full effect to those provisions, if necessary of its own motion to set aside any conflicting provisions of national legislation, even if adopted subsequently.

The CoJ ruled that directly effective provisions of Community law preclude the valid adoption of new legislative measures to the extent that they would be incompatible with Community provisions. Any inconsistent national legislation recognised by national legislatures as having legal effect would deny the effectiveness of the obligations undertaken by the member state and imperil the existence of the Community.

▶ CROSS REFERENCE

Simmenthal is considered further in section 5.1.2 in respect of constitutional practice.

Therefore, the voluntary limitation of sovereignty and the need for an effective and uniform EU law requires supremacy. To give effect to subsequent national law over and above the EU legal system that member states have accepted would be inconsistent.

In **Case 213/89 *Factortame (No. 1)***, the CoJ, building on the principle laid down in ***Simmenthal*** that a provision of EC law must be implemented as effectively as possible, held that a national court must suspend national legislation that may be incompatible with EC law until a final determination on its compatibility has been made. Thus, national rules that prevent a national court from issuing an interim injunction suspending the application of a national statute during a dispute whilst considering the existence of alleged rights under Community law must be set aside. It was later held, in **Case C-221/89 *Factortame (No. 2)***, that the UK law did in fact breach Community law.

▶ CROSS REFERENCE

Discussed in Chapter 8, section 8.3.

Finally, in this context, it is worth mentioning the consequence of a member state not giving primacy to EU law when it should have done, in that liability on the part of the state will be incurred. This principle was first established by the CoJ in Cases C-6 and 9/90 *Francovich* and later confirmed in Case 213/89 *Factortame (No. 3)* and other cases.

So far, the national legislation considered has been so-called 'ordinary' domestic national legislation and the CoJ has maintained a consistent position on supremacy. What about provisions of a member state's constitution? It is in this respect that the most serious conflicts between the views of the national judiciaries and the Court have arisen.

5.1.2 **Supremacy and member state constitutional law**

The CoJ's view in respect of national constitutional law differs little from that in respect of 'ordinary' national law.

> **Case 11/70 *Internationale Handelsgesellschaft*** concerned the claim that Community levies were contrary to the German Constitution (Articles 2.1 and 14 *Grundgesetz* (GG)) and thus, as far as the national court was concerned, inapplicable. On referral to the CoJ, it held that national courts do not possess the power to review Community law. However, in diffusing the question, the Court held that there had been no breach by Community law of constitutional rights in the case.

The important question arising from *Internationale Handelsgesellschaft* was whether the CoJ was in a position to declare supremacy over national constitutional law and thereby, in effect, review that law. In doing so, it would effectively deny national courts the right to ignore the distinction or separation of the national and EU law legal systems, but nevertheless do so itself. In other words, national courts could not question the supremacy of Community (now EU) law, but the CoJ would be able to determine that national constitutional law was not in conformity with Community (now EU) law, something clearly of great concern to national supreme courts.

> This distinction is termed 'the autonomy of jurisdictions'.

The second case arises from a conflict between the Italian Constitution and Community law. In Italy, the constitutional practice existed that the power to disregard or declare invalid a provision of national law was the sole right of the Italian Constitutional Court.

> In **Case 106/77 *Simmenthal***, a lower court was faced with inconsistency between a Community law provision and a national provision. The national court was aware that a reference to the Italian Constitutional Court would have the effect of subrogating Community law to national legal practice, inconsistent with existent Community case law on the matter, as was evident from the earlier Case 6/64 *Costa* v *ENEL*. However, disregarding the national law was contrary to Italian constitutional requirements. The Italian magistrate referred to both courts, but asked the CoJ whether subsequent national measures that conflict with the Community must be disregarded without waiting until those measures are set aside by legislative or other constitutional means.
>
> The CoJ first declared that the doctrine of direct effects of Community legislation was not dependent on any national constitutional provisions, but a source of rights in itself. Therefore, national courts must give full effect to those rights, including a refusal to apply conflicting national legislation. The Court also ruled that directly effective provisions of Community law preclude the valid adoption of new legislative measures to the extent that they would be incompatible with Community provisions. The national court should disregard the inconsistent national law. The Court established that if there was no violation of Community fundamental rights, the Community measures were acceptable and there should be no reference to national constitutions to test their validity.

It held that:

> The law stemming from the treaty, an independent source of law, cannot because of its very nature be overridden by rules of national law, however framed, without being deprived of its character as Community law. Therefore the validity of a Community measure or its effect within a Member State cannot be affected by allegations that it runs counter to either fundamental rights as formulated by the Constitution of that State or the principles of a national constitutional structure.

The CoJ has not been so expressly forthright since *Simmenthal*. The conclusion following this case is that any inconsistent national legislation recognised by national legislatures as having legal effect would, in the Court's view, deny the effectiveness of the obligations undertaken by the member states and, in particular, the good faith clause Article 10 EC (now 4(3) TEU), and thus imperil the very foundations of the Community. In its widest interpretation, the judgment holds that 'Inconsistent national measures of any sort which are introduced by member states are effectively invalid from their adoption.' However, if the same national law were also applicable to purely domestic situations, there is not a requirement to set it aside and it remains valid in that circumstance. It is only to be set aside in respect of its inconsistent application to situations governed by EU law. See Cases C-10–22/97 *IN.CO.GE.'90*.

 CROSS REFERENCE

This is further reviewed from the German perspective in section 5.3.1.

> **THINKING POINT**
>
> Did the CoJ go too far in declaring supremacy over member states' constitutional law? If your answer was yes, what are the consequences of deciding it had?

The stance taken by the CoJ is in sharp contrast to the initial stance by some of the member states' courts. Indeed, the *Internationale Handelsgesellschaft* case produced a head-on clash between the CoJ, the German Federal Constitutional Court, and the German Constitution.

> **Case C-213/89 *Factortame (No. 1)*** is a further confirmation that national constitutional practices or rules, in this case the important constitutional doctrine of parliamentary sovereignty in the UK, must not be allowed to stand in the way of a Community law right. It was previously the position in the UK under the doctrine of parliamentary sovereignty that the courts had no power to set aside or not to apply an Act of Parliament. The CoJ held that even if the Community law rule were still in dispute, the national procedure should be changed so as not, even potentially, to interfere with the full effectiveness of the Community law right.

This case is also a witness to EU law incursion into national procedure. The CoJ is therefore clear that Community and now EU law is supreme over all types of national law. Case C-399/11 *Melloni* provided yet another opportunity for the CoJ to re-confirm its uncompromising position on the supremacy of EU even over national constitutions. This was notwithstanding an interpretation of Article 53 of the EU Charter of Fundamental rights, which seemed to suggest that where the standards of national constitutions are higher than EU standards, then the national standard should prevail. The case concerned the European Arrest Warrant (Framework Decision 2002/84) and the

CROSS REFERENCE

Considered further in Chapter 8, section 8.4.

arguably higher standard offered by the Spanish Constitution for its application. The CoJ made clear that the primacy of EU law cannot be undermined, even by national constitutional law, but that any application of national law can only be done in the light of the interpretation of the Charter by the CoJ and when the primacy, unity, and effectiveness of the EU is not compromised. The measure in question was held by the CoJ to conform with EU fundamental rights and was thus applicable without reference to national standards.

The foregoing cases are only the leading cases on supremacy—those that expressly declare EU law primacy. Many other cases imply EU law supremacy; for example, all cases that declare direct effects must also acknowledge supremacy. If EU law were not supreme over national law, especially subsequent law, direct effects would be denied. Conversely, if direct effects were denied where they fulfil the criteria, supremacy would therefore also be denied because national law would be seen to prevail.

5.1.3 Supremacy and international law

The relationship between EU law and provisions of international law has been considered in a number of the judgments of the CoJ. The type of international law must be distinguished between, on the one hand, those entered into by a/the member state(s) alone, and also whether entered into before or after EU accession; and on the other hand, those entered into by the EU. Generally, member states are bound by the provisions of international agreements concluded by the EU: see Case C-239/03 *Commission* v *France*. However, in Case C-162/96 *Racke* v *Hauptzollamt Mainz*, the CoJ did concede that an EU Regulation could be held to be invalid where found to be contrary to international law.

5.1.3.1 International agreements entered into by member states

These agreements are now essentially governed by Article 351 TFEU, which provides:

Article 351 TFEU

The rights and obligations arising from agreements concluded before 1 January 1958 or, for acceding States, before the date of their accession, between one or more Member States on the one hand, and one or more third countries on the other, shall not be affected by the provisions of the Treaties.

To the extent that such agreements are not compatible with the Treaties, the Member State or States concerned shall take all appropriate steps to eliminate the incompatibilities established.

This means that supremacy of EU law does not apply to agreements made before accession to the EU. However, agreements made or those modified to the extent that the CoJ would regard them as new agreements after accession are subject to the general rule of EU law supremacy that, where they are inconsistent with EU law, they should give way to EU law.

An example of a modified agreement can be found in **Case C-466/98 *Commission* v *UK***, which concerned the 'open sky' agreements with the United States concluded originally by the UK under the Bermuda I Agreement in 1946 but modified extensively under the Bermuda II Agreement in 1977. When challenged by the Commission, the CoJ held that the new agreement was essentially a new agreement and thus not covered by Article 351. Any inconsistencies would therefore be subject to EU law.

In the Bilateral Investment Treaties (BITs) cases, **Cases 205/06, C-249/06**, and **C-118/07**, the CoJ held that the application of the EU Treaties did not disturb the duties member states owed to third countries under agreements entered into previously but that the EU itself was not so bound. Member states, though, are required, in the case of conflict, to do all they can to eliminate inconsistencies. If they cannot, they should then denounce the prior agreement as held by the CoJ in **Case C-84/98 *Commission v Portugal***. In **Case C-324/93 *Evans Medical***, the CoJ held that provisions of an agreement which were contrary to EU rules on the matter may still be applied where third parties rely on them and are still required to perform duties arising from them.

5.1.3.2 UN resolutions

The position of UN resolutions was considered in Cases C-402/05 P and 415/05 P *Kadi and Al Barakaat*.

Kadi and Al Barakaat concerned the translation into EU Regulations of United Nations (UN) measures against the support of terrorism, namely the freezing of assets of persons listed by the UN as suspected of being involved in terrorism. The applicants, Kadi and Al Barakaat, could not, of course, challenge the UN Resolution itself and the UN Resolution was not under review or challengeable before the CoJ, but they did challenge the Regulation (881/2002), which contained and was the cause of the alleged infringements of human rights, including the right to be heard and the right to an effective remedy. The issue for this chapter is whether the CoJ had the right to review or was precluded from reviewing a Regulation intended to put into effect a UN Resolution, something which, according to Article 105 of the UN Charter, is excluded.

The Court of First Instance (CFI, now General Court) and the CoJ both stated that the Community is based on the rule of law and that therefore its acts are subject to judicial review, and the Court made clear that neither the member states nor the EU institutions can avoid review of the conformity of their acts with the basic constitutional charter, the EC Treaty, which established a complete system of legal remedies and procedures designed to enable the Court to review the legality of acts of the institutions. Furthermore, a guarantee of fundamental rights forms an integral part of the Community legal order and their respect is a condition of the lawfulness of Community acts and that, as constitutional principles of the EU, this status cannot be affected by any international agreement or the fact that EU acts are based on an international obligation. A review of the validity of any Community measure in the light of fundamental rights must be considered to be the expression, in a Community based on the rule of law, of a constitutional guarantee stemming from the EC Treaty as an autonomous legal system. The Court held, therefore, that it could review the Union measures and thus indirectly the UN Resolution. The Resolution and thus the Regulation were held patently to breach the right to be heard and to an effective remedy in the inclusion in the list of the applicants' names without recourse to any form of judicial review. The Court acknowledged that security interests may justify the secret compilation of the list but would not exclude a judicial review of the lawfulness after publication. Therefore, as far as applicants were concerned, the Regulation was annulled.

Hence, the overall conclusion is that EU law in the Union takes priority over conflicting international law even where, as in the case of the UN provisions, they existed prior to EU acts.

5.1.4 **Section summary**

In summary, the Union view on supremacy is that, because of its unique nature, EU law denies the member states the right to resolve conflicts of law by reference to their own rules or constitutional provisions. EU law obtains its supremacy because of the transfer of state power and sovereignty to the Union in those areas agreed. The member states have provided the Union with legislative powers to enable it to perform its tasks. There would be no point in such a transfer of power if the member states could annul or suspend the effect of EU law by later national law or provisions of the constitutions. If that were allowed to be the case, the existence of the EU legal order and the Union itself would be called into question. A precondition of the existence and functioning of the Union is the uniform and consistent application of EU law in all of the member states. It can achieve such an effect only if it takes precedence over national law.

 THINKING POINT

Is it possible to have binding EU law that is not supreme over national law? Equally, is it possible to have EU law supremacy without it being binding in the face of conflicting national law?

The legal and logical consequences of this summary are that any provision of national law that conflicts with EU law must be overruled, regardless of its date of enactment or rank.

The CT had provided an express statement of supremacy (Article I-6), although without expressly stating that it would be supreme over the member states' constitutions. When that Treaty was abandoned, however, the member states used the opportunity to tone down significantly the clear statement previously made, but without denying this supremacy. Hence, supremacy is now dealt with in a Declaration (No. 17), which refers obliquely to the well-settled case law that established the supremacy of EU law, and further by a reference in an annex to the Final Act of the Treaty citing the Opinion of the Council Legal Service on primacy.

Council Legal Service Opinion, Council Document 11197–07 (JUR260) of 22 June 2007
It results from the case law of the ECJ that primacy of EC law is a cornerstone principle of Community law. According to the Court, this principle is inherent to the specific nature of the European Community. At the time of the first judgment of this established case law (*Costa/ENEL*, 15 July 1964, Case 6–641) there was no mention of primacy in the treaty. It is still the case today. The fact that the principle of primacy will not be included in the future treaty shall not in any way change the existence of the principle and the existing case law of the European Court of Justice (ECJ).

The following sections of this chapter consider how EU law has been received in the member states thus far.

5.2 EU law in the member states

With 28 (27) member states, it would occupy far too much space to look at the reception of EU law in all of them; therefore, only a sample of states has been chosen and in view of Brexit the consideration of the UK will be far less brief than in previous editions. Before this is undertaken, it needs to be considered how international law, as the Treaties and EU law were first thought to be, can be received into the national legal systems.

5.2.1 Theories of incorporation of international law: monism and dualism

The method of incorporation of international law into the member states' legal systems and EU law is determined initially by the particular outlook that a state has in respect of the validity of such law. There are two prevailing theories of the incorporation of external law into national legal systems that are applicable in the context of the initial incorporation of the Treaties into the member state legal systems: **monism** and **dualism**.

> **monism** Monism basically assumes that international law and national law form part of a single system or hierarchy of law; therefore, the acceptance of international law would not require formal incorporation by legislative transformation. After Treaty agreement and assent or ratification, it would be self-executing. In other words, it would be directly applicable within the state. Therefore, all that is required by such a state to achieve this is the assent to, or ratification of, an international treaty.
>
> **dualism** Dualism, on the other hand, regards international law and national law as fundamentally different systems of law that exist alongside each other. In order to overcome the barrier existing between the two systems, legislation is required to transform the rules of international law into the national legal system before they can have any binding effect within the state in such circumstances. It is for the member states to determine where the international law is then placed within the national hierarchy of laws.

》 CROSS REFERENCE

France only is a good example of a monist state. It will be considered in section 5.3.3.

Germany, Italy, and the UK are good examples of dualist states, all considered below.

Monism does not, however, determine where on the single hierarchy the international law should be placed, and this leaves open any difficulties of whether, in individual states, it takes priority over all law or only over municipal/ordinary national law and not over constitutional law.

5.2.2 EU law in the UK

In view of the ongoing Brexit negotiations with a view to exit in March 2019, this section has been radically revised to be as up to date as possible, whilst providing historical context.

》 CROSS REFERENCE

Brexit was also considered in Chapter 1, section 1.6.

For more details on this section visit the online resources.

The UK was not one of the original and founding member states of the original Communities. It had to overcome a number of difficulties in order to accommodate the duties of membership of the EEC in 1973. It had to accept all of the previous Community legislation passed, including the Treaties, Regulations, Directives, and the judicial legal developments of this established new legal order.

Here I shall only consider how entry was achieved and in a very limited way, how Community and now EU law was received by the UK courts.

5.2.2.1 UK entry and the European Communities Act (ECA) 1972

The European Communities Act (ECA) 1972 was the Act of Parliament that facilitated UK entry into the Communities. Both entry to the EC and Community law implementation in the UK initially focuses on how the ECA 1972 observes and takes account of such well-established Community law concepts as direct effect and supremacy, and the difficulties noted above in respect of dualism and sovereignty. In contrast to the earlier practice of the incorporation of international treaties, the ECA did not reproduce the whole of the European Community (EC) Treaties or subsequent secondary legislation as Acts of Parliament. If this had been done, the words of any future Act that conflicted

》 CROSS REFERENCE

Considered in section 5.2.2.4.

with Community law obligations could override the prior Treaty. Instead, the Community Treaties were adopted by a simple assent. Section 1 of the ECA 1972 was intended to future-proof the Act by allowing for subsequent EC and EU Treaties to be regarded in the same way as the original Treaties, including, of course, most recently the Lisbon Treaty and the changes that it has made to the EU and EC Treaties. The Act thus impliedly recognises the unique new legal system and started to be regarded as a special form of UK legislation, but is now the Act that must be repealed as part of the package to domesticate EU law into UK law.

5.2.2.2 Judicial reception of Community and EU law in the UK

Here we will consider recent cases and an overall view of how the UK courts regarded EU supremacy and the effect of the ECA 1972 on UK constitutional principles.

For more details on this section visit the online resources.

The ***R v Secretary of State for Transport, ex p Factortame Ltd*** litigation is a particularly important statement of the view of the House of Lords on the supremacy of Community law, which was surprising in view of the picture painted of the UK being a reluctant partner in the EU.

The procedural question referred to the CoJ by the House of Lords, was whether a UK court could or should grant interim relief against the Crown. On receipt of the ruling, the House of Lords held that if a national rule precludes a national court from granting an interim relief whilst it was being determined whether there is a conflict between national law and Community law, irreparable harm could be done. Therefore, the national court must set aside that rule. If the injunction against the Crown was not granted, the Spanish fishing companies in the case would most probably go out of business whilst waiting for the CoJ to decide the substantive issues and for that to be returned to the Queen's Bench Division and decided: a process that actually took two years and seven months. Although the substantive point of Community law in relation to the UK law had not been decided at that stage, the House of Lords nevertheless considered that if Community law rights are to be found to be directly enforceable in favour of the appellants, those rights will prevail over the inconsistent national legislation, even if later. It was held *obiter* that:

> This [section 2(4)] has precisely the same effect as if a section were incorporated into the national statute . . . which in terms enacted that the provisions . . . [of an Act] . . . were to be without prejudice to the directly enforceable Community rights of nationals of any member state of the EEC.

Lord Bridge commented on the view that the earlier decisions in favour of Community law were an attack on parliamentary sovereignty:

> If the supremacy within the European Community of Community law over the National law of member states was not always inherent in the EEC Treaty it was certainly well established in the jurisprudence of the Court of Justice long before the United Kingdom joined the Community. Thus, whatever limitation of its sovereignty Parliament accepted when it enacted the European Communities Act 1972 was entirely voluntary. Under the terms of the ECA 1972 it has always been clear that it was the duty of a United Kingdom court, when delivering final judgment, to override any rule of National law found to be in conflict with any directly enforceable rule of Community law. Thus, there is nothing in any way novel in according supremacy to rules of Community law in those areas to which they apply and to insist that, in the protection of rights under Community law, national courts must not be inhibited by rules of national law from granting interim relief in appropriate cases is no more than a logical recognition of that supremacy.

Factortame No. 2, dealing with the substantive matter, was decided in the High Court as predicted: that Community law had been breached by the UK legislation.

> Subsequently, the House of Lords confirmed in **Case C-9/91 *R v Secretary of State for Employment, ex p EOC*** the conclusion reached in *Factortame* and held that, in judicial review proceedings, UK courts could declare an Act of Parliament to be incompatible with EC law, although this does not extend to being able to annul the UK Act of Parliament, nor indeed to command a government to repeal the Act or to compel or command a minister to change the law.

The conclusion for the UK is that the courts, by and large had clearly and unambiguously accepted the supremacy of EU law even over UK Acts of Parliament and over constitutional practice. As was seen in the later cases, this is on the basis of the ECA 1972; however, the UK seemed to have gone further than some of the other member states. Certainly, the *Factortame* litigation and the conclusion at its end that, in matters of EU law, the UK courts are able not to apply UK Acts of Parliament, does introduce a form of constitutional review by the courts, hitherto not the case in the UK, and therefore impacts and undermines the doctrine of parliamentary sovereignty, at least as far as EU law is concerned. However, this will be purely of academic interest if, as planned, the UK exits the EU at the end of March 2019.

5.2.2.3 The withdrawal of the UK from the European Union Act

On 23 June 2016, those voting in the Referendum voted by a small majority to leave the EU.

The formal process of leaving the EU required the triggering of Article 50 TEU. Prior to 2009, there was no EU Treaty Article facilitating the exit of a member state from the EU; however, Article 50 TEU has now provided that and following a two-year negotiation period to agree the terms of withdrawal, the member state will exit.

To start the process, the UK government thus triggered Article 50 on 29 March 2017 and the two-year clock started ticking. The terms of withdrawal still have to be agreed with the EU, with negotiations led by the Commission under Article 218(3) TFEU and then subject to the approval of the Council of Ministers by a qualified majority and the consent of the European Parliament (EP), although representatives of all three have been participating in the negotiating process. The two years on paper—i.e. as envisaged in Article 50—may not prove long enough and more time, possibly a few years longer, may be needed. In the meantime, and up to formal withdrawal, all EU Treaties and laws remain legally binding and in force in the UK. If the withdrawal terms are agreed before the expiry deal, the departure can be facilitated earlier, as agreed; however, at the time of writing (April 2018) this is still far from certain The UK requested a transition period post exit and which has been approved by the European Council to provide for an extension period during which most EU law will still apply and be binding on the UK until the end of 2020.

5.2.2.4 The internal exit process

In order to arrange the exit internally, the UK has to repeal the most important Act of Parliament standing in its way. This is the European Communities Act 1972, the Act which facilitated accession and membership. The proposed Great Repeal Bill is now formally called the European Union (Withdrawal) Bill. As this is rather complicated and only affects the UK, suffice it to say that it seeks to nationalise EU law in one go but will leave the highly difficult task of sorting out which pieces of EU can be easily converted and which need amendment or removal until after exit.

In order to repeal an Act of Parliament, a repealing Act of Parliament must be enacted and, as should be clear, this can only be done by Parliament, and the European Union (Withdrawal) Bill is presently

> **CROSS REFERENCE**
> This has been considered in Chapter 1, section 1.6.6.

> **CROSS REFERENCE**
> See Chapter 1, section 1.6.7 for further details on Article 50 TEU.

For more details on this section visit the online resources.

on its way through Parliament, having been approved for second reading by MPs in September 2017 by 326 to 290 votes. It went to the full house committee stage for eight days of debate starting 14 November 2017 and concluding 16 December. It was be given its third reading on 16 January 2018 and is now before House of Lords for possible amendment.

However, that is only one vote that may be needed and despite earlier statements that the terms of the exit agreement will not be put to Parliament, it has been announced and decided, partially by an amendment to the above bill, that the eventual agreement with the EU will be put within another bill, presently entitled The Withdrawal Agreement and Implementation Bill. This will then be put before the Commons and Parliament for approval or rejection. That is assumed to be sometime in early 2019.

If Parliament does approve it, then that is end game and Brexit will take place. If, however, as is speculated, a majority of MPs in the House of Commons oppose exit and/or the terms of exit, or if there is no agreement, they may well vote against the deal agreed. This will leave, if nothing else, a constitutional crisis, as the government has hinted that even if they vote against the package, the UK will still exit the EU.

❱ CROSS REFERENCE

Further details on any possible new relationship are considered in Chapter 1, section 1.6.9.

For more details on this section visit the online resources.

5.3 Reception of EU law in other member states

A majority of member states have not experienced any problems so far, although there is always room judicially for this position to change. It would be beyond this particular text to conduct a tour of all of the member states, so only the following states have been selected, which include examples of clear and qualified acceptance states.

5.3.1 **Germany**

5.3.1.1 **The German Constitution (*Grundgesetz*) (GG)**

For more details on the reception of EU law in these countries visit the online resources.

In Germany, in contrast with the UK, difficulties were experienced, especially in respect of the relationship between fundamental rights provision in the German Constitution (GG) and in the Community and EU legal order. Traditionally, Germany adopted the dualist approach to the reception of international law whereby some form of transformation or adoption of international law was necessary in order for it to have any direct application in the state. There had to be a process of incorporation by statute and, once incorporated, a law would simply rank as with other *Gesetze* (Acts of the German Parliament). If a later law were in conflict with an earlier law, the later law would prevail. Articles 24 and 25 GG provided for the peaceful cooperation of the German state with international organisations. Article 24 GG allowed for membership of international organisations and a transfer of powers to them, and was used to establish membership of the European Communities. Although Article 25 GG declared general rules of public international law to be an integral part of federal law and to take precedence over national law, it was silent as to the effect of international law on German constitutional law. In order to cater specifically for further European integration, particularly into new areas as proposed in the Maastricht Treaty and to take account of the increasing concern about possible infringements of the GG, a new Article 23 GG (the *Europa Artikel*) was added and amendments were made to other key provisions.

Joint approval was also required for the ratification of the EU Treaty and is further required for any future changes affecting the contents of the GG.

> Article 23 GG provides that sovereign powers can be transferred to the EU provided the transfer has the approval of both Houses of the German Parliament, the *Bundestag* and *Bundesrat*.

5.3.1.2 The reaction of the German courts

Previously, German courts had been divided as to the effect of Community primary law and secondary law and, at times, had refused to make a reference in cases of doubt or non-acceptance, thus denying the parties to the case the chance to see whether EC law would have affected the outcome of the case. The most important court in Germany is the Federal Constitutional Court (FCC) because of its constitutional position in the German state.

> In the ***Internationale Handelsgesellschaft*** (known in Germany as ***Solange I***), the Constitutional Court held that as long as the recognition of human rights in the EEC had not progressed as far as those provided for by the **GG**, German courts retained the right to refer questions on the constitutionality of secondary Community law to the FCC, with the possible result that Community law might be ignored if it did not have sufficient regard for basic rights.

This position has been modified by subsequent rulings of the FCC.

> In ***Wünsche Handelsgesellschaft*** (known as ***Solange II***), the FCC accepted that Community recognition and safeguards of fundamental rights through the case law of the CoJ were sufficient and of a comparable nature to those provided for by the GG. Thus, it held that as long as EC and now EU law ensures the effective provision of fundamental rights, the FCC will not review EC law in the light of the rights provisions of the Constitution. The Court also stated that it would not be prepared to accept constitutional complaints against Community law from lower courts on this basis. It is argued that a reservation of supremacy is still inherent in the ruling.

The basis for the decision is not, however, the inherent supremacy of EU law, but the fact that Article 24 GG allowed a transfer of powers to the Community, and the subsequent Accession Act obliges the German courts to accept the supremacy of Community and EU law. The decision by the FCC in *Solange II* also held that the CoJ is a statutory court within the meaning of Article 101 GG and that individuals have the right to have access to statutory courts. This effectively means that German courts can no longer refuse to make references in the last instance to the CoJ.

> This happened in the 1985 case of ***Kloppenburg***. The Federal Tax Court had denied the direct effects of Directives and refused a reference to the CoJ.
>
> The FCC held in ***Re: VAT Exemption***, the follow-up to the *Kloppenburg* case, and in the separate case of ***Re: Patented Feedstuffs***, that German courts, which are courts of last instance in terms of Article 234 EC (now 267 TFEU), would be in breach of the German Constitution if they were to fail to refer to the CoJ when necessary. The earlier judgment of the Federal Tax Court was consequently annulled.

Therefore, German courts of last instance are obliged to make a reference where a dispute as to interpretation or application of EU law exists. Applications to the FCC to question the constitutionality of Community legislation have now been declared to be inadmissible because the Court considered that such acts are not acts of German public authorities within the scope of the GG and cannot thus be complained of to the FCC. Following these cases, there would seem to be no procedural difficulty in getting EU rights at least considered in the proper forum in Germany. Any court that refuses either to follow a previous ruling of the CoJ or to make an Article 267 TFEU ruling may be subject to the review of the FCC for a breach of Article 101(1) GG.

The German Accession Act to the TEU was passed by the German Parliament in December 1992. However, as a result of considerable criticism that there had been no real debate on the Maastricht Treaty in Germany and that a referendum had not been held to test public opinion on further integration, constitutional complaints were made to the FCC as a consequence of the general perception in Germany that the EU was assuming competences it did not have the right to assume.

In its judgment in **Brunner and others v Federal Republic of Germany** (known as **Maastricht**), the FCC considered the changes to the Constitution, the constitutionality of the TEU, and generally the relationship between the EC and the German Constitution. Whilst it held that the transfer of powers was compatible with the principles of the *Grundgesetz*, future extensive transfers could not be made without the approval of the German Parliament, and the FCC would reserve to itself a right to review the compatibility of EC law fundamental rights' provisions and the range of rights exercised by the EC with the German Constitution. It further commented that, if the EU institutions acted in ways not clearly sanctioned by the Treaties, any resulting EU legislative acts would not be binding on the German legal order. As such, the judgment appeared to backtrack on its previous judgments, although this final comment was not based on any existing intrusion into national competences by the TEU or by the EU. Consequently, its validity is dubious.

Following the *Maastricht* judgment, the relationship between the CoJ and the FCC remains unclear. Even though the FCC claims that fundamental rights will be protected and upheld by a relationship of cooperation between both courts, it does not clearly explain how this protection will work in practice. It seems that the FCC has accepted the standard of basic rights protection provided by the CoJ, but reserves a right to review EU Acts that could evidently infringe basic rights under the *Grundgesetz* if the Court does not offer protection. So far, this has been a theoretical proposition.

The decision of the FCC in **Case 2BvE 2/08 Lisbon Judgment** indirectly deals with EU matters, focusing on the constitutional compatibility of German legislation with the Lisbon Treaty. Following the agreement on the Lisbon Treaty on further integration of the EU by the member states, the German *Bundestag* and *Bundesrat* passed the Transformation Act and an accompanying law extending and strengthening the rights of the *Bundestag* and the *Bundesrat* in European matters. This latter law was challenged before the FCC by German members of Parliament (MPs). The Court decided that the Lisbon Treaty and its Transformation Act were compatible with the Constitution, but that the accompanying Act strengthening the rights of the *Bundestag* and *Bundesrat* was not. It held that European integration could not be achieved by means that abolished the member states' discretion to organise or establish economic, cultural, and social conditions of life. In this respect, constitutional organs such as the *Bundestag* and *Bundesrat* had a responsibility to integrate. Thus, the participation rights of these two organs within negotiations at European level had to be elaborated in a much clearer way than had happened in the challenged statute. In the case, the issues were as much how the German constitutional procedure coped with EU integration as with its reserved power of review over the constitutionality of EU law in Germany.

Subsequently, there has been a ruling by the FCC in the *Honeywell* case which steps back to some degree from the *Lisbon* judgment by declaring that review of EU law should only take place where sufficiently qualified—this means essentially only in the most obvious and manifest cases of EU law breaching member states' competences. In any event, such a review can only take place after the CoJ has been given the chance to review the case via a preliminary ruling reference, and only by the FCC and no other court in Germany.

The FCC has made clear that it retains its competence to review any EU acts in order to ensure that they do not exceed the limits of what EU organs have been authorised to do by the member states and has thus, even in this latest case, confirmed the line taken already in the *Maastricht* case, albeit subject to the qualifications now that any breach by the EU must be manifest and that the CoJ first be given chance to adjudicate on the matter. Thus, whilst jurisprudentially possible, it is unlikely, as a result of this latest case, that the FCC will of its own accord pre-emptively strike down EU law in favour of German national law.

In support of those judgments, that the CoJ must be given a chance to comment, the FCC for the first time, made a preliminary reference to the CoJ in a case involving the Outright Monetary Trans-action (OMT) measures which were part of the package operated by the European Central Bank (ECB) to support the Euro during the Eurozone debt crisis. It was objected to by members of the *Bundestag* as being not within the competence of the ECB and more to do with the economic policy, and thus member states, and was thus contrary to EU law. The FCC was not entirely satisfied that the programme was compatible with EU law but made a reference to the CoJ, which held that the OMT came within the competence of the ECB as a part of monetary policy and that the measures were both within the scope of Article 123 TFEU legal base and proportionate, thus there was no breach of EU law but any such purchase of bonds in support of the Euro must not contravene the prohibition of monetary financing. On return to the FCC, the German Constitutional Court held that providing those conditions were met, the OMT measures would not breach the German Basic Law, nor the *Bundestag*'s right to decide on a budget. It stressed, though, that national courts continued to have a role in policing the exercise of competences by EU institutions and the interpretation of EU laws by the CoJ.

For more details on this section visit the online resources.

5.3.2 **Italy**

In Italy, the position both constitutionally and judicially was and is very similar to that in Germany, whereby both had new constitutions set up after the Second World War with strong provision for fundamental rights. Both states allowed a transfer of power to international organisations, but were silent as to its effect on constitutional law.

Article 11 of the Italian Constitution provides for the limitation of national sovereignty in favour of international arrangements to secure peace and justice between nations.

As in Germany, the focus in Italy is on its Constitutional Court. Given that two of the leading EU cases on supremacy, *Costa v ENEL* and *Simmenthal*, arose from Italy, it should certainly have been clear to the Italian Constitutional Court what was expected of it. Again, there has been a mixed reaction, also along the lines of the German Constitutional Court.

> Despite the previous less-than-enthusiastic response to Community and EU law, the supremacy of Community law was accepted in the case of **Frontini v Ministero delle Finanze** and the supremacy of the European Court was accepted in the 1984 case **Granital v Administrazione delle Finanze**. The decision was based both on the basis of an interpretation of Article 11 of the Italian Constitution, allowing for the limitation of sovereignty in favour of international organisations, and by reason of the case law of the CoJ.

The case did, however, make the reservation that Italian law should be cast aside only where directly applicable Community law exists

> A later decision in **Fragd v Administrazione delle Finanze** suggests that the Italian Constitutional Court is still prepared to review EU law in the light of the fundamental rights provision in the Italian Constitution if EU law was regarded as not respecting these rights. This stance was confirmed in **Admenta v Federfarma**, in which the Italian State Council held that fundamental rights, as protected by Italian law, could not be reviewed in the light of EU law and were therefore to be reviewed exclusively in the light of Italian constitutional law.

Thus far, this remains the situation in Italy, with the possibility for outright rejection of EU law supremacy.

5.3.3 France

The French courts are divided into two hierarchies, each with their own appeal courts and final appeal, and in addition a Constitutional Court (*Conseil Constitutionnel*). They have had, however, significantly different attitudes to EC law, despite the fact that both are subject to Article 55 of the French Constitution, which is monist and gives international law a rank above municipal law, but is silent as to the effect on the Constitution. This is the point that has led to discrepancies between hierarchies.

5.3.3.1 The French Courts of Ordinary Jurisdiction

The Courts of Ordinary Jurisdiction have had no hesitation in making Article 234 TEU (now 267 TFEU) references to the CoJ, and giving supremacy to Community and thus now EU law on the basis of Article 55 of the Constitution. The French Supreme Court of Ordinary Jurisdiction (*Cour de Cassation*) has in fact gone further and found for the supremacy of Community law without direct reference to Article 55 of the Constitution, and more on the basis of the inherent supremacy and direct effects of Community law itself.

> See **Café Vabre**, in which old Article 95 EEC was held to prevail over a subsequent national statute.

These rulings have been consistently followed by the lower courts and reference to either Article 55 of the Constitution or even the decisions is rarely made, for example *Garage Dehus Sarl v Bouche Distribution*.

5.3.3.2 **French public courts**

The French public courts deal with complaints by citizens against any acts of the state administration. The Supreme Administrative Court (*Conseil d'État*) has from time to time completely denied the supremacy of Community or now EU law, or the need to make reference to the CoJ, relying heavily on the French principle of law *acte clair*.

> *acte clair* The principle that where a provision of law is clear, there is no need to refer to a higher court, but simply to apply it.

> The leading case is **Minister of the Interior v Cohn-Bendit**, which concerned Daniel Cohn-Bendit ('Danny the Red'), who was deported from France in 1968 and in 1975 requested re-entry, but was refused. He claimed that the refusal was contrary to Free Movement Directive 64/221, previously declared directly effective by the CoJ in the *Van Duyn* case. The *Conseil d'État* held that individuals could not directly rely on Directives to challenge an administrative act, and declined to follow previous CoJ rulings or to make a reference itself.

The judgment in the *Cohn-Bendit* case has been followed by the same court and lower courts, in particular in the *Semoule* case (1970), when the *Conseil d'État* did not make a reference in a case in which there was a clear conflict between a Community Regulation and a French statute. It related to the application of law in Algeria and was thus very politically sensitive; as such, the Court claimed that it did not have the jurisdiction to decide on the constitutional priority of laws. Other cases have, though, demonstrated a much more cooperative attitude on the part of the French administrative courts.

> First, in **Nicolo**, the *Conseil d'État* reviewed the supremacy of international law, including EEC Treaty Articles, with the result that the latter was seen to take precedence over subsequent national law, largely on the basis of Article 55 of the French Constitution. The submissions of the Government Commissioner were instructive in his use and observation of the decisions from the courts of other member states and their acceptance of Community law supremacy.
>
> Secondly, in **Boisdet**, incompatible national law was declared invalid in the face of a Community Regulation. In doing so, the *Conseil d'État* followed the case law of the CoJ. In *Perreux* (2009), the court effectively reversed the previous decisions by holding that an EC Directive can be relied upon to challenge a French administrative act.
>
> The cases of **Rothmans**, **Philip Morris International**, and **Arizona Tobacco** held that not only are EC Directives to be given priority over national law, even where the Directives pre-dated the French statute, but also that an award of damages against the French authorities can be made where damage is suffered as a consequence of non-compliance with EC law, clearly following the lead of the CoJ in the *Francovich* case.

Previously receiving no direct mention in the French Constitution, the European Communities and the EU are now referred to in a new Article 88. This was introduced as a result of the *Conseil Constitutionnel* ruling that the move into new policy areas under the Maastricht Treaty would be incompatible with the Constitution. As with Article 55, the original validation of Community membership and Community law within the French legal order, Article 88 also requires **reciprocity**. As a result of the change to Article 88 of the Constitution, the French Constitutional Court has declared, in Decision 2004/496 of 10 June 2004, that it will no longer review Community and now EU law in the light of the Constitution, save in relation to express elements, which is taken to mean those protecting fundamental rights, thus retaining, in principle, a distinct reservation on its recognition of supremacy in a way similar to the German Federal Constitutional Court.

❱ CROSS REFERENCE

See also Chapter 7, section 7.1.4.5, on defences to Commission enforcement actions.

> **reciprocity** In this context, reciprocity means that in order for any international Treaty and also now the EU Treaties to be upheld and complied with in France, they must be upheld reciprocally by the other party or parties. Failure to comply by another party under the customary international law understanding of this principle would mean that France is itself no longer obliged to comply with the Treaty, or the part of it not complied with.

In a further case (Decision 2006/540), the *Conseil Constitutionnel* held that in relation to implementing EU Directives—a constitutional requirement under Article 88 of the French Constitution—an implementing law can only be found to be unconstitutional if it is clearly incompatible with a Directive. The Lisbon Treaty was also questioned before the *Conseil Constitutionnel* (Decision 2007/560), which held that whilst it introduced nothing new, it could not be subjected to constitutional review. However, if Treaty clauses did impact on French national sovereign competences, then constitutional revision would be required. The assumption, thus, from the decision is that if revisions were not made, the new Treaty competences would offend the existing French Constitution, thus, in effect, subrogating EU law to the French Constitution.

French constitutional procedural law involving the *Conseil Constitutionnel* was considered by the CoJ in Cases C-188 and 189/10 *Melki and Abdeli*. The rule that national courts must refer first to the *Conseil Constitutionnel* any questions of constitutionality, including that of EU law, appeared to undermine the rights of parties to make preliminary ruling references to the CoJ under Article 267 TFEU. The Court held, though, that the rule did not offend EU law provided that national courts remained free nevertheless to refer to the Court and to disapply any national law they considered to be contrary to EU law.

Clearly, in a Union of 28 states, this is not very practical; in any event, reciprocity was expressly excluded as a defence to a breach of EU law in Cases 90–91/63 *Commission v Belgium and Luxembourg* and C-146/89 *Commission v UK (Fishing Limits)*. However, despite the change to the Constitution and the rules more sympathetic to the supremacy of EU law, cases taking a less cooperative position are still being decided by the *Conseil d'État*.

In conclusion, the French recognition of supremacy of EU law arises as much, if not more, from the French Constitution as from the inherent supremacy of EU law but not extending to supremacy over the Constitution itself.

5.3.4 **The Czech Republic**

The Czech Republic, even though a later entrant state, is regarded as one of the EU's more sceptical members. Previously, in a case in 2004, the Czech Constitutional Court annulled national government instruments on the grounds that the Czech government did not have the competence to issue them, because the sector was one in which the competence had been transferred to the EU. However, in line with the German *Brunner* judgment, discussed in section 5.3.1, the Czech Constitutional Court in the case of Sugar quotas, Pl US 50/04, of 8 March 2006 qualified this transfer by stating that the transferred powers could be exercised by the EU only in conformity with the requirements of the Czech Constitution and constitutionality in the Czech Republic. In Case Pl US 60/04, of 3 May

2006, measures adopted under the EU third pillar dealing with the European arrest warrant caused the Czech Constitutional Court even more difficulties because, in its view, even the Court of Justice had difficulties with determining how national courts should accord primacy to third-pillar acts and whether framework decisions do, in fact, take primacy over national laws, although provided that the EU maintained a sufficient level of fundamental rights protection, it would not further review EU laws. The Czech Constitutional Court has also been asked to review the compatibility of the Lisbon Treaty with the Czech Constitution. Whilst in Case Pl US 19/08, of 26 November 2008, it held that it was compatible, it expressed views that the powers transferred to the EU and the division between national and EU competences should be made much clearer, and in similar vein to other constitutional courts, notably the German FCC, it commented that a transfer of overall competence (*Kompetenz-Kompetenz*) would be in breach of the constitutional sovereignty of the Czech Republic. In a second judgment in Case Pl US 29/09, on the Lisbon Treaty, this time dealing with the delay by the Czech president in ratifying the Treaty, the court held that there should not be undue delay, save only for constitutional challenges, but that the decision on the ultimate transfer of powers was one for the Czech Parliament and not the Czech Court.

Finally, and most significantly in 2012, in Case Pl US 5/12 (2012), the Czech Constitutional Court declared *ultra vires* a ruling of the CoJ in Case C-399/09 Landtová [2011] ECR I-415, concerned with nationality discrimination in pension payments between Czech and Slovaks. That ruling has led to an amendment of national law which the Czech Court held to be incompatible with the Czech Constitution, which allowed discrimination as part of the political settlement of the dissolution of Czechoslovakia. The long-term consequences, if any, of this rebuff have yet to reveal themselves.

> The Czech Constitutional Courts can be found here: http://www.usoud.cz/en/.

5.3.5 Denmark

Together with the UK, Norway, and Ireland, Denmark applied for membership of the EC in 1961 and 1967, but on each occasion French President de Gaulle vetoed UK membership and Denmark did not wish to enter the Community without the UK, largely because of their close trade relationship. As was noted in Chapter 1, entry negotiations were resumed after the summit meeting in The Hague in 1969, and from 1 January 1973 Denmark became a member, together with Ireland and the UK. Danish entry was preceded by a binding national referendum in which 63.3 per cent voted in favour of membership and 36.7 per cent against.

Section 2 of the Danish Constitution allows for the delegation of powers to international authorities by statute adopted by a five-sixths parliamentary majority or a simple majority in a popular vote if the former is not reached or not chosen by the Parliament, which has largely been the case in Denmark. Fundamental changes to the EU have been put to the electorate in binding referenda, with the following results:

- in 1986, 56.2 per cent voted for and 43.8 per cent against the SEA;
- in 1992, 49.3 per cent voted for and 50.7 per cent against the Maastricht Treaty;
- in 1993, 56.8 per cent voted in favour and 43.2 per cent against the Maastricht Treaty, with the opt-outs agreed in Edinburgh (including defence policy, the third phase of economic and monetary union, and a common currency, union citizenship, and in the judicial field);
- in 1998, 55.1 per cent voted for and 44.9 per cent against the Amsterdam Treaty; and
- in 2000, 53.1 per cent voted against and 46.9 per cent for Denmark's joining the Single European Currency, the euro, which of course then it did not join.

In contrast, Denmark ratified the Lisbon Treaty, without a prior referendum, by way of consent of the Danish Parliament under Article 19 of the Constitution.

Denmark enjoys the dubious reputation, almost equal with the UK, of being the most Eurosceptic EU member state, although two of the 2004 EU entrant states (the Czech Republic and Poland) would clearly rival that honour, largely through the expressed views of their presidents. However, as with the UK, Denmark also enjoys a positive track record of faithful implementation of EU laws having very few, if not the fewest, infringement proceedings before the CoJ.

> Turning briefly to the Danish courts, the Danish Accession Acts were challenged in **Case I 361/1997 Carlsen and others v Prime Minister Rasmussen** as providing too much power to the EC institutions and going beyond the transfer of powers authorised by section 20 of the Danish Constitution.
>
> The Danish Supreme Court held that ratification of the TEU did not violate the Danish Constitution and that the transfer of powers under section 20 was wide enough for the EU to act, including its perceived need to act under the general residual power of Article 308 EC (now 352 TFEU). However, two provisos were laid down: that power to adopt measures contrary to the Constitution cannot be delegated to international organisations; and that the national courts retain the power to review EU law in this light and to hold it inapplicable in the event of conflict.
>
> In 1998, the Danish Constitutional Court considered that Community law might not be applicable in Denmark if the Community or Commission had breached its delegated powers, and the issue was not satisfactorily then resolved by the CoJ, thus reflecting the reservation in other states such as Germany, Italy, and Ireland. This decision and the earlier position were confirmed in 2013 in Case 199/2012 of 20 February 2013 in respect of the ratification of the Lisbon Treaty.

5.3.6 **Spain**

For more details on this section visit the online resources.

Whilst previously having made clear its acceptance of EU law supremacy according to Article 93 of the Spanish Constitution in Judgment 132/1989, the Spanish Constitutional Court was faced head-on with the question of the supremacy of EU law when asked by the Spanish government to provide an opinion on the compatibility of aspects of the Constitutional Treaty with the Spanish Constitution. In particular, Article I-6, that Union law shall take priority over national law, was raised, along with questions about the legal basis (Article 93 Spanish Constitution) of the accession and provision for fundamental rights protection. The case in fact preceded the Spanish referendum on membership and the judgment is very much in line with the German *Brunner* case, in that—whilst accession and the Constitutional Treaty, since abandoned, were held to be acceptable under the Spanish Constitution without further amendment—the Spanish Constitutional Court reserved the right to judge Community law in light of its own constitutional protection of rights.

In 2004, there was a Spanish Constitutional Court ruling in Judgment 58/2004, that involved a failure to request an Article 234 EC (now Article 267 TFEU) ruling that was considered as a violation of the fundamental right to effective judicial protection.

CROSS REFERENCE

Further details on EU law (initial implementation and reception in the courts) in the member states can be found in the articles listed in the end-of-chapter Further reading.

The CoJ considered, in Case C-118/08 *Transportes Urbanos y Servicios Generales* (2010), a Spanish domestic procedural rule which required the exhaustion of domestic remedies before an applicant would be allowed to bring an action for damages against the Spanish state for a breach of EU law. This was not, however, a requirement when taking an action for a breach of national constitutional law. It was held by the Court thus to be a breach of the EU principle of equivalence. Following the uncompromising view of the CoJ in the *Melloni* case, which was the first case referred to the CoJ by the Spanish Constitutional Court (SCC), the Spanish Court was prepared to interpret its own case law on Constitutional guarantees in the light of EU rights provision. However, the SCC, like its German counterpart, reserved a right to step in, in the case of EU law proving irreconcilable with the Spanish Constitution, to ensure the preservation of the sovereignty of the Spanish people and of the supremacy of the Spanish constitution. However, it held that this was not applicable in the case before it.

Summary

The Communities and now Union were established by a transfer of powers by the member states to enable them to act independently of those member states and to create their own laws and legal system, which was, of course, one of the reasons for establishing them in the first place. This chapter has considered the nature of the EU law that stems from this transfer of power, which is the question of supremacy or primacy of EU law, and then its reception in the member states.

A consensus appears to be emerging from the national and constitutional courts that EU law supremacy is accepted only in so far as it does not infringe the individual rights' protection of the national constitutions, in which case the constitutional courts will exercise their reserved rights over national constitutions to uphold them over inconsistent EU law. The latest flurry of cases considering the Lisbon Treaty do, though, seem to confirm the trend that the constitutional courts will regard any transfer of competences leading to EU laws which appear to impinge on the national constitutions or sovereignty as inferior to them. Also, whilst always clear (from the *Van Gend en Loos* and *Costa* v *ENEL* cases) that competences are only transferred in limited fields, the constitutional courts are making it clear that no overall transfer of competences has taken place. Only a few states appeared to have accepted EU law unconditionally, such as Belgium and prior to Brexit, the UK. Whether it will ever come to a direct rejection of EU law supremacy by a national court is debatable. Perhaps more important is that such a direct rejection is probably avoidable if the CoJ is allowed to diffuse any possible conflict before the case reaches a constitutional court, if the question of conflict is first referred to the Court via the Article 267 TFEU preliminary ruling procedure (this procedure is considered in Chapter 6). In view of the number of constitutional courts that appear to be reserving a power of review, this is something that the member states, the Union, and the CoJ need to take seriously.

? Questions

1. Outline the reasons and logic provided by the ECJ in the *Costa* v *ENEL* case and later judgments for the supremacy of EC (now EU) law over national law.

2. Is EU law supreme over any form of conflicting national law in the UK?

3. Would your answer be any different if a UK Act of Parliament were expressly to state that it was aware of a conflict with EU law, but that the Act shall nevertheless apply, or to contain an instruction to the judges that they shall nevertheless apply the UK Act and not set it aside in favour of EU law?

For suggested approaches to answering these questions visit the online resources.

Sample exam Q&A

Is it the case that 'the doctrine of the supremacy of EU law is a logical if not a necessary inference from EU Treaties'?

For guidance on how to tackle this specimen exam question and to read a suggested model answer, visit the online resources. www.oup.com/uk/foster_directions6e/.

Further reading

Books

Bobek, M. 'The effects of EU law in the national legal systems' in Barnard, C. and Peers, S. (eds) *European Union Law*, 2nd edn, Oxford University Press, Oxford, 2017, p. 143.

Bulmer, S. and Lequesne, C. *The Member States of the European Union*, Oxford University Press, Oxford, 2005.

Fabbrini, R. *The Law and Politics of Brexit*, Oxford University Press, Oxford, 2017.

Lazowski, A. (ed.) *Brave New World: The Application of EU Law in the New Member States*, TMC Asser Press, The Hague, 2010.

Lenaerts, K. and van Nuffel, P. *Constitutional Law of the European Union*, 3rd edn, Sweet & Maxwell, London, 2010.

Articles

Albi, A. and Van Elsuwege, P. 'The EU Constitution, national constitutions and sovereignty: an assessment of a European constitutional order' (2004) 29 EL Rev 741.

Alonso Garcia, R. 'The Spanish Constitution and the European Constitution: the script for a virtual collision and other observations on the principle of primacy' (2005) 6(6) German Law Journal 1001.

Avbelj, M. 'Supremacy or primacy of EU law—(why) does it matter?' (2011) 17 ELJ 744.

Beck, G. 'The problem of Kompetenz-Kompetenz: a conflict between right and right in which there is no praetor' (2005) 30 EL Rev 42.

Bursens, P. 'Why Denmark and Belgium have different implementation records: on transposition laggards and leaders in the EU' (2002) 25 Scandinavian Political Studies 173.

Dashwood, A. 'The relationship between the member states and the European Union/European Community' (2004) 41 CML Rev 355.

Doukas, D. 'The verdict of the German Constitutional Court on the Lisbon Treaty: not guilty but don't do it again' (2009) 34 EL Rev 866.

Foster, N. 'The German Constitution and EC membership' (1994) Public Law 392.

Gaja, G. 'New developments in a continuing story: the relationship between EC law and Italian law' (1990) 27 CML Rev 83.

Giegerich, T., 'The German Federal Constitutional Court's misguided attempts to guard the European guardians in Luxembourg and Strasbourg' (2013) 1232 Der Staat im Recht 49.

Grosser, A. 'The Federal Constitution Court's Lisbon case: Germany's "Sonderweg"—an outsider's perspective' (2009) 10 German Law Journal 1263.

Hoffmeister, F. 'German *Bundesverfassungsgericht: Alcan* decision of 17 February 2000—Constitutional review of EC Regulation on bananas, Decision of 7 June 2000' (2001) 38 CML Rev 791.

Hoffmeister, F. 'Constitutional implications of EU membership: a view from the Commission' (2007) 3 CYELP 59.

Knook, A. 'The Court, the Charter and the vertical division of powers in the European Union' (2005) 42 CML Rev 367.

Komerek, J. 'Czech Constitutional Court playing with matches: the Czech Constitutional Court declares a judgment of the Court of Justice of the EU ultra vires; Judgment of 31 January 2012, Pl. ÚS 5/12, Slovak Pensions XVII', (2012) 8 EU Const 323.

Kumm, M. 'The jurisprudence of constitutional conflict: constitutional supremacy in Europe before and after the Constitutional Treaty' (2005) 11 ELJ 262.

Mehdi, R. 'French Supreme Courts and European Union law: between historical compromise and accepted loyalty' (2011) 48 CML Rev 439.

Olsen, H. P. 'The Danish Supreme Court's decision on the constitutionality of Denmark's ratification of the Lisbon Treaty' (2013) 50 CML Rev 1489.

Payandeh, M. 'Constitutional review of EU Law after Honeywell: contextualising the relationship between the German Constitutional Court and the EU Court of Justice' (2011) 48 CML Rev 9.

Roseren, P. 'The application of Community law by French courts from 1982 to 1993' (1994) 31 CML Rev 315.

Schmid, C. 'All bark and no bite: notes on the Federal Constitutional Court's "Banana Decision"' (2001) 7 ELJ 95.

Thomson, R. 'Same effects in different worlds: the transposition of EU Directives' (2009) 16(1) JEPP 1.

PART 2

PROCEDURAL ACTIONS, ENFORCEMENT, AND REMEDIES IN EU LAW

6 The preliminary ruling (Article 267 TFEU)

□ **LEARNING OBJECTIVES**

In this chapter, you will learn:

- about procedural law in the European Union legal order;
- which procedural actions were provided by the Treaty;
- which remedies were developed by the Court of Justice;
- about Article 267 TFEU—the procedure that allowed it to be developed;
- the details of Article 267 TFEU references; and
- the roles and relationship of the Court of Justice of the European Union and the national courts under Article 267 TFEU.

Introduction

This chapter and Chapters 7–9 are concerned with the procedural law of the European Union (EU) and how it is enforced, including the remedies available to ensure that EU law is upheld by the member states, by the Union institutions, or by legal and natural persons. The chapters include the actions provided by the Treaties, notably Articles 258–260, 267, 263, 265, and 340 of the Treaty on the Functioning of the European Union (TFEU) and the remedies developed by the Court of Justice of the European Union (CoJ), notably direct effects, indirect effects, and state liability.

This chapter also provides a natural link between Chapter 5 on supremacy and Chapter 8 dealing with direct effects and other remedies, as it concerns Article 267 TFEU, the vehicle that allowed the CoJ to introduce those remedies into the legal order.

The CoJ and the national courts are both involved in hearing cases in which EU law is pleaded and upheld. This position was made clear following the early intervention by the CoJ. It held that Community law was a matter not only for the member states and to be argued only before the CoJ, but also concerning individuals, giving them rights that they could argue before their own national courts. They did not have to rely on the Commission to enforce and argue Community law under the limited Treaty provisions for this, nor was Community law a matter reserved and to be heard before the CoJ only.

> ▶ **CROSS REFERENCE**
> Both elements of this dual vigilance will be considered in Chapters 7 and 8.

> The case that establishes this is **Case 26/62 _Van Gend en Loos_**: it is the leading case in EU law, which is considered in Chapter 8, section 8.1.3.1 and in other chapters.

> This development led to the phrase 'dual vigilance' being coined, which describes the situation whereby, on the one hand, the Commission ensures EU law enforcement procedures against the member states but also individuals, and, on the other hand, individuals are also empowered to pursue remedies for breaches of EU law by member states that affect their rights. Clearly, there being many more individuals in the EU than Commission officials, this increases the policing of EU law dramatically.

❯ CROSS REFERENCE

These aspects are considered in Chapter 8, section 8.4.

❯ CROSS REFERENCE

Enforcement actions are dealt with in Chapter 7; judicial developments are dealt with in Chapter 8; all of the other direct actions are considered in Chapter 9.

Central to this development is a procedural device that was included in the European Economic Community (EEC) Treaty in 1957, to facilitate both the even development of the Community and now EU legal system throughout all of the member states, and to provide a link between the CoJ and the national courts faced with EU law from time to time. This is Article 267 TFEU, which was the vehicle by which the leading principles and remedies in Community and EU law were developed by the CoJ, including direct effects in the _Van Gend_ case.

Consequently, additional means of contesting national laws were developed by the CoJ to provide remedies for individuals in circumstances in which direct effects did not exist. Of these, indirect effects and state liability are the most important. The system of remedies has developed so extensively that it has also made inroads into national procedural law because it had been witnessed how those national rules affect the equal application of EU law rights in the member states. Whilst the Treaty-provided remedies and actions precede the judicial developments of remedies, an understanding of the judicial developments is crucial; therefore, it is dealt with before we consider the direct actions before the CoJ, with the exception of the enforcement actions against the member states. The other direct actions include the judicial review of EU acts, the review of a failure to act, and the determination of liability of the institutions for damage caused by their acts.

6.1 Article 267 TFEU: the preliminary ruling procedure

Article 267 TFEU is the preliminary ruling or reference procedure, also referred to by the Article number (267 TFEU) by which the courts of the member states can refer questions to the CoJ on matters of EU law. A number of details of this procedure need to be considered to gain a true picture of how this works. The procedure provides the link or bridge between the national legal systems and the EU legal system. Under Article 267 TFEU, the courts of the member states may, or sometimes must, seek a ruling from the Court on the interpretation of all forms of EU law, including the Treaties and Protocols, international treaties, the Charter of Fundamental Rights, general principles, and even non-binding acts such as recommendations and opinions, and on the validity of all forms of EU secondary legislation and other acts, including judgments of the Court of Justice (see Case 135/77 _Bosch GmbH_ v _Hauptzollamt Hildesheim_).

> **Article 267 TFEU**
>
> The Court of Justice of the European Union shall have jurisdiction to give preliminary rulings concerning:
>
> (a) the interpretation of the Treaties;
>
> (b) the validity and interpretation of acts of the institutions, bodies, offices or agencies of the Union;
>
> . . .

Whilst the validity of the Treaties is clearly beyond the jurisdiction of the CoJ, it has nevertheless been considered in Case C-370/12 *Pringle*, whether under the Article 48 TEU, the simplified revision procedure was validly followed but without questioning the Treaty Article itself.

The main task of the CoJ is to interpret and rule on the validity of EU law so that a national court can reach a conclusion on a case involving EU law. The national courts' role in the process is to determine the facts of a case, to ask questions of the CoJ when they arise, and later, when the ruling of the Court has been sent back to the national court, to apply the ruling to the facts of the case. The Court should not concern itself with the application of the ruling that it has made or advise the national court how to apply the ruling. It is to be noted that, within the national courts, it is the right of the national court to decide whether to refer a question and not an individual right of appeal. The Lisbon Treaty has amended the previous version of Article 267 to make it clear that the Court can interpret all acts of not only the main institutions, but also all bodies, offices, and agencies of the Union. It has also extended the Court's jurisdiction to provide preliminary rulings for the 'Area of Freedom, Justice and Security', previously excluded under one of the Maastricht Treaty pillars, and international treaties agreed on the basis of a Treaty article. These references have been provided with an urgent procedure, which, along with the expedited procedure, are considered in section 6.1.6. Article 267 jurisdiction, though, is excluded from the 'Common and Security Policy' (Article 275 TFEU).

Article 267 TFEU has as its purpose the uniform interpretation and application of EU law in all of the member states and contributes to legal certainty by ensuring that EU law means the same thing in each and every member state—even more important now with a Union of 28 member states. It was designed to work with the cooperation of national courts by providing the means whereby national courts would not give their own interpretations to EU law or decide themselves on its validity. The intended relationship was of equality and cooperation, rather than hierarchy or an appeal system; therefore, the CoJ should provide only a guiding ruling and not direct the national courts. It provides for the sharing of jurisdiction over EU law between the Court and the national courts. The role of the national courts has, post Lisbon, been bolstered by the provision of Article 19(1) TFEU, which states that 'Member States shall provide remedies sufficient to ensure effective legal protection in the fields covered by Union law.'

> Article 267 TFEU (ex 177 EEC and 234 Economic Community (EC)) was the instrument that allowed the CoJ to develop the doctrines of direct effects and supremacy, vital for the development of the system of remedies that has been so helpful to individuals, for example in getting round the restrictions placed on them by the strict *locus standi* requirements of the direct actions, or where the Commission has been slow in ensuring that the member states comply with their obligations under the Treaty-provided enforcement procedure in Article 258 TFEU (ex 226 EC) (see the discussion in Chapter 7, 'Summary'). Article 267 references make up the bulk of the case law heard by the CoJ: 404 cases from 632 in total in 2012.

Having created such doctrines, the Court receives numerous questions specifically asking whether a particular provision has direct effects. At the end of this chapter, we also consider how the relationship has changed from one of equality of the CoJ and national courts to one which is now arguably looking more like a relationship of hierarchy, with the CoJ providing general rulings to be followed, not just being the referring court but all member states' courts.

 THINKING POINT

What other methods or procedures could be employed to ensure EU law remains uniform in all member states but which would reduce the additional time needed at present? (Note that an alternative will be considered at the end of the chapter.)

This section continues with the issue of which national bodies can make references that will be accepted by the Court.

6.1.1 Which bodies can refer?

The CoJ has accepted references from a varied number of bodies that are not courts in the strict sense, but which nevertheless decide legal issues based on EU law, including administrative tribunals, arbitration panels, and insurance officers.

For more details on this section visit the online resources.

The determination of what is an acceptable court or tribunal is a question for the CoJ and is not dependent on national concepts. Certain criteria have now been established by which it may reasonably be determined whether a particular body may refer to the Court for guidance under Article 267 TFEU.

> For example, it was clear from **Case 26/62 *Van Gend en Loos*** that not only judicial, but also administrative, tribunals were acceptable.

Whilst the majority of judicial or quasi-judicial bodies in the member states deciding legal matters pose no problem, it is those partially or entirely outside the state legal system that raise the question of whether they are suitable courts or tribunals for the purposes of Article 267 TFEU. The following cases have helped to define the scope of acceptable bodies.

> In **Case 61/65 *Vaassen***, a reference was received from the arbitration tribunal of a private mine employees social security fund. The Court held that because the powers to nominate members and to give approval to both the panel itself and rule changes were in the hands of a government minister and because the panel was a permanent body operating under national law and rules of procedure, it qualified as a court or tribunal in the eyes of Community law.

> **Case 246/80 *Broekmeulen* v *HRC*** concerned a reference made by the Appeal Committee of the Dutch Medical Professions Organization. This was held by the CoJ to be acceptable because it was approved and had the assistance and considerable involvement of the Dutch public authorities, its decisions were arrived at after full legal procedure, the decisions affected the right to work under Community law and were final, and there was no appeal to Dutch courts.

However, in the following cases, jurisdiction was refused.

In **Case 138/80 *Borker***, a reference from the Paris Bar Association Council on the right of a French lawyer to appear as of right before German courts was refused on the ground that there was no lawsuit in progress and the Bar Council was not therefore acting as a court or tribunal called upon to give judgment in proceedings intended to lead to a decision of a judicial nature.

In **Case 102/81 *Nordsee* v *Nordstern***, a reference from a privately appointed arbitration body was refused despite the fact that the arbitrator's decision based on law, including Community law, was binding. The CoJ held that because there was no involvement of national authorities in the process, there was not a sufficiently close link to national organisation of legal remedies and thus the arbitrator could not be regarded as a court or tribunal for the purposes of Article 234 EC (now 267 TFEU).

Jurisdiction was also refused in **Case C-24/92 *Corbiau* v *Administration des Contributions*** because a reference had been made from the office of the Director of Taxation, a body that acted in both an administrative and judicial capacity and thus lacked sufficient independence to be regarded as a court or tribunal for the purposes of Article 234 EC (now 267 TFEU).

Case C-54/96 *Dorsch* is particularly instructive because the CoJ took an opportunity to spell out the criteria to be taken into account in deciding whether the body is an acceptable one, including:

- whether the body is established by law;
- whether it is permanent;
- whether its jurisdiction is compulsory;
- whether its procedure is *inter partes* or, in other words, adversarial—that is, between two parties;
- whether it applies rules of law;
- whether it is independent; and
- whether the decision rendered is of a judicial nature.

More recently, in **Case C-53/03 *Syfait* v *GlaxoSmithKline***, a reference from a national competition authority was refused because of its close connection to the national executive and supervision by a government minister. The clear independence of the members of the authority was also questioned and the fact that, under Community competition law, the authority could be relieved of its competence to hear particular cases by the EU Commission. The case also summarised the criteria outlined above in *Dorsch*.

In view of this case law, it would seem that it is not critical to acceptance whether the body is private or there is no appeal from its decision. A strong indicator is the level of involvement by national authorities. Whether all of these criteria will be strictly applied in all cases in the future is uncertain because the lack of an appeal in a case may lead to instances in which the national body itself has to interpret EU law without guidance if the CoJ is unwilling to accept jurisdiction, something that must be less than desirable from a EU point of view.

▶ CROSS REFERENCE

The CoJ Article 267 preliminary rulings Guidelines (Official Journal (OJ) 2012 C338/01) can be found in Foster, *EU Treaties and Legislation*, Oxford University Press, Oxford, published annually.

6.1.2 Is the question relevant and admissible?

For more details on this section visit the online resources.

This section covers a number of connected issues all relating to whether or not the question raised by the member state body is one that is either relevant or an admissible question as far as the CoJ is concerned. To a degree, the response to some of the questions sent to the CoJ by member state courts has varied according to the increase in the case load of the Court. The content and form of the question must also be decided by the national court, and it is possible that this will also be considered by the CoJ.

Article 267 TFEU itself contains little guidance except to provide that if the member state court or tribunal considers that a decision on a question of EU law is necessary to enable it to give judgment, it may request a ruling from the CoJ. The relationship or partnership that is supposed to hallmark this procedure requires that, once requested, a ruling be given by the Court to complete the EU side of the procedure. Unfortunately, this is not always as clear-cut in practice and a question can arise as to who should really decide whether a preliminary ruling is necessary: the parties to the case, the national court, or the CoJ. According to the letter of the Article 267 TFEU procedure, it is for the national court to decide to refer a question. The drafters of the Treaty did not envisage this system as providing an individual remedy; however, in practice it is often regarded as the initiative of one of the parties to request that a reference be made, but it remains the case that ultimately the national court has the right to decide.

> In **Case C-344/04 *IATA***, the CoJ held that a national court is not obliged to refer a question of validity on the argument of one of the parties unless the court itself is sure that a good case for invalidity has been made and the answer to that question is necessary.

> This analysis continues to be the stated view of the CoJ as provided in **Case C-236/02 *J. Slob v Productschap Zuivel***, in which the Court held:
>
> > It should be stated at the outset that it is for the national court alone to determine the subject matter of the questions which it wishes to refer to the Court. The Court cannot, at the request of one party to the main proceedings, examine questions which have not been submitted to it by the national court.

The initial approach of the Court is described as 'come one, come all' and it was happy to correct even improperly framed references to accept them.

> For example, in **Case 16/65 *Schwarze v EVGF***, a court requested a ruling on the interpretation of Community law and the validity of national law in conflict. The CoJ concluded that the Court was concerned more with the validity of a Community act and it could therefore answer the question posed.

The CoJ has consistently refused to rule on the validity of national laws; however, it has often reformatted such questions in order to give an answer to the underlying reason for the reference, which is whether the EU law conflicts with the national law and which law should take priority. A further exception exists in respect of questions about national law, where the national law is directly and unconditionally based on or refers to EU law and is binding on the national court. See Cases C-297/88 and197/89 *Dzodzi*, noted also in section 6.1.2.3, and Case C-346/93 *Kleinwort Benson*, in which it was held that such references would be accepted provided the relationship between EU law and national law was direct and unconditional and the resulting law was binding on the national court.

Turning to further case law, the first of which cases should by now be familiar, according to the CoJ in **Case 26/62 _Van Gend en Loos_**, the finding by a national court that it needs to refer is not to be questioned by the CoJ.

This position was confirmed in **Case 6/64 _Costa v ENEL_**, in which the Court held that it is a decision of the national court alone to judge whether a decision on the question is necessary for it to give judgment.

Furthermore, in **Case 106/77 _Simmenthal_**, the Court declared that it was unable to review the facts of the case presented to it in the case—that is, it would not go behind the national decision. It also held in this case that, until a reference was withdrawn by the national court referring or if quashed by a national appeal court following an appeal against the order to refer, the CoJ would hear the case.

A slight complication of that position is **Case C-210/06 _Cartesio Oktató és Szolgáltató_**, which concerned an appeal against an order to refer from a court in Hungary. In this case, the CoJ held that it would continue to hear the case unless withdrawn by the court making the reference and not the appeal court. The Court acknowledged that the appeal procedure against the order was a matter of national law, but that the Court itself would not take direct cognisance of that appeal decision.

On the face of it, it appears that the CoJ is taking matters into its own hands; however, the judgment may be argued to be more in line with its previous stated positions, in that the Court will not go behind national decisions or procedures and will only react to the national court making the reference in the first place. The latter position is probably the correct one.

However, as the number of cases and backlog increased in the 1980s and 1990s, the CoJ was seen to be less willing to accept all references and has, from time to time, declined to give a ruling on questions referred to it on the grounds that no real question arises or that such references are an abuse or misuse of Article 267 TFEU. This is not to say that it has operated a crude quota to cut down references, because the number of cases that were regarded as irrelevant or inadmissible is actually minimal.

6.1.2.1 Rejected references: relevance, clarity, and basic information

Certain cases have, nevertheless, been rejected by the CoJ, such as those lacking basic information needed for the Court to decide, or in which information is not clearly conveyed to the Court.

In **Case 93/78 _Mattheus_**, the continuation of a disputed contract was determinable by the entry of Spain, Portugal, and Greece to the Community. When a reference was made to help to resolve the disputed contract, the CoJ held this to be a matter to be determined by the member states and the potential new states, and refused jurisdiction. The question raised must be one that is justiciable before the courts and, indeed, one raised by a national court and not as a result of a contract between private parties.

In **Case C-320/90** *Telemarsicabruzzo SpA*, the CoJ held that facts and issues must be sufficiently clearly defined. The reference, as with similar cases, was so poorly or inadequately formed or with such information lacking that the Court was unable to determine exactly either what were the questions or what was the dispute to which an answer would be helpful, or how any possible answer would help.

In **Case C-83/91** *Meilicke* v *ADV/OGA*, the Court held that the questions raised could not be answered by reference to the limited information provided in the file, so that the Court would be exceeding its jurisdiction in answering what was really a hypothetical question as it was posed by a Company law lecturer to test for academic purposes the compatibility of national law with EU law.

According to the CoJ Article 267 preliminary rulings' Guidelines (2012), the CoJ's view is that it is up to the member states' courts to determine whether a ruling is needed, and that the CoJ should answer such questions, however formed. References generally, however, should be clear and succinct, but sufficiently complete to give the Court a clear understanding of the factual and legal context of the main proceedings. National courts should explain why an interpretation is necessary in their view to enable them to give judgment (see points 20–28 of the Guidelines, and in particular point 22). After another change to the Rules of Procedure, the Court may now, after hearing from the Advocate-General (AG), seek clarification from the referring court if the question or issue is unclear (Article 101 of the 201 Rules of Procedure and points 20–28 of the 2012 guidelines).

6.1.2.2 **No genuine dispute or an abuse of the procedure**

There are two cases of special importance arising from the same sets of facts and underlying problem.

Case 104/79 *Foglia* v *Novello (No. 1)* concerned a contract for the purchase of wine between a French buyer, Novello, and the Italian supplier, Foglia. Clauses stipulated that the buyer and the carrier (Danzas) should not be responsible for any French import duties that were contrary to Community law. These were, however, charged on the French border and subsequently reimbursed by Foglia. Foglia sought to recover from Mrs Novello, who denied responsibility to pay Foglia on the basis that the duties were illegally charged by the French authorities. The Italian judge made a reference to the CoJ asking whether the French tax was compatible with the Treaty. The Court rejected the reference on the grounds that there was no genuine dispute between the parties and that the action had simply been concocted to challenge French legislation. The Court considered this to be an abuse of the Article 234 EC (now 267 TFEU) procedure, particularly as there were remedies available to dispute the tax before the French courts. However, not satisfied by this, the Italian judge made a further reference.

In **Case 244/80** *Foglia* v *Novello (No. 2)*, the Italian judge specifically pointed out that the previous case marked a radical change in the attitude of the CoJ to a national court's decision to refer. He asked the CoJ to give guidelines on the respective powers and functions of the Court and the referring court. The CoJ held that its role was not to give abstract or advisory opinions under Article 234 EC (now 267 TFEU), but to contribute to actual decisions, and that although discretion is given to the national courts, the limits of that discretion are determinable only by reference to Community law.

THINKING POINT

How does this conform with the previous statement that it is up to the national court to decide?

Whilst the *Foglia* case may be regarded as a rarity, it is not alone.

In **Case C-318/00 *Bacardi-Martini* v *Newcastle United***, a French law prohibiting the advertising of alcohol was at the centre of a dispute between Newcastle United FC and the advert-
isers, whose products had been advertised at the home game of Newcastle and unlawfully
broadcast in France. The CoJ dismissed the reference after seeking clarification from the English
High Court as to why Community law would have a bearing on the case in which the law of
another member state law was in question (alcohol advertising in France), but to which case
English law was actually applicable. The Court concluded that it did not have sufficient material
to make a ruling.

A refusal of jurisdiction on the grounds of it being an abuse of the procedure occurred also in
Case C-188/92 *TWD Textilwerke*. A Commission decision addressed to Germany was not
challenged within the two-month time limit under Article 230 EC (now 263 TFEU), but instead
via the national court. The CoJ held this to be an abuse of the procedure for not acting within
the time limit provided under (now) Article 263 TFEU for a direct challenge to Community law
before the Court.

> **CROSS REFERENCE**
>
> This is considered further in
> Chapter 9, section 9.1.12.1.

The decision appears to have been reached in contradiction to the perceived promotion of Article
267 TFEU as a vehicle for realising individual rights in the face of the continued strict application of
locus standi requirements under Article 263 TFEU (ex 230 EC).

The decision to refer is now assisted by the provision of the CoJ Article 267 preliminary rulings'
Guidelines (2012).

An order for a reference should include:

- a statement of the facts essential to a full understanding of the legal significance of the main
  proceedings;
- an exposition of the applicable national law;
- a statement of reasons for the reference; and
- a summary of the main arguments of the parties.

6.1.2.3 **Acceptances nevertheless**

The decision in *Foglia* v *Novello* has been cited as authority to the CoJ in subsequent cases as an
argument that the Court should not hear the case.

In **Case 46/80 *Vinal* v *Orbat***, which involved Italian law in Italy, the government claimed that the
case was not admissible because it was just an excuse to challenge national law under Article 234
EC (now 267 TFEU). The CoJ, after obtaining further information from the parties and assuring
itself that there was a genuine underlying dispute, accepted the reference. In **Case C-412/93
Leclerc-Siplec,** the Court accepted a reference, despite the fact that it was clear that the parties
had concocted a dispute, because the reference was to challenge French law in a French court.

The distinction between the cases was that, in the latter cases, it was the national law of the case that was questioned and not the law of another member state, although the CoJ is also concerned with whether the dispute giving rise to the reference is genuine, but not necessarily rejecting a reference if it is not. However, the combinations of a concocted dispute and the law of another member state would appear to be fatal.

> In **Case 14/86 *Pretore di Salo* v *X***, there were no actual proceedings between two parties (that is, the case was not *inter partes*), something regarded previously as one of the criteria needed to be classed as a court for the purposes of Article 234 EC (now 267 TFEU). The case involved investigative proceedings of an Italian magistrate to determine whether a criminal offence had been committed by a person or persons unknown in the case, in which a river had been found seriously polluted. Nevertheless, when a question of a possible breach of Community law was referred to the Court by the magistrate, it was held to be admissible. The Court held that it was up to the national court to decide if a reference was necessary to help it. If there had been a breach of EU law, it was worth pursuing the matter further; if not, there would be no case to answer.

> In **Cases C-297/88 and 197/89 *Dzodzi* v *Belgium*** and **C-28/95 *Leur-Bloem***, the CoJ ruled in what were essentially purely internal matters involving the application of free movement of persons rules to nationals undertaking no cross-border movement, where the national decision was based on Community law. The Court considered that if it did not do so, Community law might be interpreted differently in the member states applying it in an internal situation; therefore, for the sake of uniformity, the reference was accepted.

> Additionally, in **Case C-150/88 *Eau de Cologne* v *Provide*** in a contractual payment dispute heard before a German court, an Italian law, which was the root of the problem, was brought into question. The reference from the German court was accepted by the CoJ as it was able to distinguish the case from the earlier *Foglia* litigation. It held that the case involved a genuine dispute, therefore putting aside that particular concern.

6.1.3 The question referred: an overall view

Although these cases, and others like them, would appear to be contradictory, the case of *Foglia* v *Novello* must be viewed on its own merits. These were that the CoJ did not wish to encourage national courts to challenge the validity of the laws of other member states, especially when there existed the possibility of proceedings in the French courts to challenge the French law and from which an Article 234 EC (now 267 TFEU) reference could be launched if deemed necessary by the French judge. It may be summarised that the Court may decline to take a case under Article 267 TFEU in a number of situations, including those in which:

* the question referred is hypothetical;
* the question is not relevant to the substance of the dispute;
* the question is not sufficiently clear for any meaningful legal response; and
* the facts are insufficiently clear for the application of the legal rules.

The cases highlight that the combination of involving non-national law with a contrived dispute will almost certainly be fatal to the chances of the reference, whereas this is not necessarily the case where only one of those factors exists.

The cooperation between national courts and the CoJ still exists, but the Court no longer simply accepts anything put before it. It has begun to exercise more positive control over its own jurisdiction in a similar manner to superior national courts. This approach is reflected in the case law arising from Article 234(2) and (3) EC (now 267 TFEU).

CROSS REFERENCE

Considered in sections 6.1.6 and 6.1.7.

6.1.4 A discretion or an obligation to refer?

Whether there is a discretion or an obligation to refer a question, once raised, depends first on which sentence of Article 267 TFEU applies. Article 267(2) TFEU states that any court may refer if it considers it necessary to reach a decision in the case, whereas Article 267(3) states that courts against the decision of which there is no judicial remedy shall bring the matter before the CoJ.

Article 267(2) and (3) TFEU

(2) Where such a question is raised before any court or tribunal of a Member State, that court or tribunal may, if it considers that a decision on the question is necessary to enable it to give judgment, request the Court to give a ruling thereon.

(3) Where any such question is raised in a case pending before a court or tribunal of a Member State against whose decisions there is no judicial remedy under national law, that court or tribunal shall bring the matter before the Court.

6.1.5 The discretion of lower courts

Courts falling within Article 267(2) TFEU are not obliged to refer, but have a wide discretion to refer at any stage of the proceedings and in any sort of proceedings: see, for example, Cases 13/61 *De Geus* v *Bosch* and 29–30/62 *Da Costa en Schaake*. Part of the reasoning for this rule is that an aggrieved party can appeal to a higher court if a reference is not made.

CROSS REFERENCE

The further effects that the Article 267 TFEU procedure and rulings have had on national procedural law will be considered further in Chapter 8, section 8.4.

In **Cases 146** and **166/73 *Rheinmühlen-Düsseldorf***, the CoJ made it clear that any national court that considers that a ruling on EU law will help it to decide an issue has the discretion to decide regardless of any national rules of precedent or referral.

This was confirmed by the CoJ in **Case C-312/93 *Peterbroeck Van Campenhout* v *Belgium***, in which the Court held that a national procedural rule, which prevented a national court from raising a matter of EC law of its own motion concerning the compatibility of a national law with EC law, was itself contrary to Community law and that national courts must set aside rules of national law preventing the Article 234 EC (now 267 TFEU) procedure from being followed.

Case C-213/89 *Factortame (No. 1)* also confirms that national law rules of any status must not prevent EU law from applying. In the case itself, a constitutional doctrine was involved. This case was considered in full in Chapter 5, section 5.1.1.

6.1.6 The timing of the reference

In principle, national courts can refer at any stage of the proceedings and in any type of proceedings, as has already been noted in Cases 13/61 *De Geus*, 93/78 *Mattheus* v *Doego*, and 14/86 *Pretore di Salo*.

For more details on this section visit the online resources.

> In **Cases 36/80 and 76/80 *Irish Creamery Milk Suppliers*,** the CoJ advised that the optimum time of a reference would be when facts have been established and any questions involving national law only had been settled.

The CoJ has also provided extrajudicial guidelines about when a reference should be made, if considered necessary. The CoJ Article 267 preliminary rulings' Guidelines, points 18 and 19 suggest that this is up to the national court, but also recommends that the facts and legal context should be established and both parties' views heard before the reference is sent.

> ### CoJ Article 267 preliminary rulings' Guidelines (2012), point 19
>
> It is, however, desirable that a decision to seek a preliminary ruling should be taken when the proceedings have reached a stage at which the national court is able to define the factual and legal context of the question, so that the Court has available to it all the information necessary to check, where appropriate, that European Union law applies to the main proceedings.

Allied to the topic of the timing of the reference are two special procedures, which have been developed by the CoJ to amend the Article 267 procedure in special circumstances. These are the accelerated or expedited procedure and the urgent procedure, which are provided for under Article 23a of the Protocol on the Statute of the Court of Justice and detailed further in Articles 105–106 and 107–114, respectively, in the Rules of Procedure of the Court of Justice.

Under the expedited or accelerated procedure, a national court may request that this procedure be utilised where it is a matter of exceptional urgency and the case will be listed immediately, giving the parties 15 days to submit observations. The President of the Court will decide on a proposal from the Judge Rapporteur, after hearing the AG. From its introduction in 2008–2012, 25 applications were refused, but in the same period, eight were granted. These cases were heard between two and four months from application.

The urgent preliminary ruling procedure relates specifically to the areas of freedom, security, and justice (now Title V TFEU) and was introduced to deal quickly with cases involving the detention of persons.

> The details of the urgent procedure are now set out in Articles 107–114 TFEU and Decision 2008/79. For further information on these procedures, refer also to the latest (2012) Annual Report of the Court of Justice.

In this route, the written procedure can be omitted or undertaken electronically. From 2008 to 2012, eight were rejected and 16 were heard, with a length of proceedings of between 1.9 and 2.5 months. Whilst it is useful to know that these procedures exist, it is unlikely that you will need to know the details.

None of this impinges on the ultimate discretion of national courts provided by Article 267 TFEU to decide when to refer and which criteria are necessary to decide this question.

6.1.7 **Courts of last instance**

In this category, an initial problem exists in deciding which courts are courts of last instance for the purpose of Article 267(3) TFEU. The case law of the CoJ advises that the relevant court is the highest court for the case, rather than the highest court in the member state.

In **Case 6/64 Costa v ENEL**, there was no right of appeal from the Italian magistrates' court because the sum of money involved was so small. The CoJ held that national courts, against the decisions of which there is no judicial remedy, must refer a question of Community law to the Court.

CROSS REFERENCE

This case was also considered under the discussion of supremacy in Chapter 5, section 5.1.1.

In most instances, this is an adequate answer and Article 267(3) TFEU should apply to those proceedings that deny an appeal or judicial review and thus become last instance. However, the situation in member states may not be so easy to determine: for example, in the UK, the Court of Appeal and the House of Lords Appeal Committee (now the UK Supreme Court) can refuse leave to appeal in a case that has been decided by the Court of Appeal. This has the result that the lower of the two courts then becomes the court of last instance and results in a denial of the consideration of EU law to an applicant because the case itself has closed, cannot be reopened, and cannot then be referred.

This happened in **Magnavision v General Optical Council (No. 2)**, in which the issue of Community law was raised in the first case under this name, but was neither considered nor referred, nor was an appeal to the House of Lords allowed. The applicant then applied to the High Court, stating that the previous refusal meant that the High Court became the court of last instance for the purposes of Article 234. This application was also refused on the grounds that the case had been closed and the High Court refused to refer this question to the CoJ, thus denying a consideration of Community law points.

The same situation occurred when the Court of Appeal and the House of Lords refused leave to appeal in **Chiron Corporation v Murex Diagnostics Ltd (No. 8)**, which meant that the Court of Appeal became the last-instance court. Once again, it was too late for a reference to be lodged because the case had been decided, and appeals can be lodged and considered only once the case has finished—a point expressly acknowledged by the House of Lords Appeal Committee in the case.

Note now the reformed court structure in the UK.

The CoJ had also recognised this problem in the Swedish **Case 99/00 Criminal Proceedings against Lyckeskög**. It suggested that, in such circumstances, the Supreme Court considering the appeal should consider whether a reference might be necessary and thus be sympathetic to the application to seek leave to appeal.

In order to both overcome the unfortunate earlier UK position and to take account of the *Lyckeskög* case, a change of the appeal procedure was deemed necessary in the UK and was put into place.

6.1.8 Avoiding the obligation to refer: the development of precedent and *acte clair*

Whilst Article 267(3) TFEU provides the general rule that final courts must refer, over the years the large increase in cases referred to the CoJ led to a closer consideration by the Court as to the appropriateness of a reference. In two cases, spanning a period of 20 years, the Court has outlined the

For more details on this section visit the online resources.

circumstances in which it is not necessary to make a reference. This has arguably introduced a form of precedent to the EU legal order and may have brought about changes to the relationship between the national courts and the CoJ. The Court has held that it is no longer necessary to make a reference where the provision in question has already been interpreted by the Court or the correct application is so obvious as to leave no scope for any reasonable doubt. In the latter case, the view is that no question of EU law arises to be decided; hence, there is no need to refer.

6.1.8.1 Previous ruling on the point

> **Cases 28–32/62 *Da Costa*** raised the same question as had previously been asked in *Van Gend en Loos*. The CoJ referred to its previous judgment in the *Van Gend* case as the basis for deciding the issue and advised that a materially identical question would, if the national court wished, excuse the obligation to refer.

> See also point 12 of the CoJ Article 267 preliminary rulings' Guidelines, which states the same. For example, in 2012, 36 cases were ordered to be removed from the Register. See also Article 99 of the CoJ Rules of Procedure, which makes the same point.

6.1.8.2 The answer is obvious (*acte clair*)

The judgment of the CoJ in Case 283/81 *CILFIT* extended the decision in *Da Costa*.

> In **Case 283/81 *CILFIT***, the Italian Supreme Court, from which there was no appeal, asked the CoJ directly in what circumstances it need not refer. The Court replied that, in addition to the reason given in *Da Costa*, a court may not refer if the correct application, but not interpretation, may be so obvious as to leave no scope for any reasonable doubt that the question raised will be solved.

This has introduced into the EU legal system a variation of the French law doctrine of *acte clair* by which a lower court need not refer a case to a higher court if it thinks that the application of law is obvious. In the EU context, this means that a national court need not make a reference if it considers the answer to the question on EU law to be obvious. That, however, is not an entirely accurate representation of the judgment in *CILFIT*, which is more restrictive than a straightforward application of *acte clair*. The CoJ qualified it by stating that the national court must be convinced that the matter is equally obvious to courts of other member states, that it is sure that language differences will not result in inconsistent decisions in member states, and that EU law must be applied in light of the application of it as a whole with regard to the objectives of the EU. These criteria would be extremely difficult, if not actually impossible, to fulfil if followed to the letter, especially in a Union now made up of 28 (27) member states. The judgment was, however, arguably provided so as to maintain an appearance of the bridge of equality between EU and national legal systems but, it has been suggested, the conditions were subsequently eased in, for example, Case C-160/14 *Da Silva* v *Brito*.

> **THINKING POINT**
>
> What skills or abilities would a national court or judge have to possess if that was a strict requirement?

The CoJ Article 267 preliminary rulings' Guidelines, in point 12, are clear in describing the CoJ's policy as *acte clair*, although not expressly, and its required restrictive interpretation remains, albeit in the background.

 THINKING POINT

What, though, are the dangers of too liberal an interpretation of the *acte clair* principle?

Note: this is considered following.

6.1.8.3 Questions of validity

A question of the validity of secondary EU law must be referred to the CoJ by courts of last instance. Primary law such as the Treaty, Protocols, and the EU Charter of Fundamental Rights cannot be questioned under Article 267 TFEU.

> In **Case 314/85 *Firma Foto-Frost* v *Hauptzollamt Lübeck-Ost***, the CoJ held that national courts could not decide for themselves that Community law provisions were invalid because of the danger that otherwise uniform Community laws would be declared invalid in some member states but not in others.

If this question were to be raised and an answer not possible from previous judgments, national courts would be obliged to refer the question to the CoJ. If an appeal is still possible under national rules, this could still be done as an alternative.

> This has been written into the CoJ Article 267 preliminary rulings' Guidelines, points 15–17.

> However, in **Case 66/80 *ICC***, which involved the questioning of a Community provision that had already been declared invalid by the CoJ in a previous case, the Court makes it patently clear that although such a judgment is addressed primarily to the court that requests the original ruling, it can and should be relied on by other national courts before which the matter arises, thus obviating a need to refer the same question again.

> More recently, the point has been confirmed in **Case C-461/03 *Schul*** that only the CoJ has the authority to declare Community law to be invalid and further, in **Case C-344/04 *IATA***, that a national court is not obliged to refer a question of validity on the argument of one of the parties unless the court itself is sure that a good case for invalidity has been made.

6.1.8.4 Avoiding references by the national courts

To some extent, the fears that *acte clair* will be abused to avoid making references by national courts has been realised in some cases that have come to light.

> In ***R* v *London Boroughs' Transport Committee***, decided in 1992, the House of Lords refused to refer a question to the CoJ, claiming that the EC law was obvious, which, on the facts, appeared arguable.

In 1998, a Greek court, the Council of State, itself interpreted EC law (then Article 126(1)) in the case of **Katsarou v Greek State** against the interests of an applicant seeking mutual recognition of qualifications. As far as the Greek court was concerned, the EC was regarded as *acte clair*, thus removing any obligation to refer.

In **Case C-62/00 Marks & Spencer plc**, the Court of Appeal in the UK considered that individuals could rely on the direct effect of sufficiently precise and unconditional Community law provisions only if, and in so far as, the provision had not been properly implemented in national law. If a Directive had been properly implemented, as in this case, but perhaps applied not in the way intended by the Directive, the Directive could not be relied on. However, the CoJ held that it would be inconsistent with the legal order of the Community if individuals were able to rely on a Directive that had been incorrectly implemented, but not able to rely on it where the national authorities applied the implementing legislation in a way that was incompatible with the Directive.

These cases appear to result in injustice to the litigants affected, and even at best remove the possibility of getting a ruling from the CoJ. This denial of rights may be the price to be paid now for having a more flexible arrangement under Article 267 TFEU.

Attempts to obtain a remedy where a reference was denied have, thus far, not been successful.

In Austria, in **Case C-224/01 Köbler**, the Austrian Supreme Administrative Court had decided a point of Community law itself relating to the recognition of time spent and experience gained in another member state. The Austrian court claimed it to be clear after withdrawing a reference to the CoJ seeking a ruling on the same point. The applicant in the case then sought damages from the Austrian state for the loss that he had suffered as a result of the decision in the first case, which he claimed to be contrary to Community law. On a reference in the second case, the CoJ held that Community law at that point was not clear and that the Austrian court was not entitled to take the view that the matter was clear. However, the Austrian court's infringement for the purposes of the state liability action was not sufficiently serious for the CoJ, and Köbler lost his claim. However, the Court did make it clear that a state could be held liable for an incorrect judgment where the breach was sufficiently serious, and stated that the Austrian court, from which there was no appeal, should have made a reference and applied it. Generally, the Court held that courts of last instance must make references in order to prevent rights conferred on the individual by Community and now EU law being infringed.

As such, the judgment may represent a refinement of the *acte clair* principle in the EU legal order by removing its availability to courts of last instance. Confirmation of this is needed, however, from the CoJ before this can be stated with certainty.

The final case in this section appears to represent some further movement in favour of aggrieved applicants.

> **CROSS REFERENCE**
>
> An action against a member state for a breach of Community law is also considered under *Francovich* state liability in Chapter 8, section 8.3.

In **Case C-173/03 Traghetti del Mediterraneo SpA v Italy**, it was alleged that a company had been forced into liquidation as a result of the errors in the interpretation of Community law by the Supreme Court in Italy. Furthermore, the chance to correct those errors was denied by that court, which did not make a reference to the CoJ. In a further action by the administrator of the company, the CoJ held that it could not rule out that 'manifest errors' by a national court would lead to compensation under the principle of state liability. However, it was up to the national courts to decide in each case.

The consequence of this slight extension of liability is that liability for damage caused by courts is not limited as in *Köbler* to 'intentional fault and serious misconduct' in cases in which that standard would have excluded liability for 'manifest infringement'. In other words, it extends liability to where national courts have manifestly infringed the law in their interpretation, thus causing damage, but as yet no applicant has succeeded in obtaining damages in these circumstances.

An alternative corrective action against a court of last instance whose error in interpretation and/or failure to refer to the CoJ would be an enforcement action by the Commission under Article 258 TFEU, as occurred in Case C-154/08 *Commission* v *Spain* (see Chapter 7, section 7.1.3).

6.2 The effect of an Article 267 TFEU ruling

6.2.1 The effect on the Court of Justice

In strict terms, in the absence of a system of binding precedent in the EU legal order, a ruling by the CoJ is binding and effective in that case only and there is no further binding effect on the Court. However, although it is not restrained by any doctrine of precedent, the Court tends to follow previous decisions to maintain consistency and will cite previous judgments or parts of a judgment as a basis for a current decision.

For more details on this section visit the online resources.

In this way, a development and build-up of legal principles as in common law countries takes place. In other circumstances, the Court has been known to overrule previous decisions without much commotion when it feels that the situation warrants it.

> In Article 340 TFEU (ex 288 EC) actions for damages, see **Case 25/62 *Plaumann*** and the later overruling **Case 4/69 *Lütticke***, which decided that an Article 288 EC (now 340 TFEU) action could be mounted as an independent action and not only if preceded by an Article 230 EC (now 263 TFEU) action to annul (see Chapter 9, section 9.1.9). The *Plaumann* case was later confirmed as good precedent in **Cases C-50/00 *UPA*** and **C-263/02 P *Commission* v *Jego-Quere***.

The CoJ, however, has appeared to move in the direction of setting up a system that certainly starts to resemble a system of precedent.

6.2.2 The effect on the national courts

An Article 267 ruling is a mandatory judgment and not an advisory opinion. It was held in Cases 28–30/62 *Da Costa* and later in Case 69/85 *Wünsche* to be fully binding on the national court. A ruling of the CoJ is to be treated in each member state according to how its own system of law regards authoritative judgments. As far as the UK is concerned, national courts are bound under Treaty obligations to apply the ruling received from the CoJ to the facts of the case and, where that national court is the Supreme Court, the ruling is consequentially binding on all lower courts: see Case 12/81 *Garland* v *BREL*.

The CoJ Article 267 preliminary rulings' Guidelines, point 35, provide that the CoJ wishes to see that its judgment has been applied in the national proceedings and, to that end, it must be sent a copy of the national court's final decision.

From the UK, there is now an informative case in which the national court judge refused to apply the ruling of the CoJ because he considered the Court to have rendered an unacceptable ruling in making findings of fact in a case concerned with trade mark infringement of football merchandise. However, **Case C-206/01 *Arsenal FC v Matthew Reed*** was overruled on appeal by the Court of Appeal and the ruling of the CoJ was applied conscientiously.

❱ CROSS REFERENCE

Both of these rulings will be considered in further detail in Chapter 14.

There have been times when the CoJ has limited the temporal effect of a judgment, which under normal circumstances would reach back retroactively to the entry into force of the particular provision (see Case 61/79 *Denkavit*). In relation to Treaty provisions this could be back to 1 January 1958. Therefore, in circumstances where the result of a judgment would have given rise to previously unforeseen, extensive, and probably harmful economic consequences, the CoJ has limited the temporal effect.

For example, in **Cases 43/75 *Defrenne (No. 2)*** and **C-262/88 *Barber***, the judgments were held not to be retroactive, but only effective from the date of judgment or for claims already commenced, because they would unexpectedly have imposed on employers potentially substantial pay-outs for numerous backdated claims based on the rulings.

The CoJ, in **Case 66/80 *ICC***, held that although a declaration of invalidity was directly addressed to the referring court only, it was sufficient reason for another court to regard the declaration as generally binding; however, the discretion to refer remains.

In **Case C-453/00 *Kühne and Heitz***, the Court stated that the demands of one of the general principles of Community law, namely legal certainty, which would normally mean that final decisions reached should not be reopened, could be relaxed because of the obligation of all state authorities to apply interpretative rulings of the Court from preliminary rulings in their activities, providing the rights of third parties were not compromised.

Whilst not expressly stated, clearly included in this are the national courts, which, of course, have so much to do with the application of EU law in their activities.

6.3 Interim measures within an Article 267 TFEU reference

Interim measures may also be highly relevant to EU law questions that are the subject of a reference to the CoJ, particularly as a reference may take on average some 17 months. In that time, the lack of relief may lead to great damage and in many cases the insolvency of the companies involved. Whilst the Treaty has not directly provided interim measures, as is the case with Article 263 TFEU actions for annulment and Articles 278 and 279 TFEU, the availability of interim measures for Article 267 TFEU preliminary rulings has nevertheless been developed through case law.

The clearest and leading case on this is **C-213/89** *Factortame*, in which the CoJ held that, regardless of national rules on whether interim relief should be granted, if rights under Community law were at stake pending a ruling on a reference on the substantive question, then interim relief should be granted.

Cases **C-143/88 and 92/89** *Zuckerfabrik Süderdithmarschen AG* involved the possibility of granting interim relief in a preliminary ruling on the validity of a Community law provision. The CoJ took the opportunity to provide guidelines for the national courts along the lines of those developed already by the Court under its Article 243 EC (now 279 TFEU) interim measures' jurisdiction in direct actions. It held that relief should be granted only provided that there was sufficient evidence before the Court that serious doubts existed about the validity of the Community law in question, the case was urgent, and relief was necessary to avoid serious and irreparable damage.

The grant of interim relief was extended to positive, rather than only suspensory, measures in **Case C-465/93** *Atlanta Fruchthandelsgesellschaft*, which concerned whether a licence to import bananas should be granted whilst awaiting the ruling on whether a Community Act regulating the banana market was valid. The CoJ held that national courts could do this provided that they did so in the light of existing Community case law, the Community interest in the matter, the consequences for the Community regime, and the effect on all interested parties.

Hence, from the case law a common interim measures rule has been established that is nevertheless subject to national legal procedure where necessary, but only to the extent that the EU law right is not endangered.

> **CROSS REFERENCE**
> The effect on national procedural law is considered in further detail in Chapter 8, section 8.4.

6.4 The evolution of Article 267 TFEU references

Article 267 TFEU has allowed the CoJ to develop a system of individual remedies because cases referred from the national courts are those predominantly brought by individuals whose rights have been infringed by the member state authorities. The remedies developed include direct effects, indirect effects, and state liability, which can be secured in the member states' courts so that subsequent cases need not be referred to the CoJ. The increase in cases and growing case backlog is argued to have led to a change in attitude on the part of the Court and it is now less willing to accept all references without question. It has, in a limited number of cases, provided the national courts with the grounds for not making a reference when, under a strict reading of the Treaty, a reference would be required. As a result of the development of this system of remedies and judicial devices to avoid references, a form of precedent (the *Da Costa* case) appears to have been introduced. This means that a CoJ ruling now has a far more general importance than only for the parties in a single case and appears to have placed the Court at the apex of the systems of national courts.

Inevitably, this also appears to have changed the nature of the relationship from a symbiotic or horizontal one more to a vertical or hierarchical one, although some might describe the original understanding of a relationship of equals and cooperation as somewhat illusory. These developments have given rise to what can be described as a form of conscious, or deliberate, sectoral delegation of responsibility over EU law to the national courts. The national courts then become enforcers of EU law in their own right in cases in which there exists a CoJ precedent on which to rely. Hence, a more hierarchical relationship than was ever intended by the drafters of the Treaty or the member states has ensued. This view is supported by the change to the Court's Rules of Procedure (Article 99), which allows the Court to return cases with a reasoned order where a question is identical to a question on which the Court has already ruled, where the answer to such a question may be clearly deduced from existing case law, or where the answer to the question is not open to reasonable doubt. It sends a clear signal to the national courts that they too could have reached the same conclusion, thus strengthening further the evolution of the Article 267 TFEU procedure. A part of this evolution is the *acte clair* development, although this has caused some concern, especially when it is abused by member state courts, which results in injustice to individuals who are denied their EU law rights. The *Köbler* and *Traghetti del Mediterraneo* cases appear to narrow the scope for the application of the doctrine to last-instance courts.

6.5 Reforms and future

In the context of the growing numbers of references, many reforms have been considered and changes suggested. Apart from those most recently made (including the foregoing case law changes), which include the expansion of the General Court (formerly the Court of First Instance) jurisdiction to include Article 267 TFEU references under Article 256 TFEU and the ability to set up specialised courts (formerly judicial panels) under Article 257 TFEU, further suggestions for reform include:

(a) limiting the national courts able to make a reference by removing the right of first-instance courts to refer;

(b) only allowing novel or complex cases—that is, those involving new questions of law;

(c) permitting national courts to make suggestions as to the answer;

(d) permitting national courts to decide themselves subject to an appeal to the CoJ; and

(e) setting up regional EU courts, again with an appeal to the CoJ.

The last two suggestions represent a much more radical shake-up of the system and seem very unlikely in the short-to-medium term, especially in the light of the fact that, during the development of the Lisbon Treaty, there was a clear opportunity to change things radically, which it did not do. Note also that the ability to transfer jurisdiction for Article 267 references in particular areas to the General Court has not yet been taken up. The 2015 reform of the General Court, which primarily was one to double the number of judges over two years, did not include any change to this.

The Lisbon Treaty made a limited amendment to Article 267 worth noting here. A new paragraph is included:

If such a question is raised in a case pending before a court or tribunal of a member state with regard to a person in custody, the Court of Justice of the European Union shall act with the minimum of delay.

This gives Treaty status to the CoJ Article 267 preliminary rulings' Guidelines, and the urgent reference procedure (see section 6.1.6).

↻ Summary

Article 267 TFEU is a simple but effective device that fulfils a number of tasks. It provided the link between the CoJ and the national courts so that they could each play their own roles and cooperate to ensure the uniform interpretation and application of EU law throughout the Union. For the most part, each has stuck to its own role and the link has worked very well. From time to time, but actually very rarely, there has been some overstepping of the mark, such as national courts not doing as they should, as in the *Köbler* or *Arsenal* v *Matthew Reed* cases, or arguably the CoJ in *Foglia* v *Novello*. As was stressed a number of times, because Article 267 TFEU (ex 234 EC) provided the CoJ with many references from the national courts, it was able to develop remedies that the Treaties did not and has thus enhanced greatly the shape of the EU legal system, which is considered in Chapter 8.

Over the years, cases have built up examples of best practice and these have been drawn together in the CoJ Article 267 preliminary rulings' Guidelines.

Finally, the nature of the reference procedure has changed from one clearly between equals to one that now provides a form of precedence, which must mean that the CoJ has taken on something of the role of a higher legal authority. It may also be that when the Union was established, the Court was only one among seven highest courts; now, it is one amongst 29 and, for that, stands out much more than before. Presently, there are no further plans formally to change radically either Article 267 TFEU or the workings of it, so the slow development that has been observed is likely to continue.

For suggested approaches to answering these questions visit the online resources.

? Questions

1. What are the benefits of the Article 267 TFEU preliminary ruling procedure for the development of EU law?

2. Is there a restriction on the bodies that may refer under Article 267 TFEU?

3. In what way, if at all, has the use of Article 267 TFEU led to a system of 'precedence' being developed in the EU legal order?

4. Can you define the circumstances in which the CoJ would refuse to accept a reference under the Article 267 TFEU preliminary ruling procedure?

For guidance on how to tackle this specimen exam question and to read a suggested model answer, visit the online resources. www.oup.com/uk/foster_directions6e/.

▢ Sample exam Q&A

Essay question

Define the circumstances in which the Court of Justice would refuse to accept a reference under the Article 267 TFEU preliminary ruling procedure, and outline the guidelines for courts of last instance and other national courts in determining whether a reference should be made to the CoJ on:

(1) the interpretation of EU law

(2) the validity of EU laws.

Further reading

Books

Broberg, M. and Fenger, N. *Preliminary References to the European Court of Justice*, 2nd edn, Oxford University Press, Oxford, 2014.

Foster, N. *EU Treaties and Legislation* (latest edition), Oxford University Press, Oxford.

Articles

Anagnostaras, G. 'Preliminary problems and jurisdiction uncertainties: the admissibility of questions referred by bodies performing quasi-judicial functions' (2005) 30 EL Rev 878.

Bobek, M. 'Learning to talk: preliminary rulings, the courts of the new member states and the Court of Justice' (2008) 45 CML Rev 1611.

Broberg, M. and Fenger, N. 'Preliminary references as a right—but for whom? The extent to which preliminary reference decisions can be subject to appeal' (2011) 36 EL Rev 276.

Komarek, J. 'In the court(s) we trust? On the need for hierarchy and differentiation in the preliminary ruling procedure' (2007) 32 EL Rev 467.

Kornezov, A. 'The new format of the Acte Clair doctrine and its consequences' (2016) 53 CMLR 1317.

Lord Mance, 'The interface between national and European law' (2013) 38 EL Rev 437.

Schwensfeier, R. 'The TWD principle post-Lisbon' (2012) 37 ELR 156.

7

Treaty enforcement actions against member states

LEARNING OBJECTIVES

In this chapter, you will consider the enforcement actions that may be taken against a member state, including:

- Article 258 TFEU actions by the Commission;
- Article 260 TFEU sanctions;
- Article 259 TFEU actions by other member states;
- Articles 278–279 TFEU interim measures; and
- alternative actions to direct action.

Introduction

This chapter considers the actions brought against the member states that are commenced before the Court of Justice (CoJ) and which focus on the actions by the Commission and other member states. As a possible part of such actions, interim measures under Articles 278–279 of the Treaty on the Functioning of the European Union (TFEU) are also considered. These direct actions against the member states to ensure compliance with Community and now European Union (EU) law were the first part of the system of dual vigilance enforcement of Community and EU law. They were provided from the outset in the European Economic Community (EEC) Treaty, but were not regarded as being particularly efficient, particularly before amendment, although a number of improvements have now been made. Breaches of the member states' obligation to comply with EU law, which is imposed generally by Article 4(3) of the Treaty on European Union (TEU), are officially established by the CoJ following a procedural action against the state. Article 258 TFEU is the basis for Commission action against member states for failures to fulfil obligations under the Treaties, and in doing so the Commission is acting under its Article 17 TEU duty, as the guardian of the Treaties, to ensure that the Treaties and other EU measures are complied with.

Article 259 TFEU additionally provides for actions by one member state against another member state. Furthermore, in support of both these actions, Article 260 TFEU imposes an obligation on member states to comply with judgments of the CoJ. This was revised by the Maastricht Treaty (TEU) and now provides a system of penalties that can be imposed on member states, which are considered towards the end of this chapter.

CROSS REFERENCE
Noted in Chapter 6, 'Introduction'.

7.1 Enforcement actions by the Commission

For more details on this section visit the online resources.

In contrast to other international organisations, from the outset the EU provided a much more effective control mechanism under Article 258 TFEU to ensure compliance with its own laws by member states. The enforcement procedure, though, may also serve the purposes of re-enforcing the establishing and efficacy of the policies of the EU and clarifying EU law where its meaning and requirements are sometimes disputed.

Article 258 TFEU

If the Commission considers that a Member State has failed to fulfil an obligation under the Treaties, it shall deliver a reasoned opinion on the matter after giving the State concerned the opportunity to submit its observations. If the State concerned does not comply with the opinion within the period laid down by the Commission, the latter may bring the matter before the Court of Justice of the European Union.

In addition to the action under Article 258 TFEU, there are further actions that the Commission can take against the member state in respect of specific subject matters, including Article 108(2) TFEU in respect of infringements of state aids provisions, Article 114(9) TFEU in respect of derogations from the internal market, and Articles 346–348 TFEU in respect of emergency security measures, none of which will be covered in any further detail in this volume.

7.1.1 What constitutes a breach?

Article 258 TFEU is silent as to what constitutes a breach of a duty. The CoJ has determined that a breach can be constituted not only by an act of a member state, but also by the failure to act by a member state and even general and persistent administrative practices which infringe EU law, as identified in Case C-88/07 *Commission* v *Spain* involving administrative rules which prevented herbal products from being marketed in Spain over a period of time. A failure to act is most often seen in the form of a member state failing to implement EU legislation, mainly Directives, or failing to remove national legislation that is in conflict or inconsistent with EU legislation. Other breaches are that a member state has implemented the Directive incorrectly—deliberately or inadvertently—or that the implementation was incomplete or considerably delayed. Increasingly, now, as there are general requirements to notify technical standards to the Commission and to notify the Commission of how Directives have been implemented in national law, failure to do so will probably result in an infringement proceeding being commenced. Apart from the general good faith clause under Article 4(3) TFEU and Article 18 TFEU—the duty not to discriminate on grounds of nationality—there are more specific duties under the various chapters of the Treaty and the very detailed duties imposed by secondary legislation. Thus, breaches may arise from the Treaties, secondary legislation, international agreements, decisions of the CoJ, and general principles. There are numerous examples of breaches by a member state to be found in the chapters of this book.

Failure to remove inconsistent legislation constitutes a breach even if the authorities no longer apply the national legislation and apply the EU rules in preference.

For example, in **Case 167/73 *Commission v France***, provisions of the French Maritime Code restricted the numbers of foreign workers on French vessels, but the French authorities pleaded that the national law was not being applied. The CoJ held that this law, even if it is not being applied, might influence the behaviour of people who rely on the law being applied, and thus its non-repeal would create uncertainty.

In **Case C-265/95 *Commission v France***, France was held to be in breach of Treaty obligation when its enforcement authorities did nothing to prevent criminal damage to imported Spanish strawberries as part of a protest by French farmers. The CoJ held that doing little or nothing to prevent other persons from restricting the movement of goods when action could and should have been taken would constitute a breach of obligation. France was held to be in breach of the EU law obligation.

Ireland, in **Case C-459/03 *Commission v Ireland***, was held to be in breach of the EU law obligation under Article 344 not to submit disputes to any method of settlement other than those provided for by EU law, when it took an action against the UK about the MOX nuclear recycling plant to the Tribunal for the International Convention on the Sea.

> **CROSS REFERENCE**
> This case is also considered under the free movement of goods in Chapter 11, section 11.2.1.1.

7.1.2 Identifying and reporting breaches

A possible breach can come to light as a result of the Commission's own investigations or from the failure of the member states to notify how they have implemented EU law, as they are now required to do under secondary legislation. See the following example from Directive 2002/14.

Article 11 Transposition

(1) Member States shall adopt the laws, regulations and administrative provisions necessary to comply with this Directive not later than 23 March 2005 or shall ensure that management and labour introduce by that date the required provisions by way of agreement, the Member States being obliged to take all necessary steps enabling them to guarantee the results imposed by this Directive at all times. They shall forthwith inform the Commission thereof.

(2) Where Member States adopt these measures, they shall contain a reference to this Directive or shall be accompanied by such reference on the occasion of their official publication. The methods of making such reference shall be laid down by the Member States.

Failures to notify are automatically notified to the Commission by its monitoring software. Breaches can be reported by other member states, the European Parliament, and other institutions and agencies of the EU, or concerned or affected individual citizens or companies. Note that, with regard to these last, they are unable to force the Commission to do anything about a complaint that has been lodged. In 2010, the Commission reported that 35 per cent of cases arose from its own initiative and investigations.

See **Case 247/87 *Star Fruit Company* v *Commission***, in which a company's attempt to use the Article 232 EC (now 265 TFEU) omission-to-act proceedings to try to require the Commission to take action against France was firmly rejected by the CoJ. The Court held that the Commission was not bound to take action, but had the discretion whether or not to do so.

For more details on this section visit the online resources.

The Article 258 TFEU action was not intended to be an individual remedy but to be an instrument to encourage or enforce member state compliance. As such, whilst complaints might have been welcomed by the Commission, the right to make a complaint was as far as an individual's interest in the matter formally extended. The Commission is not under an obligation to act on a complaint, nor is it even required to inform the complaining individual of what, if anything, is being done. This was further confirmed in Case T-47/96 *SDDDA* v *Commission*, in which the General Court held that there was no right for individuals to require the Commission to adopt a particular position. Although the formal position of an individual in the matter has not changed, the Commission publicises its progress much more widely than before, usually by issuing notices in the Official Journal (OJ). The Commission has set up a complaints-handling scheme to keep complainants informed. The CHAP system registers and monitors complaints from individuals, but also keeps the complainants informed, the result of which is that many complaints are satisfied before further action might be necessary on the part of the Commission against the member states. The Commission has also providing information and a standard complaint form for individuals to notify alleged member state infringements.

7.1.3 Defendants in an Article 258 TFEU action

A breach of EU law can arise from any part of a state and is not restricted to purely governmental action or inaction.

For example, in **Case 77/69 *Commission* v *Belgium* (*Belgian Wood*)**, the government pleaded that it should not be held responsible for the negligence of the Belgian Parliament, which, being out of session, was not able to implement a Community Directive in time. The CoJ held that 'Obligations arise whatever the agency of the state whose action or inaction is the cause of the failure to fulfil its obligation even in the case of a constitutionally independent institution'.

» CROSS REFERENCE

See the discussion of this in Chapter 8, section 8.4, and Case C-99/00 *Lyckeskög*, in Chapter 6, section 6.1.7, which prompted the Commission to commence an Article 226 EC (now 258 TFEU) action for the Swedish court's failure to refer, although the action was dropped when Swedish practice was amended; and see Case C-224/01 *Köbler*, considered in Chapter 8, section 8.3.1.2.

Thus the member states are responsible for breaches caused by actions of the legislature, the executive, and local and regional authorities, and even for the failures of federal authorities (Cases C-227 –230/85 *Commission* v *Belgium*). This could include breaches by the judiciary in a member state for rendering an incorrect decision or for a failure to make an Article 267 TFEU reference to the CoJ. A state may also be found to be in breach for actions of individuals in the state that breach EU law but against which the state takes no action or for which the state is responsible.

In **Case C-129/00 *Commission* v *Italy***, the failure to repeal a law that was interpreted by the Italian courts in such a way as to make a Community law right excessively difficult to realise was held by the CoJ to be a breach on the part of the Italian state. See also **Case C-154/08 *Commission* v *Spain***, in which the Spanish state was held by the Spanish Supreme Court to be in breach for the erroneous interpretation of the Sixth VAT Directive. The court did not make a preliminary ruling reference to the CoJ. The national ruling was subsequently followed by many other Spanish courts and the national tax administration and caused considerable economic harm. The defence of the independence of the judiciary raised by Spain was rejected by the CoJ. This groundbreaking judgment, if followed in the future, allows the Commission to police the judgments of the national courts and, whilst correct in EU law, is not something one supposes the national supreme courts or governments will be too happy about.

In **C-265/95** *Commission* v *France (Spanish Strawberries)*, the actions undertaken by individuals in disrupting fruit and vegetable imports, which were not prevented by the French authorities, rendered the state in breach of Community law for its failure to act.

In **Case 249/81** *Commission* v *Ireland (Buy Irish)*, a 'Buy Irish' campaign was administered by the Irish Goods Council, a registered private company. However, because the Irish government largely sponsored the campaign to buy Irish products, appointed the management committee, and set the broad outlines of the campaign, it was held accountable for the breach of Article 28 (now 34 TFEU). This case is also considered in Chapter 11, section 11.2.1.

7.1.4 The procedure of an Article 258 TFEU action

Article 258 TFEU requires certain informal and formal stages to be completed before the matter can be brought to the CoJ.

7.1.4.1 The informal or administrative stage

The first part of Article 258 TFEU states that 'If the Commission considers that a Member State has failed to fulfil an obligation under this treaty, it shall deliver a reasoned opinion on the matter.' This means that the Commission must have reached a conclusion that the member state is probably in breach of an obligation before it can commence an action before the CoJ. Having formed a view during the pre-procedural investigations and discussions with member state officials in what are described as 'package meetings' that a state has breached its obligations, the Commission will inform the state by letter and give the state the opportunity to answer the allegation or to correct its action or inaction before the formal procedure of Article 258 begins. Allied to the CHAP system, noted in section 7.1.2 above is the 'EU Pilot' scheme, which transfers the complaints after initial investigation by the Commission to the member state for consideration and comment. Again, this has led to many complaints being solved without further action being necessary. The Commission also has a National Infringement Database (NIF), which monitors the cases being pursued formally by the Commission. The Commission labels this stage as the 'early settlement' stage.

For more details on this section visit the online resources.

In view of the discretion that the Commission enjoys under the procedure, there is no obligation on it to take action. Individuals who complain or who are concerned have been held by the CoJ not to be able to force the Commission to take action.

In **Case 247/87** *Star Fruit Company* v *Commission*, the CoJ held that the Commission is not bound to commence the proceedings under Article 258 TFEU, but has a discretion that excludes the right for individuals to require it to adopt a specific position. In view of this discretion, both the formal letter and reasoned opinion cannot be challenged in Article 263 TFEU actions, which are considered in Chapter 9. (See also **Cases 48/65** *Lütticke* v *Commission* and **246/81** *Bethell* v *Commission* which reached the same conclusions with regard to actions under Article 265 TFEU.

⟫ CROSS REFERENCE
See sections 9.1.1.2 and 9.2.1.2.

Each year, the Commission prepares a report on the application of Union law, which provides statistics for the number of cases being investigated and numbers for each of the stages of Article 258 TFEU actions, which will be used to illustrate the following sections. The formal administrative part of the procedure consists of two distinct phases, prior to any court action that may ensue in the judicial stage.

7.1.4.2 Letters of formal notice

Not every suspicion of infringement by the Commission will result in the initial formal letter of notice being sent to the member state.

> The 2008 Monitoring Report noted that over 3,400 complaints and infringement procedures were being handled, but that 68 per cent were settled before the formal stage had commenced and 94 per cent had been settled prior to the CoJ giving a ruling.

Whilst, at this stage, the process is still administrative, it is nevertheless absolutely necessary as a prerequisite for the possible later judicial process should the member state fail to take action or correct the alleged breach.

> In **Case 274/83 Commission v Italy**, the initial letter was held to be essential for the commencement of proceedings before the Court.

> In 1985, the Commission sent out 503 formal letters (1,016 in 1995 and 1,552 in 2003) stating its point of view. Generally, about half of the instances in which a formal notice has been issued are settled at that stage, although this figure varies from year to year. Despite a rise to 25 member states in 2006, there was a reduction of formal letters sent out to 1,536, but this was expected to rise. In 2010, with 27 member states, there were 1,168 formal notices.

These letters simply seek a response from the member state and do not automatically lead to the next stage, the reasoned opinion, or further to the litigation stage. Case 293/85 *Commission v Belgium (Re University Fees)* held that the Commission must allow member states a period that is reasonable to reply to the letter of formal notice.

> The Commission reported that 'At the end of 2009, around 77 per cent of complaints were closed before the first formal step in an infringement proceeding; around a further 12 per cent of the total were closed before the reasoned opinion and around a further 7 per cent before a ruling from the ECJ.'

7.1.4.3 The reasoned opinion

Following the reply from the member state to the formal notice, or after the time given by the Commission for an answer (which is usually two months or what is reasonable under the circumstances) and after which no reply has been received, the Commission will deliver a reasoned opinion that records the factual and legal reasons for the failure of the member state. The reasoned opinion is delivered to the member state and also provides a further time limit within which the member state is required to bring the alleged infringement to an end. This period was also held by the CoJ in Case 293/85 *Commission* v *Belgium (Re University Fees)* to be a reasonable period, but again, as a rule of thumb, two months would be acceptable unless there are circumstances requiring a shorter period due to urgency, or a longer period if the matter is complicated. Many of the original complaints are settled informally during this stage. The reasoned opinion is confidential and cannot be obtained by third parties during the course of investigations or where the Commission exercises its discretion and decides not to proceed further against a member state (see, e.g., Cases T-105/95 *WWF* and T-191/99 *Petrie*). However, the Commission often publishes the reasoned opinion, along with the rest of the case paperwork, after the CoJ judgment.

> The number of reasoned opinions in 1985 was 233 (192 in 1995, 533 in 2003, and 680 in 2006). There were 488 in 2010.

> In **Case 39/72 *Commission* v *Italy (Slaughtered Cows)***, the CoJ determined that if the state fails to comply with the reasoned opinion of the Commission within a reasonable time, or as stipulated by the Commission (normally two months), the Commission then has the right, which is still discretionary, to bring the matter before the Court, specifying its grounds for action.

> In terms of the total number of cases each year, about 90 per cent will have been solved by the end of this stage and about 10 per cent only of the original cases will be referred to the CoJ. The figures—107 cases were brought in 1985, 72 in 1995, 215 in 2003, and 189 in 2006— bear this out. The 2008 Monitoring Report put the percentage at 94 per cent settlement prior to the judicial stage; 2010 saw no break in the trend, with 120 referrals to the CoJ, which was about 10 per cent.

7.1.4.4 The judicial stage

The final stage of the procedure is action before the CoJ and its judgment, which is merely declaratory in that the member state is held by the CoJ to have either failed or not failed to have fulfilled an obligation under EU law. After the judgment, the state is required under Article 260 TFEU to take the necessary measures to comply. Only about 5 per cent of cases reach final judgment.

> In 1985, 23 cases were removed from the Court's register prior to judgment, the member states having complied with Community obligations. Thus, judgments rendered by the Court were only 26 in 1985, 72 in 1995, 86 in 2003, and 90 in 2006. More up-to-date statistics appear on an annual basis in the Court of Justice Annual Report.

The CoJ can proceed to judgment even if the member state has complied with the Commission's reasoned opinion, but did so outside the set time limit.

For more details on this section visit the online resources.

In **Case C-240/86 *Commission v Greece***, the CoJ held that the Commission action remained admissible despite compliance before the deadline or judgment so that the Court was still entitled to establish the breach, or where the member state has persistently failed to comply with EU law on a particular issue as in **Case C-147/03 *Commission v Austria***, which concerned qualifications required by EU citizens for entry to Austrian educational establishments.

This is important in that it allows the Commission to establish exactly what the law is or to set a precedent to control other member state behaviour. Equally, the existence of national proceedings, as in Case C-508/03 *Commission v UK*, is not a reason to hold the Commission action as inadmissible, as was confirmed by the CoJ.

In **Case 22/87 *Commission v Italy***, the breach declared by the CoJ was the basis for imposing liability on the state in **Cases C-6 and 9/90 *Francovich***.

⏩ **CROSS REFERENCE**
This established the individual claim of state liability, which is considered in Chapter 8, section 8.3.

Presently, there is approximately a 20-month delay in the Court hearing enforcement actions, but if the matter is very important, the Court is able to speed up the case. Where such a delay would cause severe difficulties, it is possible for the Commission to request and the Court to order interim measures. Interim measures are considered in section 7.2.

7.1.4.5 Defences raised by the member states

The member states have raised various defences, often acceptable in international law, but without success in the EU legal order, to justify their non-compliance with obligations. Of the more common are the following.

Force majeure or overriding necessity was raised in **Case 77/69 *Commission v Belgium (Belgian Wood)*,** in which the Belgian government pleaded that the dissolution of Parliament and the separation of powers had forced the failure to implement an EC Directive.

In **Case 101/84 *Commission v Italy***, a data-processing centre had been bombed, which might have actually allowed the defence of *force majeure* to be used if it were not for the fact that the delay in implementing it was four-and-a-half years—far too long for the Court.

Community measures being the cause of political or economic difficulties were raised by the UK in **Case 128/78 *Commission v UK (Tachographs)*,** in which the UK pleaded that the cost and interruption to industry of fitting tachographs in lorry cabs would cause extreme difficulties.

In **Case 7/61 *Commission v Italy***, Italy claimed that it could take action in the case of an emergency, but this could be done only if expressly sanctioned by the Commission, which, in this case, it was not.

The claim that direct effects had been established by the CoJ in another case was not a defence against infringements proceedings for Germany in **Case 29/84 Commission v Germany** on the grounds that there was no need to implement because individuals were already able to enforce the EC law in the national courts.

In **Cases 90 and 91/63 Commission v Belgium and Luxembourg**, the member states raised reciprocity, arguing that they were justified in not complying because the Council had failed to act; and in **Case 232/78 Commission v France**, France considered itself justified on the basis that other member states had not complied with their obligations.

Likewise, arguments that a conflicting national law is not in fact applied or that the administrative practice is in compliance, as in **Case 167/73 Commission v France (Re Merchant Seamen)**, also fail.

A threat to public order pleaded by France in **Case C-265/95 Commission v France (Spanish Strawberries)** was also rejected. The Court found that:

> the French Government has manifestly and persistently abstained from adopting appropriate and adequate measures to put an end to the acts of vandalism which jeopardize the free movement on its territory of certain agricultural products originating in other Member States and to prevent the recurrence of such acts.

About the only defences that will work, given the robust dismissal by the CoJ of virtually all other defences raised, is that the Commission erred on the facts or in law; that is, that there was no breach or that the EU legislation was unlawful, invalid, or procedurally at fault, as in the cases considered in Chapter 8 under Article 263 TFEU. The Commission's overall success rate before the CoJ historically has been about 95 per cent, but more recently the CoJ has rejected a larger number for various procedural and substantive reasons, bringing that success rate down, although the latest figures suggest the success rate trend continues in that 35 cases were decided by the CoJ in 2014 with 92 per cent in favour of the Commission.

For more details on this section visit the online resources.

7.2 Suspensory orders and interim measures

One of the criticisms of the Article 258 TFEU procedure is the length of time it takes to secure a final judgment. This is about 18 months at present to the end of the formal stage and the first judicial ruling in the proceedings, but this does not take account of the informal stage before that, which can extend the whole process by years. During this time, a member state's breach can cause consid-

CHAPTER 7 TREATY ENFORCEMENT ACTIONS AGAINST MEMBER STATES

erable economic hardship and damage to individuals affected by it. To overcome this, the Court may order a contested act to be suspended under Article 278 TFEU or, in any case before it, the Court may proscribe necessary interim measures under Article 279 TFEU, both of which have been ordered occasionally in Article 258 actions.

Article 278 TFEU

Actions brought before the Court of Justice shall not have suspensory effect. The Court of Justice may, however, if it considers that circumstances so require, order that application of the contested act be suspended.

Article 279 TFEU

The Court of Justice may in any cases before it prescribe any necessary interim measures.

A case for the requested measure must be made specifically; interim measures must be requested prior to final judgment and applied only in urgent circumstances. Interim measures are not in any strict sense a direct sanction, but they can nevertheless have the effect of rectifying the alleged breach until it has been determined by the CoJ whether the conflicting national legislation should be removed or disapplied.

In **Case 53/77 *Commission v UK (Pig Producers)***, the UK was ordered to halt subsidies to pig producers until the Court could decide whether the scheme was compatible with the rules of the Common Market.

In **Case 293/85 *Commission v Belgium (University Fees)***, the Court ordered Belgium, under Article 243 EC, to allow access on equal terms to other non-Belgian Community nationals to vocational training in Belgian universities when non-Belgians were asked to pay enrolment fees but nationals were not.

The Court also made an interim order in **Case 61/77 R *Commission v Ireland (Irish Fisheries)*** for Ireland to cease certain fishing measures that the Commission claimed were contrary to Community fishing rules.

In all three cases, the member states complied immediately.

In **Case C-195/90 *Commission v Germany***, the Court ordered that a special road tax for lorries be suspended pending the outcome of the Commission Article 226 EC (now 258 TFEU) action against Germany. In response, Germany had requested a security undertaking from the Commission in case the Commission's application was not upheld, but this was judged not to be justified by the CoJ.

In the *Factortame* litigation, **Case 246/89R *Commission v UK***, the Commission requested and was granted the suspension of the alleged incompatible UK laws that were causing, and would have caused further considerable economic damage to the Spanish fishermen in the UK. It was very notable in that case that the UK did not comply with the order without considerable delay. The UK was required in a later case in the same series of litigation to pay considerable compensation to the Spanish fisherman who had been damaged by the UK breach.

7.3 The application and effect of judgments

Other international tribunals are unable to enforce their judgments against miscreant member states, for example the International Court of Justice (ICJ) at The Hague or the European Court of Human Rights (ECtHR) in Strasbourg. The best that can really be achieved is the issue and discussion of a report on the failure or breach whilst waiting for political pressure to bear on the state concerned. Whilst in the EU legal order, the initial judgment of the CoJ is only declaratory and carries no specific sanctions, changes to Article 260 considered next now allow financial sanction to be levied against the infringing state, after a follow-up action has been taken by the Commission. In addition, the revised procedure now for a failure by a member state to notify measures transposing a Directive under Article 260(3) TFEU, considered in section 7.3.1.1, permits those sanctions to be applied without having to resort to the follow-up action.

For more details on this section visit the online resources.

7.3.1 **Article 260 TFEU**

The member states are nevertheless under a further obligation under Article 260(1) TFEU to comply with the judgment by taking the necessary measures. If they do not do this, a further action under Article 258 TFEU may lie against them by the Commission for a further breach, but this time for the breach of Article 260.

The leading instance of this is **Case 48/71 *Commission v Italy (Second Art Treasures Case)***. The Commission discerned that because Italy had not complied with the Court's judgment in **Case 7/68 *Commission v Italy (First Art Treasures Case)***, judgment should be given that Italy had also failed in its obligation under Article 228 EC (now 260 TFEU). Despite the fact that Italy complied with the original decision prior to judgment, the Court held that Italy had also failed to comply with Article 228 EC (now 260 TFEU).

This case demonstrates the unsatisfactory situation that, by not having an ultimate sanction under the original Treaty provisions to encourage compliance, this allowed matters, and indeed breach of EU law by the member states, to drag on, as, for example, in cases against France for the same infringement that spanned 20 years. These and other cases prompted the member states to reform what is now 260 TFEU.

7.3.1.1 **Sanctions under Article 260 TFEU**

The TEU amended Article 228 EC (now 260 TFEU) to enable the CoJ to fine member states for breaches of EU law. The Commission must give the state the opportunity to submit its observations and to issue a formal notice, but does not need to issue a further reasoned opinion on the continued failure, as was previously the situation prior to the Lisbon changes. The Commission must state a time limit for compliance, which, if the member state fails to meet it, will allow the matter to be referred to the CoJ, which may ultimately levy a fine. Article 261 TFEU provides that penalties will be determined by regulations to be adopted by the Council, and a penalty calculation system was established by the Commission whereby it will state what penalty, if any, it considers appropriate. The penalty can be levied in the form of a lump sum or periodic payment.

> The basic penalty is fixed at €660 per day for the periodic penalty and €220 per day for the lump sum penalty multiplied by factors reflecting the gravity and duration of non-compliance, the financial situation of the member state, and the number of votes in the Council. This figure will be adjusted for inflation every three years. The amount of a fine may also take into account the impact of breaches on individuals and affected economic operators. This is not to compensate the individuals affected or redress the balance, but to reflect the overall seriousness of the breach—that is, put crudely, to reflect how many individuals may be adversely affected, from zero to a whole industry or sector of the economy (see point 16.4 of Commission Notice SEC (2005) 1658 final).

Following Case C-304/02 *Commission v France*, the CoJ held that the basic penalty can be both a lump sum and/or a periodic payment fine. The penalty will apply from the date of judgment in the first action and not from the date of original non-compliance, although the Court has discretion to set the dates. In Cases C-278/01 *Commission v Spain*, C-304/02 *Commission v France*, and C-369/07 *Commission v Hellenic Republic*, the Court set a date after the date of judgment; hence, member states have the chance to minimise the penalty. However, following Case C-304/02, the penalty can penalise a state for the time taken to comply with its obligation.

> In **Cases C-387/97 Commission v Greece** and **C-278/01 Commission v Spain**, the CoJ held that the form of the Commission penalty request does not bind the Court, which can decide the appropriate type and amount of penalty according to the circumstances. The case against Spain involved the quality of bathing water, which was assessed only annually; therefore, the Court considered a daily penalty not appropriate and instead imposed an annual penalty based on the percentage of beaches not meeting the Directive's standards.

> **Case C-304/02 Commission v France** is the follow-up case to **Case C-64/88**, which had established that France was in breach of fishery measures. France had failed to set up adequate control measures. The CoJ agreed that France had failed to comply with the first judgment. It held that it could impose both a lump sum and a periodic fine despite the fact that this form of fine had not been requested by the Commission. It reasoned that the periodic penalty was to encourage compliance and the lump sum to penalise the adverse effects caused by the state's breach, particularly where the adverse effects had persisted over a long period of time. The Court held that it was not bound by the Commission's suggestions in respect of fines. France was thus fined €57.76 million per six months of continuing breach and a lump-sum fine of €20 million.

Following this case and because CoJ has imposed both in subsequent cases (see e.g. Case 469/09 *Commission* v *Italy* and Case C-610/10 *Commission* v *Spain*), the Commission has issued new communications on fines.

In one case a fine was requested, but not imposed by the CoJ.

In **Case C-212/99 Commission v Italy**, the Commission's request for a fine was turned down by the CoJ because the previous breach had in fact been corrected in a timely manner by Italy and the Court was of the view that a fine would serve no useful purpose.

The Lisbon Treaty adopted the Constitutional Treaty's plan to remove the need for the entire second procedure under Article 260(3) TFEU when seeking a penalty fine in the limited circumstance of when a member state had failed to notify the transposition of a Directive. The Commission can therefore request the fine in the initial Article 258 action without the need for the declaratory judgment first and the secondary Article 260 action, presumably on the basis that the failure to notify is self-evident. Furthermore, the Commission under this procedure specifies the amount of fine without the possibility of this being changed by the CoJ. This will certainly speed up the process of judicially establishing the second breach and levying a fine. According to the 2008 Monitoring Report, these cases represent approximately 50 per cent of all enforcement actions, and by the end of 2012, 11 cases had been brought under this expedited Article 260 TFEU procedure. In 2012, though, the Commission opened 35 penalty actions against member states, as opposed to only nine in 2011. Cases have been opened in similar numbers in the successive years up to and including 2014, but as yet no cases referred to the CoJ have been heard, as the member states have implemented and notified that to the Commission, albeit very late.

For more details on this section visit the online resources.

 THINKING POINT

In the light of the above procedures and changes already introduced, what further changes would you make to improve the enforcement action?

7.4 Actions brought by one member state against another (Article 259 TFEU)

Article 259 TFEU (ex 227 EC) is the basis for an action by one member state against another, when one member state considers another to have breached an obligation under EU law.

> **Article 259 TFEU**
>
> A Member State which considers that another Member State has failed to fulfil an obligation under the Treaties may bring the matter before the Court of Justice of the European Union.
>
> Before a Member State brings an action against another Member State for an alleged infringement of an obligation under the Treaties, it shall bring the matter before the Commission.
>
> The Commission shall deliver a reasoned opinion after each of the States concerned has been given the opportunity to submit its own case and its observations on the other party's case both orally and in writing.
>
> If the Commission has not delivered an opinion after three months of the date on which the matter was brought before it, the absence of such opinion shall not prevent the matter from being brought before the Court.

As Article 344 TFEU obligates the member states not to pursue other methods of dispute resolution other than that provided by the Treaty, member states must use Article 259 TFEU to resolve differences under EU law, although this is not always observed to the letter of the law. It must be noted, however, that the use of Article 259 TFEU by the member states has been minimal. The preference is almost exclusively to request the Commission to take action under Article 258 TFEU. The member states have full *locus standi* in relation to Article 259, which means that they do not have to have a specific interest in bringing an action, although in the few cases that have been brought they have had a particular interest. The procedure is set out in sections 7.4.1 and 7.4.2.

7.4.1 **The involvement of the Commission**

Before an action can take place, the member state must bring the matter before the Commission, which will ask both states to submit their observations and will then deliver a reasoned opinion on the matter. The Commission seeks to bring about a solution before Court action is necessary and may even intervene to take over the action, as it did in Case 232/78 *Commission v France*, which commenced as an action by Ireland against France, and in Case 1/00 *Commission v France*, which was commenced by the UK under Article 227 EC (now Article 259 TFEU) and concerned the French measures that continued after the Commission UK beef export ban had been lifted.

7.4.2 **Complaining state may then refer the matter to the Court of Justice**

If a settlement or solution is not reached at this stage and three months has elapsed, or if the Commission fails to submit an opinion after three months of being informed of the matter, the member state can take the matter before the Court. Judgment has been reached, up to the date of writing, in only a few actions. For example:

> In **Case 141/78 *France v UK***, France successfully challenged the UK's unilateral fishery conservation measures.

Another case brought to judgment under Article 227 was **Case C-388/95 *Belgium* v *Spain***. Belgium, without the support of the Commission, failed in its action to challenge the refusal to allow the use of the *Rioja* designation for bulk-transported wine, which was argued by Spain to protect the quality designation of cellar-bottled wine. Belgium claimed that the action was an impediment to the free movement of goods.

A third case taken to judgment was **Case C-145/04 *Spain* v *UK***, which concerned the voting rights of citizens of Gibraltar, and is thus very much tied in with the political dispute between Spain and the UK over the continued British claim to ownership of Gibraltar. Spain had objected to the UK extending the European Parliament voting franchise to Gibraltarians, as required to do under an ECtHR ruling. The CoJ found in favour of the UK.

Note that there is a further, very political case between Hungary and Slovakia (**Case C-364/10**) involving the challenge by Hungary that Slovakia, in failing to invite the Hungarian President to an official ceremony, had breached citizenship and free movement rules. The date of the ceremony coincided with the anniversary of the Soviet invasion of Czechoslovakia in 1968 (Hungarian troops had been among the Soviet pact troops entering and occupying Czechoslovakia). The action was dismissed by the CoJ as only involving the President in his diplomatic status and not individually as a citizen, and was thus to be governed by national and international law and not by EU law.

These rare cases aside, member states usually prefer to ask the Commission to bring actions under Article 258 TFEU because this is a less politically obvious and contentious manner in which to secure compliance of EU law in the interests of the member state concerned. The states can continue with friendly relations whilst the Commission investigates and pursues the action warranted. Article 259 TFEU also triggers Article 260 TFEU, where a state is held to be in breach but takes no immediate action.

Additionally, under Article 273 TFEU, member states may agree to refer any dispute relating to the subject matter of the Treaty to the CoJ for adjudication, which appears never to have been employed, presumably because a complaint to the Commission is a better alternative.

7.5 Alternative actions to secure member states' compliance

Alternative actions are considered in more detail in Chapter 8, but it is appropriate to mention such actions here because they are equally, if not a great deal more, effective in ensuring compliance with EU law obligations by member states. They include actions where individuals point to the breach of an EU obligation or duty by a member state as a defence against prosecution by that member state, or where they seek to challenge national rules that operate against their interest. The doctrine of direct effects additionally places the policing of EU law in the hands of private individuals, who often have more reason and thus more incentive to bring actions than the Commission officials. Individuals may benefit by their actions, as well as help to bring about compliance by member states, parallel to Article 258 actions.

> In **Case 152/78 *Commission v France (Advertising of Alcoholic Beverages)***, it was held that a French ban on advertising foreign spirits was discriminatory and contrary to Community law. France failed to remove its legislation and prosecuted an importer for advertising. Waterkeyn, the advertiser, referred to the previous judgment as a defence.

> In the follow-up **Cases 314–316/81 *Procureur de la Republique v Waterkeyn***, it was held that individuals could rely on such past judgments as a defence to protect their rights.

⏵ CROSS REFERENCE

Considered in Chapter 8, section 8.3.

In addition, there are possibilities for individuals to sue a state for loss caused by a breach of EU law, the breach itself being previously established in an Article 258 TFEU action against the member states, under the state liability principle established first in the case of *Francovich*. This will also play a strong part in encouraging member states to comply with EU law obligations if they find themselves having to pay out significant damages in an increasing number of cases. More recent case law on state liability shows that it is not necessary for an enforcement action by the Commission to have already demonstrated a breach, although it would always be helpful if that were the case.

⟳ Summary

The biggest criticism of the Articles 258–260 TFEU procedures remains the time taken to reach judgment, and it is certainly the case that the entire process is upward of two years; if all of the informal stages are counted, it can be four or more years. However, if due consideration is given to the fact that the vast majority of cases are solved before judgment, then a truer picture is gained on how effective the procedures can be. The other major criticism is the lack of any rights of individual complainants to the Commission. Whilst reform of the Article 258 procedure has been discussed in both academic literature and by the European Ombudsman in favour of making the process more supportive of the individuals who bring complaints, this so far has fallen on deaf ears where the member states are concerned. There was the amendment to the procedure in the Constitutional Treaty, which carried on into the Lisbon Treaty, with the removal of the need for the entire second Commission action in Article 258 TFEU actions against a member state for failing to notify how Directives had been implemented. Further, the removal of the second reasoned opinion in all other enforcement actions will certainly speed up actions that have progressed that far. In addition, the various monitoring and communication schemes that have been set up, noted in section 7.1.4.1, have both highlighted breaches by member states and informed concerned individuals about progress with getting compliance by the member states. However imperfect, the procedures nevertheless provide a means whereby, ultimately, member states may find themselves before the CoJ for a breach for which they can be fined. The actions and processes do help to uphold EU law. The thirtieth Monitoring Report for 2012 shows a further reduction in the number of infringement procedures opened by the Commission.

For more details on this section visit the online resources.

⏵ CROSS REFERENCE

See the 'Further reading' listed at the end of the chapter for some of this literature.

Questions

1. What arguments have been raised by the member states in defence of Article 258 TFEU infringement proceedings against them? What success did they meet with?

2. What remedies will an individual have in circumstances in which he or she has called upon the Commission to act under Article 258 and the Commission has declined to do so?

3. Why is Article 259 TFEU so infrequently used?

4. How effective are the actions under Articles 258 and 259?

For more details on this section visit the online resources.

Sample exam Q&A

Essay question

Discuss the effectiveness of the Article 258 TFEU procedure in ensuring compliance of EU law on the part of member states.

For guidance on how to tackle this specimen exam question and to read a suggested model answer, visit the online resources. www.oup. com/uk/foster_ directions6e/.

Further reading

Books

Anderson, S. *The Enforcement of EU Law: The Role of the European Commission*, Oxford University Press, Oxford, 2012.

Hartley, T. *The Foundations of European Community Law*, 6th edn, Clarendon Press, Oxford, 2007 (Chapter 10).

Smith, M. *Centralised Enforcement, Legitimacy and Good Governance in the EU*, Routledge Press, Abingdon, 2010.

Articles

Harlow, C. and Rawlings, R. 'Accountability and law enforcement: the centralised EU infringement procedure' (2006) 31 EL Rev 447.

Jack, B. 'Article 260(2) TFEU: an effective judicial procedure for the enforcement of judgments?' (2013) 19 ELJ 404.

Kilbey, I. 'Financial penalties under Art 228(2) EC: excessive complexity?' (2007) 44 CML Rev 743.

Kilbey, I. 'The interpretation of Article 260 TFEU (ex 228 EC)' (2010) 35 EL Rev 370.

Peers, S. 'Sanctions for infringement of EU law after the Treaty of Lisbon' (2012) 18 EPL 33.

Prete, L. and Smulders, B. 'The coming of age of infringement proceedings' (2010) 47 CML Rev 9.

Smith, M. 'Inter-institutional dialogue and the establishment of enforcement norms: a decade of financial penalties under Article 228 EC (now Article 260 TFEU)' (2010) 16 EPL 547.

Taborowski, M. 'Infringement proceedings and non-compliant national courts' (2012) 49 CML Rev 1881.

Wenneras, P. 'A new dawn for Commission enforcement under Articles 226 and 228 EC: general and persistent (GAP) infringement, lump sums and penalty payments' (2006) 43 CML Rev 31.

Wenneras, P. 'Sanctions against member states under Article 260 TFEU: alive, but not kicking?' (2012) 49 CML Rev 145.

8

Remedies: direct and indirect effects and state liability

◻ **LEARNING OBJECTIVES**

In this chapter, you will learn about the remedies developed by the Court of Justice, concentrating on the following issues:

- the concepts of direct applicability and direct effects;
- direct effects of Treaty Articles, Regulations, Directives, Decisions, and international agreements;
- the distinction between vertical and horizontal direct effects;
- the problems resulting from this distinction and solutions to resolve them;
- expanding the concept of the state;
- indirect effects;
- the principle of state liability;
- the use of general principles and incidental effects; and
- the impact on national procedural law.

Introduction

This chapter considers the remedies that have been developed by the Court of Justice (CoJ). It was relatively early in the life of the Union that it was presented with cases in which individuals were confronted with two sets of laws applicable to their situation—one national and the other European Community (EC) law—but which conflicted in some way. As will be seen in the series of cases that follow in this chapter, the very significant starting point for this development was that the CoJ held that Community law concerned not only the member states, but also directly concerned individuals. From this relatively simple concept, the doctrine of direct effects arose. This development was, however, just the starting point for the development of a number of remedies that contribute to the system of dual vigilance, including, most notably, indirect effects and the principle of state liability, all developed by the CoJ in favour of individuals in the absence of express individual rights against the member states within the Treaties. In addition, this chapter considers the concept of direct applicability, found now in Article 288 of the Treaty on the Functioning of the European Union (TFEU), to distinguish it from direct effects. This chapter provides an

▶ CROSS REFERENCE

Dual vigilance is considered briefly in the introduction to Chapter 6.

explanation and review of the development of the doctrine of direct effects through case law. It includes the problems generated by this development in certain circumstances.

> **Direct effects**
>
> Direct effects (in the plural) is the way in which this term was first introduced by the CoJ in Case 26/62 **Van Gend en Loos** and, for this reason, is used throughout in this work. At page 13 of the original judgment, it was stated: 'It follows from the foregoing considerations that, according to the spirit, the general scheme and the wording of the treaty, article 12 must be interpreted as producing direct effects and creating individual rights which national courts must protect.' 'Directly applicable' is the term found in Article 288 TFEU (ex 249 EC, originally 189 Treaty of the European Economic Community (EEC)), primarily relating to an individual form of legislation possessing certain characteristics, but direct applicability is also used to describe generally the process whereby international law becomes directly available and binding within national legal orders without the need for separate or distinct implementation into domestic law.

8.1 Directly applicable and direct effects

8.1.1 Definitions and the distinction between 'directly applicable' and 'direct effects'

For more details on this section visit the online resources.

These two elements of the European Union (EU) legal system and the distinction between them are fundamental to the study and understanding of EU law. The doctrine of direct effects is a judicial development of the CoJ. It is connected and very often confused with direct applicability; however, there are fundamental differences between the two concepts. The concept of direct effects plays a central role in the EU legal order because of its link with the application and enforcement of EU law in the courts of the national legal systems. It is therefore very much related to the supremacy of EU law. Unfortunately, the terminology of the CoJ and many of the national courts has not always been consistent. This has without doubt added greatly to the difficulty in understanding these concepts. Very often, the courts did not use the term 'direct effects', but described a provision of EU law as directly applicable, but in the sense that the provision gives rise to rights enforceable by individuals before the national courts. Thankfully, such confusing use of terms is less frequent these days. Direct effects was sometimes considered to be a sub-concept of directly applicable, such that direct applicability was a prerequisite for direct effects, but that is not correct, as will be demonstrated by the cases that follow.

> In **Case 131/79 Santillo**, the CoJ spoke of Regulations that are directly applicable but that by their very nature can have direct effects, which suggests that this is automatically the case.

> In **Case 9/70 Grad**, the CoJ stated that the ability of an individual to invoke a decision before a national court leads to the same result as would be achieved by a directly applicable provision of a Regulation, again as if to suggest that the concepts are the same; hence the confusion and the need for clarification. The *Grad* case also involved a Directive, which, combined with the decision, gave rights to individuals. The case, though, is cited generally to support the result that it is not only Regulations because of their direct applicability that can give rise to direct effects, but also other forms of EU binding laws, such as Directives and decisions.

8.1.2 'Directly applicable' or 'direct applicability'

'Directly applicable', otherwise termed 'direct applicability', a term previously recognised in international law, should be used to describe the way in which some provisions of EU law have legal validity in the member states. It is therefore a mode of incorporation of law that is generally or universally binding. In the EU context, it is a concept of EU constitutional law that describes the process by which Regulations become directly applicable and legally valid within the member states without separate implementation under domestic law.

'Directly applicable' is specifically mentioned in Article 288 TFEU in relation to Regulations.

> The term 'self-executing' is also often used to describe such law, in that the legal provision itself establishes its validity in the host state.

The member states are obliged not to transform Community **Regulations** into national legislation, except where necessary under the Regulation: see Cases 39/72 *Commission* v *Italy (Slaughtered Cows)* and 128/78 *Commission* v *UK (Tachographs)*. In the latter case, the UK, by not putting into place the necessary administrative procedures for the enforcement and monitoring of tachographs, was held to be in breach of the obligations imposed by the Regulation. Regulations become law usually as specified when published or, if not specified, 20 days after publication.

| **Regulations** |
| A Regulation shall have general application. It shall be binding in its entirety and directly applicable in all member states. |

The term 'directly applicable' also applies in respect of Treaty Articles because these satisfy the criteria of directly applicable law by their automatic validity in the member states following the ratification of the Treaty. The Treaty Articles themselves are not actually transformed into national law and they are generally binding in that they also obligate individuals and not just the member states.

8.1.3 'Direct effects'

'Direct effects' is the term given to judicial enforcement of rights arising from provisions of EU law that can be upheld in favour of individuals in the courts of the member states. Provided that certain criteria are satisfied, an EU law provision will give rise to a right that is enforceable by individuals in the national courts. Whereas 'directly applicable' applies only to Regulations and Treaty Articles, direct effects have been declared by the CoJ in a series of cases in respect of Treaty Articles, fundamental rights and general principles, Regulations, Directives, Decisions, and provisions of international agreements to which the Union is a signatory.

8.1.3.1 Treaty Articles

> The first and paramount case in which this doctrine was established as a leading principle of EU law was **Case 26/62 *Van Gend en Loos***, which concerned the increase of a customs tariff by the Dutch authorities allegedly contrary to Community law—old EEC Treaty, Article 12 (now in an amended form as Article 30 TFEU)—which provided:
>
>> member states shall refrain from introducing between themselves any new customs duties on imports or exports or any charges having equivalent effect, and from increasing those which they already apply in their trade with each other.
>
> In *Van Gend en Loos*, the defendant customs authority argued that because the Treaty Article was addressed to the member state, it could not be enforced by individuals against the state.

> In support of this view, the Belgian, German, and Dutch governments and even the Advocate-General (AG) argued that the correct way in which to enforce the Treaty obligation was by formal action by the Commission under the Treaty (ex Article 169 EEC, now 258 TFEU) or by another member state, but not by individuals. The CoJ rejected this view and held that the Community had been endowed with sovereign rights, the exercise of which affects not only member states, but also their citizens, and that Community law was capable of conferring rights on individuals that become part of their legal heritage and enforceable by them before the national courts. It held that the provision (ex Article 12 EEC) was suited by its nature to produce direct effects.

To be capable of direct effects that are enforceable in the national courts, a Treaty provision must, however, satisfy the criteria established by the CoJ.

> In the words of the Court in **Case 26/62 Van Gend en Loos**:
>
> The wording of Article 12 contains a clear and unconditional prohibition which is not a positive but a negative obligation. This obligation, moreover, is not qualified by any reservation on the part of states, which would make its implementation conditional upon a positive legislative measure enacted under national law. The very nature of this prohibition makes it ideally adapted to produce direct effects in the legal relationship between member states and their subjects.

The implementation of Article 12 does not require any legislative intervention on the part of the states.

The criteria in *Van Gend en Loos* cited above, and repeated in many cases since, have been summarised in the following general terms—that the Community (and now EU) law provision in question must:

(a) be clear and precise;

(b) be unconditional (e.g. as to time limits);

(c) not require implementing measures to be taken by member states or Community (and now Union) institutions; and

(d) not leave any discretion to member states or Community (and now Union) institutions.

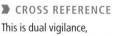 **CROSS REFERENCE**

This is dual vigilance, previously considered in the 'Introduction' to Chapter 6.

The CoJ thus enabled private parties to defend their rights arising in Community (and now EU) law in the face of inconsistent or contrary national law. In doing so, it added to the system of enforcement of EU law by empowering individuals to take action that would have the result of enforcing EU law in situations in which a member state had failed to comply with that law and in which the Commission had not taken any action. This is regarded as particularly helpful because private individuals have clear reasons of self-interest for bringing actions and, because there are so many who may be affected by EU law, the vigilance of EU law is much more widespread and effective.

 **THINKING POINT**

What was the other half of this dual vigilance?

Case 48/65 *Alfons Lütticke GmbH v Hauptzollamt Saarlouis* is an early example of the difference between Treaty Articles that could give rise to direct effects and those that could not. The case declared that old Article 95 EEC (now 110 TFEU) satisfied the criteria so as to give rise to direct effects, but that Article 97 EEC (now repealed) did not. The CoJ ruled that Article 95 had created direct effects, but that since member states had a discretion to decide whether to levy an average rate of tax, Article 97 did not produce direct effects.

Old Article 95 provided that 'No Member State shall impose, directly or indirectly . . . any internal taxation of any kind' and old Article 97 provided that 'member states . . . may, in the case of internal taxation . . . establish average rates'. (Note that old Article 97 EEC was repealed by the Treaty of Amsterdam.)

Since these early cases, direct effects have been found to arise from many Treaty Articles, which often obligate not only organs of the state as in a vertical relationship, but also other individuals in a horizontal relationship—in particular, in the EU context, employers (see Figure 8.1). It was confirmed by the CoJ that employers are obligated to comply with the requirements of a Treaty Article and that other individuals may enforce corresponding rights directly against the obligated party who has failed to comply with Community (and now EU) law.

The first case to confirm horizontal direct effects was **Case 43/75 *Defrenne v Sabena (No. 2)***, in which the rights of an air hostess for equal pay guaranteed under old Article 119 EEC (now 157 TFEU) were upheld against the employing airline Sabena (although the national airline was registered as a private company), which was in breach of the obligation. From the area of competition law, **Case C-453/99 *Courage Ltd v Crehen*** is also a very good example of a Treaty Article (Article 101 TFEU) being enforced horizontally between individuals.

Article 12 EC (now 18 TFEU)

Within the scope of application of the Treaties, and without prejudice to any special provisions contained therein, any discrimination on grounds of nationality shall be prohibited.

Article 12 EC (now 18 TFEU) on the general non-discrimination on the grounds of nationality, which is imposed on the member states, was found to be capable of horizontal direct effects in **Cases 36/74 *Walrave and Koch* and C-92/92 *Phil Collins v Imrat***. This is very important because it can be relied on by the CoJ, and indeed individuals, in many circumstances.

However, Article 10 EC (now 4(3) of the Treaty on European Union (TEU)), the good faith clause imposing a general obligation on the member states to act in conformity and not against Community (and now Union) interests, was held in **Case 44/84 *Hurd v Jones*** not to give rise to direct effects.

Figure 8.1 Vertical and horizontal direct effects

Vertical direct effects

State (or state body)

Individual (natural or legal person)

Horizontal direct effects

Individual ⟷ Individual

Article 10 EC (now 4(3) TEU)

Member States shall take any appropriate measure, general or particular, to ensure fulfilment of the obligations arising out of the Treaties or resulting from the acts of the institutions of the Union. The Member States shall facilitate the achievement of the Union's tasks and refrain from any measure which could jeopardise the attainment of Union's objectives.

Nevertheless, Article 10 EC (now 4 TEU) has been highly influential in assisting the CoJ to develop other means of enforcing Community and now EU law. See, for example, the *Von Colson* case, considered at section 8.2.2, and *Francovich*, considered at section 8.3.

Provisions of the Accession Treaties have also been held to give rise to direct effects.

See, for example, **Case C-113/89 *Rush Portuguesa* v *Office National d'Immigration***, which provided details of the rights that non-Community workers were entitled to expect whilst working outside their EC country of immigration, in another host member state.

8.1.3.2 EU Charter of Fundamental Rights

Whilst waiting for the view of the CoJ on whether provisions within the EU Charter of Fundamental Rights can produce direct effects, the Charter itself provides that it applies to obligate the EU and the member states only. It is not, therefore, to be regarded in the same way as the Treaties and Regulations which obligate everyone (see Article 51(1) of the Charter), although in view of the fact that it is primary EU law, it should therefore be regarded in the same way as Treaty Articles and in theory should be capable of giving rise to direct effects. The CoJ has, however, thus far not made any such pronouncement, although provisions of the Charter have been relied on by individuals in the face of conflicting EU and national law. The decision in Case C-176/12 *Association de Médiation Sociale (AMS)* would certainly seem to support that view, and indeed also suggest that the Charter could also provide horizontal rights. In that case, the CoJ held that despite the French private body not complying with either a directive or Article 27 of the EU Charter of Fundamental Rights, neither could give rise to horizontal effects between private parties, despite the opinion of the AG that the Article could be relied on horizontally. It may be, though, that the particular right under consideration may already be covered in existing Treaty rights or indeed in general principles, which themselves have been declared to be directly effective. However, the *AMS* case should not be read to dictate the result in any forthcoming cases considering the Charter.

8.1.3.3 **General principles**

More recent case law, in particular in the area of equality or non-discrimination law, has indicated that general principles may also give rise to vertical and horizontal direct effects and in circumstances where a Directive which focuses on particular prohibition of discrimination had not yet reached the time for its implementation. See Cases C-144/04 *Mangold* and C-555/07 *Kükükdeveci* and others which are considered further in section 8.2.3.

8.1.3.4 **Regulations**

Whilst Regulations are clearly directly applicable by reason of Article 288 TFEU (ex 249 EC) and can therefore also obligate other individuals, they are not necessarily directly effective. The question of whether they can also give rise to direct effects depends on whether they satisfy the same criteria as for Treaty Articles as laid down in *Van Gend en Loos*.

> The leading case concerning Regulations is **Case C-93/71 Leonesio v Italian Ministry of Agriculture**, in which Italian farmers were able to enforce a Regulation against the Italian state providing for compensation payments that had been subject to delays by the Italian authorities. The CoJ held that the Regulation should not be subject to delays and was immediately enforceable in the national courts.

Given that Regulations are also generally applicable in that they not only provide rights, but also apply to and impose obligations on everyone, it should not be a surprise that they are capable of giving rise to direct effects horizontally.

> For example, in **Case C-253/00 Munoz v Frumar Ltd**, the CoJ upheld the right of one individual trader to rely on the rights provided by a Regulation in a civil action against another individual not complying with the Regulation.

8.1.3.5 **Directives**

Directives have caused particular problems for the CoJ. At first, they were thought, as a general rule, not to be precise enough to give rise to direct effects because they were not directly applicable and only obligated the member states to achieve an end result.

> Article 288 TFEU provides that a Directive shall be binding, as to the result to be achieved, upon each member state to which it is addressed, but shall leave to the national authorities the choice of form and methods.

Arguably, because they often provide a wide margin of discretion, Directives were considered incapable by their very nature of ever fulfilling the *Van Gend en Loos* criteria. To allow Directives to have direct effects would, it was argued, blur the distinction between Regulations and Directives contrary to the intention of the Treaties, in that it would appear that they applied generally to everyone and would need no further implementation.

> **Case 9/70 Grad**, however, considered and allowed for the possibility that direct effects could arise from other non-directly applicable forms of Community and now EU law outside Treaty Articles and Regulations.

Case 41/74 *Van Duyn* v *The Home Office* confirmed that Directives could give rise to direct effects, provided that they also satisfied the same criteria. The provisions of the Directive would have to contain a clear and precise obligation, which they can and often do. In this case, Article 3 of Directive 64/221 was held to give rise to rights directly enforceable against the state before the national courts by Miss Van Duyn.

A further aspect of Directives that might have caused difficulty was that Directives usually allow the member states a period of time in which to implement them—two years being the most common period provided.

Case 148/78 *Publico Ministero* v *Ratti* considered this aspect. It concerned the prosecution of Mr Ratti by the Italian authorities for breaches of national law concerning product labelling. Although Mr Ratti had complied with two Community Product Labelling Directives, the expiry period for implementation of one of the two Directives had not passed. The CoJ held that Mr Ratti could rely on the Directive whose time period had expired provided it satisfied the requirements of clarity and precision etc., but could not rely on the Directive whose implementation period had not expired.

Although not expressly or directly contradicting the ruling with regard to time limits in ***Ratti***, **Case C-144/04 *Mangold*** provides that in certain circumstances the time limit for the implementation of a Directive may be less important. This is where, in addition to the specific rights contained within Directive 2000/78 in *Mangold* providing the prohibition of age discrimination, there was also a general principle prohibiting discrimination. Mangold suffered age discrimination but the Directive's implementation period had not expired. The CoJ, however, held that the discrimination also breached the general principle prohibiting discrimination, and this could not be undermined by the unexpired transposition period of a Directive. The Directive was argued to provide a more exact setting in which the pre-existing general principle could be interpreted and applied. The argument in the case was that both a strict application of Article 6 of Directive 2000/78 and the application of the general principle would have had the same result. However, if relying on the Directive only, this would have caused problems because of the non-expiry of the implementation period; thus, the Directive was incapable of producing direct effects. In order to get over those difficulties, it was better to use the general principle.

Case 51/76 *Verbond* concerned the situation in which a Directive had been implemented after the time limit had expired, but the implementation was not faithful to the requirements of the Directive. The CoJ held that to deny the rights of individuals in such circumstances would be to weaken the effectiveness of Community obligations and that, as a result, individuals helped to ensure that member states kept within the realms of the discretion granted.

▶ CROSS REFERENCE
See later in this section and section 8.2.2 for more on *Becker*.

The individual nature of the rights contained in the Directive has been stressed in a number of cases, notably **Case 8/81 *Becker***, as an element in deciding that they can be asserted against the state, although this does not form part of the required criteria. Furthermore, the *Becker* case also highlighted the wider effects of Community and now Union law as a standard by which national law should be judged and prepared the ground substantially for the CoJ to develop indirect effects in the later *Von Colson* case.

For a considerable time, the question of whether Directives could be held to give rise to horizontal direct effects and thus be enforceable against other individuals received no answer from the CoJ. At the time, further arguments against horizontal effects in addition to the apparent discretion given to the member states were that Directives did not have to be published, and this would have offended against legal certainty. Furthermore, Directives are addressed to and obligate member states and not individuals, and therefore individuals should not be obligated by them. It was argued that making Directives potentially enforceable against everyone would blur the distinction between Directives and the Regulations because they would resemble directly applicable law, something not intended under the scheme of Article 249 EC (now 288 TFEU). Arguments for horizontal direct effects of Directives are that Community and EU law should be equally actionable against the state and other individuals to ensure uniform consistency throughout the Union and to avoid giving rise to two categories of right. The discretion for Directives is not in *what* should be achieved but *how* it should be achieved; thus, the obligation or requirement is not discretional, but how it is achieved in each member state is. It is also the case that Treaty Articles are addressed to member states, but can nevertheless obligate individuals. Directives, whilst not at first publishable by compulsion, were invariably published, and indeed now must be published (see Article 297 TFEU).

Article 297 TFEU

1. Legislative acts adopted under the ordinary legislative procedure shall be signed by the President of the European Parliament and by the President of the Council . . .

    Legislative acts shall be published in the Official Journal of the European Union.

The CoJ came to a conclusion about Directives in **Case 152/84 *Marshall* v *Southampton Area Health Authority***, deciding that Directives could be enforced by individuals but only against the state or arms of the state, and not against other individuals. The case itself concerned equal treatment by the employer of men and women in retirement, but it involved vertical and not horizontal direct effects because the health authority was held to be part of the state.

This Court ruling, however, led to a whole host of problems because of the distinction created between the ability to enforce rights against public as opposed to private employers. The result of this decision is that the scope of the concept of what constitutes 'public service' as opposed to a 'private body' became crucial.

This can be seen from the later UK case of **Duke v Reliance** in which, on facts similar to those of *Marshall*, Mrs Duke lost her claim for compensation for being forced to retire earlier than men.

Two further decisions in **Cases 222/84 *Johnston* v *RUC*** and **C-188/89 *Foster* v *British Gas***showed that although the concept of public entity was wide enough to include national law enforcement agencies and nationalised industries and included any form of state control or authority, a distinction between public-sector and private-sector rights nevertheless remains.

❱ CROSS REFERENCE

The ways around the unfortunate consequences of the *Marshall* decision are explored further in section 8.2.

> **Case 8/81 *Becker*** confirmed the restriction of the direct effects of Directives as operating on the vertical axis only, but highlighted the further or wider benefits of direct effects for the Community legal order. The CoJ in this case stressed that directly effective Community law also operates in a wider sense as a standard by which national law is in effect evaluated by the Court to see if it meets the standard of EC law, rather than simply providing a narrower individual right only.

In strict terms, the CoJ has no formal right to review the validity of national law; however, the doctrine of direct effects does allow it to declare that there is an incompatibility on the part of the national law with the directly effective standard contained in the EU law. The *Becker* case thus prepares the ground for the establishment of the indirect effects, considered in section 8.2.2.

8.1.3.6 Decisions

> In **Case 9/70 *Grad v Finanzamt Traunstein***, the CoJ held that it would be contrary to the binding nature of Community law if the provisions of a Decision could not be invoked by individuals. They must also satisfy the criteria and can only be enforced against those obligated. In *Grad*, a decision addressed to the German state concerned with the harmonisation of tax regimes was held to give rise to effects that could be enforced by an individual affected by it. The Court, though, has declared in **Case C-80/06 *Carp***, that they do not give rise to horizontal direct effects between individuals from a Decision addressed to one of them (i.e. no horizontal direct effect).

8.1.3.7 International agreements

Although there is no statement in the Treaties that international agreements entered into by the Union or by the member states within the Union can give rise to direct effects, the CoJ has held that their provisions may also give rise to direct effects provided they satisfy the criteria previously established. Agreements such as association agreements between the Union and a single state, or even a number of states, are capable of producing direct effects. Indeed, due to the limited nature and scope of the agreements, they lend themselves more readily to producing direct effects than the more complex multilateral agreements, the subject matter of which may well go beyond the jurisdictional scope of the Treaties.

> For example, provisions of the EEC–Portugal Association Agreement, parts of the EEC–Morocco Agreement, and provisions of the Yaoundé Convention Agreement were held to be directly effective in **Cases 104/81 *Kupferberg*, 87/75 *Bresciani*, and C-18/90 *Kziber***, respectively.

In contrast, provisions of more complex agreements such as the General Agreement on Tariffs and Trade (GATT), which are mixed agreements involving the competences of both the Community (and now Union) and the member states, have not shown themselves to the CoJ to be so amenable to direct effects.

> For example, **Case 21–24/72 *International Fruit***, the CoJ held that the GATT provisions in question were not directly effective because they were held to be too flexible and too easily subject to change by political negotiation rather than clearly applicable in a strict and reasonably foreseeable way by the courts.

However, in line with the transition of GATT to the World Trade Organization (WTO), the CoJ has appeared to soften its stance.

The Court expressed the possibility in **Case C-280/93 *Germany v Commission*** that the GATT provisions may have direct effects, but only where the Community intended to implement a particular GATT provision or expressly referred to it in a Community Act.

See also, for example, **Case 70/87 *Fediol***, in which a reference in a Community Regulation to a commercial practice identified in the GATT would allow the Court to interpret the Community Act according to the GATT rule.

It was, however, emphasised by the CoJ in **Case C-149/96 *Portugal v Council*** that the WTO rules do not give rise to direct effects. The CoJ did not wish to tie the hands of the Community by confirming binding rules of law for the Community when those same rules are not considered to be rigidly binding by other parties.

The WTO and GATT regimes are not based on binding and immediately enforceable rules, but rules the breach of which lead first to further negotiation and even the sanctioning of reciprocal action being taken by the aggrieved state on completely different goods.

Rules emanating from the United Nations (UN) have also been considered by the CoJ. Whilst such rules, as pre-existing obligations of all the member states which are members of the UN, are thus to be respected by the EU, they appear not likely to give rise to direct effects. Thus, they join those rules from the WTO and GATT, which are not, in the view of the CoJ, capable of providing individuals with directly effective rights.

In **Case C-308/06 *Intertanko***, the CoJ held that because the UN Convention on the Law of the Sea did not create rights for individuals it could not be used by the Court to determine the validity of an EU act, alleged to be in breach of the Convention.

For more details on this section visit the online resources.

Thus, it cannot be said that there is a presumption in favour of international agreements having direct effects. It depends on their nature and whether they intend to provide rights for individuals.

8.2 Overcoming the lack of horizontal direct effect for Directives

8.2.1 **Extending the definition of 'the state'**

One way in which to avoid the unfortunate results of the *Marshall* ruling, which led to differences in treatment between state and private employees, is to expand the concept of 'public sector' to include more employers and thus more individuals capable of being able to enforce their rights vertically in the national courts through direct effects.

For more details on this section visit the online resources.

> In **Case C-188/89 *Foster v British Gas***, the House of Lords referred to the CoJ the critical question of what was meant by 'state authority'. In *Marshall*, the health authority was clearly regarded as a part of the state. *Foster* involved, at that time, a nationalised, but independently run, organisation; it was later privatised. The CoJ held that emanations of the state against which direct effects were available were those bodies that provided a public service under the control of the state and which for that purpose were granted special powers.

Direct effects are thus available against such bodies. However, although the case showed that the concept was wide enough to include nationalised industries and includes any form of state control or authority, a distinction remains between public (however widely framed) and private employers. So, it may be concluded that expanding the scope of what is meant by an 'emanation of the state' will broaden the concept and protect more people, but this still does not reach the heart of the matter. It allows a variation as between public and private employees, and because there are inevitably different situations in each of the member states as regards the public and private sector, there will also be a difference in the rights of individuals between the member states. Thus, because of this distinction, a different result can occur in each member state where national concepts of what is within the control of the state may differ. The difficulties and limits to this approach are demonstrated in a UK case.

> In ***Doughty v Rolls Royce plc***, the Court of Appeal considered that the (at the time) largely state-owned and nationalised Rolls Royce company was not a public body for the purposes of the claim to direct effects in the case, because it was not providing a public service and was not subject to special powers.

Whilst the result in the *Rolls Royce* case is probably correct, although rather narrow, it can be seen that privatisation of once-nationalised companies might also affect the rights of individuals. If decided today, *Foster* v *British Gas* would probably have a different outcome. A further case has shed a little more light on what can be included in the concept of the state.

> In **Case C-157/02 *Rieser Internationale Transporte GmbH v Autobahnen- und Schnell-straßen Finanzierungs AG***, the CoJ held:
>
> > When contracts are concluded with road users, the provisions of a directive capable of having direct effect may be relied upon against a legal person governed by private law where the State has entrusted to that legal person the task of levying tolls for the use of public road networks and where it has direct or indirect control of that legal person. The state was the sole shareholder of the company and had actual and effective overall control over both budgets and its activities.

Therefore, private companies undertaking a public duty come within the scope of the *Foster* ruling. There remains, however, no uniformity and indeed no certainty as to the application of EU law between public and private employers within and between member states. Certain individuals are thus denied rights that employees in the public sector can enforce in the face of non-compliance by member states. It has further to be observed that the state has contracted in most, if not all, member states as previous state monopoly industries are broken up for the purposes of competition or simply privatised. This means that more employees are placed into the horizontal relationship and are not able to avail themselves of the direct effects of Directives. Widening the concept is essentially swimming against a very powerful tide. The scope of the concept of public service as opposed to a private body remains a crucial, but sometimes artificial, distinction.

8.2.2 **Indirect effects**

Case 8/81 *Becker*, and its acknowledgement of a wider concept of direct effects as a standard by which the conformity of national law could in effect be reviewed by the CoJ, had already pointed EC (and now EU) law in the direction that was about to be taken in the next development.

▶ CROSS REFERENCE

Becker was considered at section 8.1.3.5.

> **Case 14/83 *Von Colson*** provided a solution where national law was not in tune with Community law and direct effects could not provide a remedy. The ruling offers an alternative for individuals defeated by the lack of horizontal direct effects. The case concerned Article 6 of the Equal Treatment Directive 76/207 and a claim against a public employer for lack of adequate compensation when discriminated against.

> At the same time, **Case 79/83 *Harz v Tradex*** was also heard by the CoJ, which involved a similar claim against a private employer. Rather than highlight the unfortunate results of the lack of horizontal direct effects of Directives against the private, but not the public, employer, the CoJ concentrated on old Article 5 EEC (now 4(3) TEU), which requires member states to comply with Community obligations.
>
> The Court held that this requirement applies to all authorities of member states, including the courts, which are obliged therefore to interpret national law in such a way as to ensure that the obligations of a Directive are obeyed, regardless of whether the national law was based on any particular Directive.

It would not, of course, have been acceptable for *Von Colson* to have succeeded under direct effects against an arm of the state but *Harz* not to have done so against a private employer; thus, an alternative solution was required.

The effectiveness of this remedy, though, depends on the willingness or ability of the member states' courts to interpret national law, if it exists, to achieve the correct result.

> However, the CoJ held in **Case 80/86 *Public Prosecutor v Kolpinghuis Nijmegen BF*** that the principle of indirect effects of a Directive could not be applied by a member state to retroactively sanction the prosecution of a Dutch firm for stocking adulterated mineral water in breach of a Community Directive. The implementation period had expired and the Netherlands should have implemented it, but had not; the CoJ held, however, that it would not, in such circumstances, give rise to indirect effects.

The decision is consistent with *Marshall* in that Directives cannot impose obligations on individuals. Thus, the sympathetic interpretation of Community and now EU law Directives required by *Von Colson* could not be used in breach of the general principles, including legal certainty and non-retroactivity. The lack of national law to interpret, however, has caused problems in furthering the principle provided by *Von Colson*. The next case required a further sleight of hand from the Court to achieve a just result that was consistent with its decision in *Marshall*.

> **Case C-106/89 *Marleasing*** concerned Directive 68/151, which had not been implemented in Spain, but which would have determined the outcome of the case. The Spanish courts wanted to know whether the Directive could nevertheless be directly upheld against an individual by

another individual. Whilst the CoJ reaffirmed that Directives do not give rise to effects between individuals, it also stressed that it was up to the courts to achieve the result required by the Directive through the interpretation of national law, whether the national law post-dated or pre-dated the Directive. The national law relevant, the Spanish Civil Code, pre-dated the Directive, but had to be interpreted in a way clearly not covered by it to conform with the later unimplemented Directive.

Such retroactive interpretation will cause severe difficulties where there is a clear conflict between the national law and an EU Directive.

This was the case in the UK House of Lords case of **Duke v GEC Reliance Systems**, in which the House of Lords refused to interpret pre-existing UK law in the light of the later Equal Treatment Directive, in spite of the decision in *Marshall*.

This difficulty was further highlighted at the Community level before the CoJ in **Case C-334/92 Wagner Miret**, which also involved Spanish legislation pre-dating a Community Directive, but which involved head-on incompatibility. The CoJ this time acknowledged the unsuitability of the *Von Colson* sympathetic interpretation for all cases, but nevertheless stressed that national courts should both presume an intention on the part of the state to comply with Community law and try as far as possible to give effect to the Community law in the case at hand.

In **Case C-168/95 Criminal Proceedings against Luciano Arcaro**, the CoJ acknowledged that the limits of the *Von Colson* principle would be overreached if there were a retroactive interpretation of national law in the light of the Directive that had not been implemented by the member states and which would have imposed criminal liability on an individual, thus confirming the limitation recognised in the *Kolpinghuis* case.

Case C-105/03 Pupino confirms much of the earlier case law. The case involved a Framework Decision (2001/220) enacted under the Police and Judicial Cooperation pillar of the EU (pre-Lisbon). The CoJ held that national courts were obliged to interpret national law in conformity with the Framework Decision by which an individual should be able to invoke the provisions (within the Decision) before the national courts, even though it was clear that the Decision, enacted under the third (intergovernmental) pillar, could not have direct effects. The CoJ held that the obligation to do so arose from general principles of Community law, in particular legal certainty and non-retroactivity, which would be offended if not respected.

⊳ CROSS REFERENCE

If you are unsure about the significance of this, refer to Chapter 1.

The case is also important in that the CoJ applied judicial reasoning and EU law principles to what was an intergovernmental part of the Union, although this latter aspect is no longer important in view of the Treaty reforms introduced by the Lisbon Treaty. The case marked a surprising extension into the intergovernmental pillar of the EU at the time and may be noted as a further example of the Court's judicial activism in the face of failure by the member states to move things forward with the Constitutional Treaty and their delay in reforming the Treaty structure of the Union.

In **Cases C-397–401/01** *Pfeiffer* **v** *Rotes Kreuz*, the CoJ, in considering how far national courts can go in applying *Von Colson*, confirmed that national courts are bound to interpret national law so far as possible in the light of a Directive to achieve the result sought by the Directive. They should also give full effectiveness to Community law, taking into account national law as a whole, as opposed to narrowly looking at a particular national implementing provision.

However, as was emphasised in **Cases C-268/06** *Impact* and **C-555/07** *Kükükdeveci* **v** *Swedex*, a national court is not expected to interpret national law contrary to its clear meaning (*contra legem*), although in **Case C-404/06** *Quelle AG*, it was held that such a difficulty facing the national court does not prevent the CoJ from nevertheless ruling that national law should in fact be interpreted according to an EU provision.

Despite the opinion of the AG in **Case C-91/92** *Faccini Dori* that horizontal direct effects of Directives should be recognised, the CoJ declined to follow this advice. It reasoned that whilst there was a case for vertical direct effects to stop states from relying on their own wrongs, recognition of horizontal direct effects would blur the distinction between Regulations and Directives contrary to the Treaty.

Instead, as it did also in **Case C-334/93** *Wagner Miret*, the CoJ expressed the view that if member states are unable to construe national law to read in conformity, which is a distinct possibility as a result either of the Court being incapable or unwilling to do so, it must be assumed that member states nevertheless intend to comply with their Community law obligations. Thus, if there is a breach, member states must compensate any loss incurred as a result of that breach according to the principles established in *Francovich*.

> **CROSS REFERENCE**
>
> See section 8.3 for more on *Francovich,* which was the EU case introducing the remedy of obtaining damages from the member states for their breach of EU law.

In other words, the failure to succeed under direct or indirect effects should not unfairly extinguish all remedies available. Individuals have, therefore, been provided with a final resort to obtain damages instead.

8.2.3 General principles and direct effects

There have been cases now that demonstrate how Directives can be influenced by a general principle of EU law to determine the result of a case between two individuals.

Case C144/04 *Mangold* **v** *Helm* concerns a German law that made it easier to offer fixed-term contracts to those over the age of 52 by conversely making it easier by reason of the fixed-term contract to end the employment relationship and not commit the employer to a permanent or long-term contract. This was an attempt to make the employment of older persons more attractive, and in this indirect way to help the employment chances of older workers. The law was challenged as contrary to the Directive 2000/78 prohibiting discrimination on the grounds of age, the implementation period of which had at the time not expired. The CoJ held that the

German legislation had gone too far and was thus contrary to the prohibition of discrimination on the ground of age, but appeared to provide for the horizontal direct effects of a Directive and, more surprisingly, even before the period of expiry of the transposition period had taken place. However, note carefully that the CoJ held that the principle of law breached by the member state was the prohibition of discrimination, which is a general principle of EU law. According to the Court, this could not be undermined by the unexpired transposition period of a Directive, which provided a more exact setting in which the pre-existing general principle could be interpreted and applied. The argument in the case was that both a strict application of Article 6 of Directive 2000/78 and the application of the general principle would have had the same result. However, if relying on the Directive only, this would have caused problems because of the non-expiry of the implementation period; therefore, in order to overcome those difficulties, it was better to use the general principle.

In other words, the use of a general principle circumvented the fact that the Directive, according to the past case law (notably the *Ratti* case), was incapable of producing direct effects due to the fact that the obligations contained within it were not yet due. The end result, as far as the CoJ is concerned, is that it remains the case that horizontal direct effects of Directives is not recognised.

Case C-212/04 *Adeneler* v *ELOG* provides some clarification of the judgment in *Mangold*. It concerned the Fixed-Term Work Directive (1999/70) to provide greater protection for fixed-term workers. It was due to be implemented by July 2002, but had not been implemented by Greece in respect of Greek employees whose then current fixed-term contracts had ended. New fixed-term contracts, according to the Directive, were only to be allowed if objectively justified. A Greek court wished to know when the obligation under the Directive should be used to interpret national law by national courts. The CoJ held that the general obligation (of the sort established in *Mangold*) arose only following the implementation period, but would apply regardless of whether the Directive was capable of direct effects for any reason.

CROSS REFERENCE
Ratti and *Von Colson* are noted at sections 8.1.3.5 and 8.2.2.

Thus far, this case takes things no further than the *Ratti* and *Von Colson* cases.

However, the Court went on to hold in **Case C-212/04 *Adeneler* v *ELOG*** that, in the period between publication of the Directive and the expiry of the implementation period, member states were nevertheless constrained (under Articles 10 and 249 EC, now 4(3) TEU and 288 TFEU) from taking any measures that would compromise attaining the requirements of the Directive.

This means that they should not, prior to the expiry of the implementation, interpret national law in a manner that might compromise the objectives of the Directive when the implementation period has then expired. This would seem almost to mean that, effective the publication date and not the expiry date, the Directive's objectives must be complied with, thus tearing up one of the remaining differences between Regulations and Directives—the implementation period.

The decision in the *Mangold* case was subsequently affirmed by the CoJ.

Case C-555/07 _Kükükdeveci_ involved a dispute as to a notice period between an employee and a private employer because a German law precluded periods of employment completed while the employee was under the age of 25 from counting towards the notice period. Ms Kükükdeveci had been dismissed with only one calendar month's notice instead of four, as claimed as a consequence of the German law that was argued to be contrary to EU law. Directive 2000/78, which prohibits discrimination on the grounds of age, had not been implemented in Germany at the material time. The preliminary ruling question was essentially, on what provision of law Kükükdeveci could rely. The CoJ held that the general principle of EU law prohibiting discrimination on the grounds of law, as expressed in Directive 2000/78, applies to preclude national law from discriminating. The CoJ held that the Directive merely gives expression to the principle of equal treatment in employment and the principle of non-discrimination on grounds of age as a general principle of EU law.

In other words, the Directive constitutes a specific application of the general principle of equal treatment and it is the general principle that applies directly between parties, not the Directive. In other words, the general principle produces direct effects that can be upheld by individuals both vertically and horizontally. Is it more controversial, though, that the general principle gives rise to horizontal direct effects or the Directive, bearing in mind that the general principle finds no clear expression anywhere in the Treaties or secondary legislation? In view of the status of general principles in the hierarchy of sources of EU law, that is probably the correct result, although the consensus appears to be that this is only possible where the general principles are backed up by specific expressions of those rights in Directives, as in the _Mangold_ and _Kükükdeveci_ cases, and not in their own right. In any event, they must also pass the criteria established in _Van Gend en Loos_.

The final category of cases that appear in some way to circumvent the inconsistencies produced by the ruling in _Marshall_ is admittedly of less importance and much more limited in scope, and may well be a category that will not attract new cases; that being so, it may well disappear altogether at some stage. For the moment, though, it does warrant brief consideration.

8.2.4 'Incidental' and 'triangular' horizontal effects

Although the opinion of the AG in Case C-91/92 _Faccini Dori_ that horizontal direct effects of Directives should be recognised by the CoJ was rejected, the Court has nevertheless given judgment in a few cases that appear to produce horizontal direct effects. The cases involve Directives that have influenced the outcome involving private parties, but in an incidental rather than a direct way and without imposing a strict obligation on any of the individual parties. The Directives are pleaded not to exert rights directly, but to overcome what would otherwise be the application of incompatible national law in a way detrimental to one of their interests. These cases also support and are supported by the wider view of direct effects put forward in Case 8/81 _Becker_, as a means by which national law is in effect reviewed by the CoJ to see if it meets the standard of EC (and now EU) law, rather than providing an individual right to assert an EU law-based right against another party.

It was claimed in the leading case in this line, **Case C-194/94 _CIA Security International SA v Signalson SA and Securitel SPRL_**, that CIA had breached the national technical standard for alarm systems. CIA pleaded the inapplicability of the national standard because of the failure of the state to notify it to the Commission, as required by Directive 83/189. The CoJ accepted this argument, which meant that CIA was assisted by the Directive. This in turn removed the obligation to meet the national standard, which would have been imposed under national law.

> The Directive relied on imposing no obligation on the other party, only on the state; therefore, there is no question of horizontal direct effects of a Directive. It is true that the other party, which had alleged that CIA had not met the standard, was affected in that its allegation was legally unfounded and it lost the action as a result. However, the national standard could be rendered lawful only by the state complying with the Directive; thus, it remained the state's obligation to ensure that its law was in compliance with Community law. This was not, therefore, an obligation imposed on an individual.

It has been noted that, following this case, the number of notifications of technical standards by the member states increased significantly, thus supporting the free movement of goods regime.

> **Case C-226/97 *Lemmens*** does not follow the trend set by the first cases, for good policy grounds. Lemmens was prosecuted for drink driving, the evidence having been obtained by the use of a breath analysis machine, the standards for which had not been notified to the Commission as required under Directive 83/189. Lemmens sought to argue the inadmissibility of that evidence for his conviction based on the failure of the state to notify the standard. In line with the *CIA* case that a party need not have to rely on a national standard that has not been notified, he argued that his prosecution should not stand. However, the CoJ held that whilst the failure to notify the standard may have hindered the marketing of such machines and as a result the free movement of goods, it did not render unlawful the use of the product as far as national prosecutions for establishing criminal wrongdoing were concerned, and could not therefore aid the defendant in his claim.

> In **Case C-443/98 *Unilever Italia SpA* v *Central Foods SpA***, the principle established in the earlier cases was extended to contractual relations between two individual parties. The Italian state had adopted a food standard before waiting for clearance under the Community Standards Directive's requirements. Unilever's supply of olive oil, which did not comply with the Italian standard, was rejected by the purchaser, Central Foods. In an action for payment, Unilever questioned the Italian legislation. The CoJ held that the Italian law should not apply, and that the case was no different in principle from the *CIA* case and did not create horizontal direct effects. No obligation had been placed on an individual; it was merely the case that un-notified national standards could not apply, regardless of the possible consequence on the contractual relations and liability between the two parties (see Figure 8.2).

Trying to rationalise these cases is not straightforward. The CoJ makes it clear that the cases do not establish the horizontal direct effect of Directives. For the most part, the cases are mainly narrowly restricted to the application of Directive 83/189 and its replacement Directive 98/34, requiring the notification of technical standards, although, as the case law has revealed, this is not the only Directive involved. More to the point is that the Technical Standards Directive essentially involves the direct relationship between the member states and the Commission, and not, as with most other Directives, an obligation on the member state which directly impacts on the relations between individuals and the state, or between individuals.

The following analysis may therefore represent the position reached. Directives are being interpreted to determine the validity of national law in an action that may affect the legal position of

Figure 8.2 Incidental horizontal effects in Case C-443/98
Unilever v *Central Foods*

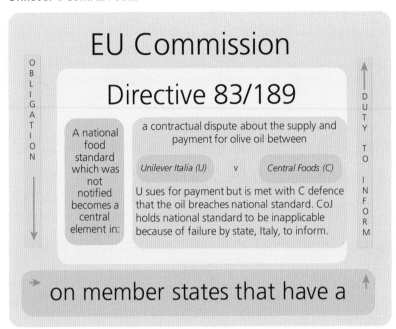

a private party to a court action. Any such incidental effect applies only to prevent reliance on national law not conforming with EU law; hence, the term or view that the effect, as far as the private parties are concerned, is incidental. The real or underlying purpose is the Court's willingness to uphold the provisions of the Directive. This translates generally as not allowing the application of non-conforming national law. As such, then, this merely enforces the public law obligations of the state rather than directly interfering with the contractual relations between parties, although, as was seen in some of the cases, those relations are affected by the obligations imposed on the member states by the Directive. Viewed in terms of estoppel, parties may rely on the Directive as a shield to estop another party from relying on national law that would otherwise harm their interests. They are not using it as a sword to attack the other party. Furthermore, it could be said that both incidental effects and indirect effects are part of the broader view of direct effects in Case 8/81 *Becker* that national law should not be allowed to apply where it does not comply with EU law.

A further form of trangularity has occurred in Cases C-37 and 58/06 *Vaimex* v *Hauptzollamt Hamburg-Jonas*, in which payments of export refunds for live animals which were authorised and set out in a Regulation, were dependent on the conditions provided in a supplementary Directive being met. An exporter was not paid for not meeting those reasons and challenged the decision, and in particular that the provisions of a directive should not be upheld against him. The CoJ held that the provisions of a Directive may be applicable by means of an express reference in a Regulation, providing that the general principle of legal certainty is observed.

An equally limited case law development which produces a similar third-party impact arising from the enforcement of a Directive is **Case C-201/02 *Wells* v *Secretary of State for Transport***, but this time in a triangular relationship. As in the cases noted previously, a Directive does not provide a direct right between individuals but instead obligates another party, which is a member state, the result of which has an impact on another individual. Directive 85/337 requires states to carry out environmental impact assessments when authorising quarrying. The UK had failed to do so and was challenged by Wells. The UK argued that if it now had to carry out the assessment, another party, the quarry owners, would have to stop operations, and thus be adversely impacted. The CoJ held that such adverse repercussions on a third party do not justify denying an individual the right to invoke the Directive against the member state. This so-called triangular effect was also confirmed in **Cases C-152–154/07 Arcor**. Of course, in *Wells* the quarry owners would be perfectly entitled to seek compensation from the state if they could attribute any losses they suffered to the failure of the state to act in accordance with the requirements of the Directive under the principle of state liability, considered in section 8.3.

The cases also serve to highlight the fact that legal difficulties between individuals can be caused by the failure of a member state to comply with an EU law Directive.

THINKING POINT

In view of the numerous developments that have taken place to get around the lack of horizontal direct effects of Directives and how some of them are construed, would it not be better to recognise horizontal direct effects of Directives?

In circumstances where which a failure by a state adversely and directly affects an individual, a further judicial remedy has been provided by the CoJ that holds the state liable to compensate the individual for any loss sustained. This is considered next.

8.3 State liability: the principle in *Francovich*

'State liability' is the term given to the action first raised and accepted by the CoJ in Cases C-6 and 9/90 *Francovich*. This case essentially condoned an action for compensation by an individual against a member state when the member state failed to comply with Community law obligations and which resulted in damage or loss to that individual. The *Francovich* case has both provided a further addition, therefore, to Commission actions against member states to enforce EU law and overcome the difficulties generated by the lack of horizontal direct effects of Directives, or indeed the entire absence of direct effects where the EU law provision fails to satisfy the *Van Gend en Loos* criteria. Instead, the state is held liable for its failure that results in damage to an individual.

Cases C-6 and 9/90 *Francovich* concerned a claim by Italian nationals against the state for a guaranteed redundancy payment granted by Directive 80/987, which had not been implemented by Italy, or alternatively for damages incurred as a result of the state failing to implement the Directive in time. Francovich and other workers were made redundant when the company employing them became insolvent. The company itself had made no payments and, as a result of the insolvency, no action was possible against the company. The CoJ had held already, following Article 226 EC (now 258 TFEU) proceedings in Case 22/87 *Commission v Italy*, that Italy had breached its obligations by its failure to implement the Directive; however, this could not help Francovich and his co-workers because the purpose of an enforcement action is to establish a breach of Community law by the member states and not to provide an individual remedy.

The CoJ held that the Directive was not capable of direct effects because of the discretion granted to the member states as to the result to be achieved. In particular, it was unclear which authority was to be responsible for setting up a compensation agency and—part of the problem for the national court in the first place—there was no national law to interpret in conformity with the Directive, nor any national procedural law to support an action against the state for compensation.

Instead, relying heavily on the fundamental doctrines of direct effects and supremacy, as out-lined in the *Van Gend en Loos, Costa* v *ENEL, Simmenthal*, and *Factortame* cases, the Court determined that the duty of the member states to ensure the full application and enforcement under Articles 10 and 249 EC (now 4(3) TEU and 288 TFEU), if breached, would give rise to li-ability. The Court rejected the defence that the liability of the state was only a matter for the national laws. It held that the protection of individuals under EU law would be weakened if they could not claim damages for loss caused by a member state's failure to comply. It con-sidered, therefore, that the principle was inherent in the scheme of the Treaty—that member states should make good any damage caused to individuals that was the consequence of a breach of Community law.

The Court held, however, that the claim required:

- that the Directive conferred an individual right;
- which could be determined by the provisions of the Directive itself; and
- that there must be a link between the breach and the damage caused.

 THINKING POINT

The ruling has been described by Bebr as the ultimate consequence of *Van Gend en Loos*. What do you think he meant by that?

The decision in *Francovich* provides individuals with a remedy that stems from the breach by the member state of the general obligations in Articles 4(3) TEU and 288 TFEU (ex 10 and 249 EC) to comply with EU law. Hence, this adds a remedy for individuals to fill the gap left where EU law provisions have not been implemented by member states or are held not to be directly effective, or because Directives are effective only on the vertical and not the horizontal axis. Damages are consequently to be assessed in accordance with national procedural rules, sub-ject, however, to overriding EU law principles, which are considered in the final section of this chapter.

The judgment in *Francovich* adds again to the effective judicial protection by providing individuals with rights against the state and deters the state from breaching EU law. It is, though, an inde-pendent action from direct and indirect effects, and provides uniform EU conditions for liability, not dependent on each national set of laws, although the assessment of the quantum of damages is for national procedural law.

> Note that the 1994 judgment in **Case C-91/92 *Faccini Dori* v *Recreb Srl*** confirmed the Court's continued opposition to horizontal direct effects. Whilst stressing the need for national courts to interpret national law wherever possible to comply with Directives, the Court pointed out that, in circumstances in which a state had caused damage caused by non-implementation of Community law, the state would be liable to compensate any loss in line with the principle established in the *Francovich* case.

Since those cases, the CoJ has had the opportunity to develop and clarify the law, starting with Cases C-46 and 48/93 *Brasserie du Pêcheur* v *Federal Republic of Germany; Factortame* v *UK (No. 3)*.

Factortame concerned the breach of a Treaty Article rather than the failure to comply with a Directive, but this was held by the CoJ to be no bar to incurring liability. The result of this case law is that the principle of state liability is applicable to all domestic acts and omissions, legislative, executive, and judicial, which are in breach of EU law, directly effective or not, and in principle by all three arms of state. Case C-424/97 *Haim* makes it clear that liability can result from a breach by any public body which breaches EU law, not just the central organs of state. There was, however, a new focus on the seriousness of the breach. *Factortame (No. 3)* introduced the revised criteria that if the state was facing choices comparable to the institutions when law-making, which essentially involves balancing many interests, the seriousness of breach also must be analogous to that applied to the EU institutions for damage caused unlawfully by legislative acts under Article 288(2) EC (now 340 TFEU).

> This is known as the '*Shöppenstedt* formula', after Case 5/71 *Zuckerfabrik Shöppenstedt*, considered in Chapter 9, section 9.3.3.

❱❱ CROSS REFERENCE

The appropriateness of this standard for member states will be considered further in section 8.4.

In order for liability to arise on the part of the member state, there must have been a sufficiently serious breach of a superior rule of law designed for the protection of individuals. This is the standard applied to damage caused by a legislative Act rather than from administrative action. As such, it is a higher standard because, according to the CoJ, the creation of legislative Acts involves choices of economic policy and is thus far more difficult to achieve.

The sufficiently serious requirement was further elaborated by the CoJ in *Factortame*. It suggested that this would be satisfied where a member state had manifestly and gravely disregarded the limits of its discretion.

The factors that should be taken into account by the national court assessing this are:

- the clarity and precision of the rule breached;
- the measure of discretion;
- whether the infringement and damage was intentional or involuntary;
- whether the error in law was excusable or inexcusable;
- whether there was any contribution to the problem by the Community institutions; and
- whether any incompatible national law was being maintained.

❱❱ CROSS REFERENCE

See Chapter 7 for the Article 260 penalty and Chapter 2 on voting in Council if you do not understand the significance of how difficult it is to reach agreement.

The cases also confirmed that liability can occur without having to establish a breach by the member state by an Article 226 EC (now 258 TFEU) action by the Commission, considered in Chapter 7. However, in cases in which the infringement is not yet clear, this could be problematic. If proven, damages arise from the date of the infringement and not the date of proving the infringement at the date of the judgment, unlike the Article 260 TFEU penalty.

At both the Union and state levels, further case law determined how serious a breach must be to incur liability.

> The CoJ initially has taken a similar approach in respect of the member states as with finding liability on the part the institutions. In **Case C-392/93 *R* v *HM Treasury, ex p British Telecom plc***, the UK government successfully argued that its incorrect implementation of a Directive was due to a misunderstanding of what the Directive required. The CoJ agreed that the Directive was capable of more than one interpretation and, as there was not a sufficiently serious breach of EU law, no liability arose.

> Likewise, in **Case C-319/96 *Brinkmann***, the incorrect application of a tax classification by Denmark, although financially damaging to a company, was not deemed sufficiently serious to incur liability because it was a mistake in the interpretation of the Directive that was also made by other states.
>
> These cases show that where discretion is introduced by the possibility of a range of interpretations of the requirements of EU law, the threshold of liability will be significantly higher and thus more difficult to achieve.

These cases comply with the analysis at the EU level in respect of the liability standards imposed on the institutions, in that where there is discretion on the part of the member state in deciding exactly what action is necessary to implement the EU law obligation or where there is an excusable error in interpretation, the standard of fault for liability will be raised, making it more difficult to obtain compensation. In line with this view, where the obligation is much clearer and the breach much more obvious, liability will be easier to impose.

> In addition to *Francovich* and *Factortame*, see, for example, in contrast, **C-5/94 *Hedley Lomas*** involving the refusal to grant an export licence which was a clear breach of a Directive under Article 29 EC (now 35 TFEU) by the UK. The UK was not required to make any legislative choices and thus had minimal discretion, if any. The mere infringement was enough to establish a sufficiently serious breach.

> See also **Case C-178/94 *Dillenkofer***, in which the simple failure to implement in time the Package Holidays Directive by Germany was in itself a sufficiently serious breach; and **Case C-140/97 *Rechberger***, which involved the incorrect interpretation and thus implementation of the Package Holidays Directive, which simply established liability on the grounds of a straightforward infringement of Community law.

> **Case C-278/05 *Robins*** confirms that the lower the degree of discretion on the part of the member state and the clearer the requirements of the Directive, the higher the chance that the member state will incur liability for a mere breach. Conversely, the more ambiguous or unclear a provision of Community law, the more discretion will be enjoyed by the member state in implementing this and the breach will correspondingly have to be much more serious before

> the member state incurs liability. In the *Robins* case, the argument hinged on the minimum level of protection required under Directive 89/987 for the protection of employees in the event of insolvency of the employer. It was argued that requirement was imprecise and that this was a view of a number of member states. The CoJ accepted this and held that, in view of the discretion to interpret the imprecise duty, the UK was not liable.

》 CROSS REFERENCE

This is considered further in Chapter 9, section 9.3.8 on damages actions under Article 340 TFEU (ex 288 EC).

> **Case C-352/98P Bergaderm** indicates an approach of the CoJ to align the rules on the finding of liability for member states and the Union institutions to that of showing that either has manifestly and gravely disregarded the limits of their discretion. So that, as with member states that have little discretion, it may be easier in future for individuals to obtain compensation from Union institutions for mere infringements that have not involved a great deal of discretion on the part of the institution.

In cases in which liability does arise, the determination of the degree of the seriousness of the breach and thus the level of damages (if any) to be awarded remain questions of national procedural law provided that remedies are not excessively difficult to obtain in the national legal systems and that damages, where applicable, are an adequate remedy. The issues arising from this are considered in section 8.4.

The principle of state liability has been extended in scope or potential scope to the private sector and to national courts.

8.3.1 The extension of *Francovich*

8.3.1.1 Extension to the private sphere

> **Case C-453/99 Courage Ltd v Crehan** was a dispute between two private parties involving a claim that a breach of competition law Article 81 EC (now 101 TFEU) by another private party caused loss to the applicant. Building on the foundation cases of *Van Gend en Loos, Costa v ENEL*, and *Francovich*, the CoJ reasoned that the extension of the principle of state liability was required by the new legal order and for the effective protection of rights, which would be undermined if it were not open to any individual to claim damages for loss caused to him by a contract or by conduct liable to restrict or distort competition.

Francovich liability therefore has been extended to determine liability between private parties and not only against member states where one has caused loss to the other by a breach of EU law.

> This has since been followed up in **Cases C-295–298/04 Manfredi,** making it clear that individuals must be able to obtain full compensation as a result of loss caused by a breach of EU competition rules.

8.3.1.2 Extension to the national courts

Whilst previous case law under *Francovich* has indicated that the CoJ holds the view that state liability is applicable to all branches of government, there was some reticence that this might apply to the judicial branch given the respect for the independence of the judiciary accorded in representative liberal democracies.

The next case introduced the possibility that state liability applies also to breaches of EU law rights by the judiciary, in which case the member state would have to compensate.

> In **Case C-224/01 *Gerhard Köbler* v *Republic of Austria***, the CoJ held that the state may also, potentially at least, be liable for the breaches of Community (and now EU) law by the national courts of last instance provided that they were manifest and sufficiently serious. It was held, however, in the particular case that the breach complained of was not serious enough, despite the opinion of AG Leger that the error of Community law made by the Austrian Administrative Court was not an excusable error. The CoJ regarded it, though, as a misreading or misinterpretation of the existing law.

▶ CROSS REFERENCE

This case was also considered in Chapter 6, section 6.1.8.4.

The *Köbler* case has now been followed up.

> In **Case C-173/03 *Traghetti del Mediterraneo SpA* v *Italy***, it was alleged that a company had been forced into liquidation as a result of the errors in interpretation committed by the Supreme Court in Italy. Furthermore, the chance to correct those errors was denied by that court, which did not make a reference to the CoJ. In a further action by the administrator, the CoJ held that it could not rule out that 'manifest errors' by a national court would lead to compensation under the principle of state liability. However, it was held that it was up to the national courts to decide in each case.

The consequence of this slight extension of liability is that liability for damage caused by courts is not limited as in *Köbler* to 'intentional fault and serious misconduct' by a court in situations in which that standard would have excluded liability for 'manifest infringement'. In other words, it extends liability to where national courts have manifestly infringed the law in their interpretation and which has caused damage. Since that case the CoJ has held in Case C-154/08 *Commission v Spain* that the incorrect interpretation made by a supreme court and the failure to make an Article 267 reference will render the member state liable. The reluctance to go this further step appears thus to have been overcome. This case was also considered in Chapter 7.

8.4 National procedural law and the system of remedies

The development of individual remedies as established and developed by the CoJ has added a second system of vigilance to the existing direct enforcement of EU law by the Union institutions and member states. Inevitably, however, because direct and indirect effects, incidental effect, and state liability are individual remedies that are pursued before the national courts, their overall effectiveness is dependent on national rules of procedural law, which are, of course, by their very nature, outside the jurisdiction and direct influence of the Union and CoJ. These rules can affect and interfere with the realisation of EU rights at the national level. Also, in a comparison between member states, this situation can be complicated by different rules on standing, time limits, burden of proof, or because certain remedies are simply not recognised in some member states. However, because court procedural rules were not within the scope or competence of any of the Treaties, they were originally considered to be entirely within the reserved and exclusive competences of the member states. This idea is given the term 'national procedural autonomy'. However, to counter this, new principles of EU law have been developing to protect individual rights and can be referred to as principles of effective legal protection.

8.4.1 The principle of national procedural autonomy

In the absence of harmonised rules on procedure, rights conferred by EU law must be exercised before national courts in accordance with the traditions laid down by national procedural rules, which, in strict terms, are autonomous from the EU legal system. To what extent, however, should they be respected where they interfere with EU law rights? There are general arguments for and against. For example, if national procedural law were entirely respected, the rule of law and legal certainty of EU law would be undermined, or if respected in each state, differences in remedies would arise between member states, which may distort the uniformity of EU law and the realisation of the internal market and other areas of EU competence and the remedies established and developed by the CoJ including, notably, indirect effects and state liability. On the other hand, some argue that it is better to leave the provision of remedies to those who know their own systems best. The position of the CoJ up to the 1980s was one that essentially respected national procedural rules, subject, however, to certain guidelines, as developed through its case law. '

> The idea that the national procedural rules were independent and beyond the influence of EU law is wrapped up within the term 'national procedural autonomy'.

> In **Case 33/76 *Rewe-Zentralfinanz***, the CoJ held that national courts were entitled to apply national procedural limits provided that national rules are no less favourable for Community law rights than for domestic situations, nor make the Community right impossible to realise.

> In **Case 45/76 *Comet***, the CoJ held that it was up to each member state to determine the procedural conditions governing those actions, but that such conditions cannot be less favourable than those relating to similar actions of a domestic nature and should ensure the protection of the rights that citizens have from the direct effect of Community law.

Thus, where an EU law right is involved, national procedural law must not deprive a litigant of his rights under EU law. Both as a consequence of this and in support of it is the general principle of Article 18 TFEU (ex 12 EC) that there be no discrimination on the grounds of nationality, which must not be breached. From the first cases and other early case law stem the principles of practical impossibility and principle of equivalence. The latter holds that EU law rights should be treated in the same way as national rights. It was seen in relation to cases in respect of supremacy such as Case 6/64 *Costa* v *ENEL* that the CoJ will not allow national rules to stand in the way of a reference to the Court or the supremacy of Community (and now EU) law. Furthermore, it was also seen in the *Simmenthal* and *Factortame (No. 2)* cases, so that it is not only national substantive laws that must give way to EU law, but also any national rules of procedure, including constitutional rules that might get in the way of the effective application of an EU law right, regardless of the origin of these rules.

However, it was clearly stated by the CoJ in **Case 158/80 Rewe v Hauptzollamt Kiel** that no new remedies were intended to be created in the national courts to ensure the observance of Community law over and above that already existing in national law. Equally, however, it became clear that in some cases, further intervention was necessary.

The alternative would be the agreement of the member states to harmonise national procedural rules or to replace them with common Union rules. However, this is neither politically acceptable, because member states do not wish to hand over control of their legal systems to the EU, nor practically possible, due to the very different and nationally idiosyncratic legal systems in existence. It would not be an impossible task, but one that would be exceedingly difficult and time-consuming.

8.4.2 Further intervention by the Court of Justice

Whilst the principle of equivalence would ensure the non-discriminatory application of national rules, this does not go far enough to remedy the situation in all cases. National remedies must, however, also provide an effective remedy. Any rule that actually prevents individuals from relying on an EU law right would be incompatible with the principle of effective legal protection.

> **CROSS REFERENCE**
> This case is also discussed in section 8.2.2 in relation to indirect effects.

In **Case 14/83 Von Colson**, the compensation offered by the national court for the discrimination suffered was the payment of the rail fare home. This was held not to be a dissuasive and adequate remedy. The remedy, according to the Court, must guarantee real and effective judicial protection and must have a real deterrent effect.

Case C-213/89 Factortame highlighted just how radical the solution had to be to ensure the effective protection of Community (and now EU) law rights in the national courts, including, in this case, the right to interim relief against the UK Crown, something that was not constitutionally possible previously.

Case C-208/90 Emmott concerned a national three-month time limit in which to bring benefits claims. The time ran from the date on which the claim arose according to the relevant legislation, in this case the entry-into-force date of a Community Directive. However, it was not clear, due to the faulty transposition of a Community Directive, that the applicant's claim was valid and the claim was rejected in any event as being out of time. The CoJ held that whilst reasonable time limits are acceptable in respect of a claim based originally in Community law, time can only run from the date on which the Directive is implemented properly and where the applicant's rights are clear.

In **Case C-271/91 Marshall II**, the award of compensation to Ms Marshall for discrimination she had experienced was set at a statutory ceiling, which was much lower than the real loss of earnings suffered. The CoJ held that unlawful dismissal based on a Community right should be subject to full compensation including interest, despite the interpretation of the Court of Appeal that, under national law, damages could not include interest.

In a much more interventionist mode, EC law has also required national courts to provide specific and new forms of remedy, most notably in Case C-6/90 *Francovich* and the establishment of the right to damages from the state where liable, discussed in section 8.3.

Thus, national rules are respected to the extent that they do not hinder an EU law right, but where they prevent an EU law right from being realised or applied in some way, the national procedural law must give way. This period of judicial activism and creativeness on the part of the CoJ—particularly the *Emmott* case, which took things surprisingly far—gave way to a less intrusive period as generally the Court was reacting to being criticised for its overt judicial activism. It is, though, still one that engages the CoJ.

In **Case C-118/08 *Transportes Urbanos y Servicios Generales***, the CoJ considered a Spanish domestic procedural rule which required the exhaustion of domestic remedies before an applicant would be allowed to bring an action for damages against the Spanish state for a breach of EU law. This was not, however, a requirement when taking an action for a breach of national constitutional law. It was held by the CoJ to be a breach of the EU principle of equivalence.

8.4.3 A more balanced approach

A more balanced approach was shown by the CoJ in the next case.

In **Case C-339/91 *Steenhorst-Neerings***, a Dutch national procedural law concerned the restriction of retroactive claims to benefits to one year. This was held to be acceptable by the CoJ.

This apparent step back from *Emmott* means that reasonable time limits are acceptable even though these can vary from state to state. However, *Steenhorst-Neerings* was distinguished from the rule in *Emmott*, which applied after a three-month deadline expired to prevent bringing an action at all. It was held that the state itself had contributed to the failure of the applicant to comply with the strict time limit by advising a wait-and-see attitude to another case concerning the same rule, which had also questioned similar rights to equal treatment in payments. The rule in *Steenhorst-Neerings*, in contrast, permitted a claim, but limited the retrospective payments under it to one year.

In **Case C-188/95 *Fantask***, the CoJ gave general grounds for accepting time limits that could result in differences between the member states. It held that national time limits would continue to apply even in situations in which the Directive had not been properly implemented into national law for reasons of legal certainty and to protect the national taxpayer and authorities. The case itself concerned a five-year limitation period for the recovery of debts, which was held to be acceptable—that is, there was to be no Community (now EU) rule for the recovery of tax payments.

Two similar cases concerned more closely with procedure were decided differently, although both concerned a variation of a national procedural rule stating that it is up to the parties to introduce legal arguments and not the courts. However, if EU law, which may be relevant, is not introduced, a party may suffer as a result. In these circumstances, it was argued in the cases that the national court must either introduce the EC law itself or at least make a reference to the CoJ, thus infringing the national rule. Questions were referred as to whether indeed the national procedural law must give way.

> In **Case C-312/93 *Peterbroeck van Campenhout***, the CoJ held that national procedural laws should not prevent references being made.

> This was seemingly contradicted by **Cases C-430 and 431/93 *Van Schijndel***, in which a similar procedural rule, which prevented a reference from taking place, was upheld as acceptable because the rule was also applied in similar domestic circumstances and was there to ensure legal certainty and clarity. In other words, the national procedural rules could not be seen to be applied in two different ways according to whether EU or national substantive laws were concerned.

Somewhat unhelpfully in *Van Schijndel*, the CoJ held that each rule of procedural law and thus each case has to be judged on its merits, taking into account the rights of defence, legal certainty, and the role of the national procedure before determining whether it renders the application of Community law impossible or excessively difficult. This would seem only to provoke further references to the Court each time a slightly new procedural law is brought into question.

> In **Case C-326/96 *Levez* v *Jennings***, the CoJ considered a UK procedural law that limited the period of claim for damages in sex discrimination cases to a period not exceeding two years running backward from the date of commencement of proceedings. The CoJ acknowledged that, in the absence of a Community regime on the matter, it was for member states to determine procedural rules governing Community law rights provided they were equivalent to similar domestic actions and were effective. A limit of two years was not criticised. However, Ms Levez had been misinformed or deliberately misled by the employer as to the higher earnings of a male predecessor and had only learnt the truth on leaving her job. Under such circumstances, the CoJ held that, if applied, the rule would serve to deprive an employee from effective enforcement of Community law because it would be almost impossible to obtain arrears of remuneration and to enable employers to avoid paying damages by deceit. In such circumstances, the rule would be manifestly incompatible with the principles of EC law.

Following the *Emmott* case, each case requires a clear demonstration that the particular facts of the case will lead to a particular unjust result, but this is not very helpful in general terms to determine whether in future cases the national procedural law will upset EU law rights. The cases previously considered in section 8.3 on *Francovich* state liability are relevant to this discussion in that they also demonstrate the impact on the national legal systems of remedies developed by the CoJ and the extension of those remedies both against other individuals under EU law and the courts of the member states. These EU law remedies were simply not available previously, although some member states may have had national remedies that would have achieved the same result.

The next case considers and summarises the scope of the EU law remedy.

> **Case C-432/05 *Unibet*** was referred to the CoJ by the Swedish Supreme Court about the compatibility of a Swedish law on lotteries with Community law. In order to determine this, the national court enquired specifically about the scope of the principle of effective judicial protection and whether Community law required a member state's legal order to provide a

》 CROSS REFERENCE

Cases 33/76 *Rewe*, and
45/76 *Comet* are considered
at section 8.4.1.

self-standing action for a declaration that a provision of its national law conflicted with Community law and whether, in waiting for the determination, interim relief had to be granted. The CoJ held that the principle of effective judicial protection is a general principle of Community law stemming from the constitutional traditions common to the member states, which is also enshrined in Articles 6 and 13 of the European Convention on Human Rights (ECHR) and which has been affirmed by Article 47 of the EU Charter of Fundamental Rights. It confirmed that Article 10 EC (now 4(3) TEU) required member states to ensure judicial protection of individuals' rights and refer to its earlier case law on this, including Cases 33/76 *Rewe*, 45/76 *Comet*, and C-312/93 *Peterbroeck*.

The CoJ held in this case, though, that, in the absence of a Community rule, the member states were left to decide according to their own procedural rules. Consequently, the principle of effective judicial protection does not require the national legal order of a member state to provide for a free-standing action for an examination of whether national provisions are compatible with Article 49 EC (now 56 TFEU), provided that other effective legal remedies, which are no less favourable than those governing similar domestic actions, make it possible for such a question of compatibility to be determined as a preliminary issue. Furthermore, the principle of effective judicial protection of an individual's rights under EU law must be interpreted as requiring it to be possible in the legal order of a member state for interim relief to be granted until the competent court has given a ruling on whether national provisions are compatible with EU law, where the grant of such relief is necessary to ensure the full effectiveness of the judgment to be given on the existence of such rights.

This essentially confirms the position previously laid down in Case C-213/89 *Factortame*, which provides that this should be no more difficult to obtain than the application for interim relief in cases concerned with domestic law. The principle of effective judicial protection thus ensures that, regardless of the existence of national law remedies, EU law rights are subject to protection before the national courts.

8.4.4 **Section summary**

National procedural autonomy is still the general rule and is still respected under the EU legal order, but the CoJ has intruded into the area by developing the demands for effectiveness and equivalence or by providing new remedies in the member states with the aim of ensuring a balance between the objective to protect the national procedural autonomy and at the same time to protect the effectiveness of EU law. Until there is an agreement by all member states to try to harmonise procedural law—a very difficult task at best—the ad hoc development of the case law that we have witnessed is not likely to change. The only change in this respect, which was introduced by the Constitutional Treaty and retained in the Lisbon Treaty, is modest. New Article 19(1) TEU provides as a general statement that member states must provide remedies sufficient to ensure effective legal protection in the fields covered by Union law, which merely reflects, but in far simpler language, the *Unibet* case.

 Summary

The original provision of remedies in the EU legal order was largely of those provided by the Treaty and included the direct remedies and the Article 234 EC (now 267 TFEU) preliminary ruling procedure. It can be seen, however, that these provide only half the picture and, more importantly from the perspective of individuals, are the series of remedies that have been introduced and developed by the CoJ. Some of these can be regarded as necessary to plug a gap in the first set of remedies—that is, direct effects—developed to supplement and provide an alternative to the Treaty-based remedies and other Court-established remedies, to further develop and plug gaps in the Court-developed remedies—that is, indirect effects, incidental horizontal effects, and state liability. It should be clear that a study of the Treaties alone does not provide the complete picture of remedies in the EU legal order and that the remedies in this chapter are equally important, constituting as they do the second half of the system of dual vigilance that has developed, as outlined at the beginning of this chapter and Chapter 6.

> **CROSS REFERENCE**
Remedies are also considered in Chapter 6, 7, and 9.

? Questions

1. Are regulations necessarily directly effective? Give reasons for your answer.

2. Has the application of the doctrine of direct effects blurred the distinction between Regulations and Directives? If so, does it matter?

3. Look at Articles 35 and 60 TFEU. Are they capable of direct effects? Explain why or why not, as appropriate.

4. Distinguish between horizontal and vertical direct effects. Do these terms apply to all forms of EU law? If not, why not?

5. How far have the drawbacks that resulted from the denial of horizontal direct effects of Directives been overcome by the CoJ's decisions in subsequent case law?

6. What are indirect effects and how are they supposed to assist individuals in realising EU legal rights?

7. What difficulties may be faced by national courts in trying to operate indirect effects? Cite case law to support your answer.

8. To what extent does the doctrine of 'state liability', first established in the *Francovich* case, add to the range of individual remedies in EU law?

9. What criteria must be satisfied before a claim under state liability will succeed and how is this judged?

10. To what extent is the principle of national procedural autonomy respected in the EU legal order? To what extent should it be?

For suggested approaches to answering these questions visit the online resources.

Sample exam Q&A

Essay question

Does the distinction between vertical and horizontal direct effects cause difficulties for individuals in actions involving EU law? If so, what has been done to mitigate these difficulties?

For guidance on how to tackle this specimen exam question and to read a suggested model answer, visit the online resources. www.oup.com/uk/foster_directions6e/.

☰ Further reading

Books

Albors-Llorens, A. 'Judicial protection before the Court of Justice of the European Union' in Barnard, C. and Peers, S. (eds) *European Union Law*, 2nd edn, Oxford University Press, Oxford, 2017, p. 262.

Lenaerts, K., Arts, D., and Maselis, I. *Procedural Law of the European Union*, 3rd edn, Sweet & Maxwell, London, 2012.

Prinssen, J. M. and Schrauwen, A. (eds) *Direct Effect: Rethinking a Classic of EC Legal Doctrine*, 2nd edn, Europa Law Publishing, Groningen, 2004.

Ward, A. *Judicial Review and the Rights of Private Parties in EU Law*, 2nd edn, Oxford University Press, Oxford, 2007.

Articles

Arnull, A. 'The principle of effective judicial protection in EU law: an unruly horse?' (2011) 36 EL Rev 51.

Anagnostaras, G. 'The quest for an effective remedy and the measure of protection afforded to putative Community law rights' (2007) 32(5) EL Rev 727.

Bebr, G. 'Case note on *Francovich*' (1992) 29 CML Rev 557.

Beutler, B. 'State liability for breaches of Community law by national courts: is the requirement of a manifest infringement of the applicable law an insurmountable obstacle?' (2009) 46 CML Rev 773.

Brinkhorst, L. 'Case note on the *Grad* and *SACE* decisions' (1971) 8 CML Rev 380.

Broberg, M. '*Acte clair* revisited: adapting the *acte clair* criteria to the demands of the times' (2008) 45 CML Rev 1383.

Cabral, P. and Neves, R. 'General principles of EU law and horizontal direct effect' (2011) 17 EPL 437.

Craig, P. 'The legal effect of Directives: policy, rules and exception' (2009) 34 ELR 349.

Davis, R. 'Liability in damages for breach of Community law: some reflections on the question of who to sue and the concept of "the state"' (2006) 31 EL Rev 69.

Dougan, M. 'When worlds collide: competing visions of the relationship between direct effect and supremacy' (2007) 44 CML Rev 931.

Drake, S. 'Scope of courage and the principle of "individual liability" for damages: further development of the principle of effective judicial protection by the Court of Justice' (2006) 31 EL Rev 841.

Granger, M.-P. 'National applications of *Francovich* and the construction of a European administrative *ius commune*' (2007) 32(5) EL Rev 157.

Jans, J. H. 'The effect in national legal systems of the prohibition of discrimination on grounds of age as a general principle of Community law' (2007) 34 LIEI 53.

Leczykiewicz, D. 'Horizontal application of the Charter of Fundamental Rights' (2013) 38 EL Rev 479.

Lock, T. 'Is private enforcement of EU law through state liability a myth? An assessment 20 years after *Francovich*' (2012) 49 CML Rev 1675.

Nassimpian, D. ' . . . And we keep on meeting: (De)fragmenting state liability' (2007) 32 EL Rev 819.

Prechal, S. 'Member state liability and direct effect: what's the difference after all?' (2006) 17 EBL Rev 299.

Prechal, S. and De Vries, S. 'Seamless web of judicial protection in the internal market' (2009) 34(1) EL Rev 5.

Schermers, H. 'No direct effect for Directives' (1997) 3(4) EPL 527.

Steiner, J. 'From direct effects to *Francovich*: shifting means of enforcement of Community law' (1993) 18 EL Rev 3.

Vajda, C. 'Liability for breach of Community law: a survey of the ECJ cases post *Factortame*' (2006) 17 EBL Rev 257.

Von Bogdandy, A. 'Pluralism, direct effect, and the ultimate say: on the relationship between international and domestic law' (2008) 6(3–4) ICON 397.

Winter, J. 'Direct applicability and direct effect: two distinct and different concepts in Community law' (1972) 9 CML Rev 425.

Direct actions before the Court of Justice

In this chapter, you will focus on the following direct actions against the European Union institutions before the Court of Justice of the European Union:

- the judicial review of acts of the institutions (Article 263 TFEU);

- actions against the institutions for a failure to act (Article 265 TFEU);

- actions for damages for loss caused as a result of an act of the institutions (Articles 268 and 340 TFEU); and

- incidental challenges to EU Acts (Article 277 TFEU).

Introduction

This chapter concerns actions provided for by the original Treaties, although in some cases in amended versions, which are heard directly before the Court of Justice (CoJ) or the General Court. The most important are the Article 263 of the Treaty on the Functioning of the European Union (TFEU) action to annul acts of the institutions that have been enacted unlawfully in some way, and Article 340 TFEU, which is an action for damages for loss caused by the unlawful actions of the institutions. In both of these actions, individuals have found it very difficult to succeed, even with cases that on their face show great merit; the reasons for this are explored in this chapter. The chapter also discusses Articles 265 and 277 TFEU, which have not been the subject of many actions before the CoJ and as a result are far less frequently included in European Union (EU) law courses. They have, though, been included for the sake of completeness.

9.1 Actions to annul EU acts

Article 263 TFEU is the action to annul legislative acts of the Union that are defective in some way.

It was held in **Case 294/83 *Parti Ecologiste Les Verts* v *EP*** that the European Community (EC) is a Community based on the rule of law in as much as neither its member states nor its institutions can avoid a review of the question whether the measures adopted by them are in conformity with the basic constitutional charter, the Treaty.

Thus, Article 263 TFEU provides for actions to be brought before the CoJ to allow it to review the validity of acts of the Union institutions. The General Court (formerly the Court of First Instance, or CFI) has jurisdiction to hear direct-action applications brought by natural or legal persons against acts of Union institutions, which are addressed to them or directly concerning them as individuals.

Article 263 TFEU

The Court of Justice shall review the legality of legislative acts, of acts of the Council, of the Commission and of the European Central Bank, other than recommendations and opinions, and of acts of the European Parliament and of the European Council intended to produce legal effects vis-à-vis third parties. It shall also review the legality of acts of bodies, offices or agencies of the Union intended to produce legal effects vis-à-vis third parties.

If found to be invalid, the CoJ has the sole right to declare those acts void. This action helps to ensure that the Union institutions comply with all requirements of EU law when they adopt acts. This section considers the two main aspects of this action: admissibility, which has four sub-parts, and the merits or substance of the action. After these elements have been covered, we also consider the amendments made by the Lisbon Treaty and, briefly, suggestions that have been made for more radical reform of Article 263 TFEU, particularly to its previous form as Article 230 EC, due to its apparent strictness. Finally, alternative actions to Article 263 TFEU are considered briefly.

9.1.1 Admissibility

The issue of the admissibility of Article 263 TFEU has to be addressed first. Failure to satisfy all four requirements of admissibility will result in the case being rejected by the CoJ. Admissibility includes the questions of which institutions are subject to review, which acts can be reviewed, the time limit for challenging acts, and the applicants who can bring an action. All of these are considered in turn, but the latter aspect has been the greatest barrier in practice to individual applicants and understandably demands most emphasis in case law and thus also textbooks. One of the problems in getting to grips with this topic in the past has been the wide choice of relevant cases. Many cases are difficult to reconcile with others and an attempt to do so can be frustrating because the decisions of the CoJ are very often policy-driven to achieve a just result in cases that merit it but the rejections of admissibility appear deliberately to discourage applications by individuals challenging general legislation. The changes introduced by the Lisbon Treaty will help rationalise the jurisprudence, as is discussed in this chapter.

9.1.1.1 The institutions whose acts are reviewable

Article 173 of the European Economic Community (EEC) (now 263 TFEU), as originally constituted, stated that the acts of the Commission and Council were subject to review, but case law extended the power of review additionally to acts of the European Parliament (EP). Over a series of cases, the CoJ justified this on the basis that, as the EP's powers grew, it should be responsible for acts that create legally binding effects in respect of third parties and these should therefore be open to review.

> See **Cases 230/81** *Luxembourg* **v** *EP* in respect of the choice of the EP's seat, **294/83** *Parti Ecologiste Les Verts* **v** *EP* in respect of a challenge to the apportionment of election campaign funds, and **34/86** *Council* **v** *European Parliament (Budgetary Procedure)* with regard to budgetary decisions of the President of the EP.

❯❯ CROSS REFERENCE
The democratic deficit debate is considered in Chapter 2, section 2.4.3.1.

The development is thus very much allied to the democratic deficit debate. As the EP's role in making law—that is, its rights—increased, so correspondingly should have its duties and obligations, to include the duty to make decisions and legal acts lawfully. Thus, there should be a right to challenge decisions of the EP that breach the legal standards required by the Treaties and in general principles of law. This is reflected in the further amendments extending the range of institutions expressly, which were included in the new Article 263 TFEU by the Lisbon Treaty, which now provides as follows.

> **Article 263 TFEU**
>
> The Court of Justice of the European Union shall review the legality of legislative acts, of acts of the Council, of the Commission, of the European Central Bank, other than recommendations and opinions, and of acts of the European Parliament and of the European Council intended to produce legal effects vis-à-vis third parties.

❯❯ CROSS REFERENCE
See Chapter 2, section 2.2.6, for further details on COREPER.

The CoJ has held that, to be subject to a challenge, an institution must be empowered under the Treaty to enact binding measures; therefore, this does not include, for example, the Committee of Permanent Representatives (COREPER; see Case C-24/94 *Commission* v *Council*). The Lisbon Treaty amended this Article to make clear that all Union institutions or combinations of them that enact both legislative acts per se and those that are intended to produce legal effects are bodies whose acts can be challenged under Article 263 TFEU. The inclusion of the European Council is significant, because this subjects for the first time the political-policy driving force of the EU to legal judicial control and, as such, bolsters the claim of the EU that it too respects the rule of law.

9.1.1.2 Reviewable acts

Prior to the Lisbon Treaty reforms, the jurisdiction of the CoJ under Article 230 EC applied to the legally binding acts of the institutions listed in Article 249 EC, which are Regulations, Directives, and Decisions, and does not therefore include recommendations or opinions or, strictly applied, anything else. However, the term 'Act' and the definition of what constitutes an act or a decision had been given a very wide interpretation by the CoJ so as to bring many other forms of acts within review that would not, on the face of it, be admissible. The reasoning for such an extension was that because these can create binding legal effects or affect the legal status of third parties, they should be subject to review and, as will be noted following, Article 263 TFEU has been amended to reflect this case law development by expressly including not only legislative acts, but also all acts intended to produce legal effects for third parties. Hence, the previous case law, which demonstrated the variety of acts that could then be challenged but not named in the Treaty Article, now merely serves as examples of what can be challenged, including a letter, the minutes of a Council meeting, a budget decision of the EP, a press release, and a Commission Communication.

> It was held in **Cases 8–11/66** *Noordwijks Cement Accord* that the test to apply to a particular act is whether it has binding legal effects or changes the legal position of the applicant. The case involved *a letter*, which changed the immunity from prosecution of certain companies under competition law.

In **Case 22/70 *Commission* v *Council (ERTA)*** it was held that Article 249 EC (now 288 TFEU) was not exhaustive and special acts such as the *minuted discussions of the Council*, which essentially set down detailed policy decisions and the Community stance for the European Road Transport Agreement, could also be challenged. The reasoning for this was that despite being negotiated by the member states as an international agreement, this was a Community competence and was thus within the review jurisdiction of the CoJ.

Case 294/83 *Parti Ecologiste Les Verts* v *European Parliament* and the EU Treaty extended the list of reviewable acts to those of the EP that give rise to legally binding effects on the position of third parties, in this case concerning *a budget decision of the Parliament* sharing out of the budget among the party groupings.

In **Case C-106/96 *UK* v *Commission***, the Council had decided not to support 'Poverty 4', a programme to combat poverty and social exclusion, but the Commission decided nevertheless to fund a number of projects amounting to an expenditure of ECU 6 million and issued a *press release* to advertise this. If the last case looked a bit like sharp practice, this one looks even more deliberate and helps us to understand why the Commission is criticised in some quarters. The CoJ held that the Commission lacked the competence to commit the expenditure and the decision was annulled. However, in view of the fact that much of the expenditure had already taken place, the Court decided, in the interests of legal certainty, to exercise the discretion given to it under Article 231 EC (now 264 TFEU) and rule in favour of the payments made or promised.

In **Case C-57/95 *French Republic* v *Commission***, the CoJ ruled on a French action to annul a *Commission Communication*, which, it was argued, imposed new obligations on the member states. It held that the challenged Communication, which was published in the Official Journal (OJ) 'C' Series and was not a legislative Act envisaged by Article 249 EC (now 288 TFEU), was a measure that could be the subject of an annulment action. The content of communication was considered and the CoJ thought that the Communication had 'imperative wording' and that its content was the same subject matter as a withdrawn draft Directive that had not found approval in Council. Hence, it held that the Communication constituted an act intended to have legal effects on its own, distinct from the Treaty provisions, and an action to annul it could be upheld.

There remain exceptions to this in that there are some acts that create legal effects that cannot be the subject of challenge.

In **Case 7/61 *Commission* v *Italy***, it was held that the reasoned opinion given by the Commission under the Article 226 EC (now 258 TFEU) proceedings did not constitute an act that could be subject to review under Article 230 EC (now 263 TFEU).

> Similarly, in **Case 48/65 *Lütticke* v *Commission***, the applicants had requested the Commission to take action against the German Federal Republic regarding a breach of Community law, but the Commission refused. Lütticke applied under Article 230 EC (now 263 TFEU) to annul the decision not to act, but it was held that the refusal to act was not a legally binding act and therefore not reviewable. Equally, the reasoned opinion of the Commission with regard to the possible member state breach was also held not to be reviewable.

In addition, applicants cannot challenge a decision to prosecute.

> In **Case C-131/03 P *Reynolds Tobacco Holdings and others***, the Commission took a decision to commence legal proceedings against the US company, which it suspected of smuggling cigarettes into the EU. Reynolds challenged that decision, but the CFI and CoJ held that the decision to take legal action was not a reviewable act. The decision had legal effects, but not ones that satisfied the test for Article 230 EC because the decisions did not determine definitively per se the obligations of the parties to the case. That determination can result only from the judgment of the Court. The CoJ confirmed that only acts that were binding on, and capable of affecting the interests of, the applicant by bringing about a distinct change in his legal position could be challenged. In this case, the decision to take legal action would not affect the legal position, while the judgment of the Court would—but, of course, that would be subject to an appeal by the party.

Hence, a wide array of measures can be subject to review, dependent on the legal effects that they produce or their nature and not only the three formal acts listed in Article 288 TFEU.

9.1.1.3 **Time limits**

Article 263(6) TFEU provides that the applicant has two months from:

- the date of publication of the measure; or
- the date of notification; or
- in the absence of publication or notification, the date on which it came to the notice of the applicant, as the case may be,

to institute proceedings. These time limits apply regardless of the status of the applicant.

> Note that the third ground applies only where the act was not published or notified, which, although clearly not impossible with some of the documents that have been held to be subject to challenge, is certainly rare.
>
> The time limit for challenging a Regulation has been determined to run from the end of the fourteenth day following publication: see Articles 50–51 of the Rules of Procedure of the Court of Justice and Article 102(1) of the Rules of Procedure of the General Court; and with both sets of rules an additional 10 days can be added due to the distance of the applicant from the Court in Luxembourg (Article 51 of the Rules of Procedure). This is to allow time for the dispatch from the Luxembourg Official Publications Office of the OJ to the furthest parts of the EU, as it was then. Today, this seems less necessary, if not entirely, unnecessary, with online publication.

In **Case T-79/89 BASF v Commission**, the time limits were held by the CFI (now the General Court) not to apply where there are such serious defects in the measure that it is to be re-garded as non-existent. Thus, if it never existed, time cannot start to run, although on appeal the CoJ held that the defects were not so serious but that nevertheless it should be annulled (Case C-137/92P).

THINKING POINT

Why might this very short time limit be justified? If it were, say, 12 months or two years, what consequence would a successful challenge have—for example, to the parties who have been relying on the provision?

9.1.2 *Locus standi*: who may apply?

The question of who may apply relates to what is known as the *locus standi* of applicants.

locus standi Literally meaning 'the place of standing', it relates to the recognition of a legal interest in a matter that produces the right to mount a legal challenge against a legal provision.

No standing means no right to challenge; hence, this is absolutely crucial to an applicant's chances.

There are three categories of applicant: privileged, semi-privileged, and non-privileged.

9.1.2.1 Privileged

Privileged applicants are named by Article 263 TFEU as the member states, the Council, and the Commission, and, following the Treaty of Nice, the EP, all of which have the right to attack any act. Notably, despite its elevation to a full institution by the Lisbon Treaty in Article 13 of the Treaty on European Union (TEU), the European Council is not included. It may be, as with the EP previously, that the CoJ has to step in to provide that right should the European Council seek to bring an action under Article 263 TFEU, although, of course, any of the members of the European Council could bring an action in their own right as a member state.

9.1.2.2 Limited or semi-privileged

Semi-privileged applicants comprise a category first established in case law for the EP by the CoJ; but, following its elevation to a full Union institution, named in Article 7 EC (now 13 TEU), the EP moved out of this category. The Treaty of Amsterdam added to the semi-privileged category the Court of Auditors, which has the right to challenge acts of the institutions, but only for the purpose of protecting its prerogatives. The right was extended to the European Central Bank (ECB) by the TEU. The term 'protection of prerogatives' is one that was essentially developed in case law and means 'where their interests are clearly affected'.

See, for example, **Case 138/79 Maizena (Roquette Freres) v Council**, as confirmed in **Cases C-70/88 EP v Council (Chernobyl)** and **C-295/90 EP v Council (Students Residence Dir-ective)**, in which the challenge by the EP to the legal base used by the Council was successful.

This limited right of challenge is now confirmed in Article 263 TFEU. The original *locus standi* reflected the original much lesser and more limited law-making and participatory role of the EP, and the extensions over time to the EP and now to the Court of Auditors and ECB reflect the fact that the decision-making of those bodies can also have far-reaching consequences. The Lisbon Treaty has added the Committee of the Regions (CoR) to the category of semi-privileged applicants, but oddly, in the light of the latter change, it does not add the European Economic and Social Committee (EESC) or even the European Council, which, as a self-standing institution, is thus excluded from any privileged applicant status. The member states individually, though, still possess full privilege.

All other persons are non-privileged applicants, who must satisfy certain conditions before their right of access to the CoJ will be recognised.

9.1.3 **Non-privileged applicants'** *locus standi*

For more details on this section visit the online resources.

Article 263(4) TFEU provides for circumstances in which non-privileged applicants can bring actions for judicial review.

Article 263(4) TFEU

Any natural or legal person may, under the conditions laid down in the first and second paragraphs, institute proceedings against

[i] an act addressed to that person

[ii] or which is of direct and individual concern to them,

[iii] and against a regulatory act which is of direct concern to them and does not entail implementing measures.

The first thing to note is that all three conditions have been changed in some way by the Lisbon Treaty, as will be explained in the sections following.

The content of this Article represents a distinct change from the former version contained in Article 230 EC, which provided that proceedings could be instituted against a decision addressed to that person or against a decision that, although in the form of a Regulation or a decision addressed to another person, is of direct and individual concern to the former.

9.1.4 **Acts addressed to the applicant**

This first situation has been revised in a subtle way, the impact of which will become clear only if and when the Court is asked to rule on it. 'Decisions' in Article 230 EC has been replaced by 'acts' in Article 263 TFEU, which is not defined and thus suggests that, provided something is addressed to the applicant, whatever its form, it may be subject to review. Hence, where the applicant is directly addressed, he or she will have automatic standing and this is most likely to occur in specific circumstances in which, for example, the applicant has been the subject of a formal Decision of the Commission under the competition rules of Articles 101–102 TFEU and Regulation 1/2003. For the purposes of the addressee mounting a challenge, there is no barrier to admissibility provided the time limit has been observed. 'Natural or legal person' was interpreted to include non-member states in Case C-298/89 *Gibraltar* v *Council*.

In **Case T-138–89** *BBV v Commission*, it was held by the CFI that it was not possible to challenge a potential decision (in other words, a decision that might be made, but which had not actually been made at the time of the challenge to the claim that the potential decision would affect the applicant's interest). The applicant cannot be seen to be 'jumping the gun' by challenging a claim that will be heard in court before that claim goes to court.

The next two situations or categories have reformulated significantly the circumstances under which individuals may challenge acts of EU institutions and bodies that have not been addressed to them.

9.1.5 An act that is of direct and individual concern to the applicant

This condition reflects previous case law, to which this section will thus refer, that demonstrating 'individual' was and is the most important aspect of the application and thus admissibility.

This condition concerns any acts addressed to another person. The new Article 263 TFEU no longer specifically mentions 'Decision' or 'Regulations', but instead refers generally to 'acts', which is not then defined. The case law of the CoJ and General Court following these changes, whilst presently limited, defines this as referring to legislative acts—that is, those defined in Article 288 TFEU (ex 249 EC). This view is confirmed by the interpretation of the third circumstance for challenge, which refers to 'regulatory acts', which term is defined as non-legislative acts. These are considered in section 9.1.7. Therefore, the focus of this section turns on the requirements to demonstrate 'direct and individual concern'. 'Individual' remains the most important aspect, just as it was in the previous case law developed by the Court in establishing the circumstances in which individuals could challenge Regulations, which, by their nature, are not addressed to individuals because they are acts of general application—that is, to everyone. Before looking in particular at 'individual', 'direct concern' will be considered, for which the previous case law remains relevant.

9.1.5.1 Direct concern

With 'direct concern', the general rule is that if a member state is granted discretion to act under the provision, then the Community or EU provision itself cannot by its nature give rise to direct concern. Discretion on the part of the member states means that the applicants are only indirectly concerned. This was certainly the initial view taken by the CoJ in Cases 25/62 *Plaumann* and 69/69 *Alcan* as examples of how the Court has interpreted this.

Case 62/70 *Bock v Commission (Chinese Mushrooms)* is a good example that involved the authorisation for a member state to restrict imports—that is, it had the discretion. An application was made by Bock to import Chinese mushrooms, but was refused by Germany on 11 September and only authorised by the Commission on 15 September. Hence the decision was a retroactive measure in direct response to the application from Bock. In other words, the discretion to act was already waived and Bock was therefore held to be directly concerned.

This trend was continued in **Case 11/82** *Piraiki-Patraiki v Commission*, in which the French authorities applied for, and were authorised to impose, quotas on yarn imports from Greece. In considering an application to review this decision, the CoJ held that where interested parties could be identified with certainty or a high degree of probability, direct concern would be

> satisfied, despite the theoretical discretion on the part of the member state. In other words, the country applied for permission to restrict imports and the Commission had granted it, so whilst in theory the country had the discretion to restrict imports or not, in reality, it had already exercised and therefore extinguished that discretion. It would make no sense for a country to apply for the permission to do something and then decide not to do it, though it remains possible!

The 'act' must directly affect the legal situation of the individual and leave no discretion to its addressees, who are entrusted with the task of implementing it. See, for example, Cases 41–44/70 *International Fruit* v *Commission*, in which the member states had no discretion in carrying out the requirements of a Regulation concerned with the restrictions and licensing of apple imports.

Following the reform of Article 263 TFEU, it may now be that direct concern will be subject to greater scrutiny because of the extension of the range of acts that can be challenged.

9.1.5.2 **Individual concern**

Why is there a requirement of individual concern? The emphasis on 'individual' derives essentially from the general rule restricting the ability of individuals to challenge general or normative Acts such as, in the EU legal order; Regulations. Regulations are general acts, and cannot be challenged by an individual because they are directly and generally applicable or 'normative' acts, which apply to everyone in the EU. Not everybody, of course, is necessarily interested in the regulation of some of the finer aspects of the Common Agricultural Policy (CAP), but this does not deprive them of their status as normative acts. In view of Article 288 TFEU, this general rule makes sense. This higher status of Regulations demands that they are to be regarded and protected as similar to 'primary law' such as Acts of Parliament in the UK or Gesetze in Germany, and that, because of their general applicability, they should not be easily contested by anyone affected by them.

> **CROSS REFERENCE**
>
> This issue is considered in further detail in section 9.1.5.3.

In **Case 17/62 *Fruit and Vegetable Confederation* v *Commission***, it was held that:

> The essential characteristics of a decision arise from the limitation of the persons to whom it is addressed, whereas a regulation, being essentially of a legislative nature, is applicable, not to a limited number of persons, defined and identifiable, but to categories of persons viewed abstractly and in their entirety.

In **Case 6/68 *Zuckerfabrik Watenstedt* v *Council***, the Court held:

> A measure does not lose its character as a normative act because the factual situation to which it applies makes it possible to identify, more or less accurately, the persons affected. A regulation applies to objectively determined situations and produces legal effects with regard to categories of persons defined in a general and abstract manner.

In other words, being able to see clearly whom a Regulation specifically affects does not actually deprive it of its general character, which means that we have to find some different or unusual characteristic in order for an applicant to stand out and be able to challenge it.

Previously, there were a number of reasons identified why this general rule should not apply, and a lot of the case law considered under these exceptions also helped us to understand the term 'individual concern'.

Individual concern has been very hard to demonstrate and has often been tested by the CoJ first or at the same time as direct concern to decide admissibility, as in the leading and still very much valid judgment of Case 25/62 *Plaumann* v *Commission* or in the *International Fruit* case considered in section 9.1.5.1. The fact that an applicant no longer has to demonstrate that a Regulation was, in fact, a Decision or bundle of Decisions may make life easier for applicants. The amended Article 263 TFEU now states that an act may be challenged that is of direct and individual concern to the applicant, which thus now tacitly rather than expressly includes a Regulation and indeed acts addressed to other persons which would also include Directives, although again this is not express. Both are included in the same condition. It is hoped that these points will be clarified at some stage by the General Court or CoJ.

First, however, the original case law will be considered, starting with *Plaumann*. An applicant must show some factors that distinguish themselves uniquely.

This was the position taken in the leading and still very much valid judgment of **Case 25/62 Plaumann v Commission**. A decision was addressed to the German government refusing permission to reduce duties on clementines, which was challenged by Plaumann. The test decided for individual concern was: does the decision affect the applicant by virtue of the fact that he is member of the abstractly defined class addressed by the rule, for example because he is an importer of clementines, or does it affect him because of attributes peculiar to him that differentiate him from all other persons? Plaumann was held to be one of a class of importers and not therefore individually concerned. The reasoning is that anyone could become an importer.

It was held in *Plaumann* that persons other than those to whom a decision is addressed may claim to be individually concerned only if that decision 'affects them by reason of certain attributes that are peculiar to them or by reason of circumstances in which they are differentiated from all other persons and by virtue of these factors distinguishes them individually', just as in the case of the person addressed. In *Plaumann*, the CoJ went on to state that 'the applicant is affected by the disputed decision as an importer of clementines, that is to say, by reason of a commercial activity which may at any time be practised by any person and is not therefore such as to distinguish the applicant in relation to the contested decision as in the case of the addressee'.

The next case makes this point all the more clearly and forcefully in view of its facts.

In **Case 231/82 Spijker Kwasten BV v Commission**, an import ban was imposed on Chinese brushes. Spijker Kwasten was the only importer of Chinese brushes in Holland and although it had previously requested a licence, it was held that the company could not be individually concerned. The reasoning was that the decision restricting imports was valid for the forward period of the next six months; therefore, it was possible that others could apply for licences in that period and hence there was no individual concern for Spijker Kwasten.

The judicial position on individual concern has been maintained in the post-Lisbon Treaty case law. In **Case T-49/07 Sofiane Fahas v Council of the European Union**, the General Court defined 'individual' in virtually the same words as used in *Plaumann*. Furthermore, in **Case T-18/10 Inuit** and on appeal (**Case C-583/11P) Inuit v European Parliament and Council**, both the General Court and the CoJ made clear that whilst Article 263 TFEU must be interpreted in the light of the fundamental right to effective judicial protection, such an interpretation could not go beyond the conditions expressed in Article 263. In other words, *Plaumann* continues to be good law.

9.1.5.3 Instances in which 'individual' has been recognised

There are certain categories, essentially established under the pre-Lisbon time, whereby a challenge and the establishment of 'individual' seemed easier for applicants but which were limited to finite circumstances such as past events or anti-dumping measures. It is to be noted that there is a great deal of overlap with the following categories such that, in future, they might be blended into a single, albeit more complex, category.

Past events and retroactivity

> In **Case 62/70 *Bock v Commission***, the company was individually concerned because applications made by Bock to import Chinese mushrooms were refused by Germany on 11 September, but the required authorisation by the Commission was passed only on 15 September. Hence, the decision was a retroactive measure in direct response to the application from Bock, which was held to have a vested legal interest and therefore individually concerned.

> See also **Case C-152/88 *Sofrimport v Commission*** concerning a Regulation restricting the import of Chilean apples, which was adopted whilst some apples were in transit and of which the Commission was specifically notified to take into account when the ban was enacted. Sofrimport was thus part of a closed group of companies with goods in transit when the Regulation was adopted and to which there could be no addition. It was thus individually concerned and the application was held to be admissible.

> **Case C-309/89 *Codorniu v Council (Spanish Wine Producers)*** involved a Regulation limiting the use of the 'Cremant' trade mark. Despite the CoJ confirming that the Regulation was a legislative measure applying to traders in general, it could still be of individual concern to one of them. Codorniu had distinguished itself by the ownership of a trademark for the term 'Crement' from the year 1924, which the Community had tried to reserve for French and Luxembourg producers. Codorniu was able to challenge a Regulation that prevented its use of a registered trademark 'Gran Cremant di Cordorniu', because this fact isolated it from other wine producers that had not registered this term and which were similarly restricted from using the name. Hence, it was a Regulation for some or most, but it was a decision for Cordorniu. While the others might take out a trademark now, they could not back date it to before the Regulation was enacted.

Where the identity of the natural or legal persons affected is fixed and ascertainable (the closed group category)

> In **Cases 106 and 107/63 *Töpfer v Commission***, it was held that, in order to establish individual concern, an applicant must be affected alone or as a member of a fixed and closed class. The closed group enables the identity of the natural or legal persons affected to be fixed and thus ascertainable. Töpfer was so identified because the company had applied for a licence prior to a Commission decision that retroactively empowered the refusal of licences, and Töpfer was therefore identifiable.

In **Cases 41–44/70** *International Fruit Company* **v** *Commission*, a group of fruit importers was held entitled to challenge a Regulation where the identity of the nature of legal persons affected was already known and thus fixed and identifiable. Apple importers had applied in advance for import licences and the decision to issue a limited quantity of licences was made on the basis of applications previously received, therefore finite and known. The Regulation was a response to the individuals; no new persons could be added at the time of challenge or thereafter to the list of applicants.

Other successful cases include **Case C-152/88** *Sofrimport* **v** *Commission* concerning a decision taken to restrict the import of Chilean apples whilst some were in transit and of which the Commission was specifically notified to take into account, and **Case C-389/89** *Cordorniu* **v** *Commission (Spanish Wine Producers)*, noted above.

Where the applicant is named in the Regulation

Alternatively, where the applicant is named in the Regulation, as in Cases 138 and 139/79 *Roquette Frères* v *Council and Maizena* v *Council*, the action will be held to be of direct and individual concern. The CoJ held that despite being a measure of general application, certain individuals may challenge Regulations as if decisions, especially when one of the Articles of the Regulation specifically referred to the applicant companies. This is very close to the next category.

Competition law and anti-dumping cases or where the applicant has taken part in the investigation or issue of the legislation

A number of cases are concerned with alleged breaches of competition law by other companies or the dumping of goods on the EU market. The applicants are those that have made a complaint to the Commission about the activities of another company that appear to breach competition or anti-dumping rules. As a result of an investigation of individual importers, the Commission may take action by issuing a decision seeking to correct the situation, or a general Regulation may be issued to catch all imports; thus, the complaint has led to the enactment of a Regulation, as in the following examples.

In **Case 264/82** *Timex* **v** *Commission*, the Timex company had complained about the dumping of watches on the European market, which led to an anti-dumping Regulation being imposed by the Commission. Timex was not satisfied with it as it thought the anti-dumping duty imposed was not high enough. Timex thus challenged the Regulation, which was held to be of direct and individual concern to Timex due to its prior close involvement.

Likewise, the application for review in **Case 26/76** *Metro-SB-Grossmarkte* **v** *Commission* was held to be admissible because Metro had a legitimate interest in the decision aimed at another person (SABA). Metro had made a complaint under the Competition Law Regulation 17 in respect of the exclusion from a distribution network by another company (SABA) and had thus played a part that led to the decision.

> See also **Case C-358/89 *Extramet Industrie v Council***, where a company was involved in an anti-dumping investigation and Regulation, which imposed a 22 per cent duty on imports. The CoJ accepted the special circumstances, which were that in the EU the company was the largest importer and end user of calcium from China and the Soviet Union; the only producer and other supplier in the EU was a French company and competitor, which had refused to supply Extramet. The company was also involved in the Commission investigations. A high import duty on calcium import would have affected it severely in view of the limited suppliers and manufacturers of the product. The CoJ held that the applicant had established the existence of a set of factors constituting such a situation which was peculiar to the applicant and which differentiated it, as regards the measure in question, from all other traders.

The *Extramet* case does not serve, though, as a very good precedent or example case for how future cases may be decided because of the very factual circumstances that make it unique. If it was similar to a number of other cases with the same or similar facts, by definition they would not be unique, not demonstrate individual concern, and would not succeed. However, the case does highlight that if there are unique circumstances, 'individual' will be established by reasons of those circumstances to the satisfaction of the CoJ and not by precedent or the application of *Extramet*. However, it also contrasted these special areas where standing was easier to achieve with the fate of applicants generally who were inevitably denied standing unless they were so unique. This also led to the attempt led by Advocate-General (AG) Jacobs to establish a fairer more universal test, which is considered in section 9.1.11 below.

A finding of individual concern would not include those who have merely written to the Commission to complain without their further involvement.

 THINKING POINT

Do you consider the requirements to be too demanding of individual applicants?

If so, how would you change things?

If not, why not?

9.1.6 Interest groups and party actions

Non-individual applications by their very nature may expect not to have standing. It might be anticipated that, by definition, an application from a group or party cannot be of individual concern. However, trade associations' applications have been recognised in Cases T-447–449/93 *AITEC v Commission* on the grounds that associations have standing if they represent the individual interests of some or all of their members or their own interests as an association. This position was confirmed in the later Case T-122/96 *Federolio v Commission* in which the General Court further qualified the conditions as requiring the association to have expressly had grants of authority to represent members and also be itself affected by the act.

> In contrast in **Case T-585/93 *Greenpeace v Commission***, the plea that all individuals with an environmental interest, and not only an economic interest, in the consequences of a decision should be able collectively to be represented by a group, failed. The CFI rejected this view, which was confirmed on appeal in **Case C-321/95P** by the CoJ; it held that the decision had affected individuals in an abstract and general fashion only, and that the applicants representing them were thus similarly affected and similarly without standing.

9.1.7 The challenge to regulatory acts

This third condition or circumstance is new to Article 263 TFEU (Figure 9.1), introduced with the Lisbon Treaty reforms, and provides individual applicants with a right to make an application against a regulatory act that is of direct concern to them and does not entail implementing measures. It is to be stressed that the applicant need show direct concern only, as noted in section 9.1.5.1, but there was no definition in the Treaties for a 'regulatory act'. If the second circumstance does, in fact, refer to a legislative act, then it is to be argued that this third condition refers to non-legislative acts—hence, the easier condition without the need to show individual concern for *locus standi*. Whilst legislative acts are described in Articles 288–289 TFEU, regulatory acts are not. These are therefore taken to be the delegated non-legislative acts described in Articles 290 and 291 TFEU, which are, essentially, the delegated and implementing administrative acts taken by the Commission and include acts that can nevertheless also be labelled Regulations, Decisions, or even Directives.

The condition, though, applies to regulatory acts only, not entailing implementing measures, so nothing that allows further executive or otherwise understood to be administrative acts, which would seem to rule out any act delegating powers.

> We now have assistance from the CoJ in determining this condition. In **Case T-18/10 *Inuit***, the General Court held that 'the meaning of "regulatory act" for the purposes of the fourth paragraph of Article 263 TFEU must be understood as covering all acts of general application apart from legislative acts'. This position was confirmed on appeal by the CoJ in **Case C-583/11P *Inuit v European Parliament and Council***.

This means that we have first to know what legislative acts are in order to be able to exclude them from a consideration under category [iii]. To determine whether an act is legislative, the General

Figure 9.1 Summary of Article 263 TFEU and individual non-privileged applicant *locus standi*

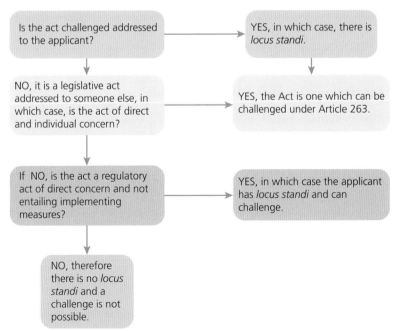

Court in *Inuit* considered what decision-making process was used. In Case T-262/10 *Microban*, the General Court considered the legal basis under which the Directive was adopted. If the challenged act was expressly adopted under Article 289 TFEU or any Article that refers to Article 289 or the ordinary or special legislative processes, it is a legislative act and thus not a category [iii] act. This is confirmed by Cases T-93-96/10 *Rütgers*. That leaves us with the conclusion that regulatory acts are indeed the general delegated and implementing acts of Articles 290 and 291 TFEU.

9.1.7.1 Implementing measures

⟩ CROSS REFERENCE
See section 9.1.5.2 above.

The regulatory act challenged must be direct and not entail any implementing measures, but again there is no definition of 'implementing measures' in the TFEU. In *Microban*, the General Court confirmed the generally understood view that implementing measures relate to any intervention by either the Commission or member states in the application of a general non-legislative act of the Commission. Any intervention would thus remove or exclude a right to challenge. Is this just an overlap with direct? Is it the same test for both elements or an additional test, perhaps put there to rule out challenges to Directives? Following the *Microban* case, Case T-380/11 *Souliotis v Commission* addressed the issue whether direct concern and not involving implementing measures amounted to the same thing or the same test. It held that direct concern, essentially relating to discretion on the part of the addressee, was different from an implementing measure, which was held by the CoJ in Case C-274/12P *Telefónica v Commission* to mean any measure at all taken or needed to be taken by the addressee of the act. If there were any measure taken by the addressee, who would in normal circumstances most likely be a member state, then the route to challenge would be via the national courts and an Article 267 reference. The problem that leaves is demonstrating that there was neither a discretion nor a need for an implementing measure; in other words, the act had to be in force without anything else happening, something arguably only applicable with any certainty to non-legislative regulations, which enter into force as they are without any implementation. Although these too could nevertheless require some form of action on the part of the member states to ensure the effectiveness of the EU measure such as in the *Tachograph* case (Case 128/78 *Commission v UK (Tachographs)*), which although involving a Regulation which does not need implementing, does though require supplementary action by the member states to set up sanctions, as in the case itself. It would seem, however, that it is an easier condition without the need to show individual concern for *locus standi* but only in respect of the administrative or implementing 'regulatory acts'; however, the broad definition given to 'implementing acts' by the CoJ in the *Telefónica* case might well mean that the easing of the condition for standing is then negated by any implementing action, thus throwing the applicant back to proving individual concern under condition [ii].

To reach firmer conclusions will require yet further interpretation by the CoJ.

9.1.8 Merits or grounds for annulment

Once admissibility has been established, the grounds or merits must be proved. These are laid down in Article 263(2) TFEU and can often overlap in individual cases.

Article 263(2) TFEU

It [the CoJ] shall for this purpose have jurisdiction in actions brought by a Member State, the European Parliament, the Council or the Commission on grounds of lack of competence, infringement of an essential procedural requirement, infringement of the Treaties or of any rule of law relating to their application, or misuse of powers.

Article 13(2) TEU

Each institution shall act within the limits of the powers conferred on it in the Treaties . . .

9.1.8.1 **Lack of competence or authority**

The lack of competence on the part of an institution to adopt a particular measure is really the equivalent of *ultra vires* and concerns the requirement that all measures must have the appropriate legal authority.

> *ultra vires*
> Meaning 'beyond the power to act'.

> **Case 9/56 *Meroni* v *High Authority*** concerned the successful challenge to decisions taken by the High Authority to which, at the time, no delegated decision-making powers had been granted.

> The High Authority was the forerunner of the Commission.

There is a degree of overlap with the fourth category—misuse of power—which is considered in section 9.1.8.4.

Further examples of a lack of competence or authority include the following.

> In **Case C-327/91 *France* v *Commission***, the Commission exceeded its competence when it concluded an international agreement with the United States because Article 300 EC (now 218 TFEU) required it to be concluded by the Council.

> **Case C-57/95 *French Republic* v *Commission*** involved a French action to annul a Commission 'Communication'. The CoJ held that the Commission had no such power to adopt an Act imposing new obligations on the member states that were not inherent in the Treaty; thus, the Commission lacked competence and the Act was annulled.

> The most important and clearest of these cases is probably **Case C-376/98 *Germany* v *EP and Council (Tobacco Advertising)*** in which a Directive banning tobacco advertising was introduced under a Treaty Article concerned with the completion of the internal market and which was held not to authorise the enactment of legislation concerned primarily with public health. The Directive was annulled.

9.1.8.2 **Infringement of an essential procedural requirement**

Specific requirements are laid down by Article 296 TFEU that all EU secondary legislation must give reasons, and refer to any proposals and opinions made in respect of the legislation. The CoJ has held that insufficient, vague, or inconsistent reasoning would constitute a breach of this ground.

> It was held in **Case 24/62 *Germany* v *Commission (Wine Tariff Quotas)*** that reasons must contain sufficient details of the facts and figures on which they are based.

In **Case 139/79 *Roquette and Maizena* v *Council***, the Council failed to consult the EP as required under old Article 43(2) EC. It had asked for an opinion, but did not wait long enough for the answer before going ahead with the Regulation, which was subsequently annulled.

In **Case C-325/91 *France* v *Commission***, it was held that there was a requirement to state the Treaty base; failure to observe this led to the annulment of the measure.

Finally, in **Case 17/74 *Transocean Marine Paint Association* v *Commission***, a measure that is not notified will deprive an applicant of the right to protest and of having its views made known or represented to the relevant institution. It was therefore held liable to annulment under Article 230 EC (now 263 TFEU).

9.1.8.3 Infringement of the Treaty or any rule relating to its application

This is the most frequently argued ground because it is capable of embracing all errors of EU law, including breaches of general principles or human rights and the EU Charter of Fundamental Rights. It thus includes such principles as non-discrimination, proportionality, legitimate expectation, non-retroactivity, and the right to a fair hearing. In the following cases, the CoJ recognised the general principles pleaded. It is allied to the general duty imposed on the CoJ under Article 19(1) to ensure that in the interpretation and application of the Treaties, the law is observed.

CROSS REFERENCE

Further examples of rules that would qualify under this subheading can be found in Chapter 4, section 4.6.1.

Case 101/76 *KSH* v *Intervention Board* considered the principle of equality, **Case 17/74 *Transocean*** was concerned with the right to be heard, and **Case 112/77 *Töpfer*** concerned legitimate expectation and legal certainty. Legitimate expectation was pleaded in a case challenging the Milk Quota Regulation in **Cases C-104/89 and 37/90 *Mulder***. Non-retroactivity was upheld in **Case 63/83 *R* v *Kirk***.

Case C-325/91 *France* v *Commission* would also be applicable here for infringing a Treaty requirement, which was the requirement to state the Treaty base.

9.1.8.4 Misuse of power by an EU institution

The basis of this ground concerns the use of power for the wrong purpose and was demonstrated very early in the life of the Communities.

In **Case 8/55 *Federation Charbonniere* v *High Authority***, the CoJ held in respect of Article 33 of the European Coal and Steel Community (ECSC) that power exercised must be related to the end result.

See also **Case 105/75 *Giuffrida* v *Council*** concerning the prearranged reappointment of a Community official, which was an abuse of the selection system.

> Case C-378/98 *Germany v European Parliament and Council (Tobacco Advertising)* would also fit in here.

❯ CROSS REFERENCE

This last case is considered at section 9.1.8.1.

This category comes very close to the first one, in that the use of power as the basis of unauthorised action is the equivalent of having no lawful basis for the action undertaken or acting beyond power. The overlap was noted, but not reformed, by the Lisbon Treaty.

9.1.9 Schematic of the admissibility and merits stages of Article 263

An Article 263 challenge comprises two main parts: admissibility and merits/grounds (see Figure 9.2).

9.1.10 The effect of a successful action and annulment

Article 264 TFEU provides that if the action is well founded, the CoJ shall declare the act concerned to be void. This ruling applies generally (*erga omnes*) and from the date of the coming into force of the measure (*ab initio*). However, Article 264(2) TFEU provides that the Court shall, if it considers this necessary, state which of the parts of an act can be considered as void and which parts not void,

Figure 9.2 Stages of Article 263

⤷ Admissibility consists of four elements:
the act challenged;
the responsible institution/s.
time limit;
the *locus standi* of the applicant.

⤷ There are three categories of applicant:
privileged;
semi-privileged;
non-privileged.

⤷ **Non-privileged applicants have three possibilities to gain *locus standi*:**
an act addressed to them;
an act addressed to another of direct and individual concern
⤷ **requires both 'direct' and 'individual' to be addressed;**

and
a regulatory act of direct concern and no implementing measure.
⤷ **requires:**
regulatory act to be defined;
meaning of 'direct'; and
meaning of 'no implementing measure'.

⤷ if successful there are four grounds of review:
lack of competence;
infringement of an essential procedural requirement;
infringement of a Treaty or any rule of law;
misuse of powers.

and can sever parts where possible. This means that the Court can specify those parts of the measure that will be annulled and those that may remain in force. The Court can also delay the date on which the annulled act becomes inoperative in order to give the institutions concerned the chance to enact a replacement where this is necessary, as in the case of Case C-295/90 *European Parliament* v *Council* on the Free Movement of Students Directive 90/366, also considered in Chapter 3.

▶ **CROSS REFERENCE**

This case is considered in section 9.1.1.2.

> In **Case C-106/96 *UK* v *Commission* (Poverty 4)**, the CoJ held that the Commission lacked the competence to commit the expenditure, and the decision in the guise of an advertisement was annulled. However, in view of the fact that much of the expenditure had already taken place, the CoJ decided, in the interests of legal certainty, to exercise the discretion given to it under Article 231 EC (now 264 TFEU) and to rule in favour of the payments made or promised.

Article 266 TFEU provides that where an act has been declared void, the institutions are obliged to take the necessary measures to comply with the judgment of the CoJ. The Court may only annul the act referred to it or dismiss the action, but cannot order an institution to pay a sum of money—that is, it cannot fine them. The institution may, though, be liable to compensate under Article 340, which is concerned with the non-contractual liability of the institutions, considered in section 9.3. The requirement to take action does not go beyond the scope of the challenge leading to the annulment or apply, for example, to parties who have not challenged the Decision imposing fines in competition proceedings. In Case C-310/97P *Assidomän Kraft*, the company and others who had not challenged a Competition Decision fine attempted to require the Commission to refund fines on the basis of a Court ruling in respect of other companies that had successfully challenged the Decision. The CoJ rejected that claim.

9.1.11 **A restrictive approach?**

The reasons for the difficulties in demonstrating *locus standi* have been subject to much debate, and policy factors feature large in this discussion. For example, there is a floodgate policy argument whereby *locus standi* requirements have been interpreted particularly restrictively by the CoJ to reduce the number of cases coming before it and the General Court. Litigants face lengthening delays to justice; thus, keeping the number of cases down will help to reduce delay. Another argument is the suggestion that there is a desire to promote the CoJ more as a supreme court of the member states and not one directly accessible as a first-instance court for individuals. In this case, it is argued that the national courts are best placed to defend individuals' interests and that, if required, cases for annulment should be referred by the national courts under Article 267 TFEU. To some extent, both of these arguments were answered by the establishment of the CFI (now the General Court) primarily to handle these cases, which elevated the CoJ into the role of an appeal court in relation to these categories of case. Other arguments revolve around discussions about balancing the interests of the Union and individuals. The decision-making procedure in the Union is a much more complex procedure and often the result of compromise, which makes legislation more difficult to enact. The inevitable economic choices of the Union are bound to affect individuals and sometimes in an adverse way, but they must be allowed to be made, otherwise the ability of the Union and Commission to operate would be undermined. Individuals' actions should not hinder the institutions' ability to operate. Comparisons with the member states may be made: for example, that such challenges nationally are also subject to equally tight *locus standi* requirements under the constitutional traditions of the member states, which often makes individual challenges to general legislative measures such as statutes entirely inadmissible and restricts individual challenges to secondary legislation only, and indeed only if they have a proven interest.

▶ **CROSS REFERENCE**

This was considered in Chapter 6, section 6.1.8, on the possible development of a system of precedent.

By contrast, in the EU legal order, there are areas in which individuals find it easier to achieve standing, such as competition law, state aids, and anti-dumping measures, and it may be argued that the often closer involvement of particular individuals makes the difference. The applicants are likely to be the ones involved in the process by informing the Commission of certain situations and supplying corroborative evidence, or can be seen clearly to be affected by the measures complained about. This then sets the applicants apart from the many other challenges, arising most frequently against legislative measures made under the CAP. Furthermore, cases that arise from the application of retroactive legislation where the applicants are seen clearly as belonging to a fixed and identifiable group and who would suffer an injustice if not allowed standing also permit standing. In other words, the system works well when it needs to.

> Arguments for a more liberalised test were made by AG Jacobs in **Case C-50/00 *Union des Pequeños Agricultores (UPA)* v *Council***, influenced by the Charter of Fundamental Rights, which provides that individuals are entitled to expect an effective judicial remedy. It was argued that the Article 230 EC (now 263 TFEU) restrictive *locus standi* test leads to a possible denial of justice because the law for individuals is complex and unpredictable. Introducing a less strict test would fit in with a general tendency to extend the scope of judicial protection in response to the growth of powers of the Community—hence the suggestion that an applicant should be regarded as individually concerned where, by reason of his or her particular circum-stances, the measure has, or is liable to have, a substantial adverse effect on his or her inter-ests. Whilst initially approved by the CFI in **Case T-177/01 *Jégo-Quéerée* v *Commission***, this was rejected by the CoJ in **Case 50/00 *UPA***, making clear that the test established in **Case 25/62 *Plaumann*** remains valid and applicable. Furthermore, the CoJ stated in the appeal **Case C-263/02 P *Commission* v *Jégo-Quéré*** that any revision to the standing rules was not for the Court, but for the member states in the context of a Treaty amendment. Thus, it overturned the CFI decision, which it held had erred in law.

Although the member states have amended Article 263 TFEU whereby the natural or legal person challenge to regulatory acts no longer need show individual concern, they have not expressly ap-proved a relaxation of the rules by which individuals may challenge legislative acts, and the CoJ too has not strayed from its interpretation of individual concern in *Plaumann* in subsequent cases, as noted in section 9.1.5.2.

For more details on this section visit the online resources.

> In **Case C-167/02 *Willi Rothley and others* v *European Parliament***, a plea for standing based on the right to judicial protection was dismissed by the CoJ, which stated that protec-tion is still available through an Article 234 EC (now 267 TFEU) reference raising a question of the validity of Community law, although there is no guarantee that such a reference will either be made by the national court or accepted by the CoJ.

CROSS REFERENCE

As noted in Chapter 6 and in section 9.1.12.1.

The overall picture remains that of a continuing restrictive *locus standi* for applicants under Article 263 TFEU, although indirect alternatives are available to individuals, albeit with mixed success.

> It may be argued that the inclusion of new Article 19(1) TEU, which requires that 'member states shall provide remedies sufficient to ensure effective legal protection in the fields covered

by Union law', reinforces the argument that the CoJ should not be a court of direct access, but that matters be filtered first by the national courts, or alternatively that the General Court or CoJ may now interpret more liberally the rights of individuals to challenge Union Acts.

Article 263 TFEU, it seems, is destined to remain a difficult action with which to get to grips and will therefore continue to be one that must be studied carefully.

9.1.12 **Alternatives to Article 263 TFEU**

9.1.12.1 **A reference under Article 267 TFEU**

The first alternative is that a reference from a national court to the CoJ for a preliminary ruling on the validity of acts of the institutions is a question that must be referred by all national courts: see Case 314/85 *Firma Foto-Frost* v *Hauptzollamt Lübeck-Ost*. In general terms, actions under Article 267 TFEU avoid the strict time limits of Article 263 TFEU and are instead subject to the national procedural rules and time limits.

> For example, in **Case 133/85 *Walter Rau* v *BALM***, a challenge to a Community decision was questioned by a national court because of the possibility that Article 230 (now 263 TFEU) could have been used. The CoJ held that if the outcome of the case depended on the validity of the decision, then a reference under Article 234 EC (now 267 TFEU) was permissible without having to decide if Article 230 EC could have been used. Hence, the possibility of an Article 263 TFEU action does not preclude an attempt to challenge a Community decision before the national courts.

> In **Case 101/76 *KSH***, a challenge to Commission Regulations had failed when raised directly before the CoJ, but was successful when made within an Article 234 EC (now 267 TFEU) reference in **Cases 103 and 145/77 *KSH* v *Council and Commission (Royal Scholten Holdings)*** before the UK courts.

However, Article 267 TFEU cannot be used simply to get around the time limits of Article 263 TFEU.

> In **Case C-188/92 *Textilwerke Deggendorf GmbH* v *Germany***, TWD was aware of a decision addressed to Germany that directly concerned it; however, it chose to challenge under Article 234 EC (now 267 TFEU) later rather than under Article 230 EC (now 263 TFEU). The CoJ held that the time limits in Article 230 EC apply equally to national court proceedings and Article 234 EC rulings on invalidity, and references will be barred if the applicant would undoubtedly have had standing under Article 230 EC, but failed to take advantage of it within the time limit.

> There are further difficulties or requirements facing individuals wishing to raise a question of validity via Article 267 TFEU, as was pointed out by the AG in **Case C-408/95 *Eurotunnel* v *SeaFrance***. There needs to be an element of national law to be able to raise a matter before the national courts.

An Article 267 TFEU reference also increases the time involved in obtaining an answer by about two years and may lead to contrived cases being concocted in the national courts in order to challenge EU legislation. Finally, the national court retains the discretion whether or not to refer and may not consider a reference necessary. Hence, Article 267 TFEU, as an alternative, is a very uncertain and unpredictable one.

9.1.12.2 The plea of illegality: Article 277 TFEU

If there are other proceedings taking place before the CoJ, a party can raise an issue of illegality of a Union act of general application, but only indirectly or incidentally and not as an independent cause of action. Thus, Article 277 TFEU is not simply a second chance to get around the strict time or *locus standi* limits of Article 263 TFEU; it is designed to overcome the strict *locus standi* requirements for private parties in cases that would otherwise be unjust.

In reflecting previous case law of the CoJ, the new Article 277 TFEU has been amended from the old Article 241 EC to apply not only narrowly to Regulations, but to all acts of general application. Article 277 TFEU is considered in section 9.4.

9.2 Action for failure to act (Article 265 TFEU)

Article 265 TFEU concerns actions against the EP, the European Council, the Council, the Commission, or the ECB, or other bodies, offices, or agencies of the Union for a failure to act and constitutes an attempt to compel the institution or institutions concerned to take action.

Article 265(1) TFEU

Should the European Parliament, the European Council, the Council, the Commission or the European Central Bank, in infringement of the Treaties, fail to act, the Member States and the other institutions of the Union may bring an action before the Court of Justice of the European Union to have the infringement established. This Article shall apply, under the same conditions, to bodies, offices and agencies of the Union which fail to act.

The action is designed to tackle the failure of an institution to act that is in violation of a Treaty duty. This clearly presupposes that there was a duty imposed on the institution to act in the first place. It complements an Article 263 TFEU action to cover inaction and can be pleaded at the same time.

In **Case 15/70 *Chevalley v Commission***, the CoJ held that it was not necessary to state which action was the subject of the application.

There are a number of similar features between the two Articles, but they were designed to cover different situations: Article 263 TFEU, illegal action; and Article 265 TFEU, illegal inaction. Both provisions, however, have as their objective the ending of a situation of illegality. Actions are heard at first instance by the General Court, with an appeal to the CoJ.

9.2.1 Admissibility and *locus standi*

9.2.1.1 Privileged applicants

The Union institutions and member states have, under Article 265(1) TFEU, a privileged right of action that is not subject to restrictions on admissibility—that is, who may bring an action before the CoJ to have the infringement of the failure to act established.

> The status of the EP as a privileged applicant was confirmed a long time ago in **Case 13/83 *EP v Council (Transport Policy)*** in which it was established that the privileged applicants can request actions requiring general legislative acts as well as decisions, without having to show any special interest.

The ECB was given the right to take action by the TEU in areas falling within its field of competence.

According to Article 265 TFEU, all of the institutions of the Union have the right to commence an action. These are now defined in Article 13 TEU and include the European Council and the Court of Auditors.

9.2.1.2 Non-privileged applicants

Individuals, on the other hand, have a restricted, more clearly defined, right of *locus standi* under Article 265(3) TFEU. There is no equivalent of direct and individual concern; instead, individuals have to be potential addressees.

> **Article 265(3) TFEU**
>
> Any natural or legal person may, under the conditions laid down in the preceding paragraphs, complain to the Court that an institution, body, office or agency of the Union has failed to address to that person any act other than a recommendation or an opinion.

> In **Case 246/81 *Lord Bethell v EC Commission***, it was held that to challenge under Article 232 EC (now 265 TFEU), an individual must have been legally entitled to make a claim for action as a potential addressee. The case involved a complaint of a failure to act on price fixing by the airlines, but it was held that any potential act would have been addressed to the airlines and not to Lord Bethell.

This strict view of the *locus standi* requirements has, however, been tempered by the CoJ in case law introducing requirements analogous to the direct and individual concern of Article 230 EC (now 263 TFEU).

> See, for example, **Case C-68/95 *T Port v Bundesanstalt für Landeswirtschaft und Ernährung***, in that a potential act should have concerned an applicant in a direct and individual manner.

9.2.2 Acts subject to an Article 265 TFEU action

In many cases, the CoJ has rejected applications by individuals for measures of general legislative content.

> Hence, it was held in **Cases 15/70 *Chevalley* v *Commission*** and **42/71 *Nordgetreide* v *Commission*** that applications are restricted to decisions only; also in the *Chevally* case, it further held that a demand for an opinion is not admissible.

Regulations cannot be requested because, by their nature, they are not capable of being addressed to specific individuals only. Directives are addressed to the member states; as such, on the face of it, only Decisions are capable of being addressed to individuals. There must be an obligation under the Treaty to adopt a reviewable act that is enforceable on the part of the institution. Following the reforms to Article 263 TFEU, the assumption is that the third condition relating to 'regulatory acts requiring no implementing measures' will also now apply to Article 265, although this is without judicial confirmation thus far.

> **Case 13/83 *European Parliament* v *Council (Transport Policy)*** holds, however, that the acts requested need not be spelled out in detail, but must be sufficiently identified.

9.2.3 Procedural requirements

9.2.3.1 The invitation to act

There is a preliminary procedural step that must be taken before court action can ensue.

> **Article 265(2) TFEU**
>
> If, within *two months* of being so called upon, the institution, body, office or agency concerned has not defined its position, the action may be brought within a further period of two months. The action shall thus be admissible only if the institution concerned has first been called upon to act.

The applicant must request the institution to take a specific action as legally required and advise that failure to do so will result in a court action under Article 265 TFEU. The invitation to act need not follow any precise form to qualify for the purposes of Article 265 TFEU, but should be made in a reasonable time.

Only if the institution fails to define its position within the two-month period can the matter be brought before the CoJ. The application to the Court must be made within a further two-month period from the end of the initial two-month period.

> In **Case 302/87 *European Parliament* v *Council (Comitology)***, it was held that if the institution complies with the request to act, the CoJ will not allow the action to proceed.

9.2.3.2 Definition of position

This requirement has been seen to defeat most actions because where the institution has explained its refusal to act already—that is, has defined its position—further action is inadmissible.

> In **Case 48/65 *Lütticke* v *Commission***, the applicants had requested the Commission to take action against the German Federal Republic regarding a breach of Community law. The Commission was of the opinion that there had been no breach, so therefore refused to take action, but also notified the applicant of this. The CoJ declared the application inadmissible on the grounds that the notification of the refusal was a definition of position.

> In **Case 8/71 *Deutscher Komponistenverband (German Composers Group)* v *Commission***, a complaint that a decision taken by the Commission was wrong did not allow an applicant to proceed under Article 232 EC (now 265 TFEU) on the basis that the right decision was not taken by Commission—that is, that it had failed to act in the right way.

> In **Case 125/78 *GEMA* v *Commission***, a competition law complaint was made to the Commission under Regulation 17 (now replaced by Regulation 2003/1) about Radio Luxembourg. When the Commission failed to take any action, GEMA attempted an Article 232 EC (now 265 TFEU) action against the Commission. It was held that the letter from the Commission to GEMA stating its decision not to take action was a sufficient definition of position to defeat GEMA's action.

> Until **Case 13/83 *European Parliament* v *Council (Transport Policy)***, a declaration by an institution of its unwillingness to act was regarded by some as constituting a sufficient definition of position for the purposes of the CoJ. However, the Court in the *Transport* case stated that in the absence of taking a formal act, the institution called upon to define its position must do more than reply stating its current position, which in effect neither denies nor admits the alleged failure, nor reveals the attitude of the defendant institution to the demanded measures.

9.2.3.3 The substantive action

The *Transport Policy* case was the first to succeed under this Article.

> In **Case 13/83 *European Parliament v Council (Transport Policy)***, the EP had complained that the Council had failed in its Treaty obligations under old Articles 3, 61, 74, 75, and 84 EC to introduce a common policy for transport, to lay down a framework for this policy, and to act on 16 specific proposals of the Commission. The CoJ held, in response to the first claim, that because the Treaty requirements were so vague, there could not be said to exist

sufficiently specific obligations as to amount to a failure to act. This was despite the fact that the obligations should have been completed long before. The Court held that the obligation of old Article 61 EC could be identified with sufficient precision as to constitute a failure on the part of the Council to lay down a framework. The second claim of failure to act on 16 proposals of the Commission was successful only in respect of the proposals regarding the freedom to provide services. The other measures were within the greater margin of discretion left to the Council by the Treaty.

9.2.3.4 **Results of a declaration of a failure to act**

The institution is required under Article 266(1) TFEU (ex 233 EC) to take the necessary measures to comply with the judgment of the CoJ within a reasonable time. A continued failure to act would be actionable under Article 265 TFEU. Article 266 states that it is without prejudice to any action for damages under Article 340 TFEU (ex 288 EC). This is considered next.

9.3 Action for damages under the non-contractual liability of the EU

The contractual liability of the Union is made subject to the jurisdiction of national law pertaining to the contract under Article 340(1) TFEU, whereas Article 268 TFEU confers jurisdiction over disputes relating to claims for non-contractual liability damages under Article 340(2) TFEU to the CoJ. The General Court hears at first-instance actions by individuals and the CoJ hears actions by the member states.

For more details on this section visit the online resources.

> **Article 268 TFEU (ex 235 EC)**
>
> The Court of Justice of the European Union shall have jurisdiction in disputes relating to compensation for damage provided for in the second paragraph of Article 340 TFEU.

Article 340(2) TFEU requires the Union to make good damage caused by the institutions or servants in the performance of their duties in accordance with the general principles common to the laws of the member states. The term 'non-contractual' is employed to take account of the different legal traditions and to ensure that the Union is responsible for all of its actions outside contractual liability. Non-contractual liability thus covers the civil wrongs caused by the legislative and administrative activities of the Union, whether committed by the institutions or servants.

9.3.1 **Admissibility**

As with Article 263 TFEU actions, there are four elements of admissibility to consider: the defendant institution, its action or inaction, a time limit, and *locus standi*. Unlike Article 263 TFEU actions, the *locus standi* aspect is much more easily satisfied and is considered first this time.

9.3.1.1 *Locus standi*

▶ CROSS REFERENCE

See section 9.3.10 as to the types of damages that can be claimed.

In contrast to Articles 263 and 265 TFEU, there is no restrictive *locus standi* imposed on individuals by either Article 268 or 340(2) TFEU. The applicant must be affected and damaged in some tangible and provable way. He or she must be able to demonstrate some degree of loss without necessarily calculating the exact amount. This can be quantified later if the action is found to be admissible and the claim upheld.

> **Case T-376/04** *Polyelectrolyte Producers Group v Council and Commission* was rejected as inadmissible by the CFI because the allegations of loss made were unsupported by any evidence of loss.

9.3.1.2 **Time limit**

Established by case law and confirmed in Article 46 of the Statute of the CoJ, there is a five-year limitation period on actions, which commences from the occurrence of the event causing the damage (Case 5/71 *Schöppenstedt* v *Council* for legislative-caused loss) or, if not discovered until later, from when the event causing the damage is discovered (Case 145/83 *Adams* v *Commission* for administrative error causing loss).

9.3.2 **The defendant institution and act**

▶ CROSS REFERENCE

This is also considered at section 9.3.12 on choice of court and in relation to Case 175/84 *Krohn* v *Commission*.

In an action against the Union, the appropriate institution that should be named as defendant is the one responsible for the legislative or administrative act or the action or inaction of which caused the damage. This can be the Commission, or the Council and EP, or both, which jointly legislate in many areas of EU law. This was confirmed originally by the CoJ in Cases 63–69/72 *Werhahn* v *Commission*. In view of the greater powers of the EP, the EP either alone or in connection with the Council can also be named as a defendant. The ECB is also named in Article 340 TFEU as an institution that can be sued. Member states are only sued where they are responsible for the implementation of Union measures and have exceeded their discretion. If there is no discretion on their part, the Commission is the proper defendant. The action under Article 340(2) TFEU does not extend to the Treaties or Accession acts which cause damage as these are acts of the member states and not the institutions (see Case 169/73 *CCT v Commission* and Case C-95/98 *Dubois v Council and Commission*).

9.3.3 **An autonomous or independent action**

The action for damages has been held by the CoJ to be an autonomous form of action, having its own particular purpose to fulfil within the Treaty system of remedies and subject to conditions on its use dictated by its specific nature.

> This is also termed the 'principle of the autonomy of remedies'.

> In **Case 4/69** *Lütticke*, damage had been suffered as a result of the Commission failing to act against Germany. The Commission argued that the action under Article 288 EC (now 340 TFEU) was an attempt to circumvent the *locus standi* requirements of a previous unsuccessful

Article 232 EC (now 265 TFEU) action. The CoJ rejected this argument and declared that the action for damages provided by Articles 235 and 288(2) (now 268 and 340 TFEU) was established by the Treaty as an independent form of action, the object of which was to compensate a party for damage sustained and not to secure the annulment of an illegal measure. The requirements to establish liability essentially follow that found in common law and delictual jurisdictions, namely, a breach of a duty, basic the duty not to act unlawfully or beach a legal measure, damage to the applicant and the causal link between them, that the breach was the cause of the damage.

Case 5/71 *Zuckerfabrik Schöppenstedt* **v** *Council* concerned an action for damages arising from a Regulation. The Council had argued that the action should be ruled inadmissible because to allow it would frustrate the system of judicial remedies provided by the Treaty by allowing a challenge to a Regulation, which is not permitted under Article 230 EC (now 263 TFEU), the reasoning being that such applications would be ruled out for lack of *locus standi* or as being outside of the short time limit. That argument was firmly rejected by the CoJ.

However, in **Case T-86/03** *Holcim (France)* **v** *Commission*, the General Court held that an action will be inadmissible if it was intended to have the same effect as an annulment action in respect of an individual administrative decision only. In such a case, it is regarded as an abuse of process as an attempt to get round the much stricter time limits of Article 263 TFEU.

Therefore, little difficulty faces applicants in respect of admissibility; the problem lies in proving that an act of the Union caused damage and that there was a sufficiently serious breach of a rule of law.

 THINKING POINT

Why is admissibility for this action so much easier to demonstrate than for actions under Article 263 TFEU?

9.3.4 The requirements of liability

Under the Article 340(2) TFEU, the liability of the Union is to be determined in accordance with the general principles common to the laws of the member states. When the CoJ looks to national laws for guidance and general principles, as in other instances of this practice, it is not required to accept the lowest common denominator, but makes a comparative review and selects principles of law appropriate to the situation. Therefore, a body of EU law is being built up in this area. From the case law, requirements have been identified to establish liability for the purpose of Article 240(2) TFEU that the Union is liable either:

- for damage caused by one of its institutions; or
- for damage caused by its servants in the performance of their duties.

There must be a wrongful act or omission on the part of the Union that has breached a duty, the applicant must have suffered damage, and there must be a causal link between the act or omission and the damage.

9.3.4.1 The standard of liability and fault

Liability can be imposed not only for administrative acts or omissions, but also in relation to legislative acts such as Regulations, Directives, or Decisions. Liability can thus be incurred as a result of failures of administration, the negligence of employees of the institutions in the performance of their duties (but not extending to personal faults of employees), and the adoption of unlawful legislative acts. The act or omission of the Union must be shown to be wrongful; however, the degree of wrongfulness or fault varies depending on whether the wrong committed was the result of an administrative act, an act of one the employees, or arose from a legislative act. Note now, however, that, since Case C-352/98 P *Bergaderm*, the CoJ has stated that a single test should apply to both administrative and legislative acts. This section, though, charts the development of the law in this area in respect of both types of act as previously developed, and returns to this new test in section 9.3.7.

9.3.5 Administrative/non-discretionary acts

While a requirement of fault is not expressly stated in the Treaty, case law indicates that this is necessary to establish liability for damage caused by administrative acts.

In **Case 14/60 *Meroni***, the CoJ ruled that liability is based on fault, for example in this case that there had to be negligence in the administration or construction of a scheme of regulation for ferrous scrap before there could be liability when the scheme malfunctioned. The CoJ held that the mere existence of errors in the administration of the scheme is not in itself evidence of a wrongful act or omission, since such errors may be caused by the fact that the problems tackled by the scheme are difficult to resolve.

In **Cases 19, 20, 25, and 30/69 *Richez Parise***, the Commission had supplied wrong information to its staff about pension rights. This information was based on an incorrect interpretation of the rules concerning rights that the staff could claim on the termination of their service. The CoJ held that only in exceptional circumstances would an incorrect interpretation constitute a wrongful act. However, in this case, the Commission was at fault by failing promptly to remedy the error of interpretation as soon as it became obvious that its interpretation was erroneous. Therefore, its failure to issue a correction within a reasonable time was of such nature as to render the Commission liable.

There is a notorious case in EU law concerning the liability of the institutions in respect of acts of its servants.

Case 145/83 *Stanley Adams v Commission* concerned the liability of the Community for a breach of the duty of care owed to its informants in the sphere of competition law. Adams claimed a breach of confidence of information by releasing documents by which Hoffmann-La Roche could identify Adams as the whistle-blower when it was investigated and fined under competition law. Article 287 EC (now 339 TFEU) imposed a duty on members of staff of institutions not to disclose information covered by professional secrecy. It was held that the Commission remained under a duty not to reveal its source even when Adams left his employment. Hoffmann-La Roche discovered his identity and the Swiss Public Prosecutor was informed. Adams was tried in his absence and convicted of industrial espionage, which is a criminal offence in Switzerland. The Commission was aware of the risk that Adams would be identified by handing over documents and failed to tell Adams of the threats to prosecute him. On return to Switzerland, Adams was arrested and jailed. His wife, who was suffering from depression, committed suicide when informed about a possible 20-year jail sentence for her husband. The Commission was held liable to make good the damage resulting from the discovery of the applicant's identity, but Adams was held to have been contributorily negligent by not informing the Commission that he could be identified from documents and failing to ask the Commission to keep him informed of progress.

The *Adams* case is an illustration of the rules relating to duty, vicarious liability, causation, and contributory negligence.

9.3.6 Liability for employees

The possibility of vicarious liability for employees was raised in an early case.

In **Case 9/69 *Sayag v Leduc***, Mr Sayag was employed by the European Atomic Energy Community (EURATOM) and, whilst showing guests of the Community around in his own car, was involved in an accident in which his passengers were injured. They sued Sayag, who claimed that the Community should be held liable. It was held that the Commission was not liable because it was not an official act of the Community: 'the Community is only liable for those acts of its servants which, by virtue of an internal and direct relationship, are the necessary extension of the tasks entrusted to the institutions of the Community'.

There was also the possible policy reason that the person's own insurance would, in any event, cover the damage.

The scope of liability is thus limited to activities of institutions or the performance of institutional tasks.

9.3.7 Liability for legislative acts

The principle that there can be liability on the part of the institutions for damage resulting from the adoption of legislative acts was established by the CoJ through case law and extended to other acts which have been created under discretionary powers of the institutions. The legislative acts of the Union are those, in view of their scope and the sheer numbers whom they can affect, which have the potential to cause great damage.

However, in the leading case that confirmed this principle, **Case 5/71 *Schöppenstedt v Council***, the CoJ laid down a strict test to be met to establish liability, which has been

> repeated often. In the case, the plaintiffs claimed that a Regulation breached the principle of non-discrimination in Article 34(2) EC (now 40(2) TFEU). The CoJ held that:
>
> > The Community does not incur liability on account of a legislative measure which involves choices of economic policy unless a sufficiently flagrant violation of a superior rule of law for the protection of the individual has occurred.
>
> It was held that the prohibition of discrimination was a superior rule of law, but that it had not been breached.

The reasoning for the strict test is very similar to the strict requirements for *locus standi* for Article 263 TFEU in that the high degree of discretion that the institutions need to carry out their economic tasks necessarily affects many persons, hence the imposition of a higher burden when choices of economic policy are involved. The point is that the act concerned is not just an administrative decision of the Commission, but a legislative act that has been brought about as the result of reaching the agreement of, if not all 28 member states in the Council, at least a significant majority of them under qualified majority voting (QMV). Therefore it is not only unlawful conduct that will attract liability, but also the degree of unlawful conduct required under the formula developed by the CoJ. All types of legislative act can be subject to an action under Article 340(2) TFEU.

The formula can be divided into two parts, although in some treatments it is divided into three parts, as follows:

(1) there must be a violation or breach of a superior rule of law (which can be linked with the next part);

(2) the rule must exist for the protection of natural or legal persons; and

(3) the violation must have been sufficiently serious.

The argument for combining the first two parts is that it is difficult to perceive a superior rule that is not for the protection of individuals or, conversely, a rule that is for the protection of individuals which is not therefore a superior rule.

❱ CROSS REFERENCE

See Chapter 8 for details on *Francovich*.

> **Case C-352/98P *Bergaderm* v *Commission*** appears to have modified the test laid down in *Schöppenstedt* in that the Court now requires there to be a sufficiently serious breach of a rule of law intended to confer rights on individuals, which is the same for member state liability as developed from the *Francovich* case. It remains the case that the causal link between the breach and the damage caused must be proved.

> This has been followed up in some, but by no means all, cases before the General Court, such as **Case T-16/04 *Arcelor***, which, following on from *Bergaderm*, focused on the degree of discretion rather than the seriousness or arbitrariness of the breach.

Whilst this development is likely to be followed because it is a logical extension of the arguments about the need for the institutions to have discretion to make the necessary choices of economic policy, there is not as yet a consistent line of authority to confirm that the more complex approach in *Schöppenstedt* has been entirely abandoned.

9.3.7.1 The rules of law covered

The rules of law include specific legal rules contained in legislation, fundamental rights, and general principles. The principles of proportionality, legal certainty, equality/discrimination, and legitimate expectation are often raised.

The rule of law accepted in the *Schöppenstedt* case was a prohibition of discrimination, which is contained in a Treaty Article; hence its acceptance as a superior rule of law.

Article 40(2) TFEU (ex 34(2) EC) provides that the CAP and measures taken under it 'shall exclude any discrimination between producers or consumers within the Union'.

In **Case 64/76 *Dumortier Freres* v Commission (Gritz and Quellmehl)**, the ending of a subsidy was held to be a breach because it was retained on starch, which was direct competition.

See also **Case 83/76 *HNL*** and **Cases 103 and 145/77 *KSH* v Council and Commission (Royal Scholten Holdings)**, which are also often cited in respect of the same rule of law.

In **Case T-166/98 *Cantina***, the rule that there should be no unjustified enrichment was breached. This was confirmed in **Case C-47/07 P *Masdar (UK)* v Commission**.

Unjustified enrichment is a principle of quasi-tort.

These rules are designed with the individual in mind; hence, in the *Bergaderm* case, the CoJ held, in order to reflect this, that there should be a move in future to deal with the rules of law required and the protection of the individual together, and in subsequent cases there has been less emphasis on the rule of law being superior.

⟩ CROSS REFERENCE

Bergaderm is considered further in section 9.3.8.

9.3.7.2 The protection of the individual

The protection of the individual, which includes natural and legal persons, has been interpreted also to include protection of classes of person, as with the importers in Cases 5, 7, 13, and 24/66 *Kampfmeyer*, in which a Regulation aimed generally at agricultural markets was held to include individuals within those markets.

Case 74/74 *CNTA* v Commission involved the general principle of legitimate expectation. The Commission was held liable to pay compensation for losses incurred as a result of a Regulation that abolished, with immediate effect and without warning, the application of compensatory amounts. This was held to be a serious breach of the principle of legitimate expectation, which was designed to provide individual protection.

See also **Case T-69/00** *Fiamm*, in which individuals were held to be affected indirectly by Community acts, but whose action was held to be admissible, although it was not successful ultimately on a damages issue.

9.3.7.3 **The breach must be sufficiently serious/flagrant**

The breach must be sufficiently serious because it is a challenge to an economic policy choice of the Union involving the exercise of wide discretion. Whilst there must be a breach of an important rule of law that is superior to more general rules of law, a mere breach is not sufficient to trigger liability; a sufficiently flagrant or serious breach is required.

In **Case 83/76** *HNL v Commission*, a Regulation requiring cattle food manufacturers to use more expensive skimmed milk than cheaper soya in their foods (to use up the 'milk lake' of the overproduction of milk) was held to be invalid, and declared null and void, because it offended the principles of proportionality and discrimination (Article 34(2) EC, now 40(2) TFEU). However, whilst in the Article 288 EC (now 340 TFEU) action the breach was acknowledged, it was held not to be a sufficiently serious or flagrant breach.

Almost inevitably in the regulation of the CAP and particular food products, a legislative decision by the Commission to allow or to restrict production will affect, often adversely, the economic position of individual farmers. To permit them to succeed in an action for damages each time would completely undermine any attempt to control the market. The Commission and Union would be rendered useless.

In **Case 83/76** *HNL v Commission*, the Court stated:

> The legislative authority . . . cannot always be hindered in making its decisions by the prospect of applications for damages whenever it has occasion to adopt legislative measures in the public interest which may adversely affect the interests of individuals.

Thus, liability is incurred only where there has been a manifest and grave disregard of the limits on the exercise of powers.

The term 'manifest and grave' was itself later interpreted in **Cases 103 and 145/77 KSH v Council and Commission** as conduct verging on the arbitrary.

Preliminary rulings in **Cases 117/76 and 16/77 Rucksdeschel** and **Cases 124/76 and 20/77 Moulins de Pont a Mousson (Maize, Gritz, and Quellmehl)** had held that Regulations providing higher production refunds for maize starch than for maize gritz were incompatible with Article 34(2) EC (now 40(2) TFEU) and thus invalid. New, lower refunds had been set for maize gritz and the companies claimed damages. The question was: had the Council of Ministers manifestly and gravely disregarded the limits of its power? Thus, in the cases known collectively as the *Maize, Gritz, and Quellmehl cases*, the CoJ held that the Council had manifestly and gravely disregarded the limits of its power because:

(1) Article 34(2) (now 40(2) TFEU) was important for the protection of individuals;

(2) only a small, defined, and closed group of commercial applicants was affected;

(3) the damage must be over and above economic risks normal in business;

(4) the equality of treatment ended without sufficient justification; and

(5) the Council ignored a Commission proposal.

The *Quellmehl* cases had the same result with regard to a discriminatory treatment by the Commission of maize starch and quellmehl, both products used in the baking industry. In both cases, damages plus interest were awarded.

Another product-specific series of cases dealt with the production of isoglucose, an artificial sweetener that competed with sugar.

Cases 116, 124, and 143/77 *Amylum and Tunnel Refineries (the Isoglucose cases)* can be typified by **Cases 124, 143, and 166/77 *Tunnel Refineries***. The production of isoglucose was heavily penalised by a Regulation, which was later annulled, but the consequence was that the producers had already suffered massive losses, including some producers going out of business. Their claims for losses failed because the breaches were not 'verging on the arbitrary'!

THINKING POINT

What would be the consequences in the EU if the applicants were easily to succeed and obtain damages for their loss? Would the Commission then be required to allow isoglucose to outsell sugar? Not to do so would result in numerous claims for loss. If so, what would be the knock-on effect on sugar production? Who and how many people in the EU are engaged in sugar production?

Factors that influence the CoJ in its determination of whether the breach is sufficiently serious include the clarity of the breach, the effect of the breach, and the manner or nature of the breach. The effect of a breach relates to its scope, the number of people affected, the type of damage caused, and if that damage was unusual. The manner or nature of the breach relates to whether it was intentional or accidental or whether it was excusable, such as the difficulty in reaching decisions in complex situations or in interpreting the legislation. Other important factors include whether there is a higher Union public interest or, as it is also termed, general economic interest involved. Another consideration is whether a particular group has been disproportionately affected. Previously, it was considered that only a small, defined, and closed group of applicants could successfully pursue a claim (see Case 152/88 *Sofrimport*) and that if large numbers were involved, this would defeat a claim.

For more details on the arguments and difficulties in finding the correct balanced solutions visit the online resources.

However, **Cases C-104/89 and 37/90 *Mulder v Council*** dealt with the application of many milk farmers who alleged damage as a result of changes to milk quota regulation. The farmers had previously been compensated for not producing milk in an attempt to reduce or prevent its over-production, a scheme that was abandoned following widespread criticism. The new regime allowed all farmers to produce a certain percentage of previous years' production only. These farmers had produced none, of course, and so were therefore disadvantaged. Hence, the CoJ suggested that a large group of applicants need not be fatal to a claim, although a serious breach still had to be demonstrated and that there was no higher public interest of the Community involved. The application in the case itself though was not successful because the Commission had not exceeded its discretion and therefore the breach was not sufficiently serious.

9.3.8 A new single test for liability?

CROSS REFERENCE

See section 9.3.9 for more on the extension to cover all acts.

According to the AG in the *Factortame* case, up to 1995 only eight awards had been made against the Community institutions, which seemed to indicate that the *Schöppenstedt* formula, as it had been applied, had been far too strict and needed to be modified.

In **Case C-352/98 P *Bergaderm* v *Commission***, the CoJ took the opportunity to modify or simplify the test laid down in *Schöppenstedt*. The Court considered the parallel developments in the cases on state liability, including, in particular, Cases C-46 and C-48/93 *Brasserie du Pêcheur* and *Factortame*, and adapted the test for liability from those cases.

The modification requires there to be a sufficiently serious breach of a rule of law intended to confer rights on individuals, and considers whether there has been a disregard of the limits of discretion by the institution involved. The slight change in emphasis from superior rules of law for the protection of individuals to those rules conferring rights and the emphasis on discretion brings into line the test for liability under state liability and Article 340 actions. The Court suggested that where the institutions and member states had manifestly and gravely disregarded the limits of their discretion, the breach would be sufficiently serious to incur liability. It also extended the test for all acts rather than only for legislative acts. Hence, as with member states, where there is no discretion, a mere infringement will suffice, but where there is discretion, it will be a matter of the degree by which the institution exceeded that discretion.

CROSS REFERENCE

See the *Bergaderm* case also discussed in Chapter 8, section 8.3, on state liability.

Whilst the new formulation has been followed up in some General Court cases and on appeal to the CoJ, there is not as yet clear authority that the more complex approach in *Schöppenstedt* has been completely abandoned.

See, for example, **Case T-212/03 *My Travel Group plc* v *Commission***, in which there were grave and manifest faults in the Commission's consideration of a proposed merger which led to the blocking of the merger and loss to My Travel Group. It was held that as a consequence of the complexity of the merger and market combined with the difficulties in applying the relevant EU law within tight time constraints and the margin of discretion enjoyed by the Commission, it was not liable. **Case T-16/04 *Arcelor*** focused on the degree of discretion enjoyed by the Commission and less on the seriousness or arbitrariness of the breach.

> However, in **Case C-282/05P *Holcim v Commission***, which applied *Bergaderm*, the sheer difficulty encountered by the Commission in investigating an extremely complex competition market was again the most important factor in holding the Commission not liable, and thus the result was the same as if the more complete *Schöppenstedt* formula had been applied.

It therefore remains very difficult to assess whether the *Bergaderm* case is actually changing how cases are analysed by the General Court or CoJ in the determination of liability, and it is submitted that at this stage further case law is required.

9.3.8.1 Individual (non-legislative) acts

The *Schöppenstedt* test was developed specifically to apply to general legislative acts and, because the subsequent *Bergaderm* case was a modification of this, it might have been expected that it would not be appropriate for specific acts applying or affecting an individual only. However, in *Bergaderm*, the CoJ also addressed this point and held that it was not material whether the act alleged to have caused damage was legislative or administrative, but whether the institution had exceeded the limits of its discretion.

> This was confirmed in the later **Case C-282/05 P *Holcim v Commission***, in which the CoJ held that the requirement to show a sufficiently serious breach should also apply to individual acts.

It would be helpful to see further cases from the CoJ supporting this development.

9.3.9 Liability for lawful acts

In a further development, the possibility that the Union may be liable, in certain circumstances, for damage caused by lawful acts has been explored.

> For example, the earlier case **C-237/98 P *Dorsch Consult v Council*** concerned the banning of trade in Iraq under an EC Regulation complying with a United Nations Resolution and resultant losses. The CoJ held that, in order for there to be liability, such losses would have to be unusual and special.

> **Case T-69/00 *FIAMM & FIAMM Technologies* and others v *Council and Commission***, and now the appeal case **C-120/06 P**, concerned Regulations enacted under the infamous Community Banana Regime, which were incompatible or alleged to be incompatible with the World Trade Organization (WTO) agreements. As a result, the United States took retaliatory measures by increasing customs duties on other products, causing the applicants loss as a result of the impact on their imports to the US. Whilst the disputed Regulations were lawful in the Community regime, internationally they were not. The CFI (now General Court) held that although the conduct was not unlawful, an action for damages could be admissible where the economic operators had borne a disproportionate burden as a result of the countermeasures

> to the Community regulation of the banana market contrary to WTO rules. The applicants still had to show actual damage, a causal link between the conduct of the Community institution and the damage, and the unusual and special nature of the damage. In the case, it was held that the conduct of the defendant institutions had led to retaliatory measures being adopted, which were the cause of the damage sustained. However, the CFI (now General Court) considered that the extent of damage suffered was neither unusual nor beyond the economic risks that might be expected in the economic sector, and the actions failed.

Whilst the case was not successful, it has widened the category of potential acts that can incur liability. On appeal, the CoJ confirmed the judgment on the facts of the CFI that no liability accrued in this case, and disapproved the principle that lawful acts could, given the appropriate facts, give rise to liability. Unless there is a subsequent change of view, the case is thus far the final word on the possibility that the Union may be liable for damage caused by lawful acts.

9.3.10 The damage

Having established the existence of an act or omission attributable to the Union, damage to the applicant must be proved. Damage can be purely economic, as in Cases 5, 7, 13, and 24/66 *Kampfmeyer* involving a cancellation fee and loss of profits, provided this is specified and not speculative, or damage can take the form of moral damage, as in Case 110/63 *Willame* v *Commission*.

> In **Case 74/74 *CNTA***, compensation for the losses caused by a sudden change to export refunds contrary to the legitimate expectations of the company was upheld, although, in the case itself, currency fluctuations meant that no actual loss was recorded.

It has been held that the damage must be over and above the risk of damage normal in business, in that it exceeds the risks inherent in the sector concerned (see Case 64/76 *Dumortier Frères* v *Council*).

> In **Case C-152/88 *Sofrimport* v *EC Commission***, which concerned Chilean apples in transit, import licences were suspended whilst the cargo was on the high seas. The applicants were successful in obtaining damages because of the complete failure of the Commission to take into account the interests of the applicants when it was required to do so. This amounted to a sufficiently serious breach of legitimate expectation. The damage went beyond the limits of economic risk inherent in business.

A claim for compensation for damage caused has also been held to include a claim for an injunction to prevent further future damage, as held by the General Court in Case T-279/03 *Galileo*. Part of the Court's reasoning was that this should be available in the same way as in national legal orders dealing with tortious or delictual claims. Similarly, contributory negligence is recognised, as was noted in the *Adams* case in section 9.3.5, and a duty to mitigate loses, as in the *Mulder* case, noted in section 9.3.7.3.

9.3.11 The causal connection

Lastly, it must be proved by the applicant that the act of the Union caused the damage with a sufficiently direct connection between the act and the injury.

> In **Cases 64 and 113/76 *Dumortier Frères v Council (Gritz and Quellmehl)***, it was held that there was no need to make good every harmful consequence, especially where remote.

Damage must be a sufficiently direct consequence of the unlawful conduct of the institution concerned.

> In **Case 169/73 *Compagnie Continentale Française***, it was held that the causal link was only established if the misleading information given would have caused an error in the mind of a reasonable person.

> In **Case 132/77 *Sugar Export***, it was held that the chain of causation may be broken by an independent act of a third party.

In summary, the damage must be certain, specific, proven, and quantifiable, and it may cover imminent foreseeable damage and lost profits: Cases 5, 7, 13, and 24/66 *Kampffmeyer*.

9.3.12 Concurrent liability/choice of court

For the most part, the application of EU legislative measures, especially in the agricultural sector, is actually administered and thus dependent on the national intervention agencies that make and receive payments. However, if a claim is based on a Union act that was wrongful, the question of whether a national court or the CoJ is the appropriate forum arises. Where a claim involves the return of sums unlawfully paid to national authorities, compensation must be sought from the national authorities before the national courts, followed, if necessary, by a reference under the Article 267 TFEU procedure (see Cases 5, 7, 13, and 24/66 *Kampffmeyer*), especially where joint liability of the member state and the EU can be proved. It is only really the conduct of the institutions or servants that would require a direct application to the CoJ or where the claims are for unliquidated damages—that is, those involving loss of profits suffered as a result of illegal action which is entirely attributable to the EU (see Cases 74/74 *CNTA* and 175/84 *Krohn v Commission*).

9.3.13 Section summary

Despite the easier-to-fulfil admissibility factors, it remains the situation that not many cases are successful. As discussed earlier, according to the AG in the *Factortame* case, up to 1995 only eight awards had been made. The same reasoning appears to apply to the merits of this action as apply at the admissibility stage of an Article 263 TFEU action to annul unlawful acts. The difficulty with which Union legislative acts are achieved is not to be easily overcome either by actions to annul or actions for damages. Both of these would undermine the ability of the Union to regulate the markets, and because Union Regulations that seek to regulate particular markets inevitably will affect individuals operating in that market, those individuals must be protected—hence the view that the strictness is not unreasonable.

9.4 The plea of illegality (Article 277 TFEU)

This action provides a right to plead the illegality of an EU Regulation in different circumstances from the direct challenge of Article 263 TFEU.

For more details on this section visit the online resources.

> **Article 277 TFEU**
>
> Notwithstanding the expiry of the period laid down in Article 263, sixth paragraph, any party may, in proceedings in which an act of general application adopted by an institution, body, office or agency of the Union is at issue, plead the grounds specified in Article 263, second paragraph, in order to invoke before the Court of Justice of the European Union the inapplicability of that act.

Article 277 TFEU is not an independent or direct cause of action to the CoJ, as confirmed in Case 33/80 *Renato Albini* v *Council and Commission*, which means that an applicant cannot simply commence an action under this Article.

> In **Cases 31 and 33/62 *Wöhrmann* v *Commission***, the CoJ held that Article 241 EC (now 277 TFEU) was available only in proceedings already brought before the CoJ under some other action and only as an incidental or indirect action.

For example, it may be that, during the course of an Article 263 TFEU challenge to a decision, it comes to light that a Regulation, which was the legal base for the decision, was for some reason unlawful, but was beyond challenge itself due to the time limit or a lack of *locus standi* under Article 263 TFEU, as considered in section 9.1. This would provide the grounds under which Article 277 TFEU might apply. It cannot be used in Article 340 TFEU actions, considered in section 9.3, nor in Article 258 TFEU actions against member states: see Case 70/72 *Commission* v *Federal Republic of Germany*.

9.4.1 *Locus standi*

An Article 277 TFEU action is available to any party, including the member states; however, it is more likely to benefit individuals who, for good reason, are unable to comply with the *locus standi* and time limit requirements of Article 263 TFEU. However, as noted above, it is not designed or intended to provide an alternative for those who have simply failed to meet the requirements of Article 263 TFEU. The conditions for *locus standi* under this action are exactly the same as Article 263 TFEU. This means that when challenging legislative acts, direct and individual concern must be demonstrated and, when challenging non-legislative acts (the delegated legislation), only direct concern need be shown but, as with Article 263 TFEU, the act must not entail implementing measures.

> In **Case 156/77 Commission v Belgium**, a Community decision was challenged directly before the CoJ; however, the Court refused the application because Belgium had allowed its right under Article 230 EC (now 263 TFEU) to expire.

Article 277 TFEU is designed more for those who either have no rights under Article 263 TFEU or were unable to meet directly the *locus standi* requirements, but who nevertheless are affected by the illegality of a Union act, usually a Decision.

> For example, in **Case 216/82 University of Hamburg v Hauptzollamt Hamburg**, the university was able to challenge a decision addressed to the German government indirectly before the national court. The reason was not because it was directly and individually concerned by it, but because the decision was not published; it was therefore unable to challenge the decision under Article 230 EC (now 263 TFEU).

9.4.2 Acts that can be reviewed

Article 277 TFEU refers to acts of general application only, which, in the EU, essentially means Regulations, which can be challenged only if they form the legal basis of the subject matter of the direct action, as in Case 9/56 *Meroni* v *High Authority*. Article 277 TFEU does not envisage the challenge of decisions or other forms of binding act that are not generally applicable.

> However, in **Case 92/78 Simmenthal v Commission**, a decision was challenged that was based generally on prior Regulations and notices. The Regulations could not be challenged directly under Article 230 EC (now 263 TFEU) because of the restrictive *locus standi* requirements, but could be challenged indirectly via Article 241 EC (now 277 TFEU). The CoJ held that it was not the form of the act that is important, but the substance. Therefore, according to the Court, other acts that are normative or general in effect should be regarded as Regulations for the purposes of making a challenge under Article 241 EC (now 277 TFEU).

This is now confirmed by the amended Article 277 TFEU, which refers to any acts of general application and makes it clear that the challenge can apply to acts adopted by any EU institution, body, office, or agency.

Addressees, though, of an individual act such as a Decision cannot challenge it indirectly in the CoJ because they should have done so directly under Article 263 TFEU within the time limits. To allow otherwise would be to render the time limit meaningless, as confirmed in Case 156/77 *Commission v Belgium*.

9.4.3 Grounds of review

The substantive grounds of the action are those listed for Article 263 TFEU.

> For example, **Case 92/78 *Simmenthal*** succeeded on its merits that the general measure had been used for purposes other than that for which it was intended—that is, improper purpose.

9.4.4 **Effect of a successful challenge**

The result of such an action is that the Regulation or act is declared inapplicable in that case and not generally void: see Case 9/56 *Meroni* v *High Authority*. Any acts based on the voidable Regulation will, however, be void and withdrawn. Also, in practice, the Regulation or act will not be applied in subsequent cases, as is the consequence in Article 267 TFEU references: for example, see Case 66/80 *ICC*.

Summary

Direct actions before the CoJ cover a number of grounds of unlawful activity, the most important of which are actions to annul an act of the Union under Article 263 TFEU and actions for damages under Article 340 TFEU. The aspects of admissibility in Article 263 TFEU and the merits in Article 340 TFEU stand out as those receiving the most attention. Less frequently visited are the actions under Article 265 TFEU for a failure to act and Article 277 TFEU, the incidental plea of illegality. However, the last two should not be entirely ignored because they may be considered as alternative actions if the main actions prove to be fruitless. Certainly, however, we should pay more attention to Articles 263 and 340 TFEU.

? Questions

For suggested approaches to answering these questions visit the online resources.

1. Is it true that admissibility is the major hurdle to a successful action under Article 263 TFEU? If so, why?

2. What must an individual show if he or she is to be recognised as having 'individual concern' for the purposes of Article 263 TFEU?

3. Is the test that the CoJ operates in Article 263 TFEU actions too strict?

4. Consider the contrasting approach of the CoJ to Article 340 TFEU and the test for *Francovich* liability. Are the same standards of liability imposed on both the Community institutions and member states?

5. What use is the plea of illegality action under Article 277 TFEU?

For guidance on how to tackle this specimen exam question and to read a suggested model answer, visit the online resources. www.oup.com/uk/foster_directions6e/.

▢ Sample exam Q&A

Essay question

How and to what extent are the rights of individuals protected in the EU legal order?

Further reading

Books

Biondi, A. and Farley, M. *The Right to Damages in European Law*, Kluwer Law International, London, 2009.

Gordon, R. *EC Law in Judicial Review*, Oxford University Press, Oxford, 2007.

Hartley, T. *The Foundations of European Community Law*, 7th edn, Clarendon Press, Oxford, 2010 (Chapter 10).

Lenaerts, K., Arts, D., and Maselis, M. *Procedural Law of the European Union*, 3rd edn, Sweet & Maxwell, London, 2012.

Türk, A. H. *Judicial Review in EU Law*, Edward Elgar Publishing, Cheltenham, 2009.

Ward, A. *Judicial Review and the Rights of Private Parties in EU Law*, 2nd edn, Oxford University Press, Oxford, 2007.

Articles

Albors-Llorens, A. 'The standing of private parties to challenge Community measures: has the European Court missed the boat?' (2003) 62 CLJ 72.

Balthasar, S. '*Locus standi* rules for challenges to regulatory acts by private applicants: the new Article 263(4) TFEU' (2010) 35 EL Rev 542.

Cortes Martin, J. M. '*Ubi ius, ibi remedium*? *Locus standi* of private applicants under Article 230(4) EC at a European constitutional crossroads' (2004) 11 MJECL 233.

Craig, P. 'The ECJ and ultra vires action: a conceptual analysis' (2011) 48 CML Rev 395.

Enchelmeier, S. 'No one slips through the net? Latest developments, and non-developments, in the European Court of Justice's jurisprudence on Art 230(4) EC' (2005) 24 YEL 173.

Gutman, K. 'The evolution of the action for damages against the European Union and its place in the system of judicial protection' (2011) 48 CML Rev 695.

Hilson, C. 'The role of discretion in EC law on non-contractual liability' (2005) 42 CML Rev 677.

Sinaniotis, D. 'The plea of illegality in EC law' (2001) 7 EPL 103.

Usher, J. 'Direct and individual concern: an effective remedy or a conventional solution?' (2003) 28 EL Rev 575.

Vogt, M. 'Indirect judicial protection in the EC law: the case of the plea of illegality' (2006) 31 EL Rev 364.

Ward, A. '*Locus standi* under Article 230(4) of the EC Treaty: crafting a coherent test for a "wobbly polity"' (2003) 22 YEL 45.

PART 3
SUBSTANTIVE LAW

10 Free movement of goods I: tariff and tax barriers

☐ LEARNING OBJECTIVES

In this chapter, you will learn about:

- the meaning and importance of the Common Market, also known as the internal market;
- the basic definitions relating to economic integration;
- the basic legislative regime for the free movement of goods;
- the prohibitions of tariff and equivalent barriers; and
- the internal tax measures that hinder free movement.

Introduction

The free movement of goods is a central part of the internal market, and is the foundation of the European Community (EC) as originally established and the Union today. It is very much concerned with the economic ideals of the Union to create a single trading bloc in which all factors of production, and particularly goods, flow freely. The free movement of goods is essential to the creation and running of the customs union and the, Common Market, as originally entitled, now the internal market. Among the prime reasons for establishing this was to create a stable trading and producing bloc capable of competing with the American and the then strongly emerging Japanese economy, and as a means of strengthening Europe both economically and politically against the rising threat of the Soviet Union. Today, we would certainly add the Brics economies to the list of rising principal economic competitors.

For more details on this section visit the online resources.

> **Brics** Brazil, Russia, India, China, and South Africa. There are now additional acronyms for rising/emerging economies—MINT, PIGS, MIST, and CIVETS—but these are overlapping and none have yet established themselves clearly.

The advantages of achieving economic integration and a large internal market allow companies to realise growth and to specialise in production. This in turn allows European companies to compete on the world economic stage. This, it is argued, creates a dynamic,

▶ **CROSS REFERENCE**

These advantages were also considered in Chapter 1, section 1.1.

competitive market for the benefit of producers, consumers, and the member states. Consumers will have wider choice and arguably more competitive prices. Hence, the broader underlying advantages are more than merely the creation of an economic community.

However, creating and maintaining the Common Market, or internal market, has proven to be much more difficult than was first envisaged in view of the member states' attempts to protect their own national producers and industries by preventing or restricting imports both by tariff and non-tariff measures.

 THINKING POINT

Before looking back at Chapter 1, section 1.1, are you able to note down other reasons now?

10.1 Legislative provisions

10.1.1 **The Treaties**

The Preamble to the former EC Treaty has proved instrumental in the rulings of the Court of Justice of the European Union (CoJ) in reaching decisions on cases involving the free movement of goods, as did Articles 2 and 3, 10 (the fidelity clause), and 12 EC (the prohibition of discrimination on grounds of nationality). The relevant Treaty Articles today are Articles 3–4 of the Treaty of the European Union (TEU) and 3–4 and 18 of the Treaty on the Functioning of the European Union (TFEU).

There are four main groups of provisions in the TFEU connected with the internal market, set out initially in Articles 26–27 TFEU:

(1) customs duties and charges having equivalent effect (Articles 28–30 TFEU);

(2) the Common Customs Tariff (Articles 31–32 TFEU);

(3) the use of national taxation systems to discriminate against goods imported from other member states (Article 110 TFEU); and

(4) quantitative restrictions or measures having an equivalent effect on imports and exports (Articles 34–36 TFEU).

As one of the cornerstones and fundamental freedoms of the European Union (EU), the free movement of goods has been stoutly defended by the CoJ, interpreting the basic provisions strictly against the member states and being equally strict in terms of any exceptions pleaded by the member states, as will be seen in the case law considered later in the chapter. The free movement of goods objectives has been set out in a revised, briefer form in Article 3 TEU than was the case previously under Articles 2–4 EC.

TEU Article 3

. . .

(3) The Union shall establish an internal market.

(4) The Union shall establish an economic and monetary union whose currency is the euro.

The internal market is now defined in Article 26(2) TFEU as 'an area without internal frontiers in which the free movement of goods, persons, services and capital is ensured in accordance with the provisions of the Treaties'.

The aim is to achieve the circulation of goods without customs, duties, charges, or financial or other restrictions, to promote unlimited trade, and to remove from the member states the control over export and import matters. The Union is solely responsible for import and export duties and tariffs by the grant of exclusive competence in this area under Article 3 TFEU.

Articles 114 and 115 TFEU are also very important Treaty Articles designed to help to achieve and maintain the single internal market. Article 114 TFEU specifically provides additional competences for the achievement of the internal market by the use of qualified majority voting (QMV) and the co-decision procedure. Article 115 TFEU provides the Council, acting unanimously, with powers to enact Directives to approximate member states' laws that directly affect the establishment or functioning of the Common Market.

> **CROSS REFERENCE**
> See the case law on these Articles in Chapter 3, section 3.3.2.1.

10.1.2 Secondary legislation

There is very little secondary legislation of direct importance in this area of EU law. Directive 70/50 is considered in Chapter 11, as is Regulation 764/2008 and Directive 98/34 and its replacement Directive 2015/1535 [2015] Official Journal (OJ) L241/1. The latter requires member states under Articles 4 and 5 to notify the Commission about any product technical standards they have applied for to their respective technical standards institutes or intend to introduce so they can be scrutinised for compatibility with the free movement of goods before being put into force. In addition to the duty to notify, the Directive imposes under Article 6 a standstill imposition of a minimum of three months on any proposals to introduce new technical standards, with the possibility of extensions to six months if there are objections raised by either the Commission or a member state.

10.2 Progress towards the Treaty goals

Whilst the goals of integration have been outlined, progression towards them is not, of course, achieved overnight, but rather comprises a series of moves. Various stages in economic integration above that of simple trade between individual sovereign states have been generally recognised, which, in crude terms, are as follows.

For more details on this section visit the online resources.

10.2.1 A free trade area

The first stage is the establishment of a **free trade area (FTA)**.

> **Free Trade Area (FTA)** This involves the removal of customs duties between member states; however, the members of a free trade area decide themselves their external policies and any duties payable by third-party countries wishing to export goods into those countries.

Different states may therefore have different external tariffs, so exporters to the FTA may target their imports on the country with lower import duties or tariffs. Any goods entering will compete with internal goods of the FTA; therefore, certification of origin and a further import duty may be required, both of which are difficult and expensive to administer.

10.2.2 A customs union

The next stage is a **customs union**, which builds on the above.

> **Customs Union** This creates a common external tariff, presenting a common position to the outside world. The same duties are imposed on goods entering the customs union regardless of from where they are imported. Once imported, the goods circulate freely as union goods throughout the union. In the EU this is governed by Article 28(1) TFEU.

10.2.3 A common market

The **common market**, which is also termed an internal or single market, is the next stage.

> **Common Market** This adds to the definitions of free trade area and customs union by providing policies and legal regimes for the free movement of the factors of production (goods, persons, and capital) and a competition policy.

10.2.4 An economic union

Next comes the **economic union**.

> **Economic Union** This involves all of the above, plus the harmonisation or unification of economic, monetary, and fiscal policies, including the creation of a common currency controlled by a central authority. An economic union is, in fact, a rare development with few historical examples.

> The BENELUX union was, however, one such example, made up of Belgium, the Netherlands, and Luxembourg, now subsumed into the EU.

The final step would then be full political union in a confederation or federal state.

10.2.5 Which stage has the EU reached?

Whilst its goals are clear, just how far has the EU progressed? Note that the EC, as originally established, was never intended to be only a free trade area; it was always intended to go much further. Articles 26 and 28–32 TFEU make it clear that a customs union should be established, which includes an internal market. The EU certainly has a customs union with a common customs tariff, which is exclusively regulated by the Commission (Article 3 TFEU). The degree to which a true common market has been achieved is more doubtful given the considerable case law still arising, which is evidence of the sheer number of obstacles, the non-tariff barriers, still in the way of the unified market. However, as from 1 January 2015, 19 countries, which now represent over half of the 28 member states and over 338 million persons, have gone further and established an economic and monetary union with a European Central Bank and a single currency, although the 'Eurozone' has not been without its difficulties.

THINKING POINT

Can you name or say where to find out the states comprising the Eurozone?

Lithuania became the nineteenth member of the Eurozone on 1 January 2015.

10.2.5.1 Internal market developments

The initial means by which the goals of the Community and now Union were to be achieved commenced with an attempt at harmonisation. In line with the original views that success or harmonisation in one area would lead to 'spill-over' to related areas, it was considered that progress would be steady; however, for various reasons, legislative stagnation set in relatively swiftly.

CROSS REFERENCE

See Chapter 1, section 1.3.1.2, for more on spill-over.

The various reasons contributing to slow progress towards the completion of the internal market included:

- the French boycott in the mid-1960s of the Community institutions and subsequent Luxembourg Accords, which led to stagnation in the decision-making process because instead of majority voting to progress matters, unanimity was effectively required, meaning each state had basically a veto;
- the economic downturn in the late 1960s;
- the oil crises and world economic recession in the 1970s; and
- the increase in the number of member states, all of which then possessed a veto over legislation that they considered not to be in their national interest.

Consider as a classic example, the Architects Harmonization Directive, which took 18 years to enact. To a certain, but necessary extent, this stagnation was countered by judicial innovation. For example, Case 26/62 *Van Gend en Loos* led to the creation of the doctrine of direct effects. Other leading cases also demonstrated that the CoJ was prepared to interpret the Treaty in a purposive way and not according to the actual words used: see, for example, Case 2/74 *Reyners*, considered in Chapter 12, section 12.4.1. However, in the 1960s and 1970s, the member states remained reluctant to carry the Common Market project forward themselves, although the CoJ, as in other areas, was making progressive judgments, as will be seen in the case law in this chapter.

From the late 1970s, however, these problems were acknowledged, and when the new Commission President Jacques Delors took office, there was sufficient support from commerce and industry and the member states for a project to be launched, which was called the 'Single Market'. This led to the Commission White Paper *Completing the Internal Market*, which was endorsed by the European Council in 1985. It set out 300 legislative measures needed to 'complete the single market' and the year 1992 was set as the target date. This also marked a shift in approach in that whilst national rules would be harmonised where needed, other means of achieving the goals were emerging. These included a shift to new, broadly construed technical harmonisation and moves towards mutual recognition, spurred on by the CoJ judgment in Case 120/78 *Cassis de Dijon*, considered in full in Chapter 11, section 11.4.1.

The first amending Treaty of the original Treaties, the Single European Act (SEA), provided the institutional and legal reforms necessary to facilitate the meeting of targets set by the '1992 Project'. This was achieved by the introduction of a new Article 95 EC (now 114 TFEU), which provided that single market measures could be enacted in Council by QMV and allowed for the greater participation of the European Parliament in the legislative process.

CROSS REFERENCE

See Chapter 2, sections 2.2.4.3 and 2.4.3.1, for further details.

In addition, other policies were put into place that were regarded as necessary to support the single market following the realisation that it could not be achieved in isolation. Therefore, an environmental policy was introduced, along with, for example, an economic and social cohesion policy. The single market was given a particular boost by the TEU, which established economic and monetary union, although only for 12 and not all of the then 15 member states. The internal market was now regarded as incorporating more than purely economic concerns. It might be argued that this demonstrates a return to functional integration or creeping federalism, in that the desire to complete the internal market led to the move to economic and monetary union and the establishment of other policies that were regarded as vital to economic and monetary union, noted in Chapter 1, section 1.3.

10.2.5.2 Integration methods

The integration of what were a number of separate national markets was and is to be achieved by two main integration strategies: namely, **negative integration** and **positive integration**.

> **Positive Integration**
> The modification of existing national laws and institutions either by harmonisation or the creation of new laws.

> **Negative Integration** The removal of existing impediments to free movement, such as striking down national rules and practices that obstruct or prevent achievement of the internal market and in particular the four fundamental freedoms.

In the EU legal order this is found in the statutory attempt to ensure the free movement of: goods (Articles 30–37 TFEU)—see, in particular, the prohibition in Article 34 TFEU; workers (Articles 44–48 TFEU); services and establishment (Articles 49–62 TFEU); and capital (Articles 67–81 TFEU). Article 34 TFEU provides: 'Quantitative restriction on imports and all measures having equivalent effect shall be prohibited between Member States.'

It is a deregulatory approach in that it is an attempt to reduce or remove rather than increase regulation to facilitate free movement and not create new European rules applying across all states. In this respect, the development of direct effects and the other developments of individual enforcement are extremely important in assisting this process by facilitating challenges to member state laws which are incompatible with the internal market and the free movement of goods. The provision and continued support of the general principle prohibiting discrimination as outlined in Article 18 TFEU also assists in combatting 'national' rules which have no place in the single market.

Discrimination can appear in the form of direct discrimination, which is usually clear and easy to spot in a difference in treatment of, or different rules being applied to, imports from that of domestic products. It is not restricted to intentional discrimination, but also unintentional discrimination, if the effect of a rule is nevertheless to discriminate against imports. The prohibition of discrimination in the EU legal order, though, also includes indirect discrimination and thus catches restrictions that, on the face of it, do not discriminate according to nationality, although the effects are the same.

Indirect discrimination has now been given statutory definition in the EU legal order.

> **Indirect Discrimination** Where an apparently neutral provision, criterion, or practice would put persons of one class at a particular disadvantage compared with persons of the other class, unless that provision, criterion, or practice is objectively justified by a legitimate aim, and the means of achieving that aim are appropriate and necessary. See for examples: Directives 2000/43 (OJ 2000 L180/22), 2000/78 (OJ 2000 L303/16), and 2006/54 (OJ 2006 L204/23).

Indirect discrimination, however, can be justified objectively. The best case to demonstrate this in the area of goods is Case 120/78 *Cassis de Dijon*, which is considered in Chapter 11 in detail; however, criteria must be satisfied to benefit from the objective justification. More recent developments in case law have gone beyond discrimination entirely and any measures nevertheless make life more difficult for exporters or importers may be caught by the free movement of goods prohibitions, considered in Chapter 11.

This is a re-regulatory approach or a return to regulation in order to ensure the equal playing field by, for example, modifying existing laws and other rules but specifically the creation of new laws to ensure that the market of the integrated area functions effectively, which may also promote other policy aims such as achieving an integrated market. Thus, positive integration often proceeds in the EU by the harmonisation of existing national laws and rules which would be the replacing of multiple and divergent national rules or gaps, where they exist, with a single EU rule which promotes free trade. It is hoped that the attempt to harmonise is undertaken with full awareness of genuine vested interests, in particular social interests, which need to be protected to avoid a 'race to the bottom' or lowest common denominator. Within the EU Treaties, there are specific legal bases for the creation of new laws; for example, for the free movement of goods (Articles 26 and 33 TFEU); workers (Articles 46 and 47 TFEU); services (Article 59 TFEU); establishment (Articles 50 and 53 TFEU); and the general legal bases for the internal market (Articles 114, 115, and 352 TFEU). The use of the latter was seen in Chapter 3 on competences. There are, however, limits to the scope and, thus, use of the general legal bases, and therefore to harmonisation itself. This was seen in Case C-376/98 *Germany* v *European Parliament and Council (Tobacco Advertising Ban Directive)*, whereby the measure was annulled for being incorrectly based on the internal market, and Article 95 EC (now Article 114 TFEU), which could not support the motive for the tobacco advertising ban because it was essentially motivated by concern for public health. However, in the second *Tobacco Advertising* case, Case C-380/03 *Germany* v *European Parliament and Council*, it appears that the CoJ leaned more in favour of harmonisation, due to the potential obstacles to the market as a result of the differing national regimes on the advertising of tobacco products.

There are different forms of harmonisation that can be undertaken, as follows.

Total or complete harmonisation

Total, or complete, harmonisation—also known as 'exhaustive' harmonisation—involves one rule being enacted for the whole Union, which precludes the member states from legislating in the same area. This means that each member state is prevented from raising an additional standard that would serve to exclude imports.

> For example, see Directives 70/156 and 76/756 on car headlights, which were considered in **Case 60/86 *Commission* v *UK (Dim-dip Headlights)***. The Directives covered all car lighting, but did not address the dim-dip facility that the UK had previously required for both imports and domestically produced cars. Following the enactment of the Directives, the UK could not impose this requirement on cars made in other EU countries that did not provide this facility.

For more details on this section visit the online resources.

This form of harmonisation requires that the standards, and thus products, must be exactly the same, with no regional variations. It is criticised largely because of the images it produces of the 'Euro-sausage' or the 'Euro-banana' and the idea that Brussels wants to harmonise everything in the EU—hence, the view that it is best used in cases in which there is compelling evidence, for safety reasons, that a single common rule is needed. Thankfully, there has been a step back from this kind of thinking recently, in that regulations banning non-standard-shape vegetable and fruit produce have been repealed.

Optional harmonisation

Optional harmonisation incorporates the idea that producers need only follow the provisions of a Directive where they intend to trade the goods across an EU member state frontier. If they do not intend to export, they can still choose to follow the Directive, but it is not regarded as very satisfactory and can lead to two differing standards in each member state. It does not take account of the fact that those products may subsequently be imported and traded in other member states, and would not then meet the appropriate and approved EU-wide standard. Also, in the home state, there would be products on the market meeting both home and EU standards, thus leading to possible confusion among consumers. Thus, it is no surprise that optimal harmonisation has been resorted to only rarely.

Minimum harmonisation

As it suggests, minimum harmonisation involves the establishment of a minimum standard, but does not mean that the member states cannot go further and insist on higher domestic standards. The latter would not apply, though, to imported goods.

> For example, Directive 89/622, now replaced, concerning tar and nicotine labelling, was considered in **Case C-11/92 *R* v *Secretary of State for Health, ex p Gallaher Ltd and others***, in which the CoJ held that the member states can retain or adopt much higher standards than the minimum standards provided in the Community legislation. In **Case C-84/94 *UK* v *Council (Working Time)***, the Court advised that 'minimum standards' does not mean *minimal* standards, as in necessarily adopting the lowest common denominator. Union minimum may be set at a fairly high level and member states remain free in any case then to set higher standards domestically.

10.2.5.3 **The new approach legislation**

The new approach legislation (including Directives 83/189 and 98/24, Regulations 764 and 765/2008, Regulation 1025/2012, and Decision 768/2008, for example) was legislation following a change of approach to harmonisation by the Commission, which was aimed very broadly at a whole industry and which provided general principles rather than detailed rules. It relies very much on the technical standards being set by private bodies—that is, those industrial bodies, especially research and standards institutes, that are in the know and are more qualified to devise appropriate technical standards, especially for consumer products and safety standards.

10.2.5.4 **Alternatives to legislative harmonisation**

Rather than harmonise, which can be a very long-winded process, an alternative method, led by judicial development, is that of the 'mutual recognition' of standards. This principle is one of two leading principles affecting the free movement of goods and was established by the CoJ and made prominent in the landmark case of *Cassis de Dijon* (Case 120/78 *Rewe-Zentrale AG* v *Bundesmonopolverwaltung für Branntwein*), which is considered in full in Chapter 11. This decision essentially holds that if a product is lawfully produced in one state and meets the safety and health standards of that state, then states into which the product is imported should accept those standards, and thus the products, as the equivalent of domestic standards and products. They should not then ban the import for not complying with different domestic standards.

Following this case, the Commission picked up the ruling as a crucial tool in completing the internal market by insisting, for example, on 'mutual recognition clauses' in national product regulations, whereby a state would be required, in setting its own standard for a product, to include a mutual recognition clause that it would accept other national standards. In Case C-184/96 *Commission* v *France (Foie Gras)*, the Court held France at fault for not including such a clause, which has now become a standard requirement as a result.

This also prompted the Commission to issue its 'Communication from the Commission concerning the consequences of the judgment given by the Court of Justice on 20 February 1979 in Case 120/78 ("*Cassis de Dijon*")' (OJ 1980 C256/2). Reproduced in Foster, *Blackstone's EU Treaties and Legislation*, Oxford University Press, Oxford, published annually.

10.3 The establishment of the internal market

10.3.1 The common commercial policy (CCP) and common customs tariff (CCT)

The common commercial policy (CCP), outlined in Articles 206–207 TFEU, is the overall driving force behind the establishment and maintenance of the common customs tariff (CCT).

The Common Market, which is a customs union, provides not only for the elimination of duties regarding goods originating in other member states, but also regarding goods originating in third countries that are in free circulation in the Common Market and on which customs duties have been paid. Under Article 31 TFEU, the external duties are fixed by the Council and Commission for the Union for goods imported from outside the Union and a single set of common tariffs is adopted in trade relations with the outside world. The CCT, which is also referred to as the common external tariff (CET), imposes a single tariff for all imports and is set by the Commission. Once a product has been imported into the EU, it is then in free circulation and further tariffs or restrictions cannot be imposed on the product (Article 29 TFEU). This aspect is now within the entire competence of the Union (Article 3 TFEU) and is ever more tied up with world developments on customs duties, most notably the General Agreement on Tariffs and Trade (GATT) and the World Trade Organization (WTO).

For more details on this section visit the online resources.

CROSS REFERENCE

The general aspects of external relations are considered in Chapter 1, section 1.7.

10.3.2 The prohibition of customs duties

The following sections concern not only customs duties in the strict sense, which are a hindrance to free trade, but also any financial barriers that have an equivalent effect, however named. Necessarily, we must also consider aspects of member states' tax regimes because these may be a disguised way of imposing additional financial burdens on imported products by making them less competitive, or even uncompetitive, in comparison with domestic products. Therefore, the TFEU also includes a provision (Article 110 TFEU) to deal with these. Note that the provisions on goods and tax are mutually exclusive sets of provisions, even though often dealing with the same factual situation. This aspect is considered more fully in section 10.4.

It is worth taking a careful note of the Treaty Article number changes that took place after the Lisbon Treaty. The Article (28 TFEU) now dealing with customs duties and charges was that previously dealing with quantitative restrictions, and it would be very easy when looking at previous case law to get these confused.

Articles 28 and 30 TFEU are aimed at the abolition of customs duties and charges having equivalent effect and at prohibiting the introduction of any such measures.

> **Article 28 TFEU**
>
> 1. The Union shall comprise a customs union which shall cover all trade in goods and which shall involve the prohibition between Member States of customs duties on imports and exports and of all charges having equivalent effect, and the adoption of a common customs tariff in their relations with third countries.
>
> . . .

This provision covers 'all trade in goods'.

> 'Goods' was defined by the CoJ in **Case 7/68 Commission v Italy (Art Treasures)**, in which Italy claimed that an export tax on art treasures was to protect the artistic heritage of Italy. The Court held goods to be 'products which can be valued in money and which are capable, as such, of forming the subject of commercial transactions'.

Article 29 TFEU expressly defines goods in free circulation as those that have complied with import formalities and customs duties in the importing state.

> The definition of goods was extended in **Case 45/87 Commission v Ireland (Dundalk Water Supply)** to include the provision of goods within a contract for the provision of services. The CoJ extended the definition of goods to include even those of no commercial value in **Case C-2/90 Commission v Belgium (Waste)**, which also involved non-recyclable waste.

Article 30 TFEU provides that 'Customs duties on imports and exports and charges having equivalent effect shall be prohibited between Member States.' Article 30 (ex 12 EEC) also specifically mentions that it applies to customs duties of a fiscal nature and was held to be directly effective in a leading Community law case.

 THINKING POINT

In which case was this?

Whilst it is relatively easy to recognise a customs duty, because it is usually designated as such and is a clear duty applied at the border, and because it is so crude and obvious, the imposition of customs duties is no longer something attempted by the member states and has as a result rarely featured in case law.

> However, **Case 26/62 Van Gend en Loos** was the leading case referred to which involved a customs duty and thus represents an exception to the paucity of case law.

It is less easy to identify 'a charge having an equivalent effect'; which was not defined in the Treaty, thus a considerable body of case law has arisen trying to define this. The total prohibition of customs duties per se means that cases of such an obvious breach rarely arise—hence the concentration on 'charges having equivalent effect', often abbreviated to CHEEs or CEEs.

In looking at this area of law and the case law, it must now be borne in mind that a lot of it took place when there were still very visible border posts and customs officials on the border stopping and checking traffic moving through. Now, and especially in the Schengen area, traffic is able to drive straight through, the border posts standing empty or increasingly having been physically removed. The overlap with tax imposition though remains very important as taxes are often applied well away from a border crossing.

For more details on this section visit the online resources.

10.3.3 A charge having equivalent effect (CHEE)

In **Cases 2 and 3/62 *Commission v Belgium and Luxembourg (Gingerbread)***, involving a tax on imported gingerbread to compensate for a domestic tax on wheat used to make gingerbread internally, the CoJ held that:

a duty, whatever it is called, and whatever its mode of application, may be considered a charge having equivalent effect to a customs duty, provided that it meets the following three criteria: (a) it must be imposed unilaterally at the time of importation or subsequently; (b) it must be imposed specifically upon a product imported from a member state to the exclusion of a similar national product; and (c) it must result in an alteration of price and thus have the same effect as a customs duty on the free movement of products.

In certain circumstances, a charge may be acceptable if it is a service rendered for the benefit of the importer, it is specifically required by EU law, or it is part of a system of internal taxation.

These criteria are all subject to further refinement by the CoJ.

In **Case 24/68 *Commission v Italy (Statistical Levy)***, a small (10-lira) levy that was imposed on imports and exports for the purpose of financing statistical surveys was held to breach Community law. Whilst there was no discrimination between imports and exports, the CoJ stressed that the purpose of using the concepts of customs duties and CHEEs was to avoid the imposition of any pecuniary charge on goods circulating within the Community by virtue of the fact that they cross a frontier. The Court stressed that any charge must be considered in the context of the achievement of one of the fundamental objectives of the EC Treaty.

In modification of its stance in *Commission v Belgium and Luxembourg*, the Court offered a definition of a CHEE to include 'any pecuniary charge, however small and whatever its designation and mode of application, which is imposed unilaterally on domestic or foreign goods by virtue of the fact that they cross a frontier'.

Such a charge is a CHEE even if it is not imposed for the benefit of the member state concerned, even if it is not discriminatory or protective in effect, and even if the product on which it is imposed is not in competition with any domestic product.

In **Cases 2 and 3/69 *Sociaal Fonds voor de Diamantarbeiders***, a levy on diamond imports was used to go towards a social fund for workers in the diamond industry and not used in any protectionary way over national products, as no diamonds are produced in Belgium, only cut and traded; hence, the levy was held nevertheless to be a charge, regardless of the purpose or motive. The effect of the charge was that imported goods became less competitive.

> The concept of crossing a frontier has also been interpreted to include the crossing of a state internal frontier where a charge is imposed purely by reason of the movement of goods to that region of the member states. In Case-363/93 *Lancry*, dock dues were charged on goods entering Réunion originating from Germany, although imported via France, but which would also apply to goods also originating in France. The CoJ held that the charges constituted a CHEE in the same was as goods entering the country despite also including French because it considered that the charges nevertheless impacted on goods coming from all other member states and imported into Réunion.

Claims by member states in relation to charges for services rendered, such as for health inspections, and warehousing fees during clearance of customs formalities, have been carefully considered by the CoJ.

10.3.3.1 The validity of charges for services rendered

In a number of cases, the CoJ has developed rules on when charges can lawfully be made for services rendered.

> In **Case 24/68 Commission v Italy (Statistical Levy)**, the levy was found to hamper the interpenetration of goods that the EEC Treaty aimed to secure and thus had an effect equivalent to a customs duty. It was further held that the levy could not be regarded as the consideration for a specific benefit actually conferred, because the advantages of the survey were so general and difficult to assess.

> In **Case 132/82 Commission v Belgium (Customs Warehouses)**, the CoJ considered the questions of whether a CHEE may be permitted when claimed to be consideration for services rendered. The Belgian authorities allowed customs formalities for goods originating or in free circulation in another member state to be completed either at the frontier or within the country. When the goods were presented for customs clearance at special stores of public warehouses, a fee fixed and levied by the municipal authorities was payable in consideration of the use by the importers of the premises made available to them to store their goods pending clearance through customs. The state did not receive the money. The only role played by the state was to fix the maximum fee payable. The CoJ held that when payment of storage charges is demanded solely in connection with the completion of customs formalities, it cannot be regarded as consideration for services actually rendered to the importer.

> In **Case 340/87 Commission v Italian Republic (Customs Posts)**, Italian legislation required importers who presented themselves at Italian customs outside normal Italian opening hours (six hours per day) to pay a fee. Article 5 of Directive 83/643 required customs offices at frontier posts to open for normal business hours of at least 10 hours per day, Monday to Friday. Therefore, in order to comply with the Directive, Italian customs officials would have to work four hours' overtime and Italian law sought to impose a charge during that four-hour period. The Italian government maintained that this was a charge for a service rendered that was commensurate to the value of the service. The CoJ said that it had already held on several occasions that a charge imposed on goods by reason of the fact that they cross a frontier might not be a CHEE to a customs duty provided that it constituted a benefit specifically or individually conferred on the economic operator concerned of an amount proportional to that service. In this case, the Court held that the charge constituted a breach of the Treaty.

In **Case 170/88** *Ford of Spain* v *Spanish State*, a claim that a charge levied by the Spanish customs for granting customs clearance at the Ford factory was a charge for services rendered and not a CHEE to a customs duty was rejected. The charge was calculated at a rate of 0.165 per cent of the declared value of the goods. The CoJ held that even if the contested charge were in fact remuneration for a service rendered to the importer, the amount charged could not be regarded as proportionate to the service. The Spanish government's argument that, in some cases, the charge would be less than the cost of carrying out the inspections only served to confirm this argument. A charge calculated on the basis of the value of the goods could not correspond to the costs incurred by the customs authorities.

The next cases help to outline the circumstances in which charges may be justified and essentially concern a genuine service being rendered.

In **Case 87/75** *Bresciani*, the CoJ held that veterinary checks and charges performed as a service are acceptable, but in that particular case they were not because they were levied in the public interest at large and not in the interest of each importer; hence, the argument is that as such it should be paid by the member state from public funds.

In **Case 46/76** *Bauhuis* v *The Netherlands*, the CoJ held that a fee for health inspections would be acceptable if required by a Community Regulation and covering the actual cost incurred only.

This was followed up in **Case 18/87** *Commission* v *Germany (Animal Inspection Fees)*, in which the CoJ held that a charge may escape classification as a CHEE. In this case, fees for inspections carried out under the requirements of Council Directive 81/389 were held to be acceptable. According to the CoJ, they satisfied the criteria that:

(1) the fees constituted a payment for a service, not exceeding the cost of the actual inspections in respect of which they were charged;

(2) the inspections in question were mandatory and uniform for all of the products in question in the Community;

(3) the inspections were provided for by Community law in the interests of the Community; and

(4) the inspections promoted the free movement of goods, in particular by neutralising the obstacles that may have resulted from unilateral inspection measures adopted under Article 30 EC (now 36 TFEU).

The fees in the case were charged by some of the German *Länder* on the importation of live animals from other member states and their purpose was to cover the cost of health inspections carried out under Council Directive 81/389. The charges in this case satisfied the conditions and were justified.

Case C-111/89 *Netherlands* v *Bakker Hillegom* extended the criteria to include the inspection requirements of international conventions.

10.3.3.2 **Where the charge is in fact a tax**

A second category in which the charge may be justified is if it is an aspect of an internal taxation system. If the charge forms part of a system of internal taxation rules that are applied systematically and under the same criteria to domestic products and imported products alike, it is a non-discriminatory tax and, if questioned, should be considered under Article 110 TFEU and not under Article 30 TFEU.

> In **Case 90/79 *Commission v France (Reprographic Machines)***, a levy was charged on all copy machines, both home-manufactured and imports, in order to compensate authors for the breaches of copyright that often occur by the use of such machines. Since very few copy machines were manufactured in France, the tax applied mainly to imports and therefore looked like disguised discrimination, but was held to be a genuine non-discriminatory tax. It served a justifiable purpose.

> This situation is sometimes referred to as the 'exotic import rules', whereby a product is available by import only and not manufactured in the importing state, although this case does not exactly fit that rule. However, in order to justify an import tax on such a product, there must be a genuine reason, as in **Case 184/85 *Commission v Italy*** where a tax on dried bananas was held not to compete with fresh table fruits. Thus, an exotic or unique product tax was held not to be contrary to Article 110(2) TFEU.

These cases highlight the often subtle difference between what is a charge and what is a genuine tax, a distinction that is considered next.

10.3.4 **The distinction between internal taxation and charges having equivalent effect**

If a charge imposed by a member state on imported goods is a measure of internal taxation that is non-discriminatory, it cannot be a CHEE and therefore cannot be caught by Articles 28–30 TFEU. It is instead governed by Article 110 TFEU dealing with internal taxation, which opens the door to member states' attempts to justify additional charges imposed on goods as instances of taxation and not charges or duties. Whilst the customs duties and CHEE mentioned in Articles 28–30 TFEU must be abolished, tax measures are allowed because, as a general principle, Article 110 TFEU allows each member state to establish the system of taxation that it considers most suitable. However, Article 110 TFEU prohibits tax from discriminating against imports and was regarded as crucial to complement the free movement of goods to prevent taxation policy from being employed by a state to circumvent the customs rules by the imposition of discriminatory internal taxes. Article 110 TFEU thus represents an early intervention into the member states' tax regimes, which is likely to become more intrusive in future but equally strongly resisted by some of the member states.

Article 30 TFEU specifically prohibits customs charges of a fiscal nature.

The difference between a charge and a tax is crucial. A charge, which is defined by the CoJ as an internal tax to which Article 110 TFEU applies, cannot at the same time be a CHEE to a customs duty and therefore be subject to Articles 28–30 TFEU.

> In **Case 78/96 *Steinlike und Weinlig v Germany***, the CoJ held that:
> Financial charges within a general system of internal taxation applying systematically to domestic and imported products according to the same criteria are not to be considered charges having equivalent effect.

It may be one thing or the other, but cannot be both. They are mutually exclusive categories. There is now a considerable body of CoJ case law on the distinction between an internal tax (to which Article 110 TFEU, might apply) and a CHEE to a customs duty (which might be prohibited by Articles 28 and 30 TFEU).

> In **Case 20/76 *Schöttle & Söhne v Finanzamt Freuenstadt***, the CoJ held that the purpose of old Article 90 EC (now 110 TFEU) is to remove disguised restrictions on the free movement of goods that may result from the tax provisions of a member state. It was held that a German tax on the transportation of goods for more than a certain distance, levied in this case on a lorry-load of gravel, was an indirect tax on the gravel itself. It would discriminate against lorries travelling from greater distances—that is, mainly affecting those from other countries.

However, this type of tax might in the future, if not now, be justified on environmental grounds, as in Case C-132/88 *Commission v Greece*, noted in section 10.4.2.

> **Case 132/78 *Denkavit v French State*** also concerned this distinction. It arose out of a charge on the importation of meat products that was the equivalent of a similar charge imposed on the slaughter of animals in French slaughterhouses. The CoJ noted that a charge could escape classification as a CHEE to a customs duty only if it related to a general system of internal dues applied systematically and in accordance with the same criteria to domestic products and imported products alike. In paragraph 8 of its judgment, the Court further emphasised that in order to relate to a system of internal taxation, the charge to which an imported product is subject must be imposed at the same rate on the same product, must be imposed at the same marketing stage, and the chargeable event giving rise to the duty must be the same for both products. It is therefore not sufficient that the objective of the charge imposed on imports is to compensate for similar charges imposed on domestic products at a production or marketing stage prior to that at which the imported products are taxed.
>
> The Court held that it was bound to regard the charge in this case as a CHEE because:
>
> - it was charged on imported goods by virtue of the fact that they had crossed a frontier;
> - the tax was imposed at a different stage of production and on the basis of a different 'chargeable event';
> - no account was taken of fiscal charges that had been imposed on the products in the member state of origin; and
> - to find otherwise would render the prohibition on charges having equivalent effect to customs duties empty and meaningless.

> Finally, in **Case 77/76 *Fratelli Cucchi***, the CoJ confirmed the mutually exclusive nature of the charges and internal taxation regimes, but stressed that because it is often difficult to tell the difference, both Articles 25 and 90 EC (now 30 and 110 TFEU) should be invoked together before the Court and the Court asked to determine which should apply.

10.4 The prohibition of discriminatory taxation

Article 110(1) TFEU provides that 'No Member State shall impose, directly or indirectly, on the products of other Member States any internal taxation of any kind in excess of that imposed directly or indirectly on similar domestic products.' This prohibits discrimination in favour of the domestic products.

Article 110(2) TFEU provides that 'Furthermore, no Member State shall impose on the products of other Member States any internal taxation of such a nature as to afford indirect protection to other products.'

> Article 90 EC (now 110 TFEU) was held to be directly effective and an indispensable foundation of the Common Market in **Case 57/65 _Lütticke v Hauptzollamt Saarlouis_**.

> Taxation was defined in **Case 90/79 _Commission v France (Reprographic Machines)_** as a general system of internal dues applied systematically to categories of product in accordance with objective criteria irrespective of the origin of the products.

Internal taxes can never be imposed solely by virtue of the fact that the goods cross a frontier. The reason for their imposition must be that domestic products are subject to taxation and that, for competition reasons, imported goods should be subject to the same tax. That Article 110 TFEU should also apply to exports, despite not being mentioned in the Article itself, was confirmed by the CoJ in Case C-234/99 _Nygard_.

10.4.1 Direct and indirect taxation (Article 101(1) TFEU)

Article 110 TFEU seeks to outlaw both directly discriminatory taxation and indirect discrimination in tax regimes. Direct discrimination occurs where imports and domestic products are deliberately treated differently and is thus automatically unlawful. Direct discrimination cannot be justified. Indirect discrimination, on the face of it, imposes the same rule on both domestic and imported products, but the result is that the import is, in fact, disadvantaged. Indirect discrimination may be objectively justified, as in Case C-196/95 _Commission v France_, in which a regional subsidy was granted to producers of sweet wines in poor growing areas. On the face of it this favoured domestic growers, but was held to be acceptable particularly as the subsidy was also open to importers who could prove similar conditions. See also Case C-132/88 _Commission v Greece (Taxation of Motor Cars)_, considered in section 10.4.2.

> In **Case 28/76 _Molkerei-Zentrale Westfalen v Haupzollamt Paderborn_**, the CoJ ruled that the words 'directly or indirectly' were to be construed broadly and embraced all taxation that was actually and specifically imposed on the domestic product at earlier stages of the manufacturing and marketing process. This means that member states cannot argue that a tax at an earlier stage on a domestic product is a lawful equivalent of a tax on imports. If it does not conform to the _Denkavit_ criteria (considered in section 10.3.4), it is unlawful.

Indirect taxation is also capable of including taxes on raw materials and the assessment of the tax.

> In **Case 20/76 *Schöttle & Söhne* v *Finanzamt Freuenstadt***, it was held that a German tax on the transportation of goods over a distance of more than 50 km, and thus more likely to affect imports, which was levied in this case on a lorry-load of gravel, was an indirect tax on the gravel itself.

> In **Case 127/75 *Bobie* v *HZA Aachen-Nord***, beer production in Germany was taxed at a level according to the quantity produced, with small producers being favoured with a lower tax. Imports were taxed on a mid-range rate not connected with the amount of production. This was held to be indirectly discriminatory against a small Belgian producer.

10.4.2 'Similar' or 'other products'

The criteria for determining whether there is discrimination differ according to whether the case is brought under Article 110(1) TFEU, concerned with similar products, or Article 110(2) TFEU, dealing with other products. The latter serves to cover imported products that may be different, but are nevertheless in competition with domestic products. In the case of Article 110(1) TFEU, the taxation on the imported product must not be higher than the tax on the similar domestic product, in which case the rule of non-discrimination has been complied with; in the case of Article 110(2) TFEU, the taxation on the imported product must not have a protectionist effect.

For more details on this section visit the online resources.

To avoid discrimination taking place in breach of Article 110(1) TFEU, not only must the rates of tax on the imported product and the domestic product be the same, but also the basis of the imposition of the tax must not lead to differences between the imported and domestic goods. The rates of tax, the basis of assessment, and the rules for levying and collecting it must all be non-discriminatory. In the case of Article 110(2) TFEU, to be caught by the prohibition on discrimination it has to be proved that the taxation has a protectionist effect. At the root of this difference is the fact that direct comparisons are possible under Article 110(1) TFEU, whereas under Article 110(2) TFEU they are not. Further case law demonstrates the differences.

> In **Case 55/79 *Commission* v *Ireland (Excise Payments)***, under Irish law, producers of beer, wine, and spirits enjoyed an extension of four to six weeks for the payment of excise duties, whereas taxes on imported beers, wines, and spirits had to be paid immediately on importation or on delivery from the bonded warehouse; hence it was discriminating in application.

So even where the level of taxation is the same, a delay in its collection in favour of domestic goods was held to be discriminatory and a breach of Article 110 TFEU.

> In **Case 112/84 *Michel Humblot* v *Directeur des Services Fiscaux***, the French authorities imposed a higher tax on cars with a higher power rating, none of which were manufactured in France, meaning that the tax applied in practice only to imported cars. The CoJ allowed for the possibility that a tax that appears to discriminate against a category of imported goods, because no goods in that category are produced domestically, will not necessarily always be in breach of Article 90 EC (now 110 TFEU). However, it held that because many of the imported cars thus taxed would still be in competition with cars produced in France taxed at the lower rate, the indirect tax was in breach of Article 90 EC (now 110 TFEU).

In contrast is **Case C-132/88 *Commission v Greece (Taxation of Motor Cars)***, in which a Greek tax on both new and second-hand cars, whether produced in Greece or imported from outside, rose steeply in respect of cars above 1800cc capacity. The cars affected were all imported because no cars above 1600cc were produced in Greece. The Court held that this measure would be indirectly discriminatory only if it were shown that the taxation had the effect of discouraging Greeks from purchasing foreign cars. On the face of it, the tax was motivated by other considerations and there was no protective effect.

Even where there may be benefits for the imported goods, a difference in the way in which a tax is levied may be held to breach Article 110 TFEU.

In **Case C-213/96 *Outokumpu Oy***, a flat rate tax on imported electricity from Sweden was held to infringe Article 90 EC (now 110 TFEU) because the tax rate on domestic electricity was calculated according to the product that was used for its manufacture for environmental reasons. The fact that only in limited circumstances would the rate of imported tax be higher was immaterial to the CoJ. The ease of administration in setting up a general system and the fact that it was extremely difficult to determine precisely the method of production of imported electricity were not accepted as grounds justifying the system adopted.

10.4.2.1 Similar products

CROSS REFERENCE

This topic of product substitution is considered in greater detail in Chapter 13.

Article 110(1) TFEU requires that if there is a difference in the way in which similar products are taxed, the levels of tax have to be equalised. First of all, in determining what constitutes 'similar products', whilst obviously including same products, the Commission and Court need to take into account various factors, including the composition, physical characteristics, and method of production of the product, as well as whether both producers meet the same consumer needs or are in competition with each other and thus substitutable.

For example, in **Case 243/84 *John Walker Ltd v Ministeriet for Skatter og Afgifter***, the question of 'whether whisky was similar to fruit wine' was posed. Whilst it was clear that both were alcoholic drinks, the CoJ held that the two drinks were not similar since they exhibited manifestly different characteristics. The wine was fruit-based and relied on natural fermentation, whereas the Scotch whisky was a cereal-based drink produced by distillation. There were also significant differences in the alcohol volume.

Organoleptic

Essentially meaning 'sensory', organoleptic refers to any sensory properties of a product, involving taste, colour, odour, and feel. Organoleptic testing involves inspection through visual examination, feeling, and smelling of products.

In **Case 184/85 *Commission v Italy (Italian Fruit)***, the similarity between bananas, on the one hand, and peaches and pears, on the other, was considered and, according to the CoJ, they were not similar. The Court referred to the **organoleptic** characteristics and the water content, which were different, and which meant that they were suited to different markets.

In **Case 106/84 *Commission v Denmark***, the CoJ held that wine made from grapes and wine made from other fruits which had very similar alcohol content and produced in the same way and substitutable were therefore similar products.

10.4.2.2 **Other products**

As far as Article 110(2) TFEU is concerned, for a tax to be caught by the prohibition on discrimination it has to be proved that the taxation has a protectionist effect to the detriment of imported goods that may be in competition with the other domestic goods. The main question focuses on whether the products can be substituted by each other.

> Probably the most important case still on Article 110(2) TFEU is **Case 170/78 _Commission v UK (Wine Excise Duties No. 2)_**, in which the CoJ held that the fact that the UK imposed a higher duty on table wines than on beer was held to give indirect protection to beer (a domestic product) over light table wines (a predominantly imported product) and contravened Article 90(2) EC (now 110(2) TFEU). The UK government had argued that wine and beer could not be regarded as competing beverages, since beer was widely consumed in public houses, whereas wine was generally drunk only on special occasions, and pointed out the difference in the alcoholic volume. The Court took the view that it was necessary not only to examine the present state of the market, but whether the two products were potentially in competition.

> See also in respect of the same pair of products, **Case C-167/05 _Commission v Sweden_**, but in this case the difference in taxation was not so great in the view of the CoJ as to influence a change of buying of the products by the consumers.

Given that the first case arose over 40 years ago, the case against the UK was a pretty shrewd judgment, because the two products are probably far more in competition with each other now than then.

The CoJ decided that such a relationship existed on the basis of volume, price, and alcoholic strength, and mentioned the thirst-quenching qualities of both products even when UK beer was then about 3 per cent alcohol and the lightest wines 8 to 9 per cent.

After such a finding, the member state may abolish discrimination either by lowering the tax on imported goods or by raising the tax on domestic products, or may use a combination of both to remove the discrimination or protection.

 ## Summary

The main aspects considered in this chapter were not customs duties, which were outlawed very early in the life of the Union and which are now extremely rare. Instead, the emphasis was more on charges having the equivalent effect to customs duties, although these too are much rarer today than in the past. The main focus of attention in the future is likely to be on taxation aspects of this topic, because taxation is still, for the most part, within the competences of the member states unless it is unfairly levied on imports in a discriminatory manner. In that case, the policy or tax provision can be reviewed by the CoJ to see if it conforms with the free movement of goods and tax provisions of the Treaty. Such taxation can, however, be justified if for a genuine reason, and taxation for environmental reasons is a likely ground for taxation in the future. It must not, however, discriminate against imports.

For suggested approaches to answering these questions visit the online resources.

? Questions

1. The four commonly recognised stages in economic integration are free trade area, customs union, common market, and economic union. Define each of these terms, and identify which stage the EU has reached.

2. What, according to the CoJ, is a charge having equivalent effect?

3. When is it acceptable to impose a charge on imported goods?

4. Under what circumstances is it possible to impose a tax on imported goods?

For guidance on how to tackle this specimen exam question and to read a suggested model answer, visit the online resources. www.oup.com/uk/foster_directions6e/.

☐ Sample exam Q&A

'However wide the field of application of Article 34 TFEU may be, it nevertheless does not include obstacles to trade covered by other provisions of the Treaty. Thus, obstacles which are of a fiscal nature or have equivalent effect and are covered by Articles 28–30 and 110 TFEU do not fall within the prohibition of Article 34 TFEU.'

Discuss.

≡ Further reading

Books

Barnard, C. *The Substantive Law of the EU: The Four Freedoms*, 5th edn, Oxford University Press, Oxford, 2016 (Chapters 2–4).

Foster, N. *Blackstone's EU Treaties and Legislation*, Oxford University Press, Oxford, published annually.

Gormley, L. W. *EU Law of Free Movement of Goods and Customs Union*, Oxford University Press, Oxford, 2009.

Oliver, P. *Oliver on Free Movement of Goods in the European Union*, 5th edn, Hart Publishing, Oxford, 2010.

Weatherill, S. *The Internal Market as a Legal Concept*, Oxford University Press, Oxford, 2017.

Articles

Banks, K. 'The application of the fundamental freedoms to member state tax measures: guarding against protectionism or second-guessing national policy choices?' (2008) 33 EL Rev 482.

Cordewener, A., Kofler, G., and van Thiel, S. 'The clash between European freedoms and national direct tax law: public interest defences available to the Member States' (2009) 46 CML Rev 1951.

Gormley, L. 'Inconsistencies and Misconceptions in the Free Movement of Goods' (2015) 40 ELR 925.

Möstl, M. 'Preconditions and limits of mutual recognition' (2010) 47 CML Rev 405.

Oliver, P. and Enchelmaier, S. 'Free movement of goods: recent developments in the case law' (2007) 44 CMLR 649.

Weatherill, S. 'Recent developments in the law governing the free movement of goods in the EC's internal market' (2006) 2 ECRL 90.

11 Free movement of goods II: non-tariff barriers

☐ **LEARNING OBJECTIVES**

In this chapter, you will consider the following aspects of the non-tariff barriers that member states have created and which hinder or prevent the free flow of goods:

- the legislative provisions applicable to non-tariff barriers;
- the definition of quantitative restrictions and measures having equivalent effect;
- the leading cases of *Dassonville* and *Cassis de Dijon*;
- the retreat from the *Dassonville* and *Cassis* cases in the case of *Keck*;
- the further explanation of what *Keck* meant in subsequent cases; and
- the developments in case law since *Keck*.

Introduction

This chapter completes the picture of the free movement of goods commenced in Chapter 10, which concerned the tariff and tax barriers to free movement by concentrating on the non-tariff barriers. Whilst these do not involve direct monetary payments, they nevertheless increase the cost to the importer to meet the requirements imposed and would put them at a competitive disadvantage if not tackled.

It is worth taking a careful note of the Treaty Article number changes that took place after both the Amsterdam and Lisbon Treaties came into force. The numbers have now swapped around two times and original Article 30 of the European Economic Community (EEC), which provided one of the basic prohibitions in this area, became Article 28 EC and is now Article 34 of the Treaty on the Functioning of the European Union (TFEU). Original Article 36 EEC, which concerned derogations, became Article 30 of the Economic Community (EC) (the old Article number for the prohibition), but is now once again Article 36 TFEU, so be extra careful when reading and referring to case law in this area: it is all too easy to slip up. Hence, in this chapter, more frequently than for other chapters, mainly when discussing previous case law, both numbers will be provided, hopefully to help to avoid confusion.

This area of law is concerned with the attempts of the member states to prevent or hinder imports and the ways in which the Commission and the European Court of Justice (CoJ) have been tackling this. It also considers where differences in national rules relating to goods are permitted, namely those that are not designed to prevent or hinder the free flow of goods.

11.1 Legislation

The main Treaty Articles applicable are Articles 34 and 36 TFEU, but also be aware of Article 35 TFEU in respect of ensuring the free movement of exports.

> **Article 34 TFEU**
>
> Quantitative restrictions on imports and all measures having equivalent effect shall be prohibited between Member States.

> **Article 35 TFEU**
>
> Quantitative restrictions on exports, and all measures having equivalent effect, shall be prohibited between Member States.

⧉ CROSS REFERENCE

Article 36 TFEU, which provides for exceptions, is considered in section 11.3.

There is very little secondary legislation of direct importance in this area of European Union (EU) law, but Directive 70/50 is considered in this chapter, as are two further enactments: Regulation 764/2008 and Directive 98/34.

11.2 Quantitative restrictions and measures having equivalent effect

Non-financial barriers to the free movement of goods are contained within the phrase 'quantitative restrictions and measures having equivalent effect'. Restrictions or obstacles to free movement are caused mainly by different national laws regulating products and trade or exacting technical standards, rather than the very crude or obvious and clearly prohibited import or export bans. Harmonisation of all products was neither a practical nor a desirable solution. The founding fathers instead adopted a means of negative integration to tackle the obstacles to free movement caused by different national laws in each member state. These become the focus of attention in this area of free movement. The phrase is not defined in the Treaty but quantitative restrictions per se are straightforward and usually found in the form of either a ban or quota.

 THINKING POINT

Why is an import ban very unlikely these days?

For more details on this section visit the online resources.

⟫ CROSS REFERENCE
See Case 8/74 *Dassonville* as a good example of this approach, considered in further depth in section 11.2.3.

The main concern, though, is about measures that fall short of a quantitative restriction. It is the extent to which member states can insist that imported products comply with national standards that can frustrate the attempt to create a genuinely unified single market and which thus requires the closest consideration.

The development of the rules on the free movement of goods reflects the general approach to the fundamental freedoms by which the CoJ has interpreted the principle of free movement liberally to promote free movement. The derogations allowed to the member states, on the other hand, are interpreted restrictively, or as narrowly as possible.

11.2.1 The general scope of the Treaty prohibition

Article 34 TFEU lays down a general prohibition on quantitative restrictions and measures having equivalent effect on imports. Article 35 TFEU extends that prohibition to exports.

Article 36 TFEU provides the member states with grounds by which they can escape the prohibitions under Articles 34 and 35 TFEU. The Article is considered in section 11.3.

Both Articles 34 and 35 TFEU have been found to be directly effective, but only vertically against measures taken by the state: see, respectively, Cases 74/76 *Ianelli and Volpi SpA* v *Meroni* and 83/78 *Pigs Marketing Board* v *Redmond*. However, measures taken by the state have been interpreted fairly liberally to include measures taken by public, semi-public, and even private bodies in certain circumstances in which there has been a fair degree of state involvement or financing. This then brings the actions of an otherwise private body within Articles 34 and 35 TFEU, thus in effect making them horizontally directly effective also.

> For example, in **Cases 266 and 267/87 *R* v *Pharmaceutical Society of Great Britain, ex p Association of Pharmaceutical Importers***, the activities of the Association, which regulated the conduct and set standards for chemists and pharmacists (who were required to be members and follow the rules set, and who were subject to disciplinary sanction) meant that it could be included.

> In **Case 249/81 *Commission* v *Ireland (Buy Irish)***, a 'buy Irish' campaign was administered by the Irish Goods Council, a registered private company. However, because the Irish government largely sponsored the campaign to buy Irish products, appointed the management committee, and set the broad outlines of the campaign, Article 28 (now 34 TFEU) was held to be applicable.

> In **Case 222/82 *Apple and Pear Development Council* v *Lewis***, a government-sponsored development council was under a duty not to run an advertising campaign to encourage the purchase of domestic fruit at the expense of imported products, although it could conduct research into the growing and development of fruit species and disseminate this information.

Without state involvement, the actions of private parties are outside the direct application of Articles 34–36 TFEU, and they would be free to advertise and promote the products of their members.

In **Case C-171/11 Fra.bo spa v DVGW**, an independent-of-state, private body, DVGW, which was responsible for certifying plumbing fittings, refused to certify copper fittings made by Fra. bo in Italy for use in Germany. There was no direct state involvement in DVGW but it regulated those goods in place of the state, which by national legislation accepted and approved DVGW's certification. When challenged, the CoJ held that Article 28 EC (now 34 TFEU) applied to the standardisation and certification activities of a private-law body, where accepted and approved by national legislation. The body then effectively restricted the marketing of products that were not certified and was thus caught by Article 34 TFEU.

The Court in *Fra.bo spa*, though, did not specifically address whether Article 34 TFEU was being applied vertical (with DVGW representing some form of extension of the state) or horizontally (with DVGW as a private party). There thus remains some scope for doubt that Article 34 TFEU does apply horizontally.

11.2.1.1 What constitutes measures for the purposes of Article 34 TFEU?

The concept of 'measures' includes not only legally binding acts, but also practices 'capable of influencing the conduct of traders and consumers' (see Case 249/81 *Commission* v *Ireland (Buy Irish)*) and may include state inaction to prevent private individuals' actions that obstruct the free movement of goods.

See **Case C-265/95 Commission v France (French Farmers/Spanish Strawberries)**, in which the state did not take effective action to stop the protests that prevented Spanish produce entering France and which involved the illegal destruction of imported products. France was held to be in breach of Article 28 EC (now 34 TFEU).

In contrast is **Case C-112/00 Schmidberger**. The lack of state action on the part of Austria in not preventing a protest that blocked the Brenner motorway pass in Austria was held to be acceptable and not a breach of Article 28 EC (now 34 TFEU). This case was distinguished on the length of protest, as a single, one-off event that was not repeated, and as a lawful protest, which was notified to and acknowledged by the Austrian state. **Case C-265/95 Commission v France** concerned instead repeated illegal sabotages of imported goods that should have been stopped, and thus was a breach of Article 28 EC (now 34 TFEU).

▶ CROSS REFERENCE

These cases are also considered in Chapter 7, section 7.1.3.

The term 'measures' has also been interpreted to include administrative practices, if they have a certain degree of consistency and generality.

For example, in **Case 21/84 Commission v France (Franking Machines)**, France had removed a law that had discriminated against imported franking machines, but the French authorities had failed to approve the import of machines from the UK. This administrative failing was held by the CoJ to come within the scope of Article 28 EC (now 34 TFEU).

The Preamble to Directive 70/50 supports this generous view of measures or rules by including non-legally binding **administrative practices**.

Administrative Practices Any standard, regularly followed procedure of a public authority, compared with recommendations, which are instruments issuing from a public authority and which, while not legally binding on the addressees thereof, cause them to pursue a certain conduct.

11.2.2 The meaning of 'quantitative restrictions'

The most obvious examples of quantitative restrictions on imports and exports are complete bans on imports or the subjection of imports or exports to quotas restricting the import or export by either quantity or value. These are clearly in contravention of Article 34 TFEU and are thus prohibited, but they are likely to be extremely rare forms of prevention of the free movement of goods these days. They would be, after all, blatantly obvious.

> **Cases 231/78 *Commission v UK (Import of Potatoes)*** and **232/78 *Commission v France (Import of Lamb)*** are straightforward examples of total bans, which are prohibited.

> In **Case 2/73 *Geddo v Ente Nationale Risi***, the CoJ held that a prohibition on quantitative restrictions covers measures that amount to a total or partial restraint of imports, exports, or goods in transit.

> In **Case 34/79 *R v Henn and Darby***, quantitative restrictions were held by the CoJ to cover measures capable of limiting imports to a finite quantity, including zero, and to include import bans.

A quantitative restriction also includes subjecting the import of goods to the condition of obtaining an import licence.

> In **Case 124/81 *Commission v UK (Imports of UHT Milk)***, the failure to obtain an import licence meant that milk could not be imported even though the requirement was a formality and licences were issued on demand. The CoJ held that import licences or other similar procedures, even if a pure formality, are precluded by Article 28 EC (now 34 TFEU).

11.2.3 Measures having equivalent effect

The concept of measures having equivalent effect (MHEEs, or also abbreviated as MQRs and MeQRs) has been defined by secondary legislation (Directive 70/50) and by the jurisprudence of the CoJ.

The Directive, which was introduced to provide guidelines at the time when the Common Market was being established, remains in the EU list of legislation in force and continues to provide guidance as to what measures may be considered a breach of the prohibition under what is now Article 34 TFEU. It defines measures having an equivalent effect on imports as including distinctly applicable measures—that is, those that apply to imports, but not domestically produced goods—and which (Article 2):

> make imports, or the disposal at any marketing stage, of imported products, subject to a condition, other than a formality, which is required in respect of imported products only, or a condition differing from that required for domestic products and more difficult to satisfy. Equally, it covers, in particular, measures which favour domestic products or grant them a preference, other than an aid, to which conditions may or may not be attached.

Basically, therefore, any measure that makes import or export unnecessarily difficult and thus discriminates between the two would clearly fall within the definition.

It also covers, under Article 3, national marketing rules that, on the face of it, are non-discriminatory or 'indistinctly applicable' (further considered in section 11.4) and:

> which deal in particular, with size, shape, weight, composition, presentation, identification, or putting up and which are equally applicable to domestic and imported products, where the restrictive effect of such measures on the free movement of goods exceeds the effects intrinsic to trade rules.

Further help in understanding this concept comes from the CoJ.

The starting point is **Case 8/74 *Procureur du Roi* v *Dassonville***, in which the term 'measures having equivalent effect' was held to include 'all trading rules enacted by a Member State which are capable of hindering, directly or indirectly, actually or potentially, intra-community trade'. The case concerned criminal proceedings in Belgium against a trader who imported Scotch whisky in free circulation in France into Belgium without being in possession of a certificate of origin from the British customs authorities (before the UK became a member state), thus infringing Belgian customs rules. The CoJ held that:

> the requirement by a Member State of a certificate of authority, which is less easily obtainable by importers of an authentic product, put into free circulation in a regular manner in another Member State, than by importers of the same product coming directly from the country of origin, constitutes a measure having equivalent effect.

The Court added that, in the absence of a Community system to guarantee a product's origin, a member state may take reasonable measures for the protection of consumers in the area of designation of origin of products without necessarily infringing Article 28 EC (now 34 TFEU).

However, this is subject to the further qualification that whether or not such measures were authorised by the derogations provided in Article 36 EEC (and TFEU), they could not constitute an arbitrary discrimination or a disguised restriction on trade between member states.

The scope of the prohibition following this definition is extremely wide and means that virtually any measure that hinders or even potentially hinders imports or exports in any way, whether or not intended, could be caught.

11.2.4 Examples of measures coming within the scope of the prohibition

11.2.4.1 National promotional campaigns

Measures that do not have a clear visible direct effect on imports may still be caught by the prohibition in Article 34 TFEU.

In **Case 249/81 *Commission* v *Ireland* (*Buy Irish*)**, the CoJ held that the activities of a company that was government-controlled, government-financed, and which carried out a government policy of promoting the sale of national products by means of an advertising campaign and promoted the use of a 'home-produced' symbol, constituted a measure having equivalent effect. It was held that it was not necessary for the government to have taken any compulsory measures and that simply encouraging the purchase of domestic products through a campaigning body was sufficient to count as a measure having equivalent effect.

The emphasis is therefore on those rules that are capable of having an effect rather than those rules actually having an effect.

In **Case 222/82 *Apple and Pear Development Council* v *Lewis***, the ruling in the ***Buy Irish*** case was qualified. The CoJ held that a member state could establish a development council for fruit production that was composed of members appointed by the minister responsible and financed only by the growers themselves as long as the activities consisted of compiling statistics, promotion, undertaking research, and giving technical advice rather than trying to get consumers to purchase only home-produced fruit and not imports.

11.2.4.2 Discriminatory national marketing rules

National marketing rules often impose restrictions on the production, packaging, or distribution of goods, which may as a consequence infringe Article 34 TFEU. Import licences, which by their nature apply to imports only, were held to be a breach of the Treaty early on in Cases 51–54/71 *International Fruit Co.* and later in Case 124/81 *Commission* v *UK (UHT Milk)*. This remains the case even if they are issued as a matter of formality, because they still represent some form of hindrance.

For example, in **Case 113/80 *Commission* v *Ireland (Metal Objects/Origin)***, the requirement to stamp the origin of goods as either Irish or foreign was held to breach the rule.

In **Case 261/81 *Rau* v *De Smedt***, the Belgian national rule that required margarine to be packed in cubes and in no other form such as tubs or rectangular blocks was held to be in breach of Article 28 EC (now 34 TFEU). It imposed an economic disadvantage on exporters to Belgium.

Price restrictions involving minimum and maximum pricing and maximum profit margins have all been found to breach Article 34 TFEU (see Cases 82/77 *Openbaar Ministerie* v *Van Tiggele*, 65/75 *Riccardo Tasca*, and 78/82 *Commission* v *Italy*).

In **Cases 266 and 267/87 *R* v *Pharmaceutical Society of Great Britain***, the rule of the Pharmaceutical Society prohibiting dispensing pharmacists from substituting for the product named on a doctor's prescription any other with identical therapeutical effect except under certain exceptional conditions was capable of coming within the operation of Article 28 EC (now 34 TFEU). It was held, however, that it was capable of being justified on the grounds of the protection of public health.

11.2.4.3 Product classification

> **Cases C-387/99 *Commission* v *Germany*** and **150/00 *Commission* v *Austria*** concerned the classification of food supplement products as medicines, which resulted in the restriction of imports where the daily doses of particular vitamins was exceeded. This practice was held to breach Article 28 EC (now 34 TFEU) and could not be justified by Article 30 EC (now 36 TFEU) because of the systematic nature of regulation rather than a case-by-case investigation. Classification by a private regulator is also now subject to Article 34 TFEU, where the results of the classification are effectively condoned by national legislation, as held in **Case C-171/11 *Fra.bo spa* v *DVGW***, noted in section 11.2.1.

11.2.4.4 Exports

> In **Case C-47/90 *Delhaize* v *Promalvin***, a ban on the export of wine in bulk was held to breach Article 29 EC (now 35 TFEU), which states that quantitative restriction on exports, and all measures having equivalent effect, shall be prohibited between member states. There was no evidence to support the contention that bottling was necessary at the source of production, especially where the wine was transported in bulk internally. The intention of the ban was almost certainly to increase the price and thus export income to the exporting state. See also **Case C-388/95 *Belgium* v *Spain* (*Rioja*)** in this respect.

The continued broad scope of *Dassonville* was confirmed as still applicable in certain circumstances in Case C-110/05 *Commission* v *Italy* involving a ban on mopeds towing trailers, which affected the trailer market, and is considered in section 11.5.3.

11.3 Article 36 TFEU derogations

Article 36 TFEU provides exceptions to the general prohibition of Article 34 TFEU.

For more details on this section visit the online resources.

> **Article 36 TFEU**
>
> The provisions of Articles 34 and 35 shall not preclude prohibitions or restrictions on imports, exports or goods in transit justified on grounds of public morality, public policy or public security; the protection of health and life of humans, animals or plants; the protection of national treasures possessing artistic, historic or archaeological value; or the protection of industrial and commercial property . . .

The application of these exceptions is subject to the limitation, set out in the second sentence of Article 36 TFEU.

> **Article 36 TFEU**
>
> . . . Such prohibitions or restrictions shall not, however, constitute a means of arbitrary discrimination or a disguised restriction on trade between Member States.

11.3.1 General purpose and scope

Article 36 TFEU provides the member states with an exhaustive list—in other words, it cannot be added to. Article 36 TFEU allows the member states to restrict the free movement of goods for certain specific reasons only. The member states must prove that the national measure is both necessary and proportionate and not fall foul of the second sentence of Article 36.

> In **Case 72/83 Campus Oil v Ministry for Industry and Energy**, the CoJ held that the purpose of Article 36 EEC (and TFEU) was not to reserve certain matters to the exclusive jurisdiction of the member states, but instead to allow national legislation to derogate from the principle of the free movement of goods to the extent to which this is and remains justified in order to achieve the objectives set out in the Article.

> In **Case 113/80 Commission v Ireland (Metal Objects)**, it was held that because the derogations were exceptions to a fundamental principle, namely the free movement of goods, they were to be construed narrowly and could not, for example, be used for economic reasons and could not be added to.

> In **Case 7/61 Commission v Italian Republic (Pigmeat Imports)**, the derogation was claimed by Italy in order to protect its own pig industry, which was suffering economic difficulties. Italy's attempt was rejected by the CoJ.

11.3.2 Public morality

The standard of morality varies from member state to member state; hence the CoJ has allowed for a margin of discretion on the part of the member states to cater for this variation within this exception.

> **Case 34/79 R v Henn and Darby** concerned a ban on the importation of pornographic magazines, despite the fact that similar magazines could be lawfully possessed in the UK, but it was noted that the enforcement of the law varied within the UK. The CoJ concluded that despite the fact that similar pornographic items could be obtained in the UK, there were, at that time, none produced in the UK; hence it was concluded that there was no lawful trade in them. The CoJ therefore ruled that a prohibition that might be stricter than the laws applicable internally, but which was not designed to discriminate in favour of the domestic product, was therefore acceptable under the public morality clause of Article 30 EC (now 36 TFEU). The Court held that it was up to member states to determine the requirements of public morality in their own state and that they therefore have a margin of discretion in this area.

This means that, provided the prohibition was not discriminatory in intent, different standards can apply. This was, however, qualified in the next case.

In **Case 121/85** *Conegate* v *HM Customs and Excise* (the infamous case concerned with the importation of 'blow-up dolls'), it was held that member states did not have complete freedom to exclude such material when similar products could be manufactured, distributed, and sold lawfully in the UK. The Court held that a member state might not rely on the ground of public morality to prohibit the importation of goods from other member states when its legislation contained no prohibition on the manufacture or marketing of such goods in its own territory. The prohibition was therefore a disguised restriction on trade and a means of arbitrary discrimination, and as such contrary to the second sentence of Article 30 EC (now 36 TFEU).

11.3.3 Public policy

The leading case in this category is **Case 7/78** *R* v *Thompson and others*, which concerned the ban on the unlawful importation into the UK of krugerrands and a ban on the export of coins, some of which were no longer legal tender and some of which were. The English coins that were no longer legal tender were held to be goods within the meaning of Article 28 EC (now 34 TFEU). However, it was held that the right to mint and thus to control coinage was a fundamental interest of the state. Therefore, a state that prohibits the destruction of coins, even when they are no longer legal tender, and imposes an export ban to prevent their destruction abroad, will be justified under Article 30 EC (now 36 TFEU) on grounds of public policy.

Other attempts by member states to invoke this exception have failed: see, for example, those cases dealing with lack of effective action by states to curb illegal protests. It has been claimed that the threat to public order that may be provoked by their action to intervene prevented them from intervening to ensure the free movement of goods.

The CoJ therefore did not accept the invocation of Article 30 EC (now 36 TFEU) to justify the lack of action in **Case C-265/95** *Commission* v *France (Spanish Strawberries)*, in which the French authorities did nothing to prevent French farmers from destroying imported Spanish strawberries.

11.3.4 Public security

The leading case dealing with security is **Case 238/82** *Campus Oil*, which concerned Irish rules requiring importers of petroleum products to purchase a certain proportion of their requirements from an Irish, state-owned refinery at prices fixed by the minister. Whilst the claim to rely on public policy failed, the CoJ held that the maintenance of essential oil supplies was covered by the public security exception and was accepted.

A further attempt to invoke Article 30 EC (now 36 TFEU) was also rejected in **Case 231/83** **_Cullet v Centre Leclerc Toulouse_**, concerned with a law imposing a minimum retail price for fuel. Lower cost imports could not realise their competitive advantage under this law. France argued that, in the absence of the pricing rules, there would be civil disturbances, blockades, and violence. The CoJ rejected this claim.

Any measures taken by member states are nevertheless subject to the principle of proportionality, considered further in section 11.4.2.

11.3.5 Protection of the health or life of humans or animals

This is a frequently argued ground for import restrictions and virtually every sort of good, especially foodstuffs, has been subjected to restrictions on health grounds, most of which have been held by the CoJ not to conform with Article 30 EC (now 36 TFEU).

In **Case 322/01** **_Deutscher Apothekerverband_**, the CoJ noted that 'the health and life of humans rank foremost among the assets or interests' protected by Article 30 EC. However, the Court has been extremely vigilant in exposing the disguised restrictions of member states.

For example, in **Case 124/81** **_Commission v UK (UHT Milk)_**, the systematic checking and re-packaging of sealed UHT cartons of milk for health checks, which dramatically increased costs to the importer, amounted to import restrictions. The CoJ held that the health of consumers would be adequately protected by the necessary controls being carried out in the country of production to meet all of the reasonable requirements of the country of import.

This case is a good example of the principle of equivalence, considered further in section 11.4.1.

Similarly, in **Case 42/82** **_Commission v France (Italian Table Wines)_**, systematic checks on three-quarters of each consignment of Italian wine, which was held up at the French border for long periods, sometimes months, was held not to be justified by Article 30 EC (now 36 TFEU). Whilst the CoJ acknowledged the right of the member states to carry out checks, it noted that the frequency of analysis of Italian wine was considerably higher than the occasional checks carried out on French wine transported within France. The CoJ held that the French authorities had no right to carry out systematic checks and, in the absence of any reasonable suspicion on the basis of specific evidence in a given case, they ought to have confined themselves to random checks.

A number of cases have now been considered by the Court concerning import bans on the grounds of protecting public health, which have focused on the content of food products and have often concerned food additives that were claimed to be hazardous to human health. The CoJ has held in these cases that, in the absence of any Community regulation of the manufacture and marketing of products, the member states are free to regulate this matter as long as they do not infringe the

Community provisions on the free movement of goods. In the cases that are concerned with an import ban raised on the grounds of protecting the health of the population from harmful additives, the CoJ takes into account the following criteria:

- whether the additives were permitted in another product; or
- whether they were lawfully permitted in another member state; or
- how they are regarded according to the results of international scientific research, in particular the work of the World Health Organization (WHO); and
- the eating habits in the country of importation.

If the additive does not constitute a real danger to public health, a ban will be a breach of Article 34 TFEU and will not be justified under Article 36 TFEU. Additionally, bans will be contrary to the principle of proportionality where there is no accessible procedure by which traders are able to request that the use of disputed additives be permitted.

> Cases include the ban on the import of beer in **Case 178/84 _Commission_ v _Germany (Beer Purity)_**, a ban on the import of sausages containing certain non-meat ingredients in **Case 274/87 _Commission_ v _Germany (Sausage Purity Law)_**, and a ban on the import of low-fat cheese in **Case 210/89 _Commission_ v _Italy_**.

However, a ban would not infringe Article 34 TFEU where the same additives are also prohibited in domestic products and where there is a system to allow the assessment and addition of additives to the list of permitted additives: see Cases 95 and 293/89 _Commission_ v _Italy and Greece_. In summary of the case law, states must make out on the basis of latest scientific data that a real risk to health exists. However, the CoJ recognises 'that such an assessment of the risk could reveal that scientific uncertainty persists as regards the existence or extent of real risks to human health'.

> However, in **Case C-192/01 _Commission_ v _Denmark_**, the CoJ stated that, in such circumstances, it must be accepted that a member state may, in accordance with the precautionary principle, take protective measures without having to wait until the existence and gravity of those risks are fully demonstrated.

> The precautionary principle has statutory form in the EU legal order in Article 191 TFEU on the environment, and permits provisional measures to be taken where a clear risk to health is identified but cannot immediately be proved beyond doubt.

> Finally, in this category is **Case C-358/95 _Tommaso Morellato_ v _Unita Sanitaria Locale_**, which focused on the contents of bread. It was claimed that imported frozen bread contravened national statutory limits by having a moisture content exceeding 34 per cent and an ash content of less than 1.40 per cent, and by containing bran, contrary to national standards for bread. France was unable to demonstrate a threat to public health and it was easy for the CoJ to reach the conclusion that the national law constituted a quantitative restriction contrary to Article 28 EC (now 34 TFEU) and was not saved by Article 30 EC (now 36 TFEU).

THINKING POINT

Why might the authorities insist on there being a minimum ash content, which does not seem a very healthy ingredient to insist on?

The answer lies in the fact that frozen bread is mass-produced and part-baked in industrial ovens heated by gas or electricity. Traditional ovens are coal- or coke-fired and some ash gets into the bread. Insisting on ash is just a way of banning mass-produced bread. Non-ash-containing bread may well be less carcinogenic and thus healthier.

An area in which the public health proviso in Article 36 TFEU is of great importance is in the importation of pharmaceutical products, for which there are often vast price differences between the retail prices in different member states.

Case 215/87 *Schumacher v Hauptzollamt Frankfurt* concerned the ban on the import of medicinal products purchased in France for personal use. The medicines in question were available in Germany without prescription, but at four times the price charged in France. The CoJ held that national rules or practices that have or are likely to have a restrictive effect on importation of pharmaceutical products are compatible with the Treaty only in so far as they are necessary for the protection of health and human life. In this case, the purchase of the goods in a pharmacy of another member state in effect gives a guarantee equivalent to that resulting from the sale of the product in a pharmacy in the member state into which it is imported. The Court ruled that the rule prohibiting the importation of the goods in this case contravened Article 28 EC (now 34 TFEU) and was not protected by Article 30 EC (now 36 TFEU).

11.3.6 **Artistic, historic, or archaeological heritage**

It was held in **Case 7/68** *Commission v Italy (Art Treasures)* that the ground of artistic heritage does not justify a tax being levied on the export of art treasures, which was therefore held to breach Article 25 EC (now 30 TFEU).

The point of this is that if Italy wants to protect art or to stop it from leaving the country, a complete ban may be justified; simply taxing it was not.

11.3.7 **The protection of industrial or commercial property**

Intellectual property (IP) rights such as patents, trade marks, and copyright can be protected even though they may often be a breach of Article 34 TFEU, as these rights are designed to restrict the complete freedom of how goods covered by them are traded. They can, though, be justified under Article 36 TFEU, but the derogation is to be read alongside Article 345 TFEU, which provides that the Treaty shall in no way prejudice the rules in member states governing the system of property ownership. Whilst most of the cases on IP are dealt with under competition law and often beyond general courses on EU law, the leading cases showing the relationship with the free movement of goods are considered here.

The leading case of **Case 78/70 *Deutsche Grammophon* v *Metro*** distinguished between the existence of the rights guaranteed by Article 345 TFEU and the exercise of those rights that often impact on the free movement of goods and Article 34 TFEU. The case also made it clear that copyright and allied rights were also covered by Article 36 TFEU.

Case 15/74 *Centrafarm* v *Sterling* dealt with the concept of the exhaustion of rights. In that case, drugs patented by Sterling and marketed in the UK and the Netherlands were bought by Centrafarm in the UK and re-sold in the Netherlands. Sterling attempted to uphold its patent to prevent the drugs from being marketed there. The CoJ held that the derogation in Article 36 TFEU served only to protect the specific subject matter, which was the exclusive right to put into circulation for the first time the products protected by the patent. However, once the goods protected have been lawfully put onto the market in more than one member state, those rights are said to be exhausted. This means that the holder cannot rely on the patent to prevent further lawful sales in another member state and importation back (known as parallel imports) into the first state of sale or manufacture.

Case 16/74 *Centrafarm* v *Winthrop* extended the same reasoning and conclusions to trade marks. The CoJ thus ensured that the exercise of patent and trade marks were not such as to prevent the lawful free movement of goods between member states.

This derogation was also considered in **Case 388/95 *Belgium* v *Spain*** and the Spanish ban on the export of Rioja wine in bulk, which was held to be a breach of Article 29 EC (now 35 TFEU), but which was justified to maintain its high quality and reputation under the Article 30 EC (now 36 TFEU) derogation for the protection of commercial property.

In view of the vast number of cases on this specialised topic, many of which are also tied up with competition law aspects, it is unlikely that you will go into any further detail on most undergraduate courses on EU law. However, the significance of a complementary competition law policy should be stressed because it is vital to the successful running of the internal market. The establishment or foundation of the EU is premised on the desire to promote integration and to create a single unified market. A competition policy within the overall Treaty regime prevents companies from setting up their own rules and obstacles to trade to replace the national rules and obstacles the EU is trying to abolish. The two go hand in hand: you cannot have one without ensuring you have the other. To have prevented the member states, on the one hand, from restricting the movement of goods only to allow private companies to do so in their agreements and practices would defeat the objectives of the first policy; on the other hand, to prevent companies from artificially dividing the markets, but to allow the member states to do so, would undermine a competition policy. Hence there is a need for both.

11.3.8 **The second sentence of Article 36 TFEU**

Article 36 TFEU provides that 'Such prohibitions or restrictions shall not, however, constitute a means of arbitrary discrimination or a disguised restriction on trade between Member States.' In addition, any measure taken by the member states to regulate products or markets must be proportionate. Proportionality is considered further in section 11.4.2.4.

Essentially, this second sentence provides a backstop for the CoJ to ensure that any claims raised by the member states under any of the grounds considered in this chapter so far do conform with the overall desire to ensure and promote the free movement of goods within the internal EU market.

> In **Case 42/82 *Commission v France (Italian Table Wines)***, the systematic checking of every consignment and subjecting inspections to very long delays of weeks, and even months, was held to be disproportionate. It simply went far beyond the alleged purposes of ensuring quality.

> Similarly, in **Case 124/81 *Commission v UK (UHT Milk)***, the requirement of an import licence was held to be a disguised restriction despite being issued automatically. In other words, it was merely a hurdle that importers had to overcome even though it was easy to obtain a licence, which actually shows that it served no quality control purpose.

> **Case C-170/04 *Rosengren*** involved a Swedish government measure prohibiting the private import of alcohol, unless sanctioned by the authorities and subject to additional import charges. The restriction was held to be contrary to Article 28 EC (now 34 TFEU), but was claimed by Sweden to be justified under the Article 30 EC (now 36 TFEU) health ground, in particular to protect young persons. The CoJ dismissed this because the measure, contained in Chapter 4(2)(1) of the Swedish Law on Alcohol, was unsuitable for attaining the objective of limiting alcohol consumption generally, and not proportionate for attaining the objective of protecting young persons against the harmful effects of such consumption. The state monopoly was not a means of restricting alcohol imports or strength of drinks, but more of preserving the state monopoly to import. The Court held therefore that it could not be regarded as being justified under Article 30 EC on grounds of protection of the health and life of humans.

If health was the overriding concern and the product constituted a clear and proven risk to health, then a complete ban would probably have been justified. So, whilst the Court is acutely aware of the health issues of alcohol abuse and consumption by young people, any measures ostensibly to address those issues must really be designed to do that. The Swedish measures were inadequate in that respect and operated only to ensure the state near-monopoly on alcohol imports.

11.3.9 **Decision 3052/95 and Regulation 764/2008**

In an attempt to regulate better the introduction by member states of measures that affect the free movement of goods, Decision 3052/95, on exchange of information about national measures derogating from the principle of free movement of goods, was adopted, now replaced by Regulation 764/2008. This required the member states to inform the Commission about any measures that may lead to the refusal of the import of goods or require the modification of goods for the market or which withdraws goods from the market. The Commission then informs the other member states to provide them with an opportunity to be able to react or express a view on them. Furthermore, the Commission may decide to seek further details or take action if it concludes that the measures actually breach Article 28 EC (now 34 TFEU). The replacement Regulation 764/2008 is also intended to assist the free movement of goods by providing procedures to assess the impact of proposed technical rules by member states, which must advise the Commission when they propose to enact any such measures.

Further details are not provided in this text, but links can be found via the online resources.

11.4 Equally applicable measures (indistinctly applicable measures)

Measures that apply to imports or exports only are called 'distinctly applicable measures'. However, Article 34 TFEU prohibits not only national rules that overtly discriminate against imported products, subject to the possibility of justification under Article 36 TFEU, but may also be used to challenge national rules that, on the face of it, make no distinction between domestic and imported goods. Measures that apply to both imports and domestic goods are termed 'equally' or 'indistinctly' applicable.

For more details on this section visit the online resources.

Article 3 of Directive 70/50 provides that measures that are equally applicable to domestic and imported goods will breach Article 34 TFEU only where the restrictive effect on the free movement of goods exceeds the effects necessary for the trade rules—that is, only those measures that are disproportionate to the aim and which thus tend to protect domestic products at the expense of the imports.

Directive 70/50, Article 3

This Directive also covers measures governing the marketing of products which deal, in particular, with shape, size, weight, composition, presentation, identification or putting up, and which are equally applicable to domestic and imported products, where the restrictive effect of such measures on the free movement of goods exceeds the effects intrinsic to trade rules. This is the case, in particular, where the restrictive effects on the free movement of goods are out of proportion to their purpose; and the same objective can be attained by other means, which are less of a hindrance to trade.

The wide definition of measures in **Case 8/74 *Procureur de Roi v Dassonville*** made no allowance for some measures introduced by member states that applied to both imports and domestic products and which might be justified on particular acceptable grounds, such as the protection of the environment. The judgment, however, did acknowledge this possibility in the statement that:

> In the absence of a community system guaranteeing for consumers the authenticity of a product's designation of origin, if a Member State takes measures to prevent unfair practices in this connection, it is however subject to the condition that these measures should be reasonable and that the means of proof required should not act as a hindrance to trade between Member States and should, in consequence, be accessible to all Community nationals.

In other words, member states can require importers to satisfy certain rules, provided Article 34 TFEU is not contravened. Thus, the case introduced the possibility that member states could restrict imports for a good reason, and marked the foundation of the so-called rule of reason.

This was developed further in a landmark decision in EU law that addressed the difficulties of indistinctly applicable measures, which may, however, be introduced by member states for arguably sound reasons. This is Case 120/78 *Rewe-Zentral AG* v *Bundesmonopolverwaltung für Branntwein*, better known as *Cassis de Dijon*.

11.4.1 **The *Cassis de Dijon* case**

Case 120/78 *Cassis de Dijon* concerned a prohibition on the marketing in the Federal Republic of Germany of spirits with less than a 25 per cent alcohol content, which included Crème de Cassis de Dijon (a blackcurrant alcoholic liqueur), which contains usually only 15–20 per cent alcohol. The ban applied to all low-alcohol liqueurs regardless of origin and did not distinguish between national and foreign drinks; hence it was indistinctly applicable. The arguments made by Germany for the ban were that lower-alcohol liqueurs would lead to alcohol tolerance, thus leading to health problems in the future, and that the lower alcohol also provided a price advantage for the imported products that was unfair and which would force down alcohol rates of drinks, and thus quality, contrary to usual manufacturing practice. However, the actual result was effectively a ban, albeit indirect, of the French imports.

The CoJ made a number of statements of importance in its judgment. It held that there was no valid reason why, provided they have been lawfully produced and marketed in one of the member states, alcoholic beverages should not be introduced without restriction into any other member state. As was seen in **Commission v UK (UHT Milk)**, this is a restatement of the principle of mutual equivalence.

The Court also held that obstacles to the free movement of goods resulting from disparities in the national laws on the marketing of products must be accepted as far as these provisions are necessary to satisfy certain mandatory requirements, considered further in the following sections.

CROSS REFERENCE

See section 11.3.5 for *UHT Milk*.

The judgment was a way of getting around too strict an application of the rule developed in the earlier *Dassonville* case. It means that measures that are equally applicable to imports and domestic products and which hinder trade may be acceptable if they are in pursuit of a reasonable special interest that the member state has the right to protect. However, they are subject to the principle of proportionality and must neither be an arbitrary discrimination nor a disguised restriction on trade. The latter two terms repeat those provided in Article 36 TFEU.

The judgment in *Cassis de Dijon* makes it clear that Article 34 TFEU also covers indirect discrimination by the reference to the words 'disparities between national laws' in the sentence 'obstacles to movement within the Community resulting from disparities between national laws relating to the marketing of the products in question'. In other words, where a national rule, although on the face of it applying equally to both imported and domestic products, acts as a hindrance or obstacle, it may also be caught by Article 34 TFEU, for example the rule in *Cassis de Dijon* itself.

The case is regarded as a very important tool for the Commission in establishing and maintaining the internal market by the creation of a simple rule that goods lawfully manufactured and sold in one member state should be able to move freely throughout the EU. Indeed, the Commission later issued a Practice Note based on its interpretation of what the *Cassis de Dijon* case meant.

> Communication from the Commission concerning the consequences of the judgments by the Court of Justice on 20 February 1979 in Case 120/78 ('*Cassis de Dijon*') (Official Journal (OJ) 1980 C256/2). Reproduced in Foster, *Blackstone's EU Treaties and Legislation*, Oxford University Press, Oxford, published annually.

11.4.1.1 Examples of acceptable mandatory measures

Examples of the types of mandatory measure required—that is, the national rules raised by the member states—suggested by the CoJ in *Cassis de Dijon* were 'the effectiveness of fiscal supervision, the protection of public health, the fairness of consumer transactions and the defence of the consumer'. The measures listed are not exhaustive and have been added to by the CoJ in subsequent cases. The following list provides a range of the additional measures and interests worthy of protection approved by the CoJ:

- environmental grounds, in Case 302/86 *Commission v Denmark (Disposable Beer Cans)*;
- cultural interests, in Cases 60 and 61/84 *Cinetheque SA v Federation Nationale des Cinemas Francais* (concerning the sale of video recordings);
- conservation of the resources of the sea, in Cases 3, 4, and 6/76 *Minister of Justice v Kramer*;
- the protection of workers, in Cases C-312/89 *Union Department des Syndicats CGT de l'Aisne v Sidef Conforama* and C-332/89 *Criminal Proceedings against Marchandise*;
- recognition of socio-cultural identity or characteristics, in Cases 60 and 61/84 *Cinetheque* and Case 145/88 *Torfaen Borough Council v B&Q plc,* although the latter case was effectively overruled by the *Keck* case, considered in section 11.5;
- the financial balance of the social security system, in Case C-120/95 *Decker*;
- maintenance of the diversity of the press, in Case C-368/95 *Vereinigte Familiapress*;
- the prevention of fraud, in Case C-426/92 *Milch-Kontor*;
- the protection of fundamental rights of freedom of speech and protest, in Case C-112/00 *Schmidberger*; and
- the protection of young persons, in Case C-244/06 *Dynamic Medien*.

 THINKING POINT

Given that *Cassis de Dijon* represents exceptions to the reasons provided by Article 36 TFEU, what is the limit of the reasons that might be raised by the member states and accepted by the CoJ?

11.4.2 Application of the rule of reason: the requirements in detail

Once it has been established that the interest comes within the rule of reason, the criteria of the rule of reason must be satisfied as follows.

11.4.2.1 There must be no EU system covering the interest in question

In other words, EU legislation must not have occupied the field and there must be no harmonising EU legislation.

In **Case 16/83 *Criminal Proceedings against Karl Prantl***, a German law provided that only certain quality wines from Franken and Baden could be marketed in the bottle known as *Bocksbeutel*. Anyone marketing any other wine in the *Bocksbeutel* committed an offence. The defendant in the main action was charged with selling quantities of Italian red wine in bottles of this type. The German authorities justified the rule under consumer protection and fair trading, and the CoJ expressly acknowledged that such mandatory requirements may be justified provided there was no applicable Community rule. In fact, wine produced in the Italian Tyrol had been produced in bottles of this type for at least a century, as have Portuguese Mateus rosé wines.

At the time of the *Prantl* case, there was in place only a partial system of EU rules governing the types of wine that might be marketed in specific types of bottle. These rules, however, had not yet been concluded to exclude national competences in respect of the shape of the bottle in question in the case at hand. Thus, it was held that, until Community rules were implemented, those adopted by the member states could be maintained so long as they did not contravene Articles 28–30 EC (now 34–36 TFEU). The Court held that the rules in question did in fact contravene Article 28 EC and were not saved by Article 30 EC (now Articles 34 and 36 TFEU).

11.4.2.2 The measure must be indistinctly applicable

The measure must apply without difference on the face of it to both imports and domestic products; otherwise it cannot be considered under the rule of reason and must fall to be considered under Article 34 TFEU and the derogations allowed under Article 36 TFEU only.

Case 113/80 *Commission v Ireland (Metal Objects)* concerned Irish legislation that required souvenirs of Ireland that were not domestically produced to bear the designation 'Foreign'. The Commission considered that the restrictions contravened Article 28 EC (now 34 TFEU) and Article 2(3)(f) of Directive 70/50 because they were measures that had the effect of lowering the value of an imported product by causing a reduction in its value or an increase in its costs. The Irish government argued that the measures were justified on grounds of consumer protection and therefore fell within the scope of the public policy derogation in Article 30 EC (now 36 TFEU).

The CoJ held that since Article 30 EC constitutes a derogation from the basic rule that all obstacles to the free movement of goods between member states are to be eliminated, Article 30 EC must be construed narrowly. Since neither the protection of consumers nor the fairness of transactions were included among the exceptions set out in Article 30 EC, it was held that they could not be relied on in connection with that Article.

The Court then considered whether the measures might be justified as necessary to meet mandatory requirements; however, the rules were not measures that applied to domestic and imported products without distinction. They applied only to imported products and were therefore discriminatory in nature. Hence, the measures were not covered by the decision in *Cassis de Dijon*, which applies only to provisions that regulate both imported products and domestic products. The rules were therefore in breach of Article 28 EC (now 34 TFEU).

11.4.2.3 The measure must be neither an arbitrary discrimination nor a disguised restriction on trade

In **Case 124/81 Commission v UK (UHT Milk)**, the requirement of an import licence requiring a second heat treatment and packaging was held to be a disguised restriction. The argument raised by the UK that there was not a Community system in place was not accepted by the CoJ, which had noted the very similar regimes applicable to UHT milk in the different member states.

▶ CROSS REFERENCE

See also the *Commission v Germany (Beer Purity Law)* case considered in section 11.4.2.4.

11.4.2.4 The measure must meet the requirements of proportionality

Apart from the *Cassis de Dijon* case itself, there are a number of other cases that serve as good examples of this point.

In **Case 113/80 Commission v Ireland (Irish Metal Objects)**, the CoJ took the view that the interests of consumers and fair trading would have been adequately protected if it were left to domestic manufacturers to take appropriate steps, such as affixing, if they so wished, their mark of origin to their own products or packaging. The Irish government requirement to stamp 'Foreign' was not reasonable; it was disproportionate.

In **Case 261/81 Walter Rau Lebensmittelwerke v De Smedt**, Belgian legislation prohibited the marketing of margarine that did not conform to a particular shape. This rule had a clear protective effect and was an obstacle to marketing to importers. The Belgian government argued that the measure was necessary for consumer protection. The CoJ ruled that if a member state has a choice between various measures to attain the same objective, it should choose the measure that least restricts the free movement of goods. In this case, consumers might have been protected and informed that the product was margarine by other measures that would have constituted less of an interference with the free movement of goods, such as labelling. Therefore, the rules contravened Article 28 (now 34 TFEU).

In **Case 16/83 Prantl**, the CoJ held that the sale of a product may not be prohibited when a labelling requirement will adequately protect the consumer from confusing the particular wine in the wine bottle sold.

▶ CROSS REFERENCE

See section 11.4.2.1 for more on *Prantl*.

The various food additives and constituent cases considered under the Article 30 EC (now 36 TFEU) derogations are also subject to the line of argument that adequate labelling will protect consumers rather than a ban, which would be disproportionate. Examples of relevant cases are considered in section 11.3.5.

See **Case 174/84 Commission v Germany (Beer Purity Law)**, concerning a German law providing that only malted barley, hops, yeast, and water could be used in the manufacture of beer, and further that only drinks complying with those provisions could be marketed under the designation 'beer'. A further law prohibited importation of beers containing additives

> unless the additives were specifically authorised. The CoJ held that whilst it was legitimate to seek to enable consumers who attribute special qualities to beer manufactured from particular raw materials to make their choice in an informed way, that end could be achieved by labelling. The prohibition went beyond what was necessary for the protection of German consumers, since such protection could easily be ensured by compulsory affixing of labels informing consumers about the nature of the product sold.

More recent cases have suggested that in determining whether a particular measure chosen by a member state is proportionate, the member state is not required to go to the extent of demonstrating beyond doubt that no other measure could have been adopted, but they must consider any suggestions made by the Commission (see Case C-28/09 *Commission* v *Austria*, both considered in section 11.5.2).

11.4.3 Technical standards and legislative intervention

CROSS REFERENCE

See Chapter 8, section 8.2.4, on incidental horizontal effects.

In order to try to regulate the free movement of goods more effectively and more comprehensively, and to avoid some of the difficulties of relying on piecemeal litigation to challenge measures introduced from time to time by the member states, the Commission introduced Directive 83/189, now updated and consolidated by Directive 98/34 (reproduced in Foster, *Blackstone's EU Treaties and Legislation*, Oxford University Press, Oxford, published annually). These require member states to notify technical standards of products before being adopted so that the Commission can consider whether they create barriers to the free movement of goods. Whilst it was not intended to create rights for individuals and merely intended to provide a channel of communication between the member states and the Commission, the Directives have nevertheless been instrumental in some cases between individuals. These cases have prompted significant use and notifications under the Directive, and have probably helped in preventing some national measures that would have created barriers.

11.4.4 Summary of *Cassis de Dijon*

The rule of reason in the *Cassis de Dijon* case either classifies measures as falling outside the scope of Article 34 TFEU or justifies measures that would otherwise have breached Article 34 TFEU because the ability given to the member states to rely on mandatory requirements provides, in effect, further derogations to Article 36 TFEU. The case certainly appeared to allow member states to maintain some rules that protected a particular interest, but it was often unclear as to whether the national mandatory requirement fell outside or would breach Article 34 TFEU. As a consequence, in some cases there has been a blurring of the distinction between distinctly and indistinctly applicable measures. Normally, the route taken would be to decide whether the measures are distinctly or indistinctly applicable and then decide if they breach Article 34 TFEU.

- If distinctly applicable, consider whether any of the derogations of Article 36 TFEU apply.
- If indistinctly applicable, consider whether any of the *Cassis de Dijon* mandatory requirements or an Article 36 TFEU derogation apply.

> Occasionally, however, as in **Case C-67/97 *Bluhme*** or **Case C-2/90 *Commission* v *Belgium* (*Walloon Waste*)**, the CoJ has entertained arguments based on mandatory requirements, although the facts related to a situation concerned essentially with a distinctly applicable rule. In both cases, environmental arguments were raised.

In the latter case, a Belgian region prohibited the transfer of waste from other regions of Belgium to Wallonia for storage, tipping, or dumping. That the rule was distinctly applicable was effectively ignored by the CoJ in both of the cases in the interests of environmental protection.

However, for the most part, the distinction remains. It is, though, necessary to consider the difference between 'equal burden' and 'dual burden' rules, a distinction that was provoked by the development of case law following *Cassis de Dijon*.

Dual burden rules, which add an additional requirement on imports, can be more easily identified and thus regarded as being in breach of Article 34 TFEU. Equal burden rules, on the other hand, which, as might be expected, impose an equal burden on imports and domestic products, are left to the national courts to decide whether the rule (the mandatory requirement) is one worthy of protection.

11.4.5 Equal burden or dual burden rules

An indistinctly applicable rule is one that applies, at least on the face of it, to imported and domestic products alike. The same rule applies and imposes an equal burden on both products. However, this is not the conclusion that should be reached if one takes into account the fact that the importer may already have satisfied a similar or slightly different rule in the state of export. Therefore, the imported product has to comply with two sets of product requirements in order to be marketed lawfully in the state of import: those operated by the state of origin and those operated by the state of importation. In this situation, the imported product is placed under an additional burden.

For example, in **Case 261/81 *Walter Rau (Margarine)***, the Belgian authorities required margarine to be packed in cube-shaped containers only, which meant that a separate production line would have to be set up for the Belgian market. If other countries adopted similar packaging requirements, maybe round for Luxembourg and so on, further types of packaging and packaging lines would have to be set up, which would not be economically viable for the manufacturer. Hence, the conclusion is that it is unfair that two sets of rules must be complied with; therefore, the additional or dual burden rule, although applying on the face of it equally, is caught by Article 34 TFEU unless justified by either Article 36 TFEU or the rule of reason mandatory requirements.

▶ CROSS REFERENCE
This case is also noted in section 11.4.2.4.

Equal burden rules in contrast should not have been considered as even coming within Article 34 TFEU because, by definition, the burden of the rule in question in the state of import falls equally on home and domestic products. The imported product suffers no discrimination or disadvantage. Unfortunately, the CoJ appeared to extend the scope of Article 28 EC (now 34 TFEU) to cover equal burden rules that applied fairly to both imported and domestic products in cases in which national measures were neither directly nor indirectly discriminatory and there was no additional burden on the imports.

For example, **Cases 60 and 61/84 *Cinetheque*** concerned the prohibition of the hire or sale of film videos in France within the first year of release in order to protect the film industry from production through to the cinemas. The rule applied equally to domestic and imported videos. The CoJ held nevertheless that the rule was a measure having equivalent effect because it did restrict the overall import of videos, although it equally restricted sales and rentals of

domestically produced videos. These, however, were fewer in number, but it could be justified for a specific reason in the case—'the protection of artistic works'—which was therefore
added to the list of mandatory requirements from *Cassis*. Otherwise, it would have breached
Article 28 EC (now 34 TFEU).

However, the extension of the scope of Article 28 EC (now 34 TFEU) prohibition to equal burden rules
had taken place. The *Cassis* case is both beneficial to the free movement of goods and, at the same
time, supports national diversity by allowing regional variations under the mutual equivalence rule.
Further, under the rule of reason and the mandatory requirements rule, additional member states'
interests and concerns covered by national rules would be recognised. However, if those equal burden
rules were also potentially a breach of Article 28 EC (now 34 TFEU), then, as proved to be the case,
all sorts of national rules and virtually any nationally imposed regulation of trade practices or commercial freedom that might have restricted in any way the level of imports were attacked by traders
who had been caught infringing the national rules. Traders claimed that their right to import goods
and sell them had been infringed. Many of the national laws challenged were concerned with sales
and marketing rules and had no impact on the access of imported goods to the national market.
Increasingly, however, national laws were questioned, not on the basis that they hindered imports
only, but because they affected the volume of trade regardless of origin: see Case 61/84 *Cinetheque*.

The Sunday trading case law and in particular **Cases 145/88 *Torfaen Borough Council* v
*B&Q plc*** and ***B&Q Ltd* v *Shrewsbury Borough Council*** serve as good examples of the
confusion that can arise. It was assumed that the national laws did affect Community trade
and were in breach of Article 28 EC (now 34 TFEU) unless justified. However, as was demonstrated in these cases, the interest worth protecting could vary. A previous ban used to exist
in the UK, which prohibited the trading of many goods on a Sunday. It was not discriminatory,
but applied to imported and domestic goods alike. However, traders claimed that it breached
Article 28 EC (now 34 TFEU) because, by reducing the volume of sales, it reduced volume
of imports and thus it was a measure having equivalent effect. The grounds stated by the
member state to justify the law were not contained in Article 30 EC (now 36 TFEU), but arguably within the mandatory requirements of *Cassis*. The case law from the UK had not been
particularly helpful, partly as a result of the CoJ deciding that national courts must determine
for themselves whether the reason for a rule was justified under the rule of reason. The ban
on Sunday trading concerned both the idea of 'keeping Sunday special' and the protection of
workers, and as a result led to contradictory decisions, depending on whether the UK courts
took into account the protection of workers, which would appear to justify a ban on Sunday
trading, and the attempt to keep Sunday special, which appeared not to justify a ban.

Before a further UK case reached the CoJ, **Cases C-312/89 *Conforama*** and **C-332/89
*Criminal Proceedings against Marchandise*** had reached the Court, which were more
instructive from the Community law point of view. In a request for preliminary rulings from
French and Belgian courts, the CoJ held that national restrictions on the opening of shops on
Sundays (the French *Code de Travail* provides for a mandatory day's rest on Sundays, whilst
the Belgian *Loi sur le Travail* prohibits the employing of retail shop workers after noon on a
Sunday) were not in breach of Community law. It was considered that this area of law was
a matter for the regulation of each individual member state. The measures were held not
designed to control patterns of trade between member states, nor were they applied so as to
discriminate against goods from other member states.

In **Case C-169/91 *Stoke City Council v B&Q plc***, which was another reference concerning Sunday trading from the UK, the CoJ held that the UK's restrictions on Sunday trading did not conflict with Community law. It held that such rules reflected 'choices relating to particular national or regional socio-cultural characteristics'.

This means that the member states have the discretion to make such choices. However, this series of cases did raise the question of whether the CoJ had gone too far in upholding the sanctity of free movement over national rules by finding that all obstacles to free movement and not merely those concerned with discrimination and protectionism were in breach of Article 28 EC (now 34 TFEU) unless justified under either Article 30 EC (now 36 TFEU) or *Cassis*. In other words, the assumption would be that anything affecting imports whatsoever would breach Article 28 EC (now 34 TFEU) unless it could be justified. Hence, the next development.

11.5 *Keck and Mithouard*: certain selling arrangements

Faced with many similar arguments by traders against national rules, when presented with a suitable occasion the CoJ was able to redefine its position.

For more details on this section visit the online resources.

Cases C-267 and 268/91 *Keck and Mithouard* concerned the French prohibition of the sale of unaltered goods at a loss. Although this was applicable to both imported and domestic products, it was argued to be a restriction of sales contrary to Article 28 EC (now 34 TFEU) as a defence to being prosecuted for a breach of the French law. France claimed that the rule was justified as a *Cassis de Dijon* mandatory exception. The CoJ stated that:

> In view of the increasing tendency of traders to invoke Article 30 EEC of the Treaty as a means of challenging any rules whose effect is to limit their commercial freedom even where such rules are not aimed at products from other member states, the Court considers it necessary to re-examine and clarify its case law on this matter.

The Court considered that traders had previously been using EU law to try to challenge laws that were not aimed at restricting imports, but which restricted the sales of all goods, domestic and imported. The Court then stated that it considered that selling or marketing arrangements did not come within the concept outlined in *Dassonville* or Article 28 EC (now 34 TFEU). The Court held that:

> contrary to what has previously been decided, the application to products from other member states of national provisions restricting or prohibiting certain selling arrangements is not such as to hinder directly or indirectly, actually or potentially, trade between member states within the meaning of the Dassonville judgment provided that those provisions apply to all affected traders operating within the national territory and provided that they affect in the same manner, in law and in fact, the marketing of domestic products and of those from other member states.

Looked at in another way, an impediment to trade is acceptable where the rule in question is merely a selling arrangement that applies to both the trade in domestic and imported products equally. It was an attempt to permit national rules that were introduced for reasons other than those intended to be a restriction on imports. Therefore, provided national rules do not impede access to markets, but merely regulate them without any form of discrimination, either in law or in fact, they will be acceptable and will not fall within Article 34 TFEU. That should have been the end of it, and such rules would not then have had to be considered either under Article 36 or *Cassis de Dijon*.

 THINKING POINT

Consider the Sunday trading rules in the UK, many of which were enacted in Victorian times. At the time of their enactment, could the authorities have had in mind Article 34 TFEU, the internal market, or even the EU itself?

However, there were problems with the *Keck* judgment because it did not provide an instant clarification of the law, most notably the questions of 'What are selling arrangements?' and 'How are they to be distinguished from product characteristics?' The scope of this expression and distinction was explored in subsequent cases.

11.5.1 Post-*Keck* case law

Selling arrangements are broadly defined as rules relating to the market circumstances in which the goods are sold. Selling arrangements are usually equal burden rules that, following the *Keck* case, now fall outside of the scope of application of Article 34 TFEU. Selling arrangements are measures dealing with where, when, how, and by whom goods may be sold. In contrast are rules relating to the product itself or its characteristics, such as those concerned with the shape, size, weight, composition, presentation, identification, packaging, or putting up (preparing for sale).

Examples of selling arrangements include, in **Case C-292/92 *Hunermund***, a rule prohibiting pharmacists from advertising para-pharmaceutical products that they sold, which was held by the CoJ not to be caught by Article 28 EC (now 34 TFEU). Similarly, **Cases C-401 and 402/92 *Tankstation 't Heustke*** involving Dutch laws about the opening times of shops at petrol outlets, **Case C-63/94 *Belgapom*** involving Belgian laws prohibiting offering products for sale at a loss, and **Case C-391/92 *Commission* v *Greece*** involving the prohibited sale of any processed milk for babies other than in pharmacies were all found to be acceptable forms of selling arrangements and not to breach Article 28 EC (now 34 TFEU). Neither did a rule that required a licence to open a new shop in **Case C-140/92 *DIP***, in view of the public interest and concern for planned commercial development. The rules involved were not concerned with the origin of goods traded.

Therefore, it appeared relatively simple to reach conclusions on particular rules that, provided a rule was classified as a selling arrangement, it should fall outside Article 34 TFEU. However, rules that at first sight may appear to be a selling arrangement, but which do have an impact on the characteristic of the product, would breach Article 34 TFEU if the rule were nevertheless shown to create a requirement physically to alter the product as in the *Mars* case, or which relate to the product, as in the *Familiapress* case (both following), unless it could be otherwise justified.

For example, in **Case C-470/93 *Mars***, a national law was challenged that prohibited the selling of Mars bars, which had been labelled as providing an extra 10 per cent free of charge. The CoJ held that the law actually concerned the product presentation, labelling, and packaging, and was thus a physical requirement, which, if upheld, meant that it imposed a dual burden. It was therefore held to be a breach of Article 28 EC (now 34 TFEU). It could, though, be justified, either under Article 36 TFEU or under the *Cassis de Dijon* rule of reason.

See also **Case C-368/95 *Vereinigte Familiapress Zeitungsverlags* v *Bauer Verlag***, which considered the difference between a selling arrangement and a physical requirement. An Austrian law prohibiting the offering of free gifts linked to the sale of goods was the basis for an Austrian publisher's action against a German magazine containing a prize crossword puzzle. The CoJ repeated its position established since *Keck* that certain national rules would not breach Article 28 EC (now 34 TFEU) unless imposing additional requirements. It held that the Austrian rules would constitute a hindrance to free movement if the content of the magazine had to be altered for the Austrian market. However, it could be justified because maintaining the diversity of the press (as coming within the *Cassis de Dijon* rule of reason and not Article 36 TFEU) was the legitimate public interest objective given by the authorities and accepted by the CoJ.

Unfortunately, the next twist in the case law was the recognition that some selling arrangements, although equal burden and not relating to physical characteristics, nevertheless had an effect that disadvantaged imports by hindering market access or which seemed to favour domestic products, in particular those in respect of advertising and sales promotion rules—that is, those that had a differential impact on the imported goods. This is then compounded by a few cases which, on the face of it, concern rules relating to the product, such as packaging, but, on closer examination by the Court, are really selling arrangements and thus to be considered as falling outside of Article 34 TFEU; hence the search for a new test to be able to classify these developments and to provide some form of predictability for the future, which is the subject of section 11.5.2.

11.5.2 **Market access or discrimination, or both?**

In the post-*Keck* case law, cases have been considered in which it was argued that Article 28 EC (now 34 TFEU) has been breached because market access had been hindered in some way or that a selling arrangement, which although equal burden, was nevertheless discriminatory in some way, or had a differential impact.

Case C-412/93 *Leclerc Siplec* concerned certain goods that could not be advertised on television, but only in the press—and in particular the local press—in order to maintain a certain level of advertising revenue for local papers and thus ensure the survival of local and independent press. Advocate-General (AG) Jacobs argued that the test should be to consider whether there was an impediment to market access and that Article 28 EC (now 34 TFEU) should catch measures that directly and substantially impede access to the market.

This was seen previously in relation to the free movement of persons in **Case C-415/93 *Union Royale Belge des Sociétés de Football Association* v *Bosman***, in which it was held that non-discriminatory rules that prevented transfers of football players and prevented market access should be outlawed.

This was taken up by the CoJ in **Cases C-34–36/95 *Konsumenten-ombudsmannen* v *De Agostini***, in which television advertising directed at children under the age of 12 was prohibited. The measure was considered to be a selling arrangement, which applied without discrimination, and thus was an equal burden. However, it was held that this would seem to have a greater impact on products from other member states because of the difficulties faced in trying to get access to the market, advertising being the only effective form of promotion. If the national court were to find that the impact of the prohibition resulted in different treatment or impact on imported goods, it would therefore breach Article 28 EC (now 34 TFEU) unless justified by Article 30 EC (now 36 TFEU) or the mandatory requirements under *Cassis*.

In a subsequent case, **Case C-405/98 *Gourmet International***, a ban on alcohol advertising was challenged under the same argument that it had a greater impact on imported products trying to gain access to the Swedish market. Without advertising, consumers would be familiar only with domestic products. Thus, it was held that the measure would be caught by Article 28 EC (now 34 TFEU) if it were to prevent access to the market by products from another state, or to impede access more than domestic products.

This could be justified under health grounds but those must be proportionate and, if health were the overriding concern, would labelling or even a total product ban better serve that concern?

Case C-416/00 *Morellato* involved packaging and the requirement that partly baked bread (known as 'bake-off' bread) be packaged by the retailer completing the baking. Thus, it appeared to be the same as the *Mars* case and concerned with product alteration, but it was held to be a selling arrangement because the rule applied only at the final stage of marketing, not physically altering the product prior to distribution.

In **Case C-254/98 *Heimdienst***, a non-discriminatory Austrian law that applied to all operators trading in the national territory (Austrian and other EU operators) required goods sold on the doorstep to come from locally established premises. It was held to be a selling arrangement, but one that impeded access to the market of the member state of importation for products from other member states more than it impeded access for domestic products. The judgment fits in with the proviso at [16] of the *Keck* judgment because, although non-discriminatory and a selling arrangement, it is the differential manner in which it affects domestic and other member state products that matters; hence, the treatment of goods is not equal in fact.

Thus, selling arrangements that either in law or in fact discriminate against non-national providers and impede or hinder market access will not escape Article 34 TFEU, but might still be justified under either Article 36 TFEU or the rule in *Cassis de Dijon*.

> A further 'bake-off' bread case, **Cases C-158 and 159/04 *Alfa Vita Vassilopoulos***, concerned the planning requirements to have a full baker's licence and all of the practical needs of a full bakery in order to sell 'bake-off' bread, which is merely thawed and reheated at the sales outlet after otherwise full preparation elsewhere, including transportation whilst frozen from other member states. The requirement, which resembled a selling arrangement in terms of who is permitted to sell a product, according to the CoJ affected part of the production of a product and was therefore, on the face of it, in breach of Article 28 EC (now 34 TFEU). It made marketing more difficult and costly, and thus was a barrier to imports.

Thus, cases involving situations that, although initially classified as certain selling arrangements, have a different burden on imported goods, albeit that some domestic goods might also be affected, breach Article 34 TFEU and, to be saved, must be justified. The differential treatment in the *Alfa Vita* case was not justified under public health grounds.

The test, as so far developed, looks at the differential manner in which a national rule affects domestic and other member state's products. Rules affecting selling arrangements that either in law or in fact discriminate against non-national providers and thus impede or hinder market access will not escape Article 34 TFEU. They may, however, still be justified under either Article 36 TFEU or the rule in *Cassis de Dijon*. This test of differential impact—that is, affecting imports more than domestic products—focuses both on market access and the fact that the effective result is discriminatory. For example, in Case C-28/09 *Commission v Austria*, in order to tackle pollution a prohibition on the use of a section of the Inn motorway in the Tirol by lorries over 7.5 tons, which applied to both the transport of national and imported goods, was held to be an MHEE because of its impact on long-distance, freight-carrying goods across Europe. It hindered access to markets. The argument that it was justified for the protection of human health and the environment, which on the face of it certainly appeared plausible, was not accepted by the CoJ because the measure itself was disproportionate. The retort for Austria was that other less disruptive measures to tackle the pollution had not been considered.

11.5.3 **Product use or residual rules cases**

Finally, or finally thus far in the post-*Keck* case law, are cases of a further development dealing with so-called 'residual rules', which concern the use of products. These have added yet another gloss on the free movement rules.

> In **Case C-265/06 *Commission v Portugal*** the fixing of tinted film on vehicle windows was banned in Portugal. It applied to both imports and domestic products, so was indistinctly applicable. The CoJ considered the market access approach as well as returning to the *Dassonville* formula, and found that the impact of the ban on potential purchasers would probably reduce imports. The products would have a smaller and less attractive market. The ban was therefore considered to be an MHEE and thus in breach of Article 34, but the argument that it could be justified on the grounds of crime prevention and road safety was not accepted by the Court.

Market access was also the favoured approach in **Case C-110/05 *Commission v Italy (Trailers)***, in which a ban on mopeds towing trailers was held to have a significant impact on the marketing and thus import of trailers and was therefore in breach of Article 34 TFEU. However, in this case the road safety argument could justify the measure especially as there were no EU common rules on this activity.

Case C-142/05 *Aklagaren v Mickelsson and Roos* concerned the Swedish ban on the use of jet-skis, which was not considered to be a selling arrangement because it concerned how a product was to be used. It was held to be an MHEE but justified on the grounds of the protection of health, life, and the environment. However, as the ban was a general one and not confined to waterways where jet-ski use constituted a threat to humans, it was held to be disproportionate.

These residual rules cases thus far appear to be with the market access group of cases and not selling arrangements. The Court did, though, categorise types of MHEEs in the *Italian Trailers* case as follows:

- rules whose object or effect is to treat imports less favourably and are distinctly applicable measures;
- indistinctly applicable product requirements rules; and
- any other measures which hinder access to the market via a differential (discriminatory) impact or residual rules not being classified as selling arrangements but which nevertheless impact on market access without discrimination.

It is because of the complexity of the types of rules and regulations that are applied to goods in the member states that finding one or more catch-all tests to tackle all of the rules employed by the member states has proved to be extremely difficult, to say the least. *Dassonville* and *Cassis de Dijon* went too far and *Keck* was not distinguishing enough. Hence, there developed the market access test and differential impact, but these did not cover situations where there was no discrimination. As such, there was a need to tackle these residual rules via a closer return to the *Dassonville* formula.

This area of law is still in need of clarification and, if possible, simplification.

Summary

Non-tariff barriers have proved to be more difficult to eradicate than the tariff barriers considered in Chapter 10 because of the huge variety of national rules that can apply and the fact that not all national rules regulating trade law should be considered as coming within Article 34 TFEU. Hence, the difficulty has been determining where to draw the line and deciding which rules offend Article 34 TFEU and which do not. We start with a perfectly sound rule (Article 34 TFEU), which seeks to ensure that there are no restrictions on the free movement of goods (see Figure 11.1). To this, we add a further statutory rule (Article 36 TFEU), which provides exceptions to the first rule because it is recognised that

Figure 11.1 Summary of scope of and exceptions to Article 34 TFEU

Article 34 TFEU prohibits the restriction of imports and all measures having equivalent effect.
A national rule which offends this Article may be justified if distinctly applicable under:

Article 36 TFEU derogations
OR, if indistinctly applicable also by:
the rule of reason from *Cassis de Dijon*.
But both of these are subject to:

the second sentence of Article 36 TFEU and the principle of proportionality, unless:

the rule is shown to be a selling arrangement under *Keck* and subsequent cases, in which case it does not offend Article 34 TFEU.
However:

if a selling arrangement adversely affects imports more than domestic products or prevents market access, it will offend Article 34 TFEU, unless:

it is justified by either:
Article 36 TFEU
Or
the rule of reason from *Cassis de Dijon*,

unless: it is a non-discriminatory 'residual rule', which will breach Article 34 TFEU under the *Dassonville* formula, unless justified by Article 36 TFEU or the rule of reason from *Cassis de Dijon*.

there are genuine circumstances in which restrictions and different treatment are justified. So far, so good . . . .

Then there are statutory guidelines (Directive 70/50) and case law, which help to determine how the rule applies and the circumstances that breach the rule or come within the exceptions. Additionally, there is a focus on the concepts of distinctly applicable measures, which can only be justified by Article 36 TFEU, which is easy to see, and indistinctly applicable measures. The indistinctly applicable measures may also come within and thus breach Article 34 TFEU, unless justified by Article 36 TFEU or a further set of justifications introduced by *Cassis* and subsequent cases (the mandatory requirements). Thus, certain national rules or laws could escape the prohibition of Article 34 TFEU because they meet either one of the

Article 36 TFEU derogations or the mandatory requirements of *Cassis de Dijon*. However, strict criteria were laid down so that member states would not be able to exploit this new possibility (the second sentence requirement of Article 36 TFEU and proportionality), which apply to both the Article 36 TFEU derogations and any national rule claimed to come with the *Cassis de Dijon* rules of reason.

> It is worth stressing again that Article 36 TFEU applies to both direct and indirect discrimination, but has an exhaustive list of exceptions, whereas *Cassis de Dijon* applies to indirect discrimination only, but has potentially a much wider range of exceptions.

Then, because it started to happen that all sorts of national rules that applied to goods might be considered to come within the ambit of the *Cassis de Dijon* case, there is another important case (*Keck*). This seeks to lay down another rule or gloss on the original rules to say that certain types of law applicable to the marketing of goods (selling arrangements) should not even be considered as coming within the original rule (that is, if you can remember it . . . Article 34 TFEU!), and there is further case law now to provide further clarifications of what was meant in *Keck*. Indistinctly applicable selling arrangements are thus presumed to be outside of Article 34 unless they introduce discrimination or prevent market access by adversely affecting imports more than domestic products (see *Heimdienst* or *Alfa Vita*), but these can be justified by Article 36 TFEU or *Cassis* (see *Familiapress*). On top of all of those now are a set of rules, known as 'residual rules', which have somehow escaped classification previously and which relate to the use of products. These rules are indistinctly applicable, are not product requirements or selling arrangements, but do appear to hinder access to markets, although not in a discriminatory way. They nevertheless, potentially if not actually, hinder imports. They will therefore breach Article 34 TFEU unless justified either by Article 36 TFEU or the rule of reason from *Cassis de Dijon*.

> It is to be noted that the 2007 Lisbon Treaty made no significant changes to this area of law.

With all this complexity, it may actually be helpful, when the occasion arises, for the member states to make statutory changes to try to regulate these continuing developments. Whether or not they do, the CoJ is sure to be involved further.

? | Questions

For suggested approaches to answering these questions visit the online resources.

1. What is a measure having equivalent effect (MHEE)? (If stuck, see Article 34 TFEU.)

2. What was the very wide definition of an MHEE in the *Dassonville* case?

3. What are distinctly applicable and indistinctly applicable measures?

4. In what circumstances can a member state lawfully restrict or prohibit the free movement of goods from another member state?

5. What are selling or marketing arrangements?

6. Distinguish between equal burden and dual burden measures.

Sample exam Q&A

Essay question

How, why, and with what success did the Court of Justice 'clarify' the scope of application of Article 34 TFEU in Cases 267 and 8/91 *Keck and Mithouard* and subsequent cases?

 For guidance on how to tackle this specimen exam question and to read a suggested model answer, visit the online resources. www.oup.com/uk/foster_directions6e/.

 Further reading

Books

Barnard, C. *The Substantive Law of the EU: The Four Freedoms*, 5th edn, Oxford University Press, Oxford, 2016 (Chapters 5–8).

Foster, N. *Blackstone's EU Treaties and Legislation*, Oxford University Press, Oxford, published annually.

Gormley, L. W. *EU Law of Free Movement of Goods and Customs Union*, Oxford University Press, Oxford, 2009.

Oliver, P. *Oliver on Free Movement of Goods in the European Union*, 5th edn, Hart Publishing, Oxford, 2010.

Articles

Connor, T. 'Accentuating the positive: the "selling arrangement", the first decade, and beyond' (2005) 54 ICLQ 127.

Davies, G. 'Can selling arrangements be harmonised?' (2005) 30 EL Rev 371.

Gormley, L., 'Inconsistencies and misconceptions in the free movement of goods' (2015) 40 ELR 925.

Hojnik, J. 'Free movement of goods in a labyrinth: can *Buy Irish* survive the crises?' (2012) 49 CML Rev 291.

Jansson, M. and Kalimo, H. '*De minimis* meets "market access": transformation in the substance and the syntax of EU free movement law?' (2014) 51 CML Rev 523.

Möstl, M. 'Preconditions and limits of mutual recognition' (2010) 47 CML Rev 405.

Oliver, P. 'Of trailers and jet skis: is the case law of Article 34 hurtling in a new direction? (2011) 33 *Fordham International Law Journal* 1470.

Oliver, P. and Enchelmaier, S. 'Free movement of goods: recent developments in the case law' (2007) 44 CMLR 649.

Snell, J. 'The notion of market access: a concept or slogan?' (2010) 47 CML Rev 437.

Wenneras, P. and Boe Moen, K. 'Selling arrangements, keeping *Keck*' (2010) 35 EL Rev 387.

Wilsher, D. 'Does *Keck* discrimination make any sense? An assessment of the non-discrimination principle within the European Single Market' (2008) 33 EL Rev 3.

12 Free movement of persons

LEARNING OBJECTIVES

In this chapter, you will:

- learn about the history and development of the free movement rights of workers, the self-employed, and the non-economically active EU residents;

- explore the concept of who may be considered an EU worker;

- learn how the rights were extensively developed for both economically active workers and members of the family;

- consider the rights of free movement of the self-employed;

- be made aware of the derogations allowed the member states;

- consider the exception for employment in the public service;

- appreciate the extension of free movement rights to general rights of free movement;

- be instructed on European citizenship and the rights provided as a result of European citizenship;

- understand the concept and meaning of the 'wholly internal' rule; and

- appreciate the rights enjoyed by independent third-country nationals.

Introduction

For more details on this section visit the online resources.

Before European citizenship was introduced as a European Union (EU) law concept and became an important source of rights itself, EU law was concerned originally with the free movement of economically active persons only, providing the direct freedom of movement for workers and self-employed persons—the latter establishing themselves or providing services in a host member state. Free movement of persons is now a much wider concept and includes the rights provided by European citizenship (considered in section 12.7.3 below). The Court of Justice of the European Union (CoJ) had, though, already expanded the range of persons who could take advantage of the Treaty provisions, and additionally, secondary EU legislation has provided rights for non-economically active members of a worker's family.

In this chapter, the free movement of workers, establishment, services, and citizenship will be dealt with together. The reasons for this are that, increasingly, case law—and in particular the new case law—applies without distinction across all of these categories, and later secondary legislation, including Directive 2004/38 and the Services Directive (2006/123), has brought much of the secondary legislation in line for all three. It therefore seems of less merit to try to maintain an increasingly irrelevant distinction. Note, though, that because the extensive law on the self-employed goes very much beyond the treatment given in many undergraduate EU law courses, it will be considered only in brief.

In contrast to previous editions, as noted, this chapter also includes citizenship, the treatment of third-country nationals (designated TCNs in the literature) and national rules which are deemed to be wholly internal and thus not subject to EU free movement rights.

CROSS REFERENCE

Directive 2006/123 is considered at section 12.4.2.1.

As ever, in considering a legal regime, the basics for each of these categories must be considered. These are now the Treaty on European Union (TEU) and the Treaty on the Functioning of the European Union (TFEU) provisions, followed by any pertinent secondary legislation and the extensive case law of the CoJ. A particular feature of this area of law are the rights that apply to the family members of EU citizens. Integrated into many of these aspects are the provisions of Directive 2004/38, which has both consolidated the previous secondary legislation and case law and introduced amended and new rules relating to those taking advantage of free movement rights.

The original Treaty Articles on free movement of persons have altered little since 1957, but their scope and our understanding of them have developed considerably since then. It is not only the original personal scope of the legislation that has been expanded by both additional statutory law and judicial interpretation, but also the consequences for the Union and national legal regimes, which are much greater than those that may have been anticipated by the member states. Free movement of persons is now a much wider concept, and has become inextricably linked with the concept of European citizenship and other wider issues of free movement, including TCNs. Therefore, in view of this substantial expansion of the law of the free movement of persons, the second part of this chapter considers those persons who are able to move and reside in other member states under the general rights of movement provided by the Treaty and secondary legislation—notably now through the citizen provisions in Articles 20 and 21 TFEU.

However, before looking at any of these particular provisions, it is useful to try to discover the original reasons and intentions behind the Treaty provision for the free movement of persons. Was the right of free movement, as originally conceived, provided in order to complete the freedom of the factors of production, along with the goods and capital for economic or capitalist development? In other words, without providing for the free movement of persons, the development of economic activities, the balanced expansion, and the accelerated raising of the standard of living referred to originally in the Preamble to the EC Treaty would not be possible. Capital (that is, employers operating productive facilities) needed to take advantage of freely movable labour without border restrictions—hence the argument that the rights were provided merely or deliberately to help to create the Common Market in the same way as for the free movement of goods. By ensuring the free movement of workers across the member countries of the Common Market, capital can easily import labour when required, which in turn ensures that economic conditions in all member states of the market are broadly similar and thus that competition is not distorted by labour shortages and higher labour costs in some parts of the market. The free movement of persons was originally contained in the economic part of the EC Treaty concerned with free movement. This provided a basic definition of the internal market,

CROSS REFERENCE

The definition of 'worker' is considered in section 12.2.2.

which is now outlined in Article 26 TFEU, and it was not originally located as part of the social policy section of the Treaty. Whilst the rights were originally restricted to those engaged in an economic activity in another member state and as a form of support for the Common Market and economic progress in the Community, as developed they have undoubtedly become a clear part of the social policy of the EU. In support of the view that social concerns now dominate, the CoJ has adopted a very liberal approach to the interpretation of the free movement of workers provisions—both the Treaty principles and the further extensions of these principles in the secondary legislation, such as the widely construed concept of 'worker'. In contrast, the exceptions to the rights granted to the member states are interpreted strictly: see, for example, the case law on Article 45(4) TFEU (ex 39(4) EC)—the public service proviso—considered at section 12.5.2.

12.1 The legal framework: primary and secondary legislation

12.1.1 Treaty provisions

Article 3(2) TEU provides as follows.

> **Article 3(2) TEU**
>
> The Union shall offer its citizens an area of freedom, security and justice without internal frontiers in which the free movement of persons is ensured . . .

Article 20(2) TFEU, which is concerned with citizenship, has been the most important more recent development in free movement rights since the original treaty provision for workers and the self-employed. Its interpretation by the CoJ means that many cases which might previously have been considered under workers only, may be and are instead considered under citizen rights. It is considered further in section 12.7.

> **Article 20(2) TFEU**
>
> Citizens of the Union . . . shall have, inter alia:
>
> (a) the right to move and reside freely within the territory of the Member States,
>
> . . .

Article 26 TFEU provides, in paragraph 2, as follows.

> **Article 26 TFEU, paragraph 2**
>
> The internal market shall comprise an area without internal frontiers in which the free movement of goods, persons, services and capital is ensured in accordance with the provisions of the Treaties.

The following Treaty Articles outline the basic requirements to facilitate the free movement of the economically active: Articles 45–48 TFEU for workers; Articles 49–55 TFEU for those wishing to establish; and Articles 56–62 TFEU for those wishing to provide services.

For workers, Article 45(1) and (2) TFEU provides as follows.

Article 45 TFEU

1. Freedom of movement for workers shall be secured within the Union.

2. Such freedom of movement shall entail the abolition of any discrimination based on nationality between workers of the Member States as regards employment, remuneration and other conditions of work and employment.

. . .

Article 39 EC (now 45 TFEU) was held to be vertically directly effective in **Case 41/74 Van Duyn v Home Office** and, later, horizontal direct effects were implied in **Case 36/74 Walrave and Koch**, which was concerned with a private body, but one established under public law. They were definitively established in **Case C-281/98 Angonese v Cassa di Risparmio di Bolzano SpA**, which involved an action by an individual against a bank.

Article 45(3) TFEU provides the basic rights for workers, but subjects those rights to the limitations on grounds of public policy, public security, or public health, amplified in Directive 2004/38. The Directive is considered in section 12.3 and throughout the chapter. The rights as listed are as follows.

Article 45(3) TFEU

. . .

(a) to accept offers of employment actually made;

(b) to move freely within the territory of member states for this purpose;

(c) to stay in the member state for the purpose of employment in accordance with the provisions governing the employment of nationals of that state laid down by law, regulation or administrative action; and

(d) to remain in the territory of a member state after having been employed in that state.

Article 45(4) TFEU provides as follows.

Article 45(4) TFEU

The provisions of this Article shall not apply to employment in the public service.

For establishment, Article 49 TFEU provides as follows.

Article 49 TFEU

Freedom of establishment shall include the right to take up and pursue activities as self-employed persons and to set up and manage undertakings, in particular companies or firms.

▶ CROSS REFERENCE

Article 49 TFEU is considered in section 12.4.

Finally, for the provision of services, Article 56 TFEU provides as follows.

> **Article 56 TFEU**
>
> Restrictions on freedom to provide services within the Union shall be prohibited in respect of nationals of Member States who are established in a Member State other than that of the person for whom the services are intended.

12.1.2 Secondary legislation

For more details on this section visit the online resources.

With regard to secondary legislation, Directive 2004/38 and the new consolidating Regulation 492/2011, which has repealed and replaced Regulation 1612/68, comprehensively cater for the rights of workers and their families in the EU. Recently, Directive 2014/54 [2014] Official Journal (OJ) L128/8 has been enacted to support and facilitate the rights provided by Article 45 TFEU and Regulation 492/2011.

12.1.3 The basic right of non-discrimination

The most basic or fundamental right in free movement is that there shall be no discrimination on the grounds of nationality. Article 18 TFEU, which prohibits discrimination on the grounds of nationality, has been highly influential in the development of this area. It has been employed by the CoJ to outlaw various discriminatory rules and practices by member states and organisations that were not a clear and direct breach of the provisions on workers, establishment, or services, but which nevertheless discriminated against non-nationals. It has been applied, inter alia, for workers in Case 59/85 *Netherlands* v *Reed*, for services in Case 2/74 *Reyners* v *Belgium*, and for establishment in Case 246/89 *Commission* v *UK (Nationality of Fishermen)*.

12.1.3.1 Indirect discrimination

The CoJ has often stressed that the concept of discrimination not only covers direct discrimination in which different rules apply to nationals and non-nationals, but also covert or indirect discrimination that leads to the prejudicial treatment of non-nationals—rules that seem to apply fairly to both, but which have an indirect discriminatory effect on non-nationals. The measure may, however, be objectively justified on other grounds. Furthermore, the prohibition of national rules has also been expanded to catch rules that hinder market access.

> Indirect discrimination was demonstrated in **Case 33/88 Alluè and Coonan v University of Venice**. The applicants, after five years of employment as foreign language lecturers, were informed that they could not be retained under a 1980 Italian decree that limited the duration of employment of foreign language lecturers. Not all of the foreign language lecturers were non-national: some 25 per cent were nationals; therefore, there was no dissimilar treatment—that is, no overt discrimination. Although the rule applied regardless of the nationality, it nevertheless mainly affected the nationals of other member states who made up 75 per cent of such language teachers. It was held by the CoJ to be discriminatory where such limitations did not exist in respect of other workers.

⟫CROSS REFERENCE

For a more detailed discussion of objective justification, see Chapter 11, section 11.4.1 on the free movement of goods and see section 12.3.2.1, where the *Schumacker* case is also considered.

The rules may also be objectively justified if there is a legitimate aim compatible with the Treaty, if the measure is justified by pressing reasons of public interest, and if the measure is proportionate. See, for example, Case C-279/93 Schumacker, in which the CoJ held that there could be objective justifications in indirect discrimination in tax regimes where the EU worker was not resident in the host country.

There are now statutory definitions of **indirect discrimination** in EU secondary legislation dealing with other forms of discrimination. See Directive 2000/43, 2000/78, or 2006/54, all Article 2, for similar definitions to the following.

indirect discrimination Arises if an apparently neutral provision, criterion, or practice would put persons of one sex, age, or nationality, etc. at a particular disadvantage compared with persons of the other sex, etc., unless that provision, criterion, or practice is objectively justified by a legitimate aim, and the means of achieving that aim are appropriate and necessary.

12.1.3.2 Hindering free movement or market access

In the same way, as will be seen for services and establishment, and indeed also in relation to goods considered in Chapter 11, there has been an attack on national rules that, although applying without discrimination to both home professionals and those establishing in the host country, are regarded as inappropriate because they are seen to hinder access in taking up opportunities and thus restrict movement.

> **CROSS REFERENCE**

Services and establishment are considered in sections 12.2.3 and 12.4, respectively, and goods in Chapter 11, section 11.5.2.

Case 415/93 *Bosman* concerns football transfer fee rules that restricted transfers, but which applied to both national and cross-border transfers; hence there was no discrimination and nationality was not a factor. The CoJ held that they were nevertheless an obstacle to movement.

The *Bosman* ruling has been applied in a number of cases since, but to give just one example in **Case C-438/00 *Kolpak v Deutscher Handballbund*** it was applied to a similarly restrictive German handball rule that limited the number of foreign players to two in each squad. The rule was held to be contrary to free movement by the CoJ and not justified on sporting grounds. It clearly limited the chances of non-Germans to enter the market.

Thus, for persons, the prohibition of harmful rules goes beyond discrimination to cover rules that impede market access.

12.2 Who may claim the rights of free movement?

This section determines who may benefit from the rules provided. The personal and material scope of the rights must be determined. In terms of the personal scope, two basic definitions have to be established: first, nationality; and, secondly, whether the person concerned is a worker or self-employed by establishing or providing services, or is otherwise entitled to enter and remain in the member state. The material scope of the rights has been determined largely by secondary legislation and concerns the actual rights provided, considered in section 12.3.

For more details on this section visit the online resources.

12.2.1 **Nationality**

For workers and the self-employed, the right to move freely and obtain other benefits, especially those rights that can be taken up by members of the worker's family, is initially dependent on them being defined as a national of one of the member states. Article 45 TFEU secures freedom for workers of the member states. 'Establishment' under Article 49 TFEU and 'services' under Article 56 TFEU refer to the right of nationals of the member states either to establish or provide services in the host member states. Establishment also includes legal persons predominantly in the form of companies, thus companies registered in one of the member states are also included within the personal scope of the rights.

The actual determination of member state nationality is a matter for each of the member states, as was expressly stated in Declaration No. 2 on nationality, which was attached to the original TEU before its removal by the Lisbon Treaty. It provided that nationality of a member state was to be settled solely by reference to the national law of the member state concerned.

> This was confirmed in **Case C-369/90 *Micheletti*** and the position was upheld in **Case C-192/99 *Manjit Kaur***, involving the attempt by a Kenyan national to obtain full British residence status rather than the limited British overseas citizen status. The CoJ confirmed that it is for each member state to lay down the conditions for the acquisition and loss of nationality.

> This was further confirmed in **Case C-135/05 *Rottmann***, in which Rottmann lost German citizenship and faced becoming stateless. His claim not to lose EU citizenship was not upheld as the CoJ had held that it was still up to the member states themselves to decide matters of nationality and statehood. That he would lose his once-entitled right as an EU citizen as a consequence was something the member state concerned had to be sure was proportionate.

It is not, however, necessary for the members of a worker's family to be member state nationals to obtain benefits, as will be seen in the secondary legislation and case law considered later in section 12.3.2.2.

12.2.2 **Union status as a worker or self-employed**

The second part of the personal scope of the law is that in order for a person to benefit personally or for his or her family to benefit from rights arising under Articles 45–62 TFEU and laws made hereunder, the person needs to be classified as a worker or self-employed person, or who enjoys another status recognised by the CoJ as coming within the concept. The definition of these concepts, as indicated in the heading, is a matter for EU law and not for each of the national legal systems to determine. For example, the persons who may rely on free movement rights under Article 45 TFEU also include an employing company (Case C-350/96 *Clean Car Autoservice*) and a recruitment agency (Case C-208/05 *ITC*). Turning first to the term 'worker', there is no definition of the term in the Treaties, but the CoJ has held from its early days that the term must have an EU meaning and cannot be the subject of differing interpretations by the courts of the member states.

> In **Case 75/63 *Hoekstra v BBDA***, the CoJ declared the reason for this view:
>
> > If the definition of this term were a matter for the competence of the national courts, it would be possible for every member state to modify the term worker and so to eliminate at will the protection afforded by the EEC Treaty to certain categories of person.
>
> In the case itself, the CoJ gave this limited definition: 'A worker is any employed person, irrespective of whether he is wage-earning or salaried, blue collar or white collar, an executive or unskilled labourer.'

THINKING POINT

Who do you think is a worker for the purposes of EU free movement of workers' law?

The CoJ has, in subsequent cases, gone on to develop the definition to include part-time workers, those seeking work under certain circumstances, those undertaking a period or course of study, and those who were effectively self-employed, but nevertheless included by the Court.

12.2.2.1 **Part-time work**

Case 53/81 *Levin* v *Minister of Justice* concerned the value of work that a person needs to do before he or she can be classed as a worker. The woman plaintiff was a British citizen working in the Netherlands as a chambermaid for 20 hours a week and whose earnings were below the subsistence level in the Netherlands. The Dutch government argued that because she was a part-time worker earning below the government-set subsistence level, she was not a 'favoured EEC citizen' and could not benefit from the provisions of EEC law guaranteeing freedom of movement of workers. The CoJ held that these considerations were irrelevant to her status as a worker, and declared that, whether she was a full-time or part-time worker, she was entitled to the status of worker provided that the work was genuine and effective, and not so infinitesimal as to be disregarded. The CoJ ruled that work would only be disregarded if it were so minimal that it did not constitute economic activity at all. The essential defining characteristic of work is that it is activity of an economic nature.

In **Case 139/85 *Kempf* v *Minister of Justice***, a German national worked as a part-time flute teacher for only 12 lessons a week. His limited income was topped up to the Dutch minimum income level with supplementary benefit under the Unemployment Benefit Act. He too was re-fused a residence permit on the grounds that he was not a 'favoured EEC citizen'. The CoJ ruled that if a person is in effective and genuine part-time employment, then he or she may not be ex-cluded from the sphere of application of the rules on freedom of movement of workers merely because the remuneration he or she derives from it is below the minimum level of subsistence set by national law. The Dutch court had found that the work was genuine and effective.

In this regard, it is irrelevant whether the supplementary means of subsistence are derived from property, from the income of another member of the family (as in *Levin*), or from public funds of the member state of residence (as in *Kempf*).

Although not expressly stated to be the situation, Case C-313/02 *Wippel* v *Peek & Cloppenburg* dealt with the common phenomenon of 'zero hours' contracts where no fixed hours are arranged and employees work only when asked to do so by the employer. The case itself concerned an equal treatment claim, and is considered in Chapter 14, but it also considered Directive 97/81 on part-time workers, hence the conclusion that even if it was not already obvious, 'zero hours' employees are considered to be workers under EU law.

The CoJ held in **Case C-357/89 *Raulin* v *Netherlands Ministry of Education and Science*** that, in considering whether work is genuine and effective, the national court should take account of all of the occupational activities of the person only in the host state and the duration of those activities. The case concerned a French national who worked for 60 hours in total as a waitress in the Netherlands, but who, whilst doing so, was granted the status of worker.

In deciding that the national courts make the final decision on the status of the person concerned according to the facts, this appears to present the member states with the discretion to define who is a worker, although the national courts are obliged to follow EU law in this respect and in particular the criteria as developed by the CoJ in its case law.

See the similar case of **Case C-413/01 *Ninni-Orasche***, which involved a person who was engaged in only two-and-a-half months' work in three years, but who would nevertheless qualify according to the CoJ to be classified as a worker, but who would not necessarily be able to take advantages of long-term rights as an EU worker. Again, however, it was up to the national authorities ultimately to decide.

In **Case 66/85 *Lawrie-Blum v Land Baden-Württemburg***, the CoJ considered the compatibility of German rules restricting access to a preparatory service stage that was necessary to become a teacher. It laid down three essential characteristics to establish an employment relationship: the provision of some sort of service, for and under the direction of another person (that is, not self-employed), and in return for remuneration.

The above ruling was applied in **Case 196/87 *Steymann v Staatssecretaris van Justitie***, whereby work in Bagwhan religious community's commercial activities, for which remuneration was paid in the form of pocket money and the meeting of material needs, was considered sufficient to be classified as a Community worker.

Some limits to the definition appear to have been found in **Case 344/87 *Bettray v Staatssecretaris van Justitie***. The CoJ held that a national of a member state employed in another member state under a social employment scheme involving therapeutic work as part of drug rehabilitation merely as a means of re-training or reintegration could not be regarded as a worker for the purposes of Community law. The activities could not be carried out as real and genuine economic activities.

Here, the position was artificially created with government money and not therefore genuine. Although carried out under supervision and remunerated, the CoJ (in contrast to its position in *Levin*) looked at the purpose of the scheme and found that Bettray was not a worker.

However, this decision may no longer hold good in view of the next decision.

In **Case C-456/02 *Trojani***, Trojani had secured accommodation in a Salvation Army hostel, where, in return for board and lodging and some pocket money, he undertook various jobs for about 30 hours a week as part of a personal socio-occupational reintegration programme.

He applied for social assistance, which was refused. The CoJ held that he had a direct right of residence under Article 18 EC (now 21 TFEU), and where such EU citizens are in possession of a residence permit, they are thus entitled, according to Article 12 EC, to social assistance on the same basis as nationals. Whilst no real decision was taken on his actual status, which was left to the national court to decide, the Court advised that the national court should have regard to factors such as whether the services performed could be regarded as a part of the normal labour market.

This case straddles both the previous *Steymann* and *Bettray* cases in terms of fact, but is one of those cases that has been caught up by the developments in European citizenship. As a result, it can be argued that the definition of worker is of lesser importance now in that if the person involved is nevertheless entitled to receive the rights or benefits claimed, his or her status becomes irrelevant, as we will see in the citizenship section at 12.7 below.

For details on another development in workers' rights relating to Frontier Workers visit the online resources.

The term 'worker' is, however, wider than only referring to those in employment and, in certain circumstances, also applies to those who are seeking work and to those who, having lost one job involuntarily, are capable of taking another.

12.2.2.2 Those seeking work

In **Case 75/63 *Hoekstra* v *BBDA***, it was established, and confirmed in the later **Case C-43/99 *Leclere and Deaconescu***, that certain rights were retained by a former worker who was in employment in the host state, but who lost his or her job, notably the right to retain the status of worker for a certain period of time and benefits derived therefrom.

⟩ CROSS REFERENCE

The Leclere case is considered in section 12.3.2.1.

Two cases follow that have considered these matters.

In **Case 316/85 *Marie-Christine Lebon***, the CoJ held that those in search of work are not entitled to receive workers' benefits (in this case, a social security support payment). Miss Lebon no longer lived with her parents, who were ex-workers; therefore, she did not qualify for benefits as a dependant of a worker. She then asked if she qualified for workers' benefits if she was looking or intended to look for work. The CoJ held that the benefits provided by legislation on free movement were only for those in actual employment and not for those who migrate in search of work and cannot find it. She could temporarily be classified as a worker, but not for the purposes of benefits.

Case C-292/89 *Antonissen* clarifies how long the temporary status entitles a person to remain to look for work. The UK wished to deport Antonissen, who had been convicted of possession and intent to supply cocaine, and asked the CoJ whether it could do so. UK legislation gave EC citizens six months in which to find employment. Antonissen was in the country for over three years without work before his imprisonment. The Court held that statements recorded in minutes regarding the acceptable time for the pursuit of work before deportation would not be allowable, have no legal significance, and cannot be used to interpret the relevant legislative provisions. A member state may deport an EC migrant worker subject to an

> appeal if he or she has not found employment after a period of six months. However, the six months' time period is to be taken as a guideline only. Where there is evidence that indicates that he or she is continuing to seek employment and that there are genuine chances of being engaged, the Court suggested that it would probably not be appropriate to deport. It would, however, be up to the national court to decide on the facts.

Therefore, after the expiry of a reasonable period, depending on the circumstances, persons may no longer be afforded the status and benefits of worker under Community law and may lawfully be deported by the member state.

▶ CROSS REFERENCE

Collins is also noted in sections 12.2.2.3 and 12.7.2.2 on citizenship; welfare rights.

> **Case C-138/02 *Collins*** has subsequently confirmed that those seeking work who do not have a sufficiently close connection to the host state may not claim benefits, whereas in **Case C23/08 *Vatsouras and Koupatantze***, the allowance was permitted because they had worked previously as EU citizens in the host state.

Article 7(3) of Directive 2004/38 makes it clear that workers and also the self-employed may retain their status and right to remain in the following circumstances:

(a) he or she is temporarily unable to work as the result of an illness or accident;

(b) he or she is in duly recorded involuntary unemployment after having been employed for more than one year and has registered as a jobseeker with the relevant employment office;

(c) he or she is in duly recorded involuntary unemployment after completing a fixed-term employment contract of less than a year or after having become involuntarily unemployed during the first 12 months and has registered as a jobseeker with the relevant employment office (in which case, the status of worker shall be retained for no less than six months); or

(d) he or she embarks on vocational training (but unless he or she is involuntarily unemployed, the retention of the status of worker shall require the training to be related to the previous employment).

 THINKING POINT

When does a person cease to be a worker for the purposes of EU free movement of persons' law?

Directive 2004/38, Article 14, further provides that residence may be retained provided that the persons concerned do not become an unreasonable burden on the social assistance of the host state. EU citizens not possessing a sufficiently close link to the host state will be ineligible for benefits according to the CoJ in Case C-138/02 *Collins*, which issues will be taken up in section 12.2.2.3.

12.2.2.3 **Worker training, education, and benefits**

A further extension of the scope of the concept of worker took place in favour of those who were employed previously but no longer in employment, but who subsequently became engaged in some form of study. This category was limited, but its boundaries may have been considerably extended by the respect now shown by the CoJ to the concept of citizenship. The new cases are very often crossover cases in that they deal with both a consideration of a specific aspect, such as whether the person is a worker, work seeker, or entitled student, but now wrapped in the context of citizenship, which is considered in section 12.7.

The leading original case is **Case 39/86 *Lair v Universität Hannover***, in which a French national employed in West Germany was refused a grant by the university for a maintenance award and training fees because she had not worked in the country continuously for at least five years. Therefore, whilst at university, she was not a worker and did not retain the status of worker. It was stated in the case that the period at university would lead to a vocational qualification and that the time at university represented a break in employment only. The CoJ held that since there was no fixed legislative definition of worker, there was nothing to say that the definition must always depend on a continuing employment relationship. Certain rights have been guaranteed to workers after employment has finished, for example the right to stay and social security rights. This could also apply to university training provided that there was a link or continuity between the previous work and university, in which case the university support could be considered one of the social rights coming within Regulation 1612/68 (now Regulation 492/2011). The status of worker was therefore retained if a link existed between the previous occupation and the studies in question.

In contrast, in **Case 197/86 *Brown v Secretary of State for Scotland***, the Scottish education department refused Brown a grant for university. He had worked for eight months in the UK prior to and as a precursor to university and gained the status of worker. The CoJ held that, whilst university training is to be regarded as mainly vocational, it is only covered by Article 12 EC (now 18 TFEU) generally outlawing discrimination. This covers tuition fees, but not the maintenance grant; therefore, a person who entered employment for eight months and who did so as a precursor or prerequisite to attending university did not retain the status of worker for the purposes of claiming a grant.

In the light of the citizenship cases considered in section 12.7.2, the *Brown* case may not be decided in the same way today or, at best, be subject to the integration requirements considered in this section.

Returning to **Case C-357/89 *Raulin***, the CoJ held that the 60 hours' work had enabled Raulin to claim the protection of Article 39 EC (now 45 TFEU), despite its very temporary nature. However, a migrant worker who then left that employment to begin a course of full-time study unconnected with the previous occupational activities did not retain the status as a worker, a finding upheld by the Dutch court. Raulin, however, did have a right of residence in the host state for the duration of the course of study, regardless of whether or not the host state had issued a residence permit.

Thus, definitions of what constitutes vocational training and the link to work are crucial for the determination of the status of a worker and the consequent benefits and rights, as is the number of weeks or hours worked. This case law is now essentially confirmed by Directive 2004, Article 7(3)(d), which provides that the status of worker is retained if the EU citizen embarks on vocational training that is related to the previous employment. Access to education services is also considered in section 12.6.1.2.

However, in **Case C-184/99 *Grzelczyk***, a French national who studied and worked on a part-time basis to help to support himself for three years in Belgium applied at the beginning of his fourth and final year of study to the Centre Public d'Aide Sociale [Public Social Welfare Centre] (CPAS) for payment of the minimex, a non-contributory minimum subsistence allowance. The CPAS granted Mr Grzelczyk the minimex, but then later denied this on the basis that he was not Belgian; hence, clear discrimination on the grounds of nationality. This case did not consider whether he enjoyed the status as a worker. The CoJ emphasised that the new citizenship provisions and new competences in education, albeit limited, allowed it to hold that Articles 12 and 17 EC (now 18 and 20 TFEU) preclude discrimination as regards the grant of a non-contributory social benefit to Union citizens where they are lawfully resident.

Note, however, that no status of worker was attributed in this case, nor indeed even a link to previous employment; however, even if a person is confirmed as a jobseeker, social assistance may be denied.

In **Case C-138/02 *Collins***, the CoJ held that, once citizenship had been established, even work seekers could claim certain benefits, in contrast to *Lebon*, but that some benefits could be restricted on objective grounds, such as the habitual residence requirement for a jobseeker's allowance, which depended on the existence of a genuine pre-existing link between the work seeker and the state.

In other words, a person such as Collins, who nevertheless enjoyed EU citizenship, could not just arrive in the UK and demand a jobseeker's allowance alongside nationals. A residence qualification period can be demanded.

A further case now appears not only to confirm *Collins*, but also to roll back slightly the previous generous interpretation of individuals' rights.

Case C-158/07 *Förster v IB-Groep* concerns Ms Förster, a German national in the Netherlands who, from 2000, worked from time to time there and qualified for a study maintenance grant, which was withdrawn when the responsible authority (IB-Groep) discovered in 2003 that she was no longer working. Her challenge to the decision failed because she was not sufficiently integrated in the Netherlands and because she had not satisfied the requirement of five years' residence. On reference to the CoJ, the Court upheld its previous decision in Case C-209/03 *Bidar* that member states were entitled to require a certain degree of integration and, in this case, a five-year period was justified and proportionate. The work–study relationship did not play a role in the Court's decision.

 THINKING POINT

Once you have completed the chapter and in particular the sections on citizenship, consider whether trying to determine if a person might come within the concept of worker, albeit with limited rights, is no longer really relevant or necessary.

Is perhaps now being a EU citizen more important?

See also Article 24(2) of Directive 2004/38, which states: 'By way of derogation from paragraph 1, the host Member State shall not be obliged to confer entitlement to social assistance during the first three months of residence or, where appropriate, the longer period provided for in Article 14(4)(b).' The latter reference refers to where EU citizens are looking for work and have genuine prospects of obtaining it, essentially the statutory rendering of the ruling in *Antonissen*, discussed at section 12.2.2.2. See also the discussion in section 12.7.2.2.

The rights of students to receive educational services and support will increasingly be assumed and, in future, considered under the expanding rights of citizenship, and is addressed in section 12.6.1.2 below.

12.2.2.4 Self-employed or worker?

In **Case C-256/01 *Allonby***, the definition of the term 'worker' was effectively extended to cover self-employed persons. The case concerned the re-employment of former college lecturers in the same establishment, but under a self-employed scheme paid by a private independent company. In considering the new relationship, the CoJ held that the formal classification of a self-employed person under national law does not change the fact that a person must be classified as a worker within the meaning of that article if his independence is merely notional.

This case is thus very important for the rights of the person concerned.

12.2.3 The scope and distinction of establishment and the provision of services

The self-employed are granted rights under the Treaty to move to another member state to establish either permanently or on a long-term basis (Articles 49–55 TFEU) or to provide services temporarily (Articles 56–62 TFEU). The definitions for the personal scope of establishment and for the provision of services are much more straightforward than for workers. The primary Treaty Articles have laid down the basic concepts.

Article 49 TFEU deals with rights of freedom of establishment as the right to enter another member state and stay on a long-term or permanent basis, to take up and pursue activities as a self-employed person, and to set up and manage undertakings. This includes legal, as well as natural, persons. Article 54 TFEU specifically mentions the application to companies.

A basic definition was given in **Case C-221/89 *Factortame*** as 'the actual pursuit of an economic activity through a fixed establishment in another member state for an indefinite period'.

In **Case C-268/99 *Jany***, the CoJ characterised self-employment as a relationship outside a relationship of subordination as would be the case with workers, and in which the remuneration earned was paid directly and in full to the self-employed person.

THINKING POINT

Consider the statement in *Jany* above and decide whether you find it a reasonable characterisation of self-employment before looking at the facts of the case.

'Services' under Article 56 TFEU envisages a temporary state of affairs, and appearance, if at all, in the host state would only be for a limited period to provide specific services. There would be no permanent personal or professional presence in the host state, or a necessity to reside. The concept of services is defined by Article 57(1) TFEU as those 'provided for remuneration, in so far as they are not governed by provisions relating to freedom of movement of goods, capital and persons'. In particular, Article 57 TFEU specifically includes activities of industrial and commercial characters, and those of craftsmen and the professions. The provision of services is potentially a much wider category and can be associated with the areas of banking, finance, insurance, and legal services. Now, with modern technology, telephone, broadcasting, and Internet services will become big services areas, notably without the need to move from the host state to provide services in other member states.

See, for example, **Case C-384/93 *Alpine Investments***, which concerned cross-frontier telephone sales calling; and **Case C-17/00 *de Coster***, which concerned the satellite transmission of television services.

The scope of the term 'services' has been held by the CoJ to include the recipients of services.

Case 186/87 *Cowan*, for example, involved a claim for criminal injury compensation by an EU citizen in France; **Case C-45/93 *Commission v Spain*** involved the right of EU nationals to visit museums without charge on the same basis as nationals; and **Case C-268/99 *Jany and others***. found that services includes prostitution.

Originally, establishment and the provision of services were regarded as, if not absolutely distinguishable, certainly clearly distinct concepts with no overlap. At times, the distinction between services and establishment can be difficult to ascertain.

In **Case 205/84 *Commission v Germany (Insurance Services)***, the provision of insurance included the setting up of offices on a long-term basis and staffing those offices with nationals of the host state. This was considered by the CoJ as establishment, even though the legal entity (owner/principal) remained in the home state.

This ruling is very important as the application of home rules may be stricter for establishment because the Treaty provision appears to be based on achieving complete equality of treatment.

Article 57 TFEU

. . . the person providing a service may, in order to do so, temporarily pursue his activity in the State where the service is provided, under the same conditions as are imposed by that State on its own nationals.

The provision of services under Article 57 TFEU, on the other hand, whilst allowing for the same conditions to be imposed by the host state, has developed on the basis that not all home rules have been found by the CoJ to be suitable or acceptable to those providing services. The distinction therefore between 'establishment' and 'services' is important. The CoJ has now advised that the provision of services may even justify the setting up of an infrastructure in the host state.

In **Case C-55/94** *Gebhard* **v** *Milan Bar Council*, the CoJ characterised 'establishment' as the right of a Community national to participate on a stable and continuous basis in the economic life of a member state other than his or her own, and 'services' by the temporary, precarious, and discontinuous nature of the services. The Court held:

> The temporary nature of the activities in question has to be determined in the light, not only of the duration of the provision of the service, but also of its regularity, periodicity or continuity. The fact that the provision of services is temporary does not mean that the provider of services within the meaning of the Treaty may not equip himself with some form of infrastructure in the host member state (including an office, chambers or consulting rooms) in so far as such infrastructure is necessary for the purposes of performing the services in question.

In this case, the setting up of chambers in Italy by a German lawyer on a long-term basis, although still practising in Stuttgart, Germany, was nevertheless held to be establishment.

The case was then in line with Case 205/84 *Commission* v *Germany*. In Case C-386/04 *Stauffer*, the CoJ stated that establishment required the permanent presence in the host state and that merely renting property from an agent to carry out activities of an Italian organisation in Germany was not establishment. In Case C-215/01 *Schnitzer*, a long-term (three-year) contract for plastering services by a Portuguese company in Germany was held by the CoJ to be exactly that, the provision of services and not establishment, which was argued to be the case by the German Skilled Trades Register. There was no intention to remain beyond the contractual period; hence, the actual classification very much depends on the view taken on the facts of the case.

As with workers, the status of self-employed is retained even if the activity ceases: see Article 7(3) of Directive 2004/38, considered in section 12.2.2.2, and the free movement rights of the self-employed, considered in section 12.4.

12.2.3.1 **The establishment of companies**

Article 49 TFEU specifically refers to the right to 'manage undertakings, in particular companies or firms within the meaning of the second paragraph of Article 54'. Article 54 TFEU, in turn, provides that those coming within the scope of Article 49 TFEU are those formed in accordance with the law of a member state and which have their registered office, central administration, or principal place of business within the Union, which includes companies or firms constituted under civil or commercial law.

Member states of original establishment may, though, impose conditions or restrictions on companies wishing to transfer, move, or split their registered office to another state. In Case C81/87 *Daily Mail*, the newspaper company attempted to move its central management to the Netherlands for tax advantages but nevertheless remain a UK company. However, it was not permitted to exit the UK by the UK Treasury. In a challenge to that decision by the *Daily Mail* under Article 49 TFEU, the CoJ held that the right of establishment was not unconditional and could be restricted lawfully by member states, particularly as company law is not harmonised and is still within the competence of the member states. In a similar case, C-210/06 *Cartesio*, a Hungarian company wanted to move its head office to Italy but continue to operate under Hungarian law.

Hungary refused to sanction this unless it ceased to operate entirely as a Hungarian company, and the CoJ held that this was acceptable under EU law. Whilst falling within this area of law, a general consideration of EU company law falls outside the scope of this book and is therefore not included.

In **Case C-212/97** *Centros Ltd*, two Danish directors registered a company in the UK and requested registration of a branch office in Denmark, which was refused on the grounds that it was an attempt to circumvent the Danish company capital requirements—particularly because there was an intention to trade only in Denmark and not in the UK. Denmark required a much higher minimum paid-up capital than the UK. Upon reference to the CoJ, the Court held that the case came within the scope of Article 43 EC (now 49 TFEU), and that any concerns that creditors would be at risk had already been catered for in national and Community law. Article 43 EC (now 49 TFEU) conveyed the right to set up companies in one member state and trade via a branch in another member state, subject to the regulation in the host state and provided that any such regulation satisfies the following requirements, observed elsewhere in free movement law, that it be: non-discriminatory; justified by imperative requirement in the general interest; and proportionate. The Court held that the complete ban by Denmark did not fulfil those conditions.

In **Case C-208/00** *Überseering*, a Dutch-registered company was transferred to Germany, but was denied legal capacity in Germany by a German court. This was argued to breach the freedom of establishment in Article 43 EC (now 49 TFEU). The CoJ agreed with this view. Both cases have been criticised for allowing companies to be registered in the state with the least restrictive requirements and thus for introducing a lowest common denominator into EU company law, resembling the Delaware clause from the United States (Delaware being the state with the regulation that is most lax). The judgments are, thus, a strong support for the free choice of company registration and free movement.

Case C-167/01 *Inspire Art* did, though, allow for the possibility that the host state could impose restrictions or conditions on an establishing company in order to protect creditors and investors, provided the restrictions or conditions were objectively justified which, in this case, they were not.

Case C-446/03 *M&S*, questioned UK tax rules, which did not allow losses from subsidiaries located in other member states to be deducted, as being an obstruction to free movement. The CoJ agreed, even though M&S, at that time, was merely contemplating setting up branches out of the UK.

Case C-411/03 *SEVIC Systems*, held that German company law rules which only allowed for mergers between companies in Germany breached Article 49 TFEU by not allowing the registration of a Germany company after merger with a company in Luxembourg acquired by the German Company. The CoJ held that such a restriction would be likely to deter the right of freedom of establishment and was not a threat to shareholder protection and other public interests. Companies should remain free to restructure in ways they wish, providing those public interest requirements are met.

12.3 The material rights of free movement

Apart from the basic rights being provided by the main Treaty Articles 45, 49, and 56 TFEU, the material rights of free movement have largely been provided in secondary law. Each of the free movement sections has its own Treaty base to empower the enactment of secondary legislation in pursuit of the Treaty objectives. Consequently, for workers under Article 40 EC (now 46 TFEU) and the self-employed under Articles 53 (now repealed), 47, and 52 EC (now 53 and 59 TFEU), the Commission was empowered to propose Directives to obtain the general objectives set out in the Treaty. The legislative function is now carried out by the European Parliament and Council on Commission proposals. To a large extent, the rights provided deal with relatively mundane things, such as paperwork in support of exit and entry rights, and only infrequently result in important new case law. Furthermore, the CoJ has been able to derive very extensive rights from the EU primary legislation, and in particular Article 12 EC (now 18 TFEU). In 2004, the secondary law underwent radical transformation, and therefore the focus of attention will turn to those provisions. The rights for workers, outlined in Article 39 EC (now 45 TFEU) of the Treaty were amplified and supplemented most importantly by three measures. Directive 64/221, Regulation 1612/68, and Directive 68/360 (now replaced by Directive 2004/38 and Regulation 492/2011) were enacted, first, to facilitate the original rights provided and, secondly, to provide genuinely new rights, particularly when it came to members of the member state national's family.

Regulation 1612/68, as repealed and replaced by Regulation 492/2011, provided for equality of access to employment for all Community nationals, equality of treatment in employment rights and housing rights, and the right for the children of Community nationals to be educated on the same terms as the children of nationals of the member state concerned.

For more details on this section visit the online resources.

> Articles 10 and 11 of Regulation 1612/68 had already been repealed and replaced by Directive 2004/38, which provided rights for a worker to be joined by his or her family.

For the self-employed, legislative intervention was used to facilitate entry and procedural rights in a similar manner to workers and also to initiate a programme of harmonisation of the various professions on a one-by-one basis by means of one or more Directives for each profession. These are too numerous for a book of this nature; thus, only the general Directives will be considered.

> For the self-employed, Directives 73/148 and 75/34 are the equivalents of Directives 68/360 and 1251/70, and they have also been repealed and replaced by Directive 2004/38.

Directive 2004/38 is now the main and most important provision of secondary legislation for the free movement of Union citizens. It has replaced most of the previous secondary legislation and covers both workers and the self-employed. It generally revises the law and has incorporated much of the previous case law of the CoJ. The Directive clarifies who should be regarded as a member of the family or person otherwise provided with rights derived from an economically active EU citizen. It also establishes permanent rights of residence for citizens after a certain period and restricts the member states' right to refuse entry on the grounds of public policy. Whilst the right of permanent residence appears new, in reality it merely reflects the previously established right to remain for many union citizens and families who have chosen to live in another member state. Its comprehensive nature has been explained in a Commission Communication (COM (2009) 313).

12.3.1 Rights of entry, residence, and exit

The rights to enter, move freely, and seek and take up employment are governed by a combination of Article 45(3) TFEU, Articles 1–5 of Regulation 492/2011 (ex Articles 1–5 of Regulation 1612/68), and Articles 4–14 of Directive 2004/38.

> Note that much of the case law is based on the repealed Directive 68/360, Articles 1–6 and 8, but it is helpful to be aware of this because you will come across references to the old Directives in the cases and literature.

Articles 1 and 2 of Regulation 492/2011 (ex Articles 1 and 2 of Regulation 1612/68) provide the right to take up employment in the host state under the same conditions as nationals without discrimination.

Article 3(1) of Regulation 492/2011 (ex Article 3(1) of Regulation 1612/68) permits member states to impose a requirement of linguistic ability on non-nationals according to the nature of the post to be filled.

> This is illustrated and interpreted by **Case 379/87 *Groener v Minister for Education***, in which the CoJ upheld an Irish requirement that teachers in Ireland should be proficient in the Irish language as part of a public policy to maintain and promote the Irish language and culture. Any requirement, however, must be proportionate.

Directive 2004/38 provides the rules to regulate the conditions by which workers can leave one member state and enter the territory of another. It prescribes the entry formalities that it is permissible for member states to impose, in particular the rules regarding the issue and withdrawal of residence permits. Cases arising under the previous Directive sought to remove the unnecessary restrictions on free movement.

Article 4 provides that exit states are obliged to allow nationals and their families with valid passports to leave with an exit visa or other formality. The exit state is obliged to issue a passport or identity (ID) card.

Article 5 provides that entrance states cannot demand an entry visa or equivalent documents from EU nationals. They can, however, require a passport or valid ID card and visas from non-Union members of the family, or, in the absence of the correct documents, unequivocal proof of the right to enter and reside (see Case C-215/03 *Salah Oulane*).

> In **Case C-68/89 *Commission v Netherlands (Entry Requirements)***, the CoJ held generally in respect of Directive 68/360 that the requirements under the Directive for documentation do not give the member state the right to further questioning regarding the purpose and duration of stay, once the correct papers have been shown.

THINKING POINT

Do you consider that whilst this is reasonable in theory, in practice it is not so likely in today's more security-conscious climate? Are the member states justified in more extensive questioning?

In **Case C-344/95 *Commission v Belgium***, a delay in issuing documents, the limited duration of residence permits, and payments demanded in excess of that comparable for national ID cards were all measures held by the CoJ to breach former Directive 68/360.

Article 6 of Directive 2004/38 permits the right to enter, travel, and reside in a host member state for a period of up to three months by an EU citizen and his or her family. It is not restricted to the economically active, but extends to any EU citizen without any conditions other than the requirement to hold valid ID and/or visa documentation, the latter covered by Articles 5 and 6. Article 24(2) of the Directive makes it clear that in that three-month period, the right to reside for those not economically active does not provide a right to social assistance or students' grants and loans. The right to reside for a period of more than three months up to five years under Article 7 is made conditional on being engaged in a gainful activity, being self-employed, being a recipient of education, or being self-sufficient with comprehensive sickness insurance cover, which again is subject to the Article 24(2) requirement. After that period, EU citizens may lose their right to remain if they become an unreasonable burden on the host state. Article 8(4) further provides that in determining the right to stay and financial self-sufficiency, the member states may not fix a minimum amount but must assess each case on its merits. However, this must not be above the threshold for national eligibility for pure safety net social assistance. As well as residence permits for family members, a registration certificate can be demanded, which must be granted to any worker who produces a passport and certificate of proof of employment. Members of the worker's family must also be afforded a registration certificate on production of a passport and proof of relationship or dependence.

In **Case C-459/99 *MRAX***, the CoJ considered that it was disproportionate and therefore prohibitive to send back a TCN married to a national of a member state who was not in possession of a valid visa where he or she was able to prove his or her identity and conjugal ties. In particular, if there were no evidence to establish that he or she represented a risk to the requirements of public policy, public security, or public health, expulsion would be excessive.

Article 8 of Directive 2004/38 reflects previous case law by providing that failure to comply with the registration requirement may render the person concerned liable to proportionate and non-discriminatory administrative sanctions only.

For example, in **Case 159/79 *R v Pieck***, Mr Pieck, a Dutch national, re-entered the UK after his original six-month entry permit had expired and he had failed to renew it. The authorities sought to deport him. The CoJ held that a failure to obtain a permit could result only in penalties for minor offences.

> In **Case 118/75 *Watson v Belman***, Miss Watson, a UK national, was acting as an au pair whilst staying in Italy with Mr Belman. Both had failed to report this to the national authorities as required, and faced imprisonment and fines under national law. In addition, Miss Watson was to be deported. The Italian magistrate asked the CoJ if the punishments were compatible with EC law. The Court held that the use of internal rules—that is, the requirement to report—was acceptable, but that the penalty must be in proportion to the offence/damage caused—that is, it should be only a small fine; therefore, any decision to deport would be contrary to the Treaty.

In line with previous case law, Article 25 of the Directive provides that the registration certificate and residence permit are not preconditions for residence, but merely evidence of the entitlement to enter and reside—that is, not the right itself, but merely the proof of it. Administrative rules requiring registration are acceptable, as is an appropriate sanction for their breach, but not deportation, which would be regarded as disproportionate.

> In **Case C-325/09 *Dias***, it was held that a residence permit is not evidence of a right to permanent residence under Directive 2004/38 particularly, as in the case, the conditions for permanent residence (five years' lawful residence under Article 7 of the Directive) had not been achieved because of absences from the state. However, the CoJ ruled that provided the absence from the state was less than two years, it should be treated as a period of absence by analogy with Article 16(4) and thus not affect the overall acquisition of the entitlement to permanent residence.

Articles 22 and 11 of Directive 2004/38 provide that the right to residence and permits must be valid for the whole territory of the member state and valid for at least five years with automatic renewal. Article 22 states, however, that 'Member States may impose territorial restrictions on the right of residence and the right of permanent residence only where the same restrictions apply to their own nationals.'

> It was confirmed in **Case 36/75 *Rutili v Minister of Interior*** that an administrative prohibition restricting movement to parts of France could only be for the entire territory of the member state and must be justified.

> As held in **Case C-100/01 *Olazbal***, however, when it comes to criminal measures being taken to restrict movement, a partial restriction of movement would be acceptable. However, the action would have to be justified and the seriousness of the crime must otherwise have led to a complete banishment. Nationals would also have to be subject to similar punitive measures.

Article 15 of Directive 2004/38 states that the expiry of the documentation does not constitute grounds for expulsion.

Temporary involuntary unemployment does not remove the employed or self-employed status (Directive 2004/38, Article 14). Whilst the period is not specified, previous case law (Case C-292/89 *Antonissen*) suggests that six months would be the limit, after which the favoured status would then be lost. Whether the host member state would then be entitled to deport the citizen concerned is doubtful in view of the case law on citizenship, unless there were serious grounds for deportation other than involuntary unemployment or the person concerned had become a burden on the state.

》 CROSS REFERENCE

The case law on citizenship is considered in section 12.7.2.

12.3.2 The rights provided by Regulation 492/2011 and Directive 2004/38

Of all of the earlier legislation, Regulation 1612/68, now repealed and replaced by Regulation 492/2011, has certainly proved to be the most supportive of free movement, in particular in the way in which Article 7 of the Regulation has been interpreted by the CoJ. The Regulation details access to employment and rights for workers, and, more importantly, as far as an extension of the rights is concerned, introduces the rights of free movement for members of the workers' family. Whilst economically active persons received confirmation that their rights extended to matters such as tax and social advantages, vocational training, trade union membership, and housing rights and benefits under Articles 7–9 of Regulation 492/2011, the most significant provisions introduced by the first expansion of the rights related to the members of the family of the EU worker or self-employed person moving. This was made even more significant by the fact that these additional rights of free movement and to take up employment or education or vocational training applied also to non-EU member state family members, termed TCNs. In respect of the extension of the rights to family members, Articles 10 and 11 of Regulation 1612/68 have been repealed, replaced, and extended by Articles 2 and 3 of Directive 2004/38, as considered in context in section 12.3.2.2.

Article 7(1) of Regulation 492/2011 (ex Article 7(1) of Regulation 1612/68), reflecting Article 18 TFEU, prohibits discrimination against workers on grounds of nationality and specifically mentions terms and conditions of employment, dismissal, and, where relevant, reinstatement.

It has been decided that, when a worker commences a job in another country that is the same as that previously undertaken in the home state, this previous service may count for advantages in the host state. The CoJ held that to ignore this is to discriminate contrary to Article 7(1).

> In **Case C-187/96 Commission v Greece**, the CoJ held that a Greek administrative regulation and practice that did not take into account periods of employment in the public service of other member states when determining seniority increments and salary grading breached Article 39 EC (now 45 TFEU) and Article 7(1) of Regulation 1612/68 (now Article 7(1) of Regulation 492/2011)—that is, that service elsewhere counts.

These rights of equality of treatment are further emphasised by Article 24 of Directive 2004/38.

> **Article 24: Equal treatment**
>
> . . . all Union citizens residing on the basis of this Directive in the territory of the host Member State shall enjoy equal treatment with the nationals of that Member State within the scope of the Treaty.

12.3.2.1 Social, tax, and other advantages

Article 7(2) of the Regulation has proved to be a provision with extremely wide scope. It refers specifically to equality in social and tax advantages, which also apply to the family of the worker.

> **Regulation 492/2011, Article 7(2)**
>
> He shall enjoy the same social and tax advantages as national workers.

'Family' is open to wide interpretation, as are the benefits under Article 7(2).

In **Case 32/75 *Fiorini aka Christini* v *SNCF***, a reduced fare entitlement was claimed by the widow of an Italian SNCF worker. Widows of French workers were allowed such a family entitlement, but it was denied to the Italian widow. The SNCF claimed that since it was not expressed in the contract of employment, it was not available to foreign workers. The CoJ was asked whether this was the kind of social advantage envisaged by Article 7. The Court held that Article 7 applies to all advantages, not only those limited to a contract of employment. It therefore applies to the family of an EC worker in the same way as for nationals.

In **Case 94/84 *ONE* v *Deak***, an unemployed Hungarian national living with his mother, an Italian national working in Belgium, was refused special unemployment benefits for non-nationals on the basis that no agreement for such benefits existed between Belgium and Hungary. The CoJ held that special unemployment benefits were a social advantage within the meaning of Article 7 and that Deak, regardless of nationality, could derive rights as the descendant of a worker; otherwise a worker might be hindered from moving if the descendants were discriminated against, thus causing financial difficulty.

In **Case 137/84 *Mutsch***, a Luxembourg national living in a German-speaking commune in Belgium was denied the use of German before a court, a right granted to the Belgian German minority. The CoJ held that right to be a social advantage under Article 7(2) despite there being no link to a contract of employment.

Article 7(2) has even been interpreted to include a grant to cover funeral expenses in **Case C-237/94 *O'Flynn***, in which nationals were provided with the same assistance.

Some limits to Article 7(2) seem, however, to have been found.

Case C-43/99 *Leclere* involved a Belgian national who was working in Luxembourg, but who was injured in an accident. He was granted an invalidity allowance by the Luxembourg authorities, but was later refused child benefits because he was no longer a worker. Whilst the invalidity benefit was regarded as linked to his former work, the child allowances were held not to be connected, and therefore could lawfully be refused.

In **Case C-385/00 *De Groot***, Article 7(2) applied to provide that there should be no discrimination in tax matters, and that any discrimination in the way in which personal and family circumstances are taken into account that results in less favourable treatment of the frontier worker amounts to an obstacle to the free movement guaranteed by Article 39 EC (now 45 TFEU). This judgment is despite—but in full recognition of—the fact that member states are ostensibly still in full competence of deciding their own tax regimes.

In another tax case, **Case C-279/93 *Schumacker***, it was held that a Belgian who worked and was taxed in Germany but continued to live in Belgium was unable to obtain married couple's tax benefits granted to German resident workers. The CoJ held that whilst different tax regimes were not to be compared due to their being applicable and relevant to the residence circumstances, the fact that Schumacker derived most of the family income from Germany made him comparable with German residents, thus there should be no discrimination in the tax regime applicable. This was confirmed in **Case C-527/06 *Renneberg***, which involved a Belgium working in Holland and deriving c. 90 per cent of his income there. The property tax relief he would have received in Belgium was only paid at a reduced rate in Holland. This was held to be a tax disadvantage and in breach of EU law, with the consequence that he was entitled to the full Dutch amount even though this was consequently much higher in Holland than in Belgium. The differences are due to the allowable disparities in tax regimes in the different member states.

It is, of course, debatable whether the presence of this provision and the social advantages do in fact figure highly in a worker's original decision to move to another member state to take up or find work, bearing in mind the facts of these cases—that is, that the dependents have mostly followed on afterwards. The CoJ, however, has not considered the relevance of this and has upheld that very wide benefit regardless. As noted already, the CoJ held in Case 316/85 *Lebon* that equal treatment with regard to social and tax advantages laid down by Article 7(2) of Regulation 1612/68 operates only for the benefit of workers and does not apply to nationals of member states who move in search of employment.

The rights under Article 7(2) of Regulation 492/2011 were summed up by the CoJ in Case 207/78 *Even* as 'all those which, whether or not linked to a contract of employment, are generally granted to national workers primarily because of their objective status as workers, or by virtue of the mere fact of their residence' in the host member state. The Court stressed that these were rights that helped facilitate the workers' mobility within the EU. However, a further right to an increased pension due to war service claimed by a French national in Belgium was not considered to be included in the understanding of social advantage as this was for a service rendered to a country and not generated by reason of the status of an EU worker.

CROSS REFERENCE

Access to education services is considered in sections 12.2.2.3 and 12.6.1.2.

Article 7(3) of Regulation 492/2011 provides that member states must permit EU workers access to vocational training under the same condition as for nationals.

Article 8 of Regulation 492/2011 provides that the no discrimination rules should apply to trade union rights.

Article 9 provides that workers shall enjoy all of the rights and benefits accorded to national workers in matters of housing, including ownership and access to local authority housing lists.

CROSS REFERENCE

The further extensive rights now enjoyed by not just workers but also EU citizens are considered in section 12.7.

12.3.2.2 Rights of family members

Directive 2004/38 provides that the rights enjoyed by a Union national under the Directive also apply to family members, which are defined generously in Article 2 as spouses, registered partners, descendants, and ascendants. Article 2 provides that partners will also be considered to be family members provided they have contracted a registered partnership in the home state and the host state treats registered partnerships as equivalent to marriage. This brings the secondary EU law in line with the case law of the CoJ in the *Reed* and *Diatta* cases considered in this section. Article 2(c) considerably widens the definition of 'the family' in providing that members of the family include the direct descendants and ascendants of the spouse and partner also. Article 3 further provides rights of entry and residence for any other family members not within the definitions in Article 2 who, in the country from which they have come, are dependents or members of the household of the Union citizen having the primary right of residence, or where there are serious health or humanitarian grounds for doing so.

Members of the family can be any nationality and include those under the age of 21 and adult children over 21 who are dependent on the worker. 'Dependency' was defined in Case 316/85 *Lebon* as a factual situation of support provided by the worker.

By way of example, in **Case 261/83 *Castelli* v *ONPTS***, the Italian mother of a retired Italian worker in Belgium claimed an old-age pension. Mrs Castelli had never worked herself in Belgium, therefore her claim was based on her status as a member of her son's family. The Belgian authorities refused to pay on the grounds that she was not Belgian and they did not have a reciprocal agreement with Italy. The CoJ held that Mrs Castelli was entitled to install herself with her son under Article 10 of Regulation 1612/68. She was also entitled to remain after her son's retirement and had a right to the pension under Article 7.

In a judgment concerned with both Articles 7 and 10 of old Regulation 1612/68, but which has now been partly overtaken by Directive 2004/38, the CoJ was required to consider whether the term 'spouse' included cohabitees.

In **Case 59/85 *Netherlands* v *Reed***, Miss Reed applied for a residence permit in the Netherlands, claiming that her right to remain was based on her cohabitation with a UK national working in the Netherlands. The Dutch government refused to recognise this. The CoJ was aware that provisions of national laws regarding cohabitees' legal rights could vary. It was unable to overcome the clear intention of Article 10, which referred to a relationship based on marriage. The Court referred instead to the social advantages guaranteed under Article 7 of the Regulation as being capable of including the companionship of a cohabitee, which could contribute to integration in the host country. The Court held that where such relationships among nationals are accorded legal advantages under national law, these could not be denied to nationals of other member states without being discriminatory and thus breaching Articles 7 and 48 EEC (now 18 and 45 TFEU).

This is a somewhat convoluted decision, but it does provide justice to free movement in the case. The cohabitee does not have rights in his or her own right, but the companionship of a cohabitee is merely regarded as one of the advantages to which workers are entitled. Hence, the case merely supports the well-established right in EU law not to be discriminated against on the grounds of nationality. Of course, in some countries, cohabitees are not afforded the same rights as married couples. The reasoning of the Court has been carried over into Article 2 of Directive 2004/38 in respect of same-sex partner rights. Where national law supports this, EU law will demand that other Union nationals are treated equally; where national law does not support such rights, EU law cannot impose them on member states. The UK does, of course, now formally recognise same-sex partnerships. The *Reed* case remains important for its wide interpretation of Article 7(2).

The rights of a spouse have been held not to be dependent on residence with the entitled worker.

In **Case 267/83 *Diatta v Land Berlin***, Mrs Diatta, a Senegalese citizen, was married to a Frenchman living and working in Berlin. She obtained work in Berlin, shortly after which the couple separated to live apart. Upon application to extend her residence permit, the German authorities refused on the ground that she was no longer a member of the family for the purposes of Regulation 1612/68. The CoJ ruled that the rights under Regulation 1612/68 were not dependent on the requirements as to how or where members of the family lived. Therefore, a permanent common family dwelling cannot be implied as a condition of the rights granted under Regulation 1612/68.

In **Case C-413/99 *Baumbast***, the CoJ confirmed that divorce will bring to an end the spousal relationship for the purposes of free movement rights. This means that the right to remain in the host state will also be brought to an end unless saved by any other reason, which was the circumstance in this case. The case is also considered in section 12.3.3.

However, under Article 13 of Directive 2004/38, also considered in section 12.3.4, in certain circumstances divorce will not affect the right to remain in the host state. These include where the spouse is a national of another member state or, if not, where the marriage or relationship has lasted at least three years, including one year in the host state, or, reflecting the *Baumbast* case, where the person is a carer of the Union citizen's children.

In reviewing a case that had the appearance of a marriage of convenience, the CoJ held in **Case C-109/01 *Akrich*** that Article 10 of the Regulation, and now, by analogy, the new Directive, applies to TCNs only if they are lawfully resident in one member state before they can move to another one. It is also not applicable where a marriage of convenience has been arranged to circumvent a member state's immigration laws. This case is also considered in section 12.9.4.

There have been cases subsequent to the *Akrich* case on related family issues.

The first of these, **Case C-01/05 *Jia***, held that Community law does not require member states to make the grant of a residence permit to TCNs who are members of the family of a Community national subject to the condition that those family members have previously been residing lawfully in another member state. See also section 12.9.

The second case, **Case C-127/08 *Metock and others***, confirms *Jia*, but this time was based on Directive 2004/38 and expressly reverses part of the judgment in *Akrich* by making clear that the Directive is not conditional on a requirement that a TCN must have been lawfully resident in another member state to stay in a member state as a spouse or member of the family of an EU citizen. The case considered numerous Articles of Directive 2004/38 and related to four TCNs who had been refused asylum in Ireland, then married EU citizens lawfully resident in Ireland. The facts of the case stated that they were not marriages of convenience. See also, section 12.9.

Article 23 of Directive 2004/38 entitles the family members of an entitled Union citizen to take up any activity as an employed person to include any activity or profession, provided the appropriate qualifications and formalities are observed.

> This was previously encapsulated in Article 11 of Regulation 1612/68.

> For example, in **Case 131/85 _Emir Gül v Regierungspräsident Düsseldorf_**, the CoJ held that this right includes the right of such concerned persons to access to employment also under the same conditions as nationals of the host state.

This was also affirmed in the case of _Diatta_ v _Land Berlin_ in favour of Mrs Diatta.

12.3.3 **Worker's family and carer rights**

Article 10 of Regulation 492/2011 (ex Article 12 of Regulation 1612/68) provides that the children of a member state host worker shall be admitted to general educational, apprenticeship, and vocational training courses under the same conditions as nationals.

> **Case 9/74 _Casagrande_** had already extended the right under Article 12 of Regulation 1612/68 to include not only access to educational facilities, but also equality of measures intended to facilitate educational attendance.

> In **Case C-7/94 _Gaal_**, the CoJ extended the right under Article 12 of Regulation 1612/68 to an independent and over-21-year-old child of a migrant worker who had been employed in another member state. Gaal was the Belgian son of an EC worker in Germany who had since died. Gaal was attending university and applied for a grant to undertake an eight-month period of study in the UK. This was refused on grounds that he was over the age of 21 and was not dependent. He was therefore denied his rights as a descendant of an EC worker. The CoJ held that he still fell within the personal scope of Article 12 of the Regulation as the definition of a 'child' was not subject to the same definition as in Articles 10 and 11. Article 12 extends to all forms of education, including university education, and must include older children no longer dependent on their parents. The case was, however, decided on the basis that the child must have lived at some time with a parent who was an EC worker and thus derived his rights in this manner.

Two cases heard together have extended the Court's view of the effect of Article 12 of Regulation 1612/68 (now Article 10 of Regulation 492/2011) to provide rights for carers of Union citizen children who are receiving education.

> In **Case C-413/99 _Baumbast; R v Home Secretary_**, the non-EU national mothers would otherwise have been deported if the Court had not held that the children had the right to be cared for even where the original basis of their right to stay in the UK had disappeared. In the cases, the original rights disappeared: one through divorce and the other because there was no longer a Community national working in the UK or indeed any member state.

It is probable that such a convoluted decision is no longer necessary under rights provided by the Directive 2004/38, considered in section 12.3.4.

The protection of carers was taken even further in **Case C-200/02 *Chen***. This involved a child born in Northern Ireland to two Chinese nationals. The baby daughter became a Community national as a result of Irish law conferring Irish nationality on anyone born in Ireland. The family had not moved from one member state to another; however, in view of the fact that the baby was an EU national with a right to remain, but was below school age and thus unable to care for herself, the Chinese nationals gained a right to remain in the UK to care for her.

⟫ CROSS REFERENCE

This case is also considered in further detail in section 12.7.2.3.

12.3.4 **Right to remain**

Article 45(3)(d) TFEU provides the right to remain after retirement or incapacity and applies also to members of the family even if a worker dies, and to whom Article 7(2) of Regulation 492/2011 (ex Article 7(2) of Regulation 1612/68) continues to apply. This is complemented by Article 7(3) of Directive 2004/38, which provides that a former worker or self-employed retains that status when the activity has ceased by reason of illness of accident, is involuntarily unemployed and registered as a job-seeker after 12 months' employment, but if less the status is retained for six months. Related vocational training also qualifies to protect that status. The CoJ has made clear, though, that the Directive does not cover all of the circumstances by which the former status may be retained. In Case C-507/12 *Jesse Saint Prix*, it held that a woman who had voluntarily given up work for three months before and after childbirth was still to be classified as a worker in that period despite the fact that she had no made herself available for work in that time, providing she was seeking and found work in a reasonable time thereafter. Article 12 of Directive 2004/38 provides that the Union citizen's death or departure from the host member state shall not affect the right of residence of his or her family members who are nationals of a member state and also non-member state family members who were living with the Union citizen for at least one year before his or her death or departure. In line with previous case law, any children also retain the right to attend educational establishments. Article 13 of Directive 2004/38 provides that divorce, annulment of marriage, or termination of partnership or relationship shall not affect the right of residence of a Union citizen's family members who are nationals of a member state and also those who are not nationals of a member state. The latter category is subject to the requirement that the marriage or partnership has lasted at least three years, one being in the host state or where the spouse or partner has custody of family children, or is warranted by particularly difficult circumstances. The rights to remain under Articles 12 and 13 are further dependent on the persons considered not being a burden on the host state (Article 14(1) of Directive 2004/38).

Article 16 of Directive 2004/38 provides that Union citizens who have resided legally for a continuous period of five years in the host member state have the right of permanent residence there and that continuity of residence will not be affected by temporary absences not exceeding a total of six months a year or by longer absences not exceeding 12 months at a time for important reasons such as compulsory military service, serious illness, pregnancy and childbirth, study or vocational training, or a work assignment in another member state or a third country. Paragraph 1 applies also to family members who are not nationals of a member state and have resided with the Union citizen in the host member state for five years. Furthermore, Article 17 provides that this period may be reduced in cases of the death or injury of the union national. Article 18 provides that family members who are not nationals of a member state acquire the right of permanent residence after residing legally for a continuous period of five years in the host member state.

This right to remain under EU law is only granted if the conditions of Directive 2004/38 are satisfied, in particular that the person is not a burden on the state, and may not be the same as an expired right of lawful residence previously granted by the member state. In Cases C-424 and 425/10 *Ziolkowski and Szeja*, two Polish nationals who had been dependent on German economic support and thus lawfully resident there until their status had changed were unable to rely on EU law to prevent deportation from Germany.

12.3.5 Directive 2014/54

This Directive is concerned with measures facilitating the exercise of rights conferred on workers in the context of freedom of movement of workers. It makes clear the procedural avenues that must be made available to workers in pursuit of the rights contained in Regulation 492/2011 such as access to judicial procedures, access to employment advice and legal advice, and generally information on workers' rights in the host state.

12.4 Free movement rights of the self-employed

For more details on this section visit the online resources.

Putting into effect the basic Treaty rights, which were considered in section 12.2.3, providing for free movement of the self-employed proved to be slower and much more difficult than the simple Treaty expression of the rights would suggest. The national rules, including rules, regulations, and conditions of the various professional organisations and bodies, were often the biggest impediments to free movement and it was at first considered by the Commission that these could be removed only by harmonisation. Both main Treaty Articles, 52 and 59 EEC, now 49 and 56 TFEU, envisaged that the basic freedoms provided would be fleshed out by the enactment of secondary legislation issued under Articles 54 and 63 EEC (now 50, 53, and 59 TFEU). Attempts by the Commission to harmonise the various professions proved to be very arduous and time-consuming, and it was not until the intervention of the CoJ in leading cases that much more rapid and expansive progress took place.

The initial approach of the Commission therefore was the harmonisation of rules by the adoption of a programme of Directives to abolish the restrictions on free movement, and the mutual recognition of qualifications in all sorts of trades and professions on an occupation-by-occupation basis. This, however, was achieved only painfully slowly by the enactment of some 40 sectoral Directives. For example, it took 18 years for the Architects Directive 85/384 to be agreed upon and finally enacted. This approach also encouraged the view throughout the EU that the only way in which these rights could be promoted and relied on was if Directives were enacted to establish them and not directly from the Treaty. Thus, little progress was made, and even prior to the issue of some Directives considered essential in the process, case law had developed the law considerably.

12.4.1 Intervention of the Court of Justice

Whilst the Commission was attempting to realise the free movement of establishment and services and the harmonisation of the various nationals' rules governing the professions by negotiation with all of the interested national bodies, cases were starting to reach the CoJ concerning self-employed persons who were facing severe restrictions in trying to practise their professions in another country. Two leading cases in particular had a considerable impact on the thinking and approach of the

Commission in trying to achieve free movement in these areas. They highlighted the slow progress and denial of the most basic rights of free movement. The cases, in which Articles 52 and 59 EEC (now 49 and 56 TFEU) were held to create direct effects by the CoJ, were decided in favour of the applicants. It was previously assumed that completing secondary legislation was necessary before the rights of free movement could be fully realised; however, the CoJ decided the cases on the basis of the Treaty Articles themselves and on the basis of the general prohibition of discrimination—Article 12 EC (now 18 TFEU).

Concerned with establishment, **Case 2/74 *Reyners v Belgian State*** involved the attempt by a suitably qualified Dutchman to gain access to the Belgian Bar, but who was refused on the grounds of nationality. The Dutch government argued that Article 52 EEC (then) was not directly effective because it was incomplete without the issue of Directives required by it. The CoJ held that the prohibition of discrimination under Article 52 EEC (now 49 TFEU) was directly effective and declared that nationality could be no barrier to appropriately qualified lawyers entering a country to practise. The Directives were simply to facilitate free movement and not to establish it, which had already been done by the Treaty by the end of the initial transition period of the Communities (1969).

In **Case 33/74 *Van Binsbergen***, it was not nationality that was the problem, but a residence requirement. The case concerned a professionally qualified Dutchman, resident in Belgium, who was refused audience rights before the Dutch courts. The CoJ held that Article 59 EEC (now 56 TFEU) was directly effective and was not conditional on the issue of a subsequent Directive in respect of the specific professions, or on a residence requirement in the Netherlands.

These decisions meant that the CoJ had opened the way for the basic Treaty rights to establish and provide services in a host state to be enjoyed without discrimination or the imposition of unnecessary requirements and on the basis of the direct effects of the Treaty Articles themselves. It was not necessary to wait for the enactment of Directives for each and every profession. Other cases soon followed that fleshed out even further the rights available under the Treaty. As with workers, free movement cases tackled the various ways in which national or professionals' rules restricted free movement either by direct or indirect discrimination and rules that were non-discriminatory, but which nevertheless prevented access.

The next case backs up the *Reyners* and *Van Binsbergen* cases.

In **Case 71/76 *Thieffry v Paris Bar Council***, the applicant was refused access to the Paris Bar despite having obtained a Belgian diploma in law, recognised by the University of Paris as the equivalent of a French diploma, and having sat and passed the French Certificate for the Profession of Advocate. The CoJ held that the relevant national authorities should apply any laws or practices that allow for the securing of freedom of establishment in accordance with the European Economic Union (EEC) policy, although no Directives may have been enacted in that particular area. Therefore, where the competent authorities have recognised a foreign diploma as equivalent to a domestic qualification, recognition of that diploma may not be refused in an individual case solely because it is not a diploma of the host state.

Moving beyond clear-cut discrimination, in **Case 205/84 *Commission v Germany (Insurance Services)***, Germany had required the providers of insurance to be resident on German soil. The CoJ held that member states were under a duty not only to eliminate all discrimination based on nationality, but also all restrictions based on the free provision of services on the grounds that the provider is established in another member state. It also emphasised that all those national rules that apply to the providers of services permanently established in a member state will not necessarily automatically apply to those 'activities of a temporary character which are carried out by enterprises established in other member states'. It was held that the residence requirement was not justified.

The CoJ has moved further in the development of a rule that prevents the restriction of services from other member states, but may still persist to limit activities of the home providers of services. The following cases also follow similar developments in moving away from prohibiting not only discriminatory rules, but also any that restrict or hinder the movement of the self-employed, unless they can be justified.

In **Case C-76/90 *Säger v Dennemeyer***, Dennemeyer wished to provide patent services in Germany, something requiring a licence, the issue of which was restricted. His right to obtain a licence was challenged by a German patent agent. Dennemeyer claimed breach of Article 59 EEC (now 56 TFEU). The rule was non-discriminatory in that it applied to all patent agents regardless of residence. The CoJ held that not only are discriminatory rules prohibited, but also any rules that are liable to prohibit or otherwise impede persons providing a service that they already lawfully do in the state of their establishment. Laws applying to the temporary provision of services must be justified by an imperative reason relating to the public interest; the public interest must not already be protected by the rules of the state of establishment, and the same result must not be able to be obtained by less restrictive means.

In view of the limited activities undertaken by the patent agents, the Court was of the view that the national measures went too far.

In **Case C-55/94 *Gebhard***, a German lawyer who had set up a second chamber in Milan was prevented from using the title *Avvocato*. No secondary law was held to apply to the situation. The issue was whether the Italian rules could be imposed on him. In principle and according to the general Treaty provision, Article 52 EEC (now 49 TFEU), he was required to comply with national rules, but the CoJ held that national measures that hinder or make less attractive the exercise of fundamental freedoms must fulfil four conditions. They must be:

- non-discriminatory in application;
- justified by imperative reason relating to the public interest;
- suitable to secure the objective sought; and
- proportionate.

In **Case 340/89 *Vlassopoulou***, a Greek lawyer who had worked in Germany and gained some partial qualifications and experience in German law had her request for admission to the German Bar rejected on the grounds that she did not have the necessary German qualifications.

On reference to the CoJ, it was held that national authorities must take into account qualifications and experience that fall short of full qualification and undertake a comparison of the qualifications to see whether they are the equivalent of the national requirements, and not dismiss them out of hand.

This was followed up in **Case C-313/01 *Morganbesser***, in which it was held that training does not constitute a regulated profession for the purposes of mutual recognition; however, member states are required to take account of all qualifications of the migrant to assess objectively what was needed to make up the shortfall.

It is left to the national courts to determine whether qualifications are equivalent; and here lies the danger in that some courts will and some will not.

The consequence of these decisions is that 'establishment' is now very close to 'services'. Perhaps this is a fair result to achieve: that it does not matter where or how you practise, either on a temporary or permanent basis, provided qualifications are roughly equivalent. Rules that seek to prevent this must satisfy the criteria or be struck out, at least as far as non-national EU citizens are concerned, and eventually this may also lead to internal pressure in member states so that the rules are also abolished in respect of nationals; otherwise, they are seen to be discriminated against in comparison with host EU free movers. Hence, as with goods and workers, the prohibited rules applying to the self-employed also include indirect discrimination and thus market access, but similarly such rules may be objectively justified.

⟩ CROSS REFERENCE

See the discussion of reverse discrimination in section 12.8.

In **Case C-384/93 *Alpine Investments***, a Dutch law that prevented financial services providers from making cold-calling telephone calls either within or outside the Netherlands was challenged as breaching Article 59 EEC (now 56 TFEU). The CoJ held that the rule was not to be equated with the selling arrangements rule established in the *Keck* and *Mithouard* cases for goods and thus outside the scope of EC law, but held instead that because the rule affects access to other markets and thus is capable of hindering intra-Community trade in services, it will breach the Treaty. Such measures can be objectively justified by imperative reasons of public interest that are necessary and proportionate. In the case itself, it was decided that the Dutch government's arguments of consumer protection and safeguarding the reputation of Dutch financial markets satisfied those criteria; therefore, the prohibition did not offend Article 59 EEC (now 56 TFEU).

In **Case C-438/05 *ITWF & FSU v Viking***, the right to establish was balanced with the rights of workers to strike. The Viking line wanted to re-register a Finnish ship under the Estonian flag to employ lower-paid Estonians, to reduce costs, and to increase competitiveness with other lines plying the same route, but was prevented from doing so by the threat of strike action and a general boycott of Viking line ships by the unions International Transport Workers' Federation (ITWF) and the Finnish Seaman's Union (FSU). Viking's claim that this was a breach of Article 43 EC (now 49 TFEU) was recognised by the CoJ between the two private parties, but the right to strike was a fundamental right and a public interest right that could be a justified breach of Article 43 EC (now 49 TFEU) provided action was necessary to safeguard jobs and that any action was proportionate. It is for the national courts to undertake the final balancing of those rights according to the facts.

This case also makes it clear that Article 43 EC (now 49 TFEU) can also be relied on horizontally against non-state organisations.

In a similar case, **C-341/05 *Laval***, concerned with the provision of cross-border services, a Swedish union and workers attempted to require a Latvian company, undertaking work in Sweden but employing lower-paid temporary workers, to observe the Swedish collective bargaining terms and conditions. The Court held that, provided the conditions observed by the company were lawful, which they were, the attempt to force higher standards represented a breach of Article 49 EC (now 56 TFEU).

Case C-17/00 *de Coster*, concerned strictly with a domestic tax regime, was eligible to be considered under EU law, in the view of the CoJ, because the taxation applied to the installation of satellite television dishes, which received broadcasts from other member states, but there was no equivalent tax on apparatus receiving domestic broadcasts only.

The interpretation of the rights of the freedoms to establish or provide services has thus been as extensively fundamentally upheld by the CoJ as for the freedom of workers.

12.4.2 Legislative developments

Even as a result of the early case law, the Commission realised that the previous harmonisation approach was not the best solution with which to realise free movement, and commenced work on a new approach to achieving free movement that was applicable to many professions across the board.

12.4.2.1 Mutual recognition

For more details on this section visit the online resources.

A change of tactic was undertaken by the Commission to overcome the problems of tackling one profession at a time, which involved the enactment of mutual recognition Directives to apply to many professions. The new approach was prompted by the slow progress on specific professions. Following the *Reyners* and *Van Binsbergen* cases, the Commission decided that it was not necessary to issue Directives for each individual trade and profession. The Directives that had already been worked on and ones in the pipeline were not rendered redundant and were, in cases before the CoJ, held to be amplifications or guidelines to the requirements of the Treaty Articles, although work on a number was abandoned. The first general Directive was the Mutual Recognition of Diplomas Directive 89/48, which applied to numerous professionals (except those subject to specific Community Directives) who had completed a period of a minimum of three years' post-secondary education and professional training, and who were regulated under national law or subject to the requirement of a diploma or other similar professional qualifications equivalent to a diploma. It applied to professionally qualified persons as opposed to those who had completed only the university or college element of instruction and included workers, not only the self-employed. It has now been replaced by Directive 2005/36, which has incorporated both the general and specific professions Directives. This has now been supplemented by Directive 2013/55 OJ 2013 L354/132, which extends the scope of the 2005 Directive to apprentices and trainees; it confirms the three routes of recognition of automatic, mutual, and easing documentation required for the temporary of services. No further details will be provided in this introductory text on EU law.

Likewise, the Provision of Services Directive 2006/123 needs only to be noted. This was designed to consolidate further the freedoms to provide services and to establish in the new, much-liberalised markets of the member states, but seems instead to have maintained and possibly increased the distinction between them. Unfortunately, this new Directive is ridden with exceptions and will overlap with existing Directives; thus, in view of its comprehensiveness and complexity, it is unlikely to be covered in any detail in general and introductory courses on EU law and no further details will be provided here.

12.4.3 The free movement of lawyers

Whilst not dealing with any other professions, as an exception in a book on EU law it is appropriate to consider briefly the legislative provisions affecting the legal professions. It was considered necessary, against the trend of moving away from sectoral Directives, to issue a Directive to realise the freedom to provide services and establishment for lawyers. Indeed, the profession is an exception within the EU regime on the professions as remaining regulated as a single profession and not incorporated with the other liberal professions under the umbrella of the general Professions' Directive.

12.4.3.1 The provision of services by lawyers

Directive 77/249 is limited to the recognition of practising lawyers from member states, who must be accepted based on an understanding that the training of lawyers in other member states is no less strict than that in the host state. Article 4(1) dispenses with residence and registration requirements for 'the representation of a client in legal proceedings'. Article 4(2) provides that lawyers providing services in judicial proceedings are required to observe both sets of rules of professional conduct of the home and host states. Article 4(4) states that, where justifiable, the same rules apply to those providing services as nationals. Article 5 provides that:

> for the pursuit of activities relating to the representation of a client in legal proceedings, a member state may require lawyers . . . to work in conjunction with a lawyer who practises before the judicial authority in question and who would, where necessary, be answerable to that authority . . .

The requirements of Directive 77/249 have been specifically considered by the CoJ.

In **Case 427/85 Commission v Germany (Lawyers' Services)**, the CoJ held that local rules were acceptable, but could not go beyond the strict requirements of Community law as to become a hindrance to free movement and the requirement to have local lawyers alongside at all times, and also before courts where there was no compulsory representation and the requirement to live locally when only providing services was far too restrictive and therefore a breach of the Treaty. The rule that lawyers could operate only in strictly defined areas was not justified by Article 5 of the Directive and could not be applied to activities of a temporary nature carried out by lawyers established in another member state, although they may still apply to national lawyers.

This case is an example of reverse discrimination, whereby the rule cannot be applied to Union lawyers from other member states but can still be applied to national lawyers. Germany has now repealed the rule.

12.4.3.2 Establishment by lawyers (practice under home title)

The Lawyers Home Title Directive 98/5 provides, under Article 2, that any lawyer shall be entitled to be recognised in any other member state under his home country professional title as an independent or salaried lawyer on a permanent basis. Lawyers need only register with the competent authority in the host state on the basis of their registration in the home member state (Article 3).

For more details on this section visit the online resources.

Article 5 provides that the host lawyer may give advice on the law of his or her home member state, on EU law, on international law, and on the law of the host member state. He or she must comply with the rules of procedure applicable in the national courts.

This so-called 'third approach' provides an easier way of acquiring the professional title of the host member state and, in effect, circumvents the necessity under the Mutual Recognition Directive 89/48 and its replacement Directive 2005/36 to undertake the aptitude test to establish in another member state. The reason given for providing this is that it was primarily directed at experienced professionals, for whom an aptitude test would constitute an obstacle on account of the time that has elapsed since they obtained their qualifications, but it is hard to see how it would not be used by lawyers of any length of service.

In **Case C-313/01 *Morgenbesser***, the CoJ ruled that the refusal to recognise paid trainee lawyers because their prior academic legal qualifications were obtained in other member states was unjustified. Hence the Court held that national authorities are obliged to compare the applicant's professional knowledge, as certified by his or her qualifications or acquired through professional experience either in the member state of origin or in the host member state, with the professional knowledge required by national law. If the comparison reveals that these correspond only partially, the host member state is entitled to require the person concerned to show that he or she has acquired the knowledge that is lacking.

When Luxembourg required non-national lawyers to take linguistic tests, not to act on behalf of companies, and to show annual proof of professional registration with their home state, it was taken before the CoJ by the Commission (Case C-193/05 *Commission* v *Luxembourg*). The CoJ found Luxembourg to have breached EU law for all of those requirements.

12.5 Derogations from the free movement regimes

12.5.1 **Procedural safeguards**

For more details on this section visit the online resources.

Before considering the substantive grounds that member states may invoke in order either to refuse entry in the first place or to justify deportation, it makes sense first to consider any procedural rights that persons may have who are faced with such decisions. If immediate deportation can be prevented, there is more time in which to consider the substantive grounds given. Article 31 of Directive 2004/38 provides a number of procedural rights that further support free movement by providing for non-discriminatory rights of appeal, rights to remain to hear the appeal result, rights to be given reasons for deportation, and rights to the judicial review of decisions.

There is a right to remain in the member state pending a decision either to grant or refuse a residence permit, other than in emergency situations. Article 30 of Directive 2004/38 provides that the grounds for deportation must be precisely and comprehensively stated. The concerned person has a right to be informed of the grounds of refusal or deportation unless security is at stake.

These rights were developed previously in case law, notably in **Cases 115 and 116/81 Adoui and Cornauille v Belgian State**, in which two French women euphemistically described by the CoJ as 'waitresses' had their residence permits withdrawn by the Belgian authorities on the grounds that their personal conduct justified the invocation of the public policy proviso. The conduct was described by the court as 'Displaying themselves in windows in scant dress and being able to be alone with clients'. Basically, Belgium was trying to clamp down on the number of French prostitutes settling in Belgium. A reference was made to the CoJ, which held that the public policy proviso does not allow expulsion where similar conduct by nationals does not incur penalty or repressive measures. However, it does not require illegality to be invoked. It was noted that Belgian prostitutes were tolerated and not prosecuted. The CoJ held also that the reasons for expulsion must be sufficiently detailed to allow a migrant to defend his or her interests and be drafted in such a way and language as to enable the person to comprehend the content or effect.

Article 30(3) provides the right to be notified of any decision to expel or the refusal of a permit and the decision should also state the minimum period given to leave the country, which cannot be less than one month in any circumstance. Article 31 provides that there should also be a system for appeal against decisions on their merits as well as legality.

THINKING POINT

Avoid February! Why?

Previously, **Case C-175/94 Gallagher** considered the body hearing the appeal. Gallagher, who had been convicted of the possession of rifles for unlawful purposes in Ireland, had been deported from the UK. In questioning this decision, he was interviewed in Ireland, before the case was heard by the Home Secretary. He challenged these bodies as not being independent. The CoJ held, however, that it was a matter for the national courts to decide whether the body hearing an appeal was independent, but that the Directive did not specify how it should be appointed. It should, however, be genuinely independent.

In **Case 98/79 Pecastaing v Belgian State**, a French prostitute was asked by the Belgian authorities to leave on grounds of personal conduct. She claimed under Articles 8 and 9 of Directive 64/221 that she should be able to stay in the country whilst the decision was being reviewed, which could be up to three years during the course of an Article 234 EC (now 267 TFEU) reference. The CoJ held that, even under Article 234 EC (now 267 TFEU), the right of appeal is not to be diluted and only in cases of emergency should automatic expulsion take place; however, the urgency could finally be determined only by the member states.

Articles 8 and 9 of the now repealed Directive did not expressly grant rights to remain in the host state pending hearing as long as the person could obtain a fair hearing and full facilities even whilst out of the country: see now Article 31 of Directive 2004/38.

12.5.2 **Restrictions on the grounds of public policy, security, and health**

Member states are able to restrict entry and deport EU nationals on the grounds set out under Article 45(3) TFEU, which are public policy, security, and health. Under Directive 2004/38, these apply expressly now to workers and the self-employed.

> Articles 52 and 62 TFEU subject establishment and provision of services to the same derogations as workers.

> These grounds have been held to be exhaustive in **Case 352/85 *Bond van Adverteerders and others* v *The Netherlands State***, in which economic grounds were pleaded in support of a decision not to allow broadcasts by non-national organisations, but rejected by the CoJ.

Article 27 of Directive 2004/38 has consolidated both the previous statutory law and the case law of the CoJ, setting out what the member states can or cannot do under the derogations.

> ### Directive 2004/38, Article 27(2)
>
> Measures taken on grounds of public policy or public security shall comply with the principle of proportionality and shall be based exclusively on the personal conduct of the individual concerned.
>
> Previous criminal convictions shall not in themselves constitute grounds for taking such measures.
>
> The personal conduct of the individual concerned must represent a genuine, present and sufficiently serious threat affecting one of the fundamental interests of society. Justifications that are isolated from the particulars of the case or that rely on considerations of general prevention shall not be accepted.

Personal conduct may not be considered a sufficiently serious threat unless the member state concerned takes serious enforcement measures against the same conduct on the part of its own nationals.

> ### Directive 2004/38, Article 28
>
> Before taking an expulsion decision on grounds of public policy or public security, the host Member State shall take account of considerations such as how long the individual concerned has resided on its territory, his/her age, state of health, family and economic situation, social and cultural integration into the host Member State and the extent of his/her links with the country of origin.

Under Article 28(2), removal decisions cannot be taken against Union citizens or family members, irrespective of nationality, who have the right of permanent residence within its territory or against family members who are minors. Article 28(3) increases the seriousness of the grounds needed for deportation for EU citizens who have resided for more than 10 years in the host state and for minors. In these cases, the decision to deport must be based on 'imperative' grounds of public security. Furthermore, any deportation orders that are taken must be subject to review for possible lifting under Article 32 at least three years after being made.

Most of the case law thus far relating to this part of the Directive relates to the previous legislation.

'Personal conduct' was defined in **Case 67/74 Bonsignore v Köln**, in which an Italian national faced deportation as a general preventative measure after conviction for fatally shooting his brother in a firearms accident for which he did not possess a permit. The CoJ held that measures adopted on grounds of public policy and for the maintenance of public security against the nationals of member states of the Community cannot be justified on grounds extraneous to the individual case, and that only the personal conduct of those affected by the measures is to be regarded as determinative.

As a departure from the rules concerning the free movement of persons and thus an exception that must be strictly construed, the concept of 'personal conduct' expresses the requirement that a deportation order may be made only for breaches of the peace and public security that might be committed by the individual affected.

In the earlier judgment in **Case 41/74 Van Duyn v The Home Office**, the CoJ held that restrictions on the grounds of public policy must be interpreted very strictly and be subject to judicial review. In this case, a Dutch woman obtained a position as secretary with the Church of Scientology in the UK, but was refused entry by the Home Office on the grounds that public policy declared the Church to be socially harmful. The CoJ held that to rely on public policy, the member state must have defined its position with regard to the organisation and have taken administrative but not necessarily legislative measures against it, which the UK had in fact done. The UK could therefore rely on the public policy exception. Additionally, Miss Van Duyn claimed that the refusal was not made on the basis of personal conduct, but the conduct of the group. The CoJ held that personal conduct must be an act or omission to act on the part of the person concerned and must be voluntary. It need not, however, be illegal or criminal to offend public policy. However, the Court then further held that present association reflecting participation in the activities and identification with the aims of a group may be considered a voluntary act and could therefore come within the definition of conduct, which hands back some of the discretion to the member states to determine whether an individual's association in a group constitutes personal conduct.

This part of the judgment is now suspect in the light of later case law and Directive 2004/38.

In **Cases 115 and 116/81 Adoui and Cornaille**, French prostitutes facing expulsion from Belgium on public policy grounds could not be denied residence on the basis of their personal conduct when similar conduct on the part of nationals did not attract similar repressive measures to combat such behaviour. The proviso was therefore unavailable to Belgium.

Concerning previous criminal convictions, which, according to Article 27 of the Directive, should not be taken into account, **Case 30/77 *R* v *Bouchereau*** involved a Frenchman who had been convicted in the UK on a number of occasions for drugs possession. The UK magistrate asked the CoJ whether he could be deported to stop him committing acts in the future. The Court held that it was not possible to look at past records to decide future conduct unless it constituted a present threat. Public policy measures could be relied on only where conduct and criminal convictions were a genuine and sufficiently serious threat affecting one of the fundamental interests of society.

See also the case of *Antonissen*, whereby the lack of employment and any serious chance of obtaining it would justify expulsion. The case was considered in section 12.2.2.2.

In **Case C-348/96 *Donatella Calfa***, a Greek rule of automatic life expulsion from Greek territory was applied following conviction and imprisonment for certain offences, including prohibited drugs in the case itself. As an exemption, the CoJ held that it must be interpreted restrictively and that, where a person has been convicted, expulsion could be based only on personal conduct outside of the conviction itself; in any event, a life ban was disproportionate. Indeed, it would now not conform with the requirement in Directive 2004/38 for a review of the expulsion after a minimum of three years (Article 32).

The public security proviso was specifically considered in **Case C-100/01 *Otieza Olazabal***, which involved the French imprisonment and ban on residence for activities undertaken for ETA, the Basque separatist movement. This was challenged, but upheld by the CoJ as coming within the public security proviso.

A case that has considered Article 27 is **Case C-33/07 *Jipa***, dealing with expulsion, in which it was held that, in deciding on the matter, member states could not simply rely on a previous expulsion or information from the home states, but that both could be considered in the context of the overall decision provided personal conduct was also considered and judged to be a threat to society. The case is therefore in line with previous judgments on personal conduct.

Articles 27 and 28 were considered by the CoJ in **Case C-145/09 *Land Baden-Württemberg* v *Tsakouridis***, in which Article 28(3) was considered requiring imperative grounds for deportation. The case involved the criminal activity of dealing in narcotics with an organised crime gang. The CoJ held that, as a deliberate raising of strictness, the measures taken under Article 28(3) had to be exceptional. Whilst the Court concluded that organised drug trafficking could be such an exceptional circumstance, the member states nevertheless still had to consider the personal conduct of the individual, as required by Article 27(2) of Directive 2004/38, and that any decision must be proportionate having regard to the time spent and degree of integration in the host state, especially where the person had spent most—even all—of his childhood in the host state. The national court must also consider the sentence passed on conviction and have account of fundamental rights in both the EU Charter of Fundamental Rights and the European Convention on Human Rights and Fundamental Freedoms (ECHR). The Court, though, defined public security as 'A threat to the functioning of the institutions and essential public services and the survival of the population, as well as the risk of a serious disturbance to foreign relations or to the peaceful co-existence of nations, or a risk to military interests', thus emphasising its internal and external aspects.

A national court thus has quite a balancing act to come to a decision on whether authorities can lawfully, under EU law, deport an EU citizen of more than 10 years' residence in a host state.

Public health measures are given further definition in Article 29 of the Directive and, rather than listing particular diseases as was the previous practice, the Directive now provides as follows.

Directive 2004/38, Article 29

The only diseases justifying measures restricting freedom of movement shall be the diseases with epidemic potential as defined by the relevant instruments of the World Health Organization and other infectious diseases or contagious parasitic diseases if they are the subject of protection provisions applying to nationals of the host Member State.

To justify expulsion, the public health proviso can only be used on entry or within three months of arrival and not thereafter and must only apply to diseases attracting emergency measures in respect of nationals.

12.5.3 Public service exemptions

Article 45(4) TFEU exempts employment in the public service from the provisions of Article 45 TFEU. The initial difficulty was that there is no Treaty definition of 'public service', which can vary considerably from state to state, and thus its understanding in different member states could vary considerably and could be claimed by the member states to apply to a vast range of workers employed by the state. Hence the CoJ has constantly stressed the need for a strict interpretation of this Article. It has been held to apply to entry and not to conditions of employment.

In **Case 152/73 *Sotgui* v *Deutsche Bundespost***, Mr Sotgui, an Italian national, was already employed by the German Post Office, but was not paid the same travel allowance as German nationals on the basis of the public service proviso. This was held to be discrimination contrary to Article 39(1) EC and was not excused by Article 39(4) EC (now 45 TFEU).

In **Case 149/79 *Commission* v *Belgium* (Public Employees)**, the CoJ held that public service derogation applies only to typical public service posts that exercise powers conferred by public law and which are there to safeguard the interests of state, regardless of the actual

> status in each of the member states. Belgium had reserved all manner of jobs across the public sector to Belgium nationals. This case, which was actually two cases, required Belgium to discuss and negotiate with the Commission the scope of those jobs that fell within and without the exception and thus helped develop the Commission guidelines, noted following.

The CoJ has, on this basis, excluded from the scope of Article 45(4) TFEU:

* nurses, in Case 307/84 *Commission v French Republic*;
* trainee secondary school teachers, in Case 66/85 *Lawrie-Blum v Land Baden-Württemberg*;
* secondary school teachers, in Case C-4/91 *Bleis v Ministry of Education*; and
* university lecturers, in Case 33/88 *Alluè and Coonan v University of Venice*.

In order to try to clarify the posts that the member states claim to come within Article 45(4) TFEU, the Commission has issued a notice (Official Journal (OJ) 1988 C72/2), confirmed by a 2002 Commission Communication (COM (2002) 694 final), of those sector positions that it thinks would rarely be covered by the public service proviso. These include public health care, teaching in state educational establishments, non-military public research, and public administration of commercial activities.

Occasionally, restrictions are accepted by the CoJ, as in Case C-47/02 *Anker and others*, in which restricting the appointment of ships' masters to Germans by private vessel owners was held to be acceptable in view of the public duties that had to be undertaken by the masters of ships. These included the maintenance of safety and exercise of police powers. However, the Court advised that such duties should not be a minor part of the activity of a master and should be exercised regularly, which, in *Anker*, was not the case.

For more details on this section visit the online resources.

There is the equivalent of the public service exception for establishment in Article 51 and by extension Article 62 TFEU, but only on the more tightly defined ground of 'positions concerned with the exercise of official authority'. The CoJ held, in the case of *Reyners*, that the derogation was more concerned with the exercise of the prerogative power of the state than with preventing particular occupations from exercising rights under EU law. In Case C-438/08 *Commission v Portugal*, for example, vehicle-testing inspectors acting under public law but working for private companies were held not to be connected with the exercise of public power. Equally the office of notary in six countries could not be reserved for nationals under the exception as they had argued (Cases C-47, 50, 52–54, and 61/08 *Commission v (Belgium, France, Portugal, Luxembourg, Austria, and Germany)*).

12.6 The extension of free movement rights

For more details on section 12.6 visit the online resources.

》 CROSS REFERENCE

Citizenship is considered in section 12.7.

Rights under the freedom of movement of persons was extended to persons other than those who were very clearly workers or self-employed to include those receiving services, as opposed to providing services, and educational services. This meant that the rights of free movement were no longer anchored to an active economic contribution. This was initially addressed by three general Directives, then by the introduction of a citizenship section into the EC Treaty, and now additionally by Directive 2004/38, which has replaced the three general rights of movement Directives. In the following sections, those receiving services and those having a right to move not based on an active economic contribution are considered.

12.6.1 Receiving services

The concept of services has been expanded to those who do not actively pursue an economic activity, but instead more or less actively or passively receive services of an economic nature. Whilst there is nothing to confirm this category within the Treaty, it was expressly mentioned in Article 1 of Directive 64/221 (now repealed), but has not been mentioned in its replacement, Directive 2004/38, probably due to the fact that establishment citizenship will secure those rights without discrimination in any case. Services can be received either by movement to another member state or by receiving services from another state in the home state. Initially, cases that confirmed this arose from the areas of educational provision and tourist travel.

12.6.1.1 Tourist services

In **Case 286/82 *Luisi and Carbone* v *Ministero del Tesauro***, two Italian nationals were prosecuted under Italian currency regulations for taking money out to pay for tourist and medical provisions abroad. These were held by the CoJ to be payments for services and thus to come under the provisions of the EEC Treaty, payments also being a fundamental freedom of the Community, and the case was covered by Articles 59, 60, and 7 EEC (now 56, 57, and 18 TFEU).

Case 186/87 *Cowan* confirms that tourists travelling and receiving services bring themselves within the protection of EC law not to be discriminated against even in areas, as in the case itself, such as participation in the French criminal injuries compensation scheme.

12.6.1.2 Educational services

In **Case 293/83 *Gravier* v *City of Liège***, a decision to charge foreign students a fee for vocational training courses, but not nationals, was claimed to be contrary to Community law Articles 6, 59, and 128 EEC (now 18, 56, and 166 TFEU). This was upheld.

It was made clear in two cases, **Cases 24/86 *Blaizot* v *University of Liège*** and **263/86 *Belgium* v *Humbel***, that university study was, for the most part, vocational training in EC law terms and that Community nationals had a right to equal access to receive it under equal conditions as nationals even where fees were financed by the host state.

In **Case C-281/98 *Angonese***, it was the activity of receiving educational services that triggered other citizenship rights, including—under Article 12 EC (now 18 TFEU)—the right not to be discriminated against on the grounds of nationality.

Case C-109/92 *Wirth* involved a question from a German court regarding whether courses available in an institute of higher education had to be classified as services under Article 50 EC (now 57 TFEU). A German national was attempting to obtain a grant from German authorities to study in the Netherlands. The CoJ held that courses given in a university or institute of higher education that is financed essentially out of public funds do not constitute services within the meaning of Article 50 EC. However, it noted that many courses were financed by the students themselves paying fees, with the aims that the course generates profit; they could, in these circumstances, be regarded as coming within the concept of services.

In many countries, payment by students of university fees has become the norm.

In **Case C-147/93 *Commission v Austria***, Austria was held to account for imposing more demanding entry conditions of university entry on other EU nationals in comparison with Austrian students in order to restrict access. The CoJ stressed the EU desire to promote the mobility of students and their right to receive education. The measure was not justified by the argument that, by not imposing stricter requirements, it would lead to a flood of non-Austrian students swamping the universities and resources, because Austria had offered no evidence on this. The CoJ held that access to education under the same conditions was the very essence of the free movement of students.

The conclusion from this case law is that access to institutions and tuition fees are subject to EU law; the earlier judgments did not, however, extend to establishing a right to grants or other social assistance whilst studying. More recent case law seems to indicate that this is no longer the case.

In **Case C-209/03 *Bidar***, Bidar, a French person residing in the UK decided to undertake study and applied for a student loan, which was refused on the grounds that Bidar was not 'settled' in the UK for the purposes of obtaining a student loan. The CoJ held that despite the previous case law, including the *Brown* and *Lair* cases, which excluded student maintenance grants from the scope of the Treaty, the introduction of the citizenship Article and a chapter on education and training meant that student assistance can now be counted as falling within the scope of the Treaty. As such, as in the previous cases, Articles 12 and 18 EC (now 18 and 21 TFEU) in combination provided Bidar with the right to equal treatment in loans. However, in building on the *Collins* case, which is considered in section 12.7.2.2, a member state could require a certain amount of integration before awarding a loan. However, national laws that completely exclude the possibility of students from other member states of obtaining the status of a settled person would be incompatible with Article 12 EC (now 18 TFEU).

In **Case C-73/08 *Bressol***, mass migration to Belgium to take up courses in medicine by Austrian students, who had difficulty in gaining a place in Austria, was restricted on the grounds that they were not resident in Belgium at the time of registration. Whilst the CoJ held the rule to be discriminatory and a breach of EU law, it also held that it was up to the Belgium authorities to see whether the rule could objectively be justified on the grounds that Belgium was entitled to reserve a certain minimum of finite places for Belgium nationals to ensure the provision of medical services in certain parts of Belgium—an argument that could be expanded into other areas of the economy, no doubt with some relief on the part of national authorities.

The rights of students to receive educational services and support will increasingly be assumed and is considered under Citizenship in section 12.7.2.2.

12.6.1.3 Receiving services without movement

It is increasingly accepted that the receipt of services can also be 'metaphysical', such as receiving services over the telephone or, more probable these days, the Internet. Such argument does, of course, raise the question, not yet decided by the CoJ and certainly not express in any legislative provision, of whether receiving services in such a manner is within the concept of engaging in an economic activity. If the simple receipt of services, irrespective of the manner of their delivery, triggers the application of EU law, then it could be argued that potentially any receipt of services will do, regardless of how minimal, such as telephoning another country to obtain advice or other services or downloading advice packages from a computer server in another member state. The *de Coster* and *Mobistar* cases lend some support to this view that receiving cross-border metaphysical services will trigger EU law rights, and are considered in the summary to this chapter.

In view of the ease by which EU law rights may be triggered for persons otherwise not entitled to those more extensive rights, the Advocates-General (AGs) in the *Carpenter, Angonese*, and *Collins* cases had suggested a new test to determine whether EU law is triggered, which relates specifically to the connection to the state of the person concerned. In other words, an economically determined level of activity could be set, below which EU rights would not be triggered for the reason that the services received were marginal. The extent to which the CoJ took up this new test will be considered later in section 12.7.2.

The receipt of services is governed also by the Services Directive 2006/123, but will not be considered further here.

12.6.2 The general free movement Directives

The three general free movement Directives (Directives 90/364, 90/365, and 93/96) have now been repealed and replaced by Directive 2004/38 and are mentioned here only in respect of the case law generated by them. Indeed, the Directives were soon overtaken by the introduction of the citizenship rights and other developments in EU law. The Directives allowed for free movement not linked to an economic activity in the same way now as provided by the new Directive 2004/38. In place of an economic activity, proof of self-sufficiency was instead required (Article 7(1)(b) of Directive 2004/38).

The CoJ confirmed, in **Case C-424/98 *Commission v Italy***, that member states may ask for evidence of self-sufficiency, but cannot dictate what that evidence should consist of.

'Unreasonable burden' were the qualifying words used in the Preamble to the Directives rather than simply 'burden', which appeared in the Article itself. In other words, a reasonable burden on the state, particularly if temporary in nature, would be acceptable, which is quite a different matter and category.

The CoJ held, in **Case C-184/99 *Grzelczyk***, that it may be possible to make a claim on the social funds of a member state provided the burden on the state is not unreasonable.

The decision leaves open who should define reasonableness in similar circumstances. Is it a matter for the CoJ or the member states? Presumably, in line with the CoJ's comments in *Grzelczyk*, this would be within the member states' courts' discretion.

> The CoJ also considered Directive 90/364 in **Case C-413/99 *Baumbast***. It held, in view of the facts, that Baumbast and family were not a burden on UK social security. They had German insurance cover, albeit not for emergency treatment; therefore, the requirement for all-risks insurance did not have to include emergency insurance, which the Court noted was provided as a matter of course in the UK.

The new Directive does not use 'unreasonable' in Article 7, but, as with the previous Directives, includes it in the Preamble and in Article 14 in respect of retaining an existing right of residence; thus, the same CoJ qualification should apply.

12.7 The Maastricht Treaty and European citizenship

The TEU signed at Maastricht introduced a small section on European citizenship to the European Community (EC) Treaty. It is introduced in Article 9 TEU and outlined in Articles 20 *et seq*. TFEU.

> **Article 20 TFEU**
>
> Citizenship of the Union is hereby established. Every person holding the nationality of a member state shall be a citizen of the Union. Citizenship of the Union shall complement and not replace national citizenship.

Furthermore, Article 21 TFEU provides as follows.

> **Article 21 TFEU**
>
> Every citizen of the Union shall have the right to move and reside freely within the territory of the Member States, subject to the limitations and conditions laid down in the Treaties and by the measures adopted to give them effect.

The rights provided by the Treaty under citizenship, as those under the earlier general free movement Directives, remove the economic activity requirement of the original free movement of persons regime. However, its true importance was not immediately obvious and has only become clearer as a result of CoJ judgments. It must also be noted that the right of residence under Article 21 TFEU is still subject to the limitations and conditions laid down in the Treaty and by the measures adopted to give it effect—in other words, by limitations already in existence, which would include the restrictions on the grounds of public policy, security, and health provisos, stated in Article 45 TFEU and clarified in Directive 2004/38, Articles 27–29 and those that might be contained in future implementing measures. The Lisbon Treaty has reorganised the provisions on citizenship slightly by providing new, overriding, general Articles in new Article 9 TEU and Article 20 TFEU, consolidating the rights previously in Articles 19–21 EC, and then expanding those rights in new Articles 21–4 TFEU. Article 25 TFEU provides that the Council, acting under the special legislative procedure and with the consent of the European Parliament, can adopt acts that add to or strengthen the rights provided in Article 20(2) TFEU.

The Maastricht Treaty also added a number of so-called political citizenship rights including, in Article 22 TFEU, the right to vote and stand as a candidate at municipal and European Parliament elections in their host country. Article 23 TFEU provides that EU citizens have the right to diplomatic protection and assistance by the consular offices of other member states in third countries and now governed by Decision 95/533. Article 24 TFEU provides that EU citizens have a right of initiative granted by Article 11 TEU, considered in Chapter 2. Article 24 TFEU also provides for a right to petition the European Parliament in accordance with Article 227 TFEU and to apply to the European Ombudsman as governed by Article 228 TFEU. Finally, Article 24 TFEU provides that EU citizens can write to and be answered by any of the institutions, bodies, offices, or agencies in any of the official languages.

12.7.1 **The definition of 'citizenship'**

The first matter to be considered is a definition of 'EU citizenship'. Article 20 TFEU provides this definition as based and dependent on the nationality of the member states. There can be no EU definition of European citizenship and the concept can be determined only as the collective definition of citizenship from all of the member states, as was made clear by the member states in a Declaration (No. 2), which was attached to the original TEU but removed by the Lisbon Treaty. If a person is a national of a member state, then Articles 20 and 21 TFEU apply.

Building on the *Micheletti* and *Manjit Kaur* cases considered in section 12.2.1, **Case C-135/08 Rottmann v Bayern** considered whether the false/illegal acquisition of nationality nevertheless brought a person within the material scope of EU citizenship. Mr Rottmann, an Austrian, had failed to reveal pending criminal proceedings when he applied and was granted German citizenship (which necessitated the loss of his Austrian citizenship). The revocation of the German citizenship would, however, have led to him being stateless. The CoJ, not following the opinion of the AG, held that EU law did apply to him. The Court considered it had not interfered with the right of the member states to decide nationality themselves, but the consequence of withdrawing nationality by a state had the result that a once-enjoyed right, EU citizenship, was also lost. The Court rather fudged the decision, though, by concluding that, ultimately, it was up to the national court to decide whether the decision to withdraw citizenship was proportionate in view of both national law and the loss of EU citizenship, even if the citizenship was acquired by a lack of disclosure. It should also have taken into account whether Rottmann's original nationality could be recovered and the gravity of the wrong committed him, especially in view of the effect on his family.

Thus, it remains uncertain whether and how under those circumstances EU citizenship can then be lost.

The scope and restrictions of citizenship rights need to be determined.

12.7.2 **Case law on the citizenship Articles**

The first significant cases establish that citizenship provides a right of continued residence and a link to other rights, notably the right not to be discriminated against on the grounds of nationality contained in Article 12 EC (now 18 TFEU). Subsequent case law demonstrates that further rights can be realised in a number of areas (as are considered in the following sections) in which the protection from discrimination now under Article 18 TFEU is the key factor in the citizenship cases.

12.7.2.1 **Non-discrimination and residence rights**

In **Case C-274/96 *Criminal Proceedings v Bickel and Franz***, Article 18 EC (now 21 TFEU) was upheld as a right that could be pleaded in support of other rights, in this case to support the view that the refusal to allow Germans the use of German in the Italian South Tirol courts would be contrary to Article 12 EC. German-speaking Italian citizens of Austrian extract in South Tirol were allowed to use German. Two German nationals, Bickel and Franz, had lawfully entered Italy under Article 49 EC (now 56 TFEU), but were not allowed to conduct their case in German in court proceedings.

In **Case C-413/99 *Baumbast***, Mr Baumbast, a German national, was self-employed in the UK, where he resided with his Colombian wife and two children, who were being educated in the UK. He was subsequently employed by a German company and worked outside the EU. His family remained in the UK. Their residence permits were not renewed, however, and Mrs Baumbast and the children faced deportation. The case was referred to the CoJ, which emphasised the right of children of EU nationals under Regulation 1612/68 to continue their education even if the worker, from whom their rights derived, is no longer working. The Court further held that the text of the Treaty does not permit the conclusion that citizens of the Union who have lawfully established themselves in another member state as employed persons are deprived, where that activity comes to an end, of the rights that are conferred on them by virtue of that citizenship.

In the most important statement of the judgment, the CoJ held that this right to stay under Article 18(1) EC (now 20 TFEU) is conferred directly on every citizen of the Union by a clear and precise provision of the EC Treaty. Purely as a national of a member state, and consequently a citizen of the Union, Mr Baumbast therefore had the right to rely on Article 18(1) EC. The Court held (at [94]):

> The answer to the first part of the third question must therefore be that a citizen of the European Union who no longer enjoys a right of residence as a migrant worker in the host member state can, as a citizen of the Union, enjoy a right of residence by direct application of Article 18(1) EC.

Subsequent CoJ judgments also show how the Court has upheld and extended the no-discrimination rule into welfare, educational, and family rights.

12.7.2.2 **Welfare rights**

The citizenship cases appear to go further than intended by the EU legislation by establishing welfare benefits rights of EU citizens who are not supposed to be a burden on the host member state. They do, however, show the Union to be concerned with the welfare rights of EU citizens over national concerns about the possible drain on national resources.

In **Case C-85/96** *María Martínez Sala* v *Freistaat Bayern*, Sala, a Spanish national who had worked in Germany for many years, lost her job, but remained in Germany with social assistance from 1989. Her residence permit had expired, but the German authorities supplied her with certificates, stating that she had applied for an extension to her permit. The authorities refused her a child allowance because she did not have a valid residence permit, which she claimed was contrary to Article 12 EC (now 18 TFEU) because German nationals were not subject to the same condition. Her status as a worker was not determined, but the CoJ held that, in any event, she was lawfully resident in Germany. Sala thus came within the personal scope of Treaty citizenship, and that (old) Article 8(2) EC (now 21 TFEU) citizenship triggered other rights, including, most importantly, Article 12 EC—the right not to be discriminated against according to nationality. This, in consequence, included the right to receive, on equal terms, social welfare benefits, including the non-contributory child allowance, which was the subject matter of the case.

Note that there was no discussion in the case as to whether the past employment could have been used as the trigger or possible justification to support the claim for welfare rights.

In **Case C-184/99** *Grzelczyk*, a French national, who studied and worked on a part-time basis to help support himself for three years in Belgium, applied at the beginning of his fourth and final year of study to the *Centre Public d'Action Sociale* [the Public Social Welfare Centre] (CPAS) for payment of the minimex, a non-contributory minimum subsistence allowance. The CPAS granted Mr Grzelczyk the minimex, but then later denied this on the basis that he was not Belgian—hence, clear discrimination on the grounds of nationality. The CoJ did not determine the possible status as a worker, but nevertheless held that the citizenship rights enable Union citizens to be treated equally. The Court emphasised the new citizenship provisions and new competences, albeit limited, in education (Articles 3(1)(q) and 149(2) EC, now 6 and 165 TFEU). Those, it reasoned, allowed it to rule that Articles 12 and 17 EC (now 18 and 20 TFEU) preclude discrimination as regards the grant of a non-contributory social benefit to Union citizens where they are lawfully resident, even though not economically active.

In **Case C-224/98** *D'Hoop*, a Belgian national had studied in France. She was refused a tide-over allowance between study and work granted to nationals by the Belgian authorities because she had studied in another member state. The CoJ had held that the tide-over allowance was a social advantage under Article 7(2) of Regulation 1612/68, but to take advantage of it the person must either have participated in the employment market or have obtained a derived right in some way. She was not a worker and her parents had remained in Belgium; therefore, she had no rights in her own right, nor derived rights from the parents. The Court referred to the new contribution to education by the EC in encouraging mobility of students and teachers (Articles 3(1)(q) and 149(2) EC, now 6 and 165 TFEU) and, citing *Grzelczyk* at [31], held that it would be incompatible with the right of freedom of movement if a citizen who had taken advantage of free movement then suffered discrimination with regard to a social benefit right as a consequence.

The Court held that such inequality of treatment is contrary to the principles that underpin the status of citizen of the Union—that is, the guarantee of the same treatment in law in the exercise of the citizen's freedom to move. The condition at issue could be justified only if it were based on objective considerations independent of the nationality of the persons concerned and were proportionate to the legitimate aim of the national provisions ([35]–[36]). The Belgian authorities offered none; hence the limiting of places of education that qualify for the tide-over allowance, according to the Court, went beyond what is necessary to attain the objective pursued.

In the *Collins* case, the claim to welfare rights appears to have been made subject to a close connection test.

In **Case C-138/02 *Collins v Secretary of State for Work and Pensions***, Collins entered the UK in 1998 on an Irish passport to seek work. He claimed an income-based jobseeker's allowance on the strength of 10 months' part-time work that he had undertaken as an American citizen from 1980 to 1981. The UK authorities refused the benefit on the grounds that he was not habitually resident in the UK. Collins claimed that this was discrimination because nationals were advantaged by automatically satisfying the time period required, whereas other Community nationals would have to fulfil this extra requirement. The CoJ held that it was permissible for member states first to require that there be a genuine link between the work seeker and the state for the purposes of claiming a jobseeker's allowance. There was indirect discrimination in that nationals could far more easily establish this link, but it was objectively justified, as the jobseeker's allowance was designed to reduce national unemployment for those living long-term in the UK.

The link requirement was confirmed in the next case, which, however, also confirms that, where appropriate, welfare rights can be claimed by EU citizens.

In **Case C-256/04 *Ioannidis***, a Greek national had spent three years in Belgium obtaining a graduate diploma, followed by a training course in France, and, on his return to Belgium to look for work, claimed a tide-over allowance (as in the *D'Hoop* case). This was refused on the grounds that he had not completed secondary education in Belgium or pursued education of the same level in another member state and was not the dependent child of a migrant worker residing in Belgium. The CoJ held that Ioannidis fell within the scope of Article 39 EC (now 45 TFEU) whilst seeking work and that, according to the citizenship provisions of the Treaty, under certain conditions, financial assistance cannot be denied to Union citizens. In line with the *Collins* case, the CoJ acknowledged that a link with the employment market could be required, but the fact that Ioannidis had completed a diploma in Belgium had already provided such a link.

In **Case C-406/04 *De Cuyper***, a Belgian national claimed unemployment benefit, but moved to France whilst continuing to claim. Once that information was revealed to the authorities, his claim was denied on the grounds that he was not in residence. The CoJ held that the requirement to reside in Belgium whilst claiming was contrary to Article 18 EC (now 21 TFEU), but that Article 18 EC (now 21 TFEU) breaches can be objectively justified. In this case, the public interest of being able to verify and monitor the right to benefit, which would be very difficult or impossible to do if the claimant were not in the country, was held to be proportionate.

In **Cases C-22 and 23/08** *Vatsouras and Koupatantze v ARGE Nürnberg*, the CoJ was asked to consider the rights to social welfare in some circumstances under Articles 18 and 21 TFEU and the ability of member states under Article 24 of Directive 2004/38 to deny social welfare to EU migrants jobseekers and their families. The Court held, in view of the Treaty Articles and previous case law, that, provided the EU citizens can establish a genuine link with the host state, such as previous employment there, a jobseeker's allowance, which was designed to facilitate access to the labour market, should be available. It was not to be regarded as safety net social assistance, which could be excluded under the Directive. The link must nevertheless be established.

Case C-333/13 *Dano v Jobseeker Leipzig*, which appears to backtrack slightly from the generous interpretation of the CoJ in previous cases and addresses the widespread member state concern about welfare or benefit to tourism. The case involved a lawfully resident (but not with permanent status) Romanian woman who lived in Germany but was non-economically active. Whilst in receipt of some social benefits, she applied for a further non-contributory cash benefit but was denied that by the authorities. This was then challenged relying on Article 18 TFEU and Article 24 of Directive 2004/38, both prohibiting discrimination and both previously seen in similar cases (*Grzelcyck, Sala, Baumbast,* and *Trojani* above in this section) of the non-economically active. In contrast to those earlier cases, in which the lawful residence status was the determinative trigger for equal treatment, the CoJ stressed that meeting the conditions of Directive 2004/38 was the criterion required to trigger equal treatment, in particular under Article 7(1) that they are not an unreasonable burden on the social assistance system of the host state. It is that requirement, according to the CoJ that allows member states to discriminate against those citizens who do not have permanent residence and who claim social benefits. The CoJ did, though, state that each case must be considered by the national court after conducting an assessment of the individual circumstances and merits. Whilst not reversing the earlier case law, it does allow the member states to focus on the 'unreasonable burden' element to deny social benefit claims.

This has been followed up in Case C-67/14 *Alimanovic* involving the claim for social security benefit (SSB) of an EU citizen in Germany who had worked temporarily for 11 months, which was originally granted but then withdrawn. In a reference to the CoJ, it held that according to Article 7(3)(c) of Directive 2004/38, EU citizens who had worked retain their status for six months and have a right to SSB during that period under Article 24(1). Thereafter, they may retain a status as a work seeker but not to SSB as per Article 24(2), so residence rights must be upheld, but not rights to benefits.

12.7.2.3 Education rights under citizenship

In **Cases C-11 and 12/06** *Morgan and Bucher*, two students moved to study abroad, but claimed the benefits to do so from their home state, which demanded that they study in the home state for at least one year. This would add a considerable disincentive by adding a year or at best complicating studies, but was insisted on by the home state to establish a clear link to the state for the purposes of receiving the benefit. The CoJ approved a need to demonstrate a sufficient level of integration with the home state in line with its previous case law. However, it held that, in the cases before it, that need was satisfied because both persons were raised and schooled in the home state. Consequently, the home state could not demand that they study there first for one year.

> **CROSS REFERENCE**
> The case law and rights under this section build on the educational rights developed under the first extensions to the rights of who were neither workers nor self-employed and which were reviewed in section 12.6.1.2.

The *Förster* case now appears not only to confirm *Collins*, but also to roll back slightly the previous generous interpretation of an individual's rights.

Case C-158/07 *Förster v IB-Groep* concerned Ms Förster, a German national in the Netherlands, who, from 2000, worked from time to time there and qualified for a study maintenance grant, which was withdrawn when the responsible authority (IB-Groep) discovered in 2003 that she was no longer working. Her challenge to the decision failed on the grounds she was not sufficiently integrated in the Netherlands and that she had not satisfied the requirement of five years' residence in Holland. On reference to the CoJ, it upheld its previous decision in Case C-209/03 *Bidar* that member states were entitled to require a certain degree of integration and, in this case, a five-year period was justified and proportionate. It seems that the student status distinguished *Förster* from the next cases following.

In **Cases C-523 and 585/11 *Prinz and Seeburger***, a minimum three-year uninterrupted residence requirement in order to receive an education grant for study abroad was held by the CoJ to be too general and disproportionate. The applicant was in fact a national of the granting state.

Thus, as far as welfare rights' entitlement and education based rights are concerned, the economic status of the person—that is, whether a worker or self-employed or even a previous worker or self-employed—is no longer an important factor. Provided there is movement in some way, even back to the home state or lawful residence in the host state, EU citizens will be entitled to be treated without discrimination compared to nationals. However, limitations on this being a universal right have appeared first in cases of a close link between the person seeking benefit and the host states or a period of residence requirement, as in the *Collins, Ioannidis, Morgan and Bucher*, and *Förster* cases, or more recently the requirement of those not permanently resident to meet the criteria of Article 7(1) of Directive 2004/38, as in *Dano* or *Alimanovic*.

The next cases are concerned, for the most part, with non-EU citizens, who are family members of an EU citizen. There is a degree of overlap with the cases considered in relation to TCNs and welfare rights, because members of the family are also those claiming additional rights.

12.7.2.4 Family and carer rights

These cases, in which a greater respect for family life has emerged, are also a product of the move from regarding free movement rights in the EU legal order as wholly dependent on the pursuit of an economic activity to recognising rights that are based on citizenship combined with fundamental freedoms and residence.

In **Case C-60/00 *Carpenter***, the CoJ was more concerned with family rights than arguments about what was the legal basis of the lawful residence of TCN members of the family. The CoJ referred to Article 49 EC (now 56 TFEU) and Regulation 1612/68, which, read strictly, did not apply to the provision of services. These provisions, according to the Court, provide rules protecting the family life of nationals of the member states in order to eliminate obstacles to the exercise of the fundamental freedoms guaranteed by the Treaty. The Court held (at [39]):

It is clear that the separation of Mr and Mrs. Carpenter would be detrimental to their family life and, therefore, to the conditions under which Mr Carpenter exercises a fundamental freedom. That freedom could not be fully effective if Mr Carpenter were to be deterred from exercising it by obstacles raised in his country of origin to the entry and residence of his spouse.

The Court considered that the rights of residence could be subject to objective restrictions, but must comply with fundamental rights and (at [42]–[43]) that:

The decision to deport Mrs. Carpenter constitutes an interference with the exercise by Mr Carpenter of his right to respect for his family life within the meaning of Article 8 of the Convention for the Protection of Human Rights and Fundamental Freedoms and does not strike a fair balance between the competing interests, that is, on the one hand, the right of Mr Carpenter to respect for his family life, and, on the other hand, the maintenance of public order and public safety. This was followed up and applied to Art 45 TFEU in Case C-457/12 S & G but with the proviso that a minimum period of cross border work may be required in order to qualify a worker's family to remain in a member state.

In **Case C-413/99 Baumbast and R v Home Office**, the UK authorities wanted to deport the American national, R. However, because her children had a right to remain and to pursue, under the best possible conditions, their education in the host member state, the CoJ reasoned that this necessarily implies that those children have the right to be accompanied by the person who is their primary carer. Accordingly, that person is able to reside with the children in that member state during their studies. To refuse to grant permission to remain to a parent who is the primary carer of the child exercising his or her right to pursue his or her studies in the host member state infringes that right.

The Court held that Regulation 1612/68, interpreted in the light of Article 8 of the ECHR, entitled the parent who is the primary carer of those children, irrespective of nationality, to reside with them in order to facilitate the exercise of that right, notwithstanding the fact that the parents have meanwhile divorced. The Court considered that the fact that only one parent is a citizen of the Union and that parent has ceased to be a migrant worker in the host member state and that the children are not themselves citizens of the Union, were irrelevant in this regard.

This derived right stems this time not directly from the worker, but from the children of the worker, who are themselves recipients of derived rights. This could be termed 'indirect derived rights'.

A further case that provides express support for family life is **Case C-459/99 MRAX**, which involved the challenge by an interest group to the Belgian authorities' application of Community law in respect of the visa requirements for TCN family members. Certainly, according to Article 3 of Directive 68/360 (now repealed), member states were entitled to demand a visa from the TCN family members. The CoJ reasoned (at [53]) that it is apparent, in particular from the Council Regulations and Directives on freedom of movement for employed and self-employed persons within the Community, that the Community legislature has recognised the importance of ensuring protection for the family life of nationals of the member states in order to eliminate obstacles to the exercise of the fundamental freedoms guaranteed by the Treaty. In this light, the CoJ considered (at [61]) that it is, in any event, disproportionate and therefore prohibitive to send back a TCN married to a national of a member state not in possession of a valid visa where he or she is able to prove his or her identity and the conjugal ties, and there is no evidence to establish that he or she represents a risk to the requirements of public policy, public security, or public health within the meaning of Article 10 of Directive 68/360 and Article 8 of Directive 73/148.

> These aspects are now covered by Articles 27–33 of Directive 2004/38.

Hence, the right to a family life protected by Article 8 ECHR has been instrumental in achieving far-reaching judgments on the rights of family members of Union citizens and is clearly beyond any strict interpretation of EU law rights.

> **Case C-109/01 *Akrich*** also concerned Article 8 ECHR, which, if the marriage in the case were determined to be genuine, would be taken into account when considering the importance of the unlawful residence of the TCN seeking to stay in the UK, although the CoJ attached no actual weight to the consideration that must be given.

The cases of *Jia* and *Metock*, also concerned with TCNs and marriage, have reinforced the weight given to family life, which, unless an abuse of fraud is present, entitles TCN family members to lawfully remain with their EU spouses in a host or home member state. The cases are also considered in section 12.9.4.

Finally in this section is a case that took the protection of EU law for the family to remarkable lengths.

> In **Case C-200/02 *Chen***, the EU citizen concerned was Catherine, the new-born daughter of a Chinese national, Mrs Chen, who was visiting the UK with her husband and who went to Belfast to give birth to Catherine. Under Irish law at the time, any person born in any part of the island of Ireland could acquire Irish nationality and Catherine was subsequently issued with an Irish passport. It was noted as a matter of record by the CoJ that this factual situation was deliberately engineered in order for the child to get EU citizenship and so that the parents could subsequently acquire a right to reside in the UK. The parents were financially self-sufficient with full private medical insurance, but their application for UK long-term residence permits had been rejected. The UK and Ireland had contended that no Community law rights should arise because there had been no movement and Catherine was not exercising any Community law rights. It was already clear that the conferring of nationality was a matter for the member states. In other words, the conferring of Irish nationality and thus EU citizenship was beyond challenge in the UK. The CoJ concluded that Article 18 EC (now 21 TFEU) and Directive 90/364 confer a right to reside for an indefinite period on a young minor who is a national of a member state, and who is covered by appropriate sickness insurance and is in the care of a parent who is a TCN having sufficient resources for that minor not to become a burden on the public finances of the host member state. In such circumstances, those same provisions allow a parent who is a minor's primary carer to reside with the child in the host member state.

❯ CROSS REFERENCE

See section 12.2.1, for more on Declaration No. 2.

The judgment was ironic because the member states expressly reserved the definition of nationality to themselves in Declaration No. 2 previously attached to the EC Treaty. Hence, once national rules had been complied with, other member states could not question the rights under EU law that arose as a consequence. The case escaped the fate of being determined as wholly internal, even though no movement out of an EU state had taken place. The particular legal circumstances of this case are no longer in place in that Ireland has repealed its generous nationality provision.

However, in **Case C-34/09 *Zambrano v ONEM***, Zambrano and his wife, Colombian nationals seeking asylum in Belgium, had two children in Belgium who acquired Belgian nationality; their own applications for Belgium residence, though, had been rejected. In the national court reviewing that decision, they asked whether Articles 12, 17, and 18 EC (now 18, 20, and 21 TFEU) conferred rights of residence in the state in which the EU citizen was born. Despite interventions by member states that the situation was wholly internal and thus beyond the scope of EU law, the CoJ held that Article 20 TFEU did indeed prevent a member state from denying residence to the parents (and carers) of an EU citizen by reason of the fact that the EU citizen dependant would otherwise be denied full exercise (or, as termed in the case, the substance) of his or her rights, including most importantly the right to reside in the EU and thus to exercise all of his or her rights under EU law.

Thus the Court (and the AG before it) upheld the sanctity of EU citizenship once acquired, in the face of member state objections.

More palatable to the member states was the ruling in **Case-434/09 *McCarthy***, which followed shortly after the *Zambrano* ruling. A UK national, who undertook no economic activity, born and living exclusively in the UK with British and, following marriage, Irish nationality, claimed citizenship and thus residence based on EU law. She had hoped to obtain that residence so that her Jamaican husband could also obtain residence under the Treaty and Directive 2004/38. The CoJ this time rejected those claims as not being based on the exercise of any movement by a national of the state in which the rights were claimed. The Court did distinguish the case from *Zambrano* on the ground that there was no fear that she would have to leave the state or residence and could still exercise her rights alone of free movement under EU citizenship. The situation was held to be confined within a single member state—in other words, wholly internal (considered in section 13.2).

Case C-256/11 *Dereci and others* may, though, add a further gloss. It involved the refusal of residence permits by Austria for five non-EU nationals living with Austrian nationals but each in different circumstances. They sought to rely on the *Zambrano* case to obtain the right to stay, but this was distinguished by the CoJ in that in *Zambrano* the derived EU rights gained by the non-EU nationals would be completely lost if forced to return to Columbia, whereas in the five situations in *Dereci*, the option of moving to another EU country and thus obtaining those rights for family members existed and thus those EU rights could be realised.

Thus, EU law does not require member states to admit non-EU spouses or family members where no such right in national law exists and the possibility of moving to another EU state exists.

In a decision, which resembles the *Dano* judgment in section 12.7.2.2 above, the CoJ in Case C-86/12 *Alopka and Moudoulou*, held that the requirement to meet the conditions of Article 7(1) of Directive 2004/38 was an important factor in determining whether a TCN who had twins prematurely (to an absconded French father) in Luxembourg had a right of residence as the carer of EU citizens. However, in line with *Chen*, above, Article 20 would apply to protect the rights of the EU citizens who would, of course, have to leave if their carer was denied the right to remain.

> **Cases C-356 and 357/11 *O, S, and L***, asked the question of the CoJ whether a TCN step-father of an EU child born to a TCN mother in a previous marriage with an EU national could derive residence rights from that child. The Court answered no, provided the substance of the rights on the EU citizen concerned (the EU child of the previous marriage) would not be denied by such a decision. Further, any decision on an application for a residence permit must under the circumstances be considered by the national court both under the family re-unification Directive 2003/86 and Articles 7 and 24 of the EU Charter on Fundamental Rights. Hence, the case is as much, if not more, to do with TCNs than derived carer rights.

> In **Case C-40/11 *Iida v Stadt Ulm***, it was argued that the rights of the child and the right to family life in the EU Fundamental Rights Charter should support a claim under the Treaty citizenship provisions to legitimise a claim by a non-EU worker in Germany to remain there, based on the derived rights from his EU child who had moved with the EU national mother to Austria. The CoJ rejected the argument that the Treaty citizenship rights could be interpreted by reference to the Charter, despite the facts that previous case law including Zambrano, which were not reliant on the Charter, would seem to support such a claim.

The cases, *Zambrano* in particular, appear to extend the reach of EU law into the national law but the *McCarthy* case appears to reaffirm it as more narrowly drawn, and *Iida* appears to step even further back from the generosity of interpretation in favour of TCN nationals by the CoJ.

12.7.3 Citizenship law summary

In summary, the citizenship law, as developed through the cases by the CoJ, would appear to be as follows. Article 21 TFEU has been declared to be directly effective and can be activated in favour of EU citizens by:

- exhausted free movement rights—that is, those once enjoyed by a member state national and which gained him or her lawful entrance and residence in the host state when exercised, but which no longer are or can be relied upon because of changed circumstances (as in the *Baumbast, Sala,* and *Grzelczyk* cases);

- the movement to another member state to receive services, which movement then triggers the general rights of citizenship, even when the EU citizen returns to his or her home state (as in the *D'Hoop* and *Ioannidis* cases); and

- acquisition of nationality of one of the member states (*Chen*), each of which has its own rules for this.

Citizenship rights obtained then further serve to protect the family of the EU citizens in circumstances that previously might have led to the expulsion of a member of the family (as in the *Chen, MRAX,* and *Baumbast* cases).

Whilst the right of residence under Article 21 TFEU continues, according to the CoJ, to be subject to the restrictions inherent in the Treaty and Directive 2004/38, Articles 20 and 21 TFEU appear, according to the Court, to ensure that, provided Union citizens are lawfully resident in a host state, this will trigger citizenship rights, the most important of which are not the political rights contained in Article 22 TFEU, but the general right to be treated without discrimination compared to nationals. However, a clear definition of what constitutes 'lawful residence' is thus far missing in EU law, with the judgments of the CoJ in *Sala* and *Grzelczyk* suggesting that, provided an EU citizen had a lawful

In **Cases 35 and 36/82 *Morson and Jhanjan***, the applicants, both Surinamese nationals, claimed the right to stay in the Netherlands with their Dutch national son and daughter working there. It was held by the CoJ that there was no application of Community law to the wholly internal situation in which national workers had not worked in any other member state. There was no movement from one member state to another by those nationals and Community law did not apply to movement from a third country by members of their family.

This was confirmed in **Cases 64 and 65/96 *Land Nordrhein-Westfalen v Uecker and Jacquet***, concerning two TCNs trying to rely on Community law as spouses of German nationals living in Germany. The case was deemed to be wholly internal and thus not within the scope of application of EC law.

If both cases had concerned, for example, Spanish nationals moving to either the Netherlands or Germany, they would have been allowed to take TCN spouses with them or have relatives join them. In some circumstances, there appears to be some softening of the wholly internal rule. Some cases look wholly internal but because there was some prior movement involved, EU law rights can be triggered against the home state. The amount of movement or degree of economic activity deemed necessary to take a situation out of being wholly internal to one in which EU law applies appears to be decreasing, as exemplified by the following cases.

In **Case C-370/90 *Surinder Singh***, an Indian spouse of a British national was able to use EC law to derive a right of residence in the UK on the basis that the spouse had previously exercised the right of free movement by providing services in another member state, but who then re-established herself in the UK.

In **Case 419/92 *Scholz***, it was held that a frontier worker who continues to live in his or her home state whilst employed in another state, but who crosses the border to work, triggers Community rights that can be claimed within the home state.

In **Case C-60/00 *Carpenter***, a Philippine national claimed a right of residence in the UK with her British spouse on the grounds that he provided services from time to time in other member states. The case is similar to ***Singh*** in as much as services had been provided in another member state before returning to the UK, except that Mrs Carpenter had not left UK soil whilst services were being provided by her husband both from the UK and travelling to other member states. The argument put forward by the applicants was that if Mrs Carpenter had also gone to another member state, both would have had rights of residence and the right to work in the other host EU states. However, she chose to remain in the UK to look after the children and thus to assist her husband in providing services in other member states.

The CoJ referred to Regulation 1612/68, which, strictly speaking, did not apply to the provision of services, but provided rules protecting the family life of national workers of the member states in order to eliminate obstacles to the exercise of the fundamental freedoms guaranteed by the Treaty. The Court held:

> It is clear that the separation of Mr and Mrs Carpenter would be detrimental to their family life and, therefore, to the conditions under which Mr Carpenter exercises a fundamental freedom. That freedom could not be fully effective if Mr Carpenter were to be deterred from exercising it by obstacles raised in his country of origin to the entry and residence of his spouse.

The CoJ noted that the marriage appeared genuine, that there were no official complaints against Mrs Carpenter, and that she looked after the children while Mr Carpenter was providing services. The Court held that Article 49 EC (now 56 TFEU), read in the light of the fundamental right to respect for family life (Article 8 ECHR), is to be interpreted as preventing a member state from refusing the TCN spouse of a provider of services established in that member state who provides services to recipients established in other member states a right to reside in its territory.

In **Case C-281/98 *Angonese***, an Italian citizen applied for a job in Italy, but was refused entry to the selection process because he did not have the appropriate local authority certificate of bilingualism, despite being accepted by the local court as perfectly bilingual and possessing certificates of language study from the University of Vienna where he had studied. The Italian government and defendant bank argued that the matter was wholly internal and had no connection with Community law. Whilst there was movement in this case, in that Mr Angonese had studied in Austria, the economic activity was the receiving of educational services. The CoJ held that the previous movement for the purposes of study had nevertheless triggered Community law rights.

A further case in this category is **Case C-403/03 *Schempp***. Divorce maintenance was being paid in another member state and the German tax regime that would normally have applied was denied. Consequently, a tax exemption on the payments was lost. It was argued by Germany and other governments that this was a wholly internal situation that had involved no movement on the part of Mr Schempp. The CoJ held, however, that the exercise of the right of free movement by the former spouse of Mr Schempp had an effect on his right to deduct tax in Germany and was therefore not a wholly internal situation, with no connection to Community law. The difference in treatment offended Article 12 EC (now 18 TFEU), although the Court stressed that, in view of the different tax regimes, Community law does not guarantee neutrality of treatment if a person takes advantage of the free movement rights under Article 18 EC (now 21 TFEU).

Case C-148/02 *Garcia Avello* looks very much wholly internal, with no movement taking place that was directly connected with the facts of the case. It involved dual nationality children of a Spanish father living in Belgium, who wished to register the children's names according to Spanish custom and practice and not Belgian. The CoJ, relying on Articles 17 and 12 EC (now 20 and 18 TFEU), held that the children's future rights to move back to Spain might be prejudiced by Belgium, contrary to the Treaty, and that by denying them the right to follow the Spanish tradition, Belgium discriminated against them on grounds of nationality.

Whilst **Case C-17/00 *de Coster*** was concerned with a national tax regime, it was nevertheless eligible to be considered under EU law. In the view of the CoJ, because the taxation was applicable only to the installation of satellite dishes that could receive television broadcasts from other member states, and not to the installation of receiving equipment capable of receiving purely domestic broadcasts, a cross-border element was produced. Television signals, which had been broadcast from another member state, could easily be received, thus introducing the cross-border element.

In similar vein, **Case C-544/03 *Mobistar*** was concerned with mobile phone masts, and also triggered the application and consideration of EU law because mobile phone signals can equally satisfy the cross-border service element.

Finally, in this context, is **Case C-200/02 *Chen***, which involved no movement from one member state to another, but, because of the particular legal rules in Ireland, nevertheless triggered the application of EU law. Ireland, at the time of the case, granted nationality to anyone born on the geographic island of Ireland, regardless of origin and nationality of parents, so when a daughter of Chinese parents was born in Northern Ireland, she became Irish and thus an EU citizen, from whom rights for the parent derived.

Thus, a factual circumstance, which on the face of it appears to be wholly internal, may nevertheless be transformed into one subject to EU law for the following reasons. If there has been some previous movement into another member state, or services have or can be received, physical or metaphysical, from another member state, or payments are made in another member state, or other facts intervene to establish some cross-border element, such as a change in legal status, then the matter is not wholly internal and is subject to EU law. This last would include the *Chen* case and the marriage of TCNs cases such as Case C-109/01 *Akrich*, considered in section 12.9.4. As can be seen from the cases, however, the dividing line between what is wholly internal and what falls within the EU citizenship rules is thin. Cases C-34/09 *Zambrano*, C-434/09 *McCarthy*, and C-256/11 *Dereci and others*, considered in section 12.7.2.4, also demonstrate this.

For more details on this section visit the online resources.

12.9 The treatment of third-country nationals (TCNs)

Nationals from third countries lawfully or unlawfully resident in a member state were not previously subject to EU law unless specifically catered for, for example as family members of EU persons taking advantage of the free-movement-of-persons rules. Independent TCNs were originally entirely a matter for national law regulation, despite the fact that there are millions of TCNs lawfully or unlawfully resident in the EU. Estimates put the figure at approximately 18.5 to 20 million TCNs lawfully resident in the 28 EU states, prior to Croatian membership. The recent migration influx of

2014–15 has no doubt swelled these numbers considerably. Whilst it may have been the case in the past that the treatment of TCNs was regarded as being below the standards of treatment to be expected from the EC, more recently the CoJ, the Commission, and the member states in the Council of Ministers have been addressing the rights of TCNs. Much attention has been directed to the immigration policies and the Schengen Agreement regarding the entry and visa regulation of TCNs, whereas less attention has been paid to the rights, including rights of free movement, of those already in the EU.

Previously, the CoJ has held, for example in Case 238/83 *Mr and Mrs Richard Meade*, that the Treaty Articles on free movement of workers apply solely to EU nationals and not therefore to TCNs.

12.9.1 Association and cooperation agreements

The first of the exceptions to the absence of EU regulation is where TCNs have been provided with rights under the various association and cooperation agreements with countries such as Turkey, Algeria, and Morocco.

12.9.2 Workers 'posted' abroad

For more details on this section visit the online resources.

Secondly, TCNs may form part of the workforce of a company established in the EU that sends workers abroad to complete a contract in another member state, which were covered by Directive 96/71, now supplemented by Directive 2014/67, noted next.

> In **Case C-43/93 *Van der Elst***, the CoJ confirmed that TCNs also have the right of free movement within the context of the right of free movement of companies that are established within the EU. This right is subject to the condition that the non-EU nationals are part of the legal labour force of the company established in the home member state and where the employer provides services in another member state.

> In **Case C-341/05 Laval**, the Posted Workers Directive was also applied in respect of industrial action to prevent Latvian workers entering Sweden to be able to undertake a contract for a Latvian company at much lower costs than negotiated between Swedish employers and employees. It was held to be a hindrance on the free movement of the Latvian posted workers and that not all host rules should be applied to posted workers undertaken work on a temporary basis, as was seen also with the cases considered under section 12.4.

In 2014, a new Posted Workers Directive (2014/67 OJ 2014 L159/11) was enacted to take into account the above case developments, so that member states could adopt measures to ensure companies could not exploit host states rules and regulations and to improve the enforcement of the rules of the first Posted Workers Directive.

12.9.3 General rights for TCNs

For more details on this section visit the online resources.

There has also now been legislative intervention in this area and further proposals have also been made. Regulation 1091/2001 was enacted, which provides limited rights of free movement for those TCNs in the EU on a long-stay visa. TCNs may also be helped by Directive 2000/43, which prohibits discrimination based on race; however, Article 3(2) of the Directive states that it is without prejudice to the provisions and conditions relating to the entry and residence of TCNs and to any treatment that arises from the legal status of TCNs. So, whilst it may prevent unequal treatment in the country of residence, it is unlikely to provide a right of free movement.

Specifically, addressing the situation of divided families with TCN family members, the institutions have enacted the Reunification Directive 2003/86, which provides that lawfully resident TCNs in member states may apply to have their family join them from a third country provided they are self-sufficient and have been in the member state for a year or more. Furthermore, Article 3 of the Directive requires that the resident TCNs must have a reasonable prospect of remaining longer. The definition of family has been restrictively drawn and member states retain much discretion in deciding whether to grant an application. The Directive does not apply to the UK, Ireland, and Denmark, which have opted out of the governing section of the Treaty (Articles 77–80 TFEU).

Article 59 EEC (now 56 TFEU) was amended by the Single European Act (SEA), and now provides that the European Parliament and the Council, acting in accordance with the ordinary legislative procedure, may extend the provisions of the Chapter to TCNs who provide services and who are established within the Union.

Directive 2003/109 permits TCNs who have been lawfully resident in the EU for a minimum of five years to apply for, and acquire, a certain status that entitles them to long-term residence in the host state and limited rights of movement within the EU. These rights are subject to the public policy and security derogations, self-sufficiency, and sickness insurance requirements, and quotas and restrictions on movements imposed by the other secondary states. The Directive extends to core family members, as defined by the Reunification Directive 2003/86, but these may not be admitted by a second EU state. Indeed, whilst the Directive does provide new rights for TCNs, it does so only without prejudice to all of the other legislative provisions already providing rights and is subject to interpretation by the member states, which may dilute some of its provisions. It came into force on 23 January 2006 and is nevertheless a welcome if, in the end, somewhat modest, improvement. Directives 2003/86 and 2003/109 do not apply to the UK, Ireland, and Denmark.

The further legislative interventions and proposals in this area are beyond most courses on EU law and will not be rehearsed here, but please visit the online resources for references.

12.9.4 Case law on TCNs

Case law has also had an impact in this area of law, although, as will be seen, some cases concerning TCNs are accommodated within the existing EU free movement regime after consideration of the facts by the CoJ. The first case, concerned with the rights of TCNs, actually contains two sets of factual circumstances, but is referred to under one name.

> **Case C-413/99 *Baumbast*** concerned 'R', an American woman who had neither personal nor derived rights to remain in the EU. Nevertheless, it was held by the CoJ that she had a right of residence under Community law and was able to resist an attempt to deport her. R moved to the UK with her French husband, who had obtained work in the UK. Later, the couple divorced and, in line with the jurisprudence of the *Diatta* and *Reed* cases, R lost her own legal right to remain in the host state as no longer coming within Article 10 of Regulation 1612/68 as a spouse. R and her children nevertheless remained in the UK. Whilst the children were granted indefinite leave to remain, R was not. The UK authorities wanted to deport her and, by necessity, her children. However, the children remained the children of an EU national, but who was no longer working in the UK. The CoJ held that Regulation 1612/68 must be interpreted as entitling the parent who is the primary carer of children, irrespective of nationality, to reside with them in order to facilitate the exercise of that right, notwithstanding the fact

> that the parents have meanwhile divorced. The fact that only one parent is a citizen of the Union who ceased to be a migrant worker in the host member state and whose children are not themselves citizens of the Union is irrelevant in this regard. According to the CoJ, to refuse to grant permission to remain to a parent who is the primary carer of the child exercising his (or her) right to pursue his (or her) studies in the host member state infringes that right (at [73] of the judgment).

Hence, there is an implied right within Article 12 of the Regulation (now Article 10 of Regulation 492/2011) that the child of a migrant worker may not only pursue his or her education in the host member state, but also that the child has the right to be accompanied by the person who is his or her primary carer. Furthermore, that person is able to reside with him or her in that member state during his or her studies.

> Case C-109/01 *Akrich* involved a Moroccan, who, after both unlawful and lawful attempts to enter and remain in the UK, married a UK national and moved to Ireland for a short period expressly in order to take advantage of EC law rights. The Secretary of State considered that Mr and Mrs Akrich's move to Ireland was no more than a temporary absence deliberately designed to manufacture a right of residence for Mr Akrich on his return to the UK and thereby to evade the provisions of the UK's national legislation. Therefore, the view was formed that Mrs Akrich had not been genuinely exercising rights under the EC Treaty as a worker in another member state. The CoJ was asked, among other questions, whether an engineered situation to evade national immigration laws was an abuse of Community law rights and, if so, whether the UK authorities could lawfully refuse entry. The CoJ held that the motive for going to Ireland was not relevant to the status of a worker, nor the decision to return to the home state. The Court did, however, acknowledge that there would be an abuse if the facilities afforded by Community law in favour of migrant workers and their spouses were invoked in the context of marriages of convenience entered into in order to circumvent the provisions relating to entry and residence of nationals of non-member states. If genuinely married, however, Article 8 ECHR should be taken into regard in considering the unlawful residence status of the TCN.
>
> The CoJ held that Article 10 of Regulation 1612/68 (now contained in Article 2 of Directive 2004/38) applies to TCNs only if they are lawfully resident in a member state before they move to another state to take advantage of the rights provided by the Regulation. It is not applicable where a marriage of convenience has been arranged to circumvent a member state's laws.

Therefore, if the marriage is genuine, despite a lack of lawful residence, member states should pay regard to Article 8 ECHR. This judgment does not provide a full answer and the main question that is left to the member state is whether or not the marriage was genuine.

> In **Case C-1/05 *Jia***, in which the scope of the *Akrich* judgment was raised, the CoJ held that neither the *Akrich* judgment nor Community law in general permitted member states to restrict the entry of a TCN relative of the spouse of a Community citizen only to where the TCN relative had first been resident in another EU country. In other words, the TCN could move directly to join her relative in the EU direct from the third country. The Court also held, though, that the proof of dependency for such moves, required previously under Directive 73/148 but now catered for by Directive 2004/38, required real proof of factual dependency from any appropriate means, not merely an undertaking from a member of the family.

A further group of claims in Case C-127/08 *Metock* confirm the *Jia* judgment and were based on Directive 2004/38.

> **Case C-127/08 *Metock and others*** considered numerous Articles of Directive 2004/38 where four TCNs who had been refused asylum in Ireland then married EU citizens lawfully resident in Ireland. In the judgment, the CoJ expressly reversed part of the judgment in *Akrich* by making clear that the Directive is not conditional on a requirement that a TCN must have been lawfully resident in another member state to stay in a member state as a spouse or member of the family of an EU citizen. The Court held that rights provided for spouses to accompany EU citizens apply irrespective of where the marriage took place and how the TCN entered the host member state. The facts of the case stated that these were not marriages of convenience, although, under Article 35 of the Directive, member states can take action to penalise those who do abuse rights or engage in fraud.

See also Cases C-356 and 357/11 *O, S, and L*, considered in section 12.7.2.3, on the rights of TCN stepfathers of EU children.

The member states are somewhat concerned as to the further consequences of this judgment.

12.9.5 **Summary of TCN rights**

The statutory and case law developments represent some slight improvement in the position of lawfully resident TCNs in the EU. The EU legislature and the CoJ are being very careful in trying to provide rules for TCNs who have a reasonable claim to reside and exercise rights of free movement, but without opening the door too widely so that unlawful residents gain a right to remain and obtain benefits against the wishes of the member state. These matters are highly politically charged in the present day. Another way of regulating TCNs and simultaneously prompting further recognition of their rights in the EU is by the policies pursued by the Schengen Agreement, which is not considered in this text.

Where TCNs are members of the family of a Union citizen who has exercised his or her rights under Community law, Articles 12 and 13 of Directive 2004/38 now provide the most secure rights with, after five years, the right of permanent residence, even in the event of the death of or divorce from the Union citizen.

The Lisbon Treaty has provided a better basis for the rights of TCNs and, under Article 67(2) TFEU, aims to frame a common policy on asylum, immigration, and external border controls that is fair towards TCNs. The provisions from both the EU and EC Treaties have been regrouped in Articles 67–74 TFEU. In order to achieve the broad objectives of Article 67, Article 75 provides for the ordinary legislative procedure to be used, which involves the co-decision procedure—a very positive move away from intergovernmentalism to supranationalism in this more controversial area of Union activity. The individual areas of border controls, asylum, and immigration are then set out respectively in Articles 77–79, the further details of which go beyond the necessary remit of this work.

Summary

The EU law provision for the free movement of persons has changed considerably from its inception. Whilst the Treaty Articles themselves have hardly changed since 1957, the scope of the rights available now to individuals has expanded considerably due to both secondary legislation and judicial interpretation.

The rights were not, in the end, employed in a way that helped to promote the economies of the EC and later Union and its member states by the mass migration of workers from one member state to another. Instead, the rights were assumed by individuals alone and consequently on a small scale. The secondary legislation and continued liberal interpretation of it by the CoJ opened up free movement for persons in the EU and their families, and it is argued that because families were granted derived rights from the workers to work and obtain various social benefits, these aspects helped further to remove the disincentives in moving to a new country in order to engage in an economic activity.

This chapter also considered the extension of free movement rights, which affect three main areas: the extension of free movement rights into European citizenship; wholly internal situations; and the position of TCNs.

Whilst any true, wholly internal situation would exclude the validity of the application of EU law, the case law on this and on the receipt of services mean that even a fairly low level of activity, or even potential activity, as in the *de Coster* case, can turn a wholly internal matter into an EU matter.

We have seen, through the case law, that TCNs may derive rights from their EU family members, including children. Even where the children are non-EU nationals, who nevertheless have rights of their own to stay in the host state, as in the case of *R*, EU nationals and TCN family members can derive further rights from those children to stay in the host state. With regard to the rights of free-standing TCNs lawfully resident in the member states, EU law developments in free movement and citizenship appear to add even more pressure for legal reform to bring their rights into line.

Where citizenship rights are established through lawful residence, Article 18 TFEU applies, and if an EU citizen is lawfully resident in another member state, there is no requirement that he or she be economically active to be entitled to equal treatment, including, for example, equal treatment in non-contributory welfare benefits on the same basis as nationals. It is even possible to be a burden on the state, albeit a reasonable one only, as in *Grzelczyk*.

It would seem that only EU citizens who do not move at any time to another member state to receive or provide services are unable to obtain these welfare and family rights unless provided for under national law.

It is clear that the legal regime regulating the free movement of persons has come a long way from the near-empty and little-used original Treaty provision for it. It is ironic, then, that at the present stage of the evolution of free movement rights, the concern is whether those rights have now actually gone too far and encroached too much on areas of the member states' own national laws, more than is universally acceptable.

THINKING POINT

Does EU citizenship and the right not to be discriminated against apply to rule out all discrimination against host EU citizens in comparison with nationals in all areas of law? Does an unemployed tourist on holiday receive services? If so, do these activate Article 20 TFEU citizenship rights? Again, if so, does this then trigger the general right of equal treatment—that is, the right to obtain benefits on the same basis as nationals if, for the sake of argument, he or she runs short of money whilst on holiday?

These dangers of an over-expansive interpretation of EU law may now mean that EU citizens who have established lawful residence in a host state will have equal rights to the full spectrum of contributory and non-contributory social benefits, and that, as such, the spectre of 'benefit tourism' has effectively been raised whereby EU nationals and their TCN family members can roam the member states in search of the 'good life'. Recent case law, however, has suggested that there is a limit to this that the member states can control by requiring a close connection to the state or a period of residence requirement, as in the *Collins, Ioannidis*, and *Förster* cases.

These issues are considered in some of the articles noted in the end-of-chapter Further reading list.

However, as is often the case with the very dynamic system of EU law, the burning questions with which we are left will only be answered by either the CoJ in future cases or by the intervention of the member states through Treaty or secondary legislative amendment.

The final comment is on Brexit. Clearly it will have some impact on the citizens of the UK and the other member states of the EU. Will the UK still be subject to the free-movement-of-persons laws as a part of continued membership of, or access to, the single market? Whilst this was agreed on 8 December 2016, that certain rights be retained, as this impacts only on a state which is exiting, strictly it thus falls outside of the substance of this chapter. Therefore, the details are not included here and I shall leave any further comments for inclusion in the online Brexit updates.

For up-to-date information on freedom of movement for UK citizens post Brexit visit the online resources.

? Questions

1. Who is a worker for the purposes of the TFEU?

2. Who is entitled to join a worker in the host state?

3. Give four case law examples of how the CoJ has interpreted social and tax advantages from Article 7(2) of Regulation 1612/68 (now Article 7(2) of Regulation 492/2011).

4. To what extent does the public service proviso allow member states to exclude all entry to public service employment in its territory?

5. For what reasons may a member state refuse entry to, or lawfully deport, an EU worker?

For suggested approaches to answering these questions visit the online resources.

6. Is European citizenship to be equated with European nationality?

7. It seems, following the case law on citizenship, that it is no longer necessary actively to engage in an economic activity to trigger valuable EU law rights. What will now trigger those rights?

8. What is meant by 'reverse discrimination'?

9. What is the 'wholly internal rule'?

Sample exam Q&A

For guidance on how to tackle this specimen exam question and to read a suggested model answer, visit the online resources. www.oup. com/uk/foster_ directions6e/.

Essay question

Discuss the extent to which free movement of persons and citizenship in the EU legal order now allows EU citizens and their families to reside and obtain equal rights in any member state of the EU.

Further reading

Books

Barnard, C. *The Substantive Law of the EU: The Four Freedoms*, 4th edn, Oxford University Press, Oxford, 2013 (Chapters 11–17).

Barnard, C. 'Free movement of natural persons and citizenship of the Union' in Barnard, C. and Peers, S. (eds) *European Union Law*, 2nd edn, Oxford University Press, Oxford, 2017, p. 369.

Barnard, C. and Snell, T., 'Free movement of legal persons and the provision of services' in Barnard, C. and Peers, S. (eds) *European Union Law*, 2nd edn, Oxford University Press, Oxford, 2017, p. 409.

Freedland, M. and Prassl, J. *Viking, Laval and Beyond*, Hart Publishing, Oxford, 2016.

Goudappel, F. *The Effects of EU Citizenship. Economic, Social and Political Rights in a Time of Constitutional Change*, Asser Press, The Hague, 2010.

Guild, E. and Peers, S. *The EU Citizenship Directive: A Commentary*, Oxford University Press, Oxford, 2014.

Nascimbene, B. and Bergamini, E. *The Legal Professions in the European Union*, Kluwer Law International, London, 2009.

Weiss, F. and Wooldridge, F. *Free Movement of Persons within the European Community*, 2nd edn, Kluwer Law International, The Hague, 2007.

Articles

Barnard, C. 'Unravelling the Services Directive' (2008) 41 CML Rev 323.

Borg-Barthet, J. 'European private international law of companies after *Cartesio*' (2009) 58 ICLQ 1020.

Costello, C. 'Metock: free movement and "normal family life" in the Union' (2009) 46 CML Rev 587.

Dautricourt, C. and Thomas, S. 'Reverse discrimination and free movement of persons under Community law: all for Ulysses, nothing for Penelope?' (2009) 34 EL Rev 433.

Dougan, M. 'The constitutional dimension to the case law on Union citizenship' (2006) 31 EL Rev 613.

Eisele, K. and van der Mei, A. P. 'Portability of social benefits and reverse discrimination of EU citizens vis-a-vis Turkish Nationals: comment on Akdas' (2012) 37 EL Rev 204.

Foster, N. 'Family and welfare rights in Europe: the impact of recent European Court of Justice Decisions in the area of the free movement of persons' (2003) 25 J Soc Wel & Fam L 291.

Hailbronner, J. 'Union citizenship and access to social benefits' (2005) 42 CML Rev 1245.

Hinarejos, A. 'Citizenship of the EU: clarifying "genuine enjoyment of the substance" of citizenship rights' (2012) 71 CLJ 279.

Hofstoetter, B. 'A cascade of rights, or who shall care for little Catherine? Some reflections on the Chen case' (2005) 30 EL Rev 548.

Jacobs, F. 'Citizenship of the European Union: a legal analysis' (2007) 13 ELJ 1591.

Johnston, A. and Syrpis, P. 'Regulatory competition in European company law after Cartesio' (2009) 34 ELR 378.

Kocharov, A. 'What intra-Community mobility for third-country workers?' (2008) 33(6) EL Rev 913.

Kochenov, D. and Plender, R. 'EU citizenship: from an incipient form to an incipient substance? The discovery of the treaty text' (2012) 37 EL Rev 369.

Kostakopoulou, D. 'European Union citizenship: writing the future' (2007) 13(5) ELJ 623.

Kostakopoulou, D. 'When EU citizens become foreigners' (2014) 20(4) ELJ 447.

Mather, J. 'The Court of Justice and the Union citizen' (2005) 11 ELJ 722.

Newdick, C. 'Citizenship, free movement and health care: cementing individual rights by corroding social solidarity' (2006) 43 CML Rev 1645.

Reich, N. 'The constitutional relevance of citizenship and free movement in an enlarged Union' (2005) 11 ELJ 675.

Reynolds, S. 'Exploring the "intrinsic connection" between free movement and the genuine enjoyment test: reflections on EU citizenship after Iida' (2013) 21 EL Rev 376.

Tryfonidou, A. 'Family reunification rights of (migrant) Union citizens: towards a more liberal approach' (2009) 15 ELJ 634.

Tryfonidou, A. 'In search of the aim of the EC Free Movement of Persons provisions: has the Court of Justice missed the point?' (2009) 46 CML Rev 1591.

Witte, F. de 'Who funds the mobile student? Shedding some light on the normative assumptions underlying EU free movement law: Commission v. Netherlands' (2013) 50 CML Rev 203.

13

An introduction to EU competition policy and law

□ **LEARNING OBJECTIVES**

In this chapter, you will learn about:

- the basics of competition law and policy in general;
- the reasons why a competition policy was adopted for the EU;
- the principal legislative competition law provisions in the EU;
- Article 101 TFEU and anti-competitive behaviour;
- Article 102 TFEU and the abuse of a dominant position;
- the enforcement of EU competition law; and
- the oversight and control of mergers in the EU.

Introduction

European Union (EU) competition law is a mature and developed area of EU law designed to ensure that there is free and fair competition in the EU and to assist in the creation and maintenance of the EU internal market. It has seen a transition from a system largely regulated by the EU Commission Competition directorate, to one that in 2003 was significantly delegated to the competition authorities of the member states. The principal rules of EU competition law, namely Articles 101 and 102 TFEU, have remained the same however. This chapter focuses on those rules for the most part, but also considers the enforcement of the competition law regime and merger regulation in the EU.

13.1 Competition policy and law

For more details on this quote visit the online resources.

Competition law applies to regulate the activities of mainly commercial undertakings to curb the excesses of the free market or to remedy situations that, in an unregulated free market, would be harmful to some parties or the system of competition itself. The idea of competition lies at the heart of the capitalist system and EU economic law. It conjures up images of the free market—a free market economy with minimal state intervention. It suggests the efficiency of the actors in the marketplace determining what should be made where and for what price and, more to the point, free from state planning or state production. An American appeal court judge summed it up in this way: 'If, as the metaphor goes, a market economy is governed by an invisible hand, competition is surely the brass knuckles by which it enforces its decisions.'

It is often commented that competition is desirable for many reasons. Competition is supposed to ensure efficiency by giving the greatest awards to the keenest in the marketplace. This efficiency is meant to provide a benefit to all in that it improves living standards, creates employment, and allows the consumer to benefit from a competitive market. Competition is therefore seen as a healthy and desirable state of affairs by economists, particularly of the right wing, who would point to the obvious failure of the planned uncompetitive economies of the communist world, which were unable to provide the gains in the standard of living achieved in the West. Thus, if competition is good, then more competition is surely better. It is therefore desirable to increase the scale over which competition can be achieved—that is, create a larger and freer market. The internal market of the EU must therefore be a good thing for the industry and economy of the member states. European-wide competition should stimulate the entire economy of the EU for both the domestic and world markets. The Commission in one of its notices on competition law has made it clear it regards competition rules as necessary to enhance consumer welfare and to ensure the efficient allocation of resources (Offiial Journal (OJ) [2004] C101/97). To a large degree, in contrast to previous judgments, this is supported now by the Court of Justice (CoJ) as expressed in Case C-209/10 *Post Denmark*.

However, unfettered competition does not maintain the status quo and, left unregulated, it is ultimately self-destructive. The most efficient undertakings will finally drive other competition out of business, leaving a monopoly that can then exploit the market to the detriment of consumers and the economy generally. So, in order to retain fair competition, some form of intervention on the part of a state is required. To continue to reap the benefits of competition, given that perfect competition is well nigh impossible, a state between perfect competition and oligopoly or monopoly must be maintained. For this, certain criteria must be fulfilled. There must be no discrimination between buyers, sellers, and producers. This is actually a requirement of the Common Agricultural Policy (CAP) (see Article 40(2) TFEU). There should be a supply of homogeneous commodities—that is, the same or at least very similar products must be available and, thus, in competition with each other. There should be a large number of buyers and sellers. Where there are a limited number (known as an **oligopoly**) or only one or two (**monopoly** or **duopoly**), the market can be severely affected or influenced by these companies.

> **Monopoly/duopoly** Where there is/are only one or two participants in the market.

> **Oligopoly**
> Where there are only a limited or few participants in the market.

There should be close and free contact between buyers and sellers in all parts of the market—that is, no artificial obstacles to trade, by tariffs or geography, etc. Without these, the market distorts or becomes imperfect, with the upper hand being achieved by one side or the other; today this is usually, but not always, the producer or seller rather than the consumer or buyer. Very large supermarket chains, though, have been known to be very demanding of their suppliers.

13.2 Competition policy and law in the EU

Competition law regulation was regarded as a necessary and essential element in the building and functioning of the Community and Union.

> A view confirmed by the Court of Justice (CoJ) in **Case C-126/97 *Eco Swiss China Time Ltd***
> (at [36]): 'Article 85 of the Treaty (now Article 101 TFEU) constitutes a fundamental provision
> which is essential for the accomplishment of the tasks entrusted to the Community and, in
> particular, for the functioning of the internal market.'

Apart from the previously noted general reasons, the EU needed an integrated competition policy to complement and ensure the maintenance of the internal market—the whole establishment or foundation of the EU is premised on the desire to promote integration and create a single unified market. One of the wider aims of the internal market is to establish and maintain European-wide competition to stimulate the entire economy of the EU for both the domestic and world markets. A competition policy within the overall Treaty regime prevents companies from setting up their own rules and obstacles to trade to replace the national rules and obstacles the EU is trying to abolish. It was clearly stated by the CoJ in Cases 56 and 58/64 *Consten* and *Grundig* that the desire on the part of the Community to remove barriers to trade and create a Common Market would not allow undertakings to restore national divisions or reconstruct barriers to trade.

The two go hand in hand; you cannot have one without ensuring that you have the other. To have prevented the member states on the one hand from restricting the movement of goods just to allow private companies to carve up the EU into national territories or dictate terms and conditions in those divided territories by their agreements and practices would defeat the objectives of the first policy. Conversely, to prevent companies from artificially dividing the markets but to allow the member states to do so would undermine a competition policy. It is worth noting that some multinational companies are in a better position to divide the market and have the same or greater turnover than the gross or national domestic product of some states. Without regulation, it would be the companies and not the member state deciding on trade flows. In order to retain fair competition in the EU, some form of intervention on the part of EU is therefore required.

The broad EU policy objective remains to maintain and encourage competition for the benefit of the EU and its citizens, to achieve an open and unified market and the integration of the EU, to encourage economic activity among small and medium-sized enterprises, and to maximise economic efficiency by allowing the free flow of goods and resources. Following the 2003 reforms, consumer welfare has also been highlighted as one of the objectives of a competition policy.

Much of the basis of EU competition policy has been borrowed from the US experience of the concentration in too few hands of power over the marketplace and also, to some extent, post-war German concern to combat the power of the large firms and cartels that obtained not only too much economic power but consequently undemocratic political power in the Weimar Republic and in Hitler's Germany.

Thus, in the period following the Second World War, German attitudes to competition were adopted in Europe. Attitudes were also influenced by the desire to protect emerging and expanding industries and companies and to encourage the rebirth of European industry after the devastation of the war.

The EU is interventionist in order to outlaw abuses of industry to the detriment of consumers and the market. However, too much intervention hinders growth and results in inefficient, small-scale production, which cannot benefit from the economies of scale. Therefore, the EU must tread a middle path. One of the fundamental positions of competition law to be established was that there should be no barriers to entry to the market of new companies and industries to ensure fairness and equality among businesses. It was also considered vital to promote European business to compete with US and Japanese capital and business ventures (now the **BRICS** economies), which already benefit from having a huge internal market on their doorsteps).

BRICS

Brazilian, Russian, Indian, Chinese, and South African economies.

So, the competition policy and rules chosen should also promote the integration of European business, especially small and medium-sized business; but at the same time, it must be ensured that companies do not become too competitive or over-concentrate and able to eliminate competition, thereby starting to dominate a market, or to cooperate in such a way as to act as one unit in the EU to the detriment of consumers and smaller firms. In the EU, regulatory action has been focused more on the larger players in the market than the small and medium-sized business enterprises.

One of the problems with EU competition policy is in respect of the multiple objectives that exist. If they are complementary there is no conflict, but if they are in fact different—objectives that require different approaches to achieve them—some difficulties, not least at the legal level, will be experienced.

The overall policy is underpinned by conflicting ideologies of why—or even how—it is to be achieved. On the one hand, a market-oriented approach defines the problems of competition as barriers to free trade which must be removed. This approach presupposes that there is formal equality of all individuals (undertakings) in the market and the Commission is merely interested in the regulation of the market per se and not on any particular interest. This leads to difficulties in satisfying all objectives, especially in the area of merger policy. On the other hand, the 'structural approach' concerns changes to the market structure because the inequality of the actors has been recognised. Therefore, the Commission is entitled to regulate and structure the market in order to achieve the goals set by the inclusion of competition policy in the EU, which can lead to difficulties in rationalising all the decisions. Thus, it is argued, you can easily achieve single objectives such as a competition policy, which has the simple aim of preventing distortion in the market. The actual prevention of this may not be simple, but the goal is unambiguous and not confused or subject to conflicting priorities. Or, you can have an industry policy to encourage small and medium-sized EU firms, or a customs policy to discourage external imports or rules to ensure the free movement of goods, or a consumer protection policy which seeks to ensure that consumers are not harmed by the activities of undertakings and that any intervention is designed to enhance the choice of consumers in the marketplace. However, when all these various policies are pursued within one supposed clear objective called competition policy, it will lead to difficulties because there is a need to regulate all of them with an eye on the others. In some quarters, this is seen as one of the steps on the way to political unity—that is, functionalism or the interrelatedness of everything. Furthermore, the particular aims pursued can change from time to time. Sometimes, the structural approach has the upper hand and is criticised because it is regarded as applying more overtly political than economic motives, in that it gives too much encouragement to small and medium-sized business and is too heavy on large-scale industry, which is the only one capable of competing on the world markets with the US, Chinese, Indian, South Korean, and Japanese industries. Then, at other times, there seems to be more concentration on larger companies or on consumer protection. Thus, the Commission may be interpreting the competition rules to meet changing objectives as politically required, for example to make the rules lighter to promote certain industries so that they can compete worldwide, or tighter to discourage entry by others, or to take account of state-imposed distortions, as with the French tobacco industry, or to protect certain agricultural products vital for the CAP. Worker protection and environmental considerations may also play their part. The point of all of this is that if you are not aware that this is happening and only seek to learn the rules, you will have difficulty in rationalising rules between cases when rationality does not exist or has been undermined by conflicting policy objectives. Hence, the approach here is not to present all the rules in competition policy, but just to demonstrate the most important in the context of the leading cases.

13.2.1 **Legislative outline**

EU competition rules are generally designed to intervene to prevent agreements that fix prices, conditions, or the supply of products, to prohibit agreements that carve up territories, and to prevent abuses of market power that have the effect of removing real competition and controlling mergers, which would also remove competition. As with the free movement of goods, the rules cover all items capable of forming the subject of commercial transactions. The aims are set out in the Preamble to the Treaty on the Functioning of the European Union (TFEU) and Article 3 in both Treaty on European Union (TEU) and TFEU.

The Preamble to the TFEU states that the 'removal of existing obstacles calls for concerted action in order to guarantee steady expansion, balanced trade and fair competition'. Article 3 TEU refers to a 'highly competitive social market' and Article 3(1)(b) TFEU lists among the exclusive competences of the EU 'the establishing of competition rules necessary for the functioning of the internal market'. The previous formulation found in Article 3(g) EC, containing the requirement that there should be 'a system ensuring that competition in the internal market is not distorted', has been relegated to Protocol No. 27 attached to the Treaties.

Protocol No. 27 on the Internal Market and Competition

The High Contracting Parties,

CONSIDERING that the internal market as set out in Article 3 of the Treaty on European Union includes a system ensuring that competition is not distorted,

HAVE AGREED that: To this end, the Union shall, if necessary, take action under the provisions of the Treaties, including under Article 352 of the Treaty on the Functioning of the European Union.

Given that protocols enjoy the same status as the Treaties under Article 51 TEU, this would seem to make no difference to the overall regime and approach to competition law regulation in the EU.

The member state fidelity clause, now contained in Article 4(3) TEU (ex 10 European Community (EC)), has also been pleaded with Articles 3(1)(b) and 101 TFEU (ex 3(1)(g) and 81 EC) as a general principle of law supporting the argument that competition law also applies in respect of the member states and not just undertakings so that they are prohibited from encouraging or requiring acts or conduct by companies which may distort competition in the EU.

The broad aims are then expanded in three sets of rules: one relating to the activities of legal persons—that is, the business undertakings, which now includes rules on concentrations and mergers; one relating to anti-dumping measures; and, finally, one relating to the activities of the member states, principally state aid. The rules concerned with private undertakings are further subdivided into: Article 101 TFEU for agreements between cartels involving more than one entity; Article 102 TFEU, concerned with dominant positions, dealing predominantly with one entity but also applicable to one or more undertakings; and the rules applicable to concentrations and mergers. The rules are designed to prevent a number of abuses, which are considered in detail in the course of this chapter.

This chapter concentrates on the main competition rules of Articles 101 and 102 TFEU applicable, for the most part, to private companies and individuals and the relationship between these two Articles. It is also concerned with the mergers policy of the EU and briefly with the procedural law of competition and merger law.

13.2.2 Application and interpretation

The Commission is given the task under Article 105 TFEU and Regulation 1/2003 to ensure that competition in the EU is not distorted. The establishment of competition rules is an exclusive competence of the EU (Article 3(1)(b) TFEU). The application of the rules by the Commission and the interpretation of the rules of the CoJ have not been done in isolation by looking at the provision alone, but have been applied in light of the objectives of competition policy, and the rules are applied in light of the general objective of the Treaty.

> In **Cases 6 and 7/73 *Commercial Solvents* v *Commission***, the CoJ held:
>
> The prohibitions of Articles 85 and 86 EEC (now Arts 101 and 102 TFEU) must be interpreted and applied in the light of Article 3(f) of the EC Treaty (now Art 3(1)(b) TFEU), which provides that the activities of the Community shall include the institution of a system ensuring that competition . . . is not distorted, and Article 2 of the EC Treaty which gives the Community the task of promoting 'throughout the Community harmonious development of economic activities'.

Presumably if the CoJ feels the need to resort to the general principles to justify a particular ruling it would now simply refer to Protocol No. 27, mentioned in section 13.2.1.

Case 26/76 *Metro* v *Saba (No. 1)* is a good example, whereby the Commission, in pursuit of a goal, also relied on Article 2 of the European Economic Community (EEC) to justify particular decisions reached. The agreements in the case were deemed to satisfy competition rules because they helped to maintain employment. The case serves as an example of where the Commission, in carrying out its tasks in relation to competition law, is also required to balance this policy with other policies, such as regional development or concern for unemployment, and which may cause it to modify its position on the behaviour of companies. The general economic climate also influences the Commission, particularly in respect of merger policy, in that in times of poor economic growth, the Commission may treat mergers as being more acceptable because of the efficiency gains to be achieved and the greater ability the emerging company will have in the world market.

13.3 Article 101 TFEU (anti-competitive behaviour)

Article 101 TFEU is designed to tackle the agreements and collusion between companies that result in restrictive practices and anti-competitive behaviour. It applies to both horizontal and vertical agreements, as considered in the sections following. It sets out the prohibitions and details of the consequences of failure to observe the prohibition. Finally, it provides a framework by which exemptions from the prohibitions can be obtained.

> **Article 101(1) TFEU**
>
> 1. The following shall be prohibited as incompatible with the internal market: all agreements between undertakings, decisions by associations of undertakings and concerted practices which may affect trade between the member states and which have as their object or effect the prevention, restriction, or distortion of competition within the internal market.

Article 101(2) TFEU provides that any agreements or decisions prohibited pursuant to Article 101 TFEU shall be automatically void. Article 101(3) TFEU concerns the exemptions to the basic rules but lays down criteria for them that must be met. The agreements must also not be too small such that they are not considered under the *de minimis* rule. Article 101 TFEU has been subject to some considerable definition in the jurisprudence of the Court and was held to be capable of producing direct effects in Case 127/73 *BRT* v *SABAM*.

This section considers in turn the basic definitions. In particular it considers what is meant by these key terms: 'agreements', 'undertakings', 'decisions by associations of undertakings', 'concerted practices', 'object or effect', and 'effect on trade'.

13.3.1 Article 101(1) TFEU definitions

13.3.1.1 Agreements

The term 'agreements' is not limited to written and legally enforceable agreements only, and it is not the form of the agreement that is important from the Commission's point of view but its effect on competition. Therefore, a broad interpretation is given to the term 'agreement, decision, and concerted practice' and includes non-binding agreements, as in, for example, the *Polypropylene Decision*, noted in section 13.3.1.2.

The terms apply to both horizontal (where the parties are at the same level of the economic process) and vertical (where the parties are at different levels of the economic process) agreements, as is illustrated by the rulings of the CoJ in Cases 56 and 58/64 *Consten and Grundig* v *Commission* and Case 56/65 *Société Technique Minière* v *Maschinenbau Ulm* (the *STM* case). A gentleman's agreement consisting of an oral or tacit agreement with nothing committed to writing is, thus, included in this definition: see Case 28/77 *Tepea* v *Commission*. In Cases C-25 and 26/84 *Ford* v *Commission*, the Ford Motor Company's refusal to supply right-hand-drive cars to German dealers, to stop them being imported into the UK at a lower cost, was held to be an agreement or concerted practice with its contractual partners, the dealers. The CoJ judgment in the appeal Case C-199/92P *Hüls AG* v *Commission*, held that to be a concerted practice, there is no need to demonstrate either conduct in the market or restricted competition, but it is sufficient merely to demonstrate that there was participation, which is similar to showing an intent to do something. Unilateral action, though, on the part of a supplier, which either has to be followed by distributors, as in Case C-2 and 3/01P *Commission* v *Bayer*, or is followed voluntarily, as in Case C-74/04 P *Commission* v *Volkswagen*, does not amount to an agreement for the purposes of Article 101 TFEU. The terms are, according to the case law, capable of being interpreted very widely.

13.3.1.2 'Undertakings'

For more details on this section visit the online resources.

The term 'undertakings' has been interpreted to include both natural and legal persons as independent or complementary economic actors. According to the Commission in Commission Decision *Polypropylene Cartel Community* v *ICI*, this includes any entity engaged in economic or commercial activities and regardless of how it is financed (Case C-41/90 *Höfner and Elser*). Any form of business undertaking is included: artists, in *Unitel*; an opera singer in Decision 78/516; an inventor in *AOIP* v *Beyrard*; groups of companies in *Re Kodak*; and public bodies if operated for profit in Case C-113/07 P *SELEX*.

If, however, the activity is more in support of public or social services, it is likely to be held not to be an undertaking carrying out an economic activity under Article 101 (or, indeed, Article 102) TFEU, especially where it is non-profit-making (see Cases C-364/92 *SAT* v *Eurocontol*, C-264/01 *AOK Bundesverband*, and C-205/03 P *FENIN*).

Groups of companies have caused problems, not least in deciding whether Article 101 or 102 TFEU should apply. As far as Article 101 TFEU is concerned, the CoJ addressed this in Case C-75/95 P *Viho Europe BV* v *Commission* (also known as the *Parker Pen* case). The problem is that if a group of companies, consisting of a parent and a number of wholly owned subsidiaries, are deemed to be one entity, then by definition Article 101 TFEU does not apply. Article 102 may have to be applied, but requires the fulfilment of the criteria for such application (considered in section 13.7).

In the **Viho** case, Viho in the Netherlands was refused supply of Parker Pens by the German Parker Co. and was referred to the Dutch Parker Co. The Court held the Parker Group to be a single entity and that the subsidiaries did not enjoy any real autonomy from the controlling parent company and, whilst their refusal to supply did effectively divide the market, Article 81 EC (now 101 TFEU) did not apply to a single entity. The Court, though, acknowledged that it might breach Article 82 EC (now 102 TFEU). However, a group-controlling or group-owning parent company may nevertheless be held liable for the anti-competitive activities of 100-per-cent-owned subsidiaries that breach Article 101 TFEU.

The Court assumed in **Case C-97/08 P AKZO Nobel v Commission** that the 100-per-cent-owning parent company exercised a decisive influence over the conduct of the subsidiary unless proved otherwise, and could then be lawfully fined by the Commission.

This applies also if the parent company is based outside the EU, as was held in Cases 48, 49, and 51–57/69 *ICI* v *Commission (Aniline Dyes)*, and confirmed in Cases 89, 104, 114, 116, 117, and 125–1299/85 *Ahlström*, known as the *Woodpulp* cases. Ownership of less than 100 per cent is determined according to the facts and the degree of decisive influence detected or demonstrated by the Commission, as in Case C-407/08 P *KnaufGips*.

CROSS REFERENCE
These are considered also in section 13.3.1.4.

13.3.1.3 Decisions by associations of undertakings

The words 'decisions by associations of undertakings' include the coordinating activities of a trade association. In the Commission Decision relating to *AROW* v *BNIC*, the *Bureau National Interprofessionel de Cognac* was fined because it had fixed a minimum distribution price for cognac, arguing that this was necessary to guarantee quality. The Commission decided that, given all the other quality-control measures that existed in the cognac industry, this argument could not be sustained.

Non-binding recommendations made by trade associations may also amount to decisions, as held in Case 8/72 *Vereeniging van Cementhandelaren* v *Commission* (the *Cement Association* case).

For more details on this section visit the online resources.

In **Case 96/82 IAZ International Belgium NV v Commission**, an association of water supply undertakings recommended its members not to connect dishwasher machines to the mains system unless they had a label supplied by the Belgian association of dishwasher manufacturers indicating that the dishwashers complied with relevant Belgian standards. The CoJ upheld the Commission's view that this recommendation, despite the fact that it was not binding, could restrict competition, since its effect was to discriminate against appliances produced in other member states.

Professional bodies which regulate the activities of their members in a particular way may also come within the definition of associations, as was made clear by the Commission and approved by the CoJ in Case C-309/99 *Wouters*, in which the Dutch Bar Association sought to prohibit multi-disciplinary practices. This was a breach of Article 85 EC (now 101 TFEU).

There is a Commission Communication on professional services: see the online resources.

13.3.1.4 Concerted practices

The term 'concerted practice' is potentially very broad and includes many forms of informal collusion between undertakings. Such collective decision-making on prices or markets by a number of companies is often described as a cartel.

For more details on this section visit the online resources.

> An important example of a 'concerted practice' is found in **Cases 48, 49, and 51–57/69 *ICI* v *Commission (Aniline Dyes)***. ICI was the first among a number of undertakings, accounting for 85 per cent of the market, to raise prices. The companies all said that the price coordination was simply a reflection of parallel behaviour in an oligopolistic market, where each producer followed the price leader. (This is very often seen, for example, with petrol prices.) The CoJ held that this was a concerted practice arising out of coordination which became apparent from the behaviour of the participants, and which was designed to replace the risk of competition and the hazards of competitors' spontaneous reactions by cooperation constituting a concerted practice.

This case is also a precedent for the extra-territorial application of the competition rules, since the head office of ICI was in the UK, which, at the time of the facts of the case, was not a member of the EEC. Nevertheless, it was fined for activities that affected trade within the then EEC.

> In **Cases 40–48, 50, 43, 56, 11, 113, and 114 *Suiker Unie (Sugar Union)* v *Commission***, the Community's main sugar producers had made deliveries in the Netherlands only, with the assent of the producers in that country, so as to weaken considerably the competitive pressure which unrestricted sugar imports would have engendered. They said that they had not agreed to any plan to that effect, and hence there was no concerted practice. The CoJ held that there was no need for an actual plan, and that a concerted practice included:
>
> > Any direct or indirect contact between such operators, the object or effect of which is either to influence the conduct on the market of an actual or potential competitor or to disclose to such a competitor the course of conduct which they themselves have decided to adopt or contemplate adopting on the market.

A concerted practice is present when it enables the firms concerned to set positions which they have secured to the detriment of free movement of goods in the internal market and the freedom of consumers to choose their suppliers. Each trader must independently decide on the policy it proposes to follow on the internal market. This requirement does not deny traders the right to adapt their conduct to the way their competitors are behaving or are likely to behave, but it does rule out any direct or indirect contact where the object or effect is to influence the conduct of an existing or potential market competitor or to reveal to it market policy decisions or intentions.

> However, in **Cases C-89, 104, 114, 116–117/85, and 125–129/85 *Ahlström Oy and others* v *Commission*** (the *Woodpulp Cartel* cases), the CoJ held that the burden is on the Commission to prove a concerted practice by establishing 'firm, precise and consistent body of evidence' that a concerted practice existed. Parallel price increases would not satisfy this unless there was no other plausible explanation for them. Agreements which were taken by the parties within their trade association to establish recommended prices were not upheld as restricting competition contrary to Article 81(1) EC (now 101 TFEU). Here, the price increases could be explained by the fact that there was an oligopolistic market in which notification of future prices was often requested by customers, and prices were set by the limited number of producers in the market which would tend to follow each other closely, without there being any understanding or agreement.

However, even the supply of information such as future pricing strategies by one party, especially if a leading party in the market, at a meeting can amount to being an agreement of concerted practice as, in the view of the Court, the other parties could not fail to take account of the information. It would thus breach Article 101 TFEU.

The Commission has now issued guidance on how the exchange of information may be judged in 'Guidelines on the applicability of Article 101 of the Treaty on the Functioning of the European Union to horizontal co-operation agreements': General Principles on Competitive Assessment of Information Exchange (OJ 2011 C11/1), p. 13.

Article 101 TFEU applies to both horizontal and vertical agreements and concerted practices; an example of the latter can be seen in the following case. Even unilateral conduct on the part of a manufacturer has been deemed by the CoJ to be capable of amounting to an agreement or a concerted practice.

In **Cases 25 and 26/84 *Ford* v *Commission***, until May 1982, Ford of Germany supplied to its German dealers a quantity of right-hand-drive cars for sale in the Federal Republic. Since spring 1981, there had been a great increase in demand for right-hand-drive cars because German prices were considerably lower than those in the UK. Ford of Germany became concerned about the effects of this on the position of Ford Britain and notified the German dealers that, as from 1 May 1982, it would no longer accept their orders for right-hand-drive cars, and all such cars would have to be purchased in Britain. The Commission decided that the dealer agreement and the termination of deliveries contravened Article 81(1) EC (now 101 TFEU). Ford argued that the cessation of deliveries was a unilateral act not caught by Article 81(1) EC. The CoJ rejected this argument (at [21]), stating that 'such a decision forms part of the contractual relations between the undertaking and its dealers. Indeed, admission to the Ford dealer network implies acceptance by the contracting parties of the policy pursued by Ford with regard to the models to be delivered to the German market.' The instruction was held to form part of the contractual relations between the undertaking and its dealers and, hence, the restriction was held to be a breach of Article 81 EC.

A single meeting and not just a series of regular meetings will suffice to constitute a concerted practice, as held in Case C-8/08 *T-Mobile*.

13.3.2 The object or effect of restricting or distorting competition

An agreement or practice is prohibited if it has either the object or effect of preventing, restricting, or distorting competition. Separated by 'or', in practice both object *and* effect must be considered, but this is not a cumulative test; either will suffice, but whilst one element may be satisfied, the other element may not be so serious as to restrict or distort competition sufficiently to be held in breach of the Treaty. So if, as a result of a consideration of the terms of the agreement, it is clear that the object is to restrict competition, on the face of it, it will be contrary to Article 101 TFEU. However, it may still be necessary to consider the economic effects of the agreement to determine whether it is caught by Article 101 TFEU, as it may fall within the *de minimis* doctrine, considered later, or it may have no effect on trade between the member states.

 THINKING POINT

Can you define at this stage what *de minimis* means?

In Case C-8/08 *T-Mobile*, the CoJ held that when an agreement will inevitably result in an injury to normal competition, it will be regarded as having an anti-competitive object regardless of whether or not it actually restricts competition, for example price-fixing agreements. If the object is not to distort competition, it must be seen whether its effect is restrictive.

In **Case 56/65 STM**, the CoJ held that 'It must be possible to foresee with a sufficient degree of probability on the basis of a set of objective factors of law or fact that the agreement in question may have an influence, direct or indirect, actual or potential, on the pattern of trade between member states.' The Court also held that:

> Where, however, an analysis . . . does not reveal the effect on competition to be sufficiently deleterious, the consequences of the agreement should then be considered and for it to be caught by the prohibition it is then necessary to find that those factors are present which show that competition has in fact been prevented or restricted or distorted to an appreciable extent.

Alternatively, if it is not established by the Commission that the object of the agreement or practice is to restrict or distort competition, it is nevertheless still necessary for the Commission to undertake an examination of the effect of the agreement on the market.

See also the Commission Guidelines on the application of Article 81(3) [now 101 TFEU] of the Treaty (OJ 2004 C 101/97).

For more details on this section visit the online resources.

In Case 23/67 *Brasserie de Haecht* v *Wilkin*, the CoJ said that the agreement, decision, or concerted practice had to be examined in the context of the market in which it operated and in the context of the effects surrounding its implementation. This entails scrutiny of the relevant product market and the relevant geographical market, the impact of national laws upon competition, the existence of intellectual property rights, and the level of competition on the rest of the market and the behaviour of other competitors. If the effect is insignificant, it is likely to be held not to distort the market enough to breach Article 101 TFEU.

See now the Commission clarification of this *de minimis* doctrine: Commission Notice on Agreements of Minor Importance which do not appreciably restrict Competition under Article 81(1) of the Treaty establishing the European Community (now 101 TFEU) (OJ 2001 C368/13).

13.3.3 Types of prohibited agreements

Article 101(1) TFEU lists as particular examples of prohibited agreements those that have as their object the restriction of competition. The non-exhaustive list includes those that:

- 'directly or indirectly fix purchase or selling prices or any other unfair trading conditions'. (These are most often seen in the form of minimum price-fixing arrangements; see e.g. Case 8/72 *Cement Association* or the Decision in *Hennessy/Henkel*, in which minimum and maximum prices were laid down, which breached Article 81 EC (now 101 TFEU). Other trading conditions include things like requiring distributors or retailers to provide suitable premises, displays, training, minimum stocks, or to hold certain promotions. In return, the retailer may be guaranteed a specific protected area. In Case 26/76 *Metro*, it was held that such systems would not breach Article 81 EC provided selection of dealers was done objectively. In Case

161/84 *Pronuptia* v *Schillgalis*, even a requirement that 80 per cent of wedding dresses were purchased from Pronuptia was held to be acceptable in order to protect the know-how and reputation of the franchisor);

- 'limit or control production, markets, technical development, or investment'—most often seen in market-sharing agreements (see e.g. market partitioning in Cases 56 and 58/64 *Consten and Grundig* and *Quinine Cartel*);

- 'share markets or sources of supply' (see also *Consten and Grundig*);

- 'apply dissimilar conditions to equivalent transactions with other trading parties, thereby placing them at a competitive disadvantage' (see e.g. Case 26/76 *Metro* v *Commission*, where a difference in prices could be justified by objective factors such as volume of purchases or transport costs); and

- 'make the conclusion of contracts subject to the acceptance by the other parties of supplementary obligations which, by their nature or according to commercial usage, have no connection with the subject of such contracts'. (An example of the last of the conditions listed would be the imposition by a producer on a distributor of an export ban (see the *Henessy/Henkel* Decision, in which a clause prohibiting the sale of competing products was held to be acceptable but not a clause prohibiting the sale of any other product).)

13.3.4 Agreements that may affect trade between member states

To be caught by the provisions of Article 101 TFEU, the practice complained of must be capable of affecting EU trade. Trade is given a wide definition and encompasses the production and distribution of goods, trade in agricultural produce, and the services sector (including banking insurance and professional services). Even opera singers have been held to be involved in trade.

In **Cases 56 and 58/64 *Consten and Grundig***, the CoJ stated that the phrase 'capable of affecting EU trade' is intended to set the boundary between the areas covered by Community law and the law of the member states. It held that the question to be asked is whether it is probable in law or fact that the agreement in question may have an influence, direct or indirect, actual or potential, on the pattern of trade between member states to hinder the attainment of a single market. The case was concerned with exclusive territorial sales licences, which served to encourage the volume of trade. Consten Grundig had granted a distributor a sole representation agreement for the whole of France, Saar, and Corsica. The distributor undertook not to sell similar articles liable to compete with the goods of the contract and not to deliver, either directly or indirectly, for or to other countries from the contract territory. An analogous prohibition was imposed on concessionaires from other territories. The result was to grant absolute territorial protection, and to insulate the French market against parallel imports. The result in this case was that it actually promoted trade. The CoJ held that the fact that an agreement encourages an increase, even a large one, in the volume of trade between states is not sufficient to exclude the possibility that the agreement may affect trade between member states. Although this may seem strange, the requirement that the agreement must affect inter-state trade goes to the jurisdiction of EU law. The contract between Grundig and Consten, on the one hand by preventing undertakings other than Consten from importing Grundig products into France, and on the other by prohibiting Consten from re-exporting those products to other countries of the Common Market, indisputably adversely affected the flow of trade between the member states. These limitations on the freedom of trade were enough to satisfy the requirement in question.

In Case 56/65, the *STM* case, the CoJ provided the basic test that if the agreement may have an influence, direct or indirect, actual or potential, it would satisfy this requirement. This is similar to the *Dassonville* formula in respect of the free movement of goods, discussed in Chapter 11.

In **Case 23/67 *Brasserie de Haecht SA* v *Wilkin and Wilkin***, a brewery had entered into a contract whereby it had furnished the Wilkins' cafe and had granted several loans. The agreement stipulated that the Wilkins were obliged to obtain all their supplies of liquor, beer, and soft drinks for the cafe and for their own personal use exclusively from the de Haecht brewery. They had purchased supplies of liquor from other undertakings and the brewery had sought to rescind the contract and claim repayment of the loans, return of the furniture, and damages. The Tribunal de Commerce asked the CoJ whether to judge the agreement on its own or in light of all such agreements. The Court ruled that the 'economic and legal context' had to be taken into account, such as in this case the fact that the arrangement tying the cafe proprietors to receiving their beer and other drink supplies from one brewery was one which was extensively used, and the extensive use of such contracts would adversely affect competition in the Community at large. The Court further ruled that in order to satisfy the 'capable of affecting trade between member states' requirement:

> it must be possible for the agreement, decision or practice, viewed objectively to appear to be capable of having some influence, direct or indirect on trade between member states, partition the market, and hampering the economic interpenetration sought by the Treaty. When this point is considered the agreement, decision or practice cannot therefore be isolated from the others of which it is one.

Therefore, if it forms a series of agreements, a single contract should not just be considered on its own.

In **Case 8/72 *Vereniging van Cementhandelaren* v *Commission***, the members of a Dutch cement dealers association argued that since the cartel was purely national in its activities, limited to the territory of the Netherlands, it could not be caught by Article 81(1) EC (now 101 TFEU). The CoJ upheld the Commission decision, declaring that an agreement extending over the whole of the territory of a member state, by its very nature, has the effect of reinforcing the compartmentalisation of markets on a national basis. Therefore, one country on its own can be used to establish an effect on trade between member states.

The Commission has issued a Guideline: The effect on Trade Concept Contained in Articles 101 and 102 TFEU (OJ 2004 C101/81).

13.3.5 Exemptions from Article 101(1) TFEU

Apart from the justification considered in section 13.6 under Article 101(3) TFEU, certain agreements have been deemed by the CoJ and Commission not to fall within the category of a 'restriction of competition'. These judicial exemptions from the application of Article 101 have been referred to as a type of 'rule of reason' in competition law, in that the General Court will balance the effects of an agreement to see whether the alleged benefits outweigh the anti-competitive effects. However, the Court of First Instance (CFI) clearly ruled this out in Case T-112/99 *Metropole Television* v *Commission* whilst confirming, nevertheless, that the Court's approach is to take account of the actual conditions and economic context in which the agreement operates. Any exemption, though, is only to be granted under Article 101(3) and not a rule of reason. Prior case law has discussed a number of circumstances which may, however, be taken into account in assessing whether a particular agreement which may have the effect of restricting competition does not breach Article 101 TFEU.

13.3.5.1 Objective necessity

There are cases where the restrictions are objectively necessary for the performance of a particular type of contract, as in franchising agreements. In Case 161/84 *Pronuptia de Paris* v *Schillgalis*, the CoJ held that the compatibility of distribution franchise agreements with Article 81(1) EC (now 101 TFEU) depended on the clauses contained in the agreements and on the economic context in which they are included.

Clauses which are indispensable to prevent the know-how and assistance provided by the franchisor from benefiting competitors and clauses which implement the control necessary for the preservation of the identity and reputation of the organisation represented in the trade mark do not constitute restrictions on competition within the meaning of Article 81(1) EC. The fact that the franchisor has communicated suggested prices to the franchisee does not constitute a restriction on competition, on condition that there has not been a concerted practice between the franchisees with a view to effective application of those prices. However, clauses that fix prices or affect a partitioning of markets between franchisor and franchisee or between franchisees and are capable of affecting trade between member states constitute restrictions on competition contrary to Article 81(1) EC. Very many of these franchise agreements, including Pronuptia's, were granted individual exemption under Article 81(3) EC (now 101 TFEU) before the modernisation in 2004 of this area of competition law.

13.3.5.2 High commercial risks

The CoJ has held that where the commercial risk undertaken by a distributor, licensee, or franchisee is great, some exclusivity must be conferred on him to induce him into the market.

Case 55/65 *STM* v *Maschinenbau Ulm* is an example of this. In this case, the French company La Société Technique Minière (STM) purchased 37 earth-levelling machines and was given exclusive sales rights for the territory of France. The agreement with the producers, Maschinenbau Ulm, stipulated that STM could only sell other goods to compete with these levelling machines with the consent of Maschinenbau Ulm. The agreement left STM entitled to export the machines. The CoJ held that in order to assess the effect of the agreement on competition, examination should take place of the severity of the clause granting the exclusive right; the nature and quantity of the products which were the subject matter of the agreement; the position of the grantor and the concessionaire on the market for the products in question; the number of parties to the agreements; and the possibilities left for other commercial currents upon the same products by means of re-exports and parallel imports. The Court held that due to the high cost and specialised nature of the product, the agreements would not offend Article 81 EC (now 101 TFEU).

13.3.5.3 Quality control

Cases involving selective distribution systems, such as Case 26/76 *Metro* v *Commission*, to ensure the quality of sales and service, to benefit the consumer in terms of safety of electrical goods, and to maintain employment in an important industry, would not breach Article 81 EC (now 101 TFEU), even though that might mean that supplies to other low-price distributors might be restricted and higher prices maintained. Price competition was recognised as not the only form of competition in the market. The restrictions could promote other forms of competition such as service and after-sales commitment, particularly as the consumer still had sufficient choice of supplier.

13.4 The *de minimis* doctrine/ agreements of minor importance

For more details on this section visit the online resources.

The doctrine of *de minimis* means that some agreements affecting competition may nevertheless not be caught by Article 101 TFEU because they do not have an appreciable effect on intra-Community trade.

> This was first formulated in **Case 5/69 *Volk* v *Vervaecke***, where Volk granted an exclusive dealership to Vervaecke for washing machines in the Belgian and Luxembourg market. Vervaecke undertook to place a monthly order for 80 appliances, and Volk undertook to protect Vervaecke's sales territory against parallel imports. There was a dispute as to agreement and the CoJ held that an agreement falls outside the scope of Article 81(1) EC (now 101 TFEU) when it has only an insignificant effect on the market, taking into account the weak position which the parties concerned have on the market of the product in question.

Consequently, an exclusive dealing agreement, even with absolute territorial protection, may, having regard to the weak position of the persons concerned on the market in question in the area covered by the absolute protection, escape the prohibition; that is, it represents too small an effect significantly to affect competition and, thus, does not fall within Article 101(1) TFEU. A strict reading of the Article does not support this, but other motives may also underpin the policy of the Commission and the judgment of the Court, for example not to suppress small and medium-sized businesses from expanding, or only restricting small business when predatory.

> In 2014, the Commission provided an updated 'Notice on Agreements of Minor Importance which do not appreciably restrict competition', setting out the criteria that will be used in determining whether a practice may affect trade between member states. This follows a CoJ ruling in Case 226/11 *Expedia*, in which the CoJ essentially stressed that any agreement which had an appreciable effect on competition, regardless of its concrete effect on the market, would breach EU law and not be saved by the *de minimis* doctrine.

▶ CROSS REFERENCE

The same pressures also led to the enactment of the block exemptions, which are discussed in section 13.6.3.

This seemed to have undermined the previous Commission *de minimis* notices issued in 1997 and 2001. However, the basic criteria in the new notice were not changed. Thus any agreement between undertakings which are actual or potential competitors who together have less than a 10 per cent market share in the EU as a whole will not contravene EU competition law. In line with a general concern that had arisen and has been responded to by the Commission, the threshold for vertical agreements was raised to 15 per cent of market share which remains the case (10 per cent for horizontal agreements). Market share below this removes agreements from the scope of Article 101 TFEU, unless, now made clear by the 2014 Notice and the *Expedia* case, they are serious or intended breaches of the competition rules or they fix prices or limit output or sales, or allocate markets or customers or breach the restrictions in the block exemptions. Even above these thresholds, small and medium-sized enterprise agreements will be considered leniently by the Commission. Although such notices are not binding in law and certainly cannot amend the Treaty provisions, they are a clear indication that, provided an agreement falls within the exception allowed, the Commission will not take action under the competition rules. There is general concern about the rigidity of the present application of the rules to vertical agreements (see *Consten and Grundig*).

Finally, in respect of a number of the issues noted earlier, Case C-234/89 *Delimitis v Henniger Bräu* should be considered. In this case, a tied-in contract between Delimitis and a brewery, which on its own would certainly fall within the *de minimis* doctrine, was argued to be part of a network of similar agreements and thus subject to Article 81 EC (now 101 TFEU). The Court observed the benefits to both parties of tied agreements and concluded that the object was not to restrict competition but that the cumulative effect, when all such agreements were taken into account, might be to restrict competition and make market entry difficult, if not impossible, unless within a tied relationship. In those circumstances, the 2001 minor importance Notice reduces the market share to 5 per cent to reflect such reasoning. Hence, regardless of whether there is a rule of reason, all the consequences of an agreement, whether or not restrictive, will form part of the analysis of whether the agreement breaches Article 101.

13.5 Article 101(2) TFEU and the consequence of a breach

Article 101(2) TFEU provides that 'Any agreements or decisions prohibited pursuant to this Article shall be automatically void.' In Case 56/65 *STM* v *Maschinenbau Ulm*, the CoJ held that this provision only applies to those parts of the agreement affected by the prohibition in Article 81(1) EC (now 101 TFEU) or to the agreement as a whole if those parts are not severable from the agreement itself. This case was considered in section 13.3.5.2. Cases 56 and 58/64 *Consten and Grundig* are also good authority for this point.

13.6 Article 101(3) TFEU exemptions

In advance of the CoJ-developed grounds, whereby certain agreements have been held not to constitute a restriction of competition, considered under section 13.3.5, the Treaty had provided in Article 101(3) certain circumstances where Article 101(1) will not apply to an agreement or concerted practice. They are most likely to apply to individual agreements but can also apply to types of agreement in the same way as block exemptions as they both incorporate the criteria with which agreements may be judged to comply or are contrary to the competition law provisions. All elements of the requirements for exemption must be satisfied. Thus, an agreement may be exempted:

> which contributes to improving the production or distribution of goods or to promoting technical or economic progress, while allowing consumers a fair share of the resulting benefit, and which does not:
>
> (a) impose on the undertakings concerned restrictions which are not indispensable to the attainment of these objectives;
>
> (b) afford such undertakings the possibility of eliminating competition in respect of a substantial part of the products in question.

⫸ CROSS REFERENCE
Examples of such benefits can be seen in the CoJ cases noted in section 13.3.5.

13.6.1 **Individual notification**

Previously—and for most of the life of the Communities it was the first and main way to obtain an exemption—parties to an agreement must have made an individual notification to the Commission. Failure to notify meant that the agreement was void and the parties liable to fines. Once notified, the Commission considered whether the agreement could have been exempted and issued an official decision, which could be challenged under Article 230 EC (now 263 TFEU) before the CFI (now the General Court). However, because the Commission could not investigate and come to a decision on all the applications made, it dealt with them very often by the so-called 'comfort letter', which provided an immunity from fines and is considered in section 13.6.2. This led to the revision of this procedure, which was contained in Regulation 1/2003 on enforcement of competition law, which came into force on 1 May 2004 and which abolished the individual notification. This was done to remove the drain on Commission resources under this procedure and coincided with 10 new member states joining the EU in 2004, which would have imposed even greater demands on the Commission. The decision-making was handed over to the national competition law authorities and was facilitated by expressly making Article 81(3) EC (now 101 TFEU) directly effective so that any disputes could be adjudicated in the national courts. Essentially, the private parties will decide if their agreement falls within the legal exceptions (rather than the previous exemptions) in Article 101 TFEU, which decision can then be challenged and defended in the national courts. To assist parties in this, the Commission has issued Guidelines on the application of Article 81(3) EC (now 101 TFEU) of the Treaty. Novel and uncertain cases may still find their way to the Commission for a decision in a procedure under Article 10 of Regulation 1/2003.

> See Notice on informal guidance relating to novel questions concerning Articles 81 and 82 of the EC Treaty that arise in individual cases (Guidance letters) (OJ 2004 C 101/78).

A further policy initiative that was undertaken to deal with the quantity of applications was the issuing of block exemptions, which, provided undertakings ensured that their agreement was in compliance, exempted the application of Article 101 TFEU to those agreements. These are considered in section 13.6.3.

13.6.2 **Negative clearance and comfort letters**

Although the following no longer applies, it is very useful to know. The previous notification regime prompted the Commission, as an alternative to taking every individual application for exemption through to a decision, frequently to settle cases informally by way of a so-called comfort letter. This was simply a notification to the parties that, in the Commission's opinion, the agreement did not infringe Article 101(1) TFEU or that it qualified for exemption. The Commission then closed the file, after sending the comfort letter. These comfort letters did not bind the national courts or produce legal effects in national law or EU law. This was made clear in a series of cases involving perfume manufacturers, Cases 253/78 and 1–3/79 *Guerlain SA, Rochas SA, Lanvin SA, and Nina Ricci SA*. Clearly, a statement of this nature from the Commission would be of persuasive authority, but a national court would not necessarily be bound by it. In an action by French shops that were unable to get supplies from Lancôme and Guerlain, the CoJ rejected the view that the comfort letters provided a defence to such actions against the refusal to supply. This, too, has now been replaced by the system of assuming that the agreement constitutes a legal exception by the parties, subject to a possible challenge in the national courts and reference to the General Court where relevant. As such, comfort letters will no longer be needed or issued.

Whilst to some extent of historical interest only, there remain a lot of previous agreements still subject to comfort letters or provisional validity. This was considered in Case C-39/96 *Koninklijke*

Vereeniging ter Bevordering van de Belangen des Boekhandels v *Free Record Shop BV*, and concerns competition agreements that were concluded prior to Regulation 17 and notified to the Commission prior to the deadline of 1 November 1962. Normally such agreements would carry provisional validity until the Commission had either given positive clearance or had taken a negative decision holding them to be contrary to EC law. Many agreements similar to this one, which concerned the retail price maintenance for books, have continued in this legal limbo ever since. The Commission is simply unable to investigate all of them and many are left without interference. The agreement in question, however, had been challenged as contrary to Article 81 EC (now 101 TFEU) by a shop selling below the imposed retail price. Having lain dormant for so long, questions about the continued validity were raised by the national court. The CoJ held that until the Commission decides one way or the other the agreement remains provisionally valid, even if it has been amended, but only in so far as the amendments render the agreement less restrictive. More restrictive amendments would end the validity unless these were severable from the original agreement.

> It is to be noted that Article 8 of the otherwise repealed Regulation 17, which permits the Commission to amend or revoke previous decisions, remains in force. See Foster, *Blackstone's EU Treaties and Legislation*, Oxford University Press, Oxford, published annually.

From May 2004, individual companies must decide whether an agreement complies with the four conditions specified in Article 101(3) TFEU and, if they conclude that they do, there is no need to take any further action or to notify the Commission or national competition authorities. However, in case of doubt a new procedure, not too dissimilar to the negative clearance and comfort letter of old, has been introduced by which guidance on grey-area agreements can be sought from the Commission. The Commission may issue this guidance in a 'guidance letter', but only if the situation is genuinely novel and not coming within any previous case law, decision, or block exemptions, considered next.

13.6.3 Block exemptions

In order to avoid unnecessary work for all involved—companies and the Commission—it was decided that certain categories of common or typical types of commercial agreement, which were considered not to infringe free and fair competition, could be exempted from the prohibition in Article 81(2) EC (now 101 TFEU) by virtue of a block exemption, sometimes applicable to particular industries or areas. Prior to the 2004 reform, if there was an applicable block exemption, there was no need to apply for individual notification. In particular, vertical agreements were considered as more beneficial than harmful to competition in that they often increase investment in the specialisation and knowledge of certain products, which is of benefit to the ultimate consumers of the products.

For more details on this section visit the online resources.

The block exemptions set out types of restriction or provision that do not infringe Article 101(1) TFEU or would be exempted. The following are now the main block exemptions and guidelines following the revision and reissue in 2010–11.

> Principal block exemptions
>
> - Regulation 330/2010 on vertical supply and distribution agreements.
> - Regulation 1217/2010 on research and development agreements.
> - Regulation 1218/2010 on specialisation agreements.
> - Regulation 461/2010 on distribution agreements in respect of motor vehicles.
> - Regulation 772/2004 on technology transfer agreements.

There are a number of guides now published by the Commission that help to clarify the block exemptions.

THINKING POINT

How do block exemptions assist the Commission and commercial entities and how do they help achieve the aims of the EU competition policy?

The pattern of these block exemptions is to provide examples of agreements and clauses that are permitted, those which are expressly forbidden, and those which, depending on the actual details contained within, may or may not offend competition law. The first category means that there is no need to take any action or inform the Commission. Agreements of clauses coming within the second category render the entire agreement in breach of Article 101 TFEU and liable to a fine, and the third type under the previous regime required notification and clearance from the Commission and are those which would now probably fall to be considered as to whether they come within the new concept of the legal exception.

Most of the Regulations listed are replacements for previous regulations that were revised in light of practical application and in response to criticisms made by the various industries and companies affected. The new Regulations now focus more on market share and market power in relation to the particular agreements rather than the agreement themselves. For example, for companies with less than a 30 per cent market share, Regulation 330/2010 removes the need to make an assessment as to whether their agreements fall within the competition law rules, thus further reducing the bureaucratic workload on the part of companies and the Commission. Without going into unnecessary detail in this introduction, the Regulation provides in:

- Article 1—definitions of what is meant by vertical agreements covered by the block exemption;
- Article 2—that vertical agreements meeting this are exempt from Article 101;
- Article 3—the 30 per cent market share threshold for both seller and buyer;
- Article 4—the hard-core restrictions which do not receive exemption, such as those aimed at price, supply, and market fixing; and
- Article 5—that certain clauses of long-term (over five years) or indefinite duration that restriction competition are prohibited.

Any restrictions that fall within Article 4 render the agreement void and unenforceable, whereas those which offend Article 5 can be severed or amended. In what is now, with the various exemptions in place, a rare case, Case T-67/01 *JCB v Commission*, JCB was found to infringe Article 81 EC (now 101 TFEU) by its restrictive distribution agreement and was not exempted by Regulation 2790/1999 (now 330/2010) because its market share was between 40 and 45 per cent.

13.7 Article 102 TFEU and the abuse of a dominant position

Article 102 TFEU applies where individual organisations have a near-monopoly position or share an oligopolistic market with a small number of other companies and take unfair advantage of this position to the detriment of the market, other companies, and the end consumers. Companies with a large market share—about 40 per cent—do not infringe Article 102 TFEU by that fact alone, but are at the position where their behaviour needs to be closely monitored in case their practices stray into abuse. Such large and larger market shares bring with them a responsibility under competition law to act only in ways which do not distort or restrict the competitive market in which their large share or dominance exists.

Article 102 TFEU

Any abuse by one or more undertakings of a dominant position within the internal market or in a substantial part of it shall be prohibited as incompatible with the internal market in so far as it may affect trade between member states.

Article 102 TFEU then goes on to give specific examples of such abuse, considered later in section 13.7.1.6.

13.7.1 Article 102 TFEU requirements

For Article 102 TFEU to be applicable, there must be domination of the internal market or a substantial part of it by one or more undertakings. This requires a definition of the relevant market by reference to both the product and the geographical area, and to a lesser extent the temporal market. The necessary requirements are that a dominant position exists within a relevant market, and that there has been abuse of the dominant market position that has affected trade between member states. The leading and best case for many of the points and issues arising from Article 102 TFEU is Case 27/76 *United Brands* v *Commission*, which will be referred to frequently in the following sections.

Article 102 TFEU contains three essential elements. There must be:

- an undertaking (or undertakings) in a dominant position;
- in the relevant markets;
- the 'abuse' of that dominant position;
- which affects or has the potential to affect trade between member states.

13.7.1.1 Definition of undertakings

The meaning of the term 'undertaking' is the same as under Article 101 TFEU but, rather than just concerning an individual company, the definition for Article 103 TFEU has been extended. The CFI (now the General Court) confirmed in Cases T-68 and 77–78/89 *Re Italian Flat Glass* that Article 82 EC (now 102 TFEU) could apply to activities of more than one undertaking where the companies together could constitute a dominant position. Furthermore, oligopolies (a small number of competing companies in a particular market) may also find their activities being considered under the Mergers Regulation, considered in section 13.11.1.

13.7.1.2 A dominant position

The **United Brands** case arose out of a complaint by a number of banana importers about the activities of United Brands Co. (UBC). Some of the facts of this case are as follows (they might put you off bananas!). Bananas are picked and transported whilst green and only begin to ripen after they have been gassed, which usually takes place when they reach the country in which they are to be sold. UBC grew, shipped, and distributed bananas, requiring its distributors/ripeners not to sell on bananas whilst still green (the green banana clause). It charged distributors in different member states different prices, sometimes by as much as 138 per cent without objective justification. UBC had also refused to supply a Danish company with Chiquita bananas because they had advertised another brand. As a result of these activities (and others), the Commission considered UBC to have infringed Article 82 EC (now 102 TFEU) and imposed a fine of 1 million Units of account (the forerunner of the European currency unit (ECU) and the Euro). UBC sought the annulment of the decision and fine before the CoJ.

The issues for the CoJ were the proof of dominance in the market and abuse of this position, which affected trade. It defined a dominant position as:

> a position of economic strength enjoyed by an undertaking which enables it to hinder the maintenance of effective competition on the relevant market by allowing it to behave to an appreciable extent independently of its competitors and customers and ultimately of consumers.

This takes us immediately on to the next points regarding the relevant market. Required are definitions of the product market, the geographical market area, and, sometimes, the temporal market, in which dominance must have existed over a period of time. This is more relevant in markets that change over time, which most markets do not (Cases 6 and 7/73 *Commercial Solvents*). These are important questions, as the definition is very often crucial to determining whether dominance exists. More recently, and along with the general reforms to competition law, in addition to raw market share other factors are taken into account, such as the position of competitors, if any, the ability of new companies to enter the market, and the overall market structure.

13.7.1.3 **The relevant product market**

The test for the relevant product market is the interchangeability of the products or product substitution. A number of factors can influence this. For example:

(a) Cross-elasticity, which is also referred to as product substitutability—that is, if the price of one product rises, will consumers change to another, for example lager for beer, frozen vegetables for fresh vegetables, margarine for butter, artificial sweeteners for sugar, Pepsi for Coke or other fizzy soft drinks? This can change over time according to fashion.

(b) Physical characteristics that are similar—these are factors that mean that a product may not be unique and be capable of being replaced by something else. This is referred to as supply substitutability.

The Commission must pay close attention to the definition of the market for the purposes of competition law. As a result of the case law of the CoJ, in 1997 the Commission published a Notice on the Definition of the Relevant Market, which provides a summary of the case law and Commission methodology for determining the relevant markets.

 THINKING POINT

What was the relevant product market in the *UBC* case?

In the *United Brands* case, UBC said the product market was fruit. The Commission said that it was bananas, clearly a difference. UBC controlled 40–45 per cent of the banana market, but argued that bananas were only a small part of a larger market in fresh fruit, and that although they might occupy a dominant position in the banana market, they did not occupy a dominant position in the fruit market. Which market was pertinent?

The Commission argued, and the Court considered, the special characteristics of the banana (sounds like a joke) and stated that the relevant product market turned on whether the banana could be 'singled out by such special features distinguishing it from other fruits that it is only to a limited extent interchangeable with them and is only exposed to their competition in a way that is hardly perceptible'.

It then identified a number of characteristics of the banana that would help to determine whether the banana had a market of its own:

(a) its physical appearance, chemical composition, taste, shape, softness, and vitamin content;

(b) the fact that it is functional, easy to eat, hygienic, convenient, has high nutritional value, and is easily digestible; and

(c) the fact that it is economic, in that the constant level of production maintained throughout the year lends itself to advance planning of sales.

All that in a banana!

The Commission and Court actually went further and identified a special sub-market of the old, young, and infirm who rely on bananas.

 THINKING POINT

You may ask why and come to the conclusion that the common characteristic might be the absence of teeth!

The CoJ held that 'a very large number of consumers being in constant need for bananas are not noticeably or even appreciably enticed away from the consumption of this product by the arrival of other fruit on the market'. Therefore, other fruits were not substitutable and the relevant product market for the Court was the banana market. It is easier to demonstrate dominance the more narrowly the relevant product market is defined. Hence, companies will seek to widen that definition as much as possible so that there are more potential competing products, and consequently dominance will be much more difficult to establish. The next case considered the supply substitutability side of the issue, which refers to the ease by which other suppliers or producers can enter the market of the product under investigation.

In **Case 6/72 *Europemballage and Continental Can v Commission***, the CoJ stressed the crucial importance of defining the relevant product market and, because the Commission had failed to define the product market properly or consider supply substitutability, the decision was quashed. The Commission had said that the companies had a dominant position in the market for cans for meat, cans for fish, and metal tops. It did not explain why these markets were separate from each other, or from the general market in cans and containers, which

> could be supplied by other manufacturers switching production. The CoJ held that it is necessary to identify the 'characteristics of the products in question by virtue of which they are particularly apt to satisfy an inelastic need and are only to a limited extent interchangeable with other products'. This is known as supply side substitutability, whereby it is questioned that if a manufacturer increases the price of products, whether other manufacturers can switch to produce competing products at minimal changeover cost.

In Cases 6 and 7/73 *ICI Commercial Solvents* v *Commission*, ICI was found to have a dominant market in one possible product raw material used for the manufacture of drugs. Although others were available, the Court held that the difficulty of substitution was a deciding factor in determining dominance. The concept of non-interchangeability is an important test which is applied by the Commission in identifying the relevant product market; see, for example, Case 85/76 *Hoffmann-La Roche*. The same product may, in fact, be classified into different markets; for example, in Case 322/81 *Michelin* v *Commission*, replacement tyres were held by the CoJ to constitute a different market from the same tyres when supplied to the car production factories.

The key feature in determining product demand substitution, and one incorporated into the 1997 Commission Notice on the relevant market, is the 'small but significant non-transitory increase in price (SSNIP)' test, whereby if a product price was raised permanently by between 5 and 10 per cent, and as a result a significant number of customers bought another similar competing product, this would show that those products are in the same market and interchangeable, such that even a dominant company would be unlikely to raise prices much or undertake other forms of abuse in fear of losing customers. This does not always work, though, especially with products with a very strong customer brand loyalty such as Coke and Pepsi.

 THINKING POINT

Is Pepsi substitutable for Coke or vice versa?

For more details on this section visit the online resources.

> A US journal paper (noted in Further reading: Articles) looked at this very question and, on the basis of the SSNIP test alone, it would seem that Coke and Pepsi are not in the same product market and not substitutable, certainly for a significant number of their loyal customers. Strange but true!

13.7.1.4 The relevant geographical market

In *United Brands*, the CoJ held that this required consideration of the opportunities for competition 'with reference to a clearly defined geographical area in which the product is marketed and where the conditions are sufficiently homogeneous for the effect of the economic power of the undertaking concerned to be able to be evaluated'—in other words, it should be plain to see where and how the competition is affected.

The whole or at least a substantial part of the EU is required, but whatever market is demonstrated, it must be drawn to show market dominance. In a narrowly drawn geographical market, a firm that operates on a comparatively localised basis may possess adequate market power to occupy a dominant position, but if the market is too narrowly drawn, it will not be sufficiently large to be a substantial part of the internal market. This problem should be seen in the context of the decision in case *Suiker Unie*, whereby the CoJ held that dominance of the sugar market in Belgium and Luxembourg, then only about 10–15 per cent of the Community, was dominance of a substantial part of the Common Market. In Case T-83/91 *Tetra Pak* v *Commission*, the geographic market was defined as the whole Community.

In *United Brands*, the area was agreed to be six (from the then nine) states, hence a substantial part in which trading conditions were similar. The market and supply conditions in the three countries (France, Italy, and the UK) were held to be significantly different to be excluded. Paragraphs 44–46 of the 1997 Commission Notice on the relevant market are also helpful in determining this, similar prices being one of the most important factors, but also taking account of exchange rate movements (not the case now in the Eurozone of 18 countries), taxation, language, culture, and lifestyle.

The temporal market

The temporal market is rarely investigated but was considered in the *United Brands* case as UBC argued that banana sales were subject to seasonal changes, particularly when summer fruits competed with them, thus trying to show that a seasonal variation widened the market. This was not accepted, as banana sales remained steady throughout the year.

13.7.1.5 **Market share and dominance**

After determining the relative markets for both product and territory, the market share or degree of market power must be considered. Whilst this is an important consideration for determining dominance, it is not definitive. In Case 85/76 *Hoffmann-La Roche*, Hoffmann-La Roche had market shares of 70–80 per cent in some drugs; in Case 6/72 *Continental Can*, Continental Can had 70–80 per cent share of the can market in Germany; in Cases 6 and 7/73 *ICI Commercial Solvents*, ICI had a virtual monopoly of the raw material; and in *Suiker Unie* the Sugar Union had 85 per cent of the Belgian production. A market share of 50 per cent or over will, though, raise a presumption of dominance (Case 62/86 *AKZO* and the headline case of Case T-201/04 *Microsoft*, in which a market share of over 90 per cent was identified).

If not clearly dominant, the particular share must also be considered in the light of the market structure overall. United Brands had only a 40–45 per cent share of the banana market, but the share of the nearest competition becomes relevant. In this case, the next company had only about 16 per cent of the market. Other factors were also critical in the *United Brands* case, such as its control of production, shipping, and dock facilities, which made market entry for any new companies very costly and thus difficult. It also ensured the ability of UBC to act independently of other banana producers and distributors. In *United Brands*, dominance was therefore satisfied.

The Commission suggested in its *Tenth Report on Competition Policy* that in the case of a highly fragmented market, a share of 20–40 per cent might constitute dominance; and in Case T-219/99 *Virgin/British Airways* the CFI (now General Court) upheld the Commission's finding that British Airway's 39.7 per cent share of total airline sales in the UK was sufficient to establish dominance. Very important in this decision was the share of the nearest rival, Virgin, which was just 5.5 per cent. The Commission subsequently published its Guidance on the Commission's enforcement priorities in applying Article 82 of the EC Treaty to abusive exclusionary conduct by dominant undertakings (OJ, 2009 C45/7), which reveals that 40 per cent is the rule-of-thumb bar on the likelihood of dominance, below which dominance is unlikely, but not impossible. At 50 per cent it is very likely that dominance exists unless there are other overriding contradictions, and between 70 and 80 per cent there is a very strong presumption of dominance, but it is still not conclusive on its own.

For more details on this section visit the online resources.

The position of potential competitors or the ability of other competitors to enter the market is taken into account by the Commission to provide a fuller context for determining dominance in the market. Various entry barriers may be present which hinder or prevent market entry, such as the length of time a company has been dominant. This was considered in the *United Brands, Continental Can*, and *Tetra Pak* cases, among others. In Case 85/76 *Hoffmann-La Roche*, the ability of competitors to enter the vitamins market to compete was all but non-existent, such was the very high cost of investment and Hoffmann's existing dominance. Market entry is now especially relevant, with leading firms in areas such as IT technologies, where they possess, or indeed own, significant financial resources, technical know-how, access to markets and to raw materials, and legal barriers including various intellectual property rights such as patents and trade marks—hence the temptation to take advantage of an existing dominant position, such as in the *Microsoft* case and Case T-286/09 *Intel* v *Commission* under appeal in Case C-413/14P.

Dominance, or in this case near-total domination (also called super-dominance) in one market, in the particular example for drinks containers, may be enough to lead to abuse in an associated market for containers (even though dominance in the associated market has not been demonstrated, or does not exist) where the products, manufacturers, and consumers were largely the same in both markets: see Case 333/94P *Tetra Pak International* v *Commission (No. 2)*. In *Continental Can*, the CoJ held that the acquisition of a position of dominance through takeover or merger could amount to an abuse of a dominant market position, although that is the same behaviour that establishes the dominance in the first place.

13.7.1.6 **Collective dominance**

Collective or joint dominance has also now been established where two or more companies act sufficiently closely as to present themselves on a particular market as a collective entity, although legally independent, as held first in Cases C-395 and 396/96 P *Compagnie Maritime Belge SA* v *Commission*. Article 102 TFEU allows for joint dominance in the phrase 'one or more undertakings'. To be considered under Article 102 TFEU, rather than approaching the situation that the companies may have reached an agreement that would breach Article 101 TFEU, it is the fact that the combined market share of the companies involved established dominance. In Case T-342/99 *Airtours plc v Commission*, the Court identified three conditions required to establish joint dominance, which included mutual awareness of trading and operating policy, the tacit agreement that they maintain the status quo, and no other effective competition. Joint dominance is also considered under merger control (see section 13.11).

13.7.1.7 **Abuse of the dominant position**

Dominance on its own is not a problem; it must be abused to breach Article 102 TFEU.

Abuse was defined in Case 85/76 *Hoffmann-La Roche* as follows:

> behaviour of an undertaking in a dominant position which is such as to influence the structure of the market where, as a result of the very presence of the undertaking in question, the degree of competition is weakened and which, through recourse to methods different from those which condition normal competition in products or services on the basis of transactions of commercial operators, has the effect of hindering the maintenance of the degree of competition still existing in the market.

Article 102 TFEU provides four categories of example abuses, dealing essentially with unfairness, prejudice, discrimination, and unnecessary conditions. These categories, though, are not exhaustive and other forms of abuse can be found. The four categories, along with cases that fit within those categories, are now discussed, followed by a more detailed look at two cases:

- 'directly or indirectly imposing unfair purchase or selling prices or unfair trading conditions': for example, unfair low prices—sometimes termed predatory pricing, loss leaders, or unfair high prices as in *United Brands, Hoffmann-La Roche*, Case C-62/86 *AKZO Chemie*, and *Tetra Pak*;

- 'limiting production, markets or technical development to the prejudice of consumers': for example, restrictions on exports in the *Sugar* cases; restrictions on resale in *United Brands*; refusal to supply, which might eliminate competitors in *Commercial Solvents*;

- 'applying dissimilar conditions to equivalent transactions with other trading parties, thereby placing them at a competitive disadvantage': as in *United Brands*; and

- 'making the conclusion of contracts subject to acceptance by the other parties of supplementary obligations which, by their nature or according to commercial usage, have no connection with the subject of such contracts': for example, the green banana clause in the *United Brands* case or tying-in clauses in *Hoffmann-La Roche*. A more recent case in this category is that of Microsoft in Case T-201/04 *Microsoft* v *Commission* and its bundling or tie-in of Windows Media Player with the Windows operating system, which was found to be an abuse of its super-dominant position.

In the *United Brands* case, the company had been found to have infringed Article 82 EC (now 102 TFEU) in that it had required its distributors not to sell bananas whilst still green (the green banana clause) and had charged distributors in different member states different prices, sometimes by as much as 138 per cent, without objective justification. UBC had also refused to supply a Danish company with Chiquita bananas because they had advertised another brand. In the *Continental Can* case, the CoJ held that 'Abuse may therefore occur if an undertaking in a dominant position strengthens such a position . . . that the degree of dominance reached subsequently fetters competition.'

Case 7/97 *Oscar Bronner GmbH & Co. KG* v *Mediaprint Zeitungs- und Zeitschriftenverlag GmbH & Co.* helps to define, perhaps in a more positive way, the boundaries of what may be regarded as the abuse of a dominant position, in that this was not found to be the legal position from the facts. A media undertaking holding a clear dominant position (46.8 per cent circulation) in one market was not obliged to allow access to a home delivery scheme, the only one in the market, to a smaller rival newspaper which could not economically set up its own scheme. There was, in other words, no breach of Article 82 EC (now 102 TFEU), although there was a dominant position in the market. The case stresses that the exploitation of the advantages achieved by reaching a dominant position does not necessarily amount to unlawful abuse.

The concept of exploitative abuse is one recognised in Article 102 actions as in Commission Decision *1998 Football World Cup* and the original ticket distribution system, which restricted the sale of tickets to those applicants with a postal address in France. The Commission stated that the unfair trading rules was exploitative behaviour, which worked to the prejudice of the consumer without a French postal address.

For more details on this section visit the online resources.

> The Commission approach and priorities in respect of Article 102 TFEU enforcement have been set out in a guidance document (OJ [2009] C45/7), along with a comprehensive volume on antitrust enforcement.

13.7.1.8 Effect on trade between member states

The effect on trade is virtually taken as read under Article 102 TFEU if abuse has been found, and the principles developed in Article 101 TFEU cases also apply here.

For more details on this section visit the online resources.

> In **Cases 6 and 7/73 *ICI Commercial Solvents***, ICI claimed that the company to which it had refused to supply raw materials sold 90 per cent of its production of a tuberculosis drug made from those materials outside the EC and, in particular, in the developing countries. ICI therefore argued that the abuse of the dominant position would not come within the ambit of the prohibition in Article 82 EC (now 102 TFEU) because it did not have an effect on trade between member states. The Court held that the expression could not be interpreted so as to limit the sphere of application of the prohibition to industrial and commercial activities supplying the member states.

By prohibiting the abuse of a dominant position within the market in so far as it may affect trade between member states, Article 102 TFEU therefore covers abuse that may directly prejudice consumers, as well as abuse that indirectly prejudices them by impairing the effective competitive structure. The Commission must consider all the consequences of the conduct complained of without distinguishing between production intended for sale within the market and that intended for export. When an undertaking in a dominant position within the internal market abuses its position so that a competitor within the internal market is likely to be eliminated, the area of trade is unimportant once it has been established that this will have repercussions on the competitive structure within the internal market. In *United Brands*, the higher prices and the various restrictions were the equivalent of a prohibition on exports and held to have an appreciable effect on trade between member states. This element is also covered in the 2009 Commission guidance on enforcement priorities relating to Article 102 TFEU, noted at section 13.7.1.5.

13.7.2 Consequences of breaching Article 102 TFEU

Unlike Article 101 TFEU, which pronounces agreements in breach of that Article as being void, Article 102 TFEU is silent as to the consequences, although subsequent enforcement legislation provides for fines that can be very substantial. See, for example, the fine of €1.06 billion imposed on Intel for abusing its dominant market position! This is Case T-286/09 *Intel* v *Commission* and presently on appeal in Case C413/14P.

13.8 The relationship between Articles 101 and 102 TFEU

Articles 101 and 102 TFEU are not mutually exclusive categories and both may be considered as applicable to the same set of facts where, for example, dominant companies abuse their strength by forcing unfair and restrictive agreements on their customers: see Case 85/76 *Hoffmann-La Roche*.

Case 6/72 *Europemballage Corp. and Continental Can* concerned an attempt by the Commission to use Article 86 EEC (now 102 TFEU) to tackle a merger that, in its view, resulted in anti-competitive behaviour. The Commission failed to establish the relevant markets in a case in which a merger had created dominance and therefore also failed to establish an abuse of a dominant position. The Court's views in the case were, however, instructive in respect of the relationship between Articles 101 and 102 TFEU and the restrictive approach to the problem adopted by the Commission, in that, by refusing to consider the use of Article 81 EC (now 101 TFEU) for mergers, it had handicapped itself.

The CoJ held that Articles 85 and 86 EEC (now 101 and 102 TFEU) seek to achieve the same aim on different levels, i.e. the maintenance of effective competition within the Common Market:

> The restraint of competition which is prohibited if it is the result of behaviour falling under Art 85 EEC (now Art 101 TFEU), cannot be permissible by the fact that such behaviour succeeds under the influence of a dominant undertaking and results in the merger of the undertakings concerned. In the absence of explicit provisions, one cannot assume that the Treaty, which prohibits in Art 85 EEC certain decisions of ordinary associations of undertakings restricting competition without eliminating it, permits in Art 86 EEC (now Art 102 TFEU) that undertakings after merging into an organic unit, should reach such a dominant position that any serious chance of competition is practically rendered impossible. Such diverse legal treatment would make a breach in the entire competition law which could jeopardize the proper functioning of the common market.

In other words, mergers cannot avoid the application of Article 101 or 102 TFEU to concerted actions of companies. The Court further held that Articles 85 and 86 EEC (now 101 and 102 TFEU) cannot be interpreted in such a way that they contradict each other, because they serve to achieve the same aim.

This was the first attempt to use the Treaty provision to tackle the effect on competition resulting from mergers. The Commission then realised that a new approach was required to tackle the problems of concentrations and, after some delay, a Mergers Regulation (Regulation 4064/89) was enacted, considered in section 13.11.1.

> The difficulties in dealing with the realities of complex commercial cross-holding were highlighted by **Cases 142 and 156/84 *BAT and Reynolds* v *Commission*.** The CoJ had to determine whether the Commission decision that the acquisition of a minority holding in a competing company was not an infringement of Articles 81 and 82 EC (now 101 and 102 TFEU). Two applicant competitive companies objected to this decision. The original companies remained independent after the agreement, therefore Article 81 EC, which the Court considered could apply to mergers, was considered first. The Court upheld the Commission decision that no anti-competitive object or effect had been established and there was no control, thus there was no case under Article 82 EC either. However, although an acquisition itself might not restrict competition, it may influence conduct to restrict or distort competition.

The case is an example of the need to consider both Articles in such complex situations.

The CoJ has, though, held that an agreement within the meaning of Article 101(1) TFEU between legally separate undertakings may nevertheless result in undertakings being so linked that they become and act as a collective entity as far as their competitors and customers are concerned. As such, it can lead to a position of collective dominance, which is then capable of being abused. See Cases C-395 and 396/96 P *Compagnie Maritime Belge Transports*. However, in a later case the CoJ considered that the Mergers Regulation is more suitable to situations of collective dominance than Article 82 EC (now 102 TFEU). See Cases C-68/94 *France* v *Commission* and C-30/95 *Société Commerciale des Potasses et de l'Azote (SCPA)* v *Commission* and comments in Chapter 10, and section 13.11 on mergers.

Therefore, some circumstances need to be considered in the light of both Articles 101 and 102 TFEU and the Mergers Regulation.

13.9 Enforcement of EU competition law

Under Article 103 TFEU the Council was provided with the power to adopt any appropriate measures to give effect to and ensure the effectiveness of Articles 101 and 102 TFEU. In addition, the Commission was given extensive independent enforcement powers by the Treaty (Article 105 TFEU). Early in the life of the Communities, Council Regulation 17 was the first Regulation to be enacted in support of Articles 85 and 86 EEC (now 101 and 102 TFEU) and provided further clarification of the powers enjoyed by the Commission in support of its role in investigating and enforcing EU competition law. As was outlined in section 13.6.1, the system of enforcement of a competition law was changed from a centralised to a devolved system, relying far more on the member states. As a result, the supportive legislation had to be extensively amended and Regulation 17 was replaced (with the exception of

Article 8 which is still in force—see Article 43 Regulation 1/2003) with Regulation 1/2003, which now provides the system of enforcement. Key provisions are Articles 5 and 6, which confer on the National Competition Authorities (NCA) and the national courts, the power to enforce Article 101 and 102 and impose fines, thus making clear that Articles 101 and 102 are directly effective. Article 2 makes it clear that the burden of proof to demonstrate a breach of the competition law rules lies squarely with the authority (Commission or NCA) or other person alleging the breach.

13.9.1 **Regulation 1/2003**

Regulation 1/2003 empowers the Commission to carry out its function of ensuring that the provisions of the TFEU are applied, to address undertakings, decisions, and recommendations for the purpose of bringing to an end infringements of Articles 101 and 102 TFEU, and to enforce these by way of fines and periodic payments. It sets out the powers and duties of the Commission in the conduct of investigations of competition law abuses, which can be prompted by individuals and companies, the member states, or on the Commission's own initiative. The ethos of the new system of enforcement of competition law introduced and enabled by this Regulation is that of cooperation between the Commission and national competition authorities and the respective courts. The main details of the Regulation follow. However, as this new Regulation replaced Regulation 17, much of the case law arising from the previous Regulation 17 remains relevant—in particular the rights of parties to be heard and present their view of matters. Therefore, the case law still needs to be considered here as analogous authorities for the new Articles in Regulation 1/2003. The existence of Regulation 773/2004 should be noted as it provides details on how proceedings under Article 101 and 102 TFEU enforcement proceedings should be conducted; however, no details are provided here.

Regulation 1/2003, Articles 1–16 are mainly concerned with the respective powers of the Commission and national authorities, interim measures, cooperation between the Commission and national authorities, and the procedure of the declarations by the Commission that the agreement either infringes the Treaty Articles or is exempt from the Treaty provisions.

Articles 17–21 concern the powers of the Commission in conducting investigations; Articles 23–28 concern sanctions available to the Commission in the case of infringements which have been established by it and the rights of the parties under investigation; and Articles 17–18 concern requests for information. The Regulation generally empowers the Commission to request information to assist its investigations from both the authorities of the member states and the undertakings. The owners of undertakings or their representatives are obliged to supply the information requested. If this is not forthcoming, the Commission can adopt a formal decision requiring the information to be supplied (Article 18(3)). Penalties may then be imposed for non-compliance with the terms of the decision.

Article 20 empowers the Commission to undertake all necessary investigations, including the right of its officials to examine books, take copies of records and books, ask for oral explanations, and enter the premises of undertakings, including now extended powers under Article 21 to search the homes of directors, managers, and other members of staff where there is a reasonable suspicion that records relevant to the investigation are stored there. This power can be exercised without the consent of the undertaking involved provided it is specifically authorised in advance by the Commission: see Case 136/79 *National Panasonic*. Alternatively, a formal Decision may be adopted for a mandatory investigation. There is no need to approach the company in advance and the Commission should not be subjected to a delay before the investigation can take place. The investigations authorised under this provision include the infamous 'dawn raids' on the premises of companies under investigation. In Decision 80/334 *Fabbrica Pisana*, it was established that a duty of the company existed to assist the Commission to find documents. In Cases 46/87 and 227/88 *Hoechst*, the authority to raid was challenged on the ground that it lacked precision, but the CoJ held that it was acceptable provided the Commission indicated clearly its suspicions rather than have to supply full information; however, force cannot be used by Commission officials to gain entry and examine documents, and assistance to gain entry must be obtained via the national authorities: Case 85/87 *Dow* v *Commission* and Case 374/87 *Orkem* v *Commission*. In the latter case, it was held by the CoJ that the power to compel the production of information does not extend to requiring the company to admit breaches of the competition rules and, thus, incriminate itself. In effect, a company can be obstructive but may suffer the penalty of fines being imposed on it under Article 23. This can be up to 1 per cent of the previous year's turnover, where a company has misled the Commission: see Cases 40–48/73 *Sugar Union*. Article 23(1) covers a number of situations of not supplying information or supplying false, misleading, or incomplete information, books, or records. In 2012, the Commission fined E.ON Energie €38m for breaking a seal placed on a door during a dawn raid by Commission Officials.

Previously largely established by case law but now contained within the Regulation, Articles 27 and 28 concern the conduct of hearings, the rights of individuals and companies in those hearings, and the rights of confidentiality and professional secrecy. The types of document which are subject to legal privilege and professional secrecy have been the subject of case law. Legal privilege is recognised and covers correspondence between the company and an independent lawyer: see Case 155/79 *AM & S*. In-house lawyers do not enjoy such privilege, so it depends on the nature of the correspondence. Case T-30/89 *Hilti* decided that the privilege extends to in-house lawyers' reports of the independent lawyers' findings. In Case C-36/92P *Samenwerkende*, a refusal to hand over documents considered to be confidential was held to be unjustified in light of the existing protections in Community law under which the Commission is required to notify undertakings of the documents they intend to release to the national authorities and, thus, give the undertakings the chance to seek judicial review to protect these documents. As such, refusal to supply would be unjustified. In the end, the General Court and CoJ must be the arbiters of what is privileged. Case T-30/89 *Hilti* decided that the privilege extends also to an in-house lawyer's reports of an independent lawyer's findings, but not the stand-alone work of an in-house lawyer.

The principle of professional secrecy does not apply to allow a company to protect documents from the Commission but to ensure that information received by the Commission in an investigation is not disclosed to competitors: see Articles 27 and 28, Cases 209–215 and 218/78 *Dow Benelux and Van Landewyck*, and Case 53/85 *AKZO*.

> In **Case C-36/92 P *Samenwerkende***, a refusal to hand over documents considered to be confidential was held to be unjustified in the light of the existing protections in Community law under which the Commission is required to notify undertakings of the documents that it intends to release to the national authorities and thus give the undertakings the chance to seek judicial review to protect these documents. As such, the refusal to supply was unjustified.

> **Case C-550/07 P *AKZO*** was appealed on various points to the CoJ, which confirmed the earlier case of Case 155/79 *A M and S* v *Commission*, to the extent that the Court confirmed that the principle of legal privilege does not extend to in-house lawyers. It held that it made no difference, even if the in-house lawyer was a member of the relevant national Bar or Law Society and was subject to the same rules of professional conduct and discipline as an independent lawyer.

For a substantive breach of Article 101 or 102 TFEU, Article 23 provides the Commission with the right to fine an undertaking not exceeding 10 per cent of the total turnover of the preceding business year, which, given the huge turnover of some multinational companies, means that fines can be substantial. In Case T-51/89 *Tetra Pak Rausing SA* v *Commission*, the company was fined 75 million ECU, which was upheld by the CoJ in Case C-333/94P *Tetra Pak Rausing SA v Commission*. In Commission Decision 98/273 and case, Volkswagen were fined 102 million ECU, which was about £67 million, but which was reduced before the CFI (now General Court) to 90 million ECU in Case T-62/98. This was topped in 2003, when the Commission fined a number of companies that had been operating a vitamin cartel a total of €855.22 million in Decision 2003/2, with Hoffmann-La Roche in that case fined €462 million. Records were also set in March 2004, when Microsoft was fined €497 million and in 2009, when Intel was fined €1.06 billion (Case T-286/09 *Intel v Commission* and under appeal in Case C-413/14P). A fine of €1.38 billion was levied against glass manufacturers in Cases T-56/09 and T-73/09.

For more details on this section visit the online resources.

> **THINKING POINT**
>
> What is the maximum amount that Inter, or indeed any other commercial enterprise can be fined?

13.9.2 Leniency notice

To encourage informant companies, a policy of leniency in fining was partly formalised in a system of so-called leniency notices, whereby companies which cooperated with the Commission in cartel investigations could have their fines drastically reduced by up to 100 per cent if they were the first company in a cartel to provide information to either launch an investigation into a previously undetected cartel or information to secure a prosecution in an ongoing investigation which lacked evidence.

> There is now a revised leniency notice covering this area: Commission Notice on Immunity from fines and reduction of fines in cartel cases (OJ 2006 C298/17).

The leniency regime appeared to have been undermined by a ruling of the CoJ in Case C-360/09 *Pfleiderer*, in which it held that documents voluntarily surrendered under a leniency application were not necessarily immune from disclosure to third parties. However, following a reference from the German court seized with the question, the CoJ held that the balance of immunity and disclosure was a matter for the national courts along national procedural law, providing that EU law was not made impossible or excessively difficult to implement. The German court ordered the disclosure of some of the documents included in the leniency application which, if this became commonplace, might deter companies from revealing possible competition law infringements. As a consequence of this case, the Commission proposed a Directive on private enforcement of EU competition law and leniency, which has now been enacted, noted under section 13.9.4 following.

13.9.3 Judicial review of enforcement

All decisions taken by the Commission under Regulation 1/2003 are subject to review by the General Court under Article 263 TFEU, with the possibility of a further appeal to the CoJ. Article 261 TFEU provides the Court with unlimited jurisdiction to review such penalties as may be imposed by the Commission under EU law provisions.

13.9.4 Private enforcement

As with other areas of EU law, enforcement of the EU rules can also take place by individuals before the national courts via the vehicle of direct effects. This is particularly important now that, as was noted earlier, the new Regulation 1/2003 has made Article 101(3) TFEU, concerned with exemptions, directly effective, which was previously not the case. If the other areas of EU law are anything to go by, this will greatly complement the Commission's power to enforce competition law—which because of its stretched resources is limited—by the vigilance of thousands of individuals who may be affected by anti-competitive practices. The Commission has also noted in paragraph 16 of its Notice on the handling of complaints by the Commission under Articles 81 and 82 of the EC Treaty (OJ 2004 C101/65) that actions before the national courts are possible and may be advantageous to aggrieved parties.

A leading case explored this development. Case C-453/99 *Courage v Crehan* concerned a pub tenant party to an agreement which tied him in to buying beer from a particular brewery, Courage plc. He claimed this was in breach of Article 81 EC (now 101 TFEU) and claimed damages. As a party thus also tainted by the agreement, the UK court was minded to dismiss the claim, but nevertheless made a reference to the CoJ under Article 234 EC (now 267 TFEU). The CoJ, in looking back at the importance of securing enforcement rights for individuals and the effectiveness of Community law (Cases 26/62 *Van Gend en Loos* and C-6/90 and 9/90 *Francovich*), held that the competition law rules were fundamental rules in the EC, and if the agreement was in breach of Article 81 EC (now 101 TFEU) and not able to be exempted, it was void and could not be relied on by anyone, including a party to the agreement.

The Court also held, in line with case developments in other areas, that in order to ensure the effectiveness of Community law, the procedural rules of the member states should not deprive individuals of rights in the absence of a Community regime. That matter was ultimately up to the member states' courts, but there should be no absolute bar to an action where a contract is held to breach Article 101 TFEU. Hence, *Courage* v *Crehan* can be relied on for a breach of Article 101 TFEU and an applicant should not be barred from seeking damages for any loss incurred as a result. However, national law can exclude a claim where the party him- or herself is also responsible for the agreement in breach. The party in this case did win damages and there is no doubt that this case and many others will assist Commission enforcement of competition law significantly.

In support of the ability of private parties to pursue claims in the national courts, Directive 2014/104 on anti-trust damages actions has been enacted to iron out some of the differences and difficulties in the member states. The Directive seeks to both encourage private enforcement of EU competition law and ensure that Companies are encouraged to use the leniency programme. Specifically, it includes a prohibition on the release of any documents submitted during a leniency or settlement proceedings (Article 6(6)) by the national courts. In further support of national courts quantifying damages in private enforcement actions, the Commission has issued a Guide document for the national authorities and courts.

For more details on this section visit the online resources.

▶ CROSS REFERENCE
See the details in Chapter 8.

13.10 Conflict of EU and national law

In theory, the division between EU and national law should be easy—one or more companies' activities will only come within EU competition law jurisdiction if they also affect trade between member states, otherwise it will be up to the member states' competition authorities to prosecute the breach. However, the question of the resolution of potential conflicts between EU and national competition law and the problem of double jeopardy was initially addressed in Case 14/68 *Walt Wilhelm* v *Bundeskartellamt*. The Federal Cartel Authority in Germany and the Commission had instituted proceedings against Walt Wilhelm for breach of competition rules. Walt Wilhelm submitted that the Bundeskartellamt could not maintain proceedings for an offence that was at the same time the object of investigation by the Commission. The CoJ ruled that conflicts between Community law and national law in the matter of cartels must be resolved by applying the principle that Community law takes precedence. This was subsequently confirmed in Case 13/77 *GB-INNO-BM*, which considered a clash between Belgian law and EC competition law in which the CoJ held that the member states had a duty not to adopt or retain any national measures which might deprive, in this case, Article 82 EC of its effectiveness. In order to clarify the procedure and assist national courts in considering cases that involve issues of EU competition law, the Commission had issued a Notice to national courts on the application of Articles 81 and 82 EC setting out the procedure that should be followed. The notice also indicated that national courts should take notice of 'comfort letters', although these remain non-binding. However, Regulation 1/2003 has now taken over the field in this area to govern the relationship between the national courts and the Commission. It provides under Article 16 that if a decision has been reached by the Commission on a competition law matter, the national authorities and courts can no longer reach their own conclusion if it conflicts with that decided by the Commission, or even that in the process of being decided by the Commission. This means, in practice, that they must wait for the Commission conclusion before taking any action. Article 15 allows for a cross-flow of information between the Commission and national competition authorities to assist both in investigations.

Regulation 1/2003, though, has made other changes that affect the relationship. By scrapping, at least on the face of it, the individual notifications procedure and by making Article 101 TFEU directly effective, the legal exceptions to Article 101 can be the subject matter of national court adjudication. However, the bottom line is that any decision reached cannot run contrary to established or pending EU law and Commission Decisions dealing with the same matter. The national courts must apply EU law where relevant.

13.11 EU merger control

It was in the area of mergers and acquisitions, or, as termed in the EU, concentrations, that the relationship of Articles 81 and 82 EC (now 101 and 102 TFEU) with each other previously came under closest scrutiny. Originally, the Commission was of the view that Article 81 EC would not apply to concentrations. Thus, if competition was restricted or distorted by a concentration of companies, Article 82 EC was the appropriate measure with which to tackle it. This policy was pursued by the Commission in Case 6/72 *Continental Can*, whereby the Commission tried to remedy an abuse of a dominant position which had been achieved by takeovers and substantial holdings in European companies by a US company. It was the first attempt at merger control by the Commission. It was not successful, mainly because the Commission failed to establish the relevant markets, rather than a failure to show abuses by the concentration. The CoJ's views in the case were, however, instructive in respect of the relationship of Articles 81 and 82 EC and the restrictive approach to the problem adopted by the Commission—that by refusing to consider the use of Article 81 EC for mergers it had handicapped itself. (See further, in section 13.7.1.5, Case 6/72 *Europemballage Corp. and Continental Can* and the CoJ's view on the aims of Articles 81 and 82 EC (now 101 and 102 TFEU).)

The Court further held that Articles 81 and 82 cannot be interpreted in such a way that they contradict each other, because they serve to achieve the same aim.

In Case T-51/89 *Tetra Pak* v *Commission*, Tetra Pak was found to be in breach of Article 82 EC (now 102 TFEU) following the acquisition of another company which held an exclusive licence to manufacture sterilised milk cartons. Whilst the acquisition itself did not offend Article 82 EC, the consequent dominant position, which was immediately abused, did so.

The difficulties in dealing with the realities of complex commercial cross-holding were highlighted by Cases 142 and 156/84 *BAT and Reynolds* v *Commission*. The CoJ had to determine whether the

Commission decision that the acquisition of a minority holding in a competing company was not an infringement of Articles 81 and 82 EC. Two applicants, competitive companies, objected to this. The original companies remained independent after the agreement, therefore Article 81 EC, which the Court considered could apply to mergers, was considered first. The Court upheld the Commission decision that no anti-competitive object or effect had been established and there was no control, thus there was no case under Article 82 EC either. However, although an acquisition itself might not restrict competition, it may influence subsequent conduct to restrict or distort competition. The case is an example of the need to consider both in such complex situations.

13.11.1 The Mergers Regulations (4064/89 and 139/04)

It was following the *Continental Can* case that the Commission realised that a new approach was required to tackle the problems of mergers, otherwise known as 'concentrations'. The Commission put forward a proposal for a regulation on merger control, but it was 16 years later, on 21 December 1989, that the Council adopted Council Regulation 4064/89 on the control of concentrations be-tween undertakings. Under it, the Commission jurisdiction under Articles 81 and 82 EC (now 101 and 102 TFEU) and Regulation 17 was repealed in respect of concentrations. The first Mergers Regulation has now been replaced by new Mergers Regulation 139/04, which provides the legal foundation of EU policy control of mergers and acquisitions. Mergers Regulation 139/04 establishes a division between large mergers with a European dimension, over which the Commission will exercise supervision, and smaller mergers, which will fall under the jurisdiction of national author-ities. The concept of a concentration is now set out in an updated Commission Notice.

For more details on this section visit the online resources.

Article 1 states that the Regulation applies to mergers and takeovers with an EU dimension, applies where there is a worldwide turnover of more than €5,000 million, and an aggregate EU wide turn-over of each of at least two of the undertakings of more than €250 million. An EU dimension may nevertheless exist, if:

(1) the combined aggregate worldwide turnover of all the undertakings is more than €2,500 million;

(2) in each of at least three member states, the combined aggregate turnover of all the under-takings is more than €100 million;

(3) in each of at least three member states, the aggregate turnover of each of at least two of the undertakings concerned is more than €25 million; and

(4) the aggregate EU-wide turnover of each of at least two of the undertakings concerned is more than €100 million.

However, if each of the undertakings concerned achieves more than two-thirds of its aggregate EU-wide turnover within the same member state, a concentration will fall outside the scope of the Regulation, and the merger will be subject to national rather than EU control.

Article 2 provides the power of review to determine whether mergers are compatible with the Com-mon Market. The creation or strengthening of such a position will be declared incompatible with the Common Market where it would significantly impede effective competition as a whole or in a substantial part of the Common Market. In making this appraisal, the Commission is required to take into account the following matters: the need to preserve and develop effective competition within the Common Market; the structure of all the markets concerned (product and geographic markets); the actual or potential competition from undertakings located within or without the EU, and which includes the market position and economic and financial power of the undertakings concerned; suppliers' and users' access to supplies or markets; legal barriers to entry into the market; supply-and-demand trends for the relevant goods and services; the interests of intermediate and ultimate consumers; and the development of technical and economic progress provided it is to consumers' advantage and does not form an obstacle to competition.

The last requirements are similar to the exemptions under Article 101(3) TFEU.

Where a merger is found by the Commission not to impede effective competition, it will be declared compatible with the Common Market (Article 2(2)). The member states, however, retain the right in such circumstances to veto mergers in particularly sensitive areas of their economies, provided this is compatible with the general requirements of EU law. Article 2(3) states that where a merger is found by the Commission to impede effective competition, it will be declared in a decision incompatible with the Common Market. Joint ventures which act as an autonomous economic entity and which have competition and concentration issues are dealt with under Article 2(4).

Article 3 defines a concentration to include mergers, acquisitions of direct or indirect control of undertakings by persons already controlling at least one undertaking, partial mergers, and merger-like joint ventures. However, it excludes from the scope of the Regulation coordination of market behaviour of firms that remain independent of each other. Such coordination, if adverse to competition in the Common Market, would fall within the scope of either Article 101 or Article 2 TFEU, as in Cases 142 and 156/84 *BAT and Reynolds* v *Commission*. However, more recent cases would seem to contradict this view. In Cases C-68/94 *France* v *Commission* and C-30/95 *Société Commerciale des Potasses et de l'Azote (SCPA)* v *Commission*, the CoJ determined that the Merger Regulation may apply also to collective dominance. The case concerned a proposal that potash companies in Germany be concentrated, thus creating a de facto monopoly in the German market and a dominant position with the French company SCPA in the Community market. To obtain Commission approval, the parties agreed to certain conditions relating to cooperation between the dominant firms and the distribution of products in the markets identified. France objected to the Commission decision before the CoJ and SCPA before the CFI (now the General Court). As they both concerned the same decision, the CFI declined jurisdiction and the whole matter was referred to the CoJ. The decision is important because it is the first time the Court has clearly stated the Mergers Regulation to be applicable to collective dominance, despite the lack of express words to that effect in the Regulation and the doubts of the member states when the Regulation was enacted that it would apply to oligopolies. The CoJ, on the other hand, thought that there was nothing in the Regulation to exclude its application. That collective dominance was not sufficiently established by the Commission in the case itself does nothing to upset this. See also Case T-102/96 *Gencor* v *Commission*, which confirms this position.

The effect of the Regulation is described as one-stop-shopping, in that only one authority—Commission or national authority—need take action, depending on the area of dominance. It provides for the operation of a so-called principle of exclusivity whereby all decisions on EU-wide mergers are taken by the Commission, member states having undertaken not to apply their national competition rules to such cases (Article 21(1) and (2)), although there is provision for referral to national authorities in certain cases.

13.11.2 Enforcement of Regulation 139/04

Article 4(1) requires the notification of a concentration with a Union dimension within one week after the conclusion of the agreement, the announcement of the public bid, or the acquisition of a controlling interest, whichever of these occurs first. Fines for a failure to notify can be imposed up to a maximum of €50,000 (Article 14(1)).

Article 7(1) provides that a concentration with a Union dimension shall not be put into effect before notification or in the three weeks following notification. The validity of transactions in securities on stock exchanges is not affected (Article 7(5)).

Under Article 10(1) the decision to open proceedings referred to in Article 6 must be taken within one month of the day following receipt of the notification. Article 6 provides that the Commission is under a duty to examine all notifications as soon as they are received, and to notify its decision to the undertakings concerned and the national authorities without delay. If the Commission considers that the proposed concentration falls outside the scope of the Regulation, it must record that finding by way of a decision. Where it finds that the proposed concentration has a Union dimension, but does not raise serious doubts as to its compatibility with the Common Market, it must decide not to oppose it and must declare it compatible with the Common Market. Where the concentration both falls within the scope of the Regulation and raises serious doubts as to its compatibility with the Common Market, the Commission must decide to issue proceedings.

Article 10(3) requires that a decision that a concentration is incompatible with the Common Market must be taken within four months of the decision to open proceedings. During this period, the parties to the proposed concentration will be free to propose changes to their merger in order to avoid a negative decision.

Where the Commission has found a proposed concentration to be incompatible with the Common Market, it may require the separation of the undertakings brought together, or the cessation of joint control, or any other action that may be appropriate to restore the conditions of effective competition (Article 8(5)). So far, the Regulations have been sparsely used to prevent mergers, most of which have been cleared. An exception was the proposed merger of Aerospatiale, Alenia, and de Havilland (M053), which was prohibited under the Regulation for the reason that the merger would have had an unacceptable impact on customer choice and the balance of competition in the EU. Following this first blocking by the Commission, another seven mergers have been blocked.

A Commission Decision which was made to block a merger was overturned by the CFI (now General Court) in Case T-342/99 *Airtours plc* v *Commission*, when Airtours wished to take over First Choice in the UK. The reason given by the CFI was that the Commission had failed to establish clearly that a position of collective dominance would have been reached following the merger.

Article 11 provides that the Commission can request information and Article 13 confers the power to undertake 'all necessary investigations' on the Commission, including the power for officials to examine and take copies of or extracts from books and other business records, to ask for oral explanations on the spot, and to enter any premises, land, or means of transport of the undertakings concerned.

The Regulation also allows for the imposition of fines and periodic payments for failure to notify, for supplying incorrect or misleading information, and for obstructing an investigation by Commission officials (Articles 14 and 15). Where the parties intentionally or negligently fail to comply with an order to suspend the concentration or disregard a decision to stop a merger or undo a merger, the Commission may impose a fine of up to 10 per cent of the aggregate annual turnover of the undertakings (Article 14(2)).

For more details on this section visit the online resources.

 Summary

The adoption and development of an EU competition law and policy was a necessary element to ensure the creation and success of the EU internal market. Without it, companies and individuals could divide the market by their anti-competitive behaviour and defeat the attempt to create a single market.

Apart from the enforcement of all aspects of EU competition law, three main elements have been considered in this chapter:

- the prohibition of anti-competitive agreements under Article 101 TFEU;
- the prohibition of an abuse of a dominant position under Article 102 TFEU; and
- the control of mergers which would lead to an elimination of competition in the EU.

Questions

1. Why is competition law an integral and necessary part of the EU legal regime?

2. Article 101(1) prohibits certain anti-competitive agreements: what conditions must be satisfied for the prohibition to apply?

3. On what grounds or reason may agreements, etc. escape falling foul of Article 101 TFEU?

4. What conditions have to be satisfied for an undertaking to be in breach of Article 102?

5. What were the main reasons for the change in the enforcement regime in EU competition law and the enactment of Regulation 2003/1?

For guidance on how to tackle this specimen exam question and to read a suggested model answer, visit the online resources. www.oup.com/uk/foster_directions6e/.

Sample exam Q&A

Essay question

Why is competition law policy an integral and necessary part of the EU?

Further reading

Books

Colino, S. M. *Competition Law of the EU and UK*, 7th edn, Oxford University Press, Oxford, 2011.

Faull, J and Nikpay, A. (eds) *The EU Law of Competition*, 3rd edn, Oxford University Press, Oxford, 2014.

Foster, N. *Blackstone's EU Treaties and Legislation*, Oxford University Press, Oxford, published annually.

Furse, M. *Competition Law of the EC and UK*, 6th edn, Oxford University Press, Oxford, 2008.

Jones, A. 'Competition law' in Barnard, C. and Peers, S. (eds) *European Union Law*, 2nd edn, Oxford University Press, Oxford, 2017, p. 509.

Jones, A. and Sufrin, B. *EU Competition Law*, 6th edn, Oxford University Press, Oxford, 2016.

Korah, V. *An Introductory Guide to EC Competition Law and Practice*, 9th edn, Hart Publishing, Oxford, 2007.

Monti, G. *EC Competition Law*, Cambridge University Press, Cambridge, 2007.

Whish, R. and Bailey, D. *Competition Law*, 8th edn, Oxford University Press, Oxford, 2015.

Articles

Akman, P. 'The role of intent in EU case law on abuse of dominance' (2014) 39 EL Rev 316.

Bailey, D. 'Single, overall agreement in EU competition law' (2010) 47 CML Rev 473.

Bailey, D. 'Restriction of competition by object under Article 101 FTEU' (2012) 49 CML Rev 559.

Baxter, S. and Dethmers, F. 'Collective dominance under EC merger control—after *Airtours* and the introductions of unilateral effects is there still a future for collective dominance?' (2006) 27 ECLR 148.

Dethmers, F. 'Fines under Article 102 of the Treaty on the Functioning of the European Union' (2011) 2 ECLR 86.

Gerber, D. and Cassinis, P. 'The modernisation of European Community competition law: achieving consistency in enforcement' (2006) 27 ECLR 10.

Lemley, M. A. and Mckenna, M. P. 'Is Pepsi really a substitute for Coke? Market definition in antitrust and IP' (2012) 100 Georgetown Law Journal 2055.

MacGregor, A. and Gecic, B. 'Due process in EU competition cases following the introduction of the new Best Practices Guidelines on Antitrust Proceedings' (2012) 3 Journal of European Competition Law and Practice 425.

Nazzini, R. 'Administrative enforcement, judicial review and fundamental rights in EU competition law: a comparative contextual-functionalist perspective' (2012) 49 CML Rev 971.

Nebbia, P. 'Damages actions for the infringement of EC competition law: compensation or deterrence?' (2008) 33 EL Rev 23.

Whish, R. and Bailey, D. 'Regulation 330/2010: the Commission's new block exemption for vertical agreements' (2010) 47 CML Rev 1757.

Witt, A.C. 'From Airtours to Ryanair: is the more economic approach to EU merger law really about more economics?' (2012) 49 CML Rev 217.

Website

http://ec.europa.eu/competition/index_en.html

14 Discrimination law

LEARNING OBJECTIVES

In this chapter, you will learn about:

- why the discrimination provisions were originally included in the EC Treaty;

- the main legislative provisions on discrimination law and, in particular, sex discrimination law;

- the basic scope of the main Treaty provision—Article 157 TFEU;

- the meaning of 'equal pay for equal work' and 'work of equal value';

- the concepts of indirect discrimination and how comparison is made;

- equal treatment, especially relating to pregnancy and childbirth; and

- principal aspects of other discrimination law.

Introduction

For more details on this section visit the online resources.

Although discrimination law in the European Union (EU) legal order has broadened out into other areas outside of its base in discrimination on the grounds of nationality and sex, this chapter focuses mainly on sex discrimination law, which is the subject of study in many law schools, rather than a wider study of general equality or non-discrimination law. This chapter, however, also includes an overview of other forms of laws to combat discrimination as a result of the expansion of what can be termed 'EU equality law' or 'equal treatment law' in the EU legal order, for example race, age, or sexual orientation. In particular, Article 19 of the Treaty on the Functioning of the European Union (TFEU) and the legislation enacted thereunder are considered.

There are a number of examples of express prohibitions of discrimination on different grounds within the Treaty, but there is not, as such, an express general principle of non-discrimination or equality in the Treaty, although new Article 10 TFEU comes closest to it. The specific prohibitions do, however, support the establishment of a general principle in the EU legal order that is additionally confirmed by the judgments of the Court of Justice of the European Union (CoJ) and academic commentary. The Treaty Articles that seek either to prohibit discrimination or promote equality on the grounds are:

- Articles 2 and 3 of the Treaty on European Union (TEU) on equality between men and women;

- Article 8 TFEU, a so-called mainstreaming provision which requires the Union to aim to eliminate inequalities and promote equality between men and women in all activities, not just in the social field;

- Article 10 TFEU, which aims to combat discrimination based across a range of issues (see also Article 19 TFEU);

- Article 18 TFEU on equality on the grounds of nationality;

- Article 19 TFEU on the general power to prohibit discrimination across a range of issues;

- Article 40(2) TFEU concerned with equality between producers and between consumers in the Common Agricultural Policy (CAP);

- Articles 45, 49, and 56 TFEU providing for equal treatment of workers and the self-employed;

- Article 106 TFEU on public undertakings;

- Article 110 TFEU on taxation;

- Article 153 TFEU on the promotion of equality of men and women in the work environment; and

- Article 157 TFEU on equal pay and now the promotion of equality between the sexes.

Without going into details, all of these Articles support the development of a general principle of equality by the establishment of a legal culture that does not tolerate the different treatment of like or the same treatment of unequals across a range of subject matters. Added to these now, since the Lisbon Treaty, is the EU Charter on Fundamental Rights, which has provided a section (Articles 20–23) prohibiting discrimination on any ground and which is considered at the end of this chapter. Furthermore, as has been shown in very many cases, the provisions of the European Convention on Human Rights (ECHR) have often been applied in the EU legal order in support of equality in a number of areas. Hence, the existence and value of a general principle of equal treatment has been acknowledged and confirmed by the CoJ in a number of cases: recently, for example, in Case C-149/10 *Chatzi,* in which the Court held that the principle of equal treatment is one of the general principles of EU law and is now affirmed by Article 20 of the Charter on Fundamental Rights (in that case, to support the right to parental leave on an equal basis).

Apart from discrimination in the area of free movement of persons, which was considered in Chapter 12, this chapter only considers sex or gender discrimination in depth, but provides an overview of the new developing areas of discrimination law at its end. Before looking at sex discrimination provisions, the reasons for its inclusion are discussed.

Reasons for the original inclusion of sex discrimination in the Treaty

 THINKING POINT

What is your view on why an Article on sex discrimination should have originally been included in what was essentially an economic agreement?

For more details on this section visit the online resources.

The inclusion of prohibitions of discrimination in other Articles of the Treaties can be readily understood because they all relate, more or less, to nationality and therefore go to the very foundation of the establishment of the Union—that is, the removal of national barriers to the establishment of the internal market. Nationality should not play a role in the free movement of goods, persons, or capital. Non-discrimination on the grounds of sex, however, is less readily understandable in this context. On the face of it, it would appear to be essentially a socially based discrimination, and not economic.

It was, however, originally framed in the EC Treaty as a form of workplace-based discrimination for reasons of competition between member states in that if men and women did not have to be paid the same, then by paying women less, some states could gain an economic advantage. It is helpful and informative to go back to the drafting of the European Economic Community (EEC) Treaty to see why what has clearly become a social law right was included in the EU in the first place. Additionally, and viewed in the context of the initial, more limited aims of the original Communities to eliminate discrimination based on nationality, there is an odd feature to sex discrimination law.

 THINKING POINT

What do the classic freedom of movement of rights provisions require to trigger the rights that the prohibition of discrimination does not?

The right not to be discriminated against on the grounds of sex does not require a cross-state border or Union context. There needs to be no movement between member states, unlike the fundamental freedoms, goods, persons, and capital, where there does. EU sex discrimination law is applicable in wholly internal situations and if a matter is deemed to be wholly internal, it lies outside the scope of EU law, unless there has been some form of cross-border event. Given the original, more economic nature of the Community, the European Community (EC) then would seem an unlikely source of women's equality rights. Fundamentally, the EC was a vehicle to promote economic integration and development of the member states, rather than to provide equality between the sexes. However, it is now accepted that the immediate reason for including Article 119 in the EEC Treaty (now 157 TFEU) was not for reasons of social justice, but out of economic considerations—that is, the creation of level playing fields for industry and member states in terms of the application of national social laws. The Article was alleged to have been included at the request of the French, whose law provided for equality of pay between male and female workers. It was feared that French industry would be at a disadvantage if equal pay were not enforced in the other member states, in particular Germany, the post-war workforce of which relied far more heavily on women workers.

Regardless of the exact underlying motive, its inclusion would appear to be based on economic arguments, the aim of which was to ensure that similar economic conditions apply in all of the member states. There appears to be no social justification for its inclusion, but we do have the chance to see a CoJ view on the matter.

> In **Case 43/75 *Defrenne* v *Sabena (No. 2)***, the CoJ declared that Article 119 EEC also forms part of the social objectives of the Community, which is not merely an economic Union but is at the same time intended, by common action, to ensure social progress and to seek the constant improvement of the living and working conditions of their peoples, as is emphasised by the Preamble to the Treaty. It held that this double aim, which is at once economic and social, shows that the principle of equal pay forms part of the foundations of the Community.

Hence, it was regarded in 1976 as one part of a double aim, and was even promoted in subsequent judgments.

> In **Case 149/77 *Defrenne* v *Sabena (No. 3)***, a couple of years later, the CoJ declared the elimination of discrimination based on sex as part of the fundamental rights within Community law.

> More recently, the CoJ confirmed in **Cases C-324 and 325/96 *Deutsche Telekom* v *Vick*** and **C-50/96 *Deutsche Telekom* v *Schröder*** that the social aims of Article 119 EEC (now 141 TFEU) prevail over the economic aims:
>
> > It must be concluded that the economic aim pursued by Article 119 EC, namely the elimination of distortions of competition between undertakings established in different member states, is secondary to the social aim pursued by the same provision, which constitutes the expression of a fundamental human right.

Article 119 EC (now 157 TFEU) was the sole original provision for the EC to concern itself with sex discrimination. In contrast, there now exists a considerable body of EU law on the subject, in the form of Treaty additions introduced notably by the Treaty of Amsterdam, a growing body of EU Directives, and the very many progressive decisions of the CoJ.

14.1 The legislative framework

14.1.1 **Treaty Articles**

Article 157 TFEU (ex 119 EEC and 141 EC) on equal pay for equal work originally provided the only specific mention of equal treatment of the sexes in the EC Treaty, but, following amendments by the Treaty of Amsterdam, Treaty references to the promotion of equality are more extensive. In addition

For more details on this section visit the online resources.

to the main Treaty Article—Article 157 TFEU—the Treaty of Amsterdam introduced as one of the goals now outlined in Article 2 TEU, 'equality between men and women', and Article 3 TEU states the aim 'to promote . . . equality, between men and women'.

This aspiration is also repeated in Article 8 TFEU: 'In all its activities, the Union shall aim to eliminate inequalities, and to promote equality, between men and women.'

Equality between men and women in the working environment was also included in the 1989 Community Social Charter, which was brought into Article 136 EC (now 151 TFEU). The amended Article 137 EC (now 153 TFEU) provides that, inter alia, the Union shall complement and support the activities of the member states in the field of equality between men and women with regard to labour market opportunities and treatment at work.

Article 157 TFEU was expanded beyond its simple original provision to ensure that men and women should receive equal pay for equal work. The Treaty of Amsterdam amended and added two sentences to locate within a Treaty base the principles of equal pay for work of equal value and action to promote equality, but which falls short of out-and-out positive discrimination.

> These rights were previously contained in Directives only, which meant that they could not give rise to direct effects against other individuals, issues considered in full in Chapter 8, section 8.1.3.

Finally, as far as the Treaties are concerned, a new enabling power has been provided in Article 19 TFEU, which provides:

> the Council, acting unanimously in accordance with a special legislative procedure and after obtaining the consent of the European Parliament, may take appropriate action to combat discrimination based on sex, racial or ethnic origin, religion or belief, disability, age or sexual orientation.

▶ CROSS REFERENCE

Article 19 is considered briefly at section 14.6.

Added to the Treaty Articles now must be included the section in the EU Charter on Fundamental Rights, Articles 20–23, which prohibits discrimination on any grounds in Article 21. It is beginning to be referred to by the CoJ and will no doubt feature much more in case law in the future.

14.1.2 Secondary legislation

The first secondary legislative interventions in this area were enacted following the publication of a social action programme in 1974 by the Commission. Three Directives concerned with equality between men and women were adopted:

- the Equal Pay Directive 75/117;
- the Equal Treatment Directive 76/207; and
- the Social Security Directive 79/7.

> A second social action programme was commenced in 1982, which led to the enactment of Directive 86/378 on equal treatment in occupational pensions and Directive 86/613 on equal treatment of the self-employed and protection of self-employed women during pregnancy and motherhood (now replaced by Directive 2010/41).

Following the amendment of the EC Treaty by the Single European Act (SEA) in 1986, another action programme was launched in 1989 and resulted in the enactment of the Pregnancy and Maternity Directive 92/85.

The new initiatives introduced by the Maastricht Treaty led to the enactment of further Directives, including the Parental Leave Directive 96/34 (repealed and replaced now by Directive 2010/18), the Burden of Proof in Sex Discrimination Cases Directive 97/80 (now absorbed into Directive 2006/54), and the Part-time Workers Directive 97/81.

While the last Directive is not directly aimed at addressing sex discrimination, it will have this effect because it aims to reduce the inequality between full-time workers and part-time workers, the majority of part-time workers being women and thus likely to be indirectly discriminated against, which is considered in section 14.2.4.

The more recent secondary legislation includes Directive 2004/113 on equality in the access to and the supply of goods and services, Directive 2010/41 on equal treatment between self-employed men and women, and Directive 2010/18 on parental leave.

Article 157 TFEU and the early legislation in particular have been subject to very liberal interpretation by the CoJ, far beyond a literal reading of the provisions, due in large part, no doubt, to the fact that, for the first 20 years of the Communities' life, there was only Article 119 EEC (now 157 TFEU) to provide for equal treatment and that was confined to equal pay. During the subsequent 10 years, this was supplemented by only the first three Directives dealing with equal treatment. The CoJ had to be inventive in order to make any progress. Whilst greater effort is being shown now by the EU institutions and the member states by the setting up of various fora in which to promote equality, in the beginning action was more likely to be taken by individuals, sometimes with the support of the national equality agencies, such as the Equal Opportunities Commission (EOC) in the UK, rather than the Commission in enforcement actions.

CROSS REFERENCE
See, for example, the *Defrenne, Garland,* and *Marshall* cases, considered in this chapter.

This chapter concentrates on the core aspects of sex equality law in the EU, notably Article 157 TFEU, Directives 75/117 and 76/207, and the case law generated by them, both of which have now been replaced by the new consolidating Directive 2006/54 on equal treatment between men and women. They will still be referred to in this chapter, with either the new or old Directive Article numbers in parentheses, according to the context, and particularly because the case law, for the moment, derives largely from those old Directives.

The consolidating Directive carries an extended concept of discrimination. Article 2 of Directive 2006/54 provides as follows.

Directive 2006/54, Article 2

. . . discrimination includes:

(a) harassment and sexual harassment, as well as any less favourable treatment based on a person's rejection of or submission to such conduct;

(b) instruction to discriminate against persons on grounds of sex;

(c) any less favourable treatment of a woman related to pregnancy or maternity leave within the meaning of Directive 92/85/EEC.

14.2 Article 157 TFEU and the scope of the principle of equal pay

For more details on this section visit the online resources.

Article 157 TFEU originally provided for equal pay for equal work only, but was amended by the Treaty of Amsterdam to refer to 'equal pay for work of equal value' by the Lisbon Treaty, a concept that was first introduced by Directive 75/117.

Article 157(1) TFEU

Each member state shall ensure that the principle of equal pay for male and female workers for equal work or work of equal value is applied.

Secondly, it attempts to define what equal pay actually means. Article 157(2) TFEU narrowly defines 'pay' as 'the ordinary basic or minimum wage or salary or any other consideration, whether in cash or in kind, which the worker receives either directly or indirectly, in respect of his employment, from his employer'.

Article 157(2) TFEU defines equal pay without discrimination to mean the following.

Article 157(2) TFEU

. . .

(a) that pay for the same work at piece rates shall be calculated on the basis of the same unit of measurement; and

(b) that pay for the same work at time rates shall be the same for the same job.

Payment by piece rates is not so common now and basically means that a person is paid per unit or piece of a product that is made. It was previously common in factory work for producing many component parts or in home working, such as the assembling of biro parts. The more assembled or made, the more is paid.

It took a long time, however, before the principle of equal pay was properly realised. Much of the delay was due to a deliberate postponing of the application of the principle by the member states and it was only action by individuals that allowed the CoJ to step in and provide for the application of the principle.

Case 43/75 *Defrenne v Sabena (No. 2)* was the first significant case under Article 119 EC (now 157 TFEU) and concerned an applicant who was previously unsuccessful in challenging a discriminatory national pension system that was held to be outside Community law competence. However, she commenced a second action to challenge unequal pay. Gabrielle Defrenne was paid at a substantially lower rate than her male colleagues for the same work and claimed compensation for the damage suffered from February 1963 until February 1966. The case was sympathetically received by the CoJ and Gabrielle Defrenne was successful. The Court held that the principle of equal pay was sufficiently clear and precise to have direct effects. However, in response to the fears expressed by employers and the interventions of some member states about the costs to industry if the judgment were backdated to 1957 (that is, all of the back pay that would have to be paid), the Court declared the ruling to be prospective only, from the date of the original litigation commenced by Defrenne and any cases in the pipeline.

This prospective-only ruling is a type of ruling that is rare, but it is repeated again in equality law in the *Barber* case, considered in section 14.2.1.1.

With *Defrenne* having opened the gate, many more cases were referred to the CoJ, which was then able to refine the definition of pay and thus the scope of Article 119 EC (now 157 TFEU).

14.2.1 **The meaning of 'pay'**

Although, previously, Case 80/70 *Defrenne* v *Belgium (No. 1)* seemed to rule out a wider definition of 'pay' to exclude pension benefits in retirement, the term 'pay' has been progressively defined.

In **Case 12/81 Garland v British Rail Engineering**, Article 119 EEC was held to include concessionary rail travel facilities for the family of an ex-employee. The CoJ held that the travel facilities in question were granted in kind by the employer to the retired male employee or his dependents directly or indirectly in relation to his employment, and could be regarded as an extension of travel facilities granted during employment.

Pay, as interpreted by the CoJ, also includes:

- rules by which seniority/loyalty payments are achieved in favour of full-time employees in Case C-184/89 *Nimz* v *Hamburg*;
- sick pay, even though part of a statutory scheme, in Case 171/88 *Ingrid Rinner-Kuhn* v *FWW Spezial-Gebaudereiningung*;
- a severance grant in Case C-33/89 *Kowalska* v *Hamburg*; and
- compensation for lost wages for attendance on training course for works council members in Case C-360/90 *Arbeiterwohlfahrt der Stadt Berlin* v *Monika Botel*.

Unfair dismissal compensation and redundancy pay were also held to come within Article 141 EC (now 157 TFEU) in Case C-167/97 *Seymour-Smith and Perez*.

Hence, 'pay' is given a very wide meaning, and any payments and benefits that arise from the employment relationship may be held to be pay under Article 157 TFEU. One particular problem was the status of pensions because of the link that exists with retirement and the fact that the EC secondary legislation at the time appeared to preserve this whole area within the competence of the member states, and not the Union.

14.2.1.1 The concept of pay and its relationship to pensions

This topic has particular complications not only because the concept of pay is being stretched, but also because it straddles the very grey area of the boundary between the jurisdiction of the member states and that of the EU and CoJ. In particular, Article 7 of Directive 79/7 provides as follows.

Directive 79/7, Article 7

This Directive shall be without prejudice to the right of Member States to exclude from its scope:

(a) the determination of pensionable age for the purposes of granting old-age and retirement pensions and the possible consequences thereof for other benefits;

(b) . . .

It was the meaning of the latter part of the Article, 'the possible consequences for other benefits', which caused the uncertainty due to its vagueness.

❯ CROSS REFERENCE

Defrenne (No. 1) is considered in section 14.2.1.

Prior to a definitive judgment on this point, the CoJ had previously decided in Case 152/84 *Marshall* that the retirement age itself should not be linked to the pension age, but had to be equal for men and women for it to comply with Community law. Hence, a clear distinction was drawn between retirement and pensions. In *Defrenne (No. 1)*, it was held that contributions into a statutory pension or social security scheme were not to be considered as coming within the concept of pay under Article 119 EEC (now 157 TFEU). As a result, it was widely assumed that this ruling was good for all forms of pension schemes.

 THINKING POINT

Why should there have been a difference in pension or indeed retirement age of men and women? After all, life expectancy of women has been historically and continuingly higher than men.

The reasons for the allowance in EU law for a difference in pension ages are starting to become lost in time. Essentially, the difference stemmed from the fact that many states provided that women retired earlier and obtained their state pensions at an earlier age.

However, many pension arrangements are now the result of private and contractual negotiation. How are these regarded by the CoJ?

In **Case 69/80 Worringham and Humphries v Lloyds Bank**, the defendant bank operated an arrangement whereby male workers under the age of 25 were paid 5 per cent more than their female counterparts to enhance a pension. The total enhanced payment package, however, formed the basis of calculation of other social advantages and welfare benefits. The bank argued that the enhancement was linked to pensions; therefore, it could lawfully discriminate. The CoJ ruled that such a contribution, which determined other benefits linked to salary paid by the employer, is pay within the meaning of Article 119 EEC (now 157 TFEU), even if the contributions are deducted at source and paid on behalf of the employee—that is, the employee never sees them directly.

This could include anything supplied by the employer to or on behalf of the employee on a pro rata basis, such as annual bonuses. Thus, in this case, the pension itself was not considered to be pay, but not all of the linked consequences could be excluded automatically under Article 7a of Directive 79/7.

Case 170/84 *Bilka Kaufhaus* v *Karin Weber Van Hartz* concerned different access rules to a pensions scheme for full-time and part-time workers, the part-timers being mainly female. It was held that where supplements were made by the employer to the basic state pension under a contractual agreement and where the amount was linked to pay (that is, as a proportion or percentage), it was pay for the purposes of Article 119 EEC. Furthermore, if access to this scheme was discriminatory, as it was proved to be in the case, it also breached Article 119 EEC (now Article 157 TFEU).

The next case was, like *Defrenne (No. 2)*, highly significant in the EU legal order because of the impact it had on employers.

In **Case C-262/88 *Barber* v *Guardian Royal Exchange (GRE) Assurance Group***, Barber was made redundant by GRE at the age of 52. There was an agreed contracted-out—that is, private—pensions scheme. His redundancy package included a statutory redundancy payment, and an ex gratia payment (a top-up), but entitlement to his occupational pension was deferred until the agreed pension age under the scheme of 62 for men and 57 for women. There was an agreement in the redundancy package that if, within ten years of the state pension ages, the pension could be obtained earlier, a redundant woman aged 52 would be entitled to immediate access to her pension because she was within 10 years of the statutory pension age, whereas Barber and other male employees were not (because they were 10 or more years adrift). It was this discrepancy between the treatment of the two sexes that was the basis for the claim of unlawful discrimination.

The defence claimed that there was a link to the pension age and the case therefore fell under the Directive 79/7 exemption, in which case it was lawful discrimination. The UK government, intervening, claimed that the scheme, which replaced the state scheme, should be regarded as coming within social security and not Article 119 EEC (now 157 TFEU). The CoJ concluded that the statutory redundancy pay and the benefits from his contracted-out occupational pension scheme—that is, the pension itself—were 'pay' within Article 119 EC. The deciding factor is whether the rules and thus payment of the specific scheme are a part of the employment contract even by the voluntary inclusion of the employer. Only if entirely to do with the compulsory state pension does a case now fall outside Article 157 TFEU. The Court emphasised (at [25]) the importance of the fact that the occupational scheme was funded without any contribution being made by the public authorities.

The *Barber* decision gave rise to severe concern. It was not expected that pensions should be pay; indeed, *Defrenne (No. 1)* suggested that they were not. It would mean that there would be unlawful discrimination not previously thought to be the case, for which huge amounts of compensation, not previously contemplated, would be payable. This would not have been taken account of in the actuarial calculations, and the pensions schemes would have had severe difficulties in making payments not previously foreseen. Hence the CoJ declared Article 119 EEC to be directly effective for pensions from the date of judgment only—that is, 17 May 1990—and for any cases in the pipeline. In other words, like the second *Defrenne* judgment on the direct effects of Article 119 EEC before it, the judgment was prospective only, applying from the date of judgment and not validating any backdated claims for equal treatment, which would have cost the industry dearly. Indeed, the member states were so concerned about the judgment and possible future interpretations of it that they attached a specific Protocol (No. 2) to the TEU, which has now been replaced by a Protocol (No. 33) attached to the Treaties by the Lisbon Treaty.

Protocol concerning Article 157 of the Treaty on the Functioning of the European Union

THE HIGH CONTRACTING PARTIES,

HAVE AGREED UPON the following provision, which shall be annexed to the Treaty on European Union and to the Treaty on the functioning of the European Union:

For the purposes of Article 157 of the Treaty on the Functioning of the European Union, benefits under occupational social security schemes shall not be considered as remuneration if and in so far as they are attributable to periods of employment prior to 17 May 1990, except in the case of workers or those claiming under them who have before that date initiated legal proceedings or introduced an equivalent claim under the applicable national law.

This means that the judgment applies to benefits payable for service after 1990. This prospective-only judgment, like the *Defrenne (No. 2)* judgment, was to overcome the economic effect on employers in the case of a retroactive application of the ruling. Thus, the period of earnings before the *Barber* judgment does not give rise to a claim.

The Protocol clarified the judgment and was expressly accepted by the CoJ in Case C-109/91 *Ten Oever*, which also extended the *Barber* ruling to pension benefits payable to the pension holder's survivors; it was further confirmed by the CoJ as coming within Article 141 EC in Case C-117/01 *KB* v *NHS Pensions*.

The *Barber* case, however, prompted many more cases seeking to establish its exact meaning and consequences, only one or two of which are considered here.

It also led to the extensive amendment of Directive 86/378 on occupational social security schemes, which is not considered further in this text.

In **Case C-152/91 *Neath* v *Hugh Steeper***, it was held that inequality in employees' contributions arising from actuarial factors such as life expectancy, which differed according to sex, would not be caught by Article 141 EC (now 157 TFEU). The case involved a conversion of a periodic payment to a lump sum payment. In this case, the male applicant received less and claimed that this was unlawful discrimination; however, according to the CoJ, the difference in treatment was objectively justified as a result of the actuarial factors.

Whilst benefits and lump sum payments must be regarded as pay, this is not the case for the contributions that determine the size of the fund, because factors other than a simple difference in sex are involved. The funding system to provide the amount of pension to be available does not come under Article 157 TFEU (ex 141 EC). The amount needed for a pension is determined by actuaries. They base their figures on the fact that women live longer after retirement, and in the past and at the time of the case they had a right to a pension at an earlier age; thus, they needed more capital to be paid into the scheme to supply this. If they work for the same length of time, they must pay more. This becomes clear when converted to a lump sum: women will receive more.

It has subsequently been established that the time limit in *Barber* and Protocol No. 33 does not apply to discrimination in relation to the right to join—that is, access to an occupational pension scheme—which is governed by the judgment in *Bilka Kaufhaus*, noted in section 14.2.4.1 and confirmed in Case C-57/93 *Vroege v NCIV Instituut*.

There are still many cases arising from this very complex relationship between pay and pensions. It is complicated because there remains a lawful discrimination on the part of member states as to when females and males receive state pensions. Any difference that relates to the amount paid in or out to achieve a pension is in law entirely acceptable unless, according to *Barber*, the payments have become part of the contractual relationship by the intervention of an agreement between the employer and employee. It is then pay, it comes within Article 157 TFEU, and the employer cannot lawfully discriminate.

14.2.2 The original Equal Pay Directive (Directive 75/117)

The Equal Pay Directive added little to that interpreted for old Article 119 EEC, but did extend the principle of equal pay to 'work to which equal value is attributed' and extended the equality requirement to 'all aspects and conditions of remuneration' (Article 1), which Article 119 EEC at the time did not. This is now contained in the new Article 157 TFEU.

THINKING POINT

What difference does including equal value in Article 157 TFEU make? Hint: think about the employment relationship covering most sex equality issues.

Article 157 TFEU
Each Member State shall ensure that the principle of equal pay for male and female workers for equal work or work of equal value is applied.

By including equal value in the Treaty Article, it makes the situation much easier for claimants who work for a private employer—that is, the vast majority of workers. It was with these concerns in mind that many of the cases that were originally raised in respect of Directive 75/117 alone or in combination with the Treaty Article were decided upon by the CoJ with reference to the Treaty Article only. If the CoJ was not able to bring the case circumstances within the scope of Article 141 EC (now 157 TFEU), there would have been severe difficulties for many of the applicants because of the absence of horizontal direct effects in Directives. A more concise equal pay principle is now to be found in Article 4 of Directive 2006/54, although, of course, the case law still relates to the previous Directive and Treaty Article. The definition of pay in Article 157 TFEU is also contained in Article 2(1)(e) of Directive 2006/54.

14.2.3 The basis of comparison

In most situations in which there is direct discrimination, it is usually clear and obvious that there is discrimination; for example, it is easy to compare a man and woman who are doing the same job in the same workplace for the same employer, but are being paid differently. There are, however, complications where the comparison is not so obvious, where the times of work differ or the job differs slightly, or the workplace differs. It then becomes important that there is a valid comparator.

> In **Case 129/79 *Macarthy's* v *Wendy Smith***, Smith was employed from March 1976 at a salary of £50 per week, and complained of discrimination because her predecessor, a man, had received a salary of £60 per week. The CoJ held that although the work actually performed by employees of different sex must be within the same establishment, the employees need not be employed at the same time. However, the Court was careful to point out that:
>
> > It cannot be ruled out that the difference in pay between two workers occupying the same post but at different periods in time may be explained by the operation of factors which are unconnected with any discrimination on grounds of sex.

This is a question of fact for the national courts to decide. The CoJ had therefore expressly left open the possibility of a genuine material factor defence. Hence, the scope of the concept of equal pay for equal work (same work) could not be restricted by a requirement by member states that the person whose work was being compared be contemporaneously employed.

Comparison can also be made with members of the other sex who do work of a lesser value to ensure that a woman doing work of higher value cannot be paid less than the male comparator.

> This was held in **Case 157/86 *Mary Murphy An Bord Telecom Éireann***, which was decided by the CoJ on the basis of old Article 119 EEC, even though it was an equal value claim, and Article 119 EEC only covered equal pay claims on the basis that it would be even more of an infringement to pay the higher value work less than the lower value work.

The CoJ had also expressed the view in the *Macarthy's* case that it would not entertain a hypothetical comparator. Equally, it held in Case C-313/02 *Wippel* v *Peek & Cloppenburg* that a woman who was working only when required (a form of zero hours contract) who claimed unfair treatment because her working hours had not been specified could not be compared with a male working full time. The reason given was that no worker working full time had a contract the same or similar to Wippel; in other words, whilst EU legislative provisions on equal treatment—Directive 76/207—and part-time workers—Directive 97/81—would apply, the case was distinguished on the facts.

There is now a statutory definition of direct discrimination in the Equality Directives (Directives 2000/43 and 2000/78) and also now Directive 2006/54, which defines this concept.

> **Directive 2006/54, Article 2**
> 'direct discrimination': where one person is treated less favourably on grounds of sex than another is, has been or would be treated in a comparable situation.

Comparison, or the lack of it, has become a crucial factor in cases that have arisen from the compulsory competitive tendering schemes that were imposed on local authorities in the UK, requiring them to contract out jobs to outside private companies in order to achieve cost savings. In these schemes, some members of staff (predominantly women) were removed from direct employment by the local authority and then re-employed by an independent employer. They were then returned to the same job, but on less money than their (mainly) male counterparts doing the same job or work previously evaluated to be of equal value.

> For example, in **Case C-320/00 *Lawrence v Regent Office Care Ltd*,** dinner ladies who were previously employed directly by the local authority had their contracts taken over by a private company. They continued to work in the same job, but were paid less in comparison with male colleagues who were retained by the local authority, but who had been rated to be doing work of equal value. The CoJ held that whilst Article 141 EC was not restricted to employees working for the same employer in the same place, it could not apply where there was not a single overall authority responsible for deciding pay.

> Similarly, in **Case C-256/01 *Allonby*,** teachers who were mainly female had been made redundant by a college, but were taken on by an agency in a self-employed capacity and returned to work in the same college. However, they were paid less than an alleged male comparator employed by the college. The CoJ held that because there was not a single source that led to the unequal pay, the work and the pay of those workers could not be compared on the basis of Article 141 EC.

With the CoJ having held twice now that an indirect comparison is not possible, the conclusion is that there can be no factual, yet alone illegal, discrimination, because there is no single employer responsible to make the pay adjustment if inequality were found to be unlawful. These cases would appear to open up a very big loophole that permits unequal pay for women by condoning the hiving-off of employment contracts according to sex, thus either directly or indirectly discriminating against women. However, with the new Directive definition, it is now arguable that 'would be' in the text opens the door for a hypothetical comparator test to be used by the CoJ in view of the unfortunate consequences of those earlier cases.

> Legislative intervention to correct this has not happened, despite the fact that recital (10) of Directive 2006/54 states that 'The Court of Justice has established that, in certain circumstances, the principle of equal pay is not limited to situations in which men and women work for the same employer'; however, those words did not appear in the body of the Directive. Thus, it appears that suitable cases will need to come along for the CoJ to make its own correction, perhaps encouraged by recital (10)?

These cases have also involved an issue that occurs a great deal in discrimination law, that of indirect discrimination, which is considered next.

14.2.4 Part-time work and indirect discrimination

It is in the area of part-time work that the concept of indirect discrimination has been most thoroughly explored by the CoJ. Direct discrimination on the grounds of sex can arguably never be justified: either it is discriminatory and thus contrary to EU law, or it is not. Indirect discrimination, however, can be justified, but is more difficult to determine. It covers cases in which a class of persons is mainly or entirely constituted of one sex (usually women), and a difference is drawn between that class and another class, which can consist of members of both sexes. In either class, no direct discrimination takes place—that is, both genders are treated the same—but, in comparison with the other class, a rule or measure operates in a discriminatory manner against the predominant sex, which can be either women or men. Whether the discrimination is actually unlawful is often dependent on the motives behind it and whether it can be justified objectively by those motives.

There is a statutory definition of 'indirect discrimination' contained in Directive 2006/54.

Directive 2006/54, Article 2(1)(b)

'indirect discrimination': where an apparently neutral provision, criterion or practice would put persons of one sex at a particular disadvantage compared with persons of the other sex, unless that provision, criterion or practice is objectively justified by a legitimate aim, and the means of achieving that aim are appropriate and necessary.

Even with the statutory definition, it is still useful to see how this was developed by the CoJ in a number of cases concerning pay differences between full-time and part-time workers. These are also usually combined with objective justifications as elements of the cases.

In **Case 96/80 *Jenkins* v *Kingsgate***, the employer paid full-time workers 10 per cent more per hour than part-time workers, in order, it was claimed, to discourage absenteeism and to achieve a more efficient use of their machinery. All but one of the part-time workers were women. The CoJ held that a difference in rates of remuneration between full-time and part-time employees did not offend against Article 119 EEC (now 157 TFEU), provided the difference was attributable to factors that were objectively justified and did not relate directly or indirectly to discrimination based on sex. If it is established that a considerably smaller percentage of women than men performs the number of hours necessary to be a full-timer, the inequality will contravene Article 119 EEC. In particular, in the light of the difficulties encountered by women in arranging to work the minimum number of hours per week, the pay policy of the undertaking cannot be explained by factors other than the discrimination based on sex.

 THINKING POINT

For what reasons is it more likely that women will seek part-time work?

It is more likely that women will find it harder to work full time and may have to seek part-time work because of commitments to family and home, but this does not make it lawful to discriminate against them.

14.2.4.1 Objective justifications

The existence or not of an objective justification is crucial, but, as observers of the cases, we do not, for the most part, see this, because this is usually a matter of factual consideration for the national court. For example, the justification given by an employer may be that the company needs to encourage the recruitment of full-time employees, in which case the national court could require evidence that demonstrates the relative number of full-time and part-time vacancies and applications for those posts, to see whether the facts bear out the claim made by the company. Where there is no plausible explanation to account for the difference in pay, it is likely to be discrimination contrary to Article 157 TFEU.

In **Case 170/84 *Bilka Kaufhaus* v *Karin Weber Van Harz***, a store gave all full-time employees a non-contributory pension on retirement, whereas part-timers qualified only if they had been employed permanently for at least 15 years. The undertaking claimed that the store needed to pay more and offer further benefits to full-timers to attract them in sufficient numbers. The CoJ ruled that Article 119 EEC (now 157 TFEU) is infringed where a company excludes part-time workers from its occupational pension scheme and where that exclusion affects a far greater number of women than men, unless the undertaking shows that the exclusion is based on objectively justified factors unconnected with discrimination based on sex.

The Court went on to consider the question whether the undertaking could justify that disadvantage on the ground that its objective is to employ as few part-time workers as possible. It held that, in order to show that the discrimination was objectively justified, the employer must show that the measures giving rise to the difference in treatment:

- correspond to a genuine need of the enterprise;
- are suitable for attaining the objective pursued by the enterprise; and
- are strictly necessary for that purpose—that is, proportionate.

A further requirement laid down by the Court was that it was for the company to show that the discrimination was not based on sex rather than the complainant having to prove discrimination.

This was part of a move by the CoJ to shift the burden of proof to the company, which it advanced over a number of cases. In the particular case, the German court applying the ruling held that the difference was not objectively justified.

In **Case C-171/92 *Rinner-Kuhn***, the CoJ suggested that an objective factor that was based on a national social policy might be acceptable, but not the reason for a difference in pay in the case based on the assumption that part-time workers were not integrated into the business in the same way as full-time workers, even where based on national law.

In **Case C-167/97 *Seymour Smith and Perez***, the CoJ held that national courts should look at both the numbers of men and women who can and cannot satisfy a particular requirement, such as full-time work, to determine whether there is a disproportionate effect on one sex, in which case discrimination will be assumed unless justified.

Part-time work and overtime were considered in two cases in which indirect discrimination was claimed, both involving a clear majority of women in the part-time group of workers.

> In **Case C-399/93 *Helmig***, part-time workers were not paid overtime rates for work in excess of their part-time hours but only, as with full-time workers, when they worked more hours than full-time workers.

> In **Case C-300/06 *Vob***, the part-time workers were paid less for overtime than full-time workers regardless of the overall number of hours worked.

> The CoJ was satisfied that in *Helmig* there was no discrimination, as pay rates were the same. However, in *Vob*, pay rates were reduced for part-time overtime but it was left open whether they could be justified objectively within the national court.

The case law on part-time work has essentially been put into statutory form by Directive 97/81.

Section 14.2.5 considers equal value claims, but is also instructive in terms of the investigation that the national court should undertake to assess the grounds for the indirect discrimination.

14.2.5 **Work of equal value**

Work of equal value claims cause further difficulties because it is not often clear that two jobs are of the same value and an appraisal has to be done, either by the national court or using a formal job evaluation scheme.

> **Case C-127/92 *Enderby* v *Frenchay Health Authority*** involved an equal value claim and the comparison of lower-paid speech therapists, comprising mainly women, with higher-paid pharmacists and clinical psychologists, comprising mainly men. The CoJ held that it was for the national court to determine, if necessary by applying the principle of proportionality, whether and to what extent the shortage of candidates for a job and the need to attract them by paying higher pay constituted an objectively justified ground for the difference in pay between jobs of equal value. The Court held that it was up to the national court to decide whether the available statistics are representative enough to provide sufficient evidence to judge the justifications given. The difficulty with indirect discrimination is that there is often higher demand for lower-paid, but flexible, jobs, especially where this demand is created by women seeking such jobs. This can be argued by the employer to constitute evidence that it needs to pay at a premium less flexible and thus less attractive jobs, occupied mainly by men.

> In **Case 157/86 *Mary Murphy* v *An Bord Telecom Éireann***, an employee claimed equal pay for her work, which was considered to be of even higher value than her comparator. The CoJ held that Article 119 EEC (now 157 TFEU) must be interpreted as covering the case in which a worker who relies on that provision to obtain equal pay is engaged in work of higher value than that of the person with whom a comparison is to be made.

The conclusion that has to be drawn from the case was that Article 119 EEC (now 157 TFEU) could also be applied to equal value claims, although not expressly stated in the Article at the time. Under the amended Article 157 TFEU, it is expressly covered.

The Court reasoned in the *Murphy* case that whilst it was true that Article 119 EEC (now Article 157 TFEU) applies only in the case of equal work, nevertheless if that principle forbids workers of one sex engaged in work of equal value to be paid a lower wage than the other sex, it prohibits such a difference in pay much more strongly where the lower-paid category of workers is engaged in work of higher value.

Interestingly, in this case, the defendant was a public body and, if it had so wished, the CoJ could have resolved the case under Directive 75/117, because it would have involved vertical direct effects.

 THINKING POINT

Why might it have done that? What advantages from doing so accrued?

It chose instead to widen the scope of Article 119 EC, which, in the long run, would assist more potential litigants than the Directive.

14.2.5.1 Job evaluation schemes and the burden of proof

In order to back up the principle of equal pay for work of equal value, Article 1 of Directive 75/117, now reproduced in Article 4 of Directive 2006/54, provided that 'where a job classification system is used for determining pay, it must be based on the same criteria for both men and women and so drawn up as to exclude any discrimination on grounds of sex'.

In a number of cases, the CoJ has ruled that any job evaluation schemes used must not be based on criteria that values one sex only and has to be transparent, so that a claimant can see how particular wages are achieved.

For example, in **Case 237/85 *Rummler* v *Dato-Druck***, a job evaluation scheme that was based on muscular effort, fatigue, and physical hardship was held by the CoJ not to be in breach of Article 1 of Directive 75/117 as long as the following condition was met: it must, in so far as the nature of the tasks carried out in the undertaking permits, take into account criteria for which workers of each sex show particular aptitude. The CoJ said that criteria based exclusively on the values of one sex contain a 'risk of discrimination'.

Additionally (as was noted in the *Bilka* and *Enderby* cases), the CoJ shifted the burden of proof so that the employer had to prove that there was no discrimination, direct or indirect, rather than the employee having to show that there was discrimination—something that would be much harder for the employee.

See, for example, **Case 109/88 *Handels- og Kontorfunktionaerernes Forbund i Danmark* v *Dansk Arbejdsgiverforening (Danfoss)***, which involved a pay structure so complex that it was impossible for a woman to identify the reasons that led to a difference in pay between her and a man doing the same job.

The results of this case law were consolidated into the Burden of Proof Directive (Directive 97/80), which has now been replaced and incorporated into Article 19 of Directive 2006/54.

Danfoss also made it clear that a length-of-service criterion for higher pay was acceptable with special justification.

> This was clearly confirmed in **Case C-17/05 *Cadman***, in which a significant difference in pay between men and women existed based on length of service. It would be only in the case of doubt that the burden would fall on the employer to justify the difference.

14.2.6 **Enforcement and remedies**

The remedies and enforcement procedures have been consolidated in Directive 2006/54 for all of the Directives that it has replaced. Member states are required, under Articles 17 and 18 of Directive 2006/54 (ex Article 2 of Directive 75/117), to ensure that judicial or conciliation procedures are available with adequate compensation measures.

Article 17(1) of Directive 2006/54 (replacing Article 2 of Directive 75/117) requires member states to provide the legal means by which all employees who consider themselves discriminated against are able to pursue a claim.

> **Directive 2006/54, Article 17(1)**
>
> Member States shall ensure that, after possible recourse to other competent authorities including where they deem it appropriate conciliation procedures, judicial procedures for the enforcement of obligations under this Directive are available to all persons who consider themselves wronged by failure to apply the principle of equal treatment to them, even after the relationship in which the discrimination is alleged to have occurred has ended.

Article 23 of Directive 2006/54 (ex Article 4 of Directive 75/117) requires member states to take the necessary measures to ensure that any provisions in collective agreements, wage agreements, or in individual contracts that breach the principles of the Directive are to be null and void or to be removed. Article 24 of Directive 2006/54 (ex Article 5 of Directive 75/117) requires the member states to take measures to protect employees against dismissal as a result of a complaint made by them of discrimination to an employer or where the employee takes legal proceedings aimed to enforce the principles provided by the Directive. The member states were required, under Article 6 of Directive 75/117, to take the necessary measures to ensure that the principle of equal pay is applied and to see that effective means are available to take care that the principle is observed. This requirement has not been carried over verbatim and has been consolidated with the overall requirement to ensure equal treatment in Articles 1 and 4 of Directive 2006/54.

14.3 Equal treatment

For more details on this section visit the online resources.

The original Equal Treatment Directive 76/207 went well beyond the original scope of Article 119 EEC (now 157 TFEU), which was concerned only with pay; therefore, the Directive had to be enacted under the general legislative power of Article 235 EEC (now 352 TFEU). It extended the prohibition of discrimination on the grounds of sex into many facets of the employment relationship including, inter alia, access, appointment, dismissal, retirement, training, and working conditions. It has now been repealed and replaced by Directive 2006/54, which was enacted under the amended Article 141(3) EC (now 157(3) TFEU) allowing for direct intervention under a dedicated Treaty legal base.

Article 14(1) of Directive 2006/54 (ex Article 1 of Directive 76/207) refers to equal treatment for men and women, which is required to be applied to working conditions, access to employment (including promotion), and vocational training. A previous Article 1a of Directive 76/207 (now Article 23 of Directive 2006/54) sets out what is known as 'gender mainstreaming'. It requires member states actively to take into account the objective of equality between men and women when formulating and implementing laws, regulations, administrative provisions, policies, and activities in the areas referred to in all of the new Directives.

14.3.1 The concept of equal treatment/no discrimination on the grounds of sex

The concept of equal treatment, which was defined in Directive 76/207 as no discrimination on the grounds of sex directly or indirectly by reference, in particular, to marital or family status, has not been carried over into Directive 2006/54, which has adopted the extended definitions of discrimination and harassment noted in section 14.1.2. The now single exception to the principle of equal treatment is that relating to particular occupational activities previously contained in Article 2(6) and now to be found in Article 14(2) of Directive 2006/54, which will be considered after the cases that previously helped to determine the extent of discrimination covered by the earlier Directive.

The concepts of equal treatment and non-discrimination are largely treated as being synonymous, but any existing distinction took on greater significance because of the much greater subject matter coverage of the earlier Directive 76/207. Does equal treatment mean more than non-discrimination? Case law has considered the scope of the protection provided for by these provisions in so far as what is meant by the right to equality within the framework agreed by the member states and interpreted by the CoJ.

> For example, in **Case C-13/94 P v S and Cornwall County Council**, a male-to-female transsexual was dismissed from employment in an educational establishment after informing the employers about the forthcoming gender reassignment. The CoJ moved away from a simple interpretation of no discrimination on the grounds of sex simply to mean a comparison of how each gender is treated, and held that the dismissal was unlawful discrimination on the grounds of sex because it was 'based, essentially if not exclusively on the sex of the person concerned'.

One of the difficulties in sex discrimination law is that the need to find a comparator is not always convenient or helpful in determining whether discrimination has been suffered (this is also a difficulty in relation to the pregnancy cases, considered in section 14.3.5.1). In the *P v S* case, if this is discrimination based on sex, as the CoJ held, with whom can a comparison be made? There is no direct comparator as such, for example a female-to-male transsexual.

 THINKING POINT

Which comparator: a female-to-male transsexual? All other workers, male or female? The male-to-female transsexual with herself?

The CoJ held that where a person is dismissed on the ground that he or she intends to undergo, or has undergone, gender reassignment, he or she is treated unfavourably by comparison with persons of the sex to which he or she was deemed to belong before undergoing gender reassignment. Therefore, the Directive appeared to remove any discrimination where sex, in a wider sense, was concerned, not limited only to a difference in treatment between genders! The question that was raised after this case was whether the concept of no discrimination on the grounds of sex had been transformed into no discrimination on the grounds of sexuality, or even no sexual-orientation discrimination. However, in the next case, the limits of EC equality law at that time were found.

In **Case C-249/96 *Grant v South West Trains***, South West Trains' regulations specifically excluded benefits for same-sex partnerships. Whereas opposite-sex partners were included even when they were not married, provided a stable relationship was established, same-sex partners were excluded. The CoJ held that this was not discrimination based on sex because the rule would apply also using a direct comparison to male same-sex relationships. This was discrimination based on sexual orientation. The Court discussed a number of points in connection with this and found that, in some member states, such a relationship would, but only for a limited range of rights, be treated the same as an opposite-sex relationship and, in other states, such relationships were not recognised in any particular way. The Court referred to the then new Article 13 EC (now 19 TFEU) by which the member states in Council were empowered to take action to outlaw sexual orientation discrimination, but stated that the law in the EC at that time did not equate same-sex relationships with opposite-sex ones; therefore, the discrimination in respect of sexual orientation, although present, was not contrary to Article 141 EC (now 157 TFEU) or the Directive (now also within Article 14 of Directive 2006/54).

The CoJ confirmed this stance in **Case 125/99P *D and Sweden v Council***.

In both cases, the CoJ decided to leave the response to this form of discrimination to the legislative intervention of the member states, which have now responded, with Directive 2000/78 providing a framework for combating discrimination on grounds of sexual orientation.

However, **Case C-117/01 *KB v NHS Pensions***, although decided on the basis of Article 141 EC and not the Directive, is worthy of a brief note here because of the much more sympathetic judgment given by the CoJ in a case involving transsexual rights under the existing Community legislation at the time of the case. The case concerned the inability to nominate a transsexual partner as a pension beneficiary because national legislation required the partner to be an opposite-sex spouse. National legislation would not allow the original sex of a partner to be altered to enable him or her to marry and thus satisfy the pension law requirement. The Court held that national legislation must be regarded as being, in principle, incompatible with the requirements of Article 141 EC on the grounds that it had already been found to be in breach of the ECHR, and prevented a couple such as KB and R from fulfilling the marriage requirement, necessary for one of them to be able to benefit from part of the pay of the other. However, the Court was not specific as to exactly how Article 141 EC might be offended, apart from the fact that Article 141 would regard the benefit as pay. The Court acknowledged, however, that it was up to the member state to determine the conditions under which legal recognition is given to the change of gender of a person in R's situation and it would be up to the national court to decide whether KB could rely on Article 141 EC (now 157 TFEU).

Equal treatment in this case, then, has been given a very wide scope to include the right to have a change in sex officially testified. Quite where a comparison fits in is difficult to see. Now that same-sex civil partnerships have been given statutory recognition in the UK and other countries in the EU, this would no longer be a problem.

> Finally in **Case C-423/04 *Richards***, it was held that the correct comparator for a male-to-female transgendered person when determining pensionable ages was a female who had not undergone gender reassignment. Article 4(1) of Directive 79/7 was held not to permit a distinction in national law as to how a pension was determined.

Directive 2006/54 adds a little light to this area.

> **Directive 2006/54, recital (3)**
>
> The Court of Justice has held that the scope of the principle of equal treatment for men and women cannot be confined to the prohibition of discrimination based on the fact that a person is of one or other sex. In view of its purpose and the nature of the rights which it seeks to safeguard, it also applies to discrimination arising from the gender reassignment of a person.

This is not, however, addressed in the body of the Directive.

14.3.2 **The scope of equal treatment**

The scope of the prohibition of discrimination within Directive 2006/54 is spelled out in detail in Article 14(1) (ex amended Article 3 of Directive 76/207), which has consolidated much of the previous case law in the process. It provides that the application of the principle of equal treatment means that there shall be no direct or indirect discrimination in the public or private sectors, including public bodies, in relation to:

(a) conditions for access to employment, to self-employment or to occupation, including selection criteria and recruitment conditions, whatever the branch of activity and at all levels of the professional hierarchy, including promotion;

(b) access to all types and to all levels of vocational guidance, vocational training, advanced vocational training, and retraining, including practical work experience;

(c) employment and working conditions, including dismissals, as well as pay as provided for in Article 157 TFEU (ex 141 EC);

(d) membership of, and involvement in, an organisation of workers or employers, or any organisation whose members carry on a particular profession, including the benefits provided for by such organisations.

Now, Article 23 of 2006/54 requires member states to take the necessary measures to ensure that:

(a) any laws, regulations and administrative provisions contrary to the principle of equal treatment are abolished;

(b) provisions contrary to the principle of equal treatment in individual or collective contracts or agreements, internal rules of undertakings or rules governing the independent occupations and professions, and workers' and employers' organisations or any other arrangements, shall be, or may be, declared null and void, or be amended . . .

The scope of application can be avoided for specific reasons given in the Directive only, considered next.

14.3.3 Equality with regard to employment access, working conditions, dismissal, and retirement ages

Article 14 of Directive 2006/54 provides that there shall be no direct or indirect discrimination relating to all aspects of employment, and notably access to jobs and conditions of employment. Situations that were considered under the previous Directive—notably Article 5, which required equality of treatment in working conditions and conditions governing dismissal—are now covered also by Directive 2006/54.

Most cases have concerned retirement and pensions. In **Case C-177/88 *Dekker* v *VJM Centram***, VJM (a social training centre) refused to employ Mrs Dekker because she was pregnant and this would mean that insurance law, which did not recognise pregnancy as a reason for paying insurance money, would not reimburse the employers during her maternity leave. As a social institution, VJM argued that it could not afford to hire a replacement for her. The CoJ held that the employer had directly discriminated in contravention of Articles 2(1) and 3(1) of Directive 76/207 by its refusal to employ, even though national rules forced this situation. Furthermore, it was pointed out by the Court that direct discrimination removed the need to compare the treatment with a man.

In **Case C-312/86 *Commission* v *France (Protection of Women)***, French legislation allowed certain privileges for women, including extended maternity leave, reduction in working hours of women aged 59, bringing forward retirement age, time off for sick children, an extra day's holiday each year per child, a day off on the first day of a school term, and others. The CoJ considered that these special provisions only for women discriminated against men, contrary to the Directive. They were not justified by Article 2(3) (now Article 14 of Directive 2006/54), which protects women during pregnancy and maternity, because the reasons given for the protection applied equally to male and female workers.

Turning to dismissal and retirement, we know from section 14.2.1.1 on equal pay that member states can, under Article 7 of Directive 7/79, exclude the determination of pensionable age for the purposes of granting old-age and retirement pensions and the possible consequences thereof for other benefits. It was thought and argued that this meant that any differences concerning either pensions entitlements or pensionable ages were excluded, and thus that retirement and dismissal ages were also excluded.

In **Case 151/84 *Roberts* v *Tate and Lyle***, Mrs Roberts was aged 53 and a redundancy scheme allowed access to a redundancy for both men and women at the age of 55. Roberts claimed unlawful discrimination because men could gain access 10 years before their pensionable age, but women only five. The CoJ held that access to a redundancy scheme was concerned with dismissal and therefore covered by Article 5 and not excluded by Article 7 of Directive 79/7. Access was not linked to the state security system. The Court held that Article 5(1) of

Directive 76/207 must be interpreted as meaning that a contractual provision that lays down a single age (55) for the dismissal of men and women under a mass redundancy involving the grant of an early retirement pension, where the normal retirement age is different for men and women, does not constitute discrimination on grounds of sex contrary to Community law.

In the leading case concerned with retirement, **Case 152/84 Marshall**, the compulsory earlier retirement of women was considered. National legislation allowed employers to retire women earlier than men. The CoJ held, however, that retirement also came within the scope of working conditions, including dismissal, and was thus covered by the Directive. When the Court came to consider whether the retirement age was linked to pensions, it decided relatively easily that the enforced earlier retirement for women than men did not fall within the justification of Article 7 of Directive 79/7 and was therefore direct discrimination.

Directive 76/207 was held by the CoJ to be directly effective, but only vertically; therefore, other means of enforcement must be pursued if a private employer is involved.

Case C-136/95 Thibault is notable for the clear statement from the CoJ about how Community (now EU) law on equal treatment should be regarded and thus applied. Pay rises and promotion were assessed on the basis of the previous six months' work presence, which was argued clearly to discriminate against women on maternity absence, who lost the chance to be assessed for pay increases or promotion. The Court held that this amounted to unlawful discrimination contrary to Articles 2(3) and 5(1) of Directive 76/207 (as they were then).

These provisions, in the view of the CoJ, required substantive and not only formal equality—that is, real rights, not only those on paper!

Finally in this section, **Case C-116/94 Meyers** is worth noting because it extended the scope of the Directive to the social security benefit, family credit, something that reasonably might be considered to come under the Social Security Directive 79/7 and not Directive 76/207. The credit was designed to supplement low-paid workers in an attempt to persuade them to remain in work, thus satisfying the CoJ that it could be construed under the terms of access to employment and working conditions, covered by Articles 3 and 5 (then of Directive 76/207), because it would encourage employees to take up job offers and also to be considered to be a condition of work. Working conditions thus apply to all aspects of the working relationship and not just those contained within the contract of employment.

Having regarded the widening scope of the principle of equal treatment, we now need to consider the derogations or exemptions that are provided under the Directive to exclude certain circumstances or situations from being subject to the principle of equal treatment. The first provision seeks to take out of the application of the principle of equal treatment circumstances in which factors other than sex allow discriminatory treatment. The second provision was designed to take account of the unique circumstance of pregnancy, and the third to allow for the possibility of promoting equality for women.

14.3.4 Exempt occupations

Article 14(2) of Directive 2006/54 replaced Article 2(6) of Directive 76/207, and provides the member states with the ability to exempt certain occupations from the application of the equal treatment principle where a characteristic not related to sex itself is a factor. The characteristic must constitute a genuine and determining occupational requirement in order not to constitute unlawful discrimination on the grounds of sex. Previously, cases showed that the member states were perhaps permitted a greater degree of discretion than more recently.

> For example, in **Case 165/82 Commission v UK (Equal Treatment for Men and Women)**, the restriction of access of males to midwifery was held to be acceptable, but, in such cases, member states are required to assess the restrictions periodically in order to decide, in the light of social developments, whether there is justification for maintaining the exclusions concerned. They must notify the Commission of the results of this assessment under Article 9(2) of Directive 76/207.

> Indeed, it is now the case that male midwives are common in the UK and other countries.

In the same case, a blanket exemption from the provisions of the Directive that applied to all companies with less than six workers was held by the CoJ not to be sanctioned by the exemption and thus contrary to the Directive.

> In **Case 222/84 Johnston v Chief Constable of the RUC**, the RUC did not renew the contracts of a number of female police officers and justified this under Article 2(2) of Directive 76/207 because of a policy decision that women could not carry firearms. The CoJ held that the exception might apply to certain activities carried out by police officers, but not to police activities in general. The member states might therefore restrict such specific activities and the training for that activity to men, provided the situation was reviewed regularly to ensure that the restrictions remained justified and complied with the principle of proportionality. The CoJ suggested that women could do other duties not involving use of firearms, rather than be dismissed outright.

Recent case law concerning employment in the armed forces, however, questions the restriction permitted in *Johnston*.

> In **Case C-273/97 Angela Sirdar v The Army Board**, the CoJ said that although EC law can also apply to employment in the army, in that case the exclusion of a woman as a cook in the Royal Marines was acceptable because of the Marines' requirements of interoperability and front-line duties—that is, the unit's cook was expected to undertake all duties and also be

involved in front-line duties. Therefore, sex was a determining factor and the UK could rely on the exemption. Sirdar, who was previously a cook for a commando regiment not having these same requirements, could not be a cook for the Marines.

In **C-285/98** *Kreil* **v** *Germany*, a case resembling *Johnston*, but dealing with the army rather than the police force, the CoJ did not accept a general exclusion from military posts that meant that all armed units could remain exclusively male. The Court held that the national authorities contravened the principle of proportionality in taking the general position that the composition of all armed units in the *Bundeswehr* had to remain exclusively male. By rejecting the application by Ms Kreil to the weapons electronics maintenance service of the Federal German Army out of hand, the German authorities had unlawfully discriminated against her.

The armed forces are thus categorically included, but with discretion preserved for the member states to discriminate for particular circumstances, as in *Sirdar*.

Finally, in this trio of army cases is **Case C-186/01** *Dory*, in which the compulsory military service for males only in Germany was challenged. The CoJ held that, while 'the Equal Treatment Directive applies to equality in the access to posts, it does not govern the member states' choices of military organisation for the defence of their territory or of their essential interests'. Germany's choice of compulsory male-only military service, enshrined in its Constitution, was immune from Community law scrutiny. The negative consequences for males as a result of their time spent in military service, such as a delay in comparison to females in arriving at the job market, can therefore be remedied only by the national authorities and courts.

> **CROSS REFERENCE**
> See, however, the *Schnorbus* case in section 14.3.6.

14.3.5 The protection of women regarding childbirth and maternity

Article 28(1) of Directive 2006/54 (replacing Article 2(3) and (7) of Directive 76/207) provides as follows.

Directive 2006/54, Article 28(1)
This Directive shall be without prejudice to provisions concerning the protection of women, particularly as regards pregnancy and maternity.

This is another derogation from the principle of equal treatment. It means that a different legal regime can apply, but this time specifically to protect women. However, these provisions should not be used to disguise discrimination. Article 15 of Directive 2006/54 (ex Article 2(7) of Directive 76/207) provides as follows.

Directive 2006/54, Article 15
A woman on maternity leave shall be entitled, after the end of her period of maternity leave, to return to her job or to an equivalent post on terms and conditions which are no less favourable to her and to benefit from any improvement in working conditions to which she would be entitled during her absence.

Directive 2006/54 repeats the prohibition that 'Less favourable treatment of a woman related to pregnancy or maternity leave within the meaning of Directive 92/85/EEC shall constitute discrimination within the meaning of this directive.' Thus, another piece of EU secondary legislation needs to be introduced at this time and read alongside Directive 2006/54.

Directive 92/85 concerns the protection of pregnant and breastfeeding workers. Its title comes across as somewhat inelegant, but it also helps to determine the rights to which women are entitled when pregnant and on maternity leave. Article 10 of the Directive, in combination with Article 8, designates a period of special protection, from the beginning of pregnancy to the end of maternity leave (which must be a 14-week minimum continuous period of leave), in which women are protected from dismissal for any reason connected to pregnancy. After the period has expired, the special protection is lost.

> Note that, even during the period of special protection, women can be dismissed where the reason is not connected to pregnancy, such as for theft.

In this particular area of law, the need to make a comparison is removed because of the special circumstances of pregnancy. Case law had, however, already expanded and clarified the then existing EC law ahead of Directive 92/85 coming into force.

> In a case that predates the Parental Leave Directive, **Case 184/83 *Hoffman* v *Barmer -Ersatzkasse***, a father claimed that the refusal to grant six months' paternity leave following the birth of his child while the mother went back to work was discrimination contrary to Articles 1, 2, and 5(1) of the Equal Treatment Directive 76/207. The CoJ held that the Directive was not designed to settle questions concerned with the organisation of the family, nor to alter the division of responsibility between parents, and that parental leave may therefore be reserved to the mother by the member states by virtue of Article 2(3).

The case makes it clear that Article 2(3) was an exception to the general principle of equal treatment established by the Directive exclusively in favour of women.

> Note, now, that the protection against dismissal during a period of parental leave is extended to workers of both sexes by the Parental Leave Directive (Directive 96/34 and as replaced by Directive 2010/41), but because this is not usually the subject of study in most EU courses, it is not considered further here.

It is to be noted that the requirement of equal treatment has been extended to time off for breastfeeding for men and women because, in the view of the CoJ, that time off has been detached from the physical aspect of breastfeeding into time being spent feeding and caring for the child, time which can be carried out and enjoyed by both the father and mother. Hence, a national measure which reserved this time off exclusively for women has been held to breach both Article 157(4) TFEU and Directive 76/207 (see Case C-104/09 *Roca Alvaraz*).

The time taken for maternity leave cannot be discounted when calculating seniority, as was held in Case C-294/04 *Herrero*.

14.3.5.1 Dismissal during or after pregnancy

A series of cases has demonstrated how protective the EU legal regime is of pregnant women. The first case deals with a national law designed to protect pregnant women, albeit by excluding them from a certain type of work.

> In **Case C-421/92 *Habermann-Beltermann v Arbeiterwohlfahrt***, HB was employed on a permanent nights contract and was dismissed when discovered to be pregnant, under a national law prohibiting the night-time work of pregnant women. The employer argued that the prohibition of night work was allowed by the Directive (then Directive 76/207) and to that extent the CoJ agreed, but not to justify dismissal. The CoJ held that neither national legislation nor employment contract rules could render void an employment contract by reason of the fact that the female worker was found to be pregnant. Dismissal was clearly disproportionate and the employer should, for example, find other work for the female worker.

> In **Case C-32/93 *Webb v EMO Air Cargo (UK) Ltd***, a woman who was employed on an indefinite contract to replace her predecessor, who was on pregnancy and maternity leave, was dismissed when it was discovered that, as a replacement, she was also pregnant. The CoJ held that to be direct discrimination contrary to Articles 2(1) and 5(1) of Directive 76/207. This case arose before Directive 92/85 came into force, and was therefore decided exclusively on Directive 76/207.

It is clear that dismissal because a woman is pregnant is a clear and direct breach of the EU law.

> The clear and forthright position taken by the CoJ in *Webb* was confirmed in **Case C-207/98 *Mahlberg*** in respect of the appointment of full-time permanent employees.

In the next cases, temporary employment contracts were considered by the CoJ to determine if they are also included within the scope of the Directive.

> In **Case C-438/99 *Melgar***, a woman was employed on a series of back-to-back fixed-term contracts. Her fourth one expired, allegedly according to the employee, without being renewed or extended, as it had been in the past. Prior to that occurring, her employer learned of her pregnancy. However, the employer *had* offered a fifth contract, but the employee had refused to sign it on the basis that her last contract had not expired and she had been dismissed unfairly. The national court did not determine whether the case concerned a dismissal from an indefinite employment contract or a failure to employ on a new contract. The CoJ held that the failure to renew a fixed-term contract was not strictly a case of dismissal discrimination contrary to Article 10 of Directive 92/85. However, it considered that the non-renewal could be regarded as a refusal to employ based on pregnancy, and thus directly discriminatory and contrary to Articles 2(1) and 3(1) of Directive 76/207.

The facts in the case, however, do not seem to support the view that there was a refusal to appoint, with the employer having offered a contract.

In a case with clearer facts concerning a fixed-term contract, **Case C-109/00 *Tele -Danmark***, a post was advertised as a six months' temporary contract. Training for the post, however, required two months before the person appointed could undertake full duties usefully. Ms Brandt-Nielsen was appointed as from 1 July 1995, but, in mid-August, she informed her employer that she was pregnant and due to give birth in early November. Under Danish law, she was entitled to paid maternity leave as from 11 September 1995—that is, after two weeks' post-training work. She had not previously informed the employer that she was pregnant and was dismissed with effect from 30 September 1995. She claimed unlawful dismissal. The CoJ held that it was direct discrimination contrary to both Article 5(1) of Directive 76/207 and Article 10 of Directive 92/85. The fact that employment was fixed-term was irrelevant, because the inability to work was due to pregnancy. The duration of employment was also not a factor that would influence the result. The CoJ held: 'Had the Community legislature wished to exclude fixed-term contracts, which represent a substantial proportion of the employment relationships, from the scope of those directives, it would have done so expressly.'

Not much later, **Case C-320/01 *Busch*** involved a woman who was on parental leave after the birth of her first child, but who became pregnant a second time. Whilst pregnant, she sought to return early to work, before the full amount of paid parental leave for the first pregnancy had expired. Her employer had a vacancy and she was permitted to return to work. She was seven months' pregnant when she did so. She had not mentioned her pregnancy to her employer, nor had her employer asked whether she was pregnant. On 9 April 2001, she started work; on 10 April 2001, she informed her employer that she was seven months' pregnant and was entitled to paid maternity commencing 23 May 2001 (that is, after six weeks of work). The employer rescinded the permission to return to work (not actually dismissal) on grounds of misrepresentation and mistake as to an essential characteristic. The reason given subsequently for returning to work early by Ms Busch was that the maternity leave allowance was higher than the parental leave allowance. The CoJ held that an employee is not under an obligation to inform her employee in seeking to return to work that, because of certain legislative prohibitions, she is not able to carry out all of her duties. Furthermore, the CoJ held that an employer is not entitled to withdraw consent given to return to work because it was in error as to the employee being pregnant.

These last two cases may seem to be acting increasingly harshly on the employers. However, it is clear that the CoJ is taking a firm position on the law as it presents itself. The Court is providing substantive support for women in achieving equal treatment in circumstances in which it is impossible to compare how a man might have been treated and in which the Union has provided a special protective legal regime because of this. These laws may not have universal support from employers, but the point is that, as a society, we have decided to correct an iniquitous situation: that pregnancy is an acceptable ground for dismissal or non-appointment.

To counter the cynical preparation of a notice of dismissal prepared to be delivered after the period of protection expired, the CoJ held this to be included in the prohibition under Article 10 of Directive 92/85 in Case C-460/06 *Paquay*.

Dismissal and pregnancy by in vitro fertilisation (IVF) treatment has also come under the judicial spotlight.

In **Case C-506/06** *Sabine Mayr*, there had been a dismissal of a woman who was undergoing IVF treatment. Whilst her ova had been fertilised, they had not been re-implanted, and the national court asked whether this was to be regarded within the protected period of pregnancy under Directive 92/85. The CoJ held that, at this stage of the treatment, it did not. However, if the woman had been dismissed as a consequence of undergoing the treatment, this would amount to direct discrimination contrary to Directive 76/207. It was left to the national court in this case to determine the exact reasons for the dismissal.

14.3.5.2 **Pregnancy and illness**

Cases that involve illness resulting from pregnancy are particularly difficult to resolve and have caused the CoJ to make hard decisions on both sides of the line.

In **Case C-179/88** *Hertz v Aldi*, Mrs Hertz was dismissed because of repeated absence due to illness that originated from her prior pregnancy. The CoJ held that although pregnancy-related discrimination was a form of direct discrimination, Directive 76/207 did not apply to dismissals due to illness absence that took place outside the maternity leave time granted. In such circumstances, it was necessary to look at national legislation to consider whether there was any direct or indirect discrimination in the grounds of dismissal.

In this and similar cases, when the period of special protection has expired, it becomes possible again to make a comparison with men to see how they are treated if absent through illness over a long time.

The approach taken in *Hertz* was confirmed in Case C-400/95 *Larsson v Dansk Handel & Service* after entry into force of Directive 92/85. The Directives do not, therefore, prevent dismissals for absences due to illness attributable to pregnancy even if it is the case that the illness arose during pregnancy and continued during and after the period of maternity leave. Dismissal is prohibited and unlawful only during the period of protected maternity leave. The dismissal after the leave period is not specifically catered for by EU law. Whether such dismissal is unlawful reverts to comparing it with the dismissal of a man for illness. A woman dismissed for taking too much time off due to illness arising from pregnancy should therefore be compared with a man suffering from any illness. Therefore, pregnancy played its role as the source of the illness outside of the protected period and it is the normal comparison that determines the legal position, something that is argued represents formal equality only and not substantive equality.

This was confirmed by the CoJ in **Case C-191/03** *McKenna*, in which the Court held that pregnancy-originated illness outside of the protected period and absence by men under ordinary sick pay schemes were rightfully to be regarded as comparable.

Case C-394/96 *Brown v Rentokil* also concerned a dismissal that resulted from time off due to an illness originating during pregnancy, but before maternity leave had commenced. The CoJ made it clear that the period or protection incorporated the entire pregnancy and maternity leave.

The result in the *Hertz* and *Larsson* cases was corrected to the extent that any time off taken during pregnancy and maternity leave cannot now be taken into account in calculating the entire time off taken for the purpose of dismissal—that is, time can only start to accrue for this purpose after the period of protection has ended. A woman would therefore be best advised to take her maternity leave as late as possible to maximise the period of protection.

14.3.6 The promotion of equal opportunity by removing existing inequalities affecting opportunities

The statutory attempt to promote equal opportunity is often described as 'positive discrimination', although this is not an accurate description for what is allowed under the EU legal regime, as will be observed from the judgments of the CoJ. Both the Treaty and Directive 2006/54 contain provision for some sort of action by the member states to try to promote equality. Directive 76/207, which was first on the scene, originally provided for this in Article 2(4). Article 3 of Directive 2006/54 has replaced old Article 2(4) and provides that 'member states may maintain or adopt measures within the meaning of Article 141(4) [EC (now 157 TFEU)] with a view to ensuring full equality in practice between men and women in working life'. Hence, the Directive Article now essentially backs up the Treaty provision, but refers specifically to women, whereas the Treaty Article mentions both men and women.

> **Article 157 TFEU (ex 141 EC)**
>
> With a view to ensuring full equality in practice between men and women in working life, the principle of equal treatment shall not prevent any Member State from maintaining or adopting measures providing for specific advantages in order to make it easier for the underrepresented sex to pursue a vocational activity or to prevent or compensate for disadvantages in professional careers.

> The CoJ, in **Case C-319/03 *Briheche***, concluded that Article 141(4) EC (now 157 TFEU) and Article 2(4) of Directive 76/207 needed to be looked at separately, suggesting that their scope differed. Hence, the Directive Article now essentially backs up the Treaty provision of Article 157(4) TFEU.

Whilst the measures concerned mostly contemplate women, this is not exclusively the position, as can be observed in the case law. The extent to which the authorities of the member states can provide legislation, or indeed private employers are able to discriminate positively in favour of women by, for example, shortlisting or interviewing only female candidates or, if dismissals are required, dismissing males only, is a difficult question. Article 3 of Directive 2006/54 would seem to allow more positive action than was previously the case by the use of the term 'equality in practice'— that is, not only on paper! Cases that arose under the old Directive Article and the Treaty amendment include the following.

> In **Case 312/86 *Commission v France (Protection of Women)***, it can be seen that not all measures adopted by a member state to assist women will be considered to be fair by the CoJ. This case is also considered in section 14.3.3.

In contrast, in **Case C-218/98 *Abdoulaye v Renault***, additional or guaranteed payments for females on maternity leave over and above those paid to males on paternity leave was recognised by the CoJ as acceptable due to the occupational disadvantages suffered by women during absence and was held not to be discriminatory.

There is a series of cases concerned with appointment procedures that have been adapted to introduce an element of rebalancing in favour of the under-represented sex.

In **Case C-450/93 *Kalanke***, the CoJ ruled that a national rule, which provided that where equally qualified men and women are candidates for a position with fewer women, women are automatically to be given priority, constituted direct discrimination on the grounds of sex contrary to the Directive. According to the CoJ, the rule had gone beyond promotion and had overstepped the exception provided for in Article 2(4) of Directive 76/207.

This decision was not taken kindly in some quarters, because it seemed to undermine any possibility of providing affirmative action to improve the equality position of women; however, there was soon a refinement of the position both in the subtlety of approach by the member state authorities and the interpretation by the CoJ.

Case C-409/95 *Marschall* involved an application for a teaching post by a qualified man being rejected by the local authority according to a law that provided that women should be given priority in the event of equal suitability. However, in contrast to *Kalanke*, a 'saving clause' provided that if a particular male candidate has grounds that tilt the balance in his favour, women are not to be given priority. Thus, the CoJ was able to conclude that the provision was one that could fall within the scope of Article 2(4) of Directive 76/207 and did not offend the prohibition of discrimination. There were, however, two safety mechanisms that should be set up: the first, to avoid discrimination against men, and the second to stop the pendulum from swinging back against women. The Court considered such priority clauses to be acceptable provided the candidates are objectively assessed to determine whether there are any factors tilting the balance in favour of a male candidate, but that such criteria employed do not themselves discriminate against women.

This is a somewhat convoluted judgment, but probably gets there in the end.

Case C-158/97 *Badeck* confirms the decision in *Marschall* that such laws are not in breach of EC law provided the priority for women was not automatic and unconditional.

The amended Article 157(4) TFEU backs up the ability of the CoJ to pursue the more liberal approach adopted in *Marschall*, although the first case reaching it under the amended Treaty Article did not give the Court an opportunity to be expansive.

In **Case C-407/98 *Abrahamsson***, a woman was appointed to a university chair in preference to a man on the basis of a positive discrimination regulation and despite a clear five-to-three vote in favour of the man, based on his qualifications and his overall higher ranking even after the positive discrimination factor had been taken into account. The university contended that the difference was not so great as to breach the objectivity requirement imposed by Community law in the light of the recent case law of the CoJ. The CoJ held that EC law, primary or secondary, does not support appointments based on automatic preference for the under-represented sex irrespective of whether the qualifications are better or worse and where no objective assessment of each candidate has taken place.

It seems that only where women have equivalent or imperceptibly near qualifications will EU law permit any affirmative action to be exercised.

A case involving female-only access to childcare facilities, save in emergency, was considered under Article 2(4) of Directive 76/207.

In **Case C-476/99 *Lommers***, a government ministry restricted access to subsidised childcare to women to address the lack of affordable facilities that caused many women to give up their jobs. Whilst this was held by the CoJ to be acceptable under Article 2(4) of Directive 76/207, it could be so only provided the emergency rule that permitted single fathers to seek places was applied on the same conditions as for female workers.

It seems that there must always be a saving clause in the background to prevent positive discrimination being too positive and thus unlawfully discriminatory.

Finally, in this area is **Case C-79/99 *Julia Schnorbus v Land Hessen***, in which a national decision addressed an imbalance that had disadvantaged men. The result is one way of addressing the army case conclusions reached by the CoJ in *Dory*.

▶ CROSS REFERENCE

Dory is considered in section 14.3.4.

In Germany, military or civilian service is compulsory, but for males only. According to which service is performed, this can take between nine and 18 months, and means that men wishing to go to university enter later and all men enter the job market later. The *Land Hessen* provided rules in respect of entry to the second stage of German legal training that gave priority to men by deferring acceptance of applications by females by up to 12 months in comparison with males who applied at the same time. It argued, when challenged by a female applicant, that the rule was designed to counterbalance the disadvantage suffered by men. It was accepted by the CoJ under Article 141 EC as being a proportionate response to the situation.

The measures found to be acceptable by the CoJ represent only modest steps in providing substantive and not only formal equality for men and women. However, as with all areas of EU law, it is an area that will certainly not stand still for long, and therefore it is always wise in EU law to be looking out for new cases and the impact that they have on the development of EU law.

14.3.7 **Judicial enforcement and remedies**

Article 23 of Directive 2006/54 (ex Article 3 of Directive 76/209) requires member states to take the necessary measures to ensure that any provisions in collective agreements, wage agreements, or individual contracts that breach the principles of the Directive are to be null and void or to be removed.

Member states are required under Articles 17 and 18 of Directive 2006/54 (ex Article 6 of Directive 76/209) to ensure that judicial or conciliation procedures are available with adequate compensation measures even after the employment relationship has ended. It also provides that individuals can pursue claims for real and effective compensation without a fixed upper limit, which was the situation established previously by the CoJ in Case C-271/91 *Marshall II*, that 'damages' means full compensation not restrictively limited by national statutory rules.

> **Case 14/83** *Von Colson and Kamann* concerned the reimbursement of travel expenses as damages for discrimination. The CoJ ruled that full implementation of the Directive entails that sanctions must be such as to guarantee real and effective judicial protection and must therefore have a real deterrent effect on the employer. Where a member state chooses to penalise the breach of the prohibition of discrimination by the award of compensation, that compensation must be adequate in relation to the damage sustained and amount to more than purely nominal compensation.

The CoJ held in the case that Article 6 of Directive 76/207 was not horizontally directly effective—hence the development of the principle of indirect effect from this case.

In Case C-271/91 *Marshall II*, it was held that 'damages' means full compensation not restrictively limited by national statutory rules.

> CROSS REFERENCE

Considered in Chapter 8, section 8.4.2.

> Another notable case is **C-180/95** *Draehmpaehl v Urania*. A job was advertised to females only, contrary to both Community and German law. In the consequent claim, damages were limited to a maximum of three months' salary, but dependent on proving fault on the part of the employer. If more than one plaintiff sued, the aggregate compensation payable was limited to six months' salary. The CoJ held that liability to compensate cannot be made dependent on fault; compensation itself must guarantee real and effective judicial protection, have a real deterrent effect on the employer, and be adequate in relation to the damage suffered. Limits such as three months' salary are acceptable where the employer can prove that, notwithstanding the discrimination, a better-qualified person was appointed and the complainant would not have been appointed in any event. However, an aggregate award ceiling regardless of the number discriminated against is not acceptable under Directive 76/207 because it may have the effect of dissuading applicants so harmed from asserting their rights.

These decisions are now reflected statutorily in Directive 2006/54.

> In a mixed equal pay and treatment case, **C-185/97 Coote v Granada**, Ms Coote settled a sex discrimination claim with Granada outside of court and the employment relationship was terminated by mutual consent. She found it difficult to obtain another job due to Granada's refusal to supply an employment agency with a reference. It was claimed that this was contrary to Article 6 of Directive 76/207, under which member states should take measures to achieve the aims of the Directive and must ensure that the rights can be enforced by the individual before the national courts. The CoJ held that this right of recourse to the courts is a general principle of Community law reflected in the member states' constitutions and Article 6 ECHR. The CoJ held that Article 6 of Directive 76/207 also covers measures an employer may take as a reaction against legal proceedings of a former employee outside of dismissal, because if employees were to find it difficult to obtain other jobs, it could deter them from taking action when they considered that they had been discriminated against on the grounds of sex.

This extends the scope of EU protection beyond the protection against dismissal.

Article 24 of Directive 2006/54 (ex Article 7 of 76/207) requires member states to take the necessary measures to protect employees against dismissal by the employer as a reaction to a complaint within the undertaking or to any legal proceedings aimed at enforcing compliance with the principle of equal treatment. This had been extended by Directive 2002/73 to protect employees' representatives who act in cases involving complaints against the employer.

 THINKING POINT

But this case involves a private employer and a Directive, so are there any difficulties with this? If so, how did Ms Coote succeed?

Article 30 of Directive 2006/54 (ex Article 8 of Directive 76/207) requires the member states to ensure that provisions of implementing laws are brought to the attention of employees by all appropriate means, and Articles 20–22 of Directive 2006/54 (ex Articles 8a and 8b of Directive 76/207) have been introduced for member states to set up bodies to promote equality and to engage in research and discussion to bring forward proposals for agreements and action to achieve equality.

14.4 The Social Security Directive (Directive 79/7)

As the third instalment of the first wave of secondary legislative additions to Article 119 EC (now 157 TFEU), Directive 79/7 was enacted to apply the principle of equal treatment to the field of social security and other elements of social protection. The scope of the Directive is limited to statutory schemes, whereas private schemes and the increasing number of contracted-out schemes were catered for later by Directive 86/378 (now repealed and replaced by Directive 2006/54), but Directive 79/7 has not been replaced by Directive 2006/54. Because most courses do not deal with this in any further detail than already dealt with here in respect of Article 7 and pensions, no further treatment will be given.

> **CROSS REFERENCE**
>
> Article 7 and pensions are discussed in section 14.2.1.1.

14.5 The Pregnant and Breastfeeding Workers Directive (Directive 92/85)

The Pregnant and Breastfeeding Workers Directive (Directive 92/85) was enacted as a measure for the protection of workers under Article 118a EC (now 154 TFEU) rather than a measure of equal treatment under Article 141 EC (now 157 TFEU), which now allows general measures of equal treatment to be adopted rather than only pay, as was the case prior to amendment. Directive 92/85 is essentially, then, a health-and-safety measure to protect pregnant and breast-feeding workers, including part-time workers, in the workplace. Article 10 of the Directive has already been considered in relation to the special period of protection in relation to dismissal for pregnant women from the beginning of pregnancy to the end of maternity leave. However, what constitutes a dismissal and what constitutes a refusal to take on an employee is not necessarily a clear-cut point, as was observed in Case C-438/99 *Melgar*. This is because the practice of employment on back-to-back or fixed-term contracts, which is commonplace in industry and commerce, confuses the issue. Thus, whilst strictly concerning health-and-safety issues, the Directive is never-theless important in providing a level of protection for women in a situation that is not compar-able with men. Without such protection, women might otherwise suffer further inequality. For example, if paid time off to attend antenatal clinics was not required by Article 9, not only might the time taken off not be paid, but it also might be counted towards the amount of time absent from work for the purposes of dismissal.

Directive 92/85 has not featured in case law to any significant extent, so whilst it was originally as-sumed following its enactment that all cases concerned with dismissal during pregnancy or mater-nity would come under its provisions, the *Melgar* case shows that we still need to have an eye on Directive 2006/54 in similar circumstances. No further consideration will be given in this volume.

14.6 Article 19 TFEU: the expansion of EU equality law

The introduction of Article 13 EC (now 19 TFEU) by the Treaty of Amsterdam provided the Treaty with a new legal base for the enactment of legislation to tackle discrimination across a range of issues. However, it is to be noted that the Article does not actually prohibit anything in its own right, but empowers the Council to take action to combat discrimination based on sex, racial or ethnic origin, religion or belief, disability, age, or sexual orientation.

Directives were issued with little delay under this Treaty Article and before a further 10 member states came on board, which would have made it even more difficult to reach the unanimity required for measures under the Article. It can be said, however, in contrast with the debate about the reasons for the inclusion of the original Article 119 EEC in the first place, that there is no suggestion that Article 13 EC was included on economic grounds; instead, it is a clear representation of the social concerns of the EU and to be welcomed for this reason. Legislation to combat discrimination was enacted under Article 13 EC (now 19 TFEU).

For more details on this section visit the online resources.

14.6.1 Secondary legislation issued under Article 19 TFEU

Two Directives were enacted in 2000 that, between them and the 2006 recast Equal Treatment Directive, encompass many of the matters identified in Article 13 EC where action was deemed necessary to combat discrimination. Directive 2004/113 on equal treatment in the access to and supply of goods and services is also briefly considered following.

14.6.1.1 The Racial Equality Directive (Directive 2000/43)

This was the first Directive to be adopted under the new Article 13 EC (now 19 TFEU) and seeks to apply the principle of equal treatment to persons regardless of racial or ethnic origin in matters of employment, social protection, education, and access to public goods and services, including housing (Article 3(1)). An exception is provided that is similar to Article 14(2) of Directive 2006/54, whereby differential treatment can be justified where a certain characteristic is a genuine and de-termining occupational requirement (Article 4(1)). The Directive requires the member states to es-tablish a body to promote equal treatment on grounds of race and ethnicity and to combat discrimination in these areas (Article 13).

14.6.1.2 The Framework Employment Directive (Directive 2000/78)

This Directive, known as the 'Horizontal Framework Directive' because it applies across all sectors of employment, deals with all of the other forms of discrimination identified by Article 19 TFEU (ex 13 EC), with the exception of the matters covered by the Racial Equality Directive and Directives on equality between men and women. As part of the justification for the Directive, it makes reference to the ECHR, as cited in Article 6 TEU. It provides that there should be no discrimination, direct or indirect, on the grounds of religion or belief, disability, age, or sexual orientation. As with forms of indirect discrimination under previous Directives, indirect discrimination can be objectively justified provided it is proportionate (Article 4). An exception exists that is also similar to Article 14(2) of Directive 2006/54 whereby different treatment can be justified by a certain characteristic that is a genuine and determining occupational requirement (Article 4(1)). There is also a special exemption for access to employment in religious organisations (Article 4(2)), and further exceptions in respect of disability (Article 5) where measures to accommodate disabled persons would cause employers a disproportionate burden, along with numerous exceptions in respect of age (Article 6). There is no requirement under this Directive to establish a body to promote equality for the matters covered by the Directive, in contrast to the Equal Treatment and Racial Equality Directives.

14.6.1.3 Common characteristics

Both Directives share the definitions of equal treatment as being no direct or indirect discrimination (Article 2(1)), thus effectively removing any need for a prolonged debate as to whether these con-cepts are synonymous, similar, overlapping, or different. They both define, as does the amended recast Equal Treatment Directive, direct and indirect discrimination, as well as 'harassment'.

Neither of the Directives encroaches on the existing prohibition on the ground of nationality (Article 18 TFEU) and neither applies in favour of third-country nationals (TCNs) (Articles 3(2) in both Directives). Both contain the objective justification defence as first statutorily defined in Article 19 of Directive 2006/54. Both also contain a provision to allow for positive action in support of achieving equality of treatment (Article 5 of Directive 2000/43 and Article 7 of Directive 2002/78). Remedies and enforce-ment considerations have been provided that are similar to those provided for in Directive 76/207, as amended, replaced by Directive 2006/54 (Articles 7–12 in Directive 2002/43 and Articles 9–14 in Dir-ective 2002/78).

Whilst there is quite a bit of overlap and common ground between the Directives, there are also differences, the details of which at this stage would be too great to consider in this volume. The

Directives have already generated considerable academic comment, some of which is cited in the end-of-chapter 'Further reading' list.

In 2004, Directive 2004/113 was enacted under Article 13 EC (now 19 TFEU) to implement the principle of equality between men and women in the access to and supply of goods and services. It applies to the provision of all public- and private-sector supply of goods and services outside the sphere of private and family life transactions, and, apart from a notable derogation in the Directive dealing with insurance leading to case law and in particular a 2011 judgment in Case C-236/09 *Test Achets*, it has not provoked much attention in academic and university studies of EU law. Further details are not therefore included within this text.

In 2008, a new Directive was proposed that aimed to combat discrimination based on religion or belief, disability, age, or sexual orientation, and to put into effect the principle of equal treatment, but outside the field of employment. Its scope is social protection, including social security and health care, social advantages, education, and access to and supply of goods and services that are available to the public, including housing. However, only professional or commercial activities are covered. Following wide consultation, with reported opposition from some countries to the inclusion of sexual orientation, the proposal was made and approved with amendments by the European Parliament in 2009 and forwarded to the Committee of the Regions (CoR) for an opinion. The proposal, however, awaits further progress and the unlikely unanimous support of the Council.

> **CROSS REFERENCE**
> *Test Achets* is considered in section 14.6.1.4.

For more details on this section visit the online resources.

14.6.1.4 Selective case law from the Article 19 TFEU Directives

Whilst largely outside the main remit of undergraduate EU courses on discrimination law, a few sample cases arising from the new Directives are considered here.

> **Case C-144/04 *Mangold v Helm*** concerns age discrimination that resulted from a scheme seeking to ease the employment of older workers. It was held that a change of German law to assist older workers in finding work went beyond the objectively justified exceptions permitted in Article 6(1) of Directive 2000/78, despite the fact that the time allowed for its implementation had not expired. Mangold became subject to the change, which allowed workers over the age of 52, previously 58, to be employed on fixed-term contracts without accruing compensation rights on termination, as opposed to permanent contracts, which would allow such rights. The justification for the ruling was that non-discrimination on the grounds of age was part of the general principle of non-discrimination in Community law and thus applicable in its own right, but with reference to the norms contained in the Directive for assistance. The Court was of the view that the German law was too general and did not permit taking into account personal circumstances or the actual conditions of the labour market.

> **CROSS REFERENCE**
> See Chapter 8, section 8.2.3, for more on this case.

> In a second case concerned with age discrimination, **Case C-411/05 *Palacios de la Villa***, a general scheme of compulsory retirement at the age of 65 under national law, but reflected within a collective agreement, was questioned as to whether this amounted to age discrimination prohibited by Directive 2000/78. The age was determined by the eligibility to the national pension. It was held by the CoJ to be justified, but the measure had to be objectively and reasonably justified, in the context of a national law, with legitimate aims in regulating employment policy and the labour market, and proportionate. In view of the need for the state to regulate the labour market, the fact that the agreement to arrange for retirement at this age was part of a collective agreement and that it was set at the age by which a pension was payable were justified considerations satisfying those requirements.

The decision in the *Mangold* case was subsequently affirmed by the CoJ in **Case C-555/07 Kükükdeveci**, which involved a dispute as to a notice period between an employee and a private employer because a German law precluded periods of employment completed before the employee reached the age of 25 from counting towards the notice period. Directive 2000/78 had been implemented in Germany at the material time. The preliminary ruling question was essentially: on what provision of law could *Kükükdeveci* rely? The CoJ held that the general principle of EU law prohibiting discrimination on the grounds of age, as expressed in Directive 2000/78, applies to preclude national law, as in this case, from discriminating by reason of age.

Thus, the general principle is seen to apply directly between parties, but not the Directive. The question may be asked whether it is more controversial for the general principle to give rise to horizontal direct effects or the Directive, bearing in mind that the general principle finds no clear expression anywhere in the Treaties or secondary legislation.

Other cases concerned with age discrimination include **Case C-341/08 Petersen**, in which panel dentists for statutory health schemes were required to retire at 68, whereas other dentists were not. The rule was defended in the interests of health patients as the ability of a dentist of that age was deemed to deteriorate. Whilst the justification under Article 2(5) of the Directive was acceptable, it was disproportionate, as the reason and rule should apply to all dentists.

Automatic retirement at pension age was held to be acceptable and justified under Article 6(1) of the Directive in **Case C-45/09 Rosenbladt** by allowing the labour market to cater for younger workers looking for work, especially when the rule was only triggered when the older employee became entitled to a pension. In addition, it was possible for the older worker to re-enter the labour market subsequently.

Other grounds of discrimination have also now been considered in the following brief selection of case law.

The scope of the term 'disability' within Articles 2(1) and 3(1) of Directive 2000/78 was considered in **Case C-13/05 Sonia Navas**, in which the Spanish referring court enquired whether it extended to cover dismissal due to sickness. The CoJ held that whilst dismissal due to disability was prohibited where a person was not competent, capable, and available to perform essential functions due to a disability, this did not extend to dismissal solely on the grounds of sickness.

In **Case C-267/06 Tadao Maruko v Versorgungsanstalt der deutschen Bühnen**, a same-sex partnership survivor's claim for a pension benefit was denied on the grounds that the compulsory occupational pensions scheme did not provide for persons who were not married. As this was held to be pay, according to the CoJ, and could be considered discrimination based on sexual orientation, it clearly came within the Framework Directive 2000/78. Whilst the Directive did not provide a direct answer to the problem, it was noted that this was within a same-sex registered partnership, which, in Germany, was increasingly being equated with marital partnerships. Thus, it was left to the national court to decide the extent to which the particular right to pension entitlement was also to be equated with spousal rights. If so, it would be direct discrimination prohibited under the Directive.

A further case involves a disability discrimination claim under Directive 2000/78.

Case C-303/06 *Coleman* concerned a claim that the carer of a disabled person suffered indirect discrimination by her employer, which was upheld by the CoJ, stating that the Directive was not limited to applying only to those suffering direct discrimination, but also, as in this case, to the primary carer of a disabled person, who sought, but was not granted, flexible working arrangements to care for the disabled person.

The above cases include four mildly generous interpretations (*Mangold, Maruko, Coleman*, and *Petersen*) and three mildly conservative judgments (*Palacios, Navas*, and *Rosenbladt*), but these cases merely scratch the surface of the issues and cases that could, and probably will in the future, arise under these Directives. Whether many standard undergraduate courses will be able to deal with these in depth, or indeed at all, is uncertain, but equally unlikely. Undoubtedly, the jurisprudence of EU equality will be richly enhanced.

One of the few cases drawing attention so far under the Race Directive 2000/43 is **Case C-54/07 *Firma Feryn***, which involved an action in Belgium against a firm's owner, who expressed the view that persons of certain races would not employed by the firm. Within the reference going to the CoJ was whether the Directive covers this statement rather than discriminatory action, although this was the opinion of the Advocate-General (AG). The CoJ held that the fact that an employer states publicly that it will not recruit employees of a certain ethnic or racial origin constitutes direct discrimination in respect of recruitment within the meaning of Article 2(2)(a) of Directive 2000/43 because such statements were likely to dissuade certain candidates from submitting their applications and, accordingly, to hinder their access to the labour market. It further held that the public statements by which an employer lets it be known that, under its recruitment policy, it will not recruit any employees of a certain ethnic or racial origin are sufficient for a presumption of the existence of a recruitment policy that is directly discriminatory within the meaning of Article 8(1) of Directive 2000/43. It is for the employer to prove that there was no breach of the principle of equal treatment by showing that the undertaking's actual recruitment practice does not correspond to those statements. It is thus for the national court to verify that the facts alleged are established and to assess the sufficiency of the evidence submitted in support of the employer's contentions that it has not breached the principle of equal treatment. It was also held that Article 15 requires that rules on sanctions must be effective, proportionate, and dissuasive, even where there is no identifiable victim.

On 1 March 2011, the CoJ delivered its judgment in **Case C236/09 *Test Achets***, which concerned the application of Directive 2004/113 (equal treatment between men and women in access to and supply of goods and services) and in particular Articles of the Directive dealing with insurance contracts.

The case was brought against a Belgian law that implemented the derogation permitted under Article 5(2) of the Directive allowing for sex to be used as one of the criteria in the determination of insurance premiums. The Directive, whilst clear about the fundamental nature of the equality between men and women as outlined in various Articles of the Treaties and Directive, was conscious of the widespread use in insurance and financial services of sex as an actuarial factor to determine risk and thus premiums or pay-outs. Hence, the Directive permitted an exception from the general requirement of unisex premiums and benefits if supported by reliable and transparent data. The derogation could last up to five years after the transposition date, namely 21 December 2007 plus five years, but after that date the Directive required a re-examination of the relevant data.

The CoJ noted the wealth of general provisions aimed at the elimination of discrimination between men and women, including very specifically Articles 21 and 23 of the EU Charter of Fundamental Rights, but also noted that legislative attempts to achieve that must be undertaken taking account of the economic and social conditions and therefore allow, for limited transitional periods, derogations where appropriate; hence, the derogation in Article 5(2) of the Directive. However, the Directive failed to specify a temporal or date limit and thus there was a risk, in the view of the Court, that the derogation would be employed without limit by the member states contrary to the general rule requiring unisex premiums in Article 5(1).

The result was a simple statement making it clear that the derogation expired on 21 December 2012.

In the light of the high visibility of this ruling, which affected car insurance, pensions, and life insurance, it attracted much comment.

THINKING POINT

Given that insurance premiums are also determined based on age, should they also be subject to the age discrimination Directive?

14.6.2 The Lisbon Treaty and the EU Charter of Fundamental Rights

Gender equality and equality generally were issues discussed during the drafting of the Constitutional Treaty, which was abandoned and replaced by the Lisbon Treaty, but which dealt with these rights in a radically different way. It is worth noting that, with regard to their inclusion in the Constitutional Treaty, the burning question was not whether they should feature in the Treaty at all, but where they should be placed. The Constitutional Treaty contained in its Preamble the equality of persons as one of the European values, which was then repeated in Article I-2. The Lisbon Treaty attached the Charter of Fundamental Rights to the Treaties by way of a Declaration, but with opt-outs for Poland and the UK applying internally in those two countries, and a political deal to do the same for the Czech Republic agreed prior to its ratification of the Lisbon Treaty. These events are covered in Chapter 1.

The Charter includes a third title dealing with equality rights in Articles 20–23.

Article 20 Equality before the law

Everyone is equal before the law.

> **Article 21 Non-discrimination**
>
> 1. Any discrimination based on any ground such as sex, race, colour, ethnic or social origin, genetic features, language, religion or belief, political or any other opinion, membership of a national minority, property, birth, disability, age or sexual orientation shall be prohibited.
>
> 2. Within the scope of application of the Treaties and without prejudice to any of its specific provisions, any discrimination on grounds of nationality shall be prohibited.

> **Article 22 Cultural, religious and linguistic diversity**
>
> The Union shall respect cultural, religious and linguistic diversity.

> **Article 23 Equality between men and women**
>
> Equality between men and women must be ensured in all areas, including employment, work and pay. The principle of equality shall not prevent the maintenance or adoption of measures providing for specific advantages in favour of the under-represented sex.

As set out, the rights provided would appear not to disturb the existing provision of equality law in the EU, with the possible exceptions of Article 20, which could be argued to apply to TCNs (not presently covered by the EU equality regime) and Article 21, which provides that any discrimination based on any ground shall be prohibited. It will be interesting to see how that is interpreted by the CoJ in the EU context. Article 51 of the Charter defines the scope of the application of the Charter as not extending to the member states when not implementing EU law and that the Charter does not extend the field of application of EU law, nor modify its powers and tasks, a proviso that is repeated in Declaration No. 1 attached to the Treaties. Time and case law will determine exactly how it will be employed in the EU legal system.

Summary

> Equality law provision in the EU has developed, from limited beginnings, a number of genuine and comprehensive legal instruments for the combating of discrimination in a range of areas. Furthermore, a general principle of equality is emerging more and more visibly through the judgments of the CoJ. We also have yet to see how the new rights in the new Directives will be received by the courts of the member states. The CoJ will no doubt have opportunities to expand on the general principle endorsed, for example, in Case C-144/04 *Mangold* and Case C-555/07 *Kükükdeveci*.

Questions

1. Why was a sex equality provision (Article 119 EEC, now 157 TFEU) included in the Treaties?

For suggested approaches to answering these questions visit the online resources.

2. How, if at all, is 'pay' defined?

3. Why were pensions considered as pay when they were meant to be excluded under Directive 79/7?

4. With whom can an applicant be compared in an equal pay claim?

5. What is 'indirect discrimination'?

6. When can a difference in pay be justified?

7. When is it lawful to dismiss a woman who is pregnant or who has given birth?

8. What does 'positive discrimination' mean in the EU context?

For guidance on how to tackle this specimen exam question and to read a suggested model answer, visit the online resources. www.oup.com/uk/foster_directions6e/.

 ## Sample exam Q&A

Essay question

To what extent has the EU moved from prohibiting discrimination on the grounds of sex to the provision of much more far-reaching equality protection? What is the evidence of the elevated status of a general principle of equality?

 ## Further reading

Books

Ellis, E. and Watson, P. *EU Anti-Discrimination Law*, 2nd edn, Oxford University Press, Oxford, 2012.

Rönnmar, M., 'Labour and equality law' in Barnard, C. and Peers, S. (eds) *European Union Law*, 2nd edn, Oxford University Press, Oxford, 2017, p. 598.

Tridimas, T. *The General Principles of EC Law*, 2nd edn, Oxford University Press, Oxford, 2006 (Chapter 2).

Articles

Anagnostaras, G. 'Sex equality and compulsory military service: the limits of national sovereignty over matters of army organisation' (2003) 28 EL Rev 713.

Besson, S. 'Never shall the twain meet? Gender discrimination under EU and ECHR law' (2008) 8 HRLR 647.

Burrows, N. and Robinson, M. 'An assessment of the recast of Community equality laws' (2006) 13 ELJ 18.

Burrows, N. and Robinson, M. 'Positive action for women in employment: time to align with Europe?' (2006) 33 J L & Soc 24.

Dewhurst, E. 'Intergenerational balance, mandatory retirement and age discrimination in Europe: how can the ECJ better support national courts in finding a balance between the generations?' (2013) 50 CML Rev 1333.

Howard, E. 'The European Year of Equal Opportunities for All 2007: is the EU moving away from a formal ideal of equality?' (2008) 14 ELJ 168.

Masselot, A. 'The state of gender equality law in the European Union' (2007) 13 ELJ 152.

Möschel, M. 'Race discrimination and access to the European Court of Justice: Belov' (2013) 50 CML Rev 1433.

Sargeant, M. 'The European Court of Justice and age discrimination' (2011) 2 JBL 144.

Waddington, L. 'Future prospects for EU equality law: lessons to be learnt from the proposed Equal Treatment Directive' (2011) 36 EL Rev 163.

Index